DAVE ERWIN

D1207276

Advanced Accounting

1A2495

A Volume in the Wiley Series in Accounting and Information Systems

John W. Buckley, Editor

Advanced Accounting

Andrew A. Haried, PhD, CPA
Associate Professor of Accounting

Leroy F. Imdieke, PhD, CPA
Professor of Accounting

Ralph E. Smith, PhD, CPA
Professor of Accounting

All of Arizona State University
Tempe, Arizona

JOHN WILEY & SONS

New York   Chichester   Brisbane   Toronto

Copyright © 1979, by John Wiley & Sons, Inc.

All rights reserved. Published simultaneously in Canada.

Reproduction or translation of any part of
this work beyond that permitted by Sections
107 and 108 of the 1976 United States Copyright
Act without the permission of the copyright
owner is unlawful. Requests for permission
or further information should be addressed to
the Permissions Department, John Wiley & Sons.

Library of Congress Cataloging in Publication Data:

Haried, Andrew A
Advanced accounting.

(Wiley series in accounting and information
systems)
Includes index.
1. Accounting. I. Imdieke, Leroy F., joint
author. II. Smith, Ralph Eugene, 1941–
joint author. III. Title. IV. Series.

HF5635.H256   657'.046   78-21944
ISBN 0-471-02374-4

Printed in the United States of America

10 9 8 7 6 5 4 3 2

To Joyce, Lorraine, and Mary

About the Authors

Andrew A. Haried, PhD, CPA, received his doctorate degree in accounting from the University of Illinois. He is currently Associate Professor of Accounting at Arizona State University. He has had public accounting experience with Arthur Andersen & Co. and has acted as a continuing professional education consultant to both local and regional sized firms of public accountants. He has instructed graduate and undergraduate courses in financial accounting, reporting, and auditing. Articles by Professor Haried have appeared in the *Journal of Accounting Research, The Accounting Review,* the *Journal of Accountancy,* and other professional journals. He is a member of the American Accounting Association, The American Institute of Certified Public Accountants, The Arizona Society of Certified Public Accountants, and the Municiple Finance Officers Association and most recently has served as a member of the Auditing Standard Committee of the Arizona Society of Certified Public Accountants.

Leroy F. Imdieke, PhD, CPA, is Professor of Accounting at Arizona State University. He received his PhD in accounting from the University of Illinois. He has instructed graduate and undergraduate courses in financial accounting and reporting and has conducted many professional development seminars during his twenty-year career. Professor Imdieke's articles on financial accounting and reporting topics have appeared in *The Accounting Review,* the *Journal of Accountancy,* and other professional journals. He is a member of the American Accounting Association, the Arizona State Society of Certified Public Accountants, and the National Association of Accountants. He has served on several committees of the American Accounting Association and is currently a member of the Financial Accounting Standards Committee of the Arizona Society of Certified Public Accountants. He has served as a consultant to a number of business firms and state agencies.

Ralph E. Smith is a Professor of Accounting at Arizona State University. During his nine-year career he has instructed financial accounting courses at both the graduate and undergraduate levels. At the graduate level he has instructed graduate seminars in financial accounting theory and problems. The undergraduate courses he has instructed range from the introductory accounting course to the advanced accounting course. He has also been active in developing and conducting a number of professional development seminars.

Professor Smith received his PhD in accounting from the University of Kansas. He is a CPA in the State of Kansas and is a member of the American Accounting Association and the American Institute of Certified Public Accountants. He has served on several committees of the American Accounting Association and also holds membership in Beta Gamma Sigma and Beta Alpha Psi. He has written a number of articles that have appeared in *The Accounting Review,* the *Journal of Accountancy,* and other professional and academic journals.

Preface

This book is suitable for advanced courses dealing with financial accounting
and reporting in the following topical areas: business combinations; consolidated
financial statements; investments in nonconsolidated investees over which an
investor exercises control or significant influence; foreign currency transactions;
partnership formation, operation, and liquidation; fund accounting and accounting
for state and local governmental units.

The objective of this textbook is to provide a comprehensive treatment of
selected topics not covered elsewhere in the financial accounting sequence. Every
effort has been made to present these topics in a clear and readable manner. It is
our belief that it is preferable and more satisfying to both student and instructor to
cover a selected number of topics in depth rather than to undertake a superficial
coverage of a larger number of topics. Consequently, adequate materials are
included for a comprehensive treatment of each of the topical areas presented.
These materials include five appendixes that consist of explanations and
comparisons of alternative concepts and techniques to those emphasized in the
corresponding chapters. The most recent pronouncements and releases of the
Financial Accounting Standards Board, the Securities and Exchange Commission,
and the National Council on Governmental Accounting are reflected throughout
the text.

Problems in accounting for business combinations that result in one surviving
legal entity are presented in Chapter 1 with particular emphasis on a comparison
of the purchase and pooling of interests methods of accounting for business
combinations.

The next nine chapters deal with problems of consolidating investments
in subsidiaries that result when there is more than one surviving legal entity in
a business combination and with problems in reporting on nonconsolidated
investments using the equity method of accounting. Chapters 2 to 7 deal with
fundamental concepts, techniques, and problems relating to the preparation of
consolidated financial statements or the reporting of a nonconsolidated investment
at equity. Chapters 8 to 10 examine additional problems that may arise in the
preparation of consolidated financial statements.

In a survey of more than 100 controllers of publically held companies we found that, in addition to the equity method, the cost method is still widely used by parent companies to *record* investments in consolidated subsidiaries. Therefore, our coverage of consolidated financial statement workpaper techniques emphasizes both cost basis and equity basis eliminations. The techniques are presented in such a way that the procedural differences between cost basis and equity basis workpaper eliminations are easily reconciled by the student.

Appropriate accounting for deferred income tax effects related to timing differences that result from consolidation procedures or application of the equity method to nonconsolidated investees is covered in Chapters 3, 6, 7, and 10. However, the textual exposition and the end of chapter problems are presented in such a way that instructors may omit the treatment of deferred income tax effects in the preparation of consolidated financial statements if they desire.

Concepts and techniques in accounting for branch activities are presented in Chapter 11, preparatory to the discussion in Chapter 12 of concepts and techniques for translating into dollars the financial statements of subsidiaries and branches that are denominated in a foreign currency. Problems in accounting for foreign currency transactions including forward exchange contracts are also discussed in Chapter 12. Segmental reporting is treated in Chapter 13.

Chapters 14, 15, and 16 provide coverage of the financial accounting and reporting problems encountered in the formation, operation, change in ownership, and liquidation of a partnership. Emphasis is on comprehensive coverage in a clear and readable form. Chapters 17 and 18 provide an introduction to fund accounting and to accounting for state and local governmental units. These chapters include illustrations and descriptions of representative transactions and financial reports for each of the fund and account group entities recommended for use by state and local governmental units. These chapters have also been updated to reflect recent modifications in principles of governmental accounting and reporting as promulgated by the National Council on Governmental Accounting.

There are more topics included in this text than can be adequately covered in a one-semester or one-quarter course. We recommend that no more than fifteen chapters be included in any one term. We believe that it is preferable to treat the topics that are selected in depth rather than to attempt a superficial coverage of any of the topics included in the text. Modules of material that an instructor may consider for exclusion in any one semester or quarter include:

Chapters 8, 9, and 10—Expanded analysis of problems in the preparation of consolidated financial statements.

Chapters 11, 12, and 13—Branches, Foreign currency transactions, Segmental reporting.

Chapters 14, 15, and 16—Partnerships.

Chapters 17 and 18—Fund accounting and accounting for state and local governmental units.

It is our opinion that most topics in advanced accounting are of such complexity that it is not meaningful to distinguish between exercises and problems. Each chapter includes a full range of problems in terms of concepts covered, complexity, and length. Probably no more than one-third of the problems are necessary for adequate coverage of the topics presented. Consequently, problem assignments may be varied from term to term. Many of the problems have been adapted from problems included on the Uniform CPA Examination and have been perfected as a result of classroom testing. A set of partially completed workpapers is available in a separate publication for use in completing problem assignments from this text. These workpapers are designed to reduce the amount of time students need to spend on repetitive procedures in the preparation of consolidated financial statement workpapers.

We wish to thank the following individuals who reviewed all or a portion of the manuscript: C. David Baron, Arizona State University; John W. Buckley, University of California, Los Angeles; Ronald M. Copeland, University of South Carolina; David Goldman, Deloitte Haskins & Sells; Leon E. Hay, Indiana University; A. C. Nieminsky, California State University, Northridge; and Isaac N. Reynolds, The University of North Carolina at Chapel Hill. The first draft of the manuscript was class tested at Arizona State University for two semesters, and we are also pleased to acknowledge the helpful comments and constructive criticism that we received from many of our students. We wish to thank the following students in particular for their assistance in developing problem materials and in testing and retesting the solutions to the problems in this textbook: Esther L. Gross, Paul D. Hickman, Ralph H. Mahoney, Edward Thompson, Randy Bowman, Barry A. Goldberg, and Richard P. Rosenthal. Special thanks is also due to the production and editorial staff including John T. Crain, Donald Ford, and Jean Varven, and to Alison Wheeler and Gladys DeJarnatt who typed the manuscript.

Suggestions and comments from users of this book will be appreciated.

Andrew A. Haried
Leroy F. Imdieke
Ralph E. Smith

Contents

Chapter 14   **Formation and Operation of a Partnership**

Chapter 15   **Changes in the Ownership of the Partnership**

Chapter 16   **Partnership Liquidation**

Chapter 17   **Introduction to Fund Accounting**

Chapter 18   Introduction to Accounting for State and Local Governmental Units

1

Business Combinations

Expansion is a major objective of many business organizations. In corporate annual reports top management often lists growth among its primary goals. Growth may be slow, the result of gradual expansion of product lines, facilities, or services, or it may be rapid and dramatic, as in the mushrooming growth of conglomerates during the 1960's. Some businessmen consider growth so important to the future of their companies that they declare that they must "grow or die."

A company may achieve its goal of expansion in a number of ways. Some firms concentrate on *internal* expansion. A firm may expand internally by engaging in product research in an effort to expand the company's total market. Although this method of achieving expansion may be effective, it is generally expensive and produces results rather slowly. A firm may choose instead to engage in advertising and other promotional activities in an attempt to obtain a greater share of a given market. Such efforts do not usually expand the total market, but they may redistribute that market by expanding the company's share of it.

Other firms seek *external* expansion, that is, one firm may expand by acquiring one or more other firms. This form of expansion produces relatively rapid growth without increasing competition. Significant cost savings may result as the operations of the companies are integrated, particularly when a company acquires one of its major suppliers.

BUSINESS COMBINATIONS—AN HISTORICAL PERSPECTIVE

In the past hundred years, United States business enterprises have effected much of their expansion through business combinations. Business combinations have been defined generally as "any transaction whereby one economic unit obtains control over the assets and properties of another economic unit, regardless of the resultant form of the economic unit emerging from the combinations transaction."[1]

During the past century three rather distinct periods were characterized by business mergers, consolidations, and other forms of combinations. The first period ran from about 1880 through 1904. During this era, huge holding companies or trusts were created by investment bankers who sought to establish monopoly control over certain industries. Examples of the trusts formed during this period are J. P. Morgan's U.S. Steel Corporation and other giant firms such as Standard Oil, American Sugar Refining Company, and the American Tobacco Company. By 1904 more than 300 such trusts had been formed, and they controlled more than 40% of the nation's industrial capital.

The second period of concentrated business combination activity began during World World I and continued through the 1920's. During the war the federal government encouraged business combinations in an effort to obtain greater standardization of materials and parts and to discourage price competition. After the war, it was difficult to reverse the trend started by this policy, and business combinations continued. During this period the individual combinations were generally smaller. They were efforts to obtain better integration of operations, reduce costs, and diversify and improve competitive positions rather than attempts to establish monopoly control over an industry. Between 1925 and 1930 more than 1,200 consolidations took place, and about 7,000 companies disappeared in the process.

The third period started after World War II and continues today. Business combination activity was particularly strong during the late 1960's. During some years more than 4,000 individual firms disappeared through combinations. The characteristics of the combination movement during this period closely resemble those of the second period. In addition, this period brought great advances in technical innovation, an expensive process, the cost of which could be recovered only through large-scale operations. Business combinations provide one method of obtaining the large amounts of capital needed to finance these technological advances.

WHY BUSINESS COMBINATIONS?

In addition to rapid expansion, the business combination method, or external expansion, has several other important advantages over internal expansion:

1. Combination with an existing company provides management of the acquiring company with an established, operating unit with its own experienced personnel, regular suppliers, productive facilities, and distribution channels. Management of the acquiring company can draw upon the operating history and the related historical data base of the acquired company for planning purposes. A history of profitable operations

---

[1]Arthur R. Wyatt, *A Critical Study of Accounting for Business Combinations* (New York: American Institute of Certified Public Accountants, 1963), p. 12.

by the acquired company may, of course, greatly reduce the risk involved in the new undertaking.

2. Expanding by combination does not create new competition as does the construction of new facilities, the output of which competes with that of existing facilities.

3. Combination may enable a company to diversify its operations rather rapidly by entering new markets which it may need to assure its sources of supply or market outlets. Entry into new markets may also be undertaken to obtain cost economies realized by smoothing cyclical operations.

4. Business combinations are sometimes entered into to take advantage of income tax laws, e.g., to obtain the advantage of significant operating loss carryforwards that can be utilized by the acquiring company.

Notwithstanding its apparent advantages, business combination may not always be the best means of expansion. An overriding emphasis upon rapid growth may result in the pyramiding of one company upon another with insufficient management control over the resulting conglomerate. Too often in such cases, management fails to maintain a sound financial equity base to sustain the company during periods of recession. In order to avoid large dilutions of equity, some companies have relied upon the use of various debt and preferred stock instruments to finance expansion, only to find themselves unable to provide the required debt service during a period of decreasing economic activity. The rapid build-up of several large conglomerates during the 1960's and the near-collapse of many of them during the early 1970's are evidence of the hazards of uncontrolled or unmanaged growth stemming from business combinations.

LEGAL CONSTRAINTS ON BUSINESS COMBINATIONS

One problem encountered by business units attempting to expand by acquisition is the possibility of antitrust suits. The federal government historically has demonstrated concern for and opposition to the concentration of economic power that may result from business combinations. Two important federal statutes, the Sherman Act and the Clayton Act, have been enacted in an effort to deal with antitrust problems.

The Sherman Act (1890) prohibits any contract, conspiracy, or combination of business interests that results in restraint of trade or tends to create monopolistic powers. This act, however, was not broad enough to cover many types of business contracts, acquisitions, or mergers, even though they essentially tended to restrain or lessen competition. As a result, Congress passed the Clayton Act (1914).

Sections 3 and 7 of the Clayton Act prohibit price discrimination, tying and exclusive selling and leasing contracts, and the acquisition by one corporation of the stock of another corporation where the effect may be to lessen competition or tend to create a monopoly. Some companies, instead of acquiring the stock of another company, acquired its assets directly, and thereby bypassed the stock acquisition provision of the Act. In 1950, Congress amended the Clayton Act to prohibit one corporation from acquiring another through the acquisition of its assets if it would have been prohibited under the 1914 act from acquiring the company's stock. These two acts have been used often by the Department of Justice and the Federal Trade Commission, with varying degrees of success, in attempts to prevent the formation of business combinations (or to break up existing ones) that restrain trade.

TYPES OF BUSINESS COMBINATIONS

Business combinations have generally been classified under two schemes, one based on the structure of the combination, and the other based on the method used to accomplish the combination.

Structure

Combinations are classified by structure into three types—horizontal, vertical, and conglomerate. A *horizontal* combination is one that involves companies within the same industry that have previously been competitors; a *vertical* combination involves a company and its suppliers and/or customers; a *conglomerate* combination is one involving companies in unrelated industries having little, if any, production or market similarities.

Method of Combination

Business combinations are also classified by method of combination into three types—statutory mergers, statutory consolidations, and stock acquisitions.

A **statutory merger** results when one company acquires all of the net assets of one or more other companies through an exchange of stock, payment of cash or other property, or the issue of debt instruments (or a combination of these methods). The acquiring company survives, whereas the acquired company (or companies) ceases to exist as a separate legal entity, although it may be continued as a separate division of the acquiring company. The boards of directors of the companies involved normally negotiate the terms of a plan of merger, which must then be approved by the stockholders of each company involved. State laws or corporation bylaws dictate the percentage of positive votes required for approval of the plan.

A **statutory consolidation** results when a new corporation is formed to acquire two or more other corporations, through an exchange of voting stock; the acquired corporations then cease to exist as separate legal entities. Stockholders of the acquired companies become stockholders in the new entity. The acquired companies may be operated as separate divisions of the new corporation, just as they may under a statutory merger. Statutory consolidations require the same type of stockholder approval as do statutory mergers.

A **stock acquisition** occurs when one corporation pays cash or issues stock or debt, for all or part of the voting stock of another company, and the acquired company remains intact as a separate legal entity. When the acquiring company acquires more than 50% of the voting stock of the acquired company, a parent-subsidiary relationship results.

The stock may be acquired through market purchases or through direct purchase from, or exchange with, individual stockholders of the investee or subsidiary company. Sometimes stock is acquired through a *tender offer,* which is an open offer to purchase up to a stated number of shares of a given corporation at a stipulated price per share. The offering price is generally set somewhat above the current market price of the shares in order to provide an additional incentive to prospective sellers. The investee or subsidiary company continues its legal existence, and the investor or parent company records its acquisition in its records as a long-term investment. Accounting and reporting for this type of investment are treated in detail in later chapters of this book.

Although **business combination** is a broad term encompassing all forms of combination, and the terms *merger* and *consolidation* have technical, legal definitions, the three terms are generally used interchangeably in practice. Thus, one cannot always rely on the accuracy of the term used to identify the type of combination, but must look to the facts of the situation in determining its accounting treatment.

The accounting treatment of mergers and consolidations, where only the acquiring or new company survives, is discussed and illustrated in this chapter. Acquisitions in which the acquired company remains intact will be discussed in subsequent chapters.

Business combinations may create rather complex accounting problems. Two pre-operating problems, (1) determining price and method of payment, and (2) determining the proper accounting method for the acquisition, are discussed below. Problems arising subsequent to acquisition are treated later.

DETERMINING PRICE AND METHOD OF PAYMENT IN BUSINESS COMBINATIONS

When a business combination is effected through an open market acquisition of stock, no particular problems arise in connection with determining price or method of payment. Price is determined by the normal functioning of the stock market, and payment is generally in cash, although some or all of the cash may have to be raised by the acquiring company through debt or equity issues. Effecting a combination may present some difficulty if there are not enough willing sellers at the open market price to permit the acquiring company to buy a majority of the outstanding shares of the company being acquired. In that event, the acquiring company must either negotiate a price directly with individuals holding large blocks of shares or revert to an open tender offer. Regardless of the method used, the acquisition is recorded at its total purchase cost including expenses incurred in acquisition.

When a business combination consitutes a true consolidation and is effected by an exchange of securities (equity, debt, or a combination thereof), both price and method of payment problems do arise. In this case, the price is expressed in terms of a **stock exchange ratio,** which is generally expressed as the number of shares of the acquiring company to be exchanged for each share of the acquired company, and constitutes a **negotiated price.** It is important to understand that each constitutent of the combination makes two kinds of contributions to the new entity—net assets and future earnings. The accountant often becomes deeply involved in the determination of the value of these contributions. The problems that arise are discussed in the following sections. Although the discussion is in terms of a *consolidation,* the basic principles involved apply to other types of acquisitions as well.

Net Asset and Future Earnings Contributions

Determination of an equitable price for each constituent company, and of the resulting exchange ratio, requires the valuation of each company's net assets, as well as their expected contribution to the future earnings of the new entity. The accountant is often called upon to aid in determining net asset value by assessing, for example, the expected collectibility of accounts receivable, current replacement costs for inventories and some fixed assets, and the current value of long-term liabilities based on current interest rates. To estimate current replacement costs of real estate and other items of plant and equipment, the services of appraisal firms may be needed.

Where the constituent companies have used different accounting methods, the accountant may also need to reconstruct their financial statements on the basis of agreed-upon accounting methods in order to obtain reasonably comparable data. Once comparable data have been obtained for a number of prior periods, they must be analyzed further in the process of projecting future contributions to earnings. The expected contributions to future earnings may vary widely among constituents, and the exchange ratio should reflect this fact. The whole process of valuation, of course, requires the careful exercise of professional judgment. Ultimately, however, the exchange ratio is determined by the bargaining ability of the individual parties to the combination.

Once the overall values of relative net asset and earnings contributions have been agreed upon, the types of securities to be issued by the new entity in exchange for those of the combining companies must be determined. In some cases a single class of stock may be issued; in other cases equity may require the use of more than one class of security.

Although the concept of "equity" is subjective in nature and the ultimate stock exchange ratios are determined by the relative bargaining ability of the parties, negotiators should be aware of the basic conditions for an equitable distribution of securities. Two basic conditions should be met if all parties to the combination are to receive equitable treatment.

1. The future income earned by the new entity should be distributed to the stockholders of the combining entities in the ratio of their contributions to those earnings. If, for example, 70% of the new entity's earnings come from the operating activities contributed by X Company, 70% of the new entity earnings should be distributed to the former stockholders of X Company.

2. The stockholders of the new entity should be given preference interests in liquidation and earnings for the net assets contributed. The stockholders should retain their relative net asset positions and obtain a normal or conservative return on net assets contributed since they could have sold the net assets they contributed and invested the proceeds at some fixed rate of return.

Use of a Single Class of Stock

In one specific situation the two conditions of equity can be met by the issue of common stock only. That situation is where the earnings rates on net assets of the combining companies are the same. Shares can be issued in the ratio of net assets contributed or earnings contributed since the ratios are identical. In all other situations the use of a single class of stock would result in an inequity either in earnings distributions or in net asset credit.

To illustrate the problems encountered, assume that the stockholders of X Company and Y Company agree to consolidate and form Z Company. The current values of net asset contributions are:

	X COMPANY	Y COMPANY	TOTAL
Net assets contributed	$400,000	$600,000	$1,000,000
Percent of net assets contributed	40%	60%	

If expected earnings contributions are, say, $40,000 for X Company and $60,000 for Y Company, their earnings rates are identical at 10% of net assets, and a single class of stock may be issued.

If expected earnings contributions were $50,000 for X and $50,000 for Y, the following situation would exist:

	X COMPANY	Y COMPANY	TOTAL
Net assets contributed	$400,000	$600,000	$1,000,000
Percent of net assets contributed	40%	60%	
Net earnings contributed	$ 50,000	$ 50,000	$ 100,000
Percent of net earnings contributed	50%	50%	

Issuance of a single class of stock in the ratio of net assets contributed would retain equitable interests in net assets, but the interests in net earnings would be changed as follows:

	INTEREST IN EARNINGS		
STOCKHOLDERS OF	BEFORE CONSOLIDATION	AFTER CONSOLIDATION	INCREASE (DECREASE)
X Company	50%	40%	(10%)
Y Company	50%	60%	10%

Distribution in the earnings contribution ratio results in the distribution of Z Company stock on a 50:50 basis, which would give X Company stockholders an interest in the net assets of Z Company that is $100,000 greater than the value of X Company net assets contributed and Y Company stockholders an interest that is $100,000 less than their net assets contributed.

Use of More than One Class of Stock

The preceding analysis demonstrates that issuance of a single class of stock in a consolidation generally results in some inequity either in the distribution of profits or in maintaining net asset positions. If the original relationships in net assets and earnings are to be maintained, the new entity must issue some preferred stock (or other senior security) in addition to common stock. The following three-step approach is one means of maintaining these relationships.

1. Expected earnings contributions of the constituents should be capitalized at a rate that reflects the best estimate of normal earnings in determining the total amount of stock to be issued to each constitutent's stockholders. Although the capitalization rate selected is relatively subjective, two limits on the rate should be observed.
    (a) The rate selected should not exceed the lowest earnings rate expected by any constituent on its net assets contributed. Should the capitalization rate exceed any of the constituent's expected earnings rates on net assets, the total value of stock issued to that constitutent's stockholders will be less than its net assets contributed.
    (b) The rate selected should not be less than the preferred dividend rate on the preferred stock to be issued. Equitable allocation of earnings requires that all shares receive the same *rate* of return. If the preferred dividend rate exceeds the capitalization rate, and the actual earnings rate equals the capitalization rate, preferred stockholders will automatically get a greater return on their shares.

2. Preferred stock should be issued to constituents in an amount equal to the value of the net assets they contributed. The stock should be preferred as to assets upon liquidation and should be cumulative and fully participating so that earnings allocations will be equitable if the actual earnings rate exceeds the preferred dividend rate.

3. Common stock should be issued to each constituent for the difference between the total value computed in No. 1 above and the amount of preferred stock issued. Where these conditions are met, net asset contribution claims are preserved through the issuance of preferred stock, and the participation feature of the preferred stock permits an allocation of earnings in the earnings ratio contributed.

As an example, assume that X Company and Y Company are to consolidate into Z Company. Net asset and earnings contributions are as follows:

	X COMPANY	Y COMPANY	TOTAL
Net assets contributed	$400,000	$600,000	$1,000,000
Percent of net assets			
contributed	40%	60%	
Earnings contributions	$ 40,000	$ 90,000	$ 130,000
Percent of earnings			
contributed	30.8%	69.2%	
Earnings rate on net assets	10%	15%	13%

The constituents agree to a plan under which (1) earnings are to be capitalized at 8%, (2) $100 par, 7% cumulative and fully participating preferred stock is to be issued for net assets contributed, and (3) $10 par common stock is to be issued for remaining values. The capitalization rate of 8% reflects the best estimate of normal earnings; thus, any common stock issued is considered to represent payment for goodwill or excess earnings potential. Determination of the stock to be issued is made as follows:

	STOCKHOLDERS OF		
	X COMPANY	Y COMPANY	TOTAL
Earnings contributions	$ 40,000	$ 90,000	$ 130,000
Capitalized at 8%	÷ 8%	÷ 8%	÷ 8%
Total stock to be issued	500,000	1,125,000	1,625,000
Preferred stock for net			
assets	400,000	600,000	1,000,000
Common stock for above-			
normal earnings	100,000	525,000	625,000

Thus, X Company stockholders will receive 4,000 shares of Z Company preferred stock and 10,000 shares of Z Company common stock. If X Company had 20,000 shares of common stock outstanding, the exchange ratio would be:

.2 shares of preferred and .5 shares of common stock
of Z Company for each outstanding common share of X Company

Preferred stockholders are preferred as to assets upon liquidation and thereby maintain their relative asset contribution ratio. Computation of earnings allocations at several earnings levels below will illustrate that earnings will also be allocated equitably.

Assume, first, that earnings expectations of $130,000 are realized. Because the actual earnings rate of 8% (130,000/1,625,000) exceeds the preferred dividend rate of 7%, and preferred stock is fully participating, the stockholders of each company can simply be allocated 8% on their total stock. Allocation of $130,000 of earnings would be:

| | STOCKHOLDERS OF | | |
	X COMPANY	Y COMPANY	TOTAL
To preferred stock @ 8%	$ 32,000	$ 48,000	$ 80,000
To common stock @ 8%	8,000	42,000	50,000
Total allocation	40,000	90,000	130,000
Percent of total allocation	30.8%	69.2%	100%

Expected earnings were exactly realized; thus, as expected, the allocation of earnings would be in the same ratio as earnings contributions, and all stockholders receive the same *rate* of return.

Assume, now, that actual earnings exceed expected earnings and amount to $146,250. The allocation in this situation would be:

| | STOCKHOLDERS OF | | |
	X COMPANY	Y COMPANY	TOTAL
To preferred stock @ 7%	$28,000	$ 42,000	$ 70,000
To common stock @ 7%	7,000	36,750	43,750
Participation	10,000	22,500	32,500
Total allocation	45,000	101,250	146,250
Percent of total allocation	30.8%	69.2%	100%

The amount of participating dividends can be computed as follows:

To preferred in the ratio of its par value to the total par value of preferred and common stock:

$$\frac{1,000,000}{1,625,000} \times 32,500 = 20,000$$

	STOCKHOLDERS OF	
	X COMPANY	Y COMPANY
To preferred stockholders of X Company, 20,000 × .4 (28,000/70,000)	8,000	
To preferred stockholders of Y Company, 20,000 × .6 (42,000/70,000)		12,000
The remaining dividend to common stockholders: 32,500 − 20,000 = 12,500		
To stockholders of X Company $\frac{100,000}{625,000} \times 12,500 =$	2,000	
To stockholders of Y Company $\frac{525,000}{625,000} \times 12,500 =$		10,500
Total	10,000	22,500

Or, since the earnings rate exceeds the preferred dividend rate, and the preferred stock is fully participating, the total allocation can be computed on the basis of the total par value of stock issued to each company. Thus,

To stockholders of X Company $\frac{500,000}{1,625,000} \times 146,250 = 45,000$

To stockholders of Y Company $\frac{1,125,000}{1,625,000} \times 146,250 = 101,250$

Total 146,250

As indicated, the percentage of the total allocation of earnings to each company's stockholders remains the same as the original earnings contribution percentage, and all stockholders receive the same *rate* of return.

Assume that actual earnings were less than expected and amount to $90,000. The allocation would be:

	STOCKHOLDERS OF		
	X COMPANY	Y COMPANY	TOTAL
To preferred stock @ 7%	$28,000	$42,000	$70,000
To common stock @ 3.2%	3,200	16,800	20,000
Total	31,200	58,800	90,000
Percent of total allocation	34.7%	65.3%	100%

The percentage of earnings allocated to X Company stockholders has increased, because Y Company was expected to contribute a greater amount of above-normal earnings, earnings that were not realized. However, all stockholders have received the same rate of return on their holdings, and the allocation is, therefore, equitable at an earnings level below expectations. The return on common stock, representing goodwill, is less than anticipated, which reflects an error in the initial evaluation of goodwill. Note, however, that all common stock receives the same rate of return at 3.2% ($20,000 \div 625,000$ total common stock).

In summary, in order to allocate earnings at the same percentage rate as earnings contributed, Z Company must obtain an actual earnings rate at least equal to the preferred dividend rate, 7% in this example.

Many variations other than those mentioned may be employed in practice. Sometimes debt securities are used as a means of providing additional protection against risk of loss to constituents who have contributed relatively greater amounts of fixed assets. In other cases, two classes of voting stock, Class A and Class B, may be issued. If each class has the same dividend rights, but only one has a prior claim to assets, the original earnings contribution ratio can be maintained at any level of actual earnings. The facts of each situation must be considered carefully in determining an equitable securities allocation.

METHODS OF ACCOUNTING FOR BUSINESS COMBINATIONS

Companies that are considering a business combination must decide early in their negotiations on the accounting method they will use to record the combination. The accounting method may affect significantly the reported financial position and results of operations of the combined entity in the current and future periods, as well as the price to be paid and the form of payment (cash, other assets, stock, etc.).

Two methods of accounting—*purchase* and *pooling of interests*—are accepted in practice. Any business combination, be it a merger, consolidation, or stock acquisition, must be accounted for under one of these two methods. The two accounting methods are discussed, illustrated, and contrasted in the following sections.

Purchase Accounting

As the term implies, the purchase method treats the combination as the acquisition of one or more companies by another. The acquiring company records the acquisition at its total cost. If cash is given, the amount paid, including expenses of acquisition, constitutes cost. If debt securities are given, the present value of future payments represents costs.

An asset acquired by issuing shares of stock of the acquiring corporation is recorded at the fair value of the asset received or the stock given, whichever is more clearly evident. If the stock is actively traded, its quoted market price, after making allowance for market fluctuations, additional quantities issued, issue costs, etc. is normally better evidence of fair value than are values assigned to the net assets of an acquired company. Thus, an adjusted market price of the shares issued is normally used. Where the stock is of a new or closely held company, however, the fair value of the assets received must generally be used.

Once the total cost is determined, it must be allocated to the identifiable assets acquired (including intangibles) and liabilities assumed, both of which should be recorded at their fair values at the date of acquisition. Any excess of total cost over the sum of amounts assigned to identifiable assets and liabilities is recorded as goodwill and should be amortized over its economic life but not in excess of forty years. On occasion, the sum of the fair values of identifiable assets and liabilities may exceed the total cost of the acquired company. If so, the excess of fair value over cost should be allocated to reduce noncurrent assets (except investments in long-term marketable securities) in proportion to their fair values in determining their assigned values. If the allocation reduces the noncurrent assets to zero value, the remainder of the excess over cost should be classified as a deferred credit and should be amortized systematically to income over the period estimated to be benefited but not in excess of forty years.[2]

To illustrate, assume that on January 1, 1980, P Company acquired, in a merger, all of the outstanding common stock of S Company through an exchange of one of its shares of $15 par value common stock for every two shares of the $5 par value common stock of S Company, and that the exchange must be accounted for by the purchase method. P Company common stock, which was selling at a range of $50 to $52 per share during an extended period prior to the combination, is considered to have a fair value per share of $48 after an appropriate reduction is made in its market value for additional shares issued and for issue costs. Balance sheets for P and S Companies (along with relevant fair value data) on January 1, 1980, appeared as follows:

| | P COMPANY | S COMPANY | | |
	BOOK VALUE	BOOK VALUE	FAIR VALUE	
Cash and receivables	250,000	180,000	170,000	
Inventories	260,000	116,000	146,000	
Land	600,000	120,000	400,000	
Buildings	800,000	1,000,000	1,600,000	
Accumulated depreciation—Bldgs.	(300,000)	(400,000)	(600,000)	
Equipment	180,000	120,000	140,000	
Accumulated depreciation—Equip.	(90,000)	(40,000)	(80,000)	
Total assets	1,700,000	1,096,000		
Current liabilities	200,000	150,000	150,000	
Bonds payable, 7%, due 1/1/90, interest payable semiannually on 6/30 and 12/31	-0-	400,000	325,227 [1]	
Common stock, $15 par, 50,000 shares	750,000			
Common stock, $5 par, 60,000 shares		300,000		
Premium on common stock	400,000	100,000		
Retained earnings	350,000	146,000		
Total equities	1,700,000	1,096,000		

[2]*Opinions of the Accounting Principles Board No. 16,* "Business Combinations" (New York: AICPA, 1970), par. 91.

[1] Assuming that the yield rate on bonds with similar risk was 10% on the date of acquisition. Thus, bonds payable are valued at their present value by discounting the future payments at 10% as follows:

> Present Value of Bonds Payable:
>   Present Value of Maturity Value:
>   P. V. of 1, 20 periods @ 5% = .37689 × 400,000 = 150,756
>   Present Value of Interest Annuity:
>   P. V. of annuity of 1, 20 periods @ 5% =
>   12.46221 × 14,000 semiannual interest =   174,471
>   Total Present Value of Bonds Payable   325,227

Because the book value of the bonds is $400,000, bond discount in the amount of $74,773 ($400,000 − $325,227) must be recorded to reduce the bonds payable to their present value.

To record the exchange of stock, P Company would make the following entry:

Cash and Receivables	170,000	
Inventories	146,000	
Land	400,000	
Buildings	1,000,000	
Equipment	60,000	
Discount on Bonds Payable	74,773	
Goodwill	139,227	
Current Liabilities		150,000
Bonds Payable		400,000
Common Stock (30,000 × 15)		450,000
Premium on Common Stock (30,000 × 33)		990,000

Note that under the purchase method the net assets are recorded at cost as measured by the fair value (30,000 shares × 48 = 1,440,000) of the shares given in exchange. Common stock is credited for the par value of the shares issued, with the remainder credited to premium on common stock. Individual assets acquired and liabilities assumed are recorded at their fair values. Fixed assets are recorded net of their accumulated depreciation balances, the customary procedure for recording the purchase of assets. Bonds payable are recorded at their fair value by recording a discount on the bonds. After all assets and liabilities have been recorded at their fair values, an excess of cost over fair value of $139,227 remains and is recorded as goodwill.

A balance sheet prepared after the acquisition of S Company is presented in Illustration 1–1.

If an acquisition takes place within a fiscal period, purchase accounting requires the inclusion of the acquired company's income only from the date of acquisiton forward. Income earned by the acquired company prior to the date of acquisition is considered to be included in the net assets acquired.

ILLUSTRATION 1-1

Purchase
Accounting

P Company
Balance Sheet
January 1, 1980

Cash and receivables		$ 420,000
Inventories		406,000
Land		1,000,000
Buildings		1,800,000
Accumulated depreciation—Buildings		(300,000)
Equipment		240,000
Accumulated depreciation—Equipment		(90,000)
Goodwill		139,227
Total assets		$3,615,227
Current liabilities		$ 350,000
Bonds payable	$400,000	
Less: Bond discount	74,773	325,227
Common stock, $15 par, 80,000 shares outstanding		1,200,000
Premium on common stock		1,390,000
Retained earnings		350,000
Total equities		$3,615,227

Pooling of Interests Accounting

The pooling of interests method interprets a business combination as a process in which two or more groups of stockholders unite their ownership interests by an exchange of equity securities. No acquisition of one company or companies by another is recognized, because the combination is accomplished without disbursing resources of the constituents, (a corporation's stock is not considered an asset). No owners of former firms are bought out. Instead, the owners, because they continue to be stockholders, retain proprietary rights, however small, in the larger surviving firm. Accordingly, the net assets of the combining companies remain intact, although combined, and the stockholder groups also remain intact, but combined.

Proponents of pooling contend that the combination is essentially a transaction between the combining stockholder groups and, therefore, that it does not involve the corporate entities; therefore, the transaction neither requires nor justifies establishing a new basis of accountability for the assets and equities of the combined operations. Thus, fair values of assets and liabilities are ignored, except in the determination of an equitable exchange ratio of securities, and the assets acquired and liabilities assumed are carried forward to the new or surviving entity at their recorded (book) values. The equity of the acquired company is combined with the equity of the acquiring company. The allocation of the acquired company's equity among capital stock, additional paid-in capital, and retained earnings may have to be restructured, however, because of differences in the par value of the stock issued and the par value of the stock acquired (retired).

To illustrate, the pooling of interests method is applied to the preceding example. Under pooling, the initial exchange of stock is recorded as follows:

Cash and Receivables	180,000	
Inventories	116,000	
Land	120,000	
Buildings	1,000,000	
Equipment	120,000	
Premium on Common Stock	50,000	
Accumulated Depreciation—Buildings		400,000
Accumulated Depreciation—Equipment		40,000
Current Liabilities		150,000
Bonds Payable		400,000
Common Stock (30,000 × 15)		450,000
Retained Earnings		146,000

Notice that the entry above records the assets and liabilities of S Company on P Company's books at their preacquisition book values. Common stock is recorded at its par value to comply with incorporation laws regarding legal capital. An adjustment in stockholders' equity is required because of the difference between the par value of stock issued, $450,000, and the par value of S Company stock acquired, $300,000. Where the amount of the par or stated value of the combined entity ($750,000 + $450,000 = $1,200,000) exceeds the total of the par or stated value of the separate combining entities ($750,000 + $300,000 = $1,050,000), the excess should be deducted first from the *combined* other contributed capital and then from *combined* retained earnings.[3] Since the par value of the stock issued exceeds the par value of the stock acquired by $150,000, the excess serves to reduce S Company premium on common stock ($100,000) to zero, and the remaining $50,000 reduces P Company premium on common stock, as indicated in the entry above. As a result, all of S Company's retained earnings of $146,000 will be combined with the retained earnings of P Company to constitute the surviving entity's retained earnings.

Note that it is the combined other contributed capital of both companies that is reduced before any reduction in combined retained earnings. For example, if the par value of the stock issued by P Company was $900,000, the entire premium on common stock of P Company would be eliminated and the following entry made for the exchange of stock. (The assets and liabilities would be recorded at book values as in the previous entry. In the entries that follow, the net effect will be recorded as "net assets," so that attention can be directed toward the items that would be different, i.e., the equity structure.)

Net Assets	546,000	
Premium on Common Stock	400,000	
Common Stock		900,000
Retained Earnings		46,000

[3] *Ibid.,* par. 53.

The par value of the stock issued ($900,000) exceeds the par value of the stock acquired ($300,000) by $600,000, which serves to reduce S Company premium on common stock by $100,000, P Company premium on common stock by $400,000, and S Comapny retained earnings by $100,000. The remainder of S Company's retained earnings ($46,000) is then combined with P Company's retained earnings to constitute the total retained earnings of the surviving company.

If the par value of the stock issued is only slightly greater than the par value of the stock acquired, some of the acquired company's other contributed capital will be combined with that of the acquiring company. Assume, for example, that the par value of the stock issued in the situation above was $375,000. The following entry would be made for the exchange of stock:

Net Assets	546,000	
Common Stock		375,000
Retained Earnings		146,000
Premium on Common Stock		25,000

The par value of stock issued ($375,000) exceeds the par value of the stock acquired ($300,000) by $75,000, which serves to reduce the amount of S Company's premium on common stock by $75,000; the remaining $25,000 represents a portion of combined premium on common stock.

Where the amount of the par or stated value of the combined entity is *less* than the total of the par or stated value of the combining entities, the difference is an addition to the combined other contributed capital. No portion of the difference is ever carried to combined retained earnings. For example, if the par value of the stock issued in the situation above was $225,000, the following stock exchange entry on the books of P Company would be appropriate:

Net Assets	546,000	
Common Stock		225,000
Retained Earnings		146,000
Premium on Common Stock		175,000

In summary, combined retained earnings may be equal to or less than the total of the precombination retained earnings of the constituents, but it can never be greater than that amount.

A postacquisition balance sheet for P Company under the pooling approach, based upon the initial situation where P Company exchanged 30,000 shares of its common stock for the stock of S Company, is presented in Illustration 1–2.

If the combination had taken place within one fiscal period, the individual revenue and expense balances of S Company would also have been carried forward to be combined with those of P Company. Any corporation that applies the pooling method of accounting to a combination should report results of operations for the period in which the combination occurs as though the companies had been combined as of the beginning of the period. Results of operations for that period, therefore, is the sum of

ILLUSTRATION 1–2

Pooling Accounting	P Company Balance Sheet January 1, 1980	

Cash and receivables	$ 430,000
Inventories	376,000
Land	720,000
Buildings	1,800,000
Accumulated depreciation—Buildings	(700,000)
Equipment	300,000
Accumulated depreciation—Equipment	(130,000)
Total assets	$2,796,000
Current liabilities	$ 350,000
Bonds payable	400,000
Common stock, $15 par, 80,000 shares outstanding	1,200,000
Premium on common stock	350,000
Retained earnings	496,000
Total equities	$2,796,000

results of (1) operations of the *separate* companies as if they had been combined from the beginning of the fiscal period to the date the combination is consummated and (2) the *combined* operations from that date to the end of the period.[4] Under pooling accounting, all expenses incurred to effect a business combination are deducted in determining the net income of the resulting combined company for the period in which the expenses are incurred.

FINANCIAL STATEMENT
DIFFERENCES BETWEEN ACCOUNTING METHODS

The purchase and pooling of interests methods cannot be considered alternatives in accounting for a specific business combination. Two business combinations may be very similar, yet one may be accounted for as a purchase and the other as a pooling. By careful planning of the combination, the constituents can determine which method should be used. Therefore, it is important to understand the differences in financial statements that result from the use of the two methods.

A comparison of Illustrations 1–1 and 1–2 shows that total assets under the purchase method in the situation described exceed those under the pooling method by $819,227, of which $139,227 represents the intangible, goodwill. The remaining $680,000 reflects the excess of the fair value of the assets of S Company over their precombination book value. To the extent that this $680,000 relates to inventory or

[4]*Ibid.*, par. 56.

depreciable assets, under the purchase method, future income charges will be greater, and reported net income less. Inventory effects are normally reflected in income during the first period subsequent to combination if the first-in, first-out (FIFO) inventory method is used by the surviving entity; under the last-in, first-out (LIFO) method, the effect is not reflected unless inventory quantities are reduced sufficiently in future periods. Depreciation charges will be greater under the purchase method over the remaining useful lives of the depreciable assets. Also, goodwill and bond discount must be amortized to future periods. Thus, pooling generally reports greater future earnings per share.

The schedule below shows the amount by which income under the purchase method would be less than it would be under pooling of interests, in the situation described, for the first period subsequent to combination. Assume that the FIFO inventory method is used, the remaining economic lives of buildings and equipment are 20 and 8 years, respectively, goodwill is amortized over the maximum period allowed, 40 years, and bond discount is amortized on a straight-line basis.

	PURCHASE	POOLING	DIFFERENCE
Building Depreciation (20 years)	75,000	55,000	20,000
Equipment Depreciation (8 years)	18,750	21,250	(2,500)
Amortization of Goodwill (40 years)	3,481	-0-	3,481
Bond Discount Amortization (10 years)	7,477	-0-	7,477
Inventory Added to Cost of Sales	406,000	376,000	30,000
Total	510,708	452,250	58,458

In addition, the future sale of any S Company assets combined will normally produce a greater gain (or lower loss) under pooling of interests since the assets are carried at lower precombination book values. The stockholders' equity sections of the balance sheets are considerably different under the two methods. The purchase method reports total stockholders' equity of $2,940,000, whereas the pooling method reports $2,046,000. This combination of lower stockholders' equity and higher reported earnings under pooling tends to produce a doubling effect on return on stockholders' equity. For example, assume a reported net income of $315,000 (ignoring income taxes) under the purchase method for the first full year after combination. Computation of the return on stockholders' equity would be:

Purchase method = 315,000 ÷ 2,940,000 = 10.7%
Pooling method = 373,458 (315,000 + 58,458) ÷ 2,046,000 = 18.3%

Thus, pooling reports a significantly greater return on stockholders' equity.

PURCHASE VERSUS POOLING—AN HISTORICAL SUMMARY[5]

Prior to the 1940's, the vast majority of business combinations were accounted for as purchases, that is, as the acquisition by one company of one or more other companies. Although some recognition of the possibility of combining assets and equities at their book values existed as early as the 1920's, most combinations using this approach entailed a change in form of organization without any real change in substance. For example, two subsidiaries of a given parent company might be combined into one company, or a parent company might dissolve an existing subsidiary and make it a part of the legal structure of the parent. In such situations the overall operating entity remained the same, and there seemed little reason to change the basis of accountability, particularly in the absence of arm's-length bargaining as a basis for the establishment of new values.

The term "pooling of interests" was used in the 1940's in rate-base cases before the Federal Power Commission to describe a combination situation where the constituents were so closely related that any arm's-length bargaining was questionable. The resulting combined entity wished, for obvious reasons, to use higher current values of assets at the time of combination as the basis for establishing appropriate rates. The Commission ruled, essentially, that no new values were appropriate, since the companies had mutually agreed to pool their interests and no sale had taken place in which one party disposed of an interest and another party acquired that interest. Thus, the term "pooling of interests" was used to describe a situation or transaction rather than a method of accounting.

During the late 1940's an increasing number of business combinations were effected through an exchange of equity securities. Combinations with similar characteristics were described as poolings of interests in some situations and as purchases in others. No definitive criteria for distinguishing purchases from poolings had been developed. The Committee on Accounting Procedure of the American Institute of Accountants (the predecessor organization to the American Institute of Certified Public Accountants) studied the situation and in 1950 issued *Accounting Research Bulletin No. 40*. A pooling of interests was described as a combination in which all or substantially all of the equity interests in the predecessor companies continued in the surviving entity, essentially in proportion to their interests in the predecessor companies. In addition, *ARB No. 40* stated that a pooling would normally involve companies of relatively the same size, with continuity of management or the power to control management. Furthermore, a pooling would normally involve companies whose business activities were similar or complementary. Where these conditions did not exist, a purchase was deemed the appropriate method by which to effect a combination.

Because many combinations did not clearly meet all of the criteria for pooling, and because *ARB No. 40* provided no guide as to the relative importance of the criteria, similar combinations continued to be accounted for in different ways, sometimes as poolings and sometimes as purchases. In practice, the relative-size test

[5]This section draws heavily upon *Accounting Research Study No. 5*, "A Critical Study of Accounting for Business Combinations," by Arthur Wyatt (New York: AICPA, 1963).

gradually deteriorated as a guide to determining the proper classification of the transaction. In 1957, in an effort to clarify the pooling criteria, the Committee on Accounting Procedure issued *Accounting Research Bulletin No. 48*. In *ARB No. 48* the criteria in *Bulletin No. 40* were reiterated, except that the relative-size test was modified to permit pooling for combinations with as great a size disparity as 90%— 10% or 95%—5%. *ARB No. 48* also concluded that "no one of the factors ... would necessarily be determinative and any one factor might have varying degrees of significance in different cases; however, their presence or absence would be cumulative in effect ... determination as to whether a particular combination is a purchase or pooling should be made in light of all attendant circumstances."[6]

Because of its failure to specify the necessary degree of conformity with the pooling criteria, *ARB No. 48* had little impact on practice. In essence, a given combination could be accounted for either as a pooling of interests or as a purchase. Just as the relative-size test had deteriorated earlier, the "continuity of ownership interests" criterion also deteriorated. The notion that relative equity interests should continue in the new or surviving entity implies, for example, that common stock should be issued for common stock. If preferred stock or other types of securities were issued for common stock, continuity of ownership interests would not exist, and pooling would not be appropriate. During the 1960's the continuity-of-ownership-interests criterion deteriorated to such a degree that many combinations were treated as poolings even though a variety of securities such as convertible preferred stock and convertible bonds were exchanged for common stock, and as a result, the nature of the ownership interests substantially changed. In addition, a procedure of "partial pooling" developed. Under this procedure a combination could be consummated by an exchange of cash and stock of the surviving company for the common stock of the other constituents, and the cash portion could be accounted for as a purchase and the common stock portion as a pooling. By the latter part of the 1960's combinors had considerable freedom in practice to account for a combination by either the purchase or pooling methods, regardless of the form of the combination. Thus, the development of better criteria to distinguish between combinations that constitute purchases and combinations that constitute poolings of interests was needed. The Accounting Principles Board made the solution of this problem one of their major tasks and issued *APB Opinion No. 16*, "Busines Combinations," in August 1970.

In *Opinion No. 16* the Board concluded:

> ... that the purchase method and the pooling of interests method are both acceptable in accounting for business combinations, although not as alternatives in accounting for the same business combination. A business combination which meets specified conditions requires accounting by the pooling of interests method. A new basis of accounting is not permitted for a combination that meets the specified conditions, and the assets and liabilities of the combining companies are combined at their recorded amounts. All other business combinations should be accounted for as an acquisition of one or more companies by a corporation.[7]

---

[6]*Accounting Research Bulletin No. 48*, "Business Combinations" *(op. cit.)*, par. 7.
[7]*APB Opinion No. 16, "Business Combinations," op. cit.*, par. 8.

Thus, *Opinion No. 16* removes the purchase-pooling option. Only the interpretation of the facts of an actual or contemplated combination can determine which method is required.

In *Opinion No. 16* the Board established twelve specific conditions; if *all* are met, use of the pooling method is required. These twelve conditions are presented in the Appendix. In simplified terms, the Board holds that combinations effected by pure common-for-common stock exchanges (with no contingency clauses, unusual extra agreements, convertible or otherwise complex securities) must be accounted for as poolings; all other combinations must be treated as purchases.

Paragraphs 45–48 of *Opinion No. 16* spell out the conditions under which pooling is required. All of these conditions must prevail. The main points are summarized as follows: (a) independent ownership interests are combined to continue previously separate operations; (b) all or nearly all of the common shares of one company are acquired in exchange for another firm's common shares, and all stockholders retain the same relative and unrestricted rights, in a single transaction that involves no planned or contingent realignment of rights in the near future; and (c) an intention must exist to continue substantially all of the operations and normal stockholder relationships of the combining companies. *Opinion No. 16* drops the relative-size and management-continuity tests, attempts to define criteria clearly, removes any choice of method (other than that provided by judicious planning of a combination's terms), and prohibits partial pooling.

Advantages and disadvantages, both theoretical and practical, may be noted for both methods. Pooling is criticized on the ground that values given and received are ignored in a negotiated transaction. Under pre-*Opinion No. 16* practices, "instant earnings" are alleged to have resulted (a) from the early sale of newly pooled assets that were carried at their precombination (and often quite low) book values, and (b) from a reporting practice that required that the surviving firm report earnings for the year of combination as if it had been combined during that entire year, even though the combination may have occurred well along in that year, or even after the fiscal year-end but before publication of the financial statements.

Pooling is defended, on the other hand, on the grounds that it is more objective than the purchase method (no appraisals of assets or stock values are necessary), that it properly continues generally accepted accounting principles rather than introducing extensive appraisal-based data, and that it avoids accounting for one part of the combined company on a fair value basis and the other part on a historical cost basis.

Those who endorse the purchase method believe that one company clearly acquires another in almost every business combination, and that control passes to the dominant corporation in a transaction bargained on the basis of current fair values given and received, regardless of the nature of the consideration. However, with the purchase method problems are alleged to exist with regard to objective determination of current values and the apparent inconsistency of accounting for only part of the combined company on an updated basis. Goodwill and the related amortization charges may materially affect financial reports, although, being derived from current valuations (appraisals, etc.) of stock issued and assets received, they are less than convincing measures.

Although *Opinion No. 16* overall has improved business combination accounting and reporting, the basic purchase versus pooling controversy remains. The Financial Accounting Standards Board currently has the topic under study, and it has issued a discussion memorandum and set public hearings. Thus, new requirements may be forthcoming.

PRO FORMA STATEMENTS

Pro forma statements, sometimes called "as if" statements, are prepared to show the effect of planned or contemplated transactions. Many management decisions have a potential impact on the firm's financial statements, so it is often useful to demonstrate the effect of a proposed decision by preparing financial statements as they would appear if that decision were followed. Thus, pro forma statements have wide application in the internal decision-making process.

Pro forma statements may also be used for external purposes. They are often used for proposed business combinations. After the boards of directors of the constituents have reached tentative agreement on a combination proposal, for example, pro forma statements showing the final effect of the proposal may be prepared for distribution to the shareholders of the constituents for their consideration prior to voting on the proposal. If the proposed combination involves the issue of new securities under Securities and Exchange Commission rules, pro forma statements may be required as part of the registration statement.

When a pro forma statement is prepared, the tentative or hypothetical nature of the statement should be clearly indicated, generally by describing it as "pro forma" in the heading and including a description of the character of the transactions given effect to. Further description of any other adjustments should be clearly stated on the statement or in related notes. A pro forma balance sheet for the preceding example of P Company's acquisition of S Company that might be prepared for use by the companies' stockholders is presented in Illustration 1–3.

The normal procedure is to show the audited balance sheet as of a given date, individual adjustments for the proposed transaction, and resulting account balances.

Other types of "pro forma" presentation are required by *APB Opinion No. 16*. For example, if a business combination occurred during the year and is accounted for by the purchase method, notes to financial statements should include on a pro forma basis:

1. Results of operations for the current year as though the companies had combined at the beginning of the year, unless the acquisition was at or near the beginning of the year.

2. Results of operations for the immediately preceding period as though the companies had combined at the beginning of that period if comparative financial statements are presented.

ILLUSTRATION 1–3
P Company
Pro Forma Balance Sheet
Giving Effect to Proposed Issue of Common Stock for All of the
Common Stock of S Company Under Purchase Accounting
December 31, 1979

ASSETS	AUDITED BALANCE SHEET	ADJUSTMENTS	PRO FORMA BALANCE SHEET
Cash and Receivables	$ 250,000	$ 170,000	$ 420,000
Inventories	260,000	146,000	406,000
Land	600,000	400,000	1,000,000
Buildings	800,000	1,000,000	1,800,000
Accumulated Depreciation—Buildings	(300,000)		(300,000)
Equipment	180,000	60,000	240,000
Accumulated Depreciation—Equipment	(90,000)		(90,000)
Goodwill	–0–	139,227	139,227
Total Assets	$1,700,000		$3,615,227
EQUITIES			
Current Liabilities	$ 200,000	150,000	350,000
Bonds Payable	–0–	325,227	325,227
Common Stock	750,000	450,000	1,200,000
Premium on Common Stock	400,000	990,000	1,390,000
Retained Earnings	350,000		350,000
Total Equities	$1,700,000		$3,615,227

Such pro forma presentation for prior years is limited to the immediately preceding year. Similarly, where a business combination has taken place during the period and is accounted for by the pooling method, financial statements and financial information of the separate companies presented for prior years should be restated on a combined basis to furnish comparative information.

APPENDIX: SPECIFIC CONDITIONS FOR POOLING OF INTERESTS

I. Attributes of the combining companies:

1. Each of the combining companies is autonomous and has not been a subsidiary or division of another corporation within two years before the plan of combination is initiated.

2. Each of the combining companies is independent of the other combining companies. This condition means that at the dates the plan of combination is

initiated and consummated the combining companies hold as intercorporate investments no more than 10 percent in total of the outstanding voting common stock of any combining company.

II. Conditions relating to the exchange to effect the combination:

1. The combination is effected in a single transaction or is completed in accordance with a specific plan within one year after the plan is initiated.

2. A corporation offers and issues only common stock with rights identical to those of the majority of its outstanding voting common stock in exchange for substantially all of the voting common stock interest of another company at the date the plan of combination is consummated. Substantially all of the voting common stock means 90 percent or more for this condition.

3. None of the combining companies changes the equity interest of the voting common stock in contemplation of effecting the combination either within two years before the plan of combination is initiated or between the dates the combination is initiated and consummated; changes in contemplation of effecting the combination may include distributions to stockholders and additional issuances, exchanges, and retirements of securities.

4. Each of the combining companies reacquires shares of voting common stock only for purposes other than business combinations, and no company reacquires more than a normal number of shares between the dates the plan of combination is initiated and consummated.

5. The ratio of the interest of an individual common stockholder to those of other common stockholders in a combining company remains the same as a result of the exchange of stock to effect the combination.

6. The voting rights to which the common stock ownership interests in the resulting combined corporation are entitled are exercisable by the stockholders; the stockholders are neither deprived of nor restricted in exercising those rights for a period.

7. The combination is resolved at the date the plan is consummated and no provisions of the plan relating to the issue of securities or other consideration are pending.   NO CONTIGENCIES

III. Absence of planned transactions:

1. The combined corporation does not agree directly or indirectly to retire or reacquire all or part of the common stock issued to effect the combination.

2. The combined corporation does not enter into other financial arrangements for the benefit of the former stockholders of a combining company, such as a guaranty of loans secured by stock issued in the combination, which in effect negates the exchange of equity securities.

3. The combined corporation does not intend or plan to dispose of a significant part of the assets of the combining companies within two years after the combination other than disposals in the ordinary course of business of the formerly separate companies and to eliminate duplicate facilities or excess capacity.

Questions

1. Distinguish between internal and external expansion of a firm.

2. List five advantages of a business combination.

3. Business combinations are classified as to structure into three types. Identify and define these types.

4. Distinguish among a statutory merger, a statutory consolidation, and a stock acquisition.

5. What conditions must exist if the issuance of a single class of stock in a business combination is to result in fair treatment to all parties?

6. If expected earnings are to be capitalized in the determination of the total value of stock to be issued to the stockholders of the companies involved in a business combination, what limits should be placed on the capitalization rate selected?

7. Discuss the basic differences between the purchase method and the pooling of interest method.

8. What are pro forma financial statements? What is their purpose?

9. What is the primary legal constraint on business combinations? Why does such a constraint exist?

10. Define a tender offer and describe its use.

11. When stock is exchanged for stock in a business combination, how is the stock exchange ratio generally expressed?

12. Describe the treatment that must be applied to other contributed capital and retained earnings of constituents of a business combination under a pooling of interests, (a) when

the par value of the new company is more than the total of the par values of the constituents, and (b) when the par value of the new company is less than the total par values of the constituents.

13. In January, 1980, Conglomerate Company acquired 90% of the outstanding common stock of Beatle Company in exchange for Conglomerate Company common stock as part of a business combination plan initiated in April, 1979. Beatle Company was incorporated in February, 1978 as a new venture. At the date the combination plan was initiated, Conglomerate Company owned 5% of Beatle Company stock which it had acquired for cash during the preceding year. One of Beatle Company's major facilities is a chemical synthesis plant similar to one operated by Conglomerate Company. Conglomerate's directors see no need to maintain two such operations and plan to dispose of Beatle's plant soon after combination. Is this combination, considering only the facts given, eligible for the pooling of interests accounting treatment?

Problems

Problem 1–1

Stockholders of X Company, Y Company, and Z Company have agreed to consolidate and form a new corporation, BZ-Inc. Asset values and expected earnings contributions of the constituents just prior to combination are:

	X COMPANY	Y COMPANY	Z COMPANY
Net assets at appraised values (before goodwill)	2,000,000	1,500,000	1,000,000
Expected annual earnings contributions	180,000	150,000	120,000

Stockholders of the constituents are considering the following plan for the combination:

BZ-Inc. will issue two classes of stock, 8%, fully participating, $100 par preferred, and $20 par common. Expected earnings will be capitalized at 8% to determine the total stock to be issued. Preferred stock will be issued for net assets contributed, and common stock for the difference between total value given and the preferred stock issued. Common stock is considered payment for goodwill.

Required:

A. Compute the total number of shares to be given to the stockholders of each constituent company.
B. Prepare the journal entry that would be made on the books of BZ-Inc. for the issue of the stock.
C. Calculate the amount and percent of earnings that would be distributed to the former stockholders of X, Y, and Z Companies, assuming that BZ-Inc. has earnings of $506,250 in the first year subsequent to consolidation and that the entire earnings are distributed.

Problem 1–2

After negotiation, May Company and Peter Corporation have agreed to consolidate their companies into a new entity, Peter May, Inc. Financial information for the two companies just prior to consolidation is as follows:

FAIR MARKET VALUES	MAY COMPANY	PETER CORPORATION
Current assets	$125,500	$ 74,500
Long-term assets	530,000	410,000
Current liabilities	95,000	92,500
Long-term liabilities	217,200	184,600

During negotiations, the committee determined that estimated earnings contributions would be $110,000 for May Co. and $43,000 for Peter Corp. Under the consolidation plan, earnings are to be capitalized at 15%; $100 par, 8% cumulative, fully participating preferred stock will be issued for net assets contributed, and $20 par common stock will be issued for remaining values.

Required:

A. Determine the quantity of each class of stock to be issued.
B. If May Co. has 10,000 shares and Peter Corp. has 5,000 shares of common stock outstanding prior to consolidation, what exchange ratios will be established?
C. Explain Peter's much higher exchange ratio on common stock.
D. At the end of Year 1, Peter May, Inc. reported a net income of $175,000. Assuming that all first-year profits are to be distributed to stockholders, calculate the amount of dividends to be received by each class of stock.
E. Calculate the amount and percent of total earnings that will be distributed to the former stockholders of May and Peter Companies, assuming that the total earnings are distributed.

Problem 1–3

Condensed balance sheets for Becker Company and Crayton Company on January 1, 1980 are as follows:

	BECKER	CRAYTON
Current Assets	$ 400,000	$250,000
Plant and Equipment (net)	700,000	350,000
Total Assets	$1,100,000	$600,000
Total Liabilities	$ 180,000	$110,000
Capital Stock, $15 par	600,000	450,000
Contributed Capital in Excess of Par	170,000	70,000
Retained Earnings (Deficit)	150,000	(30,000)
Total Equities	$1,100,000	$600,000

On January 1, 1980, the stockholders of Becker and Crayton Companies agreed to a consolidation whereby a new corporation, Adel Company, would be formed to consolidate Becker and Crayton. Adel Company issued 47,000 shares of its $25 par capital stock for all of the oustanding stock of Becker and Crayton Companies.

On the date of consolidation the fair value of Becker and Crayton Companies' current assets and liabilities was equal to their book values. The fair value of plant and equipment for each company was: Becker, $880,000; Crayton, $500,000.

The investment banking house of Blythe, Packer and Company estimated that the fair value of Adel Company's stock was $40 per share.

Prepare a journal entry to record the consolidation on the books of Adel Company, assuming that:

(a) The consolidation is accounted for as a pooling of interest.

(b) The consolidation is accounted for as a purchase.

Problem 1–4

Stockholders of X Company, Y Company, and Z Company are considering alternative arrangements for a business combination. Balance sheets and the fair value of each company's assets on October 1, 1980 were as follows:

	X CO.	Y CO.	Z CO.
Assets	$2,000,000	$2,750,000	$250,000
Liabilities	$1,425,000	750,000	87,500
Capital Stock ($10 par)	750,000	500,000	125,000
Other Contributed Capital		200,000	62,500
Retained Earnings (deficit)	(175,000)	1,300,000	(25,000)
Total Equities	$2,000,000	$2,750,000	$250,000
Fair Value of Assets	$2,400,000	$3,300,000	$300,000

X Company shares have a fair value of $18. A fair (market) price is not available for shares of the other companies because they are closely held.

Prepare a balance sheet for the business combination for each of the following assumptions:

(a) X Company acquires all of the assets and assumes all of the liabilities of Y and Z Companies by issuing in exchange 150,000 shares of its stock to Y Company and 12,500 shares of its stock to Z Company. The combination is treated as a purchase.

(b) X Company issues shares as in (a) above, but the combination is treated as a pooling of interests.

(c) A new corporation, W Company, is formed to take over the assets and to assume the liabilities of X, Y, and Z Companies. The new company issues no-par stock with a stated value of $6 as follows: to X Company, 75,000 shares; to Y Company, 150,000 shares; to Z Company, 12,500 shares. The combination is treated as a pooling of interests.

Problem 1–5

Effective December 31, 1981, Wesco Corporation proposes to issue additional shares of its common stock in exchange for all of the assets and liabilities of Southco Corporation and Eastco Corporation, after which Southco and Eastco will distribute the Wesco stock to their stockholders in complete liquidation and dissolution. The plan of combination has been carefully developed so as to comply with the criteria for a pooling of interests. Balance sheets of each of the corporations immediately prior to merger on December 31, 1981 are given below. The common stock exchange ratio was negotiated to be 1:1 for both Southco and Eastco.

	WESCO	SOUTHCO	EASTCO
Current Assets	$ 2,000,000	$ 500,000	$ 25,000
Fixed Assets (net)	10,000,000	4,000,000	200,000
Total	$12,000,000	$4,500,000	$225,000
Current Liabilities	$ 1,000,000	$ 300,000	$ 20,000
Long-term Debt	3,000,000	1,000,000	105,000
Common Stock ($10 par)	3,000,000	1,000,000	50,000
Retained Earnings	5,000,000	2,200,000	50,000
Total	$12,000,000	$4,500,000	$225,000

Required:

A. Prepare Wesco's journal entries to record the combination of Wesco, Southco, and Eastco.

B. Assume that the combination fails to meet the criteria for a pooling of interests, because Eastco had not been an autonomous entity for two years prior to the combination. The identifiable assets and liabilities of Southco and Eastco are all reflected in the balance sheets (above), and their recorded amounts are equal to their current fair market values. Wesco's common stock is traded actively and has a current market price of $45. Prepare Wesco's journal entries to record the combination.

(AICPA adapted)

Problem 1–6

On January 1, 1980, Finnerty Fashions acquired all of the assets and assumed all of the liabilities of Meyers Materials and merged Meyers into Finnerty. In exchange for the net assets of Meyers, Finnerty gave its bonds payable with a maturity value of $300,000, a stated interest rate of 7%, interest payable semiannually on June 30 and December 31, a maturity date of January 1, 1990, and a yield rate of 8%.

Balance sheets for Finnerty and Meyers (in addition to fair value data) on January 1, 1980 were as follows:

| | FINNERTY | MEYERS | |
	BOOK VALUE	BOOK VALUE	FAIR VALUE
Cash	$ 140,000	$ 52,500	$ 52,500
Receivables	157,200	61,450	56,200
Inventories	374,120	110,110	134,220
Land	425,000	75,000	210,000
Buildings	370,555	165,475	187,510
Accumulated Depreciation—Bldgs.	(110,050)	(144,455)	(163,690)
Equipment	111,545	72,710	65,480
Accumulated Depreciation—Equip.	(32,600)	(55,005)	(49,535)
Total Assets	$1,435,770	$337,785	
Current Liabilities	$ 133,335	$ 41,115	$ 41,115
Bonds Payable, 8% due 1/1/98,			
interest payable 6/30 and 12/31		150,000*	
Common Stock, $10 par	500,000		
Common Stock, $5 par		100,000	
Additional Paid-in Capital	600,000	40,000	
Retained Earnings	202,435	6,670	
Total Equities	$1,435,770	$337,785	

*The yield rate on bonds with similar risk is 10% on the date of acquisition.

Prepare the journal entry on the books of Finnerty Fashions to record the acquisition of Meyers' assets and liabilities in exchange for the bonds. (*Hint:* You must first calculate the present value of the bonds given.)

Problem 1–7

Using the data in Problem 1–6, assume that Finnerty Fashions exchanged 15,000 shares of its unissued common stock for all of the outstanding common stock of Meyers Materials (instead of exchanging bonds) and that all conditions for pooling of interests accounting are met.

Record the exchange of stock on the books of Finnerty Fashions.

Problem 1–8

The boards of directors of Kessler Corporation, Bar Company, Cohen, Inc., and Mason Corporation are meeting jointly to discuss plans for a business combination. Each of the corporations has one class of common stock outstanding; Bar also has one class of preferred stock outstanding. Although terms have not been settled as yet, Kessler will be the acquiring or issuing corporation. Because the directors want to conform to generally accepted accounting principles, they have asked you to attend the meeting as an adviser.

Required:

Consider each of the following questions independently and answer each in accordance with generally accepted accounting principles.

A. Assume that the combination will be consummated August 31, 1981. Explain the philosophy underlying the accounting and how the balance sheet accounts of each of the four corporations will appear on Kessler's consolidated balance sheet on September 1, 1981, if the combination is accounted for as a
   (1) Pooling of interests.
   (2) Purchase.

B. Assume that the combination will be consummated August 31, 1981. Explain how the income statement accounts of each of the four corporations will be accounted for in preparing Kessler's consolidated income statement for the year ended December 31, 1981, if the combination is accounted for as a
   (1) Pooling of interests.
   (2) Purchase.

C. Some of the directors believe that the terms of the combination should be agreed upon immediately and that the method of accounting to be used (whether pooling, purchase, or a mixture) may be chosen at some later date. Others believe that the terms of the combination and the method to be used are very closely related. Which position is correct?

D. Kessler and Mason are comparable in size; Cohen and Bar are much smaller. How do these facts affect the choice of accounting method?

E. Bar was formerly a subsidiary of Tucker Corporation, which has no other relationship to any of the four companies discussing combination. Eighteen months ago Tucker voluntarily spun off Bar. What effect, if any, do these facts have on the choice of accounting method?

F. Kessler holds 2,000 of Bar's 10,000 outstanding shares of preferred stock and 15,000 of Cohen's 100,000 outstanding shares of common stock. All of Kessler's holdings were acquired during the first three months of 1981. What effect, if any, do these facts have on the choice of accounting method?

G. It is almost certain that Mrs. Victor Mason, Sr., who holds 5% of Mason's common stock, will object to the combination. Assume that Kessler is able to acquire only 95% (rather than 100%) of Mason's stock, issuing Kessler common stock in exchange.

(1) What accounting method is applicable?

(2) If Kessler is able to acquire the remaining 5% at some future time—in five years, for instance—in exchange for its own common stock, which accounting method will be applicable to this second acquisition?

H. Since the directors feel that one of Mason's major divisions will not be compatible with the operations of the combined company, they anticipate that it will be sold as soon as possible after the combination is consummated. They expect to have no trouble in finding a buyer. What effect, if any, do these facts have on the choice of accounting method?

(AICPA adapted)

Problem 1–9

Balance sheets for Able Company and Baker Company on December 31, 1979 appear as follows:

ASSETS	ABLE	BAKER
Cash	$ 125,000	$ 200,000
Receivables	175,000	288,000
Inventories	225,000	312,000
Fixed Assets	1,000,000	1,500,000
Total Assets	$1,525,000	$2,300,000
EQUITIES		
Current Liabilities	$ 250,000	$ 325,000
Mortgage Payable	188,000	225,000
Common Stock, $20 par	500,000	1,000,000
Premium on Common Stock	275,000	375,000
Retained Earnings	312,000	375,000
Total Equities	$1,525,000	$2,300,000

Baker Company tentatively plans to issue 40,000 shares of its $20 par stock, which has a current market value of $33 per share net of commissions and other issue costs. Baker Company then plans to acquire the assets and liabilities of Able Company for a cash payment of $1,000,000 and $500,000 in long-term 8% notes payable. Baker Company's receivables include $80,000 owed by Able Company. Baker Company is willing to pay more than the net book value of Able Company assets, because fixed assets are undervalued by $300,000 and Able Company has historically earned above-normal profits and is, therefore, considered to have some unrecorded goodwill.

Prepare a pro forma balance sheet showing the effect of these planned transactions.

2

Consolidated Statements – Date of Acquisition

In Chapter 1 attention was directed toward accounting for business combinations arising from statutory mergers and consolidations. As you recall, in those situations the acquiring company survived and the acquired company or companies ceased to exist as separate legal entities. Our concern in this chapter is with accounting practices followed in a situation in which one company controls the activities of another company through the direct or indirect ownership of a **majority** of its voting stock.

In such a situation the acquiring company is generally referred to as the **parent** and the acquired company as a **subsidiary.** Those holding any remaining stock in a subsidiary are referred to as the **minority interest.** Any joint relationship is termed an *affiliation* and the related companies are called affiliated companies. Each of the affiliated companies continues its separate legal existence, and the investing company carries its interest as an investment.

A corporate affiliation may, of course, consist of more than two companies. A parent may obtain a majority of the voting stock of several subsidiaries. If one or more of the subsidiaries owns a controlling interest in one or more other companies, a chain of ownership is forged by which the parent company controls, either directly or indirectly, the activities of the other companies. Many large American conglomerates have been formed by a variety of indirect ownerships.

Subsidiary Defined

Although the term subsidiary is used with several meanings in practice, in this text it is used to refer to a situation where a parent (and/or the parent's other subsidiaries) owns more than 50% of the voting shares of another company. The critical criterion in this definition is the percentage of ownership, more than 50%, of the voting shares. The

Securities and Exchange Commission defines a subsidiary as "an affiliate controlled by another entity, directly or indirectly, through one or more intermediaries. Control means the possession, direct or indirect, of the power to direct or cause the direction of the management and policies of another entity, whether through the ownership of voting shares, by contract, or otherwise."

The SEC distinguishes majority-owned, totally held, and wholly owned subsidiaries. The term *majority-owned* means a subsidiary more than 50% of whose outstanding voting shares are owned by its parent and/or the parent's other majority-owned subsidiaries. (The definition of subsidiary used in this book is the same as the SEC's definition of a majority-owned subsidiary.) The term **totally held** means a subsidiary (1) substantially all of whose outstanding equity securities are owned by its parent and/or the parent's other totally held subsidiaries, and (2) which is not indebted to any person other than its parent and/or the parent's other totally held subsidiaries, in an amount that is material in relation to the particular subsidiary. The term *wholly owned* means a subsidiary all of whose outstanding voting shares are owned by its parent and/or the parent's other wholly owned subsidiaries.

The Accounting Principles Board in *APB Opinion No. 18,* explains that the term *subsidiary* "refers to a corporation which is controlled, directly or indirectly, by another corporation. The usual condition for control is ownership of a majority (over 50%) of the outstanding voting stock. The power to control may also exist with a lesser percentage of ownership, for example, by contract, lease, agreement with other stockholders or by court decree."

REASONS FOR SUBSIDIARY COMPANIES

There are several advantages to acquiring the *majority* of the voting stock of another company rather than all of its resources. For example:

1. Stock acquisition is relatively simple. Stock can be acquired by open market purchases or by cash tender offers to the subsidiary's stockholders. Such acquisitions avoid the often lengthy and difficult negotiations that are required in an exchange of stock for stock in a complete takeover.

2. Control of the subsidiary's operations can be accomplished with a much smaller investment, since only a majority (more than 50%) of the stock need be obtained.

3. The separate legal existence of the individual affiliates provides an element of protection of the parent's assets from attachment by creditors of the subsidiary. A parent may sometimes establish a subsidiary by forming a new corporation rather than simply adding a division to the existing company. The limited liability characteristic of the corporate form of business organization is often the reason for doing so.

CONSOLIDATED STATEMENTS

The statements prepared for a parent company and its subsidiaries are referred to as **consolidated statements.** They include the full complement of statements normally prepared for a separate entity and represent essentially the sum of the assets, liabilities, revenue, and expenses of the affiliates after eliminating the effect of any transactions among the affiliated companies. Accountants recognize that the unconsolidated financial statements of the parent company, the *legal entity,* are insufficient to present the financial position and results of operations of the *economic unit* controlled by the parent company.

As expressed by the AICPA in *Accounting Research Bulletin No. 51,* the purpose of consolidated statements is to present, primarily for the benefit of the shareholders and creditors of the parent company, the results of operations and the financial position of a parent company and its subsidiaries essentially as if the group were a single company with one or more branches or divisions. Consolidated statements are usually presumed to be necessary for a fair presentation when one of the companies in the group directly or indirectly has a controlling financial interest in the other companies. Thus, legal aspects of the separate entities are ignored, and emphasis is placed on the economic unit under control of one management, i.e., on substance rather than on legal form.

Although consolidated statements for the economic entity are considered to be more appropriate for use by the stockholders and creditors of the parent, they cannot substitute for the statements prepared by the separate legal entities involved. Creditors of the subsidiaries must look to the statements of the individual legal entities in assessing the degree of protection related to their claims. Likewise, minority shareholders need the statements of the individual companies in determining the degree of investment risk involved and the amounts available for dividends. Regulatory agencies are generally concerned with the net resources and results of operations of the individual legal entities. Consolidated statements, therefore, complement the individual entity statements for certain purposes, but they cannot replace them.

CONDITIONS FOR THE
PREPARATION OF CONSOLIDATED STATEMENTS

Certain conditions must be met before a given subsidiary is included in the consolidated statements. The basic condition is that of **control.** Three important aspects of control should be present before a subsidiary is consolidated:

1. Control should exist in fact, that is, the parent company must own, either directly or indirectly, more than 50% of the voting stock of the subsidiary.

2. Intent of control should be permanent rather than temporary. Management of the parent should intend a long-term relationship during which they intend to actively exercise control over the subsidiary. A parent should not consolidate a subsidiary that it expects to dispose of.

3. Control should rest with the majority owners, that is, the subsidiary should not be in legal reorganization or in bankruptcy.

Even though the necessary elements of control do exist, there may be some situations, such as the following, in which the subsidiary should be excluded from consolidation and its results separately disclosed.[1]

1. The minority interest in the net assets of the subsidiary is so large, in relation to the equity of the parent, that the presentation of separate financial statements would be more meaningful and useful. For example, the subsidiary may have a large amount of preferred stock outstanding that is held entirely by outside parties.

2. The activities of a subsidiary are so unrelated to those of the other subsidiaries and the parent that it would be more informative to exclude the nonhomogeneous subsidiary from consolidation and disclose its operations separately. An example would be a finance company in a group of manufacturing companies.

3. The resources of the subsidiary, such as a bank or insurance company, are so restricted by statute that they are not generally available for use throughout the consolidated group.

4. The subsidiary is a foreign company in a country that has imposed currency restrictions such that the income of the subsidiary cannot be effectively realized by the parent.

5. The difference in fiscal periods is such that consolidation would not be meaningful. Where the difference is not more than about three months,[2] however, the fiscal statements of the subsidiary can be consolidated and disclosure made of the effect of events that materially affect financial position or results of operations occurring between the close of the fiscal period and the financial statement date. Of course, the parent, since it has control, may change the fiscal period of the subsidiary to agree with that required for consolidation.

In general, the objective of consolidation should be to provide the most meaningful financial presentation possible in the circumstances. Considerable judgment must be exercised in accomplishing this objective. For example, even though several subsidiar-

---

[1] We shall see in the discussion in Chapter 3 that most subsidiaries that are excluded from consolidation for these reasons are carried as investments on the parent's balance sheet. Such investments are ordinarily accounted for by the equity method.

[2] The Securities and Exchange Commission, in Rule 4-02, Article 4, Regulation S-X, specifies that a subsidiary may be consolidated with its parent only if the difference in their closing dates is not more than 93 days.

ies' operations are nonhomogeneous, it may be better to prepare a full consolidation than to present a large number of separate statements. On the other hand, separate statements or combined statements[3] would be preferable for a subsidiary or group of subsidiaries if such statements would be more informative to shareholders and creditors of the parent company than would the inclusion of such subsidiaries in consolidation. The consolidation policy followed should be disclosed as part of the statement of significant accounting policies required by *APB Opinion No. 22*.

LIMITATIONS OF CONSOLIDATED STATEMENTS

As noted earlier, consolidated statements may have limited usefulness for minority shareholders, subsidiary creditors, and regulatory agencies. Minority shareholders and regulatory agencies can find little information of value to them in the consolidated statements because they contain no detail about the individual subsidiaries. Then, too, creditors of a specific company have claims only against the resources of that company unless the claims are guaranteed by the parent.

In addition, consolidated statements have been severely criticized in recent years by financial analysts. The strong merger movement of the 1960's produced many highly diversified companies operating across several industries. Consolidated operating results for such companies cannot be compared with industry standards; one conglomerate cannot be compared with another. This criticism is at least partially responsible for the SEC and FASB requirements regarding segment reporting, which will be discussed in Chapter 13.

Regardless of these limitations, however, consolidated statements continue to grow in importance. The vast majority of publicly held companies own one or more subsidiaries and report on a consolidated basis. Thus, consolidated statements have assumed the position of primary statements, and the separate statements of individual subsidiaries are considered supplementary.

CONSOLIDATED BALANCE SHEETS

Business units prepare two general types of financial statements, stock statements (the balance sheet or statement of financial position) and flow statements (retained earnings statement, income statement, and the statement of changes in financial position). Affiliated companies normally prepare this full set of financial statements. As of the date of acquisition of one company by another, however, the only relevant statement is the consolidated balance sheet. This statement reports the sum of the assets and equities of a parent and its subsidiaries as if they constituted a single company. Since the parent and its subsidiaries are being treated as a single entity,

---

[3]Combined statements are discussed in a later section of this chapter.

eliminations must be made to cancel the effect of transactions among them. Intercompany receivables and payables, for example, are reciprocal in nature, so they must be eliminated to avoid double counting and to avoid giving the impression that the consolidated entity owes money to itself. Likewise, any intercompany profits in assets arising from subsequent transactions must be eliminated, since an entity cannot profit on transactions with itself. The process of eliminating these types of items will be discussed in detail in later chapters.

Investment Elimination Under the Purchase Method

An important elimination, one that is basic to the preparation of consolidated statements, is the elimination of the investment account and the related subsidiary's equity. Stock acquisitions are recorded by the parent company at their *cost* (under the purchase method) by the following entry:

Investment in Subsidiary	XXXXXXXX	
Cash (other assets, stock)		XXXXXXXX

The investment account represents the investment by the parent in the net assets of the subsidiary and is, therefore, reciprocal to the subsidiary's stockholders' equity. Since the subsidiary's assets and liabilities are combined with the parent's in the consolidated balance sheet, it is necessary to eliminate the investment account of the parent against the related stockholders' equity of the subsidiary to avoid double counting of these net assets. In effect, when the parent's share of the subsidiary's equity is eliminated against the investment account, the subsidiary's net assets are substituted for the investment account on the consolidated balance sheet.

The process of combining the individual assets and liabilities of a parent and its subsidiary at the date of acquisition is discussed and illustrated in the following order:

1. The parent's cost of its investment is equal to the book value of the subsidiary stock acquired, and
   (a) The parent acquires 100% of the subsidiary's stock;
   (b) The parent acquires less than 100% of the subsidiary's stock.

2. The parent's cost of its investment *exceeds* the book value of the subsidiary's stock acquired, and less than 100% of the stock is acquired.

3. The parent's cost of its investment is *less* than the book value of the subsidiary's stock acquired, and less than 100% of the stock is acquired.

Illustrations are based on the balance sheets as of December 31, 1979 for P Company and S Company as follows.

Balance Sheet
December 31, 1979

	P COMPANY	S COMPANY
Cash	$100,000	$ 20,000
Other Current Assets	180,000	50,000
Plant and Equipment (net)	120,000	60,000
Total Assets	$400,000	$130,000
Liabilities	$ 60,000	$ 50,000
Common Stock, $10 par	200,000	50,000
Premium on Common Stock	40,000	10,000
Retained Earnings	100,000	20,000
Total Equities	$400,000	$130,000

80,000 BOOK VALUE (handwritten, bracketing the 50,000 / 10,000 / 20,000 of S Company)

Parent's Cost of Investment Equal to Book Value of Subsidiary Stock Acquired— 100% of Subsidiary Stock Acquired   Assume that on January 1, 1980, P Company acquired all of the outstanding stock (5,000 shares) of S Company for a cash payment of $80,000, after which P Company has $20,000 in cash and $80,000 in an Investment in S Company account. Data for the preparation of formal consolidated statements are normally accumulated on a workpaper on which any required adjusting and eliminating entries are made prior to combining remaining balances. Adjusting entries are those needed to correct any accounts of the affiliates that may be incorrect or to recognize the unrecorded effect of transactions that have been recorded by one party, but not by the other. Adjusting entries must ultimately be made on the books of one or more of the affiliates. In all illustrations throughout this book, letter notation is used to identify related parts of adjusting entries, and number notation to identify related parts of eliminating entries.

ALL EQUAL TO BOOK VALUE (handwritten, right margin)

A workpaper for the preparation of a consolidated balance sheet for P and S Companies on January 1, 1980, the date of acquisition, is presented in Illustration 2–1.

The workpaper entry to eliminate S Company's stockholders' equity against the investment account, in general journal form, is:

Common Stock—S Company	50,000	
Premium on Common Stock—S Company	10,000	
Retained Earnings—S Company	20,000	
Investment in S Company		80,000

Although it is expressed in general journal form, this entry is a *workpaper only entry*. No entry is made on the books of either company.

Purchase Accounting
Cost Equals Book Value
Wholly Owned Subsidiary
Date of Acquisition

ILLUSTRATION 2–1
Consolidated Balance Sheet Workpaper
P Company and Subsidiary
January 1, 1980

	P COMPANY	S COMPANY	ELIMINATIONS DR.	ELIMINATIONS CR.	CONSOLIDATED BALANCES
Cash	20,000	20,000			40,000
Other Current Assets	180,000	50,000			230,000
Plant and Equipment	120,000	60,000			180,000
Investment in S Company	80,000			¹80,000	
Total Assets	400,000	130,000			450,000
Liabilities	60,000	50,000			110,000
Common Stock					
P Company	200,000				200,000
S Company		50,000	¹50,000		
Premium on Common Stock					
P Company	40,000				40,000
S Company		10,000	¹10,000		
Retained Earnings					
P Company	100,000				100,000
S Company		20,000	¹20,000		
Total Equities	400,000	130,000	80,000	80,000	450,000

¹To eliminate investment in S Company.

CONSOLIDATED R/E AT DATE OF ACQ IS ALWAYS R/E OF THE PARENT

Note that the investment account and related subsidiary equity have been eliminated and the subsidiary's net assets effectively substituted for the investment account. Consolidated assets and liabilities consist of the sum of the parent and subsidiary assets and liabilities in each classification. Note also that consolidated stockholders' equity is the same as the parent company's equity. This is as it should be, since the subsidiary's stockholders' equity has been eliminated against the parent company's investment account. The consolidated balance sheet is that of the *economic* entity, and the only ownership interest is that represented by P Company's stockholders, i.e., P Company owns all of S Company's stock.

Parent's Cost of Investment Is Equal to Book Value of Subsidiary Stock Acquired—Less than 100% of Subsidiary Stock Acquired Assume now that on January 1, 1980, P Company acquired only 90% (4,500 shares) of the stock of S Company for $72,000. Since P Company owns less than 100% of S Company's stock, consideration must be given to the existence of a minority interest in S Company. A workpaper for the preparation of a consolidated balance sheet at the date of acquisition in this situation is presented in Illustration 2–2.

Purchase Accounting
Cost Equals Book Value
90%-Owned Subsidiary
Date of Acquisition

ILLUSTRATION 2–2
Consolidated Balance Sheet Workpaper
P Company and Subsidiary
January 1, 1980

	P COMPANY	S COMPANY	ELIMINATIONS DR.	ELIMINATIONS CR.	CONSOLIDATED BALANCES
Cash	28,000	20,000			48,000
Other Current Assets	180,000	50,000			230,000
Plant and Equipment	120,000	60,000			180,000
Investment in S Company	72,000			¹72,000	
Total Assets	400,000	130,000			458,000
Liabilities	60,000	50,000			110,000
Common Stock					
P Company	200,000				200,000
S Company		50,000 ×90% ¹45,000 ×10% MI			5,000 M
Premium on Common Stock					
P Company	40,000				40,000
S Company		10,000 ×90% 9,000 ×10% MI			1,000 M
Retained Earnings					
P Company	100,000				100,000
S Company		20,000 ×10% MI ×90% ¹18,000			2,000 M
Total Equities	400,000	130,000	72,000	72,000	458,000

¹To eliminate investment in S Company.

(handwritten) TOTAL BV S = 80,000
%o ACQ = 90%
BV ACQ = 72,000 PAID 72000

(handwritten) MINORITY INTEREST ENOUGH
SHOWN IN ACCOUNT TOTAL
MI = 8000

The workpaper investment elimination entry is:

Common Stock—S Company (.9 × 50,000)	45,000	
Premium on Common Stock—S Company (.9 × 10,000)	9,000	
Retained Earnings—S Company (.9 × 20,000)	18,000	
Investment in S Company		72,000

In comparing Illustrations 2–1 and 2–2, it should be noted that: (1) consolidated assets are $8,000 greater in Illustration 2–2 since it took $8,000 less cash to acquire the investment, and (2) an $8,000 minority interest exists. Minority interest has been identified on the consolidated workpaper in Illustration 2–2 with the letter "M."

Only that percentage of S Company equity acquired by P Company is eliminated against the investment account; the remainder of S Company equity constitutes the minority interest. As you recall, the purpose of the consolidated balance sheet is to report the net resources under the control of a single management, and the management of P Company effectively controls all of S Company's resources. Thus, all of S Company's assets and liabilities are combined with those of P Company on the consolidated balance sheet, and the minority interest represents the minority shareholders' interest in the net assets.

Determination of the proper classification of the minority interest presents some conceptual difficulty. The minority interest does not represent a liability under the normal concept of liabilities, because it does not require a future payment by the parent company or the consolidated entity. Nor does it represent a part of stockholders' equity since the only stockholders in the consolidated entity are parent company stockholders. Minority interest exists by virtue of the fact that the subsidiary's total net assets are combined with those of the parent company. Thus, the minority interest may be thought of as an equity interest in the consolidated net assets, although actually it represents neither creditors' nor stockholders' equity.

Reporting of minority interest varies widely in practice. Sometimes it is classified as a liability, sometimes as stockholders' equity, and, most commonly, in a separate section between liabilities and stockholders' equity.[4] In addition, some companies report the minority interest in detail as to capital stock, additional paid-in capital, and retained earnings. Since, as noted earlier, minority shareholders do not look to the consolidated statements for information about their investments, the detailing of minority interest on the consolidated balance sheet would be of little value, so most companies report the minority interest between liabilities and stockholders' equity in one amount.

***Parent's Cost of Investment Exceeds Book Value of Subsidiary Stock Acquired—
Less than 100% of the Subsidiary Stock Acquired*** Assume that on January 1, 1980, P Company acquired 4,000 shares (80%) of the outstanding common stock of S Company for $74,000 cash, after which P Company has $26,000 in cash and $74,000 in an Investment in S Company. Since the book value of the equity interest acquired by P Company is only $64,000 (80% × $80,000), cost exceeds the book value of equity acquired by $10,000.

A workpaper for a consolidated balance sheet at date of acquisition in this situation is presented in Illustration 2–3.

The workpaper investment elimination entry is:

Common Stock—S Company (.8 × 50,000)	40,000	
Premium on Common Stock—S Company (.8 × 10,000)	8,000	
Retained Earnings—S Company (.8 × 20,000)	16,000	
Plant and Equipment (Land)	10,000	
Investment in S Company		74,000

When the subsidiary equity acquired is eliminated against the investment in S Company, a $10,000 balance remains. A detailed discussion of the appropriate accounting treatment of this balance is presented in Chapter 5. At this stage of our discussion we have assumed that the $10,000 excess cost relates to the undervaluation of subsidiary land and have assigned it, therefore, to "plant and equipment."

---

[4]Accountants International Study Group, *Consolidated Financial Statements*, par. 40.

Purchase Accounting
Cost Exceeds Book Value
80%-Owned Subsidiary
Date of Acquisition

ILLUSTRATION 2–3
Consolidated Balance Sheet Workpaper
P Company and Subsidiary
January 1, 1980

	P COMPANY	S COMPANY	ELIMINATIONS DR.	ELIMINATIONS CR.	CONSOLIDATED BALANCES
Cash	26,000	20,000			46,000
Other Current Assets	180,000	50,000			230,000
Plant and Equipment	120,000	60,000	¹10,000		190,000
Investment in S Company	74,000			¹74,000	
Total Assets	400,000	130,000			466,000
Liabilities	60,000	50,000			110,000
Common Stock					
P Company	200,000				200,000
S Company		50,000 ×80%	¹40,000		10,000 M
Premium on Common Stock					
P Company	40,000				40,000
S Company		10,000 × 80%	¹ 8,000		2,000 M
Retained Earnings					
P Company	100,000				100,000
S Company		20,000 × 80%	¹16,000		4,000 M
Total Equities	400,000	130,000	74,000	74,000	466,000

¹To eliminate investment in S Company.

TOTAL BV = 80,000
% ACQ = 80%
BV ACQ = 64000
PAID 74,000

EXCESS COST OVER BOOK VALUE 10,000

The parent company often pays an amount in excess of the book value of the subsidiary stock acquired. Although we have assumed here that it relates to the undervaluation of subsidiary land, any one, or a combination, of the following conditions might exist:

1. The fair, or current, value of one or more specific subsidiary tangible or intangible assets may exceed its recorded value because of appreciation. Or, the application of conservative accounting procedures under generally accepted accounting principles often results in book values that are lower than fair values for assets and higher than fair values for liabilities. Examples are (a) the current expensing of some costs that may contain future benefits, e.g., research and development expenditures, (b) the use of accelerated depreciation methods, (c) use of the LIFO inventory method, and (d) the general prohibition against recognizing unrealized asset increments.

2. The excess payment may indicate the existence of unrecorded subsidiary goodwill as reflected by its above-normal earning capacity.

3. Liabilities, generally long-term ones, may be overvalued. For example, the subsidiary may have 6% bonds payable outstanding when acquired by the parent, even though the market rate of interest is 8% at that time.

4. A variety of market factors may affect the price paid for the stock. The mere entry of one more large buyer of stock into the market would generally have the effect of increasing the stock's market price. In essence, the parent is willing to pay a premium for the right to acquire control and the related economic advantages it expects to obtain from integrated operations.

Parent's Cost of Investment Is Less than Book Value of Subsidiary Stock Acquired—Less than 100% of Subsidiary Stock Acquired Assume that on January 1, 1980, P Company acquired 4,000 shares (80%) of the outstanding common stock of S Company for $60,000, after which P Company has $40,000 in cash and $60,000 in an Investment in S Company. Since the book value of S Company equity acquired is $64,000 ($80,000 × 80%), equity acquired exceeds cost by $4,000.

A workpaper for a consolidated balance sheet at date of acquisition in this situation is presented in Illustration 2–4.

TOTAL BV = 80,000
% OF ACQ = 80%
BV = 64,000
PAID = 60,000
-4,000 EXCESS

Purchase Accounting
Book Value Exceeds Cost
80%-Owned Subsidiary
Date of Acquisition

ILLUSTRATION 2–4
Consolidated Balance Sheet Workpaper
P Company and Subsidiary
January 1, 1980

	P COMPANY	S COMPANY	ELIMINATIONS DR.	ELIMINATIONS CR.	CONSOLIDATED BALANCES
Cash	40,000	20,000			60,000
Other Current Assets	180,000	50,000			230,000
Plant and Equipment	120,000	60,000		[1] 4,000	176,000
Investment in S Company	60,000			[1] 60,000	
Total Assets	400,000	130,000			466,000
Liabilities	60,000	50,000			110,000
Common Stock					
P Company	200,000				200,000
S Company		50,000	[1] 40,000		10,000 M
Premium on Common Stock					
P Company	40,000				40,000
S Company		10,000	[1] 8,000		2,000 M
Retained Earnings					
P Company	100,000				100,000
S Company		20,000	[1] 16,000		4,000 M
Total Equities	400,000	130,000	64,000	64,000	466,000

[1] To eliminate investment in S Company.

The workpaper investment elimination entry is:

Common Stock—S Company (.8 × 50,000)	40,000	
Premium on Common Stock—S Company (.8 × 10,000)	8,000	
Retained Earnings—S Company (.8 × 20,000)	16,000	
Investment in S Company		60,000
Plant and Equipment (Land)		4,000

When the subsidiary equity acquired is eliminated against the Investment in S Company, a $4,000 credit balance remains. Although there may be several reasons for this difference, it generally reflects one or a combination of the following: (1) one or more of the subsidiary's assets is overvalued, (2) one or more of the subsidiary's liabilities is undervalued or unrecognized, (3) the parent simply made a bargain purchase. A detailed discussion of the difference and its accounting treatment is presented in Chapter 5. Here we have assumed that it relates to the overvaluation of S Company land and is, therefore, assigned to plant and equipment.

Investment Elimination Under the Pooling of Interests Method

You will recall that a primary condition for use of the pooling of interests method is an exchange of common stock for 90% or more of the common stock of the acquired company. Under the purchase method, the initial stock acquisition is recorded at its cost. Under the pooling of interests method, however, the stock acquired is recorded at an amount equal to the book value of the subsidiary's equity acquired.

Wholly Owned Subsidiary To illustrate the pooling method for a wholly owned subsidiary, assume the balance sheets for P and S Companies on December 31, 1979 that were used in the previous illustrations. On January 1, 1980, P Company exchanged 6,000 of its common shares for all of the shares (5,000) of the common stock of S Company. Assume that all conditions required for pooling of interests treatment have been met. The exchange of stock would be recorded by P Company by the following entry:

Investment in S Company	80,000	
Common Stock (6,000 × 10)		60,000
Retained Earnings		20,000

The debit to the investment account is equal to the subsidiary's equity acquired, 100%. The credit to common stock reflects the par value of P Company stock issued, which is $10,000 more than the par value of S Company stock acquired. The $10,000 difference serves to reduce S Company Premium on Common Stock to zero, and the entire amount ($20,000) of S Company retained earnings is carried forward.

A workpaper for the preparation of a consolidated balance sheet on the date of acquisition is presented in Illustration 2–5.

Pooling Accounting	ILLUSTRATION 2-5
Par Value Issued Exceeds	**Consolidated Balance Sheet Workpaper**
Par Value Acquired	**P Company and Subsidiary**
Wholly Owned Subsidiary	**January 1, 1980**
Date of Acquisition	

	P COMPANY	S COMPANY	ELIMINATIONS DR.	ELIMINATIONS CR.	CONSOLIDATED BALANCES
Cash	100,000	20,000			120,000
Other Current Assets	180,000	50,000			230,000
Plant and Equipment	120,000	60,000			180,000
Investment in S Company	80,000			¹80,000	
Total Assets	480,000	130,000			530,000
Liabilities	60,000	50,000			110,000
Common Stock					
P Company	260,000				260,000
S Company		50,000	¹50,000		
Premium on Common Stock					
P Company	40,000				40,000
S Company		10,000	¹10,000		
Retained Earnings					
P Company	120,000				120,000
S Company		20,000	¹20,000		
Total Equities	480,000	130,000	80,000	80,000	530,000

¹To eliminate investment in S Company.

The workpaper investment elimination entry is:

Common Stock—S Company	50,000	
Premium on Common Stock—S Company	10,000	
Retained Earnings—S Company	20,000	
Investment in S Company		80,000

In the elimination of the investment account against subsidiary equity, S Company common stock, premium on common stock, and retained earnings are eliminated against the investment account.

Recall from our earlier discussion of pooling of interests in Chapter 1 that when the par or stated value of the shares given exceeds that of the shares acquired, the difference is first deducted from the combined additional paid-in capital of the parent and subsidiary, after which retained earnings is reduced. For example, if P Company exchanged 7,000 of its shares for all of those of S Company, the following acquisition entry would be made:

Investment in S Company *PARENTS PREMIUM*	80,000	
Premium on Common Stock	10,000	
Common Stock (7,000 × 10)		70,000
Retained Earnings		20,000

After the appropriate eliminating entry is prepared on the workpaper, consolidated stockholders' equity on the consolidated balance sheet would be reported as:

Common Stock, $10 par (200,000 + 70,000)	270,000
Premium on Common Stock (40,000 − 10,000)	30,000
Retained Earnings (100,000 + 20,000)	120,000
Total	420,000

In the event that the par value of P Company stock issued is *less* than the par value of S Company stock acquired, premium on common stock is increased. Assume, for example, the situation in the preceding illustration except that P Company exchanged only 4,000 of its shares for all of those of S Company. In this situation, P Company would make the following acquisition entry:

Investment in S Company	80,000	
Common Stock (4,000 × 10)		40,000
Retained Earnings → *NEVER INCREASED*		20,000
Premium on Common Stock		20,000

A date of acquisition consolidated balance sheet workpaper in this case is presented in Illustration 2–6. Elimination of the investment and subsidiary equity follows the procedure used in previous illustrations.

Partially Owned Subsidiary Acquisition of less than 100% of the subsidiary's stock does not change the basic concept of pooling. The investment account is debited by the parent for the equity acquired, which is less than 100%; the common stock account is credited for the par value of the stock issued; and other equity accounts are adjusted to reflect any reclassification of equity.

Assume the preceding illustration except that P Company exchanges 5,000 of its shares of common stock for 95% (4,750 shares) of the common stock of S Company. P Company would make the following acquisition entry:

Investment in S Company (80,000 × .95)	76,000	
Common Stock (5,000 × 10)		50,000
Retained Earnings (20,000 × .95)		19,000
Premium on Common Stock		7,000

The minority interest in S Company Premium on Common Stock is $500 (5% × 10,000), and the remaining $9,500 represents P Company's interest. Since the par value of the stock given ($50,000) exceeds the par value of the stock acquired

Pooling Accounting
Par Value Acquired
Exceeds Issued
Wholly Owned Subsidiary
Date of Acquisition

ILLUSTRATION 2–6
Consolidated Balance Sheet Workpaper
P Company and Subsidiary
January 1, 1980

	P COMPANY	S COMPANY	ELIMINATIONS DR.	ELIMINATIONS CR.	CONSOLIDATED BALANCES
Cash	100,000	20,000			120,000
Other Current Assets	180,000	50,000			230,000
Plant and Equipment	120,000	60,000			180,000
Investment in S Company	80,000			¹80,000	
Total Assets	480,000	130,000			530,000
Liabilities	60,000	50,000			110,000
Common Stock					
P Company	240,000ᵃ				240,000
S Company		50,000	¹50,000		
Premium on Common Stock					
P Company	60,000ᵇ				60,000
S Company		10,000	¹10,000		
Retained Earnings					
P Company	120,000ᶜ				120,000
S Company		20,000	¹20,000		
Total Equities	480,000	130,000	80,000	80,000	530,000

¹To eliminate investment in S Company.
ᵃ200,000 + 40,000.
ᵇ40,000 + 20,000.
ᶜ100,000 + 20,000.

($47,500), the $2,500 increase in par value serves to reduce P Company's interest to $7,000 ($9,500 − $2,500). A date of acquisition workpaper for this case is presented in Illustration 2–7.

Elimination of 95% of S Company's equity against the investment account is accomplished by the following workpaper entry:

Common Stock—S Company	47,500	
Premium on Common Stock—S Company	9,500	
Retained Earnings—S Company	19,000	
Investment in S Company		76,000

Pooling Accounting
Par Value Issued
  Exceeds Acquired
95%-Owned Subsidiary
Date of Acquisition

ILLUSTRATION 2–7
Consolidated Balance Sheet Workpaper
P Company and Subsidiary
January 1, 1980

	P COMPANY	S COMPANY	ELIMINATIONS DR.	ELIMINATIONS CR.	CONSOLIDATED BALANCES
Cash	100,000	20,000			120,000
Other Current Assets	180,000	50,000			230,000
Plant and Equipment	120,000	60,000			180,000
Investment in S Company	76,000			¹76,000	
Total Assets	476,000	130,000			530,000
Liabilities	60,000	50,000			110,000
Common Stock					
P Company	250,000ᵃ				250,000
S Company		50,000	¹47,500		2,500 M
Premium on Common Stock					
P Company	47,000ᵇ				47,000
S Company		10,000	¹ 9,500		500 M
Retained Earnings					
P Company	119,000ᶜ				119,000
S Company		20,000	¹19,000		1,000 M
Total Equities	476,000	130,000	76,000	76,000	530,000

¹To eliminate investment in S Company.
ᵃ200,000 + 50,000.
ᵇ40,000 + 7,000.
ᶜ100,000 + 19,000.

SUBSIDIARY TREASURY STOCK HOLDINGS

A subsidiary may hold some of its own shares as treasury stock at the time the parent company acquires its interest. The determination of the percentage interest acquired, as well as the total equity acquired, is based on shares outstanding and should, therefore, exclude treasury shares.

For example, assume that P Company acquired 18,000 shares of S Company common stock on January 1, 1980 for a payment of $320,000 when S Company's equity section appeared as follows:

Common Stock, $10 par, 25,000 shares issued	250,000
Premium on Common Stock	50,000
Retained Earnings	125,000
	425,000
Less: Treasury stock at cost, 1,000 shares	20,000
Total Stockholders' Equity	405,000

P Company's interest is 75% (18,000/24,000 shares), and total equity acquired is 75% × $405,000, or $303,750, which results in a difference between cost and book value of $16,250 ($320,000 − $303,750).

Procedures used to account for treasury stock are normally discussed in detail in intermediate accounting. Recall that, where the cost method of accounting for treasury stock is used, the treasury stock account contains contra-elements of legal capital, additional paid-in capital, and retained earnings. (If the par value method is used, the treasury stock account contains contra-legal capital only.) In the preparation of a consolidated statements workpaper, the treasury stock account should be offset against the appropriate stockholders' equity accounts before the investment account is eliminated. The offset entry, which is a workpaper only entry, is:

Common Stock ($10 × 1,000)	10,000	
Premium on Common Stock ($2 × 1,000)	2,000	
Retained Earnings	8,000	
Treasury Stock		20,000

[handwritten: PREMIUM 50000 / 25000 # SHARES; REDISTRIBUTE TREASURY]

After the workpaper entry above is prepared, the investment account is eliminated against the *adjusted* equity balances. Thus, in this example, the eliminating entry would be:

Common Stock (.75 × 240,000)	180,000	
Premium on Common Stock (.75 × 48,000)	36,000	
Retained Earnings (.75 × 117,000)	87,750	
Difference Between Cost and Book Value	16,250	
Investment in S Company		320,000

If the par value method of accounting for treasury stock had been used, S Company's capital accounts, other than common stock, would have been adjusted in the treasury stock acquisition entry and the treasury stock account established at an amount equal to the par value of the stock reacquired. In that case, the offset entry would simply be a debit to common stock and a credit to treasury stock for $10,000. The entry to eliminate the investment account would be the same as that presented above.

Other Intercompany Balance Sheet Eliminations

Up to this point we have discussed the elimination of the parent's share of the subsidiary equity acquired against the related investment account. Balance sheet eliminations of a variety of intercompany receivables and payables are also often required. Intercompany accounts receivable, notes receivable, and interest receivable, for example, must be eliminated against the reciprocal accounts payable, notes payable, and interest payable. Cash advances among affiliated companies constitute receivables and payables and must be eliminated. Eliminations also must be made for all types of intercompany accruals for such items as rent and other services. The full amount of all intercompany receivables and payables is eliminated without regard to the percentage of control held by the parent company. This practice is consistent with the notion that the entire amount of a partially owned subsidiary's assets and liabilities is included in the consolidated balance sheet, along with the related minority interest in the net assets.

Adjustments to Statement Data

At times, workpaper adjustments to accounting data may be needed before appropriate eliminating entries can be accomplished. The need for adjustments generally arises because of in-transit items where only one of the affiliates has recorded the effect of an intercompany transaction. For example, the parent company may have recorded a cash advance to one of its subsidiaries near year-end but the subsidiary may not yet have recorded the receipt of the advance. Thus, the Advances to Subsidiary account on the parent's books would have no reciprocal account on the subsidiary's books. An adjusting workpaper entry debiting cash and crediting Advances from Parent would be required so that the asset (cash) could be appropriately included in consolidated assets and a reciprocal account established that would permit the elimination of intercompany advances. The workpaper eliminations columns are used to enter these adjusting entries. Of course, it would also be possible simply to adjust the subsidiary's statements prior to their entry on the workpaper.

A COMPREHENSIVE ILLUSTRATION— MORE THAN ONE SUBSIDIARY COMPANY

No particular problem exists where the parent company owns a direct controlling interest in more than one subsidiary. The balance sheet of each affiliate is entered on the workpaper, any adjustments needed are prepared, and all related intercompany accounts, including those between subsidiaries, are eliminated. The remaining balances are combined, and they constitute the consolidated balance sheet.

It should be useful at this point to look at an illustrative workpaper and consolidated balance sheet for a parent company, P Company, and its two subsidiaries, S

Company and T Company. Assume that on January 1, 1980, P Company acquired 90% and 80% of the outstanding common stock of S Company and T Company, respectively. Immediately after the stock acquisition, balance sheets of the affiliates were:

	JANUARY 1, 1980		
	P COMPANY	S COMPANY 90%	T COMPANY 80%
Cash	$ 82,000	$ 36,000	$ 4,000
Accounts Receivable (net)	68,000	59,000	10,000
Inventories	76,000	64,000	15,000
Advances to T Company	20,000		
Investment in S Company	250,000		
Investment in T Company	115,000		
Plant and Equipment (net)	224,000	251,000	136,000
Total Assets	$835,000	$410,000	$165,000
Accounts Payable	$ 85,000	$ 40,000	$ 25,000
Notes Payable	-0-	100,000	-0-
Common Stock, $10 par	500,000	200,000	100,000
Retained Earnings	250,000	70,000	40,000
Total Equities	$835,000	$410,000	$165,000

Other information:

1. On the date of acquisition, P Company mailed a cash advance of $20,000 to T Company to improve T Company's working capital position. T Company had not yet received and, therefore, had not yet recorded, the advance.

2. On the date of acquisition, P Company owed S Company $6,000 for purchases on open account, and S Company owed T Company $5,000 for such purchases. All of these items had been sold by the purchasing companies prior to the date of acquisition.

A workpaper, under the purchase approach, for the preparation of a consolidated balance sheet on January 1, 1980 for P, S, and T Companies is presented in Illustration 2–8.

Several items on the workpaper should be noted. The cash in transit from P Company to T Company was picked up through an adjusting entry; if it had not been, $20,000 cash would have been excluded from the consolidated balance sheet. The adjustment also provided a reciprocal account, Advance from P Company, that permitted the elimination of the intercompany transaction for advances. (The perceptive reader will have already noticed that the same net effect could have been accomplished by a combined adjusting and eliminating entry with a debit to Cash and credit to Advances to T.)

Purchase Accounting
Two Partially Owned
Subsidiaries
Date of Acquisition

ILLUSTRATION 2-8
Consolidated Balance Sheet Workpaper
P Company and Subsidiaries
January 1, 1980

	P COMPANY	S 90% COMPANY	T 80% COMPANY	ELIMINATIONS DR.	ELIMINATIONS CR.	CONSOLIDATED BALANCES
Cash	82,000	36,000	4,000	a 20,000		142,000
Accounts Receivable (net)	68,000	59,000	10,000		2 11,000	126,000
Inventories	76,000	64,000	15,000			155,000
Advance to T Company	20,000				1 20,000	
Investment in S Company	250,000				3 250,000	
Investment in T Company	115,000				4 115,000	
Plant and Equipment	224,000	251,000	136,000			611,000
Difference Between Cost and Book Value				3 7,000 / 4 3,000		10,000
Total Assets	835,000	410,000	165,000			1,044,000
Accounts Payable	85,000	40,000	25,000	2 11,000		139,000
Notes Payable		100,000				100,000
Common Stock						
P Company	500,000					500,000
S Company		200,000		3 180,000		20,000 M
T Company			100,000	4 80,000		20,000 M
Retained Earnings						
P Company	250,000					250,000
S Company		70,000		3 63,000		7,000 M
T Company			40,000	4 32,000		8,000 M
Total Equities	835,000	410,000	165,000			
Advance from P Company				1 20,000	a 20,000	
				406,000	406,000	1,044,000

aTo adjust for cash advance in transit from P Company to T Company.
1To eliminate intercompany advances.
2To eliminate intercompany accounts payable and receivable.
3To eliminate investment in S Company.
4To eliminate investment in T Company.

The elimination of all intercompany accounts receivable and accounts payable, including those between subsidiaries, was accomplished through one entry. There is no need to eliminate them individually. Notice also that the equity acquired in each subsidiary was eliminated against each individual investment account.

The formal consolidated balance sheet is prepared from the detail in the consolidated balance sheet columns of the workpaper and is presented in Illustration 2-9.

ILLUSTRATION 2–9
Consolidated Balance Sheet
P Company and Subsidiaries
January 1, 1980

ASSETS

Current Assets:

Cash	$ 142,000
Accounts Receivable (net)	126,000
Inventories	155,000
Total Current Assets	416,000
Plant and Equipment (net)	611,000

Other Assets:

Excess of Cost over Equity in Subsidiaries	10,000
Total Assets	$1,044,000

LIABILITIES AND STOCKHOLDERS' EQUITY

Current Liabilities:

Accounts Payable		$ 139,000
Notes Payable		100,000
Total Liabilities		232,000
Minority Interest in Subsidiaries		55,000

Stockholders' Equity:

Common Stock, $10 par	$500,000	
Retained Earnings	250,000	750,000
Total Liabilities and Stockholders' Equity		$1,044,000

[handwritten annotations: "NOT LIABILITY OR EQUITY" pointing to Minority Interest in Subsidiaries; "PARENTS RIE" pointing to Retained Earnings]

The balance sheet data are classified according to normal balance sheet arrangements. The difference between cost and book value is assumed here to reflect a premium paid by P Company for the right to acquire control of S and T Companies and is, therefore, simply identified as an Excess of Cost over Equity in Subsidiaries and reported as one amount.

As discussed earlier, minority interest in subsidiaries is classified in some cases as a liability, in others as a part of stockholders' equity, and in still others in a separate section. In the treatment illustrated here, which is the most widely followed, the minority interest in all subsidiaries is reported in a single amount between liabilities and stockholders' equity.

COMBINED FINANCIAL STATEMENTS

Some affiliations do not involve a parent-subsidiary relationship, i.e., there is no equity investment in one company by another. For example, the relationship among subsidiaries of the same parent company may not involve an investment by one subsidiary in another, although the subsidiaries are affiliates. The same condition exists among several companies owned by one individual. Consolidated statements are not appropriate if there is no investment by one affiliate in another to eliminate. In these situations the most meaningful presentation may be that of combined statements in which the individual balance sheet and income statement classifications are simply summed or combined into one set of financial statements. Where such combined statements are prepared for a group of related companies, intercompany transactions, balances, and profit or loss should be eliminated in the same manner as in consolidated statements.

Assume, for example, that P Company, a manufacturing company, owns several manufacturing and retailing subsidiaries, as well as four banking subsidiaries. The manufacturing and retailing subsidiaries are consolidated with P Company, but the banking subsidiaries are not consolidated because their operations are non-homogeneous. As will be discussed in Chapter 3, P Company's equity in the banking subsidiaries is included in the consolidated balance sheet as an investment, and its share of their income is included in the consolidated income statement as investment income. In order to provide detail concerning the banking operations, without including four individual sets of statements, the banking subsidiaries may be combined into one set of combined statements and included in P Company's annual report, along with the consolidated statements.

Questions

1. What are the advantages of acquiring the *majority* of the voting stock of another company rather than acquiring *all* of its voting stock?

2. What is the justification for preparing consolidated financial statements when, in fact, it is apparent that the consolidated group is not a legal entity?

3. Why is it often necessary to prepare separate financial statements for each legal entity in a consolidated group even though consolidated statements provide a better economic picture of the combined activities?

4. What aspects of control must exist before a subsidiary is consolidated?

5. Why are consolidated workpapers used in preparing consolidated financial statements?

6. Define minority interest. List three methods of reporting minority interest in a consolidated balance sheet.

7. List several reasons why a parent company would be willing to pay more than book value for subsidiary stock acquired.

8. What effect do subsidiary treasury stock holdings have at the time the subsidiary is acquired? How should the treasury stock be treated on consolidated workpapers?

9. What effect does a minority interest have on the amount of intercompany receivables and payables eliminated on a consolidated balance sheet?

10. What type of financial statements would you suggest for an affiliated group consisting of a gold mining company (the parent), two silver mining companies, a uranium mining company, and two investment firms?

Problems

Problem 2–1

The two following separate situations show the financial position of a parent and its subsidiary on November 30, 1980, just after the parent had purchased 80% of the subsidiary's stock:

	SITUATION I		SITUATION II	
	X COMPANY	Y COMPANY	X COMPANY	Y COMPANY
Current Assets	$ 450,000	$120,000	$ 400,000	$140,000
Investment in Y Company	70,000		70,000	
Long-term Assets	700,000	200,000	600,000	200,000
Other Assets	45,000	20,000	35,000	25,000
Total	$1,265,000	$340,000	$1,105,000	$365,000
Current Liabilities	$ 320,000	$135,000	$ 335,000	$130,000
Long-term Liabilities	425,000	145,000	460,000	135,000
Common Stock	300,000	80,000	300,000	80,000
Retained Earnings	220,000	(20,000)	10,000	20,000
Total	$1,265,000	$340,000	$1,105,000	$365,000

Prepare a November 30, 1980 consolidated balance sheet workpaper for each of the situations above. (Any difference between the cost of the investment and the book value of equity acquired relates to subsidiary land.)

Problem 2–2

Under the purchase approach prepare in general journal form the workpaper entries to eliminate Baxter Company's investment in Colter Company prior to the preparation of a consolidated balance sheet at date of acquisition under each of the following cases:

			COLTER COMPANY EQUITY BALANCES		
CASE	PERCENT OF STOCK OWNED	INVESTMENT COST	COMMON STOCK	PREMIUM ON COMMON STOCK	RETAINED EARNINGS
a.	100%	$345,000	$200,000	$ 60,000	$ 70,000
b.	90%	315,000	300,000	100,000	(40,000)
c.	75%	298,000	300,000	100,000	(10,000)

Any difference between cost and book value of equity acquired relates to subsidiary land.

Problem 2–3

Under a pooling approach prepare in general journal form, (a) the investment acquisition entries and (b) the workpaper entries to eliminate Dudley Company's investment in Exter Company prior to the preparation of a consolidated balance sheet at date of acquisition under each of the following cases. Dudley Company common stock is $15 par, and its only additional paid-in capital is premium on common stock with a total of $80,000.

| | | | EXTER COMPANY EQUITY BALANCES | | |
| | PERCENT OF | DUDLEY SHARES | COMMON | PREMIUM ON | RETAINED |
CASE	OWNERSHIP	ISSUED	STOCK	COMMON STOCK	EARNINGS
a.	100%	7,000	$100,000	$60,000	$ 70,000
b.	100%	11,000	100,000	60,000	70,000
c.	90%	8,000	100,000	50,000	20,000
d.	95%	6,000	100,000	40,000	(20,000)

Problem 2–4

On January 1, 1980, Trident Company purchased 7,500 shares of U-Bend Company common stock for $150,000. Immediately after the stock acquisition, the statements of financial position of Trident and U-Bend appeared as follows:

ASSETS	TRIDENT	U-BEND
Cash	$102,000	$ 40,000
Accounts Receivable	80,000	32,000
Inventory	65,000	28,000
Investment in U-Bend Company	150,000	
Plant Assets	220,000	114,000
Accumulated Depreciation—Plant Assets	(70,000)	(24,000)
Total	$547,000	$190,000
LIABILITIES AND OWNERS' EQUITY		
Current Liabilities	$ 26,000	$ 38,000
Mortgage Notes payable	50,000	–0–
Common Stock, $10 par	300,000	100,000
Premium on Common Stock	100,000	18,000
Retained Earnings	71,000	34,000
Total	$547,000	$190,000

Prepare a consolidated balance sheet workpaper as of January 1, 1980. (Any difference between the cost of the investment and the book value of equity acquired relates to subsidiary land.)

Problem 2–5

On March 1, 1980, Rearden Company acquired, as a long-term investment, 9,000 of the 10,000 outstanding common stock shares of Maxwell Mining (par $30) by issuing 20,000 shares of its own common stock (par $15). Prior to the acquisition, the balance sheets of the two companies reflected the following:

	REARDEN COMPANY	MAXWELL MINING
Cash	$ 400,000	$110,000
Inventories	320,000	190,000
Receivables (net)	60,000	65,000
Fixed Assets (net)	450,000	200,000
Patents (net)	35,000	
Total	$1,265,000	$565,000
Current Liabilities	$ 52,000	$ 51,000
Long-term Liabilities	275,000	110,000
Common Stock	600,000	300,000
Premium	150,000	90,000
Retained Earnings	188,000	14,000
Total	$1,265,000	$565,000

Required:

Assume that the acquisition meets all of the criteria for the pooling of interests method.

A. Give the entry to record the stock exchange in the accounts of Rearden Co. at date of acquisition.

B. Prepare a consolidated balance sheet workpaper immediately after acquisition.

Problem 2–6

Statements of financial position for P Company and S Company on August 1, 1980 are as follows:

	P COMPANY	S COMPANY
Cash	$ 74,000	$ 28,500
Receivables	122,000	42,000
Inventory	89,000	36,000
Investment in Bonds	102,000	-0-
Investment in S Company Stock	145,000	-0-
Plant and Equipment (net)	277,000	200,000
Total	$809,000	$306,500
Accounts Payable	$ 58,000	$ 26,000
Accrued Expenses	10,800	8,500
Bonds Payable, 1997, 8%		100,000
Common Stock	500,000	100,000
Premium on Common Stock	80,000	20,000
Retained Earnings	160,200	52,000
Total	$809,000	$306,500

Prepare a workpaper for the preparation of a consolidated statement of financial position for P Company and its subsidiary S Company on August 1, 1980, taking into consideration the following:

(a) P Company acquired 80% of the outstanding common stock of S Company on August 1, 1980 for a cash payment of $145,000.

(b) Included in the investment in bonds accounts are $20,000 par value of S Company bonds payable that were purchased at par by P Company in 1978. The bonds pay interest on April 30 and October 31. S Company has appropriately accrued interest expense on August 1, 1980; P Company, however, inadvertently failed to accrue interest income on the S Company bonds.

(c) Included in P Company receivables is a $15,000 cash advance to S Company that was mailed on August 1, 1980. S Company had not yet received the advance at the time of the preparation of its August 1, 1980 statement of financial position.

(Any difference between the cost of the investment and the book value of equity acquired relates to subsidiary land.)

Problem 2–7
The balance sheet of Newcastle Company on April 30, 1981 was as follows:

ASSETS		
Cash		$ 13,000
Accounts Receivable:		
Sturgis Company	$13,000	
Others	33,000	46,000
Inventory		50,000
Land		35,000
Machinery (net)		30,000
Buildings (net)		15,000
Copyrights		11,000
Total Assets		$200,000

EQUITIES	
Accounts Payable	$ 25,000
Notes Payable	36,500
Bonds Payable	40,000
Common Stock, 1,000 shares	80,000
Other Contributed Capital	10,000
Retained Earnings	20,000
Less: Treasury Stock at Cost (100 shares)	(11,500)
Total Equities	$200,000

On April 30, 1981, Sturgis Company acquired a controlling interest in Newcastle Company by purchasing 810 shares of its common stock for $130 per share. The trial balance of Sturgis Company immediately after the stock acquisition appeared as follows:

	DEBITS	CREDITS
Cash	$ 15,000	
Accounts Receivable	34,700	
Inventory	62,000	
Investment in Newcastle	105,300	
Land	175,000	
Accounts Payable		$ 30,000
Accounts Payable—Newcastle Company		13,000
Notes Payable		48,000
Common Stock, 5,000 shares		200,000
Other Contributed Capital		80,000
Retained Earnings		21,000
Total	$392,000	$392,000

(Any difference between cost and book value acquired relates to subsidiary land.)

Prepare a consolidated balance sheet workpaper as of April 30, 1981.

Problem 2–8

On January 1, 1980, P Company acquired, as a long-term investment, 21,375 of the outstanding common stock shares of S Company (par $10) by issuing 45,000 of its own common stock (par $6). The balance sheets of the two companies reflected the following data just prior to the acquisition:

	P COMPANY	S COMPANY
Cash	$ 150,000	$140,000
Other Current Assets	665,000	195,000
Long-term Assets	1,500,000	260,000
Other Assets	25,000	
Total Assets	$2,340,000	$595,000
Current Liabilities	$ 485,000	$ 67,000
Bonds Payable	200,000	
Common Stock	1,200,000	250,000
Treasury Stock at Par		(25,000)
Premium on Common Stock	400,000	125,000
Retained Earnings	55,000	178,000
Total Equities	$2,340,000	$595,000

Assuming that the acquisition meets all of the criteria for the pooling of interests method:
(a) Give the entry to record the stock exchange in the accounts of P Company at the date of acquisition.
(b) Prepare a consolidated balance sheet workpaper immediately after the acquisition.

Handwritten annotations:

25,000 SHARES TREAS REDUCES TO 95%
ACTUALLY ACQUIRING
225,000 = 250,000 - 25,000
225,000 × 95% = 213,750
213,750 = 56,250
270,000 - 213,750 = 118,750
125,000 × 95% = 118,750 56,250
178,000 × 95% = 169,100 67,500 62,500
PRE 125,000
R/E 178,000 × 95% = 169,100
RETIRE TREAS:
COMMON STOCK
T. STOCK
25,000 25,000
213,750 (95% × 225,000)
c/s 213,750
PRE 118,750
R/E 169,100
INV

BV 528,000
95%
501,600

501,600

Problem 2–9

On February 1, 1981, Alpha Company acquired 100% of the outstanding common stock of Beta Company, in a pooling, and purchased 75% of the outstanding common stock of Gamma Corporation with cash. Immediately prior to the two acquisitions, balance sheets of the three companies were as follows:

	ALPHA COMPANY	BETA COMPANY	GAMMA CORP.
Cash	$ 275,000	$ 75,000	$ 24,000
Accounts Receivable (net)	47,000	68,000	43,000
Notes Receivable	30,000		
Merchandise Inventory	177,000	49,000	23,000
Prepaid Insurance	22,500	4,200	500
Advances to B Company	10,000		
Advances to G Company	25,000		
Land	413,000	72,000	13,500
Buildings (net)	100,000	45,000	27,000
Equipment (net)	91,000	11,000	4,500
Total	$1,190,500	$324,200	$135,500
Accounts Payable	$ 42,500	$ 33,000	$ 17,500
Income Taxes Payable	50,000	13,000	
Notes Payable		10,000	15,000
Bonds Payable	200,000		
Common Stock: Alpha, $10 par	400,000		
Beta, $12 par		240,000	
Gamma, $10 par			70,000
Premium	250,000	20,000	50,000
Retained Earnings	248,000	8,200	(17,000)
Total	$1,190,500	$324,200	$135,500

The following additional information is relevant to this situation:

(1) One week prior to the acquisitions, Alpha Company had advanced $10,000 to Beta Company and $25,000 to Gamma Corporation. Beta Company recorded an increase to accounts payable for its advance, but Gamma Corporation failed to record the transaction. *ELIMINATE W/S*

(2) On the date of acquisition, Alpha Co. owed Beta Co. $8,000 for purchases on account, and Gamma Corp. owed Alpha Co. $5,000 and Beta Co. $4,000 for such purchases.

(3) Alpha Co. exchanged 20,000 shares of its $10 par value stock for 20,000 shares of Beta's $12 par value stock in the pooling.

(4) Alpha Co. paid $65,000 for the purchase of 75% of Gamma Corp.'s outstanding common stock.

(5) $5,000 of Beta Co.'s notes payable and $13,000 of Gamma's notes payable were payable to Alpha Co. *ELIMINATE W/S*

Required:

A. Give the entries to record the two acquisitions in the accounts of Alpha Company.

B. Prepare a consolidated balance sheet workpaper immediately after acquisition.

C. Prepare a consolidated balance sheet at the date of acquisition for Alpha Co. and subsidiaries.

(Any difference between the cost of the investment and the book value of equity acquired relates to subsidiary land.)

3

Investments Subsequent to Acquisition: Equity Method

Investments in voting stock of other companies may be consolidated, or they may be separately reported in the financial statements of the investor at cost, at the lower of aggregate cost or market, at market, or at equity. The method of reporting adopted depends on a number of factors including the degree of control exercised by the investor over the investee, the type of financial reports issued by the investor, and the marketability of equity securities. "Investor" refers to a business entity that holds an investment in voting stock of another company. "Investee" refers to a corporation that issued voting stock held by an investor.

Statement of Financial Accounting Standards No. 12, which is more fully discussed in the intermediate accounting text in this series, requires that, with certain exceptions, investments in marketable equity securities that are neither consolidated nor accounted for under the equity method of accounting be reported in the financial statements at the lower of aggregate cost or market. Investments that are not consolidated and that are not required to be reported at equity or at the lower of aggregate cost or market are ordinarily reported at cost.

Although the cost method is seldom used in **reporting** on an investment in a subsidiary, it is often used by parent companies to **record** investments in subsidiaries that are consolidated for **reporting** purposes. The consolidated balances reported will be the same without regard to the accounting method (cost, equity, or a variation thereof) that is used by the parent company to record its investment in the consolidated subsidiary. However, the eliminating entries that must be made in the consolidating workpaper in order to arrive at the appropriate consolidated balances will be significantly different if the investment is recorded at cost rather than equity on the books of the parent company. The cost and equity methods of **recording** an investment in a subsidiary are illustrated and compared in this chapter in order to provide the reader with a basis for understanding the different workpaper eliminating entries illustrated in subsequent chapters.

The equity method must be used in reporting investments in most subsidiaries that are not consolidated and certain other investments in voting stock in the financial statements. In this chapter the circumstances that require the use of the equity method of reporting and problems relating to such *reporting* are identified and illustrated.

RECORDING THE ACTIVITY OF SUBSIDIARIES SUBSEQUENT TO ACQUISITION

In this section, methods of **recording** the activities of a subsidiary are discussed and illustrated. **Reporting** methods are discussed in later sections of this chapter.

At the date an investment in a subsidiary is acquired, the investment account is charged with the cost of the investment (purchase method) or with the parent's interest in the book value of the net assets of the subsidiary on the date of acquisition (pooling method). Subsequent to acquisition, the parent company may use either the cost method or the equity method to account in its records for the activities of the subsidiary. The major differences between the cost and equity methods pertain to the period in which subsidiary income is formally recorded on the books of the parent company and the amount thereof.

Under the equity method, income is formally recorded in the books of the parent company in the same accounting period that it is reported by the subsidiary, whether or not such income is distributed to the parent company. Under the cost method, no subsidiary income is recorded in the books of the parent company unless and until it becomes available to the parent company in the form of a dividend. Under the equity method, the amount of income recorded is the parent's share of the subsidiary's reported income. Under the cost method, the amount of income recorded is the amount of dividends received from the subsidiary or, stated another way, it is the parent's share of the income distributed by the subsidiary.

Example 1—Illustration of the Cost and Equity Methods

Assume that P Company acquired 80% of the outstanding voting stock of S Company at the beginning of Year 1 for $800,000. The reported net income (loss) and dividend distributions of S Company are summarized in Illustration 3–1.

ILLUSTRATION 3–1
Net Income and Dividends Reported by S Company
End of Years (1 Through 4)

END OF YEAR	REPORTED INCOME (LOSS)[a]	DIVIDENDS DISTRIBUTED[a]	INCOME OVER (UNDER) DIVIDENDS	UNDISTRIBUTED INCOME SINCE DATE OF ACQUISITION BY P COMPANY
1	90,000 (2)	40,000 (3)	50,000	50,000
2	60,000 (4)	40,000 (5)	20,000	70,000
3	(20,000) (6)	40,000 (7)	(60,000)	10,000
4	18,750 (8)	40,000 (9)	(21,250)	–0–
Total	148,750	160,000	(11,250)	

[a]Numbers in parentheses refer to the corresponding journal entries in Example 1.

Journal entries required on the books of P Company to account in its records for its investment in S Company under the cost method and under the equity method of accounting are illustrated and explained below.

Entries in Year 1—Income Exceeds Dividends

COST METHOD   EQUITY METHOD

(1) Investment in S   800,000
      Cash   800,000   Same entry
          To record Investment.

(2) No entry   Investment in S   72,000
                                              Equity in
                                                Subsidiary Income   72,000
          To record equity in reported income of subsidiary in Year 1.

(3) Cash   32,000   Cash   32,000
      Dividend Income   32,000   Investment in S   32,000
          To record dividends received from subsidiary in Year 1.

Entries in Year 2—Income Exceeds Dividends

(4) No entry   Investment in S   48,000
                                              Equity in
                                                Subsidiary Income   48,000
          To record equity in reported income of subsidiary in Year 2.

(5) Cash   32,000   Cash   32,000
      Dividend Income   32,000   Investment in S   32,000
          To record dividends received from subsidiary in Year 2.

Various account titles other than "Equity in Subsidiary Income (Loss)" are used to record the parent's share of the subsidiary's income or loss under the equity method. Whatever the title used, however, under the equity method, the parent company records its share of the subsidiary's reported income (80% of $90,000 = $72,000 in Year 1 and 80% of $60,000 = $48,000 in Year 2), whereas under the cost method, it records its share of the income distributed by the subsidiary (80% of $40,000 = $32,000 in both Year 1 and Year 2).

In addition, the parent company may make certain adjustments to the amount of income it records under the equity method that are not illustrated above.

Illustrations and explanations in this chapter are based on the assumptions that (1) the cost of the investment is equal to the book value of the equity interest acquired in the investee, (2) there are no material transactions between the investor and the investee that involve the recognition of profit or loss, and (3) there is no change in the percentage of investee common stock owned by the investor. If these assumptions are released, adjustments must be made to the amount of income recognized by an investor reporting investee income under the equity method. Since such adjustments are also necessary in the preparation of consolidated financial statements, they will be examined in subsequent chapters at the same time that their impact on consolidated financial statements is illustrated and explained. Adjustments to give effect to amortization and depreciation of the difference between the cost and book value of the equity interest acquired in an investee are described in Chapter 5. Adjustments to give effect to the elimination of intercompany profit and loss are described in Chapters 6 and 7. The effect of changes in ownership is described in Chapter 8.

Entries in Year 3—Subsidiary Reports a Loss

COST METHOD			EQUITY METHOD		
(6) No entry			Equity in		
			Subsidiary Loss	16,000	
			Investment in S		16,000
	To record equity in reported loss of subsidiary in Year 3.				
(7) Cash	32,000		Cash	32,000	
	Dividend Income	32,000	Investment in S		32,000
	To record dividends received from subsidiary in Year 3.				

Under the equity method, the parent company records its share of subsidiary loss in the period in which it is reported. Under the cost method, reported losses are ordinarily not recognized or recorded.

Entries in Year 4—Liquidating Dividend

From the point of view of a parent company, a purchased subsidiary is deemed to have distributed a liquidating dividend when the cumulative amounts of its dividends subsequent to its acquisition by the parent company exceed the cumulative amount of its reported earnings subsequent to its acquisition. The treatment of such dividends as a return of capital is consistent with the purchase concept that subsidiary earnings prior to acquisition are purchased by the parent company at the time it acquires its interest in the subsidiary. Since, under the equity method, the parent treats its share of reported subsidiary income as an increase in its investment, all dividend distributions are routinely treated as a return of its investment and deducted from the investment account. Accordingly, under the equity method of accounting, liquidating dividends require no special treatment. Under the cost method, however, liquidating dividends must be recorded as a reduction of the investment account rather than as dividend income.

	COST METHOD		EQUITY METHOD	
(8) No entry			Investment in S 15,000	
			Equity in	
			Subsidiary Income	15,000

To record equity in the reported income of subsidiary in Year 4.

(9) Cash	32,000		Cash	32,000	
Dividend Income		23,000	Investment in S		32,000
Investment in S		9,000			

To record (liquidating) dividend received from the subsidiary in Year 4.

In this example, net income of S Company in Years 1 through 4 totals $148,750, while dividends distributed by S Company during the same period amount to $160,000 (see Illustration 3–1). Hence, the $40,000 dividend distributed in Year 4 includes a liquidating dividend of $11,250 ($160,000 − $148,750). P Company's share of the liquidating dividend is 80% of $11,250, or $9,000. Illustration 3–2 shows the amount of income recorded each year and the end-of-year balances in the investment account under both the cost and equity methods.

ILLUSTRATION 3–2
Comparison of Investment Account Balances and
Income Recorded by P Company
(Based on Assumptions In Example 1)

	INVESTMENT ACCOUNT BALANCE			INCOME (LOSS) RECORDED			
END OF YEAR	COST METHOD	EQUITY METHOD	DIFFERENCE	COST METHOD	EQUITY METHOD	DIFFERENCE	CUMULATIVE DIFFERENCE
1	800,000	840,000	40,000	32,000	72,000	40,000	40,000
2	800,000	856,000	56,000	32,000	48,000	16,000	56,000
3	800,000	808,000	8,000	32,000	(16,000)	(48,000)	8,000
4	791,000	791,000	–0–	23,000	15,000	(8,000)	–0–
				119,000	119,000	–0–	

As illustrated therein, immediately after the appropriate recording of a liquidating dividend, the balance in the investment account and the total amount of subsidiary income recorded on the books of the parent company from the date the subsidiary was acquired to the date the liquidating dividend is recorded will be the same under both the cost and equity methods. The amount of income recorded in individual accounting periods, however, may vary substantially.

Comparison of Cost and Equity Methods

Differences in the balances in the investment account and in the cumulative amount of recorded income that result from applying the equity method rather than the cost method are shown in Illustration 3–2. As demonstrated therein, the differences in the investment account balances are exactly equal to the cumulative differences in recorded income. In addition, both differences can be defined as, and are equal to, the *parent's share of the undistributed income (reported net income — dividend distribution) of the subsidiary since acquisition.* This important definition is illustrated as follows:

END OF YEAR	UNDISTRIBUTED INCOME OF S COMPANY SINCE ACQUISITION BY PARENT (ILLUSTRATION 3-1)		PARENT'S % EQUITY IN S COMPANY		PARENT'S SHARE OF UNDISTRIBUTED INCOME OF S COMPANY SINCE ACQUISITION EQUALS DIFFERENCES IN BALANCES BETWEEN COST AND EQUITY METHODS (ILLUSTRATION 3-2)
1	50,000	×	.80	=	40,000
2	70,000	×	.80	=	56,000
3	10,000	×	.80	=	8,000
4	–0–	×	.80	=	–0–

METHODS OF REPORTING ON INVESTMENTS IN SUBSIDIARIES SUBSEQUENT TO ACQUISITION

Because a subsidiary is a separate legal entity, it maintains separate accounting records. Ordinarily, such records enable the subsidiary to prepare a full set of financial statements for the subsidiary. Where there is a minority interest, such financial statements are usually prepared and distributed by the subsidiary to minority shareholders and other interested parties. In the case of wholly owned subsidiaries, financial information may be conveyed only to the parent company, and the subsidiary may or may not otherwise prepare and distribute formal financial statements.

Apart from the preparation and distribution of financial statements by its subsidiaries, however, is the parent company's reporting of its interest in and control over the resources and income of its subsidiaries in its own annual and quarterly reports to stockholders and others. The parent company may report *all* of its subsidiaries on a consolidated basis (Consolidated Financial Statements of Parent and Subsidiary(s)), it may consolidate some subsidiaries but not others (Consolidated Financial Statements of Parent and Consolidated Subsidiary(s)), or it may choose not to consolidate any of its subsidiaries in its financial statements (Financial Statements of Parent Company Only).

Consolidated Financial Statements of Parent and Subsidiary(s)

In most cases, the parent company prepares consolidated financial statements that combine its operating results, financial position, and changes in financial position with those of its subsidiaries. The method (cost or equity) used by the parent company to record its investment in its consolidated subsidiary(s) has no effect on the amounts of individual assets, liabilities, equities, revenues, expenses, sources of financial resources, or application of financial resources reported in the consolidated financial statements. Differences in the amounts recorded on the parent company's books in the investment and related income accounts that result from using the cost rather than the equity method of accounting do, however, require different eliminating entries in the consolidating workpapers. Substantial attention is given in subsequent chapters to the differing effects of the cost and equity methods of recording an investment on such workpaper entries.

Consolidated Financial Statements of Parent and Consolidated Subsidiaries

Although there is a presumption that consolidation of subsidiaries is necessary for fair presentation in the financial statements, sufficient justification may exist not to consolidate a subsidiary because of nonhomogeneous operations or for other reasons suggested in Chapter 2. Financial statements in which some subsidiaries are consolidated but others are not are referred to as consolidated financial statements, but special care must be taken to disclose the fact that not all subsidiaries have been consolidated.

The appropriate treatment of unconsolidated subsidiaries in consolidated financial statements was first dealt with on an authoritative basis in paragraph 19 of *ARB No. 51* as follows:

> There are two methods of dealing with unconsolidated subsidiaries in consolidated statements. Whichever method is adopted should be used for all unconsolidated subsidiaries, subject to appropriate modification in special circumstances. The preferable method, in the view of the committee, is to adjust the investment through income currently to take up the share of the controlling company or companies in the subsidiaries' net income or net loss, except where the subsidiary was excluded because of exchange restrictions or other reasons which raise the question of whether the increase in equity has accrued to the credit of the group. (Adjustments of the investment would also be made for "special" debits or credits shown on the income statements of the unconsolidated subsidiaries below the net income for the period, and for similar items shown in the schedule of earned

surplus.) The other method, more commonly used at present, is to carry the investment at cost, and to take up income as dividends are received; however, provision should be made for any material impairment of the investment such as through losses sustained by the subsidiaries, unless it is deemed to be temporary. When the latter method is followed, the consolidated statements should disclose, by footnote or otherwise, the cost of the investment in the unconsolidated subsidiaries, the equity of the consolidated group of companies in their net assets, the dividends received from them in the current period, and the equity of the consolidated group in their earnings for the period; this information may be given in total or by individual subsidiaries or groups of subsidiaries.

Later, in *Opinion No. 10,* the Accounting Principles Board prescribed the use of the equity method for reporting most unconsolidated domestic subsidiaries in consolidated financial statements. Finally, in *Opinion No. 18,* the application of the equity method was extended, with limited exceptions, to all unconsolidated subsidiaries (foreign as well as domestic) in consolidated financial statements. The limited exceptions apply to subsidiaries that are not consolidated because of serious question as to the parent company's ability to control the subsidiary or appropriate the benefits of its ownership (e.g., subsidiaries in legal reorganization or bankruptcy and certain foreign subsidiaries with direct limitations on their ability to transfer funds out of the foreign country). In such cases, the cost method of reporting the parent's investment is considered appropriate.

In summary, generally accepted accounting standards require that investments in subsidiaries that are not consolidated be reported using the equity method. The equity method, however, is not a valid substitute for consolidation and does not justify the exclusion of a subsidiary from consolidation when consolidation is otherwise appropriate.

Financial Statements of Parent Company Only

Although consolidated financial statements are ordinarily considered necessary for fair presentation of the results of operations, financial position, and changes in financial position of parent-subsidiary affiliations, there are circumstances where parent company statements may be prepared in which all subsidiaries are reported as investments rather than consolidated. For example, parent-company-only statements may be necessary to present adequately the position of bondholders and other creditors or preferred stockholders of the parent company. In addition, under certain circumstances, parent-company-only statements as well as consolidated financial statements are required in registration statements and in annual filings with the SEC.

Prior to the issuance of *APB Opinion No. 18,* there was a general impression that the equity method of reporting unconsolidated subsidiaries was appropriate only in consolidated financial statements, and it was not clear as to whether the equity method was appropriate in the case of parent-company-only statements. For example, if the objective of parent-company-only statements is to focus on the parent company as a separate legal entity, it can be argued that the cost method of reporting on the intercorporate investment is more consistent with that objective than is the equity method because it recognizes that a subsidiary has no legal obligation to distribute earnings until it declares a dividend.

APB Opinion No. 18 removed most of the previous uncertainty by requiring that the equity method be applied to all unconsolidated subsidiaries in parent-company financial statements prepared for *issuance to stockholders* as the financial statements of the primary reporting entity.[1] The only exceptions to applying the equity method to unconsolidated subsidiaries in such reports relate to situations in which there is serious question as to the parent-company's ability to control the subsidiary or appropriate the benefits of its ownership. In such cases, the cost method of reporting the parent company's investment is considered appropriate.

Comparison of Equity Method Presentation and Consolidation of Investments in Subsidiaries

Excerpts from the financial statements of a parent company and its 85%-owned subsidiary are presented in Illustration 3–3.

The first column illustrates the manner in which parent-company-only information would be presented. The investment in the unconsolidated subsidiary is reported in the balance sheet of the parent company as a single amount, and the parent company's share of the unconsolidated subsidiary's income (85% of $18,200 equals $15,470) is reported in the income statement as a single amount. The second column illustrates excerpts from the financial statements prepared and distributed by the subsidiary to minority shareholders and others. The third column illustrates the manner in which consolidated financial information would be presented. In the consolidated financial statements, 100% of the subsidiary's current assets, property and equipment, liabilities, sales, cost of sales, and all other expense items are combined with the corresponding items of the parent company. The minority interest in the net assets of the subsidiary (15% of $106,600 equals $15,990) is reflected as a separate amount in the consolidated balance sheet, and the minority interest in the net income of the subsidiary (15% of $18,200 equals $2,730) is reflected as a separate item in the consolidated income statement.

Comparison of Columns 1 and 3 in Illustration 3–3 verifies that the amount of retained earnings and the amount of net income reported by the parent company are the same whether the investment in the subsidiary is consolidated or is reported separately using the equity method. This is no coincidence. *APB Opinion No. 18* is specifically aimed at ensuring that the effect on reported net income and retained earnings is the same when the equity method is used as it would be if the investment were consolidated.

Thus, the general requirement that all unconsolidated subsidiaries be reported in consolidated or parent-company-only financial statements using the equity method

---

[1] In *Opinion No. 18,* the APB indicated that it had deferred for future consideration the appropriate treatment of investments in subsidiaries in parent-company-only financial statements that are not prepared for *issuance to stockholders* as the financial statements of the primary reporting entity.

ILLUSTRATION 3–3
Comparison of Consolidation and Equity Method
Presentation of an Investment in an 85%-Owned Subsidiary

	EXCERPTS FROM FINANCIAL STATEMENTS (000 OMITTED)		
BALANCE SHEET	PARENT-COMPANY-ONLY STATEMENTS: EQUITY METHOD	SUBSIDIARY COMPANY STATEMENTS	CONSOLIDATED FINANCIAL STATEMENTS
Current Assets	$ 67,710	$ 36,080	$103,790
Investment in Unconsolidated Subsidiary	90,610		
Property and Equipment (net)	135,700	100,820	236,520
Total Assets	$294,020	$136,900	$340,310
Less Liabilities	62,000	30,300	92,300
Net Assets	$232,020	$106,600	$248,010
Less Minority Interest	NA	NA	15,990
Net Assets less Minority Interest	$232,020	$106,600	$232,020
Capital Stock	$100,000	$ 70,000	$100,000
Additional Paid-In Capital	38,700	—	38,700
Retained Earnings	93,320	36,600	93,320
Total Stockholders' Equity	$232,020	$106,600	$232,020
INCOME STATEMENT			
Sales	$350,000	$180,000	$530,000
Cost of Sales	240,200	103,400	343,600
Gross Profit	$109,800	$ 76,600	$186,400
All Other Expenses	73,500	58,400	131,900
Income Before Equity in Net Income of Unconsolidated Subsidiary	$ 36,300	NA	NA
Equity in Net Income of Unconsolidated Subsidiary	15,470	NA	NA
Income Before Minority Interest in Net Income of Consolidated Subsidiary	NA	NA	$ 54,500
Minority Interest in Net Income of Consolidated Subsidiary	NA	NA	2,730
Net Income	$ 51,770	$ 18,200	$ 51,770

NA = Not Applicable in this Statement

EQUITY   THE SAME!   CONSOLIDATION

means that the amount of reported net income and retained earnings, with few exceptions, will be the same whether or not a parent company prepares consolidated financial statements or consolidates all of its subsidiaries in the consolidated financial statements. Illustration 3–3 demonstrates, however, that there are differences between consolidation and the equity method and that the major differences lie in the details reported in the financial statements. In the consolidated financial statements, each category of the subsidiary's assets, liabilities, revenues, and expenses is combined with the corresponding item of the parent company. Under the equity method, the parent company's equity in the net assets of the subsidiary is presented as a single amount in the balance sheet, and its equity in the net income of the subsidiary is presented as a single amount in the income statement. Because of these characteristics, the equity method of reporting on an investment is often referred to as a "one-line consolidation."

The major similarities and differences in the details of the financial statements that are illustrated in Illustration 3–3 (purchase method) are equally applicable to investments in subsidiaries that are accounted for as poolings of interests.

Method Used to Record Activities of Consolidated Subsidiaries

Because all items *reported* in the consolidated financial statements will be identical whether the cost method or the equity method is used to *record* the activities of a consolidated subsidiary, one may question whether one method is preferable to the other for purposes of formal record keeping. The preferable method is the one that facilitates record keeping and reporting, and it varies among companies, depending on their particular circumstances.

The recording of subsidiary income using the equity method requires more formal entries, and some companies believe that such formal entries provide a better record than do workpaper entries. The equity method also facilitates the preparation of parent-company-only statements. In addition, the equity method provides self-checking control figures in the preparation of consolidated financial statements, since, with certain exceptions, consolidated net income and consolidated retained earnings should equal the parent's recorded net income and retained earnings when the equity method is used.

On the other hand, under the equity method, the preparation of formal entries is more burdensome than under the cost method. Complicated adjustments relating to intercompany profits, intercompany bonds, and/or subsequent depreciation or amortization of the difference between cost and book value may have to be made as adjustments to the amount of income recorded using the equity method. If the subsidiary is consolidated, the parent must make these calculations both when making the periodic formal entries recording the subsidiary's income and when preparing consolidated financial statements. Hence, some companies prefer the cost method because the equity method seems inefficient and repetitious.

REPORTING ON INVESTMENTS WHEN THE INVESTOR CAN EXERCISE SIGNIFICANT INFLUENCE OVER THE INVESTEE

Prior to 1971 and the issuance of *Accounting Principles Board Opinion No. 18*, revenue recognition standards were generally interpreted as prohibiting the recognition of income from an investment in the stock of a nonsubsidiary prior to the declaration of a dividend by the investee. This interpretation was based on the perspective that (1) an investor and a less-than-50%-owned investee are separate legal and accounting entities, (2) accordingly, the investor is not entitled to recognize income on such an investment until a right to claim the income exists, and (3) such a claim occurs only when and to the extent that dividends are declared by the investee. Thus, the cost method was considered to be the appropriate method of accounting for and reporting on investments in the voting stock of less-than-50%-owned investees.

Critics of the cost method, however, maintained that revenue recognition under this method is unduly restrictive and potentially misleading and that it results in the elevation of legal form over economic substance. They argued that the cost method generally fails to reflect the economic consequences of holding an investment, because dividends received may have little relationship either in amount or in timing to the income or loss currently accruing to the investor company. And, since the investor company is often in a position to influence the dividend policy of the investee, it could, within limits, adjust the timing and amount of its own reported income.

Critics of the cost method considered the equity method to be more appropriate because it measures and reports increases and decreases in the economic resources underlying an investment in the period in which the changes occur, and because it avoids the potential abuses that can arise from reliance on the receipt of dividends as the standard of income recognition.

In paragraph 12 of *APB Opinion No. 18,* the Board reasoned that, if an investment enables an investor to influence the operating or financial decisions of an investee, "... the investor then has a degree of responsibility for the return on its investment, and it is appropriate to include in the results of operations of the investor its share of the earnings or losses of the investee."

Accordingly, the Board concluded that the equity method of accounting should be used to report on investments in voting stock when the investor has the ability to exercise significant influence over the operating and financial policies of the investee even though the investor holds less than 50% of the voting stock.

The concept of "significant influence" was elaborated on in paragraph 17 of *Opinion No. 18* as follows:

> Ability to exercise that influence may be indicated in several ways, such as representation on the board of directors, participation in policy making processes, material intercompany transactions, interchange of managerial personnel, or technological dependency. Another important consideration is the extent of ownership by an investor in relation to the concentration of other shareholdings, but substantial or majority ownership of the voting stock of an investee by another investor does not necessarily preclude the ability to exercise significant influence by the investor. The Board recognizes that determining the ability of an investor to exercise such influence is not always clear and applying judgment is necessary to assess the status of each investment.

To assist in the application of such judgments, the Board established the presumption that, in the absence of evidence to the contrary, an investor has the ability to exercise significant influence over an investee if it owns 20% or more of the voting stock of the investee and, conversely, that an investor does not have the ability to exercise significant influence if it owns less than 20% of the voting stock of an investee unless such ability can be demonstrated.

Thus, in 1971, the application of the equity method of accounting was extended by *APB Opinion No. 18* to investments in 20%-and-over-owned investees, as well as to nonconsolidated subsidiaries. More recently, it has been argued that the equity method should be used to account for all significant investments in common stock, not just those in the 20-to-50% range, when they represent long-term business relationships where consolidation is inappropriate.[2] Under this view, the investor's purpose in holding the stock, rather than its presumed ability to significantly influence the operating or financial policies of the investee, would be the appropriate criterion for use of the equity method to recognize income on nonconsolidated investments in common stock.

ACCOUNTING AND REPORTING CONSIDERATIONS IN APPLYING THE EQUITY METHOD

Application of the equity method may involve considerations other than those discussed above. Most of these additional considerations will be discussed and illustrated in this chapter; however, those relating to (1) the treatment in periods subsequent to acquisition of the difference between the cost and the book value of an investment on the date it is acquired, (2) intercompany profits, and (3) changes in the percentage of ownership are discussed and illustrated in Chapters 5, 6, 7, and 8.

Determining Ownership Percentage and Share of Earnings

For purposes of the 20% presumption the investor, in determining its percentage of **voting stock interest** in an investee, should consider **all currently outstanding voting securities** of the investee. For purposes of income determination, the investor's share of earnings or loss of the investee should be based on the number of shares of *common stock* it holds. Securities that are defined as "common stock equivalents" under *APB Opinion No. 15* should not be considered as outstanding common stock in this calculation. The investor should compute its share of earnings after deducting the amount of the current year's preferred dividends that is declared or paid by the investee or that will require declaration and payment by the investee in the future, such as dividends on cumulative preferred stock.

Classification of Investment Income

The investor's share of income or loss from its investment is normally reported in the income statement as a single amount. However, if prior-period adjustments or extraordinary items reported by the inves*tee* are material in the income statement of

---

[2]Arthur Andersen & Co., *Accounting and Reporting Problems of the Accounting Profession,* Fifth Edition (Chicago: Arthur Andersen & Co., 1976), p. 201.

the invest*or,* they should be separately classified by the investor in the same manner as they were classified by the investee. For example, the investor's share of an investee's extraordinary item would also be set out as an extraordinary item in the investor's financial statements. Similarly, if the amounts reported by the investee are material to the investor, the investor's share of the investee's cumulative effect of an accounting change *(APB Opinion No. 20)* and the investor's share of the effect of the disposal of a segment of the investee's business *(APB Opinion No. 30)* should be reported in the investor's financial statements in the same manner as those items are reported in the investee's financial statements.

Deferred Income Tax

When the investor recognizes the income of a less than 50%-owned investee using the equity method of accounting, there is ordinarily a difference between pre-tax accounting income and taxable income. This difference is equal to the investor's interest in the undistributed earnings of the investee and arises because investee income is taxable to the investor only when it is received. This same difference exists when a parent company consolidates a subsidiary or reports its share of a subsidiary's income under the equity method, unless the subsidiary is also included in a consolidated income tax return, or the affiliated group of which it is a part elects the tax-free dividend alternative. The difference between the investor's taxable and pre-tax accounting income raises two major reporting issues.

1. Is the difference a timing difference or a permanent difference? If the difference is a timing difference, then deferred income tax treatment of the tax effects of the difference is appropriate. If the difference is a permanent difference, then no provision for deferred income taxes is necessary.

2. If the difference is a timing difference, what income tax rate should be used to calculate the tax effect? The flexibility inherent in the Internal Revenue Code may permit a parent company to be taxed on the ultimate distribution of the previously undistributed income of a subsidiary at special rates, which may vary, depending on how the distribution is structured. An investor's equity in the undistributed income of a nonsubsidiary investee may ultimately be realized in the form of a dividend, or it may be realized by sale or other disposition of the investment.

The nature and timing of transactions that reverse the timing difference and the ultimate taxability of currently undistributed investee income, therefore, vary and must be estimated. In order to determine the tax rates to use to calculate tax effects on undistributed subsidiary or other investee income in the current reporting period, therefore, assumptions must be made as to the ultimate form and timing of the realization of the undistributed earnings.

The Accounting Principles Board considered these issues as well as others in *APB Opinion No. 23* (subsidiaries and joint ventures) and *APB Opinion No. 24* (investees other than subsidiaries and joint ventures) and concluded as follows:

1. Nature of the difference:

A. Subsidiaries (*Opinion No. 23,* par. 9 to 12)

The Board concludes that including undistributed earnings of a subsidiary in the pre-tax accounting income of a parent company, either through consolidation or accounting for the investment by the equity method, may result in a timing difference, in a difference that may not reverse until indefinite future periods, or in a combination of both types of differences, depending on the intent and actions of the parent company. The Board believes it should be presumed that all undistributed earnings of a subsidiary will be transferred to the parent company. Accordingly, the undistributed earnings of a subsidiary included in consolidated income (or in income of the parent company) should be accounted for as a timing difference. However, the presumption that all undistributed earnings will be transferred to the parent company may be overcome, and no income taxes should be accrued by the parent company, if sufficient evidence shows that the subsidiary has invested or will invest the undistributed earnings indefinitely or that the earnings will be remitted in a tax-free liquidation. A parent company should have evidence of specific plans for reinvestment of undistributed earnings of a subsidiary which demonstrate that remittance of the earnings will be postponed indefinitely. Experience of the companies and definite future programs of operations and remittances are examples of the types of evidence required to substantiate the parent company's representation of indefinite postponement of remittances from a subsidiary.

B. Nonsubsidiary investees (*Opinion No. 24,* par. 7)

The Board concludes that the tax effects of differences between taxable income and pre-tax accounting income attributable to an investor's share of earnings of investee companies (other than subsidiaries and corporate joint ventures) accounted for by the equity method are related either to probable future distributions of dividends or to anticipated realization on disposal of the investment and therefore have the essential characteristics of timing differences. The Board believes that the ability of an investor to exercise significant influence over an investee differs significantly from the ability of a parent company to control investment policies of a subsidiary and that only control can justify the conclusion that undistributed earnings may be invested for indefinite periods.

2. Calculation of tax effects:

A. Subsidiaries (*Opinion No. 23,* par. 10)

Problems in measuring and recognizing the tax effect of a timing difference do not justify ignoring income taxes related to the timing difference. Income taxes of the parent company applicable to a timing difference in undistributed earnings of a subsidiary are necessarily based on estimates and assumptions. For example, the tax effect may be determined by assuming that unremitted earnings were distributed in the current period and that the parent company received the benefit of all available tax-planning alternatives and available tax credits and deductions.

B. Nonsubsidiary investees (*Opinion No. 24,* par. 8)

If evidence indicates that an investor's equity in undistributed earnings of an investee will be realized in the form of dividends, an investor should recognize income taxes attributable to the timing difference as if the equity in earnings of the investee that the investor included in income were remitted as a dividend during the period, recognizing available dividend-received deductions and foreign tax credits. If evidence indicates that an investor's equity in undistributed earnings of an investee will be realized by ultimate disposition of the investment, an investor should accrue income taxes attributable to the timing difference at capital gains or other appropriate rates, recognizing all available deductions and credits.

In summary, with the significant exception of differences resulting from the **permanently invested** undistributed earnings of a subsidiary (note that this same exception is not available in the case of nonsubsidiary investees), the difference in taxable and pre-tax accounting income that results from the application of the equity method of accounting is considered a timing difference, and entries must be made on the investor's or parent company's books to reflect the tax effect of the timing difference. The calculation of the tax effect necessarily depends on estimates and assumptions as to the nature of the transaction(s) that will result in the ultimate realization of the previously undistributed earnings.

Illustration of Income Tax Allocation   Investor Company owns 40% of the common stock of Tee Company and accounts for its investment using the equity method. For the year ended December 31, 1980, Investor Company has pre-tax accounting income exclusive of income recognized on its investment in Tee Company of $8,000,000. During the same period, Tee Company reported net income of $1,000,000 and distributed dividends of $200,000. The combined federal and state income tax rate for Investor Company is 60%. Investor Company acquired its investment in Tee Company for an amount that was equal to the book value of the equity it acquired in Tee Company on that date. Both federal and state income tax laws provide for the exclusion from taxable income of 85% of dividends received from domestic corporations. Investor Company has no other timing differences than that relating to its use of the equity method. The management of Investor Company does not intend to dispose of its investment in Tee Company in the foreseeable future.

Investor Company would make the following entries to record its equity in the operating results and dividend distributions of Tee Company:

Investment in Tee Company	400,000	
Investment Income		400,000
To record share of reported net income of Tee Company (.40 × 1,000,000 = 400,000)		

Cash	80,000	
Investment in Tee Company		80,000
To record dividends received from Tee Company (.40 × 200,000 = 80,000)		

Investor Company's income tax expense, income tax payable, and deferred income tax would be calculated and recorded as follows:

Income Tax Expense	4,800,000	
Income Tax Payable		4,800,000

    To provide for income tax expense on pre-tax accounting income exclusive of investment income (.60 × 8,000,000 = 4,800,000).

Income Tax Expense	36,000	
Income Tax Payable		7,200
Deferred Income Tax		28,800

    To provide for income tax expense on recorded investment income as follows:

Investor Company's share of reported net income of Tee Company	400,000
Less dividend-received exclusion available upon distribution (.85 × 400,000)	340,000
Amount subject to income tax when distributed	60,000
Income Tax Expense (.60 × 60,000)	36,000
Income taxes payable based on dividends received in current year (.60 × [.15 × 80,000])	7,200
Deferred income taxes on Investor Company's share of the undistributed 1980 earnings of Tee Company (.60 × [.15 × 320,000])	28,800
Income Tax Expense	36,000

In this illustration, deferred income tax is calculated on the assumption that Investor Company's share of the undistributed earnings of Tee Company will ultimately be realized by Investor Company in the form of a dividend. If realization is expected through the sale of the Tee Company stock, the calculation of deferred income tax would be based on capital gain rates. If Tee Company were a subsidiary, calculations similar to those presented in the illustration would ordinarily be used to determine income tax expense, income tax payable, and deferred income tax. If, however, there were sufficient evidence that Tee Company intended to permanently reinvest its undistributed earnings, *and* if *and only if* Tee Company were a subsidiary, no deferred tax would be recorded and income tax expense would be reduced accordingly.

Income Tax Allocation in Subsequent Chapters   Unless otherwise stated, all illustrations in subsequent chapters are based on the assumption that income not distributed by a subsidiary company is permanently invested and will never be remitted to the parent company. This simplifying assumption is made so that we can concentrate on the major issues being presented in those chapters without having to repeat the deferred tax treatment discussed in detail in this chapter.

In addition, although the entries discussed in this chapter are always necessary to recognize deferred income tax on the undistributed income of less than 50%-owned equity basis investees, they are omitted from illustrations presented in subsequent chapters in order that we may concentrate on the issues presented in those chapters.

Other Than Temporary Declines in Value

An other than temporary decline in the value of an investment that is reported under the equity method should be recognized by the investor. Evidence of a permanent loss in value includes the absence of an ability to recover the carrying amount of an investment, a series of operating losses that brings into question the ability of the investee to sustain an earnings capacity that justifies the carrying amount of the investment, or a decline in the market value of the stock of an investee that can be attributed to specific adverse conditions for that particular company or industry. Except in the case of marketable securities, it is difficult to measure the "value" of an investment and changes in it. In the case of marketable securities, changes in value may be easily measured, but judgments as to whether or not declines in market value are temporary or other than temporary are still difficult to make. Under the equity method of *reporting* for both subsidiaries and nonsubsidiary investees, if an other than temporary decline in value is determined to have occurred and if the estimated value of the investment is lower than its carrying value under the equity method, the investment account is written down to the lower value, and a realized loss in the amount of the necessary write-down is recognized in the current year's income statement.

To illustrate, assume that Vestor Company purchased 30% of the outstanding common stock of Stee Company for $800,000, and that undistributed earnings of Stee Company since Vestor Company purchased its stock amount to $100,000. Near the end of the current year, the total market value of Stee Company's outstanding common stock declines precipitously to $1,800,000 after the announcement by federal regulatory authorities of a permanent injunction against the production, use, or sale of Blue Dye #4 because of the environmental and health hazards associated with the product. Blue Dye #4 previously constituted about 50% of the production and sales of Stee Company.

In this illustration, the decline in the market value of the outstanding stock of Stee Company is considered to be other than temporary because of the specific adverse circumstances that precipitated the decline in value. Since the carrying value of the investment under the equity method ($800,000 + [.30 × $100,000] = $830,000) exceeds the market value of the investment (.30 × $1,800,000 = $540,000), the investment account must be written down to $540,000 and a $290,000 realized loss (before income tax effects) recognized in the current year's income statement. Income (loss) reported and dividends received from an investee subsequent to the write-down of the investment account are recorded under the equity method in the manner previously illustrated. Subsequent recoveries in the market value of the investment, however, are not recorded on the investor's books or recognized in the investor's income statement.

Reduction of Carrying Value Below Zero

Under the equity method of reporting a nonconsolidated subsidiary or other investee, the investor's share of reported investee loss is recorded as a charge to income and a reduction in the carrying amount of the investment. What happens if the point is reached where the investor's share of the current year's loss exceeds the carrying amount of the investment? Ordinarily, when the investment is reduced to zero, the investor would discontinue the application of the equity method and no additional loss would be provided for. The investor would then resume application of the equity method only after its share of net income subsequently reported by the investee equaled its share of the net loss that was not recognized during the period the equity method was suspended.

However, if the investor has guaranteed obligations of the investee or is otherwise committed to provide further financial support for the investee, the equity method should not be suspended and the investor should continue to recognize its share of reported investee losses even when the investment account has been reduced to zero. In circumstances where the investment account has been reduced to zero, additional losses should also be provided for if the imminent return of the investee to profitable operations seems assured. The equity method would not be suspended if, for example, a material nonrecurring loss of an isolated nature reduced the investment below zero but the underlying profitable operating pattern of the investee remained unimpaired. The treatment described above applies to nonconsolidated subsidiaries as well as to other investees that are reported at equity in the financial statements.

If the investment account is reduced below zero, the resulting credit balance may be reported as a liability or as a deduction from other investments (i.e., as a contra asset). We recommend reporting the credit balance as a liability, particularly when the investor has guaranteed obligations of the investee or is otherwise committed to provide further financial support to the investee.

Questions

1. How does the treatment of a liquidating dividend differ under the cost and equity methods of accounting?

2. Describe the calculation necessary to adjust an investment balance from the cost basis to the equity basis.

3. How should nonconsolidated subsidiaries be reported in consolidated financial statements? Does your answer apply to all nonconsolidated subsidiaries? Explain.

4. How should subsidiaries be reported in parent-company-only financial statements? Does your answer apply to all subsidiaries? Explain.

5. Why might a parent company *record* an investment in a subsidiary at cost if it knows that under generally accepted accounting principles it can never *report* that investment using the cost method?

6. Under some conditions it is desirable to exclude a subsidiary from consolidated reports. List the conditions under which a subsidiary should not be consolidated in the consolidated financial statements.

7. What differences in the amount of reported net income and retained earnings would one expect to find as a result of the use of the equity method of reporting an investment in a subsidiary, as opposed to consolidating this same subsidiary?

8. Is the use of the equity method of reporting a valid substitute for consolidation of a subsidiary? Explain.

9. Was the adoption of the equity method of reporting as the required method of reporting on investments in investees over which the investor has significant influence a relaxation or a constriction of revenue-recognition criteria for investment revenue?

10. What are the guidelines for evaluating significant influence for purposes of the application of the equity method of accounting.

11. What effect, if any, should an investor give to the current-year preferred dividend obligations of an investee when computing its share of the investee's earnings?

12. Under what circumstances may the difference between the amount of investment income recognized under the equity method and the amount of investment income included in taxable income be treated as a permanent difference rather than a timing difference? Do you agree with the conclusions embodied in authoritative standards on this question? Why or why not?

13. During an era of continually improving business operations, would one expect the equity method of accounting for investments to produce a larger or a smaller amount of investment revenue than the cost method? Explain.

14. In what circumstances, if any, might the balance in an investment account be reduced below zero?

15. What problems might confront auditors in verifying investment income reported under the equity method of accounting?

Problems

Problem 3-1

On January 1, 1980, Clayton Company purchased 75,000 of the 100,000 outstanding shares of common stock of Durant Corporation as a long-term investment. The purchase price was

$2,020,500 and was paid in cash. At the purchase date the balance sheet of Durant Corporation included the following (summarized):

Current assets (net)	$1,463,275
Long-term assets (net)	1,947,265
Other assets	379,845
Current liabilities	317,614
Long-term liabilities	778,771
Common stock (par $10)	1,000,000
Premium	945,700
Retained earnings	748,300

Additional data on Durant Corporation for the four years following the purchase:

	1980	1981	1982	1983
Net income (loss)	$1,664,960	$449,400	($149,600)	($329,400)
Cash dividends paid (12/31)	500,000	500,000	500,000	500,000

Required:

A. Prepare journal entries to record the purchase and to record all subsequent required entries on the books of Clayton Company, assuming that the cost method is used to account for its investment.

B. Prepare all entries indicated, assuming that the equity method is used to account for Clayton Company investments.

Problem 3–2

On December 31, 1980, Johnston Industries acquired 80% of the outstanding stock of Marston Machinery through a cash purchase for $475,000. Income and dividend information for Marston for six years following the acquisition is as follows:

YEAR	REPORTED INCOME	DIVIDENDS DISTRIBUTED
1981	$174,000	$50,000
1982	139,000	50,000
1983	71,000	75,000
1984	47,000	75,000
1985	(59,500)	75,000
1986	(9,400)	75,000

Required:

A. Utilizing a schedule of undistributed earnings, prepare journal entries for 1985 and 1986 under both the cost and the equity methods of accounting for investments.

B. Immediately after a liquidating dividend is recorded, the balance in the investment account and the total amount of subsidiary income recorded on the books of the parent company from date of acquisition to the date of the liquidating dividend is the same under both the cost and equity methods. Prepare a schedule for Johnston Industries and its subsidiary to reconcile the income totals and investment account balances under the two accounting methods at the end of 1986.

Problem 3–3

On January 1, 1980, Adam Company purchased 20% of the 25,000 shares of common stock of Cain Company for $24 per share. At that date, the following data were available:

	CAIN COMPANY
Assets	$1,000,000
Liabilities	200,000
Preferred Stock, 5%	200,000
Common Stock ($20 par)	500,000
Retained Earnings	100,000

At the end of 1980, Cain Company reported a net income of $475,000, declared a $10,000 preferred stock dividend, and paid a $125,000 cash dividend to common stockholders.

Required:
Prepare entries to account for Adam Company's investment in Cain Company from the date of the purchase of the investment through the end of 1980, assuming that:
(a) The cost method of accounting for investments is used.
(b) The equity method of accounting for investments is used.

Problem 3–4

Select the best answer for each of the following. Briefly justify your choice for each item.

1. Under the equity method, the effect on the investor of dividends received from the investee is usually
   (a) A reduction of deferred income taxes and a reduction of investment.
   (b) A reduction of deferred income taxes and no effect on investment.
   (c) No effect on deferred income taxes and a reduction of investment.
   (d) No effect on deferred income taxes and no effect on investment.

2. Ray Company has invested in several domestic manufacturing corporations. Ray would be most likely to use the equity method to determine the amount to be reported as an investment in its consolidated balance sheet for its holding of
   (a) 2,000 of the 50,000 outstanding common shares of Locke Company.
   (b) 3,000 of the 10,000 outstanding preferred shares of Dawes Company.
   (c) 15,000 of the 60,000 outstanding common shares of Bates Company. ✓
   (d) 20,000 of the 25,000 outstanding common shares of Welch Company.

3. American Commercial Ventures, Inc., owns 25% of the common stock of an overseas corporation which has consistently operated profitably since the investment was made. Because the foreign corporation needs capital for growth, the foreign interests who own a majority of its stock have declared no dividends and evidently have no intention of declaring any in the foreseeable future. In the light of these facts, American Commercial, which uses the equity method to account for its investment,
   (a) Need not now make any provision for taxes on the foreign profits.
   (b) Must accrue a provision for taxes on the foreign profits. ✓
   (c) Can provide, on a discretionary basis, for taxes on the foreign profits.
   (d) Should recognize taxes only when and as foreign profits are remitted as dividends (with a resultant prior-period adjustment).

4. When undistributed earnings of a subsidiary company have increased the pre-tax accounting income of a parent company, because the parent consolidated the subsidiary or used the equity method to account for its investment,
   (a) Income tax allocation is necessary, because there is an invariable presumption that undistributed earnings will ultimately be transferred to the parent.
   (b) Maximum tax rates should be applied as a matter of conservatism if income tax allocation is applied.
   (c) Income taxes need not be accrued where there is evidence that the subsidiary will not remit undistributed earnings to the parent for an indefinite period.
   (d) Generally accepted accounting principles have been violated.

5. What would be the effect on the financial statements if an unconsolidated subsidiary is accounted for by the equity method, but consolidated statements are being prepared with other subsidiaries?
   (a) All of the unconsolidated subsidiary's accounts would be included individually in the consolidated statements.
   (b) The consolidated retained earnings would not reflect the earnings of the unconsolidated subsidiary.
   (c) The consolidated retained earnings would be the same as if the subsidiary had been included in the consolidation.
   (d) Dividend revenue from the unconsolidated subsidiary would be reflected in the consolidated net income.

6. The Mon Corporation acquired a 30% interest in the Soon Company on January 1, 1980 for $600,000. At that time, Soon had 2,000,000 shares of its $1 par value common stock issued and outstanding. During 1980, Soon paid cash dividends of $20,000 and thereafter declared and issued a 5% common stock dividend when the market value was $2 per share. Soon's net income for 1980 was $120,000. What should the balance in Mon's "Investment in Soon Co." account be at the end of 1980?
   (a) $570,000
   (b) $600,000
   (c) $630,000
   (d) $636,000

(AICPA adapted)

Problem 3–5

On January 1, 1975, Scott Company acquired 30% of the common stock of Delta Company for $180,000 when the common stock and retained earnings of Delta Company were $500,000 and $100,000, respectively. Scott Company considers its investment in Delta Company to be a long-term investment and accounts for it by use of the equity method. The following information is available for the two companies:

	SCOTT COMPANY PRE-TAX ACCOUNTING INCOME	DELTA COMPANY REPORTED NET INCOME (LOSS)
Accounting Income (excluding investment income):		
1980	$600,000	$150,000
1981	700,000	(40,000)
1982	800,000	60,000

Delta Company distributed $50,000 in dividends in each of the years 1980, 1981, and 1982. The retained earnings balance of Delta Company on January 1, 1980 was $200,000. The combined federal and state income tax rate for Scott Company is 60%. Dividends received from Delta Company are subject to the 85% dividends-received deduction. Scott Company has no timing differences other than those relating to its use of the equity method to account for its investment in Delta Company.

Required:
A. Calculate the balance in the investment account and in the deferred income tax account on the books of Scott Company on January 1, 1980.
B. Prepare the necessary entries in general journal form to record Scott Company's equity in the operating results and dividend distributions of Delta Company and to record Scott Company's income tax liability and expense for each of the three years 1980 through 1982.
C. Calculate the balance in the investment account and in the deferred income tax account on the books of Scott Company on December 31, 1982.

Problem 3–6

Page Company purchased 30% of the outstanding common stock of Shiprock Company on June 1, 1976 for $450,000 when Shiprock Company (a domestic corporation) had stockholders' equity of $1,500,000. Page Company records and reports its investment in Shiprock Company using the equity method. Effective income tax rates for Page Company are 40% on ordinary income and 25% on capital gains. Eighty-five percent of dividends received from domestic corporations may be excluded from taxable income. In 1981, Shiprock Company reported net income of $150,000 and distributed dividends in the amount of $30,000.

P-S CONSOLIDATE

Required:
Prepare in general journal form the necessary entries, including tax consequences, that should be DON'T PROVIDE
recorded by Page Company during 1981 to account for its investment in Shiprock Company, DEFERRED
assuming that:
(a) Page Company never intends to dispose of its investment in Shiprock Company and has established that Shiprock Company intends to permanently reinvest all income that is not distributed currently.
(b) Page Company never intends to dispose of its investment and expects to recover its interest in the undistributed income of Shiprock Company in future dividend distributions.
(c) Page Company has established that Shiprock Company intends to permanently reinvest all income that is not distributed currently and expects to recover its interest in such undistributed earnings through the future sale of its investment in Shiprock Company.

Problem 3–7

During 1980, American Corporation owned voting common stock in two companies and accounted for these investments on the equity basis. Information concerning each of these investments is supplied below. American Corporation's effective income tax rate is 50% and its capital gains rate is 30%. Assume that 85% of dividends received by American Corporation are excluded from its taxable income.

Western Warehousing Company

American Corporation purchased 7,500 shares of Western Ware-housing Company for $375,000 on January 1, 1980. The following information is pertinent to Western Warehousing Company.

1. Total common shares outstanding	10,000
2. Net income—1980	$180,000
3. Common dividends—1980	$ 50,000
4. Total stockholders' equity at 1/1/80	$500,000

5. American Corporation has established that all of Western Warehousing Company's undistributed earnings for the foreseeable future will be invested in plant expansion.

Radio Equipment Corporation

American Corporation purchased 2,500 shares of Radio Equipment Corporation on January 1, 1980 for $1,250,000. The following information is pertinent to Radio Equipment Corporation.

1. Total common shares outstanding	10,000
2. Net income—1980	$ 500,000
3. Dividends—1980	$ 100,000
4. Total stockholders' equity at 1/1/80	$5,000,000

5. American Corporation ultimately expects to realize its equity in undistributed earnings through the sale of its investment in Radio Equipment Corporation.

Required:

Prepare in general journal form the entries, including tax effects, that should be recorded by American Corporation during 1980 for each of its investments.

Problem 3–8

Platte Company accounts for and reports its investment in Sand Company using the equity method of accounting. For the foreseeable future, Sand Company plans to permanently reinvest all income not currently distributed. In 1980, Sand Company reported net income of $500,000 and paid dividends of $300,000. Platte Company's marginal income tax rate is 40% on ordinary income and 25% on long-term capital gains. Platte Company can deduct from its taxable income 85% of any dividends received from Sand Company.

Required:

A. Prepare the entry(s) on Platte Company's books in 1980 to record income tax expense on the income recognized by it on its investment in Sand Company, assuming that:
   (1) Platte Company owns 75% of the common stock of Sand Company and intends to hold it indefinitely.
   (2) Platte Company owns 30% of the common stock of Sand Company, and its interest in the undistributed income of Sand Company is expected to be realized through the sale of the Sand Company Stock.
   (3) Platte Company owns 30% of the common stock of Sand Company and intends to hold it indefinitely.

B. Describe the proper financial statement classification of the deferred income tax balance that results from the entries prepared in Part A (2) above.

Problem 3–9

On May 22, 1975, Prescott Company acquired 75% of the outstanding common stock of Showlow Company (a domestic corporation) for $900,000, at which date the book value of the stockholders' equity of Showlow Company was $1,200,000. Prescott Company records and reports its investment in Showlow Company using the equity method. Effective income tax rates for Prescott Company are 40% on ordinary income and 25% on capital gains. Eighty-five percent of dividends received from domestic corporations may be excluded from taxable income. In 1981, Showlow Company reported net income of $400,000 (including an extraordinary gain of $50,000 net of tax) and distributed dividends in the amount of $100,000.

Required:

Prepare in general journal form the entries, including tax consequences, that should be recorded by Prescott Company during 1981 to account for its investment in Showlow Company, assuming that:

(a) Prescott Company has established that all earnings not currently distributed by Showlow Company will be permanently reinvested by that company.

(b) There is insufficient evidence to determine what amount of Showlow Company's earnings will ultimately be reinvested and what amount will be included in future dividend distributions.

Problem 3–10

Several years ago, Provo Products purchased 35% of the common stock of Salt Lake Industries for $195,500, an amount equal to the equity interest acquired. Provo accounts for this investment by the equity method. For the first three years following the acquisition, the following income and dividend data were available for the two entities:

	PROVO PRODUCTS	SALT LAKE INDUSTRIES
	PRE-TAX ACCOUNTING INCOME	REPORTED NET INCOME
Accounting income (excluding investment income):		
Year 1	$2,453,500	$61,545
Year 2	1,757,625	44,360
Year 3	1,665,425	39,885
Dividend distributions:		
Year 1		$50,000
Year 2		50,000
Year 3		50,000

The combined federal and state income tax rate for Provo Products is 60%. Provo Products may exclude 85% of any dividends received from Salt Lake Industries from its taxable income in the year they are received.

Required:

A. Prepare the necessary entries to record Provo Products' equity in the operating results and dividend distributions of Salt Lake Industries and to record Provo Products' income tax liability and expense for each of the three periods.

B. How should the balance in the deferred income tax account at the end of Year 3 be classified on the balance sheet?

Problem 3–11

Petrol Company acquired a 60% interest in the common stock of Solvent Company on January 1, 1980 for $1,950,000. Petrol Company records its investment in Solvent Company using the cost method. Solvent Company follows a policy of permanently reinvesting all of its income. The unadjusted trial balance for each company on December 31, 1980 is presented in summary form below:

Trial Balance
December 31, 1980

	PETROL COMPANY	SOLVENT COMPANY
	DEBITS	DEBITS
Current Assets	$1,480,000	$1,200,000
Noncurrent Assets	3,950,000	3,000,000
Investment in Solvent Co.	1,950,000	—
Cost of Sales	1,100,000	700,000
Selling, Admin. & Tax Expense	400,000	150,000
Cumulative effect of change in accounting method (net of tax) to the beginning of year	–0–	300,000
Total	$8,880,000	$5,350,000

	CREDITS	CREDITS
Current Liabilities	$ 880,000	$ 750,000
Noncurrent Liabilities	1,000,000	–0–
Capital Stock	3,000,000	2,000,000
Additional Paid-in Capital	500,000	–0–
Retained Earnings 1/1/80	1,500,000	1,250,000
Sales	2,000,000	1,200,000
Extraordinary Item (net of tax)	–0–	150,000
Total	$8,880,000	$5,350,000

Required:

A. Prepare a balance sheet and a combined statement of income and retained earnings for the year ending December 31, 1980, under each of the following assumptions:

(1) Parent-company-only financial statements are to be prepared with the investment in Solvent Company reflected therein using the equity method of reporting a nonconsolidated subsidiary.

(2) Consolidated financial statements are to be prepared.

Problem 3–12

La Palma, Inc., a restaurant chain, acquired 80% of another smaller food chain, Tiny Burgers, six years ago, paying an amount equal to the book value of the stock acquired. Financial data for the past year, 1980, are given in the following unadjusted trial balances.

	LA PALMA DR.	LA PALMA CR.	TINY BURGERS DR.	TINY BURGERS CR.
Cash	$ 174,585		$ 36,494	
Accounts Receivable	13,168		3,296	
Supplies Inventory 12/31/80	29,455		11,675	
Other Current Assets	48,766		4,356	
Land	175,712		75,982	
Buildings (net)	308,155		200,432	
Investment in Tiny Burgers—1/1/80	172,392			
Accounts Payable		$ 67,775		$ 49,250
Taxes Payable		23,750		17,540
Mortgages Payable		175,750		55,600
Long-term Notes Payable		25,450		15,975
Common Stock		200,000		80,000
Premium		275,000		74,500
Retained Earnings—1/1/80		133,353		60,990
Sales		375,500		74,950
Cost of Goods Sold	255,454		48,550	
Miscellaneous Operating Expenses	61,117		26,653	
Administrative Expenses	26,659		13,678	
Other Expenses	11,115		7,689	
Totals	$1,276,578	$1,276,578	$428,805	$428,805

Required:

A. Prepare a parent-company-only balance sheet and income statement, assuming that the two companies were not consolidated, and that La Palma, Inc. used the equity method of accounting for its investment (ignore income tax effects).

B. Prepare a consolidated balance sheet and income statement, assuming that the two companies are consolidated (ignore income tax effects).

C. Compare the financial statement results of these two methods of reporting the investment in Tiny Burgers.

Problem 3–13

On January 1, 1980, Marshall Enterprises purchased 2,500 of the 10,000 outstanding shares of common stock of Randall Company, paying an amount equal to the book value of the shares acquired. Relevant income statement data for the two firms for 1980 follow.

	MARSHALL ENTERPRISES	RANDALL COMPANY
Gross Revenues	$4,162,755	$755,436
Cost of Goods Sold	2,986,754	485,618
Miscellaneous Operating Expense	374,932	52,784
Administrative Expense	166,693	23,347
Retained Earnings (1/1/80)	864,279	137,482

In addition to the data above, the following items are relevant to the financial operations of the two companies for 1980:

1. Randall Company suffered a $275,500 uninsured loss when one of its plants was demolished by a flash flood. Management had not carried flood insurance on the plant because of its location in a semi-arid region where no such natural disasters had ever been recorded.

2. Randall Company embarked upon a plan to dispose of all its chemical manufacturing facilities on June 30, 1980. The chemical operations accounted for 20% of Randall's revenue and 30% of costs and expenses during 1979, spread evenly throughout the year. The final disposal date was December 31, 1980, and the facilities were sold at a loss of $180,000.

3. Randall changed from the double-declining balance method to the straight-line method of depreciating its manufacturing equipment. The cumulative effect of the change on prior years was to increase income by $104,103. (The new method became effective on January 2, 1980.)

4. In previous years, Randall Company had recorded royalty income on the cash basis. Starting with 1980, royalty income was recorded when earned. The effect of this change was the recognition of additional income for prior periods in the amount of $47,565. (This change was made to comply with generally accepted accounting principles.)

5. In 1980, Marshall Enterprises had additional income of $135,400 resulting from changes in accounting principles, and an extraordinary fire loss of $452,875. (The additional income represents the cumulative effect on prior years of the change in principles.)

Assuming that all amounts are material (ignore income taxes):
(a) Prepare an income statement and statement of retained earnings for Randall Company.
(b) Prepare an income statement and statement of retained earnings for Marshall Enterprises in which its investment income is recognized by use of the equity method.

Problem 3–14

Jensen Laboratories, a drug company, manufactures and distributes a variety of nonprescription drugs, and sundry cosmetic products. Vector Company, realizing the excellent profit potential in the nonprescription drug and cosmetics business, purchased 30% of the outstanding voting common stock shares of Jensen Laboratories in 1974 for $700,000, an amount equal to the equity acquired. Undistributed earnings for Jensen from the date of acquisition to January 1, 1980, amounted to $645,000.

More than 45% of Jensen's revenues for the last five years had come from the sale of its facial cleanser products. During 1980, a federal agency found one of the ingredients of this product line to be a cancer-causing agent, and banned its use in products manufactured in the United States. Stockholders witnessed a precipitous decline in their common stock holdings during the remainder of 1980, and as of December 31, 1980, the total market value of Jensen Laboratories' outstanding common stock had decreased to $1,500,000.

Additional information related to Jensen Laboratories' performance during 1980 and 1981 is as follows:

	1980	1981
Net Income	$255,545	$395,500
Dividends Paid	150,000	150,000

Required:

A. Prepare the journal entries that would be required on the books of Vector Company during 1980. Management considers the decline in the market value of the Jensen Laboratories common stock to be permanent.

B. Early in 1981 an outstanding scientist working for Jensen Laboratories found an effective replacement for the banned ingredient, and the market responded with an increase in the total market value for the common stock of Jensen Laboratories to $2,200,000. Prepare the journal entries required during 1981.

Problem 3–15

In 1970, Prent Company acquired a 90% interest in Export Company for $70,000. Export Company is incorporated and located in a foreign country. Prent Company does not consolidate its subsidiary but reports it in its consolidated financial statements as a separate investment using the equity method.

On December 31, 1980, Prent Company reported its equity in the underlying net assets of Export Company at $100,000 and the deferred income tax credit on the undistributed income of the unconsoliated subsidiary at $12,000. The average income tax rate for Prent Company is 40%. There is no dividend exclusion or other income tax preference available to Prent Company on dividends received from Export Company. Export Company reported a loss of $250,000 for the year ending December 31, 1981. No dividends were declared by Export Company in 1981.

The requirements for this problem are based on the three independent assumptions described below. Each assumption is independent of the others.

1. Assume that Prent Company has guaranteed unpaid obligations of Export Company in the amount of $400,000.

2. Assume that the income statement of Export Company for the year ending December 31, 1981 includes an extraordinary loss (net of tax) of $300,000 and that Export Company can be expected to continue modestly profitable operations in future years.

3. Assume that the 1981 loss of Export Company is the latest in a series of loss years for that company and that Prent Company has abandoned any plans to provide (and has no obligation to provide), additional financial support to Export Company.

Required:

A. For each of the three independent assumptions described above:

   (1) Prepare entries in general journal form to record Prent Company's equity in the reported loss of Export Company for 1981 including related income tax effects (if any).

   (2) Calculate tha balance on December 31, 1981 of the investment account and of the deferred tax and/or other balance sheet accounts relating to Prent Company's investment in Export Company.

B. Export Company reports net income of $60,000 in 1982. No dividends are declared by Export Company in 1982. Prepare entries in general journal form to record Prent Company's equity in the income of Export Company and related income tax effects for the year ending December 31, 1982 if:

   (1) The same facts apply for 1981 as those in Assumption 1 above.

   (2) The same facts apply for 1981 as those in Assumption 2 above.

C. Export Company reports net income of $150,000 in 1982. No dividends are declared by Export Company in 1982. Prepare entries in general journal form to record Prent Company's equity in the income of Export Company and related income tax effects for the year ending December 31, 1982 if the same facts apply for 1981 as those in Assumption 3 above.

4

Consolidated Statements Subsequent to Acquisition

The preparation of consolidated financial statements at a date subsequent to acquisition is not materially different in concept from preparing them at the acquisition date in the sense that reciprocal accounts are eliminated and remaining balances are combined. The process is more complex, however, because time has elapsed and business activity has taken place between the date of acquisition and the date of consolidated statement preparation. On the date of acquisition, the only relevant financial statement is the consolidated balance sheet; subsequent to acquisition, a complete set of consolidated financial statements, income statement, retained earnings statement, balance sheet, and statement of changes in financial position must be prepared for the affiliated group of companies.[1] In addition, as discussed earlier, the parent company may elect to use either the cost or equity method of accounting for its investments on its records.

WORKPAPER FORMAT

Accounting workpapers are used to accumulate, classify, and/or arrange data for a variety of accounting purposes, including the preparation of financial reports and statements. Although workpaper style and technique vary among firms and individuals, we have adopted a formalized, three-section workpaper for illustrative purposes in this book. The format includes a separate section for each of the three basic financial

[1]Technically, under the pooling of interests method a full set of financial statements that combine the activities of the pooled subsidiary could be parepared for the full fiscal period ending on the date of acquisition.

statements, income statement, retained earnings statement, and balance sheet. In most cases the input to the workpaper comes from the individual financial statements of the affiliates to be consolidated, in which case the three-section workpaper is particularly appropriate. At times, however, input may be from affiliate trial balances, and the data must be arranged in financial statement form to accommodate completion of the workpaper.

The discussion and illustrations that follow are based on trial balances at December 31, 1980 for P Company and S Company given below. When modification of the data is necessary in some illustrations, the changes will be pointed out.

	DECEMBER 31, 1980			
	P COMPANY		S COMPANY	
	DR.	CR.	DR.	CR.
Cash	37,000		13,000	
Accounts Receivable (net)	64,000		28,000	
Inventory, 1/1/80	56,000		32,000	
Investment in S Company	210,000			
Plant and Equipment (net)	180,000		165,000	
Other Assets	35,000		17,000	
Accounts Payable		31,000		24,000
Other Liabilities		62,000		37,000
Common Stock, $10 par		200,000		100,000
Premium on Common Stock		40,000		50,000
Retained Earnings, 1/1/80		210,000		40,000
Dividends Declared	20,000		15,000	
Sales		300,000		160,000
Dividend Income		15,000		
Purchases	186,000		95,000	
Expenses	70,000		46,000	
	858,000	858,000	411,000	411,000
Inventory, 12/31/80	67,000		43,000	

INVESTMENT ELIMINATION UNDER
THE PURCHASE METHOD—A WHOLLY OWNED SUBSIDIARY

You will recall that there are two methods of accounting for the investment on the parent company's records, the cost method and the equity method. When the acquisition is accounted for as a purchase, the investment is recorded initially at its purchase price or cost under both the cost and equity methods. Illustrations of these two methods for a wholly owned subsidiary follow. (Throughout this chapter, any difference between the cost of the investment and the book value of equity acquired is assumed to relate to the under- or over-valuation of subsidiary land and is, therefore, assigned to plant and equipment in the elimination entry.)

Investment Carried at Cost—Year of Acquisition

Assume that P Company purchased all of the outstanding shares of S Company common stock on January 1, 1980 for $210,000, and the following entry was made:

Investment in S Company	210,000	
Cash		210,000

On June 6, 1980, S Company paid a dividend of $15,000, which was debited to a "dividends declared" account, a temporary account that is closed to retained earnings at year-end. Since P Company owns all of S Company's stock, the receipt of the dividend was recorded under the cost method as:

Cash	15,000	
Dividend Income		15,000

Note that the trial balance data reflect the effect of both the investment and dividend transactions.

A workpaper for the preparation of consolidated financial statements at December 31, 1980, the end of the year of acquisition, is presented in Illustration 4–1.

Data from the trial balances are arranged in statement form and entered on the workpaper. Consolidated financial statements should include only those balances resulting from transactions with outsiders. Eliminating techniques are designed to accomplish this end. The consolidated income statement is essentially a summary or combination of the revenue, expense, gain, and loss of all consolidated affiliates after elimination of amounts representing the effect of transactions among the affiliates. The net income resulting is reduced by the minority interest's share (if any) of the net income of subsidiaries. The remainder, which is identified as **consolidated net income,** consists of parent company net income plus or minus its share of affiliate's income or loss resulting from transactions with outside parties. The consolidated retained earnings statement consists of the normal ordering of the statement, beginning consolidated retained earnings plus consolidated net income or minus consolidated net loss, minus parent-company dividends declared. The net represents consolidated retained earnings at the end of the period.

Several observations should be noted concerning the workpaper, Illustration 4–1:

1. The total net income line from the income statement section of the workpaper is carried down to the retained earnings section; likewise, the ending retained earnings line in the retained earnings section is carried to the balance sheet section. Of course, the eliminations columns in each section do not balance, since individual eliminations made involve more than one section. The total eliminations for all three sections, however, are in balance.

2. Each section of the workpaper represents one of the three consolidated financial statements.

ILLUSTRATION 4–1
Consolidated Statements Workpaper
P Company and Subsidiary
For Year Ending December 31, 1980

	P COMPANY	S COMPANY	ELIMINATIONS DR.	ELIMINATIONS CR.	CONSOLIDATED BALANCES
INCOME STATEMENT					
Sales	300,000	160,000			460,000
Dividend Income	15,000		¹ 15,000		
Total Revenue	315,000	160,000			460,000
Cost of Goods Sold:					
Inventory—1/1/80	56,000	32,000			88,000
Purchases	186,000	95,000			281,000
	242,000	127,000			369,000
Inventory—12/31/80	67,000	43,000			110,000
Cost of Goods Sold	175,000	84,000			259,000
Other Expense	70,000	46,000			116,000
Total Cost and Expense	245,000	130,000			375,000
Net Income to Retained Earnings	70,000	30,000	15,000	–0–	85,000
RETAINED EARNINGS STATEMENT					
1/1/80 Retained Earnings					
P Company	210,000				210,000
S Company		40,000	² 40,000		
Net Income from above	70,000	30,000	15,000	–0–	85,000
Dividends Declared					
P Company	(20,000)				(20,000)
S Company		(15,000)		¹ 15,000	
12/31/80 Retained Earnings to Balance Sheet	260,000	55,000	55,000	15,000	275,000
BALANCE SHEET					
Cash	37,000	13,000			50,000
Accounts Receivable (net)	64,000	28,000			92,000
Inventory—12/31/80	67,000	43,000			110,000
Investment in S Company	210,000			²210,000	
Plant and Equipment (net)	180,000	165,000	² 20,000		365,000
Other Assets	35,000	17,000			52,000
Total	593,000	266,000			669,000
Accounts Payable	31,000	24,000			55,000
Other Liabilities	62,000	37,000			99,000
Common Stock					
P Company	200,000				200,000
S Company		100,000	²100,000		
Premium on Common Stock					
P Company	40,000				40,000
S Company		50,000	² 50,000		
Retained Earnings from above	260,000	55,000	55,000	15,000	275,000
Total	593,000	266,000	225,000	225,000	669,000

¹To eliminate intercompany dividends.
²To eliminate investment in S Company.

3. The elimination of intercompany dividends is made by a debit to dividend income and a credit to dividends declared. This elimination is needed to prevent the double counting of income, since the subsidiary's individual income and expense items are combined with the parent's in the determination of consolidated net income.

4. The elimination of the investment account is the same one that would be made at the date of acquisition for the preparation of a consolidated balance sheet.

5. Consolidated net income of $85,000 represents P Company's net income before subsidiary dividends of $55,000 ($70,000 − $15,000) plus P Company's share of S Company's income ($30,000 × 100%), of $30,000.

6. Consolidated retained earnings represent P Company's beginning retained earnings (S Company's retained earnings having been eliminated as part of the equity acquired) plus consolidated net income minus dividends declared by P Company. Or, consolidated retained earnings may be thought of as P Company's retained earnings, $260,000, plus P Company's share of the *undistributed* income of S Company since acquisition (100% × [$30,000 − $15,000]) of $15,000.

Investment Carried at Equity—Year of Acquisition

Continue the situation in the preceding illustration, but assume that P Company has elected to use the equity method in accounting for its investment in its wholly owned subsidiary, S Company. The investment is initially recorded at its cost; however, under the equity method the parent's share of subsidiary dividends and income is recorded in the investment account. Thus, P Company made the following entries during 1980 relative to its investment in S Company.

1/1/80 Investment in S Company	210,000	
Cash		210,000
6/6/80 Cash	15,000	
Investment in S Company		15,000
12/31/80 Investment in S Company	30,000	
Equity in Subsidiary Income		30,000

After these entries are posted, the investment account would appear as presented below:

INVESTMENT IN S COMPANY

1/1/80	210,000	6/6/80 Sub. Dividends	15,000
12/31/80 Sub. Income	30,000		
12/31/80 Balance	225,000		

A consolidated statements workpaper under the equity method is presented in Illustration 4–2.

Purchase Accounting
Equity Method
Wholly Owned Subsidiary
Year of Acquisition

ILLUSTRATION 4–2
Consolidated Statements Workpaper
P Company and Subsidiary
For Year Ending December 31, 1980

	P COMPANY	S COMPANY	ELIMINATIONS DR.	ELIMINATIONS CR.	CONSOLIDATED BALANCES
INCOME STATEMENT					
Sales	300,000	160,000			460,000
Equity in Subsidiary Income	30,000		¹ 30,000		
Total Revenue	330,000	160,000			460,000
Cost of Goods Sold	175,000	84,000			259,000
Other Expense	70,000	46,000			116,000
Total Cost and Expense	245,000	130,000			375,000
Net Income to Retained Earnings	85,000	30,000	30,000	–0–	85,000
RETAINED EARNINGS STATEMENT					
1/1/80 Retained Earnings					
P Company	210,000				210,000
S Company		40,000	² 40,000		
Net Income from above	85,000	30,000	30,000	–0–	85,000
Dividends Declared					
P Company	(20,000)				(20,000)
S Company		(15,000)		¹ 15,000	
12/31/80 Retained Earnings to					
Balance Sheet	275,000	55,000	70,000	15,000	275,000
BALANCE SHEET					
Cash	37,000	13,000			50,000
Accounts Receivable (net)	64,000	28,000			92,000
Inventory—12/31/80	67,000	43,000			110,000
Investment in S Company	225,000			¹ 15,000	
				²210,000	
Plant and Equipment (net)	180,000	165,000	² 20,000		365,000
Other Assets	35,000	17,000			52,000
Total	608,000	266,000			669,000
Accounts Payable	31,000	24,000			55,000
Other Liabilities	62,000	37,000			99,000
Common Stock					
P Company	200,000				200,000
S Company		100,000	²100,000		
Premium on Common Stock					
P Company	40,000				40,000
S Company		50,000	² 50,000		
Retained Earnings from above	275,000	55,000	70,000	15,000	275,000
Total	608,000	266,000	240,000	240,000	669,000

¹To reverse effect of parent-company entries during the year for subsidiary dividends and income.
²To eliminate investment in S Company.

The detail making up cost of goods sold is provided in Illustration 4–1. In future illustrations in this chapter the detail will be collapsed into one item "Cost of Goods Sold."

Observe that the only differences in the affiliates' account data from Illustration 4–1 appear in P Company's data; equity in subsidiary income of $30,000 rather than dividend income is reported in P Company's income statement, and the reported retained earnings of P Company at 12/31/80 reflects the effect of the increase in reported income.

Where the investment account is carried on the equity basis, it is necessary first to make a workpaper entry reversing the net effect of parent-company entires on the investment account for subsidiary income and dividends during the current year. The entry, in general journal form, is:

Equity in Subsidiary Income	30,000	
Dividends Declared—S Company		15,000
Investment in S Company		15,000

This reversal has two effects. First, it eliminates intercompany equity in subsidiary income. Second, it returns the investment account to its balance as of the beginning of the year. This is necessary because it is the parent's share of the subsidiary's retained earnings at the *beginning of the year* that is eliminated in the investment elimination entry. Income statement detail for the year is included separately on the consolidated workpaper. A second eliminating entry must then be made to eliminate the investment account against subsidiary equity, as follows:

Common Stock—S Company	100,000	
Premium on Common Stock—S Company	50,000	
Retained Earnings, 1/1/80—S Company	40,000	
Plant and Equipment (Land)	20,000	
Investment in S Company (225,000 − 15,000)		210,000

Completion of the workpaper follows the same process as that used under the cost method.

Comparison of Illustrations 4–1 and 4–2 brings out one important observation. The consolidated column of the workpaper is the same under both the cost and equity methods. Thus, the decision to use the cost or equity method in accounting for investments in *subsidiaries that will be consolidated* will have no impact upon the consolidated financial statements. Only the elimination process is affected.

Both previous situations dealt with the preparation of consolidated financial statements at the end of the year of acquisition. The process of preparation of consolidated statements for periods subsequent to the year of acquisition for a wholly owned subsidiary under both cost and equity methods will now be discussed and illustrated.

Investment Carried at Cost—Subsequent to Year of Acquisition

For illustration purposes, assume continuation of the previous example with data updated to December 31, 1981. Trial balances for P Company and its wholly owned subsidiary, S Company, at December 31, 1981 are:

	DECEMBER 31, 1981			
	P COMPANY		S COMPANY	
	DR.	CR.	DR.	CR.
Cash	54,000		36,000	
Accounts Receivable (net)	68,000		32,000	
Inventory, 1/1/81	67,000		43,000	
Investment in S Company (cost)	210,000			
Plant and Equipment (net)	220,000		185,000	
Other Assets	38,000		18,000	
Accounts Payable		52,000		30,000
Other Liabilities		70,000		45,000
Common Stock		200,000		100,000
Premium on Common Stock		40,000		50,000
Retained Earnings, 1/1/81		260,000		55,000
Dividends Declared, 8/10/81	30,000		10,000	
Sales		350,000		190,000
Dividend Income		10,000		
Purchases	215,000		90,000	
Other Expenses	80,000		56,000	
	982,000	982,000	470,000	470,000
Inventory, 12/31/81	82,000		39,000	

Note that the "Investment in S Company" account still reflects the cost of the investment, $210,000, since the cost method is being used. Also, the retained earnings balances for P and S Companies on 1/1/81 are consistent with the balances on 12/31/80 in Illustration 4–1.

A workpaper for the preparation of consolidated financial statements for P and S Companies under the cost method for the year ending December 31, 1981 is presented in Illustration 4–3.

The workpaper entries in years subsequent to the year of acquisition are essentially the same as those made for the year of acquisition (Illustration 4–1) with one major exception. Prior to the elimination of the investment account, a workpaper entry, (1) in Illustration 4–3, is made to the investment account and P Company's beginning retained earnings to recognize P Company's share of the cumulative undistributed income or loss of S Company from the date of acquisition to the beginning of the current year as follows:

Investment in S Company	15,000	
Retained Earnings—P Company		15,000

This adjustment has the effect of placing the investment account at the same balance it would have had at the beginning of the year if the equity method had been used ($225,000 in this illustration). S Company earned $30,000 during 1980, $15,000 of which was distributed to P Company in the form of a dividend and is, therefore, included in P Company's retained earnings balance. The remaining $15,000 represents P Company's share of S Company's undistributed income for 1980. The process may be thought of as simply restating the investment account and parent company retained earnings to the balances they would have had at the beginning of the current year under the equity method. The process also facilitates the elimination of the investment account against the subsidiary's equity. In addition, the adjustment to P Company's retained earnings recognizes that P Company's share of S Company's undistributed income (loss) from the date of acquisition to the beginning of the current year is properly an addition to (deduction from) beginning consolidated retained earnings.

Actually, the amount of the adjustment can be computed more readily and accurately by multiplying the parent company's percentage of ownership times the increase or decrease in the subsidiary's retained earnings from the date of acquisition to the beginning of the current year. This approach will automatically adjust for complications that might arise where the subsidiary may have made direct entries to its retained earnings for error corrections or prior-period adjustments.[2]

After the adjustment has been prepared, intercompany dividend income is eliminated and P Company's share of S Company's equity is eliminated against the adjusted investment account as follows:

---

[2]The parent's share of any prior-period adjustments or error corrections to retained earnings made by the subsidiary subsequent to acquisition that relate to periods prior to acquisition should be adjusted (1) to the difference between cost and book value under the purchase method, and (2) to the investment account and related equity accounts used in the initial investment entry under the pooling method.

ILLUSTRATION 4–3
Consolidated Statements Workpaper
P Company and Subsidiary
For Year Ending December 31, 1981

	P COMPANY	S COMPANY	ELIMINATIONS DR.	ELIMINATIONS CR.	CONSOLIDATED BALANCES
INCOME STATEMENT					
Sales	350,000	190,000			540,000
Dividend Income	10,000		² 10,000		
Total Revenue	360,000	190,000			540,000
Cost of Goods Sold	200,000	94,000			294,000
Other Expense	80,000	56,000			136,000
Total Cost and Expense	280,000	150,000			430,000
Net Income to Retained Earnings	80,000	40,000	10,000	–0–	110,000
RETAINED EARNINGS STATEMENT					
1/1/81 Retained Earnings					
P Company	260,000			¹ 15,000	275,000
S Company		55,000	³ 55,000		
Net Income from above	80,000	40,000	10,000	–0–	110,000
Dividends Declared					
P Company	(30,000)				(30,000)
S Company		(10,000)		² 10,000	
12/31/81 Retained Earnings to					
Balance Sheet	310,000	85,000	65,000	25,000	355,000
BALANCE SHEET					
Cash	54,000	36,000			90,000
Accounts Receivable (net)	68,000	32,000			100,000
Inventory—12/31/81	82,000	39,000			121,000
Investment in S Company	210,000		¹ 15,000	³225,000	
Plant and Equipment (net)	220,000	185,000	³ 20,000		425,000
Other Assets	38,000	18,000			56,000
Total	672,000	310,000			792,000
Accounts Payable	52,000	30,000			82,000
Other Liabilities	70,000	45,000			115,000
Common Stock					
P Company	200,000				200,000
S Company		100,000	³100,000		
Premium on Common Stock					
P Company	40,000				40,000
S Company		50,000	³ 50,000		
Retained Earnings from above	310,000	85,000	65,000	25,000	355,000
Total	672,000	310,000	250,000	250,000	792,000

¹To recognize P Company's share (100%) of S Company's *undistributed* income from the date of acquisition to the beginning of the current year.

²To eliminate intercompany dividends.

³To eliminate investment in S Company.

Dividend Income	10,000	
Dividends Declared—S Company		10,000
Common Stock—S Company	100,000	
Premium on Common Stock—S Company	50,000	
Retained Earnings, 1/1/81—S Company	55,000	
Plant and Equipment (Land)	20,000	
Investment in S Company		255,000

Consolidated balances are then determined in the same manner as in previous illustrations.

Investment Carried at Equity—Subsequent to Year of Acquisition

To illustrate the preparation of a consolidated workpaper for years subsequent to the year of acquisition under the equity method, assume the same data as that given in the previous illustration, but use of the equity rather than the cost method. After P Company has recorded its share of S Company's income earned ($40,000) and dividends declared ($10,000), the Investment in S Company account would appear as follows:

INVESTMENT IN S COMPANY			
12/31/80 Balance	225,000	8/10/81 Sub. Dividends	10,000
12/31/81 Sub. Income	40,000		
12/31/81 Balance	255,000		

A consolidated statements workpaper in this situation is presented in Illustration 4–4.

Observe once again that the only difference in affiliates account data from Illustration 4–3 appears in P Company's statements, the investment account showing a balance of $255,000, equity in subsidiary income rather than dividend income in P Company's income statement, and P Company's beginning and ending retained earnings reflecting the effect of recognizing its share (100%) of S Company's income.

The elimination process follows the same procedures as those in Illustration 4–2. A workpaper entry is made to reverse the effect of parent-company entries on the investment account for the current year. The effect is to eliminate P Company's share of subsidiary income recognized and subsidiary dividends declared during the year and to restate the investment account to its balance at the beginning of the year. Completion of the workpaper follows the same process as that used in the previous illustrations. Again, observe that the consolidated columns in Illustration 4–3 and 4–4 are the same; regardless of the method used, the consolidated results are unaffected.

ILLUSTRATION 4-4
Consolidated Statements Workpaper
P Company and Subsidiary
For Year Ending December 31, 1981

	P COMPANY	S COMPANY	ELIMINATIONS DR.	ELIMINATIONS CR.	CONSOLIDATED BALANCES
INCOME STATEMENT					
Sales	350,000	190,000			540,000
Equity in Subsidiary Income	40,000		¹ 40,000		
Total Revenue	390,000	190,000			540,000
Cost of Goods Sold	200,000	94,000			294,000
Other Expense	80,000	56,000			136,000
Total Cost and Expense	280,000	150,000			430,000
Net Income to Retained Earnings	110,000	40,000	40,000	–0–	110,000
RETAINED EARNINGS STATEMENT					
1/1/81 Retained Earnings					
P Company	275,000				275,000
S Company		55,000	² 55,000		
Net Income from above	110,000	40,000	40,000	–0–	110,000
Dividends Declared					
P Company	(30,000)				(30,000)
S Company		(10,000)		10,000	
12/31/81 Retained Earnings to					
Balance Sheet	355,000	85,000	95,000	10,000	355,000
BALANCE SHEET					
Cash	54,000	36,000			90,000
Accounts Receivable (net)	68,000	32,000			100,000
Inventory—12/31/81	82,000	39,000			121,000
Investment in S Company	255,000			¹ 30,000	
				²225,000	
Plant and Equipment (net)	220,000	185,000	² 20,000		425,000
Other Assets	38,000	18,000			56,000
Total	717,000	310,000			792,000
Accounts Payable	52,000	30,000			82,000
Other Liabilities	70,000	45,000			115,000
Common Stock					
P Company	200,000				200,000
S Company		100,000	²100,000		
Premium on Common Stock					
P Company	40,000				40,000
S Company		50,000	² 50,000		
Retained Earnings from above	355,000	85,000	95,000	10,000	355,000
Total	717,000	310,000	265,000	265,000	792,000

¹To reverse the effect of parent-company entries during the year for subsidiary dividends and income.
²To eliminate investment in S Company.

INVESTMENT ELIMINATION UNDER THE PURCHASE METHOD—A PARTIALLY OWNED SUBSIDIARY

Previous discussion in this chapter has been limited to consolidating wholly owned subsidiaries under the purchase method. Let us now turn our attention to the problems of consolidating a partially owned subsidiary using the purchase method. Illustrations will include subsidiaries accounted for by a parent using both cost and equity methods.

Data for illustration purposes are taken from the trial balances of P Company and S Company on December 31, 1980 as presented on page 93. However, some modification of the data is required, as indicated, to reflect the fact that P Company owns less than 100% of S Company's common stock.

Investment Carried at Cost—Year of Acquisition

When the parent company owns a controlling, but less than 100%, interest in the subsidiary, consolidated financial statements will reflect the existence of a minority interest in the subsidiary. Assume, for illustration purposes, that P Company purchased 80% (8,000 shares) of the common stock of S Company on January 1, 1980 for a cash payment of $165,000, and the cost method is followed. The following modifications of P Company's trial balance presented on page 93 are necessary:

1. The investment in S Company reflects its cost of $165,000.

2. The cash balance is $79,000 rather than $37,000, since P Company paid $45,000 ($210,000 − $165,000) less for its interest in S Company, but received $3,000 less in cash dividends during the year.

3. Dividend income is $12,000 rather than $15,000, because P Company received only 80% of the dividends declared by S Company. The remaining dividends were distributed to the minority shareholders.

The modified trial balances are reproduced below for the convenience of the reader.

DECEMBER 31, 1980

	P COMPANY		S COMPANY	
	DR.	CR.	DR.	CR.
Cash	79,000		13,000	
Accounts Receivable (net)	64,000		28,000	
Inventory, 1/1/80	56,000		32,000	
Investment in S Company	165,000			
Plant and Equipment (net)	180,000		165,000	
Other Assets	35,000		17,000	
Accounts Payable		31,000		24,000
Other Liabilities		62,000		37,000
Common Stock, $10 par		200,000		100,000
Premium on Common Stock		40,000		50,000
Retained Earnings, 1/1/80		210,000		40,000
Dividends Declared	20,000		15,000	
Sales		300,000		160,000
Dividend Income		12,000		
Purchases	186,000		95,000	
Expenses	70,000		46,000	
	855,000	855,000	411,000	411,000
Inventory, 12/31/80	67,000		43,000	

A workpaper for the preparation of consolidated financial statements at December 31, 1980 in this situation is presented in Illustration 4–5.

Purchase Accounting
Cost Method
80%-Owned Subsidiary
Year of Acquisition

ILLUSTRATION 4–5
Consolidated Statements Workpaper
P Company and Subsidiary
For Year Ending December 31, 1980

INCOME STATEMENT	P COMPANY	S COMPANY	ELIMINATIONS DR.	ELIMINATIONS CR.	MINORITY INTEREST	CONSOLIDATED BALANCES
Sales	300,000	160,000				460,000
Dividend Income	12,000		¹ 12,000			
Total Revenue	312,000	160,000				460,000
Cost of Goods Sold	175,000	84,000				259,000
Other Expense	70,000	46,000				116,000
Total Cost and Expense	245,000	130,000				375,000
Net	67,000	30,000				85,000
Minority Interest in Income					6,000	(6,000)
Net Income to Retained Earnings	67,000	30,000	12,000	–0–	6,000	79,000
RETAINED EARNINGS STATEMENT						
1/1/80 Retained Earnings						
P Company	210,000					210,000
S Company		40,000	² 32,000		8,000	
Net Income from above	67,000	30,000	12,000	–0–	6,000	79,000
Dividends Declared						
P Company	(20,000)					(20,000)
S Company		(15,000)		¹ 12,000	(3,000)	
12/31/80 Retained Earnings to						
Balance Sheet	257,000	55,000	44,000	12,000	11,000	269,000
BALANCE SHEET						
Cash	79,000	13,000				92,000
Accounts Receivable (net)	64,000	28,000				92,000
Inventory—12/31/80	67,000	43,000				110,000
Investment in S Company	165,000			²165,000		
Plant and Equipment (net)	180,000	165,000	² 13,000			358,000
Other Assets	35,000	17,000				52,000
Total	590,000	266,000				704,000

	P COMPANY	S COMPANY	ELIMINATIONS DR.	ELIMINATIONS CR.	MINORITY INTEREST	CONSOLIDATED BALANCES
Accounts Payable	31,000	24,000				55,000
Other Liabilities	62,000	37,000				99,000
Common Stock						
P Company	200,000					200,000
S Company		100,000	² 80,000		20,000	
Premium on Common Stock						
P Company	40,000					40,000
S Company		50,000	² 40,000		10,000	
Retained Earnings from above	257,000	55,000	44,000	12,000	11,000	269,000
Minority Interest					41,000	41,000
Total	590,000	266,000	177,000	177,000		704,000

¹To eliminate intercompany dividends.
²To eliminate investment in S Company.

A comparison of Illustrations 4–5 and 4–1 discloses that the primary difference is the addition of a minority interest column on the workpaper in Illustration 4–5 to accumulate their 20% interest in the net assets of the subsidiary. The total minority interest is made up of the following:

1. A $6,000 (20% × $30,000) interest in S Company income. The $6,000 is added to the minority interest and deducted from combined income in determining consolidated income.

2. An $8,000 share in the beginning balance of S Company's retained earnings. The other $32,000 was purchased by P Company and is, therefore, eliminated.

3. A $3,000 (20% × $15,000) decrease for dividends distributed to the minority shareholders during the year. The other $12,000 in dividends represents parent-company dividend income and is, therefore, eliminated.

4. A $20,000 and $10,000 interest, respectively, in the common stock and premium on common stock of S Company. The remaining common stock and premium on common stock were purchased by P Company and are, therefore, eliminated.

The sum of the minority interest column is transferred to the consolidated balance sheet since it reflects the minority shareholders' interest in the net assets of the consolidated group.

Investment Carried at Equity—Year of Acquisition

If P Company elects to use the equity method to account for its investment in its partially owned subsidiary, the preparation of the consolidated workpaper at

12/31/80, the end of the year of acquisition, follows the same procedures as those in Illustration 4–2. Because P Company owns only 80% of S Company, however, some adjustment to the data in Illustration 4–2 is needed. Under the equity method, P Company would make the following entries during 1980:

1/1/80 Investment in S Company	165,000	
Cash		165,000
6/6/80 Cash	12,000	
Investment in S Company		12,000
12/31/80 Investment in S Company	24,000	
Equity in Subsidiary Income		24,000

At December 31, 1980, the Investment in S Company account would be:

INVESTMENT IN S COMPANY

1/1/80	165,000	6/6/80 Sub. Dividends	12,000
12/31/80 Sub. Income	24,000		
12/31/80 Balance	177,000		

Thus, the account data that are different from those in Illustration 4–2 appear only in P Company data: (1) subsidiary income of $24,000 rather than $30,000, (2) Investment in S Company reflecting the balance indicated above, and (3) retained earnings at 12/31/80 reflecting the fact that P Company recognized $6,000 less income from S Company because they hold only an 80% interest in S Company.

Illustration 4–6 presents the consolidated workpaper under the equity method with an 80% investment.

INVESTMENT ELIMINATION UNDER THE POOLING METHOD—SUBSEQUENT TO DATE OF ACQUISITION

The preceding sections of this chapter discussed and illustrated use of the purchase approach under both cost and equity methods for partially and wholly owned subsidiaries for periods subsequent to the date of acquisition. Let us now turn our attention to use of the pooling of interests method in preparing consolidated financial statements, subsequent to date of acquisition. Just as two methods, cost and equity, are available for use under the purchase approach, two methods are available under pooling of interests, the book value method and the equity method.

The book value method under pooling is similar to the cost method under the purchase approach. The investment, however, is recorded initially at an amount equal to the book value of subsidiary equity acquired. Subsidiary earnings are not recorded until distributed, at which time the parent company recognizes dividend income. Thus, the investment account remains at an amount equal to the *initial* subsidiary equity acquired unless the parent company acquires additional subsidiary shares or disposes of part of its investment.

Under the equity method also the investment is recorded initially at an amount equal to the book value of subsidiary equity acquired. Accounting subsequent to

ILLUSTRATION 4–6
Consolidated Statements Workpaper
P Company and Subsidiary
For Year Ending December 31, 1980

	P COMPANY	S COMPANY	ELIMINATIONS DR.	ELIMINATIONS CR.	MINORITY INTEREST	CONSOLIDATED BALANCES
INCOME STATEMENT						
Sales	300,000	160,000				460,000
Equity in Subsidiary Income	24,000		¹ 24,000			
Total Revenue	324,000	160,000				460,000
Cost of Goods Sold	175,000	84,000				259,000
Other Expense	70,000	46,000				116,000
Total Cost and Expense	245,000	130,000				375,000
Net	79,000	30,000				85,000
Minority Interest in Income					6,000	(6,000)
Net Income to Retained Earnings	79,000	30,000	24,000	–0–	6,000	79,000
RETAINED EARNINGS STATEMENT						
1/1/80 Retained Earnings						
P Company	210,000					210,000
S Company		40,000	² 32,000		8,000	
Net Income from above	79,000	30,000	24,000	–0–	6,000	79,000
Dividends Declared						
P Company	(20,000)					(20,000)
S Company		(15,000)		¹ 12,000	(3,000)	
12/31/80 Retained Earnings to						
Balance Sheet	269,000	55,000	56,000	12,000	11,000	269,000
BALANCE SHEET						
Cash	79,000	13,000				92,000
Accounts Receivable (net)	64,000	28,000				92,000
Inventory—12/31/80	67,000	43,000				110,000
Investment in S Company	177,000			¹ 12,000 ²165,000		
Plant and Equipment (net)	180,000	165,000	² 13,000			358,000
Other Assets	35,000	17,000				52,000
Total	602,000	266,000				704,000
Accounts Payable	31,000	24,000				55,000
Other Liabilities	62,000	37,000				99,000
Common Stock						
P Company	200,000					200,000
S Company		100,000	² 80,000		20,000	
Premium on Common Stock						
P Company	40,000					40,000
S Company		50,000	² 40,000		10,000	
Retained Earnings from above	269,000	55,000	56,000	12,000	11,000	269,000
Minority Interest					41,000	41,000
Total	602,000	266,000	189,000	189,000		704,000

¹To reverse the effect of parent-company entries during the year for subsidiary dividends and income.
²To eliminate investment in S Company.

acquisition follows the same procedures as those used under the equity method with a purchase approach, with the parent company recording its share of subsidiary earnings as reported by the subsidiary and treating dividends as reductions in the investment account. One important distinction should be noted, however. Since the investment is recorded initially at the book value of equity acquired rather than at cost, no difference between cost and book value exists.

The two methods are illustrated in the following sections. The book value method is presented for a wholly owned subsidiary at the end of the year of acquisition. The equity method is presented for a partially owned subsidiary at the end of the year subsequent to the year of acquisition.

Investment Carried at Book Value of Equity Acquired—Wholly Owned Subsidiary—End of Year of Acquisition

Discussion and illustration are based on the previous trial balance data presented on page 93. For ease in following the illustration, trial balances at the end of the year of acquisition for P and S Companies are presented below as they would appear under the book value method. The trial balances and workpaper illustration are based on the assumption that P Company exchanged 9,000 shares of its common stock for all of the outstanding common stock of S Company on January 1, 1980, and that all of the conditions precedent to use of the pooling of interests method have been met.

Trial balances for P and S Companies on December 31, 1980, would appear as follows:

| | DECEMBER 31, 1980 | | | |
| | P COMPANY | | S COMPANY | |
	DR.	CR.	DR.	CR.
Cash	247,000		13,000	
Accounts Receivable (net)	64,000		28,000	
Inventory, 1/1/80	56,000		32,000	
Investment in S Company	190,000			
Plant and Equipment (net)	180,000		165,000	
Other Assets	35,000		17,000	
Accounts Payable		31,000		24,000
Other Liabilities		62,000		37,000
Common Stock, $10 par		290,000		100,000
Premium on Common Stock		100,000		50,000
Retained Earnings, 1/1/80		250,000		40,000
Dividends Declared	20,000		15,000	
Sales		300,000		160,000
Dividend Income		15,000		
Purchases	186,000		95,000	
Other Expenses	70,000		46,000	
	1,048,000	1,048,000	411,000	411,000
Inventory, 12/31/80	67,000		43,000	

On January 1, 1980, P Company made the following entry to record its investment in S Company:

Investment in S Company	190,000	
Common Stock (9,000 × $10)		90,000
Retained Earnings		40,000
Premium on Common Stock		60,000

The investment is recorded at the book value of S Company equity ($190,000), and S Company's retained earnings and premium on common stock are recorded on P Company's books. Since the par value of P Company's stock issued ($90,000) is less than the par value of S Company stock acquired ($100,000), it is necessary to record an additional $10,000 premium on common stock. Thus, the total premium on common stock recorded is $60,000 ($50,00 + $10,000).

The only other entry relevant to the investment was made by P Company to record receipt of the $15,000 dividend on August 10, 1980.

Note that the only differences between these trial balances and those presented on page 93 appear in P Company's accounts. The cash account is $210,000 greater, since the investment was acquired through an issue of stock rather than for cash, and P Company's equity accounts reflect the effect of the investment transaction presented above.

A workpaper for the preparation of consolidated financial statements for P and S Companies on December 31, 1980 is given in Illustration 4–7.

As indicated earlier, the book value method under pooling produces results similar to the cost method under purchase accounting. Comparison of Illustration 4–1 and 4–7 shows that:

Pooling Accounting
Book Value Method
Wholly Owned Subsidiary
Year of Acquisition

ILLUSTRATION 4-7
Consolidated Statements Workpaper
P Company and Subsidiary
For Year Ending December 31, 1980

INCOME STATEMENT	P COMPANY	S COMPANY	ELIMINATIONS DR.	ELIMINATIONS CR.	CONSOLIDATED BALANCES
Sales	300,000	160,000			460,000
Dividend Income	15,000		¹ 15,000		
Total Revenue	315,000	160,000			460,000
Cost of Goods Sold	175,000	84,000			259,000
Other Expense	70,000	46,000			116,000
Total Cost and Expense	245,000	130,000			375,000
Net Income to Retained Earnings	70,000	30,000	15,000	–0–	85,000
RETAINED EARNINGS STATEMENT					
1/1/80 Retained Earnings					
P Company	250,000				250,000
S Company		40,000	² 40,000		
Net Income from above	70,000	30,000	15,000	–0–	85,000
Dividends Declared					
P Company	(20,000)				(20,000)
S Company		(15,000)		¹ 15,000	
12/31/80 Retained Earnings to					
Balance Sheet	300,000	55,000	55,000	15,000	315,000
BALANCE SHEET					
Cash	247,000	13,000			260,000
Accounts Receivable (net)	64,000	28,000			92,000
Inventory—12/31/80	67,000	43,000			110,000
Investment in S Company	190,000			²190,000	
Plant and Equipment (net)	180,000	165,000			345,000
Other Assets	35,000	17,000			52,000
Total	783,000	266,000			859,000
Accounts Payable	31,000	24,000			55,000
Other Liabilities	62,000	37,000			99,000
Common Stock					
P Company	290,000				290,000
S Company		100,000	²100,000		
Premium on Common Stock					
P Company	100,000				100,000
S Company		50,000	² 50,000		
Retained Earnings from above	300,000	55,000	55,000	15,000	315,000
Total	783,000	266,000	205,000	205,000	859,000

¹To eliminate intercompany dividends.
²To eliminate investment in S Company.

1. Elimination procedures are the same except that no excess of cost over equity arises.

2. Consolidated income is the same, $85,000.

3. The consolidated retained earnings section is the same, although the final consolidated retained earnings is $40,000 greater under pooling since P Company carried over S Company's retained earnings.

4. The composition of the balance sheet is different. Total assets are $190,000 greater under pooling because no cash ($210,000) was paid out under pooling, and no excess of cost over equity acquired ($20,000) exists. In addition, the equity section of the balance sheet under pooling is $190,000 greater, reflecting the amount of equity recorded in the acquisition entry.

Investment Carried at Equity—
Partially Owned Subsidiary—Subsequent to Year of Acquisition

As mentioned earlier, the equity method may be used to account for an investment initially recorded under the pooling approach. To illustrate consolidation procedures for a period subsequent to the year of acquisition, assume the preceding situation, Illustration 4–7, except that P Company, on January 1, 1980, issued 8,100 shares of its common stock for 90% (9,000 shares) of the outstanding common stock of S Company, and all criteria for the use of pooling of interests accounting are met. In order to update data to December 31, 1981, the first year after the year of acquisition, the investment account is reproduced and the appropriate trial balances for P and S Companies at December 31, 1981, are given below:

The entry to record the initial investment for the 90% acquisition under pooling is:

Investment in S Company (.9 X 190,000)	171,000	
Common Stock (8,100 X 10)		81,000
Retained Earnings (.9 X 40,000)		36,000
Premium on Common Stock		54,000

The investment account is established at 90% of the subsidiary stockholders' equity at the date of acquisition and 90% of S Company's retained earnings and premium on common stock are recorded on P Company's books. Since the par value of S Company stock acquired ($90,000) exceeds the par value of P Company stock issued ($81,000), a $9,000 additional premium on common stock is recorded. Thus, total premium on common stock is recorded as $54,000 ($9,000 + [.9 X $50,000]).

During 1980 and 1981, P Company recognized its share of S Company income and dividends as indicated in the investment account reproduced below.

INVESTMENT IN S COMPANY

1/1/80 Initial entry	171,000	8/30/80 Sub. Dividends	13,500
12/31/80 Sub. Income	27,000		
12/31/80 Balance	184,500		
12/31/81 Sub. Income	36,000	8/10/81 Sub. Dividends	9,000
12/31/81 Balance	211,500		

Trial balances for P and S Companies on December 31, 1981 are as follows:

**Trial Balances
December 31, 1981**

	P COMPANY		S COMPANY	
	DR.	CR.	DR.	CR.
Cash	261,500		36,000	
Accounts Receivable (net)	68,000		32,000	
Inventory, 1/1/81	67,000		43,000	
Investment in S Company	211,500			
Plant and Equipment (net)	220,000		185,000	
Other Assets	38,000		18,000	
Accounts Payable		52,000		30,000
Other Liabilities		70,000		45,000
Common Stock, $10 par		281,000		100,000
Premium on Common Stock		94,000		50,000
Retained Earnings, 1/1/81		308,000		55,000
Dividends Declared	30,000		10,000	
Sales		350,000		190,000
Subsidiary Income		36,000		
Purchases	215,000		90,000	
Other Expense	80,000		56,000	
	1,191,000	1,191,000	470,000	470,000
Inventory, 12/31/81	82,000		39,000	

A workpaper for the preparation of consolidated financial statements is presented in Illustration 4–8.

Construction of the workpaper and the elimination procedures followed where the equity method is used with the pooling approach is the same as under purchase accounting. A workpaper entry is made to reverse the effect of the parent-company

ILLUSTRATION 4-8
Consolidated Statements Workpaper
P Company and Subsidiary
For Year Ending December 31, 1981

	P COMPANY	S COMPANY	ELIMINATIONS DR.	ELIMINATIONS CR.	MINORITY INTEREST	CONSOLIDATED BALANCES
INCOME STATEMENT						
Sales	350,000	190,000				540,000
Subsidiary Income	36,000		¹ 36,000			
Total Revenue	386,000	190,000				540,000
Cost of Goods Sold	200,000	94,000				294,000
Other Expense	80,000	56,000				136,000
Total Cost and Expense	280,000	150,000				430,000
Net	106,000	40,000				110,000
Minority Interest in Income					4,000	(4,000)
Net Income to Retained Earnings	106,000	40,000	36,000	–0–	4,000	106,000
RETAINED EARNINGS STATEMENT						
1/1/81 Retained Earnings						
P Company	308,000					308,000
S Company		55,000	² 49,500		5,500	
Net Income from above	106,000	40,000	36,000	–0–	4,000	106,000
Dividends Declared						
P Company	(30,000)					(30,000)
S Company		(10,000)		¹ 9,000	(1,000)	
12/31/81 Retained Earnings to Balance Sheet	384,000	85,000	85,500	9,000	8,500	384,000
BALANCE SHEET						
Cash	261,500	36,000				297,500
Accounts Receivable (net)	68,000	32,000				100,000
Inventory—12/31/81	82,000	39,000				121,000
Investment in S Company	211,500			¹ 27,000		
				²184,000		
Plant and Equipment (net)	220,000	185,000				405,000
Other Assets	38,000	18,000				56,000
Total	881,000	310,000				979,500
Accounts Payable	52,000	30,000				82,000
Other Liabilities	70,000	45,000				115,000
Common Stock						
P Company	281,000					281,000
S Company		100,000	² 90,000		10,000	
Premium on Common Stock						
P Company	94,000					94,000
S Company		50,000	² 45,000		5,000	
Retained Earnings from above	384,000	85,000	85,500	9,000	8,500	384,000
Minority Interest					23,500	23,500
Total	881,000	310,000	220,500	220,500		979,500

¹To reverse the effect of parent-company entries during the year for subsidiary dividends and income.
²To eliminate investment in S Company.

entries on the investment account for the current year, resulting in the elimination of intercompany income and the return of the investment account to its balance at the beginning of the year. Since we are working from a trial balance, the books have not been closed. Thus, the retained earnings amounts in the trial balance represent beginning of the year balances. The restatement of the investment account to its beginning of the year balance permits the elimination of the investment account against subsidiary equity as of the beginning of the year. A consolidated statement of income and retained earnings and a consolidated balance sheet in this situation are presented in Illustrations 4-9 and 4-10.

ILLUSTRATION 4-9

P Company and Subsidiary

Consolidated Statement of Income

and Retained Earnings

For the Year Ending December 31, 1981

Sales	$540,000
Cost of Goods Sold	294,000
Gross Margin	246,000
Other Expense	136,000
Operating Income	110,000
Minority Interest in Income	4,000
Net Income	106,000
Retained Earnings, 1/1/81	308,000
Total	414,000
Dividends Declared	30,000
Retained Earnings, 12/31/81	$384,000

ILLUSTRATION 4–10
P Company and Subsidiary
Consolidated Balance Sheet
December 31, 1981

ASSETS

Current Assets:		
Cash		$297,500
Accounts Receivable (net)		100,000
Inventories		121,000
Total Current Assets		518,500
Plant and Equipment (net)		405,000
Other Assets		56,000
Total Assets		$979,500

EQUITIES

Accounts Payable		$ 82,000
Other Liabilities		115,000
Total Liabilities		197,000
Minority Interest		23,500
Stockholders' Equity:		
Common Stock $10 par	$281,000	
Premium on Common Stock	94,000	
Retained Earnings	384,000	759,000
Total Equities		$979,500

SUMMARY OF WORKPAPER ELIMINATING ENTRIES

Basic consolidated financial statements workpaper eliminating entries depend upon whether:

1. The purchase or pooling of interests method was used to record the acquisition.

2. The cost (purchase), equity (purchase or pooling), or book value (pooling) method is used to account for the investment on the books of the parent company subsequent to acquisition.

3. The workpaper is being prepared at the end of the year of acquisition or at the end of a period subsequent to the year of acquisition.

In addition, the *amounts* eliminated depend upon whether the subsidiary is wholly or partially owned.

Workpaper eliminating entries for the various alternatives are summarized in Illustration 4–11.

ILLUSTRATION 4–11
Summary of Basic Workpaper Eliminating Entries

| PURCHASE ACCOUNTING | | POOLING ACCOUNTING | |
COST	EQUITY	BOOK VALUE	EQUITY
END OF YEAR OF ACQUISITION			

Dividend Income
   Dividends Declared—S
	Subsidiary Income
	   Dividends Declared—S
	   Investment in S
		Same as Cost under Purchase Accounting	Same as Equity under Purchase Accounting

To eliminate intercompany dividend income.	To eliminate intercompany income and to return the investment account to its cost at date of acquisition.	To eliminate intercompany dividend income.	To eliminate intercompany income and to return the investment account to its balance as of the beginning of the current year.

Capital Stock—S
Add. Paid-in Cap.—S
Ret. Earnings—S
Difference Between Cost
and Book Value
   Investment in S
	Same as Cost Method	Capital Stock—S
		Add. Paid-in Cap.—S
		Ret. Earnings—S
		   Investment in S
			Same as Book Value Method

To eliminate parent's share of its subsidiary's stockholders equity against the investment account.

COST	EQUITY	BOOK VALUE	EQUITY
END OF PERIOD SUBSEQUENT TO YEAR OF ACQUISITION			
Investment in S Ret. Earnings—P	No entry needed.	Same as Cost under Purchase Accounting	No entry needed.
To establish reciprocity. *RECORD UNDISTRIBUTED INCOME AS OF DATE OF ACQ.*			

Dividend Income
   Dividends Declared—S
	Subsidiary Income
	   Dividends Declared—S
	   Investment in S
		Same as Cost under Purchase Accounting	Same as Equity under Purchase Accounting

To eliminate intercompany dividend income	To eliminate intercompany income and to return the investment account to its balance as of the beginning of the current year.		

Capital Stock—S
Add. Paid-in Cap.—S
Ret. Earnings—S
Difference Between Cost *— STAYS SAME EVERY YEAR SINCE DATE OF ACQ.*
and Book Value
   Investment in S
	Same as Cost Method	Capital Stock—S
		Add. Paid-in Cap.—S
		Ret. Earnings—S
		   Investment in S
			Same as Book Value Method

To eliminate parent's share of its subsidiary's stockholders' equity against the investment account.

CONSOLIDATED STATEMENT OF CHANGES IN FINANCIAL POSITION

The procedures followed in the preparation of a statement of changes in financial position are discussed in most intermediate accounting texts. When the company is reporting on a consolidated basis, the statement of changes in financial position must also be presented on a consolidated basis. Some aspects of the statement are different when consolidated statements are issued. Examples are:

1. *APB Opinion No. 19* requires the prominent disclosure of working capital or cash provided from or used in operations of the period.[3] The normal procedure is to begin with net income for the period and add back (or deduct) any items recognized in determining that net income that did not use (or provide) working capital or cash. These adjustments normally include such things as depreciation and amortization. An additional adjustment for a consolidated statement is the add-back of minority interest in income (or deduction of the minority's share of operating loss), since no working capital or cash is used or provided.

2. Because the entire amount of the minority interest in net income (loss) is added back (deducted) from net income in determining working capital or cash provided by operations, any subsidiary dividend payments to the minority shareholders must be included with parent company dividends as a use of working capital or cash.

3. Cost of the acquisition of additional shares in a subsidiary by the parent may or may not constitute a use of working capital or cash. If the acquisition is a market purchase, it does represent such a use. If it is an acquisition directly from the subsidiary, however, it represents an intercompany transfer that does not affect the working capital or cash of the consolidated group.

As an illustration of the preparation of a consolidated statement of changes in financial position, a consolidated income statement and comparative consolidated balance sheets for P Company and its 90%-owned subsidiary, S Company, along with other information, are presented below:

---

[3]*Opinions of the Accounting Principles Board No. 19, "Reporting Changes in Financial Position"* (New York: AICPA, 1971), par. 7.

P Company and Subsidiary
Consolidated Income Statement
For the Year Ending December 31, 1981

Sales	$540,000
Cost of Sales	294,000
Gross Margin	246,000
Operating Expenses	136,000
Income from Operations	110,000
Equity in Income of Investee Companies	6,000
Total	116,000
Minority Interest in Net Income	(4,000)
Consolidated Net Income	$112,000

P Company and Subsidiary
Comparative Balance Sheets

	DECEMBER 31	
ASSETS	1980	1981
Cash	$ 60,000	$ 80,000
Accounts Receivable	92,000	100,000
Inventories	110,000	121,000
Plant and Equipment (net)	345,000	403,000
Other Assets	52,000	58,000
Goodwill	20,000	18,000
Total Assets	$679,000	$780,000
EQUITIES		
Accounts Payable	$ 60,000	$ 72,000
Other Current Liabilities	99,000	110,000
Total Liabilities	159,000	182,000
Minority Interest	20,000	22,000
Stockholders' Equity:		
Common Stock	200,000	200,000
Premium on Common Stock	40,000	40,000
Retained Earnings	260,000	336,000
Total Stockholders' Equity	500,000	576,000
Total Equities	$679,000	$780,000

Other Information:

1. Depreciation expense of $24,000 and amortization of goodwill of $2,000 are included in operating expenses.

2. Manufacturing equipment was acquired during 1981 at a cost of $82,000.

3. Other Assets includes equity investments on which $6,000 in equity income was recognized. No dividends were received during the year.

4. Minority interest in net income was $4,000. However, $2,000 was distributed to minority stockholders as dividends during the year. Thus, minority interest on the balance sheet increased by only $2,000.

5. Dividend payments totaled $38,000, of which $36,000 were to P Company stockholders (thereby reducing consolidated retained earnings) and $2,000 were to S Company minority shareholders.

The consolidated statement of changes in financial position for this situation is presented in Illustration 4–12.

ILLUSTRATION 4–12
P Company and Subsidiary
Consolidated Statement of Changes in Financial Position
For the Year Ending December 31, 1981

Working Capital was Provided by:

Operations:

Net Income			$112,000
Adjustments for Items not Affecting Working Capital:			
Depreciation Expense			24,000
Amortization of Goodwill			2,000
Minority Interest in Net Income			4,000
Equity in Income of Investee Companies			(6,000)
Working Capital Provided by Operations			$136,000

Working Capital was Used for:

Purchase of Manufacturing Equipment			$ 82,000
Payment of Dividends			38,000
Total Working Capital Used			120,000
Increase in Working Capital			$ 16,000

SCHEDULE OF CHANGES IN WORKING CAPITAL	1980	1981	CHANGE
Cash	$ 60,000	$ 80,000	$ 20,000
Accounts Receivable	92,000	100,000	8,000
Inventories	110,000	121,000	11,000
Accounts Payable	60,000	72,000	(12,000)
Other Current Liabilities	99,000	110,000	(11,000)
Increase in Net Working Capital			$ 16,000

CONSOLIDATED NET INCOME
AND CONSOLIDATED RETAINED EARNINGS

Consolidated net income and consolidated retained earnings were defined briefly in the discussion of Illustration 4–1. It may be worthwhile, however, to take a more comprehensive look at these important concepts.

Consolidated Net Income

Consolidated net income was previously calculated from a workpaper computation approach as the result of combining the revenues, expense, gain, and loss of all consolidated affiliates after elimination of amounts representing the effect of transactions among affiliates and the deduction (addition) of any minority interest share of the net incomes (loss) of subsidiaries. A more direct definition is that consolidated net income consists of the parent company's income from its independent operations plus (minus) its share of reported subsidiary income (loss). Income from the parent's independent operations excludes dividend income from subsidiaries recognized under the cost method and subsidiary income recognized under the equity method.

For an example under the cost method, refer to the workpaper data in Illustration 4–5. The computation of consolidated net income may be made as follows:

P Company net income	67,000
Less: Dividend income from S Company	12,000
P Company net income from independent operations	55,000
Add: P Company's share of S Company's income	
($30,000 × 80%)	24,000
Consolidated Net Income	79,000

Under the equity method, refer to Illustration 4–6.

P Company net income	79,000
Less: Equity in Subsidiary Income	24,000
P Company net income from independent operations	55,000
Add: P Company's share of S Company's income	24,000
Consolidated Net Income	79,000

Under the equity method, P Company net income and consolidated net income are identical, as they should be since the equity method essentially applies the analytical calculation of consolidated income. Note again that consolidated net income under the cost and equity method are identical.

Consolidated Retained Earnings

Consolidated retained earnings was previously defined as consolidated retained earnings at the beginning of the year plus (minus) consolidated net income (loss), minus parent-company dividends declared during the period. In essence, this definition says that consolidated retained earnings consists of the elements employed in constructing the standard retained earnings statement. This approach is sufficient under the equity method because parent-company income and consolidated income are identical.

Under the cost method, however, an analytical approach to the definition of consolidated retained earnings may be useful. Consolidated retained earnings may be defined as parent company's cost-basis retained earnings plus (minus) its share of the increase (decrease) in subsidiary retained earnings from the date of acquisition to the current date. For example, assume that P Company acquired 75% of the outstanding common stock of S Company on January 1, 1980. A summary of P Company and S Company retained earnings from January 1, 1980 to December 31, 1981 follows:

	P COMPANY	S COMPANY
Retained Earnings, 1/1/80	120,000	40,000
1980 — Income	60,000	20,000
Dividends	(20,000)	(5,000)
1981 — Income	75,000	15,000
Dividends	(25,000)	(20,000)
Retained Earnings, 12/31/81	210,000	50,000

Consolidated retained earnings on December 31, 1981 may be computed as:

P Company retained earnings, 12/31/81	210,000
P Company's share of the increase in retained earnings of S Company since date of acquisition ($50,000 − $40,000) × 75%	7,500
Consolidated Retained Earnings, 12/31/81	217,500

One modification to the calculation above must be made where the pooling approach is used; subsidiary retained earnings acquired by the parent on the date of acquisition must be added under either the equity or book value method in computing consolidated retained earnings.

ELIMINATION OF INTERCOMPANY REVENUE AND EXPENSE ITEMS

Discussion and illustrations to this point have emphasized the procedures used to eliminate subsidiary equity acquired against the investment account under both purchase and pooling approaches using either the cost or equity method of accounting for the investment at the end of the year of acquisition and for subsequent periods. Before proceeding with a discussion of some special topics relating to consolidated statements in succeeding chapters, it should be noted that there are several types of intercompany revenue and expense items that must be eliminated in the preparation of a consolidated income statement.

Affiliates often engage in numerous sale-purchase transactions with other affiliates. The parent company may sell merchandise or services to one or more of its subsidiaries (a downstream sale) or acquire goods or services from its affiliates (an upstream sale). Likewise, one subsidiary may buy or sell goods or services from or to another subsidiary (a horizontal transaction). The total of all such sales and related purchases is eliminated in the preparation of a consolidated income statement, regardless of the direction of the sale or the percentage of ownership by the parent company since they represent transactions within the affiliated group. (Treatment of any unrealized profit remaining in inventories on these sales is presented in Chapter 6.) As an example, assume that P Company owns 80% and 90%, respectively, of the common stock of S Company and T Company. Interaffiliate sale-purchase transactions during the current year are indicated in the following schedule:

SALES BY	SALES TO			
	P COMPANY	S COMPANY	T COMPANY	TOTAL
P Company		50,000	30,000	80,000
S Company	100,000		40,000	140,000
T Company	80,000	20,000		100,000
Total Intercompany Sales	180,000	70,000	70,000	320,000

The workpaper entry, in general journal form, to eliminate intercompany sales and purchases would be:

Sales	320,000	
Purchases		320,000

The credit in this eliminating entry may be to cost of sales in the event that the affiliates have closed purchase accounts to cost of sales. In addition, any related unpaid balances remaining in accounts receivable and accounts payable at year-end resulting from these transactions would also be eliminated.

Similar types of eliminating entries are made for such intercompany revenue and expense items as interest, rent, and professional services.

Note that these eliminations have no effect on consolidated net income because equal amounts are eliminated from both revenue and expense. The detail included in the consolidated income statement, as well as the relationship of such things as cost of sales and gross margin to sales, however, is affected by the elimination. Likewise, any ratios computed or other comparisons made using the related revenue and expense items may be affected by the elimination.

INTERIM ACQUISITIONS OF SUBSIDIARY STOCK

Discussion and illustrations to this point have been limited to situations in which the parent company acquired its interest in a subsidiary at the beginning of the subsidiary's fiscal period. That condition is unrealistic because the majority of stock acquisitions are likely to be made during the subsidiary's fiscal period. Thus, the proper treatment of the subsidiary's revenue and expense items prior to acquisition in consolidated financial statements must be considered.

Interim Acquisition Under the Purchase Method

When the purchase method of accounting is used, two acceptable alternatives for treating the preacquisition revenue and expense items of the subsidiary in the consolidated income statement are prescribed by *Accounting Research Bulletin No. 51:*

> When a subsidiary is purchased during the year, there are alternative ways of dealing with the results of operations in the consolidated income statement. One method, which usually is preferable, especially where there are several dates of acquisition of blocks of shares, is to include the subsidiary in the consolidation as though it had been acquired at the beginning of the year, and to deduct at the bottom of the consolidated income statement the preacquisition earnings applicable to each block of stock. This method presents results which are more indicative of the current status of the group, and facilitates future comparison with subsequent years. Another method of prorating income is to include in the consolidated statement only the subsidiary's revenue and expenses subsequent to the date of acquisition.[4]

As you recall from the discussion in Chapter 1, under purchase accounting, income of the acquired company is included with income of the acquiring company only from the date of acquisition forward. Both alternatives identified above accomplish this end, although through different forms. The difference is in the detail included in the consolidated income statement.

The first method, which includes the subsidiary in consolidation as though it had been acquired at the beginning of the year and makes a deduction at the bottom of the consolidated income statement for the applicable preacquisition earnings, is preferable, and it will be illustrated here. The second method, which includes only the subsidiary's revenue and expenses subsequent to acquisition, is illustrated in the Appendix using the same data given below.

To illustrate, assume that P Company acquired 90% of the outstanding common stock of S Company on April 1, 1980 for a cash payment of $290,000. P Company uses the cost method to account for its investment in S Company. The difference between cost and book value relates to the undervaluation of S Company land. Trial balances at December 31, 1980 for P and S Companies are as follows:

[4]*Accounting Research Bulletin No. 51,* "Consolidated Financial Statements" (New York: AICPA, 1959), par. 11.

	P COMPANY		S COMPANY	
	DR.	CR.	DR.	CR.
Current Assets	146,000		71,000	
Investment in S Company	290,000			
Depreciable Fixed Assets	326,000		200,000	
Land	120,000		90,000	
Liabilities		100,000		65,000
Common Stock		500,000		200,000
Retained Earnings, 1/1		214,000		80,000
Dividends Declared, 11/1	50,000		20,000	
Sales		600,000		160,000
Dividend Income		18,000		
Cost of Goods Sold	380,000		80,000	
Other Expense	120,000		44,000	
	1,432,000	1,432,000	505,000	505,000

A workpaper for the preparation of consolidated statements on December 31, 1980 is presented in Illustration 4–13.

S Company's entire income statement accounts are included on the workpaper and P Company's share of S Company's net income earned prior to acquisition is deducted as "subsidiary income purchased." Thus, the workpaper eliminating entry for the investment account, in general journal form, is:

Common Stock—S Company	180,000	
Retained Earnings—S Company	72,000	
Land	29,900	
Subsidiary Income Purchased	8,100	
Investment in S Company		290,000

In the computation of subsidiary income purchased, it is assumed that S Company's income of $36,000 was earned evenly throughout the year. Because one-fourth of the year had expired by April 1, the date of acquisition, net income purchased is computed as $36,000 \times \frac{1}{4} \times .9 = \$8,100$. If S Company earns its income unevenly throughout the year, because of the seasonal nature of its business, for example, this should be taken into consideration in estimating the amount of net income earned prior to April 1. In the event the subsidiary incurs a net loss for the year, a "subsidiary loss purchased" would be credited in the elimination entry and added to consolidated income, just as the minority interest in a net loss by the subsidiary would be reflected by a deduction in the minority interest column and an addition to consolidated income.

The preceding discussion assumed the use of the cost method. If the equity method had been used, P Company would have recognized its share of subsidiary income earned *after* acquisition. Dividends would be treated as usual as a reduction in the investment account. Thus, P Company would make the following dividend and earnings entries relative to its investment in S Company for 1980:

ILLUSTRATION 4–13

Purchase Accounting		**Consolidated Statements Workpaper**			
Interim Purchase of Stock		**P Company and Subsidiary**			
Cost Method		**For the Year Ended December 31, 1980**			

	P	S	ELIMINATIONS		MINORITY	CONSOLIDATED
INCOME STATEMENT	COMPANY	COMPANY	DR.	CR.	INTEREST	BALANCES
Sales	600,000	160,000				760,000
Dividend Income	18,000		¹ 18,000			
Total Revenue	618,000	160,000				760,000
Cost of Goods Sold	380,000	80,000				460,000
Other Expense	120,000	44,000				164,000
Total Cost and Expense	500,000	124,000				624,000
Net	118,000	36,000				.136,000
Subsidiary Income Purchased			² 8,100			(8,100)
Minority Interest					3,600	(3,600)
Net Income to Retained Earnings	118,000	36,000	26,100	–0–	3,600	124,300
RETAINED EARNINGS STATEMENT						
1/1 Retained Earnings						
P Company	214,000					214,000
S Company		80,000	² 72,000		8,000	
Net Income from above	118,000	36,000	26,100	–0–	3,600	124,300
Dividends Declared						
P Company	(50,000)					(50,000)
S Company		(20,000)		¹ 18,000	(2,000)	
12/31 Retained Earnings to						
Balance Sheet	282,000	96,000	98,100	18,000	9,600	288,300
BALANCE SHEET						
Current Assets	146,000	71,000				217,000
Investment in S Company	290,000			²290,000		
Depreciable Fixed Assets (net)	326,000	200,000				526,000
Land	120,000	90,000	² 29,900			239,900
Total	882,000	361,000				982,900
Liabilities	100,000	65,000				165,000
Common Stock						
P Company	500,000					500,000
S Company		200,000	²180,000		20,000	
Retained Earnings from above	282,000	96,000	98,100	18,000	9,600	288,30.
Minority Interest					29,600	29,60.
Total	882,000	361,000	308,000	308,000		982,900

¹To eliminate intercompany dividends.

²To eliminate investment in S Company.

Cash	18,000	
Investment in S Company		18,000
(Subsidiary Dividends)		
Investment in S Company	24,300	
Equity in Subsidiary Income (.9 × 27,000)		24,300
(Subsidiary Income)		

Workpaper eliminating entries at the end of 1980 under the equity method would be:

Equity in Subsidiary Income	24,300	
Dividends Declared—S Company		18,000
Investment in S Company		6,300
Common Stock—S Company	180,000	
Retained Earnings—S Company	72,000	
Subsidiary Income Purchased	8,100	
Land	29,900	
Investment in S Company		290,000

In subsequent years under the cost method, the establishment of reciprocity is based on the parent's share of the change in subsidiary retained earnings from the date of acquisition, April 1, 1980, to the beginning of the appropriate year. S Company's retained earnings on April 1, 1980 were $89,000, consisting of the 1/1/80 balance of $80,000 plus the $9,000 income earned from January 1 to April 1, 1980. Thus, the December 31, 1981 workpaper entry to establish reciprocity, for example, would be:

Investment in S Company	6,300	
Retained Earnings—P Company		6,300
.9 (96,000 − 89,000)		

Regardless of whether the cost or equity method is used, consolidated income and consolidated retained earnings can be verified as follows:

CONSOLIDATED INCOME

P Company Income from its independent operations (118,000 − 18,000 dividends)	100,000
P Company's share of S Company's income since acquisition (27,000 × .9)	24,300
Consolidated Net Income	124,300

CONSOLIDATED RETAINED EARNINGS

P Company's reported cost-basis retained earnings	282,000
P Company's share of the *undistributed* income of S Company since date of acquisition (27,000 − 20,000 × .9)	6,300
Consolidated Retained Earnings	288,300

Likewise, the verification of the difference between cost and book value may be made as follows:

Cost of Investment		290,000
Book Value of Equity Acquired:		
Common Stock	200,000	
Retained Earnings (80,000 + 9,000)	89,000	
Total	289,000 × .9	260,100
Difference between cost and book value		
(Assigned to land on workpaper)		29,900

Note that the retained earnings figure represents the amount that would be in the retained earnings account of S Company if its books had been closed on April 1, the date of acquisition.

Interim Acquisition Under the Pooling Method

Under the pooling of interests method, the revenue and expense accounts of the acquired company are combined with those of the acquiring company for the entire year in which the combination takes place. As a result, the investment is recorded as if the combination had taken place at the beginning of the year of acquisition. Because consolidated net income includes the parent's share of the subsidiary's net income for the entire period in which the acquisition occurs, no deduction is needed for "net income purchased."

To illustrate, assume the preceding situation except that P Company acquired 90% of S Company's stock in exchange for 10,000 shares of its $15 par value common stock and that all conditions for pooling accounting have been met. The exchange of shares would be recorded by P Company through the following entry:

Investment in S Company (.9 × 280,000)	252,000	
Common Stock (10,000 × 15)		150,000
Retained Earnings (.9 × 80,000)		72,000
Premium on Common Stock		30,000

The par value of S Company stock acquired of $180,000 (.9 × 200,000) exceeds the par value of P Company stock issued ($150,000) by $30,000, which is credited to premium on common stock.

A workpaper for the preparation of consolidated financial statements on December 31, 1980 under pooling and assuming use of the book value method is presented in Illustration 4–14.

ILLUSTRATION 4–14

Pooling Accounting
Interim Acquisition
Book Value Method

Consolidated Statements Workpaper
P Company and Subsidiary
For the Year Ended December 31, 1980

INCOME STATEMENT	P COMPANY	S COMPANY	ELIMINATIONS DR.	ELIMINATIONS CR.	MINORITY INTEREST	CONSOLIDATED BALANCES
Sales	600,000	160,000				760,000
Dividend Income	18,000		¹ 18,000			
Total Revenue	618,000	160,000				760,000
Cost of Goods Sold	380,000	80,000				460,000
Other Expense	120,000	44,000				164,000
Total Cost and Expense	500,000	124,000				624,000
Net	118,000	36,000				136,000
Minority Interest					3,600	(3,600)
Net Income to Retained Earnings	118,000	36,000	18,000	–0–	3,600	132,400
RETAINED EARNINGS STATEMENT						
1/1 Retained Earnings						
P Company	286,000					286,000
S Company		80,000	² 72,000		8,000	
Net Income from above	118,000	36,000	18,000	–0–	3,600	132,400
Dividends Declared						
P Company	(50,000)					(50,000)
S Company		(20,000)		¹ 18,000	(2,000)	
12/31 Retained Earnings to						
Balance Sheet	354,000	96,000	90,000	18,000	9,600	368,400
BALANCE SHEET						
Current Assets	436,000	71,000				507,000
Investment in S Company	252,000			²252,000		
Depreciable Fixed Assets (net)	326,000	200,000				526,000
Land	120,000	90,000				210,000
Total	1,134,000	361,000				1,243,000
Liabilities	100,000	65,000				165,000
Common Stock						
P Company	650,000					650,000
S Company		200,000	²180,000		20,000	
Premium on Common Stock	30,000					30,000
Retained Earnings from above	354,000	96,000	90,000	18,000	9,600	368,400
Minority Interest					29,600	29,600
Total	1,134,000	361,000	270,000	270,000		1,243,000

¹To eliminate intercompany dividends.
²To eliminate investment in S Company.

APPENDIX: ALTERNATIVE METHOD OF ACCOUNTING
FOR AN INTERIM ACQUISITION—PURCHASE METHOD

As indicated earlier, another method of prorating income is to include in the consolidated income statement only the subsidiary's revenue and expenses subsequent to the date of acquisition. Thus, assuming the interim purchase situation discussed earlier, because the purchase of stock took place on April 1, only three-fourths of S Company's sales, cost of goods sold, and other expense is included in the consolidated income statement as if S Company's books had been closed on April 1, 1980. A workpaper for the preparation of consolidated financial statements on December 31, 1980 is presented in Illustration 4–15.

The workpaper entry to eliminate the investment account is:

Common Stock—S Company	180,000	
Retained Earnings—S Company (.9 × 89,000)	80,100	
Land	29,900	
Investment in S Company		290,000

Note that S Company's beginning retained earnings is $9,000 greater than in Illustration 4–13, reflecting the implied effect of the closing to retained earnings of income earned during the first three months. Minority interest in net income included in combined income is 10% of $27,000, or $2,700, and the minority interest's share of beginning retained earnings of S Company is $900 greater. Note, however, that consolidated net income, consolidated retained earnings, and the consolidated balance sheet are identical to those in Illustration 4–13. Only the detail included in the consolidated income statement is different.

Questions

1. If a parent company elects to use the equity method rather than the cost method of accounting for its investments in subsidiaries, what effect will this choice have on the consolidated financial statements?

2. How are dividends declared and paid by a subsidiary during the year eliminated in the consolidated workpapers under the equity method? Under the cost method?

3. Define: Consolidated net income; consolidated retained earnings.

4. At the date of an 80% acquisition, a subsidiary had common stock of $100,000 and retained earnings of $16,250. Seven years later, at December 31, 1980, the subsidiary retained earnings had increased to $461,430. If the parent company records its investments by the cost method, what adjustment will have to be made on the consolidated workpaper at December 31, 1981 to recognize the parent's share of the cumulative undistributed profits (losses) of its subsidiary? Why?

ILLUSTRATION 4–15

Purchase Accounting	**Consolidated Statements Workpaper**
Interim Purchase of Stock	**P Company and Subsidiary**
Cost Method	**For the Year Ended December 31, 1980**

	P	S	ELIMINATIONS		MINORITY	CONSOLIDATED
INCOME STATEMENT	COMPANY	COMPANY	DR.	CR.	INTEREST	BALANCES
Sales	600,000	120,000				720,000
Dividend Income	18,000		¹ 18,000			
Total Revenue	618,000	120,000				720,000
Cost of Goods Sold	380,000	60,000				440,000
Other Expense	120,000	33,000				153,000
Total Cost and Expense	500,000	93,000				593,000
Net	118,000	27,000				127,000
Minority Interest					2,700	(2,700)
Net Income to Retained Earnings	118,000	27,000	18,000	–0–	2,700	124,300
RETAINED EARNINGS STATEMENT						
Beginning Retained Earnings						
P Company (1/1/80)	214,000					214,000
S Company (4/1/80)		89,000	² 80,100		8,900	
Net Income from above	118,000	27,000	18,000	–0–	2,700	124,300
Dividends Declared						
P Company	(50,000)					(50,000)
S Company		(20,000)		¹ 18,000	(2,000)	
12/31 Retained Earnings to						
Balance Sheet	282,000	96,000	98,100	18,000	9,600	288,300
BALANCE SHEET						
Current Assets	146,000	71,000				217,000
Investment in S Company	290,000			²290,000		
Depreciable Fixed Assets (net)	326,000	200,000				526,000
Land	120,000	90,000	² 29,900			239,900
Total	882,000	361,000				982,900
Liabilities	100,000	65,000				165,000
Common Stock						
P Company	500,000					500,000
S Company		200,000	²180,000		20,000	
Retained Earnings from above	282,000	96,000	98,100	18,000	9,600	288,300
Minority Interest					29,600	29,600
Total	882,000	361,000	308,000	308,000		982,900

¹To eliminate intercompany dividends.

²To eliminate investment in S Company.

5. On a consolidated workpaper for a parent and its partially owned subsidiary, the minority interest column accumulates the minority interests' share of several account balances. What are these accounts? What does the minority interest on the consolidated balance sheet represent?

6. Illustrations 4–4 and 4–6 show that, under the equity method, parent company net income equals consolidated net income and parent company retained earnings equals consolidated retained earnings on the balance sheets. Since this is the case, why are consolidated financial statements considered superior to parent-company financial statements when the parent uses the equity method?

7. Identify and briefly describe two methods for accounting for a subsidiary subsequent to acquisition under the pooling of interests method.

8. In the preparation of a consolidated statement of changes in financial position, what adjustments are necessary because of the existence of a minority interest?

9. Describe two methods for treating the preacquisition revenue and expense items of a subsidiary acquired during a fiscal period under the purchase method.

·10. How are preacquisition revenue and expense items of a subsidiary acquired during a fiscal period treated under the pooling of interests method?

11. A principal limitation of consolidated financial statements is their lack of separate financial information about the assets, liabilities, revenues, and expenses of the individual companies included in the consolidation. Identify some problems which the reader of consolidated financial statements would encounter as a result of this limitation.

(CPA adapted)

Problems

Problem 4–1

Pestcott Corporation acquired a 100% interest in Stainless Company on January 1, 1980, paying $300,000. The cost method is used to account for the investment. Financial statement data of the two companies for the year ended December 31, 1980 are presented below:

INCOME STATEMENT	PESTCOTT	STAINLESS
Sales	$780,000	$386,000
Cost of Goods Sold	499,500	304,000
Other Expense	113,300	73,600
Dividend Income	5,000	
RETAINED EARNINGS STATEMENT		
Balance, 1/1/80	190,000	60,000
Net Income	172,200	8,400
Dividends Declared	45,000	5,000

BALANCE SHEET

Cash	148,000	72,000
Accounts Receivable	103,000	105,400
Inventories	133,200	121,000
Investment in Stainless Company	300,000	
Accounts Payable	67,000	35,000
Common Stock	300,000	200,000
Retained Earnings	317,200	63,400

Prepare a workpaper for the preparation of consolidated financial statements on December 31, 1980. (Any difference between the cost of the investment and the book value of equity acquired relates to subsidiary land.)

Problem 4–2

Trial balances for Utah Company and its wholly owned subsidiary, Arizona Company, are presented below. The parent acquired its interest in the subsidiary on January 1, 1980 for $300,000 and accounts for this investment by the equity method.

DEBITS	UTAH	ARIZONA
Cash	$ 160,000	$ 96,000
Accounts Receivable	139,000	56,000
Inventories	170,000	180,000
Land	30,000	18,000
Investment in Arizona Company	319,000	
Dividends Declared	24,000	8,000
Cost of Goods Sold	492,000	236,000
Other Expense	83,000	61,000
	$1,417,000	$655,000

CREDITS		
Accounts Payable	$ 115,000	$ 41,000
Common Stock	300,000	140,000
Premium on Common Stock	100,000	100,000
Retained Earnings, 1/1	100,000	50,000
Sales	775,000	324,000
Equity in Subsidiary Income	27,000	
	$1,417,000	$655,000

Prepare a workpaper for the preparation of consolidated financial statements on December 31, 1980. (Any difference between the cost of the investment and the book value of equity acquired relates to subsidiary land.)

Problem 4–3

Condensed financial information for Lupine Company and Butler Company is given below:

Balance Sheet Data
December 31, 1981

	LUPINE	BUTLER
Current Assets	$ 87,973	$ 35,570
Investment in Butler Company	230,465	
Other Assets	330,000	180,000
Total Assets	$648,438	$215,570
Liabilities	$ 63,710	$ 16,269
Common Stock	300,000	160,000
Retained Earnings	284,728	39,301
Total Equities	$648,438	$215,570

Retained Earnings Data

	LUPINE	BUTLER
Balance, 1/1/80	$113,480	$ 9,450
1980 Net Income	64,110	30,050
1980 Dividends Declared	(30,000)	(21,000)
1981 Net Income	172,138	40,801
1981 Dividends Declared	(35,000)	(20,000)
Balance, 12/31/81	$284,728	$ 39,301

Income Statement Data
1981

	LUPINE	BUTLER
Sales	$436,500	$301,555
Subsidiary Income	40,801	
Total Revenue	477,301	301,555
Cost of Goods Sold	230,416	179,595
Other Expense	74,747	81,159
Total Cost and Expense	305,163	260,754
Net Income	$172,138	$ 40,801

Lupine Company purchased all of Butler Company's common stock at the beginning of 1980 and uses the equity method to account for its investment.

Prepare a workpaper for the preparation of consolidated financial statements on December 31, 1981. (Any difference between the cost of the investment and the book value of equity acquired relates to subsidiary land.)

Problem 4–4

Braden Company purchased 90% of the capital stock of Carter Company on January 1, 1978 for $130,000, when the latter's capital stock and retained earnings were $100,000 and $20,000, respectively. The difference between cost and book value relates to Carter Company land holdings. Trial balances as of December 31, 1981 were as follows:

	BRADEN	CARTER
Cash	$ 26,000	$ 20,000
Receivables	42,000	34,000
Inventory, 1/1	30,000	16,000
Investment in Carter Company	130,000	
Plant and Equipment	120,000	100,000
Land	50,000	36,000
Dividends Declared	20,000	10,000
Purchases	180,000	40,000
Other Expense	30,000	14,000
Total Debits	$628,000	$270,000
Accounts Payable	$ 31,000	$ 20,000
Capital Stock, $10 par	200,000	100,000
Retained Earnings, 1/1	158,000	70,000
Sales	230,000	80,000
Dividend Income	9,000	
Total Credits	$628,000	$270,000
Inventory, 12/31	$ 60,000	$ 20,000

Prepare a workpaper for the preparation of consolidated financial statements on December 31, 1981.

Problem 4–5

Camelback Company purchased 80% of the common stock of Peoria, Inc. on January 1, 1981 for $175,000. Trial balances at the end of 1981 for the companies were:

	CAMELBACK	PEORIA
Cash	$ 31,408	$ 34,000
Accounts and Notes Receivable	108,000	104,260
Inventory, 1/1	34,680	9,840
Investment in Peoria, Inc.	203,108	
Other Assets	150,802	106,637
Dividends Declared	15,000	10,000
Purchases	151,500	81,400
Selling Expense	18,541	9,667
Other Expense	7,444	6,398
	$720,483	$362,202
Accounts and Notes Payable	$ 42,239	$ 16,270
Other Liabilities	6,400	7,143
Common Stock	100,000	50,000
Premium on Common Stock	150,000	75,000
Retained Earnings	111,176	67,499
Sales	274,560	146,290
Subsidiary Income	36,108	
	$720,483	$362,202

Inventory balances on December 31, 1981 were $11,260 for Camelback and $6,150 for Peoria, Inc. Peoria's accounts and notes payable contained a $2,500 note payable to Camelback.

Prepare a workpaper for the preparation of consolidated financial statements on December 31, 1981. (Any difference between the cost of the investment and the book value of equity acquired relates to subsidiary land.)

Problem 4–6

Purchase Company acquired an 80% interest in Sell Company on March 1, 1980. Trial balances for the two companies on February 28, 1981 were:

	PURCHASE	SELL
Cash	$ 84,627	$ 28,119
Accounts and Notes Receivable	117,749	91,113
Advances to Sell Company	25,000	
Inventory, 12/31	67,269	62,911
Investment in Sell Company	110,000	
Other Assets	103,749	70,000
Dividends Declared	19,000	16,000
Sales Returns	10,000	3,000
Cost of Goods Sold	246,736	137,458
Other Expense	99,691	76,988
	$883,821	$485,589
Accounts and Notes Payable	$133,927	$ 43,089
Advances from Purchase Company		25,000
Common Stock	250,000	170,000
Retained Earnings	66,394	(32,500)
Sales	416,000	280,000
Dividend Income	17,500	
	$883,821	$485,589

Purchase Company's accounts and notes payable include $13,000 due to Sell Company, whereas $7,540 of Sell Company's accounts and notes payable were due to Purchase Company.

Prepare a workpaper for the preparation of consolidated financial statements for the year ended February 28, 1981. (Any difference between the cost of the investment and the book value of equity acquired relates to subsidiary land.)

Problem 4–7

On January 1, 1980, Deadwood Enterprises acquired 92% of the outstanding common stock of Black Hills Company by exchanging 2,000 shares of its own common stock in a pooling of interests. Summary financial data are presented below for 1980:

INCOME STATEMENT	DEADWOOD	BLACK HILLS
Sales	$ 790,808	$264,983
Cost of Goods Sold	423,337	161,930
Selling Expense	41,966	21,128
Administrative Expense	30,941	23,004
Total Cost and Expense	496,244	206,062
Net	294,564	58,921
Subsidiary Income	54,207	
Net Income	$ 348,771	$ 58,921

RETAINED EARNINGS STATEMENT

Balance, 1/1	$ 564,192	$111,213
Net Income	348,771	58,921
Dividends Declared	(175,000)	(50,000)
Balance, 12/31	$ 737,963	$120,134

BALANCE SHEET

Cash	$ 114,294	$ 74,210
Accounts Receivable	211,677	71,326
Inventory	283,922	99,417
Investment in Black Hills Company	299,123	
Land	565,410	78,000
Buildings	420,817	95,864
Equipment	603,369	99,800
	$2,498,612	$518,617
Accounts Payable	$ 110,649	$ 94,166
Notes Payable	125,000	50,000
Other Liabilities	122,084	49,317
Common Stock, $100 par	900,000	150,000
Premium on Common Stock	400,600	55,000
Retained Earnings	840,279	120,134
	$2,498,612	$518,617

On December 31, 1980, Black Hills owed Deadwood $14,560 on open account.

Required:

A. Reconstruct the entries Deadwood made on its records to record the acquisition and subsequent events relating to its investment during 1980.

B. Prepare a consolidated workpaper for the year ended December 31, 1980.

C. Assume that Deadwood used the book value method to record its investment. Give, in general journal form, the eliminating entries for a consolidated workpaper on December 31, 1980.

Problem 4–8

Price Company purchased 51,000 shares of the outstanding voting stock of Stride Company on January 2, 1976 for $480,000 cash. At that time Stride Company had the following stockholders' equity:

Capital Stock, $5 par	$300,000
Other Contributed Capital	120,000
Retained Earnings	88,000
Total	$508,000

Trial balances for Price and Stride Companies on December 31, 1980 were:

	PRICE	STRIDE
Current Assets	$ 398,000	$ 187,000
Investment in Stride Company	480,000	
Plant and Equipment (net)	561,000	429,000
Land	300,000	112,000
Dividends Declared	75,000	40,000
Cost of Goods Sold	1,140,000	560,000
Other Expense	380,000	220,000
Total	$3,334,000	$1,548,000
Liabilities	$ 228,000	$ 90,000
Capital Stock	600,000	300,000
Other Contributed Capital	240,000	120,000
Retained Earnings, 1/1	532,000	168,000
Sales	1,700,000	870,000
Dividend Income	34,000	
Total	$3,334,000	$1,548,000

Prepare a consolidated statements workpaper at December 31, 1980. (Any difference between cost and book value acquired relates to subsidiary land.)

Problem 4–9
On January 1, 1980, Pride Company acquired 90% of the common stock of Stacy Company for a cash payment of $130,000. Trial balances on December 31, 1980 were:

	PRIDE	STRIDE
Current Assets	$ 398,000	$164,000
Investment in Stacy Company	121,000	
Other Assets	665,000	72,000
Dividends Declared	50,000	
Cost of Goods Sold	442,000	334,000
Other Expense	110,000	96,000
Equity in Subsidiary Loss	9,000	
	$1,795,000	$666,000
Liabilities	$ 167,000	$ 92,000
Common Stock	600,000	200,000
Retained Earnings, (deficit)	348,000	(46,000)
Sales	680,000	420,000
	$1,795,000	$666,000

Prepare a consolidated statements workpaper at December 31, 1980. (Any difference between cost of the investment and the book value acquired relates to subsidiary land.)

Problem 4–10
Bethel Company purchased an 80% interest in Crane Company on May 1, 1980 for a cash payment of $206,880. December 31, 1980 trial balances for Bethel and Crane Companies were as follows:

	BETHEL	CRANE
Current Assets	$ 195,300	$ 89,600
Treasury Stock at Cost, 500 shares		16,000
Investment in Crane Company	206,880	
Plant and Equipment (net)	667,000	281,000
Cost of Goods Sold	630,500	292,000
Expenses	242,000	121,000
Dividends Declared		20,000
	$1,941,680	$819,600
Accounts and Notes Payable	$ 116,000	$ 62,000
Dividends Payable		20,000
Capital Stock, $10 par	500,000	100,000
Additional Paid-in Capital	182,000	45,000
Retained Earnings	157,680	104,600
Sales	970,000	485,000
Dividend Income	16,000	3,000
	$1,941,680	$819,600

Crane Company declared a $20,000 cash dividend on December 20, 1980, payable on January 10, 1981 to stockholders of record on December 31, 1980. Bethel Company recognized the dividend on the declaration date.

Prepare a workpaper for the preparation of consolidated financial statements at December 31, 1980, assuming that revenue and expense amounts of Crane Company are included with those of Bethel Company for the entire year.

Problem 4–11

Using the data given in Problem 4–10, prepare a workpaper for the preparation of consolidated financial statements at December 31, 1980 under the assumption that Crane Company's revenue and expense accounts are included in the consolidated income statement from the date of acquisition only. (Round to the nearest dollar.)

Problem 4–12

The consolidated income statement for the year ending December 31, 1980 and comparative balance sheets for 1979 and 1980 for Pacer Company and its 80 percent owned subsidiary Sally Company are as follows:

PACER COMPANY AND SUBSIDIARY
Consolidated Income Statement
For the Year Ending December 31, 1980

Sales		$513,000
Cost of Goods Sold		252,000
Gross Margin		261,000
Depreciation Expense	$ 45,000	
Other Operating Expenses	153,000	198,000
Income from Operations		63,000
Equity in Income of Unconsolidated Affiliate		12,000
Combined Net Income		75,000
Minority Interest in Net Income		6,000
Consolidated Net Income		$ 69,000

PACER COMPANY AND SUBSIDIARY
Consolidated Balance Sheets
December 31, 1979 and 1980

	1980	1979
Cash	$ 72,000	$ 75,000
Receivables	156,000	180,000
Inventory	252,000	147,000
Property, Plant and Equipment (net of depreciation)	465,000	450,000
Investment in Unconsolidated Affiliate	81,000	78,000
Goodwill	111,000	120,000
Total Assets	$1,137,000	$1,050,000
Accounts Payable	$ 135,000	$ 120,000
Accrued Expenses	60,000	45,000
Bonds Payable, July 1, 1997	240,000	300,000
Total Liabilities	$ 435,000	$ 465,000
Minority Interest	$ 63,000	$ 60,000
Common Stock	$ 375,000	$ 300,000
Retained Earnings	264,000	225,000
Total Stockholders' Equity	639,000	525,000
Total	$1,137,000	$1,050,000

Other Information:

1. Pacer Company recognized $12,000 income and received a $9,000 dividend on its investment in its unconsolidated affiliate.

2. Sally Company distributed a $15,000 dividend during 1980 of which $3,000 were paid to minority stockholders.

Prepare a consolidated statement of changes in financial position using a working capital approach.

5

Accounting for the Difference Between Cost and Book Value of an Investment

When the acquisition of an investment is accounted for as a purchase, there is ordinarily a difference between the fair value of the consideration given up (cost of the investment) and the book value of the equity interest acquired in the investee. In most cases, the investor's cost exceeds the book value of the stock acquired. In some instances, however, the book value of the stock acquired may exceed its cost. Circumstances that may give rise to such differences were discussed in Chapter 2.

This chapter contains a detailed discussion and illustration of the allocation of this difference to assets and liabilities in the consolidated balance sheet and of the amortization and depreciation of the difference in the consolidated income statement. In addition, the impact of the difference between cost and book value on the determination of income from nonconsolidated investees under the equity method is described and illustrated.

CONSOLIDATING WORKPAPERS: INVESTMENT RECORDED AT COST

An excess of cost over the book value of subsidiary stock acquired implies that there are unrecorded or undervalued assets and/or overstated liabilities on the books of the subsidiary. Conversely, an excess of book value of subsidiary stock acquired over the cost of acquiring that stock implies that there are overvalued assets and/or undervalued or unrecorded liabilities on the books of the subsidiary. When consolidated financial statements are prepared, assets and liability values must be adjusted by allocating the difference between cost and book value to specific unrecorded or recorded tangible and intangible assets and/or liabilities. This allocation is made on the consolidating workpaper, since generally accepted accounting standards would ordinarily prohibit a subsidiary from recording on its own books increases in net asset valuations implied by the amount paid for the purchase of a controlling interest in its stock. However, if, and only if, the difference between cost and book value reflects accounting errors on the books of the subsidiary in the valuation of assets or liabilities, appropriate adjustments should be recorded on the subsidiary's books prior to preparation of the consolidating workpapers.

Adjustment of Assets and Liabilities: Wholly Owned Subsidiaries

The treatment in the consolidated financial statements of the difference between cost and book value of an investment in a wholly owned subsidiary is analogous to the allocation of the cost of an acquired company to the assets acquired and liabilities assumed in a business combination as described in Chapter 1. The process is different, however, in that the book values of individual assets and liabilities must be adjusted to their fair values in the consolidating workpapers each year, as contrasted with the one-time recording of these assets and liabilities at their fair values when there is only one surviving legal and accounting entity.

In the case of a wholly owned subsidiary, the difference between cost and book value is first applied to the adjustment of individual assets and liabilities to their fair values on the date of acquisition. If, after adjusting identifiable assets and liabilities to fair values, a residual amount of difference remains, it is treated as follows: When cost exceeds the aggregate fair values of identifiable assets and liabilities, the residual amount will be positive (a debit balance). A positive residual difference is evidence of an unspecified intangible and is accounted for as goodwill and generally referred to as "consolidated goodwill." It is preferable, however, to give this positive residual difference an operational description in the consolidated financial statements such as "unamortized excess of cost over fair value of subsidiary net assets acquired."

If the total fair values of identifiable subsidiary assets less liabilities exceeds acquisition cost, the residual amount of difference will be negative (credit balance). In *APB Opinion No. 16* (par. 91), the Accounting Principles Board takes the position that "the value assigned to net assets acquired should not exceed the cost of an acquired company because the general presumption in historical cost based accounting is that net assets acquired should be recorded at not more than cost." Accordingly, *Opinion No. 16* (par. 91) provides that a negative residual difference should be allocated to reduce proportionately the values initially assigned to noncurrent assets (except noncurrent marketable securities) in determining their fair values. If noncurrent assets are reduced to zero by this allocation, any remaining residual negative difference should be classified as a deferred credit and amortized to consolidated income over a period not to exceed forty years.

In all subsequent illustrations, *"difference between cost and book value"* is used to designate the total difference between acquisition cost and the parent's equity in the book value of the net assets of the subsidiary on the date it acquires its interest in the subsidiary. *"Excess of cost over fair value"* is used to designate the excess of acquisition cost over the parent's equity in the *fair value* of the net assets of the subsidiary on the date the parent acquires its interest in the subsidiary. *"Excess of fair value over cost"* is used to designate the excess of the parent's equity in the *fair value* of the net assets of the subsidiary on the date it acquires its interest over the cost of its investment in the subsidiary. *"Deferred excess of fair value over cost"* is used to designate that portion, if any, of the "excess of fair value over cost" that remains after the noncurrent assets of the subsidiary (excluding marketable securities) have been reduced to zero.

Where the difference between cost and book value is assigned to depreciable or amortizable assets or to discount or premium on long-term debt, entries must be made in the consolidating workpapers to account for current and prior-year depreciation and amortization relating to this difference. Workpaper entries are necessary when the parent company uses the cost method, since neither the parent nor the subsidiary company records or reports the amortization or depreciation, as such, in their own records or financial statements.

Example 1—Workpaper Adjustments and Eliminations (Cost Method)

Assume that P Company acquires a 100% interest in S Company on January 1, 1980 for $2,300,000 when the stockholders' equity of S Company had a book value of $1,700,000 as follows:

Capital Stock	1,000,000
Retained Earnings	700,000
Stockholders' Equity	1,700,000

P Company accounts for its investment in S Company at cost. Each year, the investment-eliminating entry in the consolidating workpaper will result in a debit to the "difference between cost and book value" in the amount of $600,000, as follows:

Beginning Retained Earnings—S Company	700,000	
Capital Stock—S Company	1,000,000	
Difference Between Cost and Book Value	600,000	
Investment in S Company		2,300,000

Assume further that differences between fair values and book values of S Company's identifiable assets and liabilities on January 1, 1980 are as follows:

ITEM	BOOK VALUE	FAIR VALUE	DIFFERENCE
Property & Equipment	1,600,000	2,200,000	600,000
Accumulated Deprec.	(480,000)	(660,000)	(180,000)
Property & Equipment (net)	1,120,000	1,540,000	420,000
Inventory	300,000	320,000	20,000
Land	500,000	570,000	70,000
Bonds Payable			
(par value $500,000)	(500,000)	(424,184)	75,816
Other Assets &			
Liabilities (net)	280,000	280,000	–0–
Unspecified Intangible			
(unallocated balance)	–0–	14,184	14,184
Total	1,700,000	2,300,000	600,000

If a consolidated balance sheet was prepared on January 2, 1980, the difference between cost and book value of $600,000 would be reclassified with a workpaper entry as follows:

Property & Equipment	600,000	
Inventory	20,000	
Land	70,000	
Unamortized Discount on Bonds Payable	75,816	
Excess of Cost Over Fair Value	14,184	
Accumulated Depreciation		180,000
Difference Between Cost and Book Value		600,000

Workpaper entries necessary in subsequent years because of the assignment of the difference between cost and book value to each of the items above are illustrated and explained below.

Assignment of the Difference Between Cost and Book Value to Depreciable Assets Workpaper entries on December 31, 1980 to account for the amount of difference between cost and book value assigned to equipment are as follows:

Property & Equipment	600,000	
Accumulated Depreciation		180,000
Difference Between Cost and Book Value		420,000
Depreciation Expense	60,000	
Accumulated Depreciation		60,000

These entries are based on the assumptions that on January 1, 1980 the equipment was 30% depreciated, had an estimated remaining useful life of 7 years, and is depreciated by S Company using straight-line depreciation.

The rationale for the second entry is that depreciation in the consolidated income statement should be based on the value assigned to the equipment in the consolidated balance sheet. Since neither the parent nor the subsidiary records the equipment write-up on its books, neither the parent nor the subsidiary will record depreciation on the $420,000 net difference ($600,000 gross difference) between cost and book value assigned to the equipment in the consolidated balance sheet. Accordingly, workpaper adjustments must be made each year if the additional depreciation associated with the difference is to be appropriately recognized in the consolidated financial statements. In this illustration, the equipment had an original life of 10 years and a remaining life of 7 years on the date a controlling interest was acquired in the subsidiary. Additional annual depreciation is accordingly calculated as $60,000 (600,000/10 = 60,000 or 420,000/7 = 60,000).

It is also assumed that accumulated depreciation on property and equipment will be separately disclosed in the consolidated financial statements. Allocation of the $420,000 difference assigned to property and equipment (net of accumulated depreciation) separately to property and equipment (gross) and to accumulated depreciation requires knowledge of the reproduction cost new and the sound value of the property and equipment as shown in the appraisal report, or it may be implied as follows: If the property and equipment is 30% depreciated on January 1, 1980, the $420,000 difference between the sound value and the book value of the property and equipment is 70% of the difference between the replacement cost new and the acquisition cost of the property and equipment.[1] Therefore, the difference between replacement cost new and acquisition cost is $600,000 (420,000/.70 = 600,000). Accumulated depreciation on the difference between replacement cost new and acquisition cost is 30% of $600,000, or $180,000.

Workpaper entries required at the end of the second, third, and seventh year subsequent to acquisition are presented below:

	12/31/81	12/31/82	12/31/86
Property & Equipment	600,000	600,000	600,000
Accumulated Depreciation	180,000	180,000	180,000
Difference Between Cost			
and Book Value	420,000	420,000	420,000
Beginning Retained Earnings—			
Parent (Beginning Consolidated			
Retained Earnings)	60,000	120,000	360,000
Depreciation Expense	60,000	60,000	60,000
Accumulated Depreciation	120,000	180,000	420,000

Beginning consolidated retained earnings must be adjusted each year for the cumulative amount of additional depreciation deducted from consolidated income in previous years. By reducing previously reported consolidated net income, these workpaper depreciation adjustments also reduced previously reported consolidated retained earnings. Accordingly, the amounts indicated by the account balances on the

---

[1]Sound value is replacement cost new less accumulated depreciation based on replacement cost new from the date of the acquisition of the asset to the date of the appraisal.

books of the affiliated companies must be adjusted for the cumulative effect of the depreciation entries that have been made only on the consolidating workpapers. The reduction of beginning consolidated retained earnings is accomplished by a debit to the beginning retained earnings of the parent company in the consolidating workpapers.

Assuming that the subsidiary abandons the property and equipment at the end of its estimated useful life, the workpaper entry necessary on December 31, 1987 and in all subsequent years is:

Beginning Retained Earnings—Parent		
(Beginning Consolidated Retained Earnings)	420,000	
Difference Between Cost and Book Value		420,000

The reduction of consolidated retained earnings by $420,000 appropriately reflects the fact that consolidated net income in prior years has been reduced by a workpaper adjustment of $60,000 each year for seven years.

Premature Disposal of Depreciable Asset by Subsidiary   Assume that three years after its acquisition by P Company, S Company sells for $800,000 all of the property and equipment to which the $420,000 difference was assigned. The carrying value of the property and equipment on the books of the subsidiary and from a consolidated point of view on January 1, 1983 (the date of the sale) are as follows:

	S COMPANY	DIFFERENCE	CONSOLIDATED
Cost	1,600,000	600,000	2,200,000
Accumulated Depreciation	960,000	360,000	1,320,000
Undepreciated Basis	640,000	240,000	880,000
Proceeds	(800,000)		(800,000)
(Gain) Loss on Sale	(160,000)	240,000	80,000

S Company will report a gain of $160,000 on the disposal of the equipment. From the point of view of the consolidated entity, however, there is a loss of $80,000. The workpaper entry necessary to adjust the amounts in the consolidated financial statements is as follows:

Beginning Retained Earnings—Parent		
(Beginning Consolidated Retained Earnings)	180,000	
Gain on Disposal of Equipment	160,000	
Loss on Disposal of Equipment	80,000	
Difference Between Cost and Book Value		420,000

The effect of the entry is to reduce beginning consolidated retained earnings for the $180,000 additional depreciation charged to consolidated net income in the three years prior to the sale; to eliminate the gain of $160,000 reported by S Company in the year of the sale; and to recognize the consolidated loss on the disposal of the equipment of $80,000. In all future years, the necessary eliminating entry will be:

Beginning Retained Earnings—Parent
  (Beginning Consolidated Retained Earnings)   420,000
    Difference Between Cost and Book Value   420,000

The $420,000 reduction of consolidated retained earnings reflects the reduction of consolidated net income by a total of $180,000 for additional depreciation recognized in 1980, 1981, and 1982, and by an additional $240,000 in the year of the sale when the gain of $160,000 reported by the subsidiary was converted to a consolidated loss of $80,000 on the consolidating workpaper.

Depreciable Assets Used in Manufacturing When the difference between cost and book value is assigned to depreciable assets used in manufacturing, workpaper entries necessary to reflect additional depreciation may be more complex, because the current and previous year's additional depreciation may have to be allocated between work in process, finished goods on hand at the end of the year, and cost of goods sold. In practice, such refinements are often ignored on the basis of materiality, and all of the current year's additional depreciation is charged to cost of sales.

Assignment of the Difference Between Cost and Book Value to Inventory The treatment of the amount of difference between cost and book value assigned to inventory ($20,000 in this illustration) depends on the inventory cost flow assumption followed by the subsidiary. If the subsidiary company uses the first-in, first-out (FIFO) assumption, the workpaper entry on December 31, 1980 is:

Cost of Goods Sold   20,000
  Difference Between Cost and Book Value   20,000

The presumption implicit in this entry is that the undervalued inventory of the subsidiary was sold during the year. Since S Company will not have included the additional $20,000 assigned to inventory in its reported cost of goods sold, consolidated cost of goods sold must be increased by a workpaper entry. In all future years the eliminating entry would be:

Beginning Retained Earnings—Parent
  (Beginning Consolidated Retained Earnings)   20,000
    Difference Between Cost and Book Value   20,000

The workpaper increase in consolidated cost of goods sold in 1980 decreased consolidated net income and consolidated retained earnings at December 31, 1980 by $20,000. Accordingly, an adjustment to consolidated retained earnings is necessary in all subsequent years, since the $20,000 reduction of consolidated net income will not have been reflected in the accounts of either the parent or the subsidiary.

If the subsidiary uses the last-in, first-out (LIFO) assumption in pricing its inventory, the workpaper entry each year will be as follows, so long as there is no reduction in inventory quantities between years:

Inventory	20,000	
Difference Between Cost and Book Value		20,000

If there is a reduction in inventory quantities, all or a pro rata portion of the $20,000 must be allocated to cost of goods sold in the year of the reduction and to beginning consolidated retained earnings in subsequent years by appropriate workpaper entries.

Assignment of the Difference Between Cost and Book Value to Land The amount of the difference between cost and book value assigned to nondepreciable, nonamortizable assets poses no particular problems in consolidation. The following workpaper entry is made each year until the land is disposed of by the subsidiary:

Land	70,000	
Difference Between Cost and Book Value		70,000

If and when the land is disposed of by the subsidiary, any gain (loss) recognized on the subsidiary's books will be reduced (increased) by $70,000 in determining the amount of gain or loss to be reported in the consolidated income statement in the year of the sale. In all years subsequent to the disposal of the land by the subsidiary, the following workpaper entry would be necessary:

Beginning Retained Earnings—Parent		
(Beginning Consolidated Retained Earnings)	70,000	
Difference Between Cost and Book Value		70,000

Assignment of the Difference Between Cost and Book Value to Long-Term Debt Notes payable, long-term debt, and other obligations of an acquired company should be valued for consolidation purposes at the present value of amounts to be paid in the future. The present value should be determined using appropriate market rates of interest *at the date of acquisition.*

Assume, for example, that S Company has outstanding $500,000 in 6%, 20-year bonds that were issued at par on January 1, 1965, and that interest on the bonds is paid annually. Assume further that on January 1, 1980, when S Company is acquired by P Company, the yield rate on bonds with similar risk is 10%. The present value of S Company's bonds payable determined at the effective yield rate on the acquisition date is calculated as follows:

Interest Payments ....$30,000 \times 3.79079^1 = 113,724$
Principal Payments ....$500,000 \times .62092^2 = \underline{310,460}$
Present Value of Future Cash Payments Discounted at 10% $\underline{424,184}$

[1]Present value of an annuity of 1 for five periods discounted at 10%.
[2]Present value of an amount of 1 received five periods hence discounted at 10%.

From the point of view of the consolidated entity, bonds payable are overstated on January 1, 1980 by $75,816 (500,000 − 424,184), and a corresponding amount of the total difference between cost and book value on the date of acquisition must be assigned to "unamortized discount on bonds payable." In years subsequent to acquisition, interest expense reported by the subsidiary will be understated for consolidation purposes. Thus, workpaper entries must also be made to amortize the discount in a manner that will reflect consolidated interest expense as a constant rate on the carrying value of the liability to the consolidated entity. An amortization schedule for this purpose is presented in Illustration 5–1. Workpaper entities necessary in the first five years subsequent to P Company's acquisition of S Company are summarized below (credits are shown in parentheses).

| | DECEMBER 31 | | | | |
	1980	1981	1982	1983	1984
(1) Unamortized Discount on Bonds Payable	75,816	75,816	75,816	75,816	75,816
Difference Between Cost and Book Value	(75,816)	(75,816)	(75,816)	(75,816)	(75,816)
(2) Beginning Retained Earnings—Parent (Beginning Consolidated Retained Earnings)	—	12,418	26,078	41,104	57,633
Interest Expense (Illustration 5–1)	12,418	13,660	15,026	16,529	18,183
Unamortized Discount on Bonds Payable	(12,418)	(26,078)	(41,104)	(57,633)	(75,816)

In 1986, the bonds will be redeemed at par value ($500,000), which now is also the carrying value to the consolidated entity. In all future years, the appropriate workpaper eliminating entry relating to the bond discount will be:

Beginning Retained Earnings—Parent
  (Beginning Consolidated Retained Earnings)   75,816
    Difference Between Cost and Book Value   75,816

ILLUSTRATION 5–1
Bond Discount Amortization Schedule

DATE	INTEREST EXPENSE RECORDED BY S	CONSOLIDATED INTEREST EXPENSE	DISCOUNT AMORTIZATION	CONSOLIDATED CARRYING VALUE
1/ 1/1980	-0-	-0-	-0-	424,184
12/31/1980	30,000	42,418 [a]	12,418 [b]	436,602 [c]
12/31/1981	30,000	43,660 [d]	13,660	450,262
12/31/1982	30,000	45,026	15,026	465,288
12/31/1983	30,000	46,529	16,529	481,817
12/31/1984	30,000	48,183	18,183	500,000
	150,000	225,816	75,816	

[a] $.10 \times 424,184 = 42,418$
[b] $42,418 - 30,000 = 12,418$
[c] $424,184 + 12,418 = 436,602$
[d] $.10 \times 436,602 = 43,660$

Excess of Cost Over Equity in Fair Value of Subsidiary Assets Acquired The amount of difference between cost and book value not assigned to specific identifiable assets or liabilities is treated in the consolidated financial statements as an unspecified intangible and must be amortized (straight-line method recommended) over a period not to exceed forty years, in accordance with *APB Opinion No. 17*. Assuming that the excess of cost over fair value of $14,184 in this illustration is to be amortized over forty years, workpaper entries necessary one, two, three, and forty years subsequent to the acquisition of S Company by P Company are as follows:

	12/31/80	12/31/81	12/31/82	12/31/2020
(1) Excess of Cost Over Fair Value	14,184	14,184	14,184	14,184
Difference Between Cost and Book Value	14,184	14,184	14,184	14,184
(2) Beginning Retained Earnings— Parent (Beginning Consolidated Retained Earnings)	-0-	355	710	13,829
Amortization of Excess of Cost Over Fair Value	355	355	355	355
Excess of Cost Over Fair Value	355	710	1,065	14,184

At the end of forty years, the excess of cost over fair value will have been fully amortized against consolidated net income. In all future years the only necessary workpaper entry will be:

Beginning Retained Earnings—Parent (Beginning Consolidated Retained Earnings)	14,184	
Difference Between Cost and Book Value		14,184

Income Tax Effects   The adjustments to consolidated net income that result from the allocation, amortization and depreciation of the difference between cost and book value are not allowable adjustments to taxable income. They therefore result in a permanent difference between financial and taxable income. Thus, it is not necessary to apply deferred income tax procedures to the effects of the amortization and depreciation of the difference between cost and book value.

Comprehensive Illustration (Cost Method)   Consolidating workpapers for the years ended December 31, 1980 and December 31, 1981 that reflect the workpaper entries necessary for the allocation, depreciation, and amortization of the $600,000 difference analyzed above are presented in Illustration 5–2 and Illustration 5–3. It is assumed that S Company uses FIFO to account for its inventory. Particular attention should be given to the adjustments to the beginning retained earnings row of P Company in Illustration 5–3. As previously discussed, these adjustments are necessary so that the amount of consolidated retained earnings reported at the beginning of the year is equal to the amount of consolidated retained earnings reported at the end of the previous year ($1,808,227 in Illustration 5–2).

It should also be noted that, in the workpapers, the allocation of the difference between cost and book value to individual assets and liabilities is made in one entry (Entry No. 3 in Illustration 5–2 and Entry No. 4 in Illustration 5–3). Workpaper elimination entries illustrated in Illustrations 5–2 and 5–3 are summarized in general journal form beginning on page 155.

Purchase Accounting
Cost Method
Wholly Owned Subsidiary
Year of Acquisition

ILLUSTRATION 5–2
Consolidated Statements Workpaper
P Company and Subsidiary
For Year Ending December 31, 1980

INCOME STATEMENT	P COMPANY	S COMPANY	ELIMINATIONS DR.		ELIMINATIONS CR.	CONSOLIDATED BALANCES
Sales	3,100,000	2,200,000				5,300,000
Dividend Income	20,000		2	20,000		
Total	3,120,000	2,200,000				5,300,000
Inventory—1/1/80	500,000	300,000	3	20,000		820,000
Purchases	1,680,000	1,370,000				3,050,000
	2,180,000	1,670,000				3,870,000
Inventory—12/31/80	480,000	310,000				790,000
Cost of Goods Sold	1,700,000	1,360,000				3,080,000
Depreciation	380,000	210,000	4	60,000		650,000
Interest	120,000	30,000	5	12,418		162,418
Amortization of Excess of Cost over Fair Value			6	355		355
Other Expenses	624,000	475,000				1,099,000
Total	2,824,000	2,075,000				4,991,773
Net Income to Retained Earnings	296,000	125,000		112,773	–0–	308,227

	P COMPANY	S COMPANY	ELIMINATIONS DR.	ELIMINATIONS CR.	CONSOLIDATED BALANCES
RETAINED EARNINGS STATEMENT					
1/1/80 Retained Earnings					
P Company	1,650,000				1,650,000
S Company		700,000	¹ 700,000		
Net Income from above	296,000	125,000	112,773	–0–	308,227
Dividends Declared					
P Company	(150,000)				(150,000)
S Company		(20,000)		² 20,000	
12/31/80 Retained Earnings					
to Balance Sheet	1,796,000	805,000	812,773	20,000	1,808,227
BALANCE SHEET					
Inventory	480,000	310,000			790,000
Other Current Assets	620,000	550,000			1,170,000
Investment in S Company	2,300,000			¹2,300,000	
Difference Between Cost					
and Book Value			¹ 600,000	³ 600,000	
Land	1,250,000	500,000	³ 70,000		1,820,000
Property and Equipment	3,800,000	2,100,000	³ 600,000		6,500,000
				³ 180,000	
				⁴ 60,000	
(Accumulated Depreciation)	(1,520,000)	(840,000)			(2,600,000)
Excess of Cost over Fair Value			³ 14,184	⁶ 355	13,829
Total Assets	6,930,000	2,620,000			7,693,829
Current Liabilities	634,000	315,000			949,000
Bonds Payable	1,500,000	500,000			2,000,000
(Unamortized Discount on					
Bonds Payable)			³ 75,816	⁵ 12,418	(63,398)
Capital Stock					
P Company	3,000,000				3,000,000
S Company		1,000,000	¹1,000,000		
Retained Earnings from above	1,796,000	805,000	812,773	20,000	1,808,227
Total Liabilities & Equity	6,930,000	2,620,000	3,172,773	3,172,773	7,693,829

¹To eliminate investment account.

²To eliminate intercompany dividends.

³To assign the difference between cost and book value to specific assets and liabilities.

⁴To depreciate the amount of difference between cost and book value assigned to depreciable assets.

⁵To amortize the amount of difference between cost and book value assigned to unamortized discount on bonds payable.

⁶To amortize the amount of the difference between cost and book value assigned to unspecified intangible.

Purchase Accounting
Cost Method
Wholly Owned Subsidiary
Subsequent to Year of Acquisition

ILLUSTRATION 5–3
Consolidated Statements Workpaper
P Company and Subsidiary
For Year Ending December 31, 1981

INCOME STATEMENT	P COMPANY	S COMPANY	ELIMINATIONS DR.	ELIMINATIONS CR.	CONSOLIDATED BALANCES
Sales	3,534,000	2,020,000			5,554,000
Dividend Income	60,000		³ 60,000		
Total	3,594,000	2,020,000			5,554,000
Inventory—1/1/81	480,000	310,000			790,000
Purchases	2,070,000	1,250,000			3,320,000
	2,550,000	1,560,000			4,110,000
Inventory—12/31/81	510,000	360,000			870,000
Cost of Goods Sold	2,040,000	1,200,000			3,240,000
Depreciation	380,000	210,000	⁵ 60,000		650,000
Interest	120,000	30,000	⁶ 13,660		163,660
Amortization of Excess of Cost over Fair Value			⁷ 355		355
Other Expense	600,000	440,000			1,040,000
Total	3,140,000	1,880,000			5,094,015
Net Income to Retained Earnings	454,000	140,000	134,015	–0–	459,985
RETAINED EARNINGS STATEMENT					
1/1/81 Retained Earnings					
P Company	1,796,000		⁴ 20,000 ⁵ 60,000 ⁶ 12,418 ⁷ 355	¹ 105,000	1,808,227
S Company		805,000	² 805,000		
Net Income from above	454,000	140,000	134,015	–0–	459,985
Dividends Declared					
P Company	(150,000)				(150,000)
S Company		(60,000)		³ 60,000	
12/31/81 Retained Earnings to Balance Sheet	2,100,000	885,000	1,031,788	165,000	2,118,212

	P COMPANY	S COMPANY	ELIMINATIONS DR.	ELIMINATIONS CR.	CONSOLIDATED BALANCES
BALANCE SHEET					
Inventory	510,000	360,000			870,000
Other Current Assets	610,000	530,000			1,140,000
Investment in S Company	2,300,000		¹ 105,000	²2,405,000	
Difference Between Cost and Book Value			² 600,000	⁴ 600,000	
Land	2,000,000	750,000	⁴ 70,000		2,820,000
Property and Equipment	3,800,000	2,100,000	⁴ 600,000		6,500,000
				⁴ 180,000	
(Accumulated Depreciation)	(1,900,000)	(1,050,000)		⁵ 120,000	(3,250,000)
Excess of Cost over Fair Value			⁴ 14,184	⁷ 710	13,474
Total Assets	7,320,000	2,690,000			8,093,474
Current Liabilities	720,000	305,000			1,025,000
Bonds Payable	1,500,000	500,000			2,000,000
(Unamortized Discount on Bonds Payable)			⁴ 75,816	⁶ 26,078	(49,738)
Capital Stock					
P Company	3,000,000				3,000,000
S Company		1,000,000	²1,000,000		
Retained Earnings from above	2,100,000	885,000	1,031,788	165,000	2,118,212
Total Liabilities & Equity	7,320,000	2,690,000	3,496,788	3,496,788	8,093,474

¹To establish reciprocity as of 1/1/81 ([805,000 − 700,000] × 100% = 105,000).
²To eliminate the investment account.
³To eliminate intercompany dividends.
⁴To assign the difference between cost and book value to specific assets and liabilities.
⁵To depreciate the amount of the difference between cost and book value assigned to depreciable assets.
⁶To amortize the amount of the difference between cost and book value assigned to unamortized discount on bonds payable.
⁷To amortize the amount of the difference between cost and book value assigned to unspecified intangible.

December 31, 1980 workpaper entries in general journal form (Illustration 5–2)

(1) Beginning Retained Earnings—S Company	700,000	
Capital Stock—S Company	1,000,000	
Difference Between Cost and Book Value	600,000	
Investment in S Company		2,300,000
To eliminate the investment account.		
(2) Dividend Income	20,000	
Dividends Declared		20,000
To eliminate intercompany dividends.		

(3) Property and Equipment   600,000
    Cost of Goods Sold (Beginning Inventory)   20,000
    Land   70,000
    Unamortized Discount on Bonds Payable   75,816
    Excess of Cost over Fair Value   14,184
        Accumulated Depreciation   180,000
        Difference Between Cost and Book Value   600,000
        To assign the difference between cost and book value to specific assets and liabilities.

(4) Depreciation Expense   60,000
    Accumulated Depreciation   60,000
        To depreciate the amount of difference between cost and book value assigned to depreciable assets.

(5) Interest Expense   12,418
    Unamortized Discount on Bonds Payable   12,418
        To amortize the amount of difference between cost and book value assigned to unamortized discount on bonds payable.

(6) Amortization of Excess of Cost over Fair Value   355
    Excess of Cost over Fair Value   355
        To amortize the amount of difference between cost and book value assigned to unspecified intangible.

December 31, 1981 workpaper entries in general journal form (Illustration 5–3)

(1) Investment in S Company   105,000
    Beginning Retained Earnings—P Company   105,000
        To establish reciprocity as of January 1, 1981.

(2) Beginning Retained Earnings—S Company   805,000
    Capital Stock—S Company   1,000,000
    Difference Between Cost and Book Value   600,000
        Investment in S Company   2,405,000
        To eliminate investment account.

(3) Dividend Income   60,000
    Dividends Declared   60,000
        To eliminate intercompany dividends.

(4) Property and Equipment   600,000
    Beginning Retained Earnings—P Company   20,000
    Land   70,000
    Unamortized Discount on Bonds Payable   75,816
    Excess of Cost over Fair Value   14,184
        Accumulated Depreciation   180,000
        Difference Between Cost and Book Value   600,000
        To assign the difference between cost and book value to specific assets and liabilities.

(5) Beginning Retained Earnings—P Company   60,000
    Depreciation Expense   60,000
      Accumulated Depreciation   120,000
        To depreciate the amount of difference between cost and book value assigned to depreciable assets.

(6) Beginning Retained Earnings—P Company   12,418
    Interest Expense   13,660
      Unamortized Discount on Bonds Payable   26,078
        To amortize the amount of difference between cost and book value assigned to unamortized discount on bonds payable.

(7) Beginning Retained Earnings—P Company   355
    Amortization of Excess of Cost over Fair Value   355
      Excess of Cost over Fair Value   710
        To amortize the amount of difference between cost and book value assigned to unspecified intangible.

Example 2—Treatment of Excess of Fair Value over Cost

Assume the same facts as those in Example 1 except that P Company acquires its 100% interest in S Company for $2,045,816, rather than $2,300,000, and that the "other assets and liabilities (net)" of S Company with a fair value and a book value of $280,000 are constituted as follows:

Other Current Assets	110,000
Deferred Charge	290,000
Current Liabilities	(120,000)
Other Assets & Liabilities (net)	280,000

The calculation and allocation of the difference between the cost of the investment in S Company and book value of the equity in the net assets of S Company acquired is presented in Illustration 5–4. The difference between cost and book value is $345,816 (2,045,816 − 1,700,000). However, the fair value of the net assets of S Company exceed the cost of the investment resulting in an excess of fair value over cost of $240,000 (2,285,816 − 2,045,816).

ILLUSTRATION 5–4
Adjustment of Difference Between Cost and Book Value for Excess of Fair Value over Cost
(Based on Assumptions in Example 2)

ITEM	(1) BOOK VALUE	(2) FAIR VALUE	(3) INITIAL DIFFERENCE ALLOCATION	(4) ALLOCATION OF EXCESS OF FAIR VALUE OVER COST[a]	(5) ADJUSTED DIFFERENCE ALLOCATION
Property and Equipment	1,600,000	2,200,000	600,000	(220,000)	380,000
Accumulated Depreciation	(480,000)	(660,000)	(180,000)	66,000	(114,000)
Property and Equipment (net)	1,120,000	1,540,000	420,000	(154,000)	266,000
Land	500,000	570,000	70,000	(57,000)	13,000
Deferred Charge	290,000	290,000	–0–	(29,000)	(29,000)
Total Noncurrent Assets	1,910,000	2,400,000	490,000	(240,000)	250,000
Inventory	300,000	320,000	20,000	–0–	20,000
Other Current Assets	110,000	110,000	–0–	–0–	–0–
Current Liabilities	(120,000)	(120,000)	–0–	–0–	–0–
Long-term Debt	(500,000)	(424,184)	75,816	–0–	75,816
Net Assets	1,700,000	2,285,816			
Excess of Fair Value over Cost		(240,000)	(240,000)	240,000	–0–
Cost	1,700,000	2,045,816	345,816	–0–	345,816

[a](240,000/2,400,000) × fair value of each noncurrent asset item (excluding marketable securities).

The workpaper entry to eliminate the investment account is as follows:

(1) Beginning Retained Earnings—S Company	700,000	
Capital Stock—S Company	1,000,000	
Difference Between Cost and Book Value	345,816	
Investment in S Company		2,045,816

Allocation of the difference between cost and book value to specific assets and liabilities based on their fair values is calculated in Column 3, "Initial Difference Allocation," of Illustration 5–4, and may be summarized in general journal form as follows:

(2) Property and Equipment	600,000	
Land	70,000	
Beginning Inventory	20,000	
Unamortized Discount on Bonds Payable	75,816	
Accumulated Depreciation		180,000
Excess of Fair Value over Cost		240,000
Difference Between Cost and Book Value		345,816

The amount of excess of fair value over cost set up in this entry must, however, be eliminated by allocating it on the consolidating workpaper to reduce proportionally the *fair values* (not book values) initially assigned to noncurrent assets (excluding marketable securities).

Total noncurrent assets of S Company (excluding marketable securities) amount to $2,400,000. The proportionate reduction of individual assets based on this denominator is presented in Column 4, "Allocation of Excess of Fair Value over Cost," of Illustration 5–4, and may be summarized in general journal form as follows:

(3) Excess of Fair Value over Cost	240,000	
Accumulated Depreciation	66,000[a]	
Property & Equipment		220,000[b]
Land		57,000[c]
Deferred Charge		29,000[d]

[a]$(660,000/2,400,000) \times 240,000 = (240,000/2,400,000) \times 660,000 = (66,000)$.
[b]$(2,200,000/2,400,000) \times 240,000 = (240,000/2,400,000) \times 2,200,000 = 220,000$.
[c]$(570,000/2,400,000) \times 240,000 = (240,000/2,400,000) \times 570,000 = 57,000$.
[d]$(290,000/2,400,000) \times 240,000 = (240,000/2,400,000) \times 290,000 = 29,000$.

As a matter of efficient workpaper procedure, it is preferable to prepare a schedule similar to Illustration 5–4 and combine workpaper entries (2) and (3) above into one entry. See Column 5, "Adjusted Difference Allocation," of Illustration 5–4.

Allocation of the excess of fair value over cost as a reduction of noncurrent assets will change the amounts of workpaper adjustments to depreciation and amortization made necessary because of the assignment of the difference between cost and book value to specified assets and liabilities. After allocating the excess of fair value over cost, the amount of difference between cost and book value assigned to property and equipment (gross) is $380,000, rather than $600,000. Hence, a workpaper entry adjusting depreciation by $38,000, rather than $60,000, will be necessary each year subsequent to acquisition.

In addition, any amortization of the deferred charge must now also be adjusted by a workpaper entry, since the amount of the deferred charge from the point of view of the consolidated entity is $29,000 *less* than its carrying value on the books of S Company. Assuming that the deferred charge is being amortized over ten years from January 1, 1980, workpaper entries one and two years subsequent to the acquisition of S Company by P Company will be as follows:

	12/31/80	12/31/81
Deferred Charge	2,900	5,800
Amortization of Deferred Charge	2,900	2,900
Beginning Retained Earnings—P Company	–0–	2,900

Amortization of the amount of difference between cost and book value assigned to unamortized discount on bonds payable and treatment of the amount of difference assigned to inventory are as explained in Example 1.

Adjustment of Assets and Liabilities:
Less Than Wholly Owned Subsidiaries

In the case of less than wholly owned subsidiaries, a question arises as to what value to assign to subsidiary assets and liabilities in the preparation of consolidated financial statements. To illustrate, assume that in Example 1, P Company acquired a 75% interest in S Company for $1,725,000, rather than a 100% interest for $2,300,000. The total book value of the net assets of S Company is $1,700,000, the same as in Example 1. The implied fair value of the net assets of S Company is still $2,300,000 (1,725,000/.75), and the difference between the implied total fair value and the book value of the net assets is $600,000 (2,300,000 − 1,700,000). Should the net assets of S Company be written up by $600,000 or by 75% of $600,000 for presentation in the consolidated financial statements? The alternative selected depends on whether an entity approach or a proprietary approach is adopted.

An entity theory approach would result in a write-up of the net assets of S Company in the consolidating workpaper by $600,000 to $2,300,000 on the theory that consolidated financial statements should reflect 100% of the net asset values controlled by the parent company without regard to the parent company's percentage interest therein.

The proprietary theory approach restricts the write-up of the net assets of S Company in the consolidating workpaper to $450,000 (.75 × 600,000) on the theory that the write-up of the net assets of S Company should be restricted to the amount actually paid by P Company in excess of the book value of the interest it acquires (1,725,000 − [.75 × 1,700,000] = 450,000).

Under the entity theory approach, then, on the date of acquisition the net assets of the subsidiary (individually and in total) are included in the consolidated financial statements at their book value ($1,700,000) plus the *entire difference* between their fair value and their book value ($600,000) or at a total of $2,300,000. Minority interest is reported at its percentage interest in the *fair value* of the net assets, or $575,000 (.25 × 2,300,000).

In contrast, under the proprietary theory approach, the net assets of the subsidiary (individually and in total) are included in the consolidated financial statements at their book value ($1,700,000) plus the *parent company's share* of the difference between fair value and book value (.75 × 600,000 = 450,000) or at a total of $2,150,000. Minority interest is reported at its percentage interest in the *book value* of the net assets, or $425,000 (.25 × 1,700,000).

In either case, the majority interest in the net assets is the same and is equal to their cost to the parent company, as is demonstrated below.

	PROPRIETARY THEORY	ENTITY THEORY
Net Assets of S Company Included in Consolidation	2,150,000	2,300,000
Less Minority Interest	425,000	575,000
Majority Interest (Cost)	1,725,000	1,725,000

Although the entity theory approach is conceptually appealing, the proprietary theory approach is generally followed in practice and will be used in this text. Major differences between the proprietary theory and entity theory approaches in the preparation of the consolidating workpaper and the consolidated financial statements are illustrated in the Appendix to this chapter.

It must be stressed that, under the proprietary approach, the amount of difference between cost and book value that is assigned to any specific asset or liability is equal to the *parent company's share* of the difference on the date of acquisition between the fair value and the book value of the specific asset or liability. To illustrate, in Example 1, if P Company acquired a 75% interest in S Company for $1,725,000, the amount of the difference between cost and book value assigned to specific assets and liabilities would differ from the amount assigned when a 100% interest was acquired. See Illustration 5–5.

ILLUSTRATION 5–5
Assignment of Difference Between Cost and Book Value
75%-Owned Subsidiary

PRACTICALLY WILL ALWAYS COME OUT RIGHT

ITEM	(1) BOOK VALUE	(2) FAIR VALUE	(3) DIFFERENCE BETWEEN FAIR VALUE AND TOTAL BOOK VALUE	(4) DIFFERENCE BETWEEN COST AND BOOK VALUE (75% OF COLUMN 3)
Property & Equipment (net)	1,120,000	1,540,000	420,000	315,000
Inventory	300,000	320,000	20,000	15,000
Land	500,000	570,000	70,000	52,500
Bonds Payable	(500,000)	(424,184)	75,816	56,862
Other Identifiable Assets & Liabilities (net)	280,000	280,000	–0–	–0–
Total Identifiable Net Assets	1,700,000	2,285,816	585,816	439,362
Unallocated Balance	–0–	14,184	14,184	10,638
Total Net Assets	1,700,000	2,300,000[a]	600,000	450,000[b]

[a]The total fair value of $2,300,000 is implied by the fact that P Company paid $1,725,000 for a 75% interest in S Company (1,725,000/.75 = 2,300,000).
[b]1,725,000 − (.75 × 1,700,000) = 450,000.

Thus, when a 75% interest is acquired, $315,000 rather than $420,000 will be assigned to Property and Equipment (net), $15,000 rather than $20,000 to Inventory, etc. In addition, when a 75% interest is acquired, the workpaper adjustments to depreciation and amortization will be based on the amount of the difference assigned to depreciable or amortizable assets. Thus, in this example, depreciation expense will be adjusted by $45,000 (315,000/7) rather than $60,000 (420,000/7) in each of the seven remaining years of the life of the property to which a portion of the difference between cost and book value is assigned.

In Illustration 5–5, $10,638 of the difference between cost and book value which cannot be assigned to specific assets or liabilities is carried to "Excess of Cost over Fair Value" in the consolidating workpaper. As defined earlier, this amount is equal to the excess of acquisition cost (1,725,000) over the parent company's equity in the fair value of the identifiable net assets of the subsidiary (.75 × 2,285,816 = 1,714,362), or $10,638 (1,725,000 − 1,714,362) in this example.

NONCONSOLIDATED INVESTMENTS REPORTED USING THE EQUITY METHOD

The cost of an investment in common stock of an investee that qualifies for use of the equity method of reporting may differ from the underlying equity acquired in those net assets. *APB Opinion No. 18* requires the investor to account for this difference as if the investee were a consolidated subsidiary. *Opinion No. 18* also requires footnote disclosure in the investor's financial statements of the difference between the amount at which an investment is reported and the amount of underlying equity in the net assets of the investee.

Since the amount of the investment and the amount of investee income recognized each appear as one amount in the investor's financial statements, the effect of this provision is to require an adjustment to the amount reported as the investment balance and to the amount of investee income that would otherwise be recognized by the investor.

Nonconsolidated Subsidiaries

To illustrate, assume that the wholly owned subsidiary in Example 1 (above) will not be consolidated and is accounted for in the records and reported in the financial statements of the parent company using the equity method. Pertinent information from Example 1 is presented below.

	JAN. 1 1980	YEAR ENDED DEC. 31	
		1980	1981
Cost of Investment (Wholly Owned)	2,300,000		
Difference Between Cost and Book Value	600,000		
Reported Income of Subsidiary		125,000	140,000
Dividends Received from Subsidiary		20,000	60,000

Calculation of the adjustments to the reported income of the subsidiary for the years ended December 31, 1980 and December 31, 1981 is as follows:

	DIFFERENCE BETWEEN COST AND BOOK VALUE	DECREASE IN NET INCOME RESULTING FROM DEPRECIATION, AMORTIZATION, & INVENTORY ADJUSTMENTS	
		1980	1981
Property & Equipment (net)	420,000	60,000	60,000
Inventory (FIFO)	20,000	20,000	-0-
Land	70,000	-0-	-0-
Unamortized Discount on Bonds Payable	75,816	12,418	13,660
Unspecified Intangible	14,184	355	355
Total	600,000	92,773	74,015

* Entries made on the books of the parent company to reflect the activities of the subsidiary for each year are as follows:

	1980	1981
(1) Investment in S Company	125,000	140,000
Equity in Subsidiary Income	125,000	140,000

To record equity interest in reported income of wholly owned subsidiary.

	1980	1981
(2) Equity in Subsidiary Income	92,773	74,015
Investment in S Company	92,773	74,015

To record adjustment to equity in subsidiary income relating to assignment, amortization, and depreciation of the difference between cost and book value.

These two entries could obviously be combined into a single entry to be recorded each year if so desired.

	1980	1981
(3) Cash	20,000	60,000
Investment in S Company	20,000	60,000

To record the receipt of dividends from the subsidiary.

Amounts reported in the financial statements of P Company for the carrying value of the investment and its equity in the income of S Company will be as follows:

DECEMBER 31,	1980	1981
Investment in Nonconsolidated Subsidiary	2,312,227[a]	2,318,212[b]
Equity in Income of Nonconsolidated Subsidiary (Income Statement)	32,227[c]	65,985[d]

[a] 2,300,000 + (125,000 − 92,773) − 20,000 = 2,312,227

[b] 2,312,227 + (140,000 − 74,015) − 60,000 = 2,318,212

[c] 125,000 − 92,773 = 32,227

[d] 140,000 − 74,015 = 65,985

If the nonconsolidated subsidiary is less than wholly owned, the calculation of adjustments to the parent company's share of the reported income of the subsidiary is based on the depreciation, amortization, or allocation of the *parent company's share* of the difference between the fair value and the book value of specific assets and liabilities on the date of acquisition (see Illustration 5–5).

Less Than 50%-Owned Investees Reported at Equity

Similar adjustments to the amount of investee income recognized by the investor because of a difference between the carrying value and the underlying equity in the net assets of the investee must be made for investments in less than 50%-owned investees accounted for using the equity method.

Assume, for example, that Investor Company acquires a 30% interest in the common stock of Investee Company for $390,000 on January 1, 1980 when the book value of the stock of Investee Company is $1,000,000. Assume further that (1) the $90,000 difference between cost and book value is attributed to the fact that the fair market value of land owned by the investee is $100,000 more than its recorded value, and (2) the appraisal value of property and equipment with a remaining useful life of 10 years is $200,000 in excess of its carrying value on the books of the investee. This information may be summarized as follows:

	DIFFERENCE BETWEEN FAIR VALUE AND BOOK VALUE	INVESTOR'S EQUITY IN DIFFERENCE (30%)	ADJUSTMENTS TO INCOME 1980	1981
Land	100,000	30,000	–0–	–0–
Property and Equipment	200,000	60,000	6,000	6,000
Total	300,000	90,000	6,000	6,000

If the investee declares no dividends and reports income of $70,000 in 1980 and $80,000 in 1981, the investor's equity in the investee would be recorded and reported as follows:

ENTRIES ON BOOKS:	1980		1981	
(1) Investment in Investee Company	21,000		24,000	
Equity in Investee Income		21,000		24,000
To record equity in reported income of Investee Company.				
(2) Equity in Investee Income	6,000		6,000	
Investment in Investee Company		6,000		6,000
To record adjustment because of the difference between the carrying value of the investment and the equity in the underlying net assets of the investee.				

REPORTED IN FINANCIAL STATEMENTS:	DECEMBER 31,	
	1980	1981
Equity in Investee Income (Income Statement)	15,000	18,000
Investment in Investee Company (Balance Sheet)	405,000	423,000

An investor may find that it is impracticable to determine on the day it acquires its investment the fair values of the investee's assets and liabilities as a basis for determining the appropriate assignment of the difference between cost and book value and the related adjustments to reported investee income. Generally accepted accounting standards require that a reasonable effort at such a determination be made. As a practical matter, however, the investor may elect to amortize the total amount of difference between cost and book value as an adjustment to income in equal amounts over a reasonable period not to exceed forty years. Frequently, the selection of a reasonable amortization period is based on the average remaining life of the depreciable assets of the investee.

CONSOLIDATING WORKPAPERS: INVESTMENT RECORDED AT EQUITY

A parent company may consolidate an investment which it has accounted for on its books using the equity method. When the investment in a subsidiary is recorded at equity on the books of the parent company, the amount of difference between cost and book value recorded in the consolidated financial statements workpaper entry eliminating the investment account against the equity accounts of the subsidiary will become progressively smaller each year. The amount of difference between cost and book value recognized in this entry may be considered to be a residual or balancing figure. Since the investment account is periodically reduced on the parent company's books by the amortization of the original difference between cost and book value, this residual is necessarily reduced by a like amount and represents the unamortized difference between cost and book value at any particular point in time.

In addition, under the equity method the retained earnings of the parent company will be equal to consolidated retained earnings. Accordingly, no adjustments to the parent's beginning retained earnings are necessary in the workpaper to arrive at beginning consolidated retained earnings.

Because of these two factors, *the only procedural change in the workpaper entries relating to the elimination of the difference between cost and book value is that adjustments that are debited or credited to the beginning retained earnings of the parent company in cost-basis consolidating workpapers are debited or credited to the difference between cost and book value in equity-basis workpapers.* The equity-basis consolidating workpapers for the years ended December 31, 1980 and December 31, 1981 presented in Illustration 5–6 and Illustration 5–7 are based on the information and assumptions as to the $600,000 difference between cost and book value presented in Example 1. The workpaper eliminations entries in Illustrations 5–6 and 5–7 are presented in general journal form following each illustration for the convenience of the reader.

Purchase Accounting
Equity Method
Wholly Owned Subsidiary
Year of Acquisition

ILLUSTRATION 5–6
Consolidated Statements Workpaper
P Company and Subsidiary
For Year Ending December 31, 1980

	P COMPANY	S COMPANY	ELIMINATIONS DR.	ELIMINATIONS CR.	CONSOLIDATED BALANCES
INCOME STATEMENT					
Sales	3,100,000	2,200,000			5,300,000
Equity in Subsidiary Income	32,227		¹ 32,227		
Total	3,132,227	2,200,000			5,300,000
Inventory—1/1/80	500,000	300,000	³ 20,000		820,000
Purchases	1,680,000	1,370,000			3,050,000
	2,180,000	1,670,000			3,870,000
Inventory—12/31/80	480,000	310,000			790,000
Cost of Goods Sold	1,700,000	1,360,000			3,080,000
Depreciation	380,000	210,000	⁴ 60,000		650,000
Interest	120,000	30,000	⁵ 12,418		162,418
Amortization of Excess of Cost over Fair Value			⁶ 355		355
Other Expenses	624,000	475,000			1,099,000
Total	2,824,000	2,075,000			4,991,773
Net Income to Retained Earnings	308,227	125,000	125,000	–0–	308,227
RETAINED EARNINGS STATEMENT					
1/1/80 Retained Earnings					
P Company	1,650,000				1,650,000
S Company		700,000	² 700,000		
Net Income from above	308,227	125,000	125,000	–0–	308,227
Dividends Declared					
P Company	(150,000)				(150,000)
S Company		(20,000)		¹ 20,000	
12/31/80 Retained Earnings to Balance Sheet	1,808,227	805,000	825,000	20,000	1,808,227
BALANCE SHEET					
Inventory	480,000	310,000			790,000
Other Current Assets	620,000	550,000			1,170,000
Investment in S Company	2,312,227			¹ 12,227 ²2,300,000	
Difference Between Cost and Book Value			² 600,000	³ 600,000	
Land	1,250,000	500,000	³ 70,000		1,820,000
Property and Equipment	3,800,000	2,100,000	³ 600,000		6,500,000
(Accumulated Depreciation)	(1,520,000)	(840,000)		³ 180,000 ⁴ 60,000	(2,600,000)
Excess of Cost over Fair Value			³ 14,184	⁶ 355	13,829
Total Assets	6,942,227	2,620,000			7,693,829

	P COMPANY	S COMPANY	ELIMINATIONS DR.	ELIMINATIONS CR.	CONSOLIDATED BALANCES
Current Liabilities	634,000	315,000			949,000
Bonds Payable	1,500,000	500,000			2,000,000
(Unamortized Discount on Bonds Payable)			³ 75,816	⁵ 12,418	(63,398)
Capital Stock					
P Company	3,000,000				3,000,000
S Company		1,000,000	²1,000,000		
Retained Earnings from above	1,808,227	805,000	825,000	20,000	1,808,227
Total Liabilities & Equity	6,942,227	2,620,000	3,185,000	3,185,000	7,693,829

¹To establish reciprocity as of 1/1/80 and to eliminate subsidiary income.
²To eliminate the investment account.
³To assign the difference between cost and book value to specific assets and liabilities.
⁴To depreciate the amount of the difference between cost and book value assigned to property and equipment.
⁵To amortize the amount of the difference between cost and book value assigned to unamortized discount on bonds payable.
⁶To amortize the amount of the difference between cost and book value assigned to unspecified intangible.

December 31, 1980 workpaper entries (Illustration 5–6).

(1) Equity in Subsidiary Income (125,000 − 92,773)   32,227
    Dividends Declared   20,000
    Investment in S Company   12,227
      To adjust the investment account to the beginning-of-year balance and to eliminate subsidiary income.

Equity in subsidiary income equals the reported income of S Company of $125,000 less amortization and depreciation adjustments relating to the difference between cost and book value in the amount of $92,773 (see preceding calculations under the heading "Nonconsolidated Subsidiaries").

(2) Beginning Retained Earnings—S Company   700,000
    Capital Stock—S Company   1,000,000
    Difference Between Cost and Book Value   600,000
      Investment in S Company   2,300,000
      To eliminate the investment account.

(3) Property & Equipment   600,000
    Cost of Goods Sold (Beginning Inventory)   20,000
    Land   70,000
    Unamortized Discount on Bonds Payable   75,816
    Excess of Cost over Fair Value   14,184
      Accumulated Depreciation   180,000
      Difference Between Cost and Book Value   600,000
      To allocate the amount of difference between cost and book value at the date of acquisition to specific assets and liabilities.

(4) Depreciation Expense   60,000

    Accumulated Depreciation   60,000

       To depreciate the amount of the difference between cost and book value assigned to property and equipment.

(5) Interest Expense   12,418

    Unamortized Discount on Bonds Payable   12,418

       To amortize the amount of the difference between cost and book value assigned to unamortized discount on bonds payable.

(6) Amortization of Excess of Cost over Fair Value   355

    Excess of Cost over Fair Value   355

       To amortize the amount of difference between cost and book value assigned to unspecified intangibles.

Purchase Accounting
Equity Method
Wholly Owned Subsidiary
Subsequent to Year of Acquisition

ILLUSTRATION 5–7
Consolidated Statements Workpaper
P Company and Subsidiary
For Year Ending December 31, 1981

INCOME STATEMENT	P COMPANY	S COMPANY	ELIMINATIONS DR.	ELIMINATIONS CR.	CONSOLIDATED BALANCES
Sales	3,534,000	2,020,000			5,554,000
Equity in Subsidiary Income	65,985		¹ 65,985		
Total	3,599,985	2,020,000			5,554,000
Inventory—12/31/81	480,000	310,000			790,000
Purchases	2,070,000	1,250,000			3,320,000
	2,550,000	1,560,000			4,110,000
Inventory—12/31/81	510,000	360,000			870,000
Cost of Goods Sold	2,040,000	1,200,000			3,240,000
Depreciation	380,000	210,000	⁴ 60,000		650,000
Interest	120,000	30,000	⁵ 13,660		163,660
Amortization of Excess of Cost over Fair Value			⁶ 355		355
Other Expenses	600,000	440,000			1,040,000
Total	3,140,000	1,880,000			5,094,015
Net Income to Retained Earnings	459,985	140,000	140,000	–0–	459,985
RETAINED EARNINGS STATEMENT					
1/1/81 Retained Earnings					
P Company	1,808,227				1,808,227
S Company		805,000	² 805,000		
Net Income from above	459,985	140,000	140,000	–0–	459,985
Dividends Declared					
P Company	(150,000)				(150,000)
S Company		(60,000)		¹ 60,000	
12/31/81 Retained Earnings to Balance Sheet	2,118,212	885,000	945,000	60,000	2,118,212

	P COMPANY	S COMPANY	ELIMINATIONS DR.	ELIMINATIONS CR.	CONSOLIDATED BALANCES
BALANCE SHEET					
Inventory	510,000	360,000			870,000
Other Current Assets	610,000	530,000			1,140,000
Investment in S Company	2,318,212			[1] 5,985 [2] 2,312,227	
Difference Between Cost and Book Value			[2] 507,227 [3] 20,000 [4] 60,000 [5] 12,418 [6] 355	[3] 600,000	
Land	2,000,000	750,000	[3] 70,000		2,820,000
Property and Equipment	3,800,000	2,100,000	[3] 600,000		6,500,000
(Accumulated Depreciation)	(1,900,000)	(1,050,000)		[3] 180,000 [4] 120,000	(3,250,000)
Excess of Cost over Fair Value			[3] 14,184	[6] 710	13,474
Total Assets	7,338,212	2,690,000			8,093,474
Current Liabilities	720,000	305,000			1,025,000
Bonds Payable	1,500,000	500,000			2,000,000
(Unamortized Discount on Bonds Payable)			[3] 75,816	[5] 26,078	(49,738)
Capital Stock					
P Company	3,000,000				3,000,000
S Company		1,000,000	[2] 1,000,000		
Retained Earnings from above	2,118,212	885,000	945,000	60,000	2,118,212
Total Liabilities & Equity	7,338,212	2,690,000	3,305,000	3,305,000	8,093,474

[1] To establish reciprocity as of 1/1/81 and to eliminate subsidiary income.
[2] To eliminate investment account.
[3] To assign the original difference between cost and book value to specific assets and liabilities.
[4] To depreciate the amount of the difference between cost and book value assigned to property and equipment.
[5] To amortize the amount of the difference between cost and book value assigned to unamortized discount on bonds payable.
[6] To amortize the amount of the difference between cost and book value assigned to unspecified intangible.

December 31, 1981 workpaper entries (Illustration 5–7).

(1) Equity in Subsidiary Income   65,985
    Dividends Declared   60,000
    Investment in S Company   5,985
      To adjust the investment account to the beginning-of-year balance and to eliminate subsidiary income.

(2) Beginning Retained Earnings—S Company   805,000
    Capital Stock—S Company   1,000,000
    Difference Between Cost and Book Value   507,227
    Investment in S Company   2,312,227
      To eliminate investment account.

Notice that the residual amount debited to "difference between cost and book value" has been reduced by the amount of the original difference that has been amortized, depreciated, or otherwise charged to income of prior years on the books of P Company (600,000 − 92,773).

(3) Property & Equipment	600,000	
Difference Between Cost and Book Value	20,000	
Land	70,000	
Unamortized Discount on Bonds Payable	75,816	
Excess of Cost over Fair Value	14,184	
Accumulated Depreciation		180,000
Difference Between Cost and Book Value		600,000

     To allocate the amount of the difference between cost and book value at the date of acquisition to specific assets and liabilities.

Notice that the original amount of difference ($600,000) is allocated without regard to the residual amount set up in Entry (2) ($507,227 in the 12/31/81 workpaper). The $20,000 debit to "difference between cost and book value" results from the fact that the amount of the difference assignable to inventories was charged to consolidated cost of sales (i.e., fully amortized) in the prior year.

(4) Difference Between Cost and Book Value	60,000	
Depreciation Expense	60,000	
Accumulated Depreciation		120,000

     To depreciate the amount of the original difference between cost and book value assigned to property and equipment.

(5) Difference Between Cost and Book Value	12,418	
Interest Expense	13,660	
Unamortized Discount on Bonds Payable		26,078

     To amortize the amount of the original difference between cost and book value assigned to unamortized discount on bonds payable.

(6) Difference Between Cost and Book Value	355	
Amortization of Excess of Cost over Fair Value	355	
Excess of Cost over Fair Value		710

     To amortize the amount of the original difference between cost and book value assigned to unspecified intangible.

    The net result of Entries (2), (3), (4), (5), and (6) is to debit the difference between cost and book value for $600,000 (507,227 + 20,000 + 60,000 + 12,418 + 355) and to credit it for the same amount (Entry (3)). A comparison of the consolidated balances in Illustrations 5–2 and 5–3 with the consolidated balances in Illustration 5–6 and 5–7, respectively, will confirm that the consolidated financial statements are not affected by the method (cost or equity) used by the parent company to account for its subsidiaries.

CONSOLIDATED NET INCOME AND CONSOLIDATED RETAINED EARNINGS: REFINED ANALYTICAL DEFINITIONS

In the preceding chapter, definitions were developed to provide an analytical approach to the calculation of consolidated net income and consolidate retained earnings. These definitions must now be refined to accommodate the effect on these calculations of the allocation, amortization, and depreciation of the difference between cost and book value.

Consolidated net income is now defined as the parent company's income from its independent operations plus (minus) its share of reported subsidiary income (loss) minus (plus when acquisition cost is less than the book value of the interest acquired) adjustments for the period relating to the allocation, depreciation, and amortization of the difference between cost and book value. On the basis of Illustration 5–2 and/or Illustration 5–6, the calculation of consolidated net income for the year ending December 31, 1980, using the analytical approach, may be demonstrated as follows:

P Company's net income from its independent operations			276,000[a]
P Company's share of the reported income of S Company (100%)		125,000	
Allocation, depreciation, and amortization for the period of the amount of the difference between cost and book value assigned to:			
Inventory	20,000		
Property and Equipment	60,000		
Discount on Bonds Payable	12,418		
Excess of Cost over Fair Value	355	(92,773)	32,227
			308,227

[a]Cost method (Illustration 5–2): $296,000 (reported net income of P Company) − $20,000 (subsidiary dividend income) = $276,000. Equity method (Illustration 5–6): $308,227 (reported net income of P Company) − $32,227 (equity in subsidiary income) = $276,000.

This, of course, is the same amount of consolidated net income as that calculated in the consolidated financial statement workpapers presented in Illustrations 5–2 and 5–6.

Consolidated retained earnings is now defined as the parent company's cost-method retained earnings plus (minus) the parent company's share of the increase (decrease) in reported subsidiary retained earnings from the date of acquisition to the current date minus (plus when acquisition cost is less than the book value of the interest acquired) the cumulative effect of adjustments to date relating to the allocation, depreciation, and amortization of the difference between cost and book value. As was indicated in Chapter 4, an analytical approach to the calculation of retained earnings is useful only where the parent records its investment using the cost method. On the basis of Illustration 5–3, the calculation of consolidated retained earnings on December 31, 1981, using the analytical approach, may be demonstrated as follows:

	1980	1981	CUMULATIVE	
P Company's retained earnings on December 31, 1981				2,100,000
P Company's share (100%) of the increase in S Company's retained earnings from January 1, 1980 to December 31, 1981 ([885,000 − 700,000] × 1.00)				185,000
Cumulative effect to December 31, 1981 of the allocation, depreciation, and amortization of the difference between cost and book value assigned to:				
Inventory	20,000		20,000	
Property and Equipment	60,000	60,000	120,000	
Discount on Bonds Payable	12,418	13,660	26,078	
Excess of Cost over Fair Value	355	355	710	
	92,773	74,015	166,788	(166,788)
Consolidated Retained Earnings on December 31, 1981				2,118,212

This, of course, is the same amount of consolidated retained earnings as that calculated in the consolidated financial statement workpaper presented in Illustration 5–3.

The purpose of this chapter has been to explain and illustrate the treatment of the difference between the cost of an investment and the book value of the equity interest acquired in the investee. The reader is reminded that this discussion is, therefore, applicable only to investments accounted for as a purchase. Where an investment is accounted for as a pooling of interest, no difference between cost and book value arises.

APPENDIX—COMPARISON OF APPROACHES TO THE ASSIGNMENT OF VALUES TO SUBSIDIARY NET ASSETS IN THE PREPARATION OF CONSOLIDATED FINANCIAL STATEMENTS

As was indicated earlier in this chapter, in the case of less than wholly owned subsidiaries, the values assigned to subsidiary assets and liabilities in the preparation of consolidated financial statements depends on whether the entity or proprietary theory approach is adopted.

To illustrate, assume that P Company acquires a 60% interest in S Company for $960,000 when the book value of the net assets and of the stockholders' equity of S Company is $1,000,000. The book value and the fair value of the net assets of S Company on the date P Company acquires its interest in S Company are the same except for the book value of depreciable assets with a remaining life of 20 years, which is $600,000 less than their fair value.

The differences between the entity theory approach and the proprietary theory approach is the preparation of consolidated financial statement workpapers and consolidated financial statements one year subsequent to the acquisition of S Company by P Company are presented in Illustrations 5–8 and 5–9 and compared in Illustration 5–10. The workpaper entries in Illustrations 5–8 and 5–9 are presented in general journal form on the next page.

Purchase Accounting
Cost Method
60%-Owned Subsidiary
Proprietary Theory

ILLUSTRATION 5–8
Consolidated Statements Workpaper
P Company and Subsidiary
Year Ending One Year Subsequent to Acquisition

	P COMPANY	S COMPANY	ELIMINATIONS DR.	ELIMINATIONS CR.	MINORITY INTEREST	CONSOLIDATED BALANCES
INCOME STATEMENT						
Revenue	350,000	200,000				550,000
Expense	310,000	120,000	³ 18,000			448,000
	40,000	80,000				102,000
Minority Interest (.40 × 80,000)					32,000	(32,000)
Net Income to Retained Earnings	40,000	80,000	18,000	–0–	32,000	70,000
RETAINED EARNINGS STATEMENT						
P Company—January 1	300,000					300,000
S Company—January 1		200,000	¹ 120,000		80,000	
Net Income from above	40,000	80,000	18,000	–0–	32,000	70,000
Retained Earnings to Balance Sheet	340,000	280,000	138,000	–0–	112,000	370,000
BALANCE SHEET						
Specified Assets (net of accumulated depreciation)	1,440,000	1,100,000	² 360,000	³ 18,000		2,882,000
Investment in S Company	960,000			¹ 960,000		
Difference Between Cost and Book Value			¹ 360,000	² 360,000		
	2,400,000	1,100,000				2,882,000
Liabilities	60,000	20,000				80,000
Capital Stock						
P Company	2,000,000					2,000,000
S Company		800,000	¹ 480,000		320,000	
Retained Earnings from above	340,000	280,000	138,000	–0–	112,000	370,000
Minority Interest					432,000	432,000
	2,400,000	1,100,000	1,338,000	1,338,000		2,882,000

¹To eliminate investment account.
²To assign the difference between cost and book value to specified depreciable assets.
³To depreciate the difference between cost and book value assigned to specified depreciable assets.

Consolidating workpaper entries under proprietary theory (Illustration 5–8).

(1) Beginning Retained Earnings—S Company	120,000	
Capital Stock—S Company	480,000	
Difference Between Cost and Book Value	360,000	
Investment in S Company		960,000
To eliminate investment account.		
(2) Specified Assets	360,000	
Difference Between Cost and Book Value		360,000
To assign the difference between cost and book value to specified assets.		
(3) Depreciation	18,000	
Specified Assets (Accumulated Depreciation)		18,000
To recognize additional depreciation on the difference between cost and book value assigned to specified depreciable assets.		

Consolidating workpaper entries under entity theory (Illustration 5–9).

(1) Beginning Retained Earnings—S Company	120,000	
Capital Stock—S Company	480,000	
Difference Between Cost and Book Value	360,000	
Investment in S Company		960,000
To eliminate the investment account.		
(2) Specified Assets	600,000	
Difference Between Cost and Book Value		360,000
Minority Interest		240,000
To write up specified assets to reflect total fair values implied by the cost of the investment.		
(3) Depreciation	30,000	
Specified Assets (Accumulated Depreciation)		30,000
To depreciate write-up of specified assets.		

Purchase Accounting
Cost Method
50%-Owned Subsidiary
Entity Theory

ILLUSTRATION 5–9
Consolidated Statements Workpaper
P Company and Subsidiary
Year Ending One Year Subsequent to Acquisition

	P COMPANY	S COMPANY	ELIMINATIONS DR.	ELIMINATIONS CR.	MINORITY INTEREST	CONSOLIDATED BALANCES
INCOME STATEMENT						
Revenue	350,000	200,000				550,000
Expense	310,000	120,000	³ 30,000			460,000
	40,000	80,000				90,000
Minority Interest						
(.40 × [80,000 − 30,000])					20,000	(20,000)
Net Income to Retained Earnings	40,000	80,000	30,000	–0–	20,000	70,000
RETAINED EARNINGS STATEMENT						
P Company—January 1	300,000					300,000
S Company—January 1		200,000	¹ 120,000		80,000	
Net Income from above	40,000	80,000	30,000	–0–	20,000	70,000
Retained Earnings						
to Balance Sheet	340,000	280,000	150,000	–0–	100,000	370,000
BALANCE SHEET						
Specified Assets (net of						
accumulated depreciation)	1,440,000	1,100,000	² 600,000	³ 30,000		3,110,000
Investment in S Company	960,000			¹ 960,000		
Difference Between Cost						
and Book Value			¹ 360,000	² 360,000		
	2,400,000	1,100,000				3,110,000
Liabilities	60,000	20,000				80,000
Capital Stock						
P Company	2,000,000					2,000,000
S Company		800,000	¹ 480,000		320,000	
Retained Earnings from above	340,000	280,000	150,000	–0–	100,000	370,000
Minority Interest				² 240,000	420,000	660,000
	2,400,000	1,100,000	1,590,000	1,590,000		3,110,000

¹To eliminate investment account.
²To write up specified depreciable assets to reflect fair values implied by the cost of the investment.
³To depreciate the write-up of specified depreciable assets.

ILLUSTRATION 5–10
Comparison of Consolidated Financial Statements
Using a Proprietary Approach and an Entity Approach
To the Valuation of Subsidiary Net Assets

(000 OMITTED)

CONSOLIDATED INCOME STATEMENT	PROPRIETARY THEORY (ILLUSTRATION 5–8)	ENTITY THEORY (ILLUSTRATION 5–9)	DIFFERENCE
Revenues	$ 550	$ 550	$ –0–
Expense	448	460	12
Combined Income	$ 102	$ 90	$ 12
Less Minority Interest	32	20	(12)
Net Income	$ 70	$ 70	$ –0–
CONSOLIDATED BALANCE SHEET			
Specified Assets (net of accumulated depreciation)	$2,882	$3,110	$ 228
Liabilities	80	80	$ –0–
Minority Interest	432	660	228
Capital Stock	2,000	2,000	–0–
Retained Earnings	370	370	–0–
	$2,882	$3,110	$ 228

A comparison of consolidated balances under each method is presented in Illustration 5–10. As demonstrated therein, consolidated net income and consolidated retained earnings will be the same under either approach. The major differences between the two approaches are in the amounts of individual assets, liabilities, and revenue and expense items reported in the consolidated financial statements, in the amount of total consolidated assets and liabilities, in the amount of combined income, and in the amount of minority interest reported in the consolidated income statement and in the consolidated balance sheet. As a practical matter, these differences rarely have a material effect upon the consolidated financial statements.

Questions

1. Distinguish among the following concepts:
   a. Difference between cost and book value.
   b. Excess of cost over fair value.
   c. Excess of fair value over cost.
   d. Deferred excess of fair value over cost.

2. In what account is "the difference between cost and book value" recorded on the books of the investor? In what account is the "excess of cost over fair value" recorded?

3. In most cases the allocation of the difference between cost and book value to specific assets and/or liabilities is accomplished in the consolidated statements workpaper. When, if ever, might this adjustment be made directly on the books of the subsidiary?

NON CONSOLIDATED INVESTMENT EQUITY METHOD

4. Describe the difference between the entity and proprietary theory approaches to the reporting of subsidiary assets and liabilities in the consolidated financial statements.

ENTITY - ALL
PROPRIETARY - PARENTS SHARE

5. How is the amount of the "difference between cost and book value" to be assigned to a specific asset of a less than wholly owned subsidiary determined?

PROPRIETARY OR ENTITY

6. The parent company's share of the fair value of the net assets of a subsidiary may exceed acquisition cost. How must this excess be treated in the preparation of consolidated financial statements?

REDUCE PROPORTIONALLY THE FAIR VALUES ASSIGNED TO NONCURRENT ASSETS

7. Why are marketable securities excluded from the noncurrent assets to which any excess of fair value over cost is to be allocated?

FAIR VALUE IS READILY DETERMINABLE

8. "Under the cost method, the amount of difference between cost and book value initially recognized in the investment elimination entry on the consolidated statements workpaper will be the same each year from the date of acquisition to the date the subsidiary is disposed of." Do you agree or disagree? Explain.

AGREE   NO CHANGES ON BOOKS OF PARENT IN THE INVESTMENT ACCOUNT

9. P Company acquired a 100% interest in S Company. On the date of acquisition the fair value of the assets and liabilities of S Company was equal to their book value except for land which had a fair value of $1,500,000 and a book value of $300,000. At what amount should the land of S Company be included in the consolidated balance sheet? At what amount should the land of S Company be included in the consolidated balance sheet if P Company acquired an 80% interest in S Company rather than a 100% interest?

1,500,000
ENTITY - 1,500,000
PROPRIETARY - 1,200,000

10. Corporation A purchased the net assets of Corporation B for $80,000. On the date of A's purchase, Corporation B had no long-term investments in marketable securities and $10,000 (book and fair value) of liabilities. The fair values of Corporation B's assets, when acquired, were:

Current assets	$ 40,000
Noncurrent assets	60,000
Total	$100,000

How should the $10,000 difference between the fair value of the net assets acquired ($90,000) and the cost ($80,000) be accounted for by Corporation A?

a. The $10,000 difference should be credited to retained earnings.

b. The noncurrent assets should be recorded at $50,000.

c. The current assets should be recorded at $36,000, and the noncurrent assets should be recorded at $54,000.

d. A deferred credit of $10,000 should be set up and then amortized to income over a period not to exceed forty years.

11. Assume that Corporation A paid $110,000 for Corporation B's net assets, and that all other information given in No. 10 remains the same. What is the minimum annual

difference between financial accounting income and tax income because of this purchase?

a. Zero.

b. $500.

c. $2,000.

d. Cannot be determined from the information given.

12. Meredith Company and Kyle Company were combined in a purchase transaction. Meredith was able to acquire Kyle at a bargain price. The sum of the market or appraised values of identifiable assets acquired less the fair value of liabilities assumed exceeded the cost to Meredith. After revaluing noncurrent assets to zero, there was still some "negative goodwill." Proper accounting treatment by Meredith is to report the amount as

a. An extraordinary item.

b. Part of current income in the year of combination.

ⓒ A deferred credit and amortize it.

d. Paid-in capital.

13. From a procedural point of view, what is the essential difference between cost-basis and equity-basis workpaper eliminations to allocate, depreciate, and amortize the difference between cost and book value?

14. How does the recording in the consolidated statements workpaper of the increase in depreciation that results from the allocation of a portion of the difference between cost and book value to depreciable property affect the calculation of minority interest in combined income?

15. How do the considerations in this chapter differ when applied to a consolidation reported as a pooling of interest rather than as a purchase?

16. What problems may auditors encounter in verifying the investment revenue reported under the equity method because of the considerations discussed in this chapter?

17. How does the inventory cost flow assumption utilized by a subsidiary affect the treatment of the difference between cost and book value assigned to inventory?

Problems

Problem 5–1

On January 1, 1978, Cost Company purchased an 80% interest in the capital stock of Funding Company for $820,000. At that time, Funding Company had capital stock of $500,000 and retained earnings of $100,000. The difference between cost and the book value of the 80% interest acquired was attributed to specific assets of Funding Company as follows:

100,000	to equipment of Funding Company that had a 5-year remaining life (original life of 10 years) at the date of acquisition.
50,000	to land held by Funding Company.
30,000	to inventories of Funding Company. Funding Company uses the FIFO cost flow assumption in pricing its inventory.
160,000	amount that could not be assigned to specific assets or liabilities of Funding Company (amortized over 40 years).
340,000	Total _80% of EXCESS_ _PROPRIETARY_ _COST METHOD_

The adjusted trial balances of Cost Company and Funding Company on December 31, 1980 are presented below.

December 31, 1980
Adjusted Trial Balance

	COST COMPANY	FUNDING COMPANY
Cash	80,000	50,000
Accounts Receivable	250,000	170,000
Inventory 12/31/80	230,000	150,000
Investment in Funding Co.	820,000	—
Land	—	300,000
Property & Equipment	600,000	400,000
Cost of Goods Sold	850,000	180,000
Other Expense	100,000	70,000
Dividends Declared	100,000	50,000
Total	3,030,000	1,370,000
Accumulated Depreciation	250,000	150,000
Accounts Payable	160,000	100,000
Notes Payable	50,000	20,000
Capital Stock	1,000,000	500,000
1/1/80 Retained Earnings	480,000	200,000
Sales	1,050,000	400,000
Dividend Income	40,000	—
Total	3,030,000	1,370,000

Required:

A. Prepare a consolidated financial statements workpaper for the year ending December 31, 1980.

B. Describe the effect on the consolidated balances if Funding Company uses the LIFO cost flow assumption in pricing its inventory and there has been no decrease in ending inventory quantities since 1978.

Problem 5–2

On January 1, 1978, Equity Company purchased an 80% interest in the capital stock of Funding Company for $820,000. At that time, Funding Company had capital stock of $500,000 and retained earnings of $100,000. The difference between cost and the book value of the 80% interest acquired was attributed to specific assets of Funding Company as follows:

100,000	to equipment of Funding Company with a 5-year remaining life on January 1, 1978 (original life of 10 years).
50,000	to land held by Funding Company.
30,000	to inventory of Funding Company. Funding Company uses the FIFO convention in pricing its inventory.
160,000	that could not be assigned to specific assets or liabilities of Funding Company (amortized over 40 years).
340,000	Total

Equity Company accounts for its investment in Funding Company using the equity method of accounting. The adjusted trial balances of Equity Company and Funding Company are presented below:

December 31, 1980
Adjusted Trial Balances

	EQUITY COMPANY	FUNDING COMPANY
Cash	80,000	50,000
Accounts Receivable	250,000	170,000
Inventory 12/31/80	230,000	150,000
Investment in Funding Company	878,000	—
Land	—	300,000
Property & Equipment	600,000	400,000
Cost of Goods Sold	850,000	180,000
Other Expense	100,000	70,000
Dividends Declared	100,000	50,000
Total	3,088,000	1,370,000
Accumulated Depreciation	250,000	150,000
Accounts Payable	160,000	100,000
Notes Payable	50,000	20,000
Capital Stock	1,000,000	500,000
1/1/80 Retained Earnings	482,000	200,000
Sales	1,050,000	400,000
Equity in Subsidiary Income	96,000	—
Total	3,088,000	1,370,000

Required:

A. Prepare in general journal form the entries required on the books of Equity Company during 1980 to account for its investment in Funding Company.

B. Prepare a consolidated financial statements workpaper for the year ending December 31, 1980.

C. Compare the consolidated balances in the workpaper with those in Problem 5–1.

D. Prepare a consolidated balance sheet and a consolidated income statement.

Problem 5–3

On January 1, 1980, Pringle Company purchased an 80% interest in Sugar Company for $2,800,000, at which time Sugar Company had retained earnings of $1,000,000 and capital stock of $500,000. On the date of acquisition, the fair value of the assets and liabilities of Sugar Company was equal to their book value, except for property and equipment (net) which had a fair value of $1,500,000 and a book value of $600,000. The property and equipment had an estimated remaining life of 10 years. Pringle Company amortizes the excess of cost over fair value over 20 years. Pringle Company reported net income from its independent operations of $400,000 in 1980 and $425,000 in 1981. Sugar Company reported net income of $300,000 in 1980 and $400,000 in 1981. Neither company declared or paid dividends in 1980 or 1981.

Required:
A. Prepare in general journal form the entries required on the books of Pringle Company in 1980 and 1981 to account for its investment in Sugar Company:
    (1) Under the cost method of accounting.
    (2) Under the equity method of accounting.
B. Prepare in general journal form the workpaper entries necessary in the consolidating workpapers for the years ending December 31, 1980 and 1981:
    (1) Assuming that the investment in Sugar Company is accounted for using the cost method of accounting.
    (2) Assuming that the investment in Sugar Company is accounted for using the equity method of accounting.
C. Prepare in good form a schedule showing the calculation of consolidated net income for the years ending December 31, 1980 and December 31, 1981.

Problem 5–4
On January 1, 1980, Post Company purchased a 70% interest in Sand Company for $1,300,000, at which time Sand Company had retained earnings of $500,000 and capital stock of $1,000,000. On January 1, 1980, the fair value of the assets and liabilities of Sand Company was equal to their book value except for Bonds Payable. Sand Company had outstanding a $1,000,000 issue of 6% bonds that were issued at par and that mature on January 1, 1985. Interest on the bonds is payable annually, and the yield rate on similar bonds on January 1, 1980 is 10%. Post Company amortizes the excess of cost over fair value over 16 years. Post Company reported net income from its independent operations of $300,000 in 1980 and $250,000 in 1981. Sand Company reported net income of $100,000 in 1980 and $120,000 in 1981. Neither company paid or declared dividends in 1980 or 1981.

Required:
A. Calculate the amount of income recorded by Post Company because of its affiliation with Sand Company for each of the years 1980 and 1981:
    (1) Under the cost method of accounting.
    (2) Under the equity method of accounting.
B. Prepare in general journal form the workpaper entries necessary in the consolidating workpapers for the years ending December 31, 1980 and December 31, 1981:
    (1) Assuming that the investment in Sand Company is accounted for using the cost method of accounting.
    (2) Assuming that the investment in Sand Company is accounted for using the equity method of accounting.
C. Prepare in good form a schedule showing the calculation of consolidated net income for the years ending December 31, 1980 and December 31, 1981.

Problem 5-5

On January 1, 1980, Pump Company purchased an 80% interest in Sound Company for $2,100,000, at which time Sound Company had retained earnings of $375,000 and capital stock of $750,000. On the date of acquisition, the fair value of the assets and liabilities of Sound Company was equal to their book value except for property and equipment (net) which had a fair value of $1,875,000 and a book value of $1,500,000, and inventory which had a fair value of $600,000 and a book value of $450,000. The estimated remaining life of the equipment on January 1, 1980 was five years. One-half of the inventory was sold in 1980 and the remaining half was sold in 1981. Pump Company amortizes the excess of cost over fair value over 20 years. Pump Company reported net income from its independent operations of $525,000 in 1980 and $600,000 in 1981. Sound Company reported net income of $450,000 in 1980 and $375,000 in 1981. Neither company declared or paid dividends in 1980 or 1981.

Required:

A. Prepare in general journal form the entries required on the books of Pump Company in 1980 and 1981 to account for its investment in Sound Company:
  (1) Under the cost method of accounting.
  (2) Under the equity method of accounting.
B. Prepare in general journal form the workpaper entries necessary in the consolidating workpapers for the years ending December 31, 1980 and December 31, 1981:
  (1) Assuming that the investment in Sound Company is accounted for using the cost method of accounting.
  (2) Assuming that the investment in Sound Company is accounted for using the equity method of accounting.
C. Calculate consolidated net income for the years ending December 31, 1980 and 1981.

Problem 5-6

On January 1, 1980, Bates Company acquired a 100% interest in Mass Marketers at a cost of $530,000. At the purchase date, Mass Marketers' stockholders' equity consisted of the following:

Common Stock	$300,000
Retained Earnings	179,000

The excess of cost over book value of Bates' investment is attributable partially to undervalued assets. Financial statement data for 1980 are presented below.

	BATES COMPANY	MASS MARKETERS
Sales	$ 590,000	$ 310,000
Cost of Sales	410,225	203,375
Gross Margin	$ 179,775	$ 106,625
Depreciation Expense	24,000	31,500
Other Expenses	62,225	29,400
Income from Operations	$ 93,550	$ 45,725
Equity in Subsidiary Income	37,800	
Net Income	$ 131,350	$ 45,725

Retained Earnings, 1/1/80	$ 274,600	$ 179,000
Add: Net Income	131,350	45,725
	$ 405,950	$ 224,725
Deduct: Dividends	110,000	35,000
Retained Earnings, 12/31/80	$ 295,950	$ 189,725
Cash	$ 90,750	$ 47,600
Accounts Receivable	221,400	187,675
Inventories	205,505	188,715
Investment in Mass Marketers	532,800	
Equipment	410,350	210,000
Accumulated Depreciation—Equipment	(205,000)	(84,000)
Building	340,000	175,000
Accumulated Depreciation—Building	(160,050)	(105,000)
Total Assets (12/31/80)	$1,435,755	$ 619,990
Accounts Payable	$ 124,395	$ 30,265
Notes Payable	365,410	100,000
Bonds Payable	150,000	
Common Stock	500,000	300,000
Retained Earnings	295,950	189,725
	$1,435,755	$ 619,990

Additional Information—Date of Acquisition:

Mass Marketers' equipment had an original life of 15 years, a remaining useful life of 10 years, and a fair value of $150,000. Its building had an original life of 10 years, a remaining useful life of 5 years, and a fair value of $120,000. No new assets have been purchased since the acquisition date. (Straight-line depreciation is assumed.) The excess of cost over fair value, if any, is amortized over 20 years.

Required:
Prepare a consolidated financial statement workpaper for the year ending December 31, 1980.

Problem 5–7
On January 1, 1980, P Company purchased a 100% interest in S Company for $200,000. On this date, S Company had common stock of $45,000 and retained earnings of $105,000.

An examination of S Company's assets and liabilities revealed that their book value was equal to their fair value except for the equipment.

	BOOK VALUE	FAIR VALUE
Equipment	$180,000	$225,000
Accumulated Depreciation—Equipment	60,000	75,000

The equipment had an expected remaining life of 6 years and no salvage value. Straight-line depreciation is used. P Company has decided to amortize any excess of cost over fair value over a period of 10 years.

During 1980 and 1981, P Company reported net income from its own operations of $40,000 and paid dividends of $25,000 in each year. S Company had income of $20,000 each year and paid dividends of $15,000 on each December 31. P Company accounts for its investment using the cost method.

Required:

A. Prepare eliminating entries for the consolidated financial statement workpaper for the year ending December 31, 1980.

B. On January 1, 1981, S Company sold all of its equipment for $110,000. Prepare the eliminating entries for the consolidated financial statement workpaper for the year ending December 31, 1981.

Problem 5–8

Champion Motors purchased 80% of the common stock of Rotary, Inc. in the open market on January 1, 1979, paying $31,000 more than the book value of the interest acquired. The difference between cost and book value is attributable to land. During the first three years following the purchase, Rotary, Inc. had cumulative earnings of $175,000 and paid dividends totaling $80,000. The consolidated balance sheet at December 31, 1981 revealed a minority equity in the net assets of Rotary, Inc. totaling $65,000. The parent company accounts for its investments on the equity basis.

Required:

A. What workpaper entry is required each year until the land is disposed of?

B. Calculate the cost of the investment.

C. Calculate the investment carrying value on 12/31/81.

D. Assume that the land is sold on 1/1/82 and that Rotary, Inc. recognizes a $50,000 gain on its books. What amount of gain will be reflected on the 1982 consolidated income statement? In all years subsequent to the disposal of the land, what workpaper entry will be necessary?

Problem 5–9

On January 1, 1980, Nemo Corporation purchased a 75% interest in Galena Company for $300,000. A summary of Galena's balance sheet at date of purchase follows.

	BOOK VALUE	FAIR VALUE
Equipment	$240,000	$330,000
Accumulated Depreciation—Equipment	(80,000)	(110,000)
Other Assets	150,000	150,000
	$310,000	
Liabilities	$ 85,000	$ 85,000
Common Stock	100,000	
Retained Earnings	125,000	
	$310,000	

The equipment had an original life of 15 years and a remaining useful life of 10 years. Any excess of cost over fair value will be amortized over the maximum period allowable.

During 1980, Nemo Corporation reported income of $79,000 and paid dividends of $50,000. Galena Company reported net income of $41,000 and paid dividends of $40,000. Nemo Corporation uses the equity method of accounting for investments in subsidiaries.

Required:
A. Reconstruct in general journal form the entries that Nemo Corporation recorded during 1980 in respect to its investment in Galena Company.
B. Prepare the workpaper elimination entries for the consolidated financial statement workpaper on December 31, 1980.
C. Assume that Galena Company disposed of all its equipment on January 1, 1982 for $150,000.
  (1) What amount of gain (loss) will Galena Company report?
  (2) What is the consolidated gain (loss)?
  (3) Prepare the workpaper entry necessary to adjust the amounts in the consolidated financial statements as a result of the sale.
  (4) What workpaper adjustment will be necessary in future years?

Problem 5-10
On January 1, 1980, P Company acquired a 100% interest in S Company for $300,000. At this date, S Company had common stock of $47,500 and retained earnings of $97,500.

An examination of S Company's assets and liabilities revealed that their book value was equal to their fair value except as follows:

	BOOK VALUE	FAIR VALUE
Inventory (FIFO)	$30,000	$ 40,000
Equipment (net)	60,000	150,000
Land	30,000	50,000

The equipment had an expected remaining life of 9 years. P Company will amortize any excess of cost over fair value over 20 years.

During 1980 and 1981, P Company reported net income from operations of $45,000. S Company's income was $35,000 in 1980 and $38,000 in 1981. S Company paid dividends of $20,000 in 1980 and $28,000 in 1981.

P Company specialized in steel production while S Company was engaged in the retail sale of fast foods. It was not considered appropriate, therefore, to issue consolidated financial statements. P Company accounts for its investment by use of the equity method.

Required:
A. Prepare in general journal form the entries that P Company would have made in 1980 and 1981 with respect to its investment in S Company.
B. What amounts will be reported in the financial statements of P Company for the carrying value of the investment and its equity in the income of the subsidiary for 1980 and 1981?

Problem 5–11

On January 1, 1980, Paney Company acquired 80% of the outstanding common stock of Stretz Company for $216,000, at which time Stretz Company had stockholders' equity in the amount of $160,000. On January 1, 1980, the book value of the assets and liabilities of Stretz Company was equal to their fair value except as follows:

	BOOK VALUE	FAIR VALUE
Inventory (FIFO)	$45,000	$ 60,000
Equipment (net)	90,000	140,000
Land	40,000	75,000

The equipment had an expected remaining life of 5 years on that date and Paney Company amortizes any excess of cost over fair value over 16 years.

During 1980 and 1981, Stretz Company did not declare any dividends and reported net income of $30,000 and $25,000, respectively. Paney Company manufactures truck frames, whereas Stretz Company is engaged in the custom binding of books and manuscripts. Paney Company records and reports its investment in Stretz Company using the equity method of accounting.

Required:

Prepare in general journal form the entries necessary in 1980 and 1981 to record Paney Company's equity in the net income of Stretz Company.

Problem 5–12

On January 1, 1980, Ajax Company acquired a 25% interest in the common stock of Klenzer Company for $142,500 when Klenzer Company had capital stock in the amount of $300,000 and retained earnings in the amount of $150,000. On January 1, 1980, the average remaining life of the depreciable assets of Klenzer Company was 10 years. Although it was not practicable for Ajax Company to determine the fair values of the specific noncurrent assets of Klenzer Company on January 1, 1980, it was determined that the book value of the current assets and liabilities of Klenzer Company was equal to their fair value except for inventory which had a book value of $150,000 and a fair value of $190,000. Klenzer Company prices its inventory using the FIFO method and reported net income of $250,000 in 1980 and $200,000 in 1981. Klenzer Company also distributed dividends of $100,000 in each year.

Required:

A. Calculate the amount of equity in investee income to be reported by Ajax Company in 1980 and 1981. Justify the assumptions (if any) that you must make.
B. Calculate the balance in the investment in Klenzer Company account reported by Ajax Company on December 31, 1980 and December 31, 1981.

Problem 5–13

On January 1, 1980, Tidwell Company acquired 30% of the outstanding common stock of Andrews Company for $450,000, at which time Andrews Company had total stockholders' equity in the amount of $1,000,000. On January 1, 1980, the average remaining life of the depreciable assets of Andrews Company was 15 years. Although it was not practicable for Tidwell Company to determine the fair value of the specific noncurrent assets of Andrews Company on January 1, 1980, it was determined that fair value of the current assets and liabilities of Andrews Company was equal to their book value, except for inventory which had a fair value of $260,000 and a book value of $200,000. Andrews Company prices its inventory at the lower of FIFO cost or market and reported net income of $280,000 in 1980 and $220,000 in 1981.

Required:

Calculate the amount of equity in investee income to be reported by Tidwell Company in 1980 and 1981. Justify the assumptions, if any, that you must make.

Problem 5–14

Pasture Company acquired an 80% interest in Service Company on January 1, 1980 for $2,600,000. The book value and fair value of the assets and liabilities of Service Company on that date were as follows:

	BOOK VALUE	FAIR VALUE
Current Assets	$ 575,000	$ 575,000
Property & Equip. (net)	1,500,000	2,000,000
Land	625,000	1,000,000
Deferred Charge	200,000	200,000
Total Assets	$2,900,000	$3,775,000
Less Liabilities	400,000	400,000
Net Assets	$2,500,000	$3,375,000

The property and equipment had a remaining life of 10 years on January 1, 1980, and the deferred charge was being amortized over a period of 5 years from that date. Pasture Company records investments in its subsidiaries using the cost method.

Required:

A. Prepare in general journal form the December 31, 1980 workpaper entry to eliminate the investment account.

B. Prepare in general journal form the December 31, 1980 workpaper entry(s) necessary to assign the difference between cost and book value to specific assets and/or liabilities.

C. Prepare in general journal form the December 31, 1980 and December 31, 1981 workpaper entries necessary to adjust the balances of depreciation, amortization, etc. reported by Service Company to the balances to be reported in the consolidated financial statements on those dates.

Problem 5–15

On January 1, 1980, Pueblo Company acquired all of the outstanding common stock of Sun Company for $556,000 in cash. Financial data relating to Sun Company on January 1, 1980 are presented below.

	BALANCE SHEET	
	BOOK VALUE	FAIR VALUE
Cash	104,550	104,550
Receivables	123,000	112,310
Inventories	220,000	268,000
Buildings	331,000	375,000
Accumulated Depreciation—Buildings	(264,800)	(300,000)
Equipment	145,000	130,000
Accumulated Depreciation—Equipment	(108,750)	(97,500)
Land	150,000	420,000
Total Assets	700,000	1,012,360
Current Liabilities	106,000	106,000
Bonds Payable, 8% due 1/1/98, interest payable on 6/30 and 12/31	300,000[a]	
Common Stock	200,000	
Premium on Common Stock	80,000	
Retained Earnings	14,000	
Total Equities	700,000	

[a]Sun Company would expect to pay 10% interest to borrow long-term funds on the date of acquisition.

During 1980, Sun Company wrote its receivables down by $10,690 and recorded a corresponding loss. Sun Company accounts for its inventories at lower of FIFO cost or market. Its buildings and equipment had a remaining estimated useful life on January 1, 1980 of 10 years and 2½ years, respectively. No dividends were declared by Sun Company in 1980.

Required:

A. Assume that Pueblo Company accounts for its investment in Sun Company at cost. Prepare in general journal form the December 31, 1980 workpaper elimination entries necessary to eliminate the investment account and to allocate, amortize, and depreciate the difference between cost and book value.

B. Assume that Pueblo Company accounts for its investment in Sun Company using the equity method and that Sun Company reports net income of $80,000 in 1980. Prepare in general journal form the entry(s) necessary to record Pueblo Company's equity in the net income of Sun Company for the year ended December 31, 1980.

C. Assume that Sun Company reports net income in 1980 of $80,000, and Pueblo Company's net income from its independent operations amounts to $500,000. Calculate consolidated net income for 1980.

Problem 5–16

On June 30, 1980, Vasquez, Inc. purchased 100% of the outstanding common stock of Santos, Inc. for $4,100,000 cash. At the date of purchase, the book and fair values of Santos' assets and liabilities were as follows:

	BOOK VALUE	FAIR VALUE
Cash	$ 160,000	$ 160,000
Accounts Receivable (net)	910,000	910,000
Inventory	860,000	860,000
Furniture & Fixtures	3,000,000	2,550,000
Accumulated Depreciation—		
Furniture & Fixtures	(2,000,000)	(1,700,000)
Buildings	9,000,000	7,250,000
Accumulated Depreciation—		
Buildings	(3,450,000)	(2,779,166)
Intangible Assets (net)	150,000	220,000
	$ 8,630,000	
Accounts Payable	$ 580,000	580,000
Note Payable	500,000	500,000
5% Mortgage Note Payable	4,000,000	3,710,186
Common Stock	2,900,000	
Retained Earnings	650,000	
	$ 8,630,000	

As of June 30, 1980, Santos, Inc.'s furniture and fixtures and buildings had an estimated remaining life of 8 and 10 years, respectively. All intangible assets had an estimated remaining life of 20 years. All depreciation and amortization is to be computed using the straight-line method.

As of June 30, 1980, the 5% mortgage note payable had eight equal annual payments remaining, and the next payment was due June 30, 1981. The fair value of the note was based on a 7% rate.

Many of the management functions of the two companies have been consolidated since the merger. Vasquez charges Santos a $30,000 per month management fee. Vasquez also sold $200,000 in merchandise to Santos during the last half of 1980, all of which has been resold by Santos to nonaffiliates by December 31, 1980.

At December 31, 1980, Santos owes Vasquez two months' management fees and $18,000 for merchandise purchases.

Required:

Complete the worksheet for the preparation of a consolidated balance sheet and income statement for Vasquez, Inc. and its subsidiary, Santos, Inc., for the year ended December 31, 1980. Provide computations in good form where appropriate to support entries. The first two columns of the consolidated financial statement workpaper are presented below:

Consolidated Statement Workpaper
Vasquez, Inc. and Subsidiary
For Year Ended December 31, 1980

INCOME STATEMENT	VASQUEZ INC.	SANTOS INC.
Sales	$ 26,000,000	$ 6,000,000
Management Service Income	180,000	
Dividend Income	210,250	
Total Revenue	$ 26,390,250	$ 6,000,000
Cost of Goods Sold	18,000,000	3,950,000
Expenses:		
Selling & Administrative	3,130,000	956,000
Management Services		180,000
Depreciation	3,701,000	340,000
Amortization Expense		3,750
Amortization of Excess of		
Cost over Fair Value		
Interest Expense	662,000	100,000
Total Cost & Expense	$ 25,493,000	$ 5,529,750
Net Income to Retained		
Earnings	$ 897,250	$ 470,250
RETAINED EARNINGS STATEMENT		
Retained Earnings		
Vasquez, Inc. 1/1/80	$ 1,930,500	$
Santos, Inc. 6/30/80		650,000
Net Income from above	897,250	470,250
Dividends Declared		
Vasquez, Inc.	(450,000)	
Santos, Inc.		(210,250)
12/31/80 Retained Earnings		
to Balance Sheet	$ 2,377,750	$ 910,000
BALANCE SHEET		
Cash	$ 112,000	$ 200,750
Accounts Receivable	1,790,000	817,125
Inventory, 12/31	2,031,000	1,009,500
Investment in Santos	4,100,000	
Difference Between Cost		
and Book Value	–0–	–0–
Furniture & Fixtures	4,200,000	3,000,000
Accumulated Depreciation—		
Furniture & Fixtures	(2,000,000)	(2,062,500)
Buildings	17,000,000	9,000,000
Accumulated Depreciation—		
Buildings	(6,000,000)	(3,727,500)
Intangible Assets (net)		146,250
Excess of Cost over Fair Value	–0–	–0–
Total	$ 21,233,000	$ 8,383,625

Accounts Payable	$ 2,295,750	$ 473,625
Interest Payable	200,500	100,000
Mortgage Notes Payable	6,786,500	4,000,000
Bonds Payable	4,900,000	
Common Stock:		
Vasquez, Inc.	4,672,500	
Santos, Inc.		2,900,000
Retained Earnings from above	2,377,750	910,000
Total	$ 21,233,000	$ 8,383,625

Vasquez' profit and loss figures are for the 12-month period while Santos' are for the last six months.

(AICPA adapted)

Problem 5–17
Park Company acquired an 80% interest in the capital stock of Sedler Company on January 1, 1980 for $840,000. The trial balances for each company on December 31, 1980 are presented below.

	PARK COMPANY	SEDLER COMPANY
Current Assets	$ 350,000	$ 448,000
Investment in Sedler Company	1,008,000	
Equipment (net)	581,000	282,000
Land	119,000	250,000
Dividends Declared		70,000
Cost of Goods Sold	364,000	245,000
Expense	126,000	105,000
	$2,548,000	$1,400,000
Liabilities	$ 84,000	$ 70,000
Capital Stock	700,000	420,000
Retained Earnings	840,000	280,000
Sales	700,000	630,000
Equity in Subsidiary Income	224,000	
	$2,548,000	$1,400,000

The entire difference between cost and book value is allocated to land.

Required:
Prepare a consolidated balance sheet as of December 31, 1980 and a consolidated income statement for the year then ended:
(a) Using the entity theory approach.
(b) Using the proprietary theory approach.

Problem 5–18

The following account balances were taken from the December 31, 1980 trial balance of Advance Corporation:

Common Stock—$50 par	$200,000
Retained Earnings, 1/1/80	45,660
Sales	756,800
Cost of Sales	475,860
Expenses	214,950
Dividends Declared	25,000

Pleasant Valley, Inc. acquired 80% of the common stock of Advance Corporation on January 1, 1980 for $220,000. The difference between cost and book value was attributable to several small computers owned by Advance, who, anticipating a faster than experienced advance in computer technology, had depreciated the computers too rapidly. These computers had been acquired by Advance on January 1, 1975, and were being depreciated over a six-year estimated life on the straight-line basis.

Required:

Applying the entity theory approach, compute:

(a) The minority interest in the net income of Advance Corporation for 1980.

(b) The minority interest in the net assets of Advance Corporation on December 31, 1980.

6

Elimination of Unrealized Profit on Intercompany Sales of Inventory

Affiliated companies may engage in intercompany sales of inventory or other assets. Ordinarily, the selling affiliate recognizes and reports a profit on such sales. From the point of view of the consolidated entity, however, such profit should not be recognized until the inventory or other assets acquired by the purchasing affiliate have been sold to parties outside the affiliated group (third parties). Profit (loss) that has not been realized from the point of view of the consolidated entity through subsequent sales to third parties is defined as *unrealized intercompany profit (loss)* and must be eliminated in the preparation of consolidated financial statements. In addition, when investee income is reported using the equity method, the effects of unrealized intercompany profit (loss) must be removed therefrom. The elimination of unrealized profit resulting from intercompany sales of inventory is examined in this chapter. The elimination of unrealized profit resulting from intercompany sales of property and equipment will be examined in Chapter 7.

Consolidated sales and consolidated cost of sales should include only those amounts that relate to sales of merchandise to nonaffiliates. In addition, consolidated inventories should be stated at cost to the consolidated entity. Thus, in cases where there have been intercompany sales of merchandise, workpaper entries are necessary to adjust the reported amounts of sales, cost of sales (or components thereof), and ending inventory to the amounts that should be reported in the consolidated financial statements.

In this chapter, entries that are necessary in consolidated financial statement workpapers when an investment in a subsidiary is recorded at cost are presented first. Next, the effect of the elimination of intercompany profit on the recording and reporting of an investment under the equity method of accounting is considered. Finally, consolidated financial statement workpaper entries that are necessary when an investment in a subsidiary is recorded at equity are described and illustrated. In order to concentrate on intercompany profit eliminations and adjustments, reporting complications relating to accounting for the difference between acquisition cost and book value are avoided in all illustrations by assuming that all acquisitions are made at the book value of the acquired interest in net assets and that the book value of the subsidiary net assets equals their fair value on the date the parent's interest is acquired.

CONSOLIDATING WORKPAPER—INVESTMENT RECORDED AT COST

The basic workpaper eliminating entries required because of intercompany sales of merchandise are illustrated using the following simplifying assumptions:

1. P Company sells all goods it manufactures to its wholly owned subsidiary, S Company, at 125% of cost.

2. During the first year of this arrangement, goods that cost P Company $200,000 are sold to S Company for $250,000.

3. During the same year, S Company sells all of the goods purchased by it from P Company to third parties for $270,000.

Purchase
Accounting
Cost Method
Wholly Owned
Subsidiary

ILLUSTRATION 6–1
Partial Consolidated Statements Workpaper
Elimination of Intercompany Sale of Inventory
No Unrealized Profit

	P COMPANY	S COMPANY	ELIMINATIONS DR.	ELIMINATIONS CR.	CONSOLIDATED BALANCES
INCOME STATEMENT					
Sales	250,000	270,000	¹250,000		270,000
Cost of Sales	200,000	250,000		¹250,000	200,000
Gross Profit	50,000	20,000			70,000
BALANCE SHEET					
Inventory	–0–	–0–			–0–

¹To eliminate intercompany sales.

Sales, cost of sales, and inventory balances reported by the affiliated companies are presented in Illustration 6–1. The workpaper entry in the year of the sale to eliminate intercompany sales of merchandise takes the following form:

(1) Sales	250,000	
Cost of Sales (Purchases)		250,000

No unrealized intercompany profit exists, since all goods sold by P Company to S Company have been resold to third parties. After the elimination of intercompany sales, consolidated sales of $270,000 equals the amount of sales of the affiliated group (S Company) to third parties, and consolidated cost of sales of $200,000 equals the cost to the affiliated group (P Company) of manufacturing the goods sold.

Failure to eliminate intercompany sales would result in an overstatement of sales ✳ and of cost of sales in the consolidated financial statements. Since both sales and cost of sales would be overstated by the same amount, consolidated net income is not affected by the failure to eliminate intercompany sales. However, the gross profit rate and other financial ratios would be distorted if the elimination were not made.

Purchase	ILLUSTRATION 6-2				
Accounting	Partial Consolidated Statements Workpaper				
Cost Method	Elimination of Intercompany Sale of Inventory				
Wholly Owned	Unrealized Profit in Ending Inventory				
Subsidiary					

	P	S	ELIMINATIONS		CONSOLIDATED
INCOME STATEMENT	COMPANY	COMPANY	DR.	CR.	BALANCES
Sales	250,000	135,000	¹250,000		135,000
Cost of Sales	200,000	125,000	² 25,000	¹250,000	100,000
Gross Profit	50,000	10,000			35,000
BALANCE SHEET					
Inventory	–0–	125,000		² 25,000	100,000

¹To eliminate intercompany sales.
²To eliminate unrealized intercompany profit in ending inventory.

Assume now that S Company sells only one-half of the goods purchased from P Company to third parties prior to the end of the current year. Sales, cost of sales, and inventory balances reported by each of the affiliated companies are presented in Illustration 6–2. Entry (1) to eliminate sales and cost of sales is the same as explained above. However, unrealized intercompany profit in the amount of $25,000 (125,000 − [125,000/1.25]) resides in the ending inventory balance of S Company. When, at the end of the accounting period, some of the merchandise remains in the inventory of the purchasing affiliate, the intercompany profit recognized thereon must be excluded from consolidated net income and from the inventory balance in the consolidated balance sheet. The workpaper entry to accomplish this elimination is as follows:

(2) Cost of Sales   REDUCES INCOME
        (Ending Inventory in Income Statement)   25,000
              Inventory   25,000

The form of the entry eliminating intercompany sales, Entry (1), implicitly assumes that there is no unrealized intercompany profit. Accordingly, either that entry must be adjusted or this second entry must be made to remove the unrealized intercompany profit from the ending inventory and to reduce the excessive credit to cost of sales. The first and second eliminating entries could be combined and one entry prepared as follows:

Sales	250,000	
Cost of Sales (Purchases)		225,000
Inventory		25,000

As a practical matter, two entries are conventionally prepared as shown in Illustration 6–2. In either case, after adjustment, consolidated sales of $135,000 equal the amount of sales of the affiliated group (S Company) to third parties. Consolidated cost of sales of $100,000 equals the cost to the affiliated group (P Company) of manufacturing the goods sold ($\frac{1}{2} \times 200,000$), and the consolidated inventory balance of $100,000 equals the cost to the affiliated group (P Company) of manufacturing the goods held by S Company at the end of the year.

Purchase Accounting	ILLUSTRATION 6–3
Cost Method	**Partial Consolidated Statements Workpaper**
Wholly Owned	**Elimination of Intercompany Sale of Inventory**
Subsidiary	**Intercompany Profit in Beginning and Ending Inventories**

| | P | S | ELIMINATIONS | | CONSOLIDATED |
	COMPANY	COMPANY	DR.	CR.	BALANCES
INCOME STATEMENT					
Sales	500,000	405,000	¹500,000		405,000
Cost of Sales	400,000	375,000	² 50,000	¹500,000	300,000
				³ 25,000	
Gross Profit	100,000	30,000			105,000
RETAINED EARNINGS STATEMENT					
Beginning Retained Earnings					
P Company (Consolidated)	XXX		³ 25,000		XXX
BALANCE SHEET					
Inventory	–0–	250,000		² 50,000	200,000

¹To eliminate intercompany sales.
²To eliminate unrealized intercompany profit in ending inventory.
³To recognize intercompany profit in beginning inventory realized during the period and reduce beginning consolidated retained earnings for unrealized intercompany profit at the beginning of the year.

Assume now that in the next period P Company sells merchandise to S Company in the amount of $500,000 (cost $400,000) and that S Company sells all of its beginning inventory ($125,000) and one-half of its current purchases from P Company ($250,000) to third parties for $405,000. Sales, cost of sales, and inventory balances reported by the affiliated companies are presented in Illustration 6–3. Unrealized intercompany profit in the amount of $50,000 (250,000 − [250,000/1.25]) resides in the ending inventory of S Company. Workpaper eliminating entries (1) and (2) are similar to those discussed in the preceding example. Assuming a first-in first-out

(FIFO) inventory cost flow, intercompany profit in inventories excluded from consolidated net income in one period will be realized by sales to third parties in the next period. The form of the workpaper entry to recognize profit in the buying affiliate's beginning inventory that is realized during the current period is as follows:

(3) Beginning Retained Earnings—Parent
    (Beginning Consolidated Retained Earnings)   25,000
        Cost of Sales (Beginning Inventory in Income Statement)   25,000

The credit to cost of sales (beginning inventory) in Entry (3) is necesssary in order to recognize in consolidated income the amount of profit in the beginning inventory that has been confirmed by sales to third parties during the current period. S Company charged cost of sales for its cost of $125,000, whereas the cost to the affiliated group of the beginning inventory of S Company is only $100,000. Accordingly, cost of sales must be decreased by $25,000, which increases consolidated net income by $25,000.

The rationale for the debit of $25,000 to beginning retained earnings of P Company (beginning consolidated retained earnings) is as follows. In the previous year, P Company recorded $50,000 in profit on intercompany sales and transferred it to its retained earnings as part of the normal accounting process. Since, at the beginning of the year, one-half of that amount has not been realized by sales to third parties it must be eliminated from the beginning retained earnings of P Company (and from beginning consolidated retained earnings). The debit to beginning retained earnings may also be explained in the following manner. In determining consolidated net income and ending consolidated retained earnings in the prior year, $25,000 was deducted from the reported income and retained earnings of the affiliated group by a workpaper entry. Therefore, in the current year, the amount indicated by the beginning account balances on the books of the affiliated companies must be reduced by a workpaper entry in the amount of $25,000 in order that beginning consolidated retained earnings of the current year will be reported at an amount equal to that reported for ending consolidated retained earnings in the previous period.

Consolidated sales of $405,000 are equal to the amount of sales of the affiliated group (S Company) to third parties. Consolidated cost of sales of $300,000 equals the cost to the affiliated group (P Company) of manufacturing the goods sold and is calculated as follows:

Cost of one-half of goods transferred to S Company in prior year ($\frac{1}{2} \times 200,000$)	100,000
Cost of one-half of goods transferred to S Company in current year ($\frac{1}{2} \times 400,000$)	200,000
Cost of goods sold to third parties during the current year	300,000

Consolidated inventory of $200,000 equals the cost to the affiliated group (P Company) of manufacturing the goods on hand at the end of the year ($\frac{1}{2} \times 400,000$).

Over two consecutive periods, assuming a FIFO flow of inventory costs, differences between the net income recorded on the books of the individual affiliates and consolidated net income offset each other, as does the effect of the differences on beginning retained earnings.

If an inventory cost flow assumption other than FIFO is used, unrealized intercompany profit in beginning inventory balances may continue to be included in the ending inventory. In that case, to the extent that unrealized intercompany profit at the beginning of the year remains unrealized, the increase in consolidated net income that would otherwise result from the credit to cost of sales in Entry (3) is offset by a portion of the debit to cost of sales in Entry (2). Thus, as a matter of workpaper procedure, there is no need to be concerned in formulating Entry (3) as to whether or not unrealized intercompany profit in the beginning inventory is also included in the ending inventory.

Individual components (beginning inventory, purchases, ending inventory) of cost of sales are shown parenthetically in the entries illustrated above. If the detail of cost of sales is to be presented in the consolidated income statement, workpaper entries must be made so as to adjust the individual components as indicated rather than aggregate cost of sales.

Determination of the Amount of Intercompany Profit

In the preceding examples, the amount of intercompany profit subject to elimination was calculated on the basis of the selling affiliate's *gross profit rate*. This is the concept that is normally applied in practice. An alternative would be to determine intercompany profit on the basis of the selling affiliate's profit after deducting selling and administrative expense. The effect of this approach, as compared with the gross profit method, would be to reduce the amount of profit subject to elimination and increase consolidated inventory balances by the amount of the selling and administrative expense associated with the goods still held by the affiliated group. Support for the gross profit approach is based on the proposition that consolidated inventory balances should include manufacturing costs only and that generally accepted accounting standards normally preclude the capitalization of selling and administrative costs.

Inventory Pricing Adjustments

Assume that: (1) P Company sells S Company goods costing $200,000 for $250,000; (2) at the end of the year, all of these goods remain in the ending inventory of S Company and are written down from $250,000 to $215,000 on that company's books; (3) the write-down on the books of S Company results from the application of the lower of cost or market rule in pricing its ending inventory; and (4) the related loss is included in the cost of sales of S Company. What amount of intercompany profit is subject to elimination in the preparation of consolidated financial statements? Since the gross profit of $50,000 recognized by P Company is offset by the reduction of gross profit of $35,000 recognized by S Company, only the remaining $15,000 is still subject to elimination in the preparation of consolidated financial statements. The deduction of the amount of the current year's write-down of intercompany inventory from the amount of intercompany profit otherwise subject to elimination also results in the presentation of intercompany inventory at cost to the affiliated group (215,000 − 15,000 = 200,000). In summary, the amount of intercompany profit subject to elimination should be reduced to the extent that the related goods have been written down by the purchasing affiliate.

100% Versus Partial Elimination of Intercompany Profit

It is clear that unrealized intercompany profit should not be included in consolidated net income or assets. However, two alternative views of the amount of intercompany profit that should be considered as "unrealized" exist. The elimination methods associated with these two points of view are generally referred to as *100%* (total) *elimination* and *partial elimination*.

Proponents of 100% elimination regard *all* of the intercompany profit associated with assets remaining in the affiliated group to be unrealized. Proponents of partial elimination regard only the parent company's share of the profit recognized by the *selling affiliate* to be unrealized. Stated another way, they regard the minority interest's share of the *selling affiliate's* profit on intercompany sales to be realized.

Under 100% elimination, the entire amount of unconfirmed intercompany profit is eliminated from combined income and the related asset balance. Under partial elimination, only the parent company's share of the unconfirmed intercompany profit recognized by the *selling affiliate* is eliminated.

One hundred percent elimination is consistent with the entity approach to the preparation of consolidated financial statements. This approach emphasizes reporting consolidated assets at cost to the consolidated entity and views minority interest as a separate equity interest in consolidated net assets. One hundred percent elimination is also supported by the position that the full effect of transactions that do not result from arms-length bargaining should be eliminated in consolidation. The presumption is that transactions between affiliates controlled by a majority stock interest rarely, if ever, result from arms-length bargaining.

Partial elimination is consistent with the proprietary approach to the preparation of consolidated financial statements. Thus, only the parent's (proprietary) interest in profits recognized by the selling affiliate is eliminated. Under this approach, minority interest is considered to be the same as any other creditor and is deemed to be entitled to its share of the reported profit of the subsidiary regardless of whether the profit results from sales to affiliates of the subsidiary or to third parties.

Generally accepted accounting standards *require* 100% elimination of inter-company profit *in the preparation of consolidated financial statements*. This standard was originally promulgated in paragraph 14 of *ARB No. 51* as follows:

The amount of intercompany profit or loss to be eliminated . . . is not affected by the existence of a minority interest. The complete elimination of the intercompany profit or loss is consistent with the underlying assumption that consolidated statements represent the financial position and operating results of a single business enterprise.

Because generally accepted accounting standards currently require total elimination of intercompany profit in the preparation of consolidated financial statements, all illustrations of consolidating workpapers in this text are based on 100% elimination of intercompany profit. The reader needs to be aware, however, that there is support in the accounting literature for partial elimination of intercompany profit. Accordingly, partial elimination is illustrated and compared with 100% elimination in the appendix to this chapter.

As is demonstrated therein, the method used to eliminate unrealized intercompany profit does not affect the amount of reported consolidated net income or consolidated retained earnings. However, when 100% elimination is used, asset balances resulting from intercompany sales are reported in the consolidated financial statements at the cost of the asset to the selling affiliate. When partial elimination is used, such balances are reported at the cost of the asset to the selling affiliate plus an amount equal to the minority interest in the profit recognized by the selling affiliate on the intercompany sale. The increase in asset balances reported under partial elimination is exactly offset by an increase in the amount of minority interest in consolidated net assets reported in the consolidated balance sheet.

Income Tax Effects (Investment Recorded at Cost)

If the selling affiliate files a separate income tax return, it records taxes on unrealized intercompany profit in the year of the sale. Since the recognition of such profit is deferred in the consolidated financial statements, the related income tax must also be deferred by a separate workpaper entry. For example, assume that on December 31, 1980, there is $500,000 in unrealized intercompany profit residing in the ending inventory of the affiliates and that the average income tax rate is 40%. Entries in the December 31, 1980 and December 31, 1981 workpapers relating to the intercompany profit in the December 31, 1980 inventory are as follows:

DECEMBER 31, 1980

Cost of Sales	500,000	
Inventory		500,000
To eliminate unrealized intercompany profit in ending inventory.		
Deferred Income Tax	200,000	
Income Tax Expense		200,000
To defer recognition of income tax paid on unrealized intercompany profit. (.4 × 500,000 = 200,000).		

Beginning Retained Earnings—Parent (Beginning		
Consolidated Retained Earnings)	500,000	
Cost of Sales		500,000

        To recognize profit in beginning inventory realized by the consolidated entity through sales to third parties during the year and to reduce consolidated retained earnings at the beginning of the year for the gross effect of the prior-year workpaper reduction of consolidated income.

Further adjustment to beginning retained earnings for the tax effects of these amounts is accomplished in the following entry.

Income Tax Expense	200,000	
Beginning Retained Earnings—Parent (Beginning		
Consolidated Retained Earnings)		200,000

        To recognize income tax expense on intercompany profit considered to be realized during the current year (.4 $\times$ 500,000 = 200,000) and to adjust beginning retained earnings for the income tax effects on the unrealized intercompany profit eliminated therefrom.

Note that the net effect of the two entries is to reduce beginning retained earnings by $300,000 (500,000 − 200,000), which is the amount of unrealized intercompany profit in beginning inventory *net of tax*.

If a consolidated income tax return is filed, unrealized intercompany profit will be reported in taxable income in the same period that it is recognized in the consolidated income statement. In that case no timing difference exists, and it is not necessary to consider deferred income tax in the preparation of the consolidated financial statements.

Adjustments to Minority Interest Necessitated by 100% Elimination (Investment Recorded At Cost)

Sales from a parent company to one or more of its subsidiaries are referred to as *downstream sales*. Sales from subsidiaries to the parent company are referred to as *upstream sales*. Sales from one subsidiary to another subsidiary are referred to as *horizontal sales*.

When the selling affiliate is a less than wholly owned subsidiary and 100% of intercompany profit is eliminated, the amount of profit eliminated should be allocated proportionately between the majority (consolidated net income) and minority (minority interest in combined income) interests. If the income of a less than wholly owned subsidiary is, in effect, increased or decreased by intercompany profit workpaper entries prior to its aggregation with the income of the parent, the calculation of minority interest in the combined income should be based on the amount of subsidiary income included in the combined income of that period. Likewise, the calculation of minority interest in consolidated net assets should be based on the amount of net assets of the subsidiary included in the consolidated balance sheet.

When the 100% elimination method is used to eliminate intercompany profit, the calculation of minority interest in net income is modified as follows: Minority interest in net income = (minority interest ownership percentage) × (reported subsidiary income minus unrealized intercompany profit net of tax recognized by the subsidiary in the current period plus intercompany profit net of tax recognized by the subsidiary in the prior period(s) that is realized by sales to third parties during the current period). The calculation of minority interest may be stated more succinctly as: (the minority interest ownership percentage) × (reported subsidiary income plus unrealized profit net of tax in beginning inventory minus unrealized profit net of tax in ending inventory). The reader is reminded, however, that this modification of the calculation of minority interest is applicable only when the less than wholly owned subsidiary is the *selling affiliate* (upstream or horizontal sales). Where the parent company is the selling affiliate (downstream sale), the calculation of minority interest in the net income of a less than wholly owned subsidiary is unaffected.

On the consolidating workpaper, the amount carried to the minority-interest column from the subsidiary company's beginning retained earnings row must also be adjusted so that it is consistent with the workpaper reduction of minority interest in combined income in the previous year(s). This adjustment is accomplished when preparing the workpaper adjustments for unrealized intercompany profit in *beginning inventory* by apportioning the debits and/or credits to beginning retained earnings between the beginning retained earnings row of the parent and that of the subsidiary. For example, if in the preceding example the selling affiliate was a 70%-owned subsidiary, the cost-basis workpaper entries relating to intercompany profit in beginning inventory would be as follows:

(1) Beginning Retained Earnings—Parent (Beginning		
Consolidated Retained Earnings) (.7 × 500,000)	350,000	
Beginning Retained Earnings—Subsidiary		
(Minority Interest) (.3 × 500,000)	150,000	
Cost of Sales		500,000
(2) Income Tax Expense	200,000	
Beginning Retained Earnings—Parent (Consolidated		
Retained Earnings) (.7 × 200,000)		140,000
Beginning Retained Earnings—Subsidiary (Minority		
Interest) (.3 × 200,000)		60,000

Although 100% elimination of intercompany profit is required in the preparation of consolidated financial statements, the minority-interest adjustments described above are discretionary under current generally accepted accounting standards. This position is stated in paragraph 14 of *ARB No. 51* as follows: "The elimination of intercompany profit or loss *may* be allocated proportionately between the majority and minority interests [emphasis added]." Thus, the adjustments to the calculation of minority interest (and as a result to consolidated net income) *may* be made but are not *required* under generally accepted accounting standards. In our opinion, where the amounts are material, the allocation of intercompany profit and loss eliminations proportionately between majority and minority interests is necessary for fair presentation, and there is no justification other than expediency for permitting discretionary allocation. Therefore, appropriate adjustments to the calculation of minority interest for the effects of intercompany profit adjustments will be adhered to in all subsequent consolidating workpaper illustrations in this text.

Comprehensive Illustration: Less Than Wholly Owned Subsidiary (Investment Recorded at Cost)

Assume that P Company acquires an 80% interest in S Company for $1,360,000 on January 1, 1980, that the average income tax rate for both companies is 40%, that S Company files a separate income tax return, and that S Company sells merchandise to P Company as follows:

YEAR	TOTAL SALES OF S COMPANY TO P COMPANY	INTERCOMPANY MERCHANDISE IN 12/31 INVENTORY OF P COMPANY	UNREALIZED INTERCOMPANY PROFIT (25% OF SELLING PRICE)
1980	700,000	400,000	100,000
1981	1,000,000	500,000	125,000

P Company uses the cost method to account for its investment in S Company. Consolidated statement workpapers (cost method) for the years ending December 31, 1980 and December 31, 1981 are presented in Illustration 6–4 and Illustration 6–5, respectively. Workpaper entries in Illustrations 6–4 and 6–5 are summarized in general journal form following each illustration for the convenience of the reader.

Purchase Accounting
Cost Method
80%-Owned Subsidiary
Upstream Sale of Inventory

ILLUSTRATION 6-4
Consolidated Statements Workpaper
P Company and Subsidiary
For Year Ending December 31, 1980

	P COMPANY	S COMPANY	ELIMINATIONS DR.	ELIMINATIONS CR.	MINORITY INTEREST	CONSOLIDATED BALANCES
INCOME STATEMENT						
Sales	3,104	2,200	¹ 700			4,604
Dividend Income	16		⁴ 16			
Total Revenue	3,120	2,200				4,604
Inventory 1/1/80	500	300				800
Purchases	1,680	1,370		¹ 700		2,350
	2,180	1,670				3,150
Inventory 12/31/80	480	310	² 100			690
Cost of Goods Sold	1,700	1,360				2,460
Other Expense	927	632				1,559
Income Tax Expense	197	83		³ 40		240
Total Cost and Expense	2,824	2,075				4,259
Net	296	125				345
Minority Interest .2 (125−[100 − 40])					13	(13)
Net Income to Retained Earnings	296	125	816	740	13	332
RETAINED EARNINGS STATEMENT						
1/1/80 Retained Earnings						
P Company	1,650					1,650
S Company		700	⁵ 560		140	
Net Income from above	296	125	816	740	13	332
Dividends Declared						
P Company	(150)					(150)
S Company		(20)		⁴ 16	(4)	
12/31/80 Retained Earnings to						
Balance Sheet	1,796	805	1,376	756	149	1,832
BALANCE SHEET						
Inventory	480	310		² 100		690
Investment in S Company	1,360			⁵1,360		
Other Assets (net)	5,090	2,310				7,400
Deferred Income Tax			³ 40			40
Total	6,930	2,620				8,130
Liabilities	2,134	815				2,949
Capital Stock						
P Company	3,000					3,000
S Company		1,000	⁵ 800		200	
Retained Earnings from above	1,796	805	1,376	756	149	1,832
Minority Interest					349	349
Total Liabilities & Equity	6,930	2,620	2,216	2,216		8,130

000 OMITTED

¹To eliminate intercompany sales.
²To eliminate unrealized intercompany profit in ending inventory.
³To defer recognition of taxes paid on unrealized intercompany profit.
⁴To eliminate intercompany dividends.
⁵To eliminate the investment account.

December 31, 1980 workpaper entries (Illustration 6–4)

(1) Sales	700,000	
Purchases (Cost of Sales)		700,000
To eliminate intercompany sales.		

(2) 12/31 Inventory-Income Statement (Cost of Sales)	100,000	
Inventory		100,000
To eliminate unrealized intercompany profit in ending inventory.		

(3) Deferred Income Tax	40,000	
Income Tax Expense		40,000
To defer recognition of taxes paid on unrealized intercompany profit (.40 × 100,000).		

(4) Dividend Income	16,000	
Dividends Declared		16,000
To eliminate intercompany dividends.		

(5) Beginning Retained Earnings—S Company	560,000	
Capital Stock—S Company	800,000	
Investment in S Company		1,360,000
To eliminate the investment account.		

Since the selling affiliate is a partially owned subsidiary, the calculation of minority interest in combined income is modified by subtracting unrealized intercompany profit net of tax from reported subsidiary net income as follows:
$.2 \times (125,000 - [100,000 - .4 \times 100,000]) = 13,000.$

ILLUSTRATION 6–5
Consolidated Statements Workpaper
P Company and Subsidiary
For Year Ending December 31, 1981

	P COMPANY	S COMPANY	ELIMINATIONS DR.	ELIMINATIONS CR.	MINORITY INTEREST	CONSOLIDATED BALANCES
INCOME STATEMENT						
Sales	3,546	2,020	[1] 1,000			4,566
Dividend Income	48		[7] 48			
Total Revenue	3,594	2,020				4,566
Inventory 1/1/81	480	310		[4] 100		690
Purchases	2,070	1,250		[1] 1,000		2,320
	2,550	1,560				3,010
Inventory 12/31/81	510	360	[2] 125			745
Cost of Goods Sold	2,040	1,200				2,265
Other Expense	798	587				1,385
Income Tax Expense	302	93	[5] 40	[3] 50		385
Total Cost and Expense	3,140	1,880				4,035
Net	454	140				531
Minority Interest					25	(25·)
Net Income to Retained Earnings	454	140	1,213	1,150	25	506
RETAINED EARNINGS STATEMENT						
1/1/81 Retained Earnings				[6] 84		
P Company	1,796		[4] 80	[5] 32		1,832
S Company		805	[4] 20	[5] 8	149	
			[8] 644			
Net Income from above	454	140	1,213	1,150	25	506
Dividends Declared						
P Company	(150)					(150)
S Company		(60)		[7] 48	(12)	
12/31/81 Retained Earnings to Balance Sheet	2,100	885	1,957	1,322	162	2,188
BALANCE SHEET						
Inventory	510	360		[2] 125		745
Investment in S Company	1,360		[6] 84	[8] 1,444		
Other Assets	5,450	2,330				7,780
Deferred Income Tax			[3] 50			50
Total	7,320	2,690				8,575
Liabilities	2,220	805				3,025
Capital Stock						
P Company	3,000					3,000
S Company		1,000	[8] 800		200	
Retained Earnings from above	2,100	885	1,957	1,322	162	2,188
Minority Interest					362	362
Total Liabilities & Equity	7,320	2,690	2,891	2,891		8,575

*.2 (140 − [.6 × 125] + [.6 × 100]) = 25
[1] To eliminate intercompany sales.
[2] To eliminate unrealized intercompany profit in ending inventory.
[3] To defer recognition of income tax paid on unrealized intercompany profit.
[4] To recognize intercompany profit in beginning inventory realized during the year and to reduce consolidated retained earnings and minority interest at beginning of year for unrealized intercompany profit at the beginning of the year.
[5] To recognize tax effects on intercompany profit in beginning inventory.
[6] To establish reciprocity as of 1/1/81 (.8 [805−700] = 84).
[7] To eliminate the intercompany dividends.
[8] To eliminate the investment account.

December 31, 1981 workpaper entries (Illustration 6–5)

(1) Sales   1,000,000
    Purchases (Cost of Sales)   1,000,000
      To eliminate intercompany sales.

(2) 12/31 Inventory—Income Statement (Cost of Sales)   125,000
    Inventory   125,000
      To eliminate unrealized intercompany profit in ending inventory.

(3) Deferred Income Tax   50,000
    Income Tax Expense   50,000
      To defer recognition of income tax paid on unrealized intercompany profit (.40 × 125,000 = 50,000).

(4) Beginning Retained Earnings—P Company
    (.80 × 100,000)   80,000
    Beginning Retained Earnings—S Company
    (.20 × 100,000)   20,000
      1/1 Inventory—Income Statement (Cost of Sales)   100,000
      To recognize intercompany profit in beginning inventory realized during the year and to reduce consolidated retained earnings and minority interest at the beginning of the year for unrealized intercompany profit at the beginning of the year.

(5) Income Tax Expense   40,000
    Beginning Retained Earnings—P Company
    (.8 × 40,000)   32,000
    Beginning Retained Earnings—S Company
    (.2 × 40,000)   8,000
      To recognize income tax expense on intercompany profit considered to be realized during the current year and to adjust beginning retained earnings and minority interest for the income tax effects on the unrealized intercompany profit eliminated therefrom.

(6) Investment in S Company   84,000
    Beginning Retained Earnings—P Company   84,000
      To establish reciprocity as of 1/1/81 (.8 × [805,000 − 700,000] = 84,000).

(7) Dividend Income	48,000	
Dividends Declared		48,000
To eliminate intercompany dividends.		
(8) Beginning Retained Earnings—S Company	644,000	
Capital Stock—S Company	800,000	
Investment in S Company		1,444,000
To eliminate the investment account.		

The minority interest in the beginning retained earnings of S Company in the amount of $149,000 is equal to the minority interest's share of the reported retained earnings of S Company (.20 × 805,000 = 161,000) *reduced* by its share of the unrealized intercompany profit net of tax included therein (.20 × [100,000 − 40,000] = 12,000). The workpaper procedure to reduce the amount of minority interest in beginning retained earnings is to allocate the debits and credits to beginning retained earnings resulting from the elimination of unrealized intercompany profit *net of tax* proportionately between the parent company's row (80,000 − 32,000 = .80 × [100,000 − 40,000] = 48,000) and the subsidiary company's row (20,000 − 8,000 = .20 × [100,000 − 40,000] = 12,000). A comparison of the December 31, 1980 retained earnings row of the workpaper presented in Illustration 6–4 with the amount of January 1, 1981 retained earnings extended to the minority interest and consolidated balances columns in the workpaper presented in Illustration 6–5 should convince the reader of the necessity of this procedure. After these adjustments, January 1, 1981 consolidated retained earnings amount to $1,832,000 (Illustration 6–5) and are equal to December 31, 1980 consolidated retained earnings (Illustration 6–4). Minority interest in January 1, 1981 retained earnings is $149,000 (Illustration 6–5) and is equal to that calculated in December 31, 1980 retained earnings (Illustration 6–4). The reader may also wish to note that, after adjustment, consolidated inventory amounts to $690,000 on December 31, 1980 (Illustration 6–4) and on January 1, 1981 (Illustration 6–5).

Consolidated Net Income and Consolidated
Retained Earnings: Refined Analytical Definitions

In Chapter 5 the analytical definitions of consolidated net income and consolidated retained earnings were refined to accommodate the effect of the allocation, amortization, and depreciation of the difference between cost and book value. These definitions must now be further refined to accommodate the effect thereon of unrealized intercompany profit.

Consolidated Net Income   Consolidated net income is now defined as the parent company's income from its independent operations that has been realized in transactions with third parties plus (minus) its share of reported subsidiary income (loss) that has been realized in transactions with third parties minus (plus when acquisition cost is less than the book value of the interest acquired) adjustments for the period relating to the allocation, depreciation, and amortization of the difference betwen cost and book value.

On the basis of Illustration 6–5 the calculation of consolidated net income for the year ending December 31, 1981, using the analytical approach, may be demonstrated as follows:

P Company's net income from its independent operations		406,000[1]
Amount of income not realized in		
transactions with third parties		–0–
P Company's income from its independent		
operations that has been realized in		
transactions with third parties		406,000
Reported net income of S Company	140,000	
Less unrealized intercompany profit net of tax on		
1981 sales to P Company	(75,000)	
Plus profit net of tax on 1980 sales to P Company		
realized in transactions with third parties in 1981	60,000	
Reported subsidiary income that has been realized		
in transactions with third parties	125,000	
P Company's share thereof (.8 × 125,000)		100,000
Consolidated net income		506,000

[1]From Illustration 6–5: $454,000 (reported net income of P Company) — $48,000 (subsidiary dividend income) = $406,000.

This, of course, is the same amount of consolidated net income as that calculated in the consolidated financial statement workpaper presented in Illustration 6–5.

Consolidated Retained Earnings   As was indicated in Chapter 4, an analytical approach to the calculation of consolidated retained earnings may be useful where the parent company records its investment using the cost method. For these purposes, consolidated retained earnings is now defined as the parent company's cost method retained earnings that have been realized in transactions with third parties plus (minus) the parent company's share of the increase (decrease) in reported subsidiary retained earnings that has been realized in transactions with third parties from the date of acquisition to the current date minus (plus when acquisition cost is less than the book value of the interest acquired) the cumulative effect of adjustments to date relating to the allocation, depreciation, and amortization of the difference between cost and book value.

On the basis of Illustration 6–5, the calculation of consolidated retained earnings on December 31, 1981, using the analytical approach, may be demonstrated as follows:

P Company's retained earnings on December 31, 1981		2,100,000
Amount of P Company retained earnings that have not been realized in transactions with third parties		–0–
P Company's retained earnings that have been realized in transactions with third parties		2,100,000
Increase in retained earnings of S Company from January 1, 1980 to December 31, 1981 (885,000 − 700,000)	185,000	
Less unrealized profit net of tax on sales to P Company in 1981 that has not been confirmed by sales to third parties	(75,000)	
Increase in reported retained earnings of S Company since acquisition that has been realized in transactions with third parties	110,000	
P Company's share thereof (.8 × 110,000)		88,000
Consolidated Retained Earnings on December 31, 1981		2,188,000

This, of course, is the same amount of consolidated retained earnings as that calculated in the consolidated financial statement workpaper presented in Illustration 6–5.

NONCONSOLIDATED INVESTEES REPORTED IN THE FINANCIAL STATEMENTS USING THE EQUITY METHOD

Investments that do not qualify for consolidation but that are appropriately reported in the financial statements using the equity method (see Chapter 3) may also require adjustment for the effects of unrealized intercompany profits. In paragraph 19a of *Opinion No. 18,* the Accounting Principles Board concluded that, in applying the equity method, intercompany profit and loss should be eliminated until realized by the investor or investee as if the subsidiary or other investee company that qualifies for the equity method were consolidated. This apparently straightforward position is, however, subject to different interpretations as to (1) the proportion of unrealized intercompany profit that should be eliminated when the equity method is applied, and (2) the form of the entry on the investor company's books to accomplish the elimination.

Nonconsolidated Subsidiaries Reported at Equity

Recall that the Accounting Principles Board stated in paragraph 19 of *Opinion No. 18* that ". . . an investor's net income for the period and its stockholders' equity at the end of the period are the same whether an investment in a subsidiary is accounted for under the equity method or the subsidiary is consolidated."

In addition, recall that in consolidation the proportion of unrealized intercompany profit charged to the majority interest (consolidated net income) differs as between upstream and downstream intercompany sales. In the case of upstream sales from less than wholly owned subsidiaries, although the entire amount of unrealized intercompany profit is eliminated from combined net income, proportionate allocation of the total amount eliminated to the majority and minority interests is deemed appropriate (although not required) and is the method illustrated in this chapter. In the downstream case, the entire amount of unrealized intercompany profit is treated as a reduction of the majority interest (consolidated net income), and the calculation of the amount of minority interest in combined income is unaffected.

In order for the equity method of reporting on an unconsolidated subsidiary to have the same effect on reported net income and stockholders' equity as the consolidation procedures summarized above, the parent company's net income must be reduced by the *entire amount* of unrealized intercompany profit if the sale is *downstream*, whereas only an amount equal to the *parent company's interest in the subsidiary* times the unrealized intercompany profit must be deducted from the net income of the parent company if the sale is *upstream.*[1]

Assume that P Company owns 75% of the voting stock of S Company and accounts for its investment using the equity method. S Company reports net income of $200,000 in 1980 and $300,000 in 1981. Intercompany sales of merchandise amount to $150,000 in 1980 and $200,000 in 1981. On December 31, 1980 and December 31, 1981, unrealized intercompany profit on intercompany sales of merchandise amount to $40,000 and $60,000 (50% of selling price), respectively. The average income tax rate for both companies is 40%, and separate income tax returns are filed.

Entries on the Parent Company's Books in 1980 (Equity Method)   As was indicated above, the entries recorded by the parent company differ, depending upon whether the intercompany sale is upstream or downstream.

---

[1]Generally accepted accounting standards do not always require the elimination procedures described above. If the intercompany sale is consummated on an arms-length basis, *Interpretation No. 1* of *Opinion No. 18,* "Intercompany Profit Elimination under the Equity Method," apparently permits the elimination of an amount equal to only *the parent company's interest in the subsidiary times the total unrealized intercompany profit, even in the case of downstream sales.* In addition, since *ARB No. 51 permits* charging the majority interest in consolidated statements with the entire amount of unrealized intercompany profit even in the case of upstream sales from less than wholly owned subsidiaries, under the equity method generally accepted accounting standards apparently also *permit* the reduction of the *full amount* of unrealized intercompany profit from the parent company's income in the case of *upstream sales.* Thus, the current authoritative literature in this area is at best permissive and at worst conflicting. We feel that the interpretation presented herein—full reduction in the case of downstream sales and reduction of an amount based on the parent company's interest in the subsidiary in the case of upstream sales—is consistent with the best of current practice and is sound in theory. See Thomas E. King and Valdean C. Lembke, "Reporting Investor Income Under the Equity Method," *Journal of Accountancy,* September, 1976, pp. 65–71, for a critical evaluation of the contradictions in the authoritative literature relating to this matter.

Upstream sale

(1) Investment in S Company   150,000
      Equity in Subsidiary Income   150,000
         To record P Company's share of the reported net income of S Company (.75 ×
         200,000 = 150,000).

(2) Equity in Subsidiary Income   18,000
      Investment in S Company   18,000
         To reduce P Company's equity in subsidiary income by its share of the unrealized
         intercompany profit net of tax included in the net income of S Company (.75 ×
         [.6 × 40,000] = 18,000).

In the case of an upstream sale, the intercompany profit has been recorded on the books of the subsidiary, and it is generally agreed that the appropriate entry on the parent company's books is to reduce the amount of equity in subsidiary income otherwise recorded on its books by its share of the unrealized intercompany profit net of income tax.

Downstream sale

(1) Investment in S Company   150,000
      Equity in Subsidiary Income   150,000
         To record P Company's share of the reported net income of S Company.

In the case of downstream sales, the sales revenue and gross profit on the intercompany sale are included in the sales and gross profit balances recorded and reported by the parent company. Several alternative procedures have been suggested for recording the elimination of the unrealized intercompany profit on the books of the parent company. Three of these procedures are illustrated below:[2]

(1) Sales   80,000
      Cost of Sales   40,000
      Investment in S Company   40,000
      (.50 × 80,000 = 40,000)
      Deferred Income Tax   16,000
      Income Tax Expense   16,000
      (.4 × 40,000 = 16,000)
(2) Equity in Subsidiary Income   24,000
      Investment in S Company   24,000
      (1.0 [.6 × 40,000] = 24,000)

---

[2]See King and Lembke, "Reporting Investor Income Under the Equity Method," cited above, for a more complete discussion of these and other alternatives.

(3) Unrealized Gross Profit on
     Sales to Unconsolidated Subsidiaries
     (Reduction in Income Statement)   40,000
        Income Tax Expense   16,000
        Investment in S Company   24,000
        (.4 × 40,000 = 16,000)

The rationale for the approach illustrated in Entry (1) is that all balances in the parent company's records and reports relating to the sale of goods to affiliates that have not been confirmed by sales to third parties are adjusted to eliminate the effects of such sales.

Entry (2) is the approach generally followed in practice. Supporters of this approach maintain that it (1) gives appropriate recognition to the parent company's separate activities in that all sales of the parent company are included in the income statement with appropriate disclosure of the amount and terms of sales to nonconsolidated subsidiaries and other related parties, and (2) has the practical advantage of adjusting the same accounts on the parent company's books regardless of whether the intercompany sale is upstream or downstream.

Entry (3) is supported by those who, in the case of downstream sales, object to the reduction of the parent company's equity in subsidiary income by an amount that was recorded as gross profit on the parent company's (rather than on the subsidiary company's) books. Advocates of Entry (2) counter that, since the necessity for the elimination of the unrealized gross profit arises only because of the parent/subsidiary relationship, it is entirely proper to reflect the net effect of the subsidiary company's activities on the parent company's income by reducing the parent company's reported equity in subsidiary income for unrealized intercompany profit in the ending inventory of the subsidiary company.

Note that all three approaches have the effect of reducing the parent company's net income for the full amount of the unrealized intercompany profit net of tax ($24,000). We consider each of the three approaches illustrated to be acceptable. In all subsequent illustrations, however, it is assumed that the approach illustrated in (2) is followed and that the parent company makes all intercompany profit adjustments directly to the equity in subsidiary income and investment accounts.

Entries on the Parent Company's Books in 1981 (Equity Method)

	UPSTREAM SALE		DOWNSTREAM SALE	
(1) Investment in S Company	225,000		225,000	
Equity in Subsidiary Income		225,000		225,000

       To record P Company's share of the reported net income of S Company (.75 × 300,000 = 225,000).

	UPSTREAM SALE		DOWNSTREAM SALE	
(2) Investment in S Company	18,000		24,000	
Equity in Subsidiary Income		18,000		24,000

       To record intercompany profit net of tax in beginning inventory realized during 1981 (.75 × [.6 × 40,000] = 18,000; 1.0 × [.6 × 40,000] = 24,000).

It is assumed in formulating this entry that all of the beginning inventory is sold during the current year. Since unrealized intercompany profit in ending inventory will be determined and eliminated in Entry (3) below, however, any profit recognized in this entry on merchandise in the beginning inventory that is not actually sold during the year will be removed in Entry (3). Thus, as a matter of procedure, there is no need to be concerned in formulating this entry as to whether or not all of the beginning inventory has actually been sold.

	UPSTREAM SALE	DOWNSTREAM SALE
(3) Equity in Subsidiary Income	27,000	36,000
Investment in S Company	27,000	36,000

      To eliminate unrealized intercompany profit net of tax in ending inventory (.75 $\times$ [.6 $\times$ 60,000] = 27,000; 1.0 $\times$ [.6 $\times$ 60,000] = 36,000).

Less than 50%-Owned Investees Reported at Equity

Similar adjustments to the amount of investee income recognized by the investor because of unrealized intercompany profit must be made for investments in less than 50%-owned investees appropriately accounted for using the equity method. In the case of less than 50%-owned investees, however, the percentage of unrealized intercompany profit to be eliminated under generally accepted accounting standards is clearly stated and *is the same regardless of whether the intercompany sale is an upstream or downstream sale.* In paragraph 5 of *Interpretation No. 1* of *Opinion No. 18,* the Accounting Principles Board concluded that in the case of noncontrolled investees

> . . . it would be appropriate for the investor to eliminate intercompany profit in relation to the investor's common stock interest in the investee. In these cases, *the percentage of intercompany profit to be eliminated would be the same regardless of whether the transaction is "downstream"* (i.e., a sale by the investor to the investee) *or "upstream"* (i.e., a sale by the investee to the investor) [emphasis added].[3]

To illustrate, assume that Investor Company owns 30% of the voting stock of Investee Company and accounts for its investment using the equity method. Investee Company reports net income of $500,000 in 1980. Unrealized intercompany profit in beginning and ending inventories resulting from intercompany sales of merchandise amount to $80,000 and $100,000, respectively. The income tax rate on the taxable income of both companies averages 40%.

Regardless of whether the sale of merchandise was upstream or downstream, the entries on Investor Company's books to record its equity in the income of Investor Company during 1980 are as follows:

---

[3]It has also been argued that in the case of less than 50%-owned investees, *no* unrealized intercompany profit should be eliminated from the amount of investee income reported by the investor unless the intercompany transaction did not result from arms-length bargaining, in which case *all* of it should be eliminated. See King and Lembke, "Reporting Investor Income Under the Equity Method," cited above.

(1) Investment in Investee Company   150,000

      Equity in Investee Income   150,000

          To record Investor Company's share of the net income reported by Investee Company ($.3 \times 500,000 = 150,000$).

(2) Investment in Investee Company   14,400

      Equity in Investee Income   14,400

          To record intercompany profit net of tax in beginning inventory realized during 1980 ($.3 \times [.6 \times 80,000] = 14,400$).

(3) Equity in Investee Income   18,000

      Investment in Investee Company   18,000

          To eliminate unrealized intercompany profit net of tax in ending inventory ($.3 \times [.6 \times 100,000] = 18,000$).

Notice that even if the sale is downstream, in which case Investor Company will have recognized the entire profit net of tax of $60,000 residing in the ending inventory, only 30% of that profit is considered to be unrealized ($.3 \times 60,000 = 18,000$) and subject to elimination from reported income.

CONSOLIDATING WORKPAPER—INVESTMENT RECORDED AT EQUITY

When the investment in a subsidiary is recorded at equity in the books of the parent company, unrealized intercompany profit has already been eliminated from the parent company's recorded net income and retained earnings and from the investment account. In addition, since the retained earnings of the parent company are equal to consolidated retained earnings, as a matter of workpaper procedure, no adjustments to the parent company's beginning retained earnings are necessary to arrive at beginning consolidated retained earnings. Because of these factors, the only procedural change in the workpaper entries relating to the elimination of intercompany profits is that adjustments that are debited or credited to beginning retained earnings of the parent company in *cost-basis* consolidating workpapers are debited or credited to the investment account balance in *equity-basis* workpapers.

Comprehensive Illustration: Less Than Wholly Owned Subsidiary (Investment Recorded at Equity)

Assume that P Company acquires an 80% interest in S Company for $1,360,000 on December 31, 1979, when the retained earnings and capital stock of S Company are $700,000 and $1,000,000, respectively. The reported net income of S Company is $125,000 in 1980 and $140,000 in 1981. S Company pays dividends of $20,000 in 1980 and $60,000 in 1981. The average income tax rate for both companies is 40%, separate income tax returns are filed, and S Company sells merchandise to P Company as follows:

YEAR	TOTAL SALES OF S COMPANY TO P COMPANY	INTERCOMPANY MERCHANDISE IN 12/31 INVENTORY OF P COMPANY	UNREALIZED INTERCOMPANY PROFIT (25% OF SELLING PRICE)
1980	700,000	400,000	100,000
1981	1,000,000	500,000	125,000

P Company uses the equity method to account for its investment in S Company. Entries to record subsidiary income *on the books* of P Company under the equity method, as well as *workpaper entries* necessary in the consolidating workpapers for the years ending December 31, 1980 and December 31, 1981, are summarized in general journal form below.

Entries on the Books of P Company—1980

(1) Investment in S Company   100,000

     Equity in Subsidiary Income   100,000

         To record P Company's share of the reported net income of S Company (.8 × 125,000 = 100,000).

(2) Cash   16,000

     Investment in S Company   16,000

         To record receipt of dividends from S Company.

(3) Equity in Subsidiary income   48,000

     Investment in S Company   48,000

         To eliminate P Company's share of unrealized intercompany profit net of tax in ending inventory (.8 × [.6 × 100,000] = 48,000).

Consolidating Workpaper Entries—December 31, 1980

(1) Sales   700,000

     Purchases   700,000

         To eliminate intercompany sales.

(2) 12/31 Inventory-Income Statement (Cost of Sales)   100,000

     Inventory   100,000

         To eliminate unrealized intercompany profit in ending inventory.

(3) Deferred Income Tax   40,000

     Income Tax Expense   40,000

         To defer recognition of taxes paid on unrealized intercompany profit (.4 × 100,000 = 40,000).

(4) Equity in Subsidiary Income   52,000
   Investment in S Company   36,000
   Dividends Declared   16,000
    To adjust the investment account to the beginning-of-year balance and to eliminate equity
    in subsidiary income (100,000 − 48,000 = 52,000).

(5) Beginning Retained Earnings—S Company   560,000
  Capital Stock—S Company   800,000
   Investment in S Company   1,360,000
    To eliminate the investment account.

  Entries (1), (2), and (3) are identical to corresponding cost-basis eliminating entries (see Illustration 6–4). Since the selling affiliate is a partially owned subsidiary, the calculation of minority interest in combined income is modified by subtracting unrealized intercompany profit net of tax from reported subsidiary net income as follows:

$$.2 \times (125{,}000 - [.6 \times 100{,}000]) = 13{,}000$$

Entries on the Books of P Company—1981

(1) Investment in S Company   112,000
   Equity in Subsidiary Income   112,000
    To record P Company's share of the reported net income of S Company (.8 ×
    140,000 = 112,000).

(2) Cash   48,000
   Investment in S Company   48,000
    To record the receipt of dividends from S Company (.8 × 60,000 = 48,000).

(3) Investment in S Company   48,000
   Equity in Subsidiary Income   48,000
    To record intercompany profit net of tax in beginning inventory realized during 1981
    (.8 × [.6 × 100,000] = 48,000).

(4) Equity in Subsidiary Income   60,000
   Investment in S Company   60,000
    To eliminate P Company's share of unrealized intercompany profit net of tax in ending
    inventory (.8 × [.6 × 125,000]).

Consolidating Workpaper Entries—December 31, 1981 (Illustration 6–6)

(1) Sales   1,000,000
      Purchases (Cost of Sales)   1,000,000
         To eliminate intercompany sales.

(2) 12/31 Inventory—Income Statement (Cost of Sales)   125,000
      Inventory   125,000
         To eliminate unrealized intercompany profit in ending inventory.

(3) Deferred Income Tax   50,000
      Income Tax Expense   50,000
         To defer recognition of income tax paid on unrealized intercompany profit (.4 ×
         125,000 = 50,000).

(4) Beginning Retained Earnings—S Company   20,000
      Investment in S Company   80,000
         1/1 Inventory—Income Statement (Cost of Sales)   100,000
            To recognize intercompany profit realized during the year and to reduce minority interest
            at the beginning of the year for its share of unrealized intercompany profit at the beginning
            of the year.

(5) Income Tax Expense   40,000
      Beginning Retained Earnings—S Company   8,000
      Investment in S Company   32,000
         To recognize income tax effects on intercompany profit in beginning inventories.

Recall that adjustments to minority interest in net assets at the beginning of the year
are accomplished as a matter of workpaper procedure by debiting (decrease minority
interest) or crediting (increase minority interest) the beginning retained earnings row
of the subsidiary. Note that the only difference between Entries (4) and (5) and the
corresponding cost-basis eliminating entries (see Illustration 6–5) is that in these
entries the majority's share of unrealized profit net of tax ($48,000) is debited (80,000)
and credited (32,000) to the investment balance rather than to the beginning retained
earnings of P Company.

(6) Equity in Subsidiary Income   100,000
      Investment in S Company   52,000
      Dividends Declared   48,000
         To adjust the investment account to the beginning-of-year balance and to eliminate equity
         in subsidiary income (112,000 + 48,000 − 60,000 = 100,000).

(7) Beginning Retained Earnings—S Company   644,000
      Capital Stock—S Company   800,000
      Investment in S Company   1,444,000
         To eliminate the investment account.

Entries (1), (2), and (3) are identical to corresponding cost-basis eliminating entries (see Illustration 6–5). Minority interest in combined income is calculated after subtracting end-of-year unrealized intercompany profit net of tax and adding intercompany profit net of tax realized during the current year to the net income reported by the subsidiary ($.2 \times [140,000 - 75,000 + 60,000] = 25,000$).

The consolidated financial statement workpaper for the year ending December 31, 1981 is presented in Illustration 6–6. A comparison of the consolidated balances in that illustration with those in Illustration 6–5 will confirm that the consolidated balances are not affected by the method of accounting (cost or equity) used by P Company to record its investment in S Company.

CONSOLIDATIONS ACCOUNTED FOR AS A POOLING OF INTERESTS

The practice of recognizing in the consolidated financial statements only profits resulting from the sale of goods and services to parties outside the affiliated group is the same under both pooling of interests and purchase accounting. Accordingly, workpaper entries for the elimination of unrealized profit on intercompany sales of merchandise are the same whether the consolidation is accounted for as a purchase or as a pooling of interests. Since a parent company ordinarily records its interest in a subsidiary that qualifies for pooling of interests accounting by use of the equity method, intercompany profit workpaper eliminations similar to those presented in the section on *Consolidating Workpaper—Investment Recorded at Equity* are ordinarily applicable to pooled subsidiaries. If, for some reason, the parent company maintains its investment in the subsidiary at an amount equal to the book value on the date its interest was acquired, intercompany profit workpaper eliminations similar to those presented in the section on *Consolidating Workpaper—Investment Recorded at Cost* would be appropriate.

SUMMARY OF WORKPAPER ELIMINATING ENTRIES

Consolidated financial statement workpaper entries to eliminate unrealized profit on intercompany sales of merchandise depend upon whether

1. The selling affiliate is wholly owned or less than wholly owned.

2. The investment in a subsidiary is recorded by the parent company using the cost method or the equity method of accounting.

3. The affiliates file separate income tax returns or a consolidated income tax return.

As previously explained, the form of the workpaper elimination entries for intercompany profit are the same whether the consolidation is accounted for as a pooling of interest or as a purchase.

Workpaper elimination entries for the various alternatives presented above are summarized in Illustration 6–7.

ILLUSTRATION 6-6
Consolidated Statements Workpaper
P Company and Subsidiary
For Year Ending December 31, 1981

INCOME STATEMENT	P COMPANY	S COMPANY	ELIMINATIONS DR.	ELIMINATIONS CR.	MINORITY INTEREST	CONSOLIDATED BALANCES
Sales	3,546,000	2,020,000	[1] 1,000,000			4,566,000
Equity in Subsidiary Income	100,000		[6] 100,000			
Total Revenue	3,646,000	2,020,000				4,566,000
Inventory 1/1/81	480,000	310,000		[4] 100,000		690,000
Purchases	2,070,000	1,250,000		[1] 1,000,000		2,320,000
	2,550,000	1,560,000				3,010,000
Inventory 12/31/81	510,000	360,000	[2] 125,000			745,000
Cost of Goods Sold	2,040,000	1,200,000				2,265,000
Other Expense	798,000	587,000				1,385,000
Income Tax Expense	302,000	93,000	[5] 40,000	[3] 50,000		385,000
Total Cost and Expense	3,140,000	1,880,000				4,035,000
Net	506,000	140,000				531,000
Minority Interest					25,000	(25,000*)
Net Income to Retained Earnings	506,000	140,000	1,265,000	1,150,000	25,000	506,000
RETAINED EARNINGS STATEMENT						
1/1/81 Retained Earnings						
P Company	1,832,000					1,832,000
S Company		805,000	[7] 644,000			
			[4] 20,000	[5] 8,000	149,000	
Net Income from above	506,000	140,000	1,265,000	1,150,000	25,000	506,000
Dividends Declared						
P Company	(150,000)					(150,000)
S Company		(60,000)		[6] 48,000	(12,000)	
12/31/81 Retained Earnings to						
Balance Sheet	2,188,000	885,000	1,929,000	1,206,000	162,000	2,188,000
BALANCE SHEET						
Inventory	510,000	360,000		[2] 125,000		745,000
Investment in S Company	1,448,000		[4] 80,000	[5] 32,000		
				[7] 1,444,000		
				[6] 52,000		
Other Assets	5,450,000	2,330,000				7,780,000
Deferred Income Tax			[3] 50,000			50,000
Total	7,408,000	2,690,000				8,575,000
Liabilities	2,220,000	805,000				3,025,000
Capital Stock						
P Company	3,000,000					3,000,000
S Company		1,000,000	[7] 800,000		200,000	
Retained Earnings from above	2,188,000	885,000	1,929,000	1,206,000	162,000	2,188,000
Minority Interest					362,000	362,000
Total Liabilities & Equity	7,408,000	2,690,000	2,859,000	2,859,000		8,575,000

*.2 × (140,000 − [.6 × 125,000] + [.6 × 100,000]) = 25,000

¹To eliminate intercompany sales.

²To eliminate unrealized intercompany profit.

³To defer recognition of income tax paid on unrealized intercompany profit.

⁴To recognize intercompany profit realized during the year and to reduce minority interest at the beginning of the year for its share of unrealized intercompany profit at the beginning of the year.

⁵To recognize income tax effects on intercompany profit in beginning inventories.

⁶To adjust the investment account to the beginning-of-year balance and to eliminate equity in subsidiary income.

⁷To eliminate the investment account.

(handwritten: PURCHASE – POOLING NO DIFFERENCE)

ILLUSTRATION 6–7
Intercompany Profit—Inventories
Summary of Workpaper Elimination Entries

(handwritten: ALLOCATE IF UPSTREAM)

SELLING AFFILIATE IS PARENT OR WHOLLY OWNED SUBSIDIARY		SELLING AFFILIATE IS A LESS THAN WHOLLY OWNED SUBSIDIARY	
INVESTMENT IN SUBSIDIARY IS RECORDED AT		INVESTMENT IN SUBSIDIARY IS RECORDED AT	
BOOK VALUE (POOLING) OR COST (PURCHASE)	EQUITY (POOLING) OR EQUITY (PURCHASE)	BOOK VALUE (POOLING) OR COST (PURCHASE)	EQUITY (POOLING) OR EQUITY (PURCHASE)

Sales
  Cost of Sales   **SAME**   **SAME**   **SAME**

– To eliminate intercompany sales –

Cost of Sales
  Inventory (Balance Sheet)
                         SAME   **SAME**   **SAME**

– – – – – – – – – – – – – – – To eliminate intercompany profit in **ending inventory** – – – – – – – – – – – – – – – – – –

Beg. Ret. Earn.—P	Investment in S	Beg. Ret. Earn.—P	Investment in S
		Beg. Ret. Earn.—S	Beg. Ret. Earn.—S
Cost of Sales	Cost of Sales	Cost of Sales	Cost of Sales

| To recognize intercompany profit in **beginning inventory** realized during the current year and to adjust recorded balances for the amount of unrealized profit at the beginning of the year. | | To recognize intercompany profit in **beginning inventory** realized during the year, to adjust recorded balances for the parent's share of the unrealized profit at the beginning of the year and to adjust minority interest for its share of unrealized profit at the beginning of the year. | |

If the affiliates file separate income tax returns, additional workpaper eliminations will be necessary as follows

Deferred Inc. Tax
  Inc. Tax Expense   **SAME**   **SAME**   **SAME**

To defer recognition of income tax paid on unrealized intercompany profit in **ending inventory.**

Inc. Tax Expense	Inc. Tax Expense	Inc. Tax Expense	Inc. Tax Expense
Beg. Ret. Earn.—P	Investment in S	Beg. Ret. Earn.—P	Investment in S
		Beg. Ret. Earn.—S	Beg. Ret. Earn.—S

| To recognize income tax expense on intercompany profit in **beginning inventory** considered to be realized during the current year and to adjust recorded balances for the income tax effect on the unrealized profit at the beginning of the year. | | To recognize income tax expense on intercompany profit in **beginning inventory** considered to be realized during the year, to adjust recorded balances for the parent's share of the income tax effect on the unrealized profit at the beginning of the year, and to adjust minority interest for its share of the income tax effect on unrealized profit at the beginning of the year. | |

APPENDIX—COMPARISON OF 100% AND PARTIAL ELIMINATION

Under 100% elimination, the entire amount of unrealized intercompany profit is eliminated from combined income and the related asset balance. Under partial elimination, only the parent company's share of the unrealized intercompany profit recognized by the *selling affiliate* is eliminated.

A careful reading of these two positions will help the reader understand that in the case of all downstream sales and in the case of upstream or horizontal sales where *the selling affiliate is a wholly owned subsidiary,* there is no difference in the amount of intercompany profit eliminated as between the 100% elimination and partial elimination methods. In those cases, 100% of the intercompany profit will be eliminated even where the partial elimination method is used, since the parent company's interest in the profits of the *selling affiliate* (itself or its wholly owned subsidiary) is 100%.

The two approaches will give different results, however, in the case of upstream or horizontal sales *where the selling affiliate is a less than wholly owned subsidiary.* To illustrate, assume that (1) P Company acquires a 60% interest in S Company on January 1, 1980 for $1,020,000; (2) intercompany sales from S Company to P Company amount to $1,000,000, on which S Company recognizes a gross profit of $300,000 or 30%; (3) on December 31, 1980, P Company has on hand goods it purchased from S Company for $500,000; (4) the companies file a consolidated income tax return and (5) P Company accounts for its investment in S Company at cost. Consolidated financial statement workpapers prepared using 100% elimination and partial elimination are presented in Illustration 6–8 and Illustration 6–9, respectively. The workpaper entries to eliminate intercompany sales and unrealized intercompany profit in those illustrations are summarized below:

	100% ELIMINATION		PARTIAL ELIMINATION	
Sales	1,000,000		1,000,000	
Cost of Sales		1,000,000		1,000,000
To eliminate intercompany sales.				

Intercompany sales amount to $1,000,000 and are always eliminated in their entirety under either method.

	100% ELIMINATION		PARTIAL ELIMINATION	
Cost of Sales	150,000		90,000	
Inventory		150,000		90,000
To eliminate unrealized intercompany profit in ending inventory.				

Intercompany profit on goods held by P Company on December 31 amount to $150,000 (500,000 × .30). Using the 100% elimination method, this entire amount is eliminated, whereas only the parent company's interest in the profit of the selling company (.60 × 150,000 = 90,000) is eliminated using the partial elimination method.

Purchase Accounting
Cost Method
60%-Owned Subsidiary
100% Elimination

ILLUSTRATION 6–8
Consolidated Statement Workpaper
P Company and Subsidiary
For Year Ending December 31, 1980

(000 OMITTED)

	P COMPANY	S COMPANY	ELIMINATIONS DR.	ELIMINATIONS CR.	MINORITY INTEREST	CONSOLIDATED BALANCES
INCOME STATEMENT						
Sales	3,400	2,000	²1,000			4,400
Cost of Goods Sold	2,380	1,400	³ 150	²1,000		2,930
Gross Profit	1,020	600				1,470
Other Expense	670	400				1,070
Net	350	200				400
Minority Interest .4(200 − 150)					20	(20)
Net Income to Retained Earnings	350	200	1,150	1,000	20	380
RETAINED EARNINGS STATEMENT						
1/1/80 Retained Earnings						
P Company	1,750					1,750
S Company		700	¹ 420		280	
Net Income from above	350	200	1,150	1,000	20	380
12/31/80 Retained Earnings to						
Balance Sheet	2,100	900	1,570	1,000	300	2,130
BALANCE SHEET						
Inventory	510	360		³ 150		720
Investment in S Company	1,020			¹1,020		
Other Assets	5,790	2,330				8,120
Total Assets	7,320	2,690				8,840
Liabilities	2,220	790				3,010
Capital Stock						
P Company	3,000					3,000
S Company		1,000	¹ 600		400	
Retained Earnings from above	2,100	900	1,570	1,000	300	2,130
Minority Interest					700	700
Total Liabilities & Equity	7,320	2,690	2,170	2,170		8,840

¹To eliminate investment account.
²To eliminate intercompany sales.
³To eliminate P Company's interest in unrealized intercompany profits in ending inventory.

Purchase Accounting
Cost Method
60%-Owned Subsidiary
Partial Elimination

ILLUSTRATION 6–9
Consolidated Statement Workpaper
P Company and Subsidiary
For Year Ending December 31, 1980

	P COMPANY	S COMPANY	ELIMINATIONS DR.	ELIMINATIONS CR.	MINORITY INTEREST	CONSOLIDATED BALANCES
INCOME STATEMENT				(000 OMITTED)		
Sales	3,400	2,000	² 1,000			4,400
Cost of Goods Sold	2,380	1,400	³ 90	² 1,000		2,870
Gross Profit	1,020	600				1,530
Other Expense	670	400				1,070
Net	350	200				460
Minority Interest .4(200)					80	(80)
Net Income to Retained Earnings	350	200	1,090	1,000	80	380
RETAINED EARNINGS STATEMENT						
1/1/80 Retained Earnings						
P Company	1,750					1,750
S Company		700	¹ 420		280	
Net Income from above	350	200	1,090	1,000	80	380
12/31/80 Retained Earnings to						
Balance Sheet	2,100	900	1,510	1,000	360	2,130
BALANCE SHEET						
Inventory	510	360		³ 90		780
Investment in S Company	1,020			¹ 1,020		
Other Assets	5,790	2,330				8,120
Total Assets	7,320	2,690				8,900
Liabilities	2,220	790				3,010
Capital Stock						
P Company	3,000					3,000
S Company		1,000	¹ 600		400	
Retained Earnings from above	2,100	900	1,510	1,000	360	2,130
Minority Interest					760	760
Total Liabilities & Equity	7,320	2,690	2,110	2,110		8,900

¹To eliminate investment account.
²To eliminate intercompany sales.
³To eliminate unrealized intercompany profits in ending inventory.

    The amount of minority interest in combined income to be deducted in arriving at consolidated net income is calculated as follows:

	100% ELIMINATION		PARTIAL ELIMINATION	
Minority interest in reported profit of S Company (.4 × 200,000)		80,000		80,000
Less minority interest in intercompany profit eliminated from combined income:				
Profit eliminated	150,000		90,000	
Parent company's share thereof	90,000		90,000	
Minority interest's share thereof	60,000	60,000	–0–	–0–
Minority interest in combined income		20,000		80,000

An alternative approach to the calculation of minority interest is as follows:

100% Elimination, .40 × (200,000 − 150,000) = 20,000
Partial Elimination, .40 × 200,000 = 80,000

When combined income has been reduced by the total amount of the intercompany profit recognized by the subsidiary, the minority interest therein is also reduced. However, when combined income is reduced by only the parent company's share of the intercompany profit recorded by the subsidiary, no adjustment to minority interest in combined income is necessary.

A comparison of the consolidated balances that result from the use of the two methods is presented on the following page in Illustration 6–10.

The main point to note in this comparison is that the method used to eliminate unrealized intercompany profit does not affect the amount of reported consolidated net income ($380,000) or consolidated retained earnings ($2,130,000). In the consolidated income statement the difference of $60,000 in the amount of reported combined income is exactly offset by the amount of difference in the reported minority interest in combined income. In the consolidated balance sheet, the difference of $60,000 in reported inventory balances is exactly offset by the difference in the amount of reported minority interest in net assets.

When 100% elimination is used, inventory balances resulting from intercompany sales are stated at the cost of the inventory to the selling affiliate. When partial elimination is used, such balances are stated at the cost of the inventory to the selling affiliate plus an amount equal to the minority interest in the profit recognized by the selling affiliate on the intercompany sale of the inventory.

ILLUSTRATION 6–10
Comparison of the Effect of 100 Percent and Partial Elimination of Intercompany Profit on Consolidated Balances

	(000 OMITTED)		
	100%[a]	PARTIAL[b]	DIFFERENCE
Sales	4,400	4,400	–0–
Cost of Goods Sold	(2,930)	(2,870)	60
Other Expense	(1,070)	(1,070)	–0–
Combined Income	400	460	60
Minority Interest in Income	(20)	(80)	(60)
Consolidated Net Income	380	380	–0–
1/1/80 Retained Earnings	1,750	1,750	–0–
Consolidated Net Income	380	380	–0–
12/31/80 Retained Earnings	2,130	2,130	–0–
Inventory	720	780	60
Other Assets	8,120	8,120	–0–
Total Assets	8,840	8,900	60
Liabilities	3,010	3,010	–0–
Minority Interest	700	760	60
Capital Stock	3,000	3,000	–0–
Consolidated Retained Earnings	2,130	2,130	–0–
Total Liabilities & Equity	8,840	8,900	60

[a]Source: Illustration 6–8.
[b]Source: Illustration 6–9.

Questions

1. Does the elimination of the effects of intercompany sales of merchandise always affect the amount of reported consolidated net income? Explain.

2. Why is the gross profit on intercompany sales, rather than profit after deducting selling and administrative expenses, ordinarily eliminated from intercompany inventory balances?

3. P Company sells inventory costing $100,000 to its subsidiary, S Company, for $150,000. At the end of the current year, one-half of the goods remain in S Company's inventory. Applying the lower of cost or market rule, S Company writes down this inventory to $60,000. What amount of intercompany profit should be eliminated on the consolidated statements workpaper?

4. What arguments might be used to support partial elimination as opposed to 100% elimination of intercompany profit in the preparation of consolidated financial statements?

5. What are the effects on the consolidated balance sheet if the partial elimination method rather than the 100% elimination method is used in the preparation of consolidated financial statements? Be specific.

6. B Company is a 75%-owned subsidiary of A Company. B sells goods to A at an average markup of 25% over cost. A's beginning inventory includes $500,000 of merchandise purchased from B, and its ending inventory includes $750,000 of merchandise purchased from B. A uses the FIFO cost flow assumption. In the preparation of the consolidated statements workpaper, what amount of the unrealized intercompany profit will be eliminated from B Company's beginning retained earnings, and what amount will be eliminated from A Company's ending inventory? Explain why the reduction of the beginning retained earnings of B Company is necessary.

7. Are the adjustments to minority interest for the effects of intercompany profit eliminations illustrated in this text necessary for fair presentation in accordance with generally accepted accounting principles? Explain.

8. Why are adjustments made to the calculation of minority interest for the effects of intercompany profit eliminations and not for the amortization, depreciation, and allocation of the difference between cost and book value?

9. What procedure is used in the consolidated statements workpaper to adjust minority interest in consolidated net assets at the beginning of the year for the effects of intercompany profits?

10. What is the essential procedural difference betwen cost-basis workpaper eliminating entries for unrealized intercompany profit and equity-basis workpaper eliminating entries?

11. At the end of 1980, a 75%-owned *nonconsolidated* subsidiary had on hand goods purchased from its parent for $100,000. The goods cost the parent company $60,000. The average income tax rate for the parent company is 40%. Illustrate three alternatives for adjusting the reported balances of the parent company for the effects of the unrealized intercompany profit. Which alternative do you prefer? Why?

12. What is the essential procedural difference between the workpaper eliminating entries for unrealized intercompany profit made when a consolidation is accounted for as a pooling of interest and those made when it is accounted for as a purchase?

13. What is the essential procedural difference in workpaper eliminating entires for unrealized intercompany profit made when the selling affiliate is a less than wholly owned subsidiary and those made when the selling affiliate is the parent company or a wholly owned subsidiary?

Problems

Problem 6–1

The existence of intercompany profits in consolidated inventories as a result of sales by a less than wholly owned subsidiary to its parent has given rise to the following three viewpoints as to how such profits should be treated when preparing consolidated financial statements:

1. Only the parent company's share of intercompany profits in inventory should be eliminated.

2. The entire amount of intercompany profits in inventories should be eliminated against the equities of the controlling and minority groups in proportion to their interests.

3. The entire amount of intercompany profits in inventories should be eliminated against consolidated retained earnings.

Required:
A. Give the arguments that are used to support each treatment.
B. Discuss the theoretical propriety or impropriety, as the case may be, of each treatment.

(AICPA adapted)

Problem 6–2

Major Company owns 75% of the common stock of Minor Company. Minor Company sells merchandise to Major Company at 30% above cost. During 1980 and 1981 such sales amounted to $390,000 and $546,000, respectively. At the end of each year, Major Company had in its inventory one-third of the amount of goods purchased from Minor Company during that year. Major Company reported $200,000 in net income from its independent operations in 1980 and in 1981. Minor Company reported net income of $120,000 in each year and did not declare any dividends in either year. Major Company accounts for its investment in Minor Company by use of the cost method. The affiliates file a <u>consolidated</u> income tax return. There were no intercompany sales prior to 1980.

Required:
A. Prepare in general journal form all entries necessary on the consolidated financial statement workpapers to eliminate the effects of the intercompany sales for each of the years 1980 and 1981.
B. Calculate the amount of minority interest to be deducted from combined income in the consolidated income statement for 1981.
C. Calculate consolidated net income for 1981.

Problem 6–3

Park Company owns 75% of the common stock of Swap Company. Park Company sells merchandise to Swap Company at 25% above its cost. During 1980 and 1981, such sales amounted to $375,000 and $625,000, respectively. The 1980 and 1981 ending inventories of Swap Company included goods purchased from Park Company for $150,000 and $250,000, respectively. Park Company reported $400,000 in net income from its independent operations in 1980 and $450,000 in 1981. Swap Company reported net income of $250,000 in 1980 and $300,000 in 1981 and did not declare dividends in either year. Park Company records its investment in Swap Company at cost. The income tax rate on the taxable income of each company averages 35 percent and the affiliates file separate income tax returns. There were no intercompany sales prior to 1980.

Required:

A. Prepare in general journal form all entries necessary on the consolidated financial statement workpapers to eliminate the effects of the intercompany sales for each of the years 1980 and 1981.

B. Calculate the amounts of minority interest to be deducted from combined income in the consolidated income statements for 1980 and 1981.

C. Calculate consolidated net income for 1981.

Problem 6–4

Probe Company owns all of the outstanding common stock of Space Company and 80% of the outstanding common stock of Stellar Company. The amount of intercompany profit included in the inventories of Probe Company on December 31, 1980 and December 31, 1981 is indicated below.

	INTERCOMPANY PROFIT ON		
	GOODS PURCHASED FROM		
	SPACE COMPANY	STELLAR COMPANY	TOTAL
Inventory—12/31/80	3,800	4,600	8,400
Inventory—12/31/81	4,800	2,300	7,100

The three companies reported net income from their independent operations for the year ending December 31, 1981 as follows:

Probe Company	280,000
Space Company	172,000
Stellar Company	120,000

Required:

A. Assume that the companies file a consolidated income tax return. Calculate consolidated net income for the year ending December 31, 1981.

B. Assume that the average combined federal and state income tax rate for each company is 40% and that the companies file separate income tax returns. Calculate consolidated net income for the year ending December 31, 1981.

Problem 6–5

P Company owns 90% of the outstanding stock of S Company and records its investment using the cost method. During 1980, S Company reported net income of $300,000. At the end of the year, S Company's inventory included $225,000 in unrealized profit on purchases from P Company of $800,000. The affiliates file separate income tax returns and both companies pay an average income tax rate of 40%. S Company uses the FIFO cost flow assumption for its inventories.

Required:

A. Prepare in general journal form all consolidated financial statement workpaper entries necessary at the end of 1980 and 1981 to eliminate the effects of the 1980 intercompany sales.

B. Calculate the amount of minority interest to be deducted from combined income in arriving at 1980 consolidated net income.

C. Assume that S Company uses a LIFO cost flow assumption rather than FIFO, and that one-half of the unrealized intercompany profit in the December 31, 1980 inventories was not realized in 1981. Prepare in general journal form the workpaper entries necessary at the end of 1980 and 1981 to eliminate the effects of the 1980 intercompany sales.

Problem 6-6

Union Corporation owns 90% of the common stock of Carter Company. The stock was purchased for $540,000 on January 1, 1976, when Carter Company's retained earnings were $100,000. Preclosing trial balances for the two companies at December 31, 1980, are presented below:

	UNION CORP.	CARTER CO.
Cash	$ 80,000	$ 50,000
Accounts Receivable (net)	213,000	112,500
Inventory—1/1	150,000	110,000
Investment in Carter Co.	540,000	
Other Assets	500,000	400,000
Dividends Declared	100,000	60,000
Purchases	850,000	350,000
Other Expenses	120,000	90,000
Income Tax Expense	87,000	47,500
	$2,640,000	$1,220,000
Accounts Payable	70,000	30,000
Other Liabilities	75,000	40,000
Common Stock	800,000	500,000
Retained Earnings	541,000	120,000
Sales	1,100,000	530,000
Dividend Income	54,000	
	$2,640,000	$1,220,000
Inventory—12/31	$ 140,000	$ 115,000

The January 1, 1980 inventory of Union Corporation includes $30,000 of profit recorded by Carter Company on 1979 sales. During 1980, Carter Company made intercompany sales of $200,000 with a markup of 25% on cost. The ending inventory of Union Corporation includes goods purchased in 1980 from Carter Company for $50,000.

The affiliates file separate tax returns, and the average income tax rate for both companies is 50%. Carter Company uses the FIFO cost flow assumption.

Required:
A. Prepare the entries recorded on the books of Union Corporation during 1980 relating to its interest in Carter Company.
B. Prepare consolidating workpapers for the year ended December 31, 1980.
C. Calculate consolidated net income using the analytical approach and compare your answer to the consolidated net income arrived at on the workpapers.

Problem 6-7

Assume the same information as that presented in Problem 6-6 except that the affiliates filed a consolidated income tax return rather than separate returns.

Required:

A. Prepare the entries recorded on the books of Union Corporation during 1980 relating to its interest in Carter Company.

B. Prepare consolidating workpapers for the year ended December 31, 1980.

C. Calculate consolidated net income using the analytical approach and compare your answer to the consolidated net income arrived at on the workpapers.

Problem 6–8

Several years ago, Calculator Company acquired a 60% interest in Techtronics, Inc. at book value. Techtronics has remained a nonconsolidated subsidiary since the acquisition and is accounted for under the equity method. During 1980 and 1981, intercompany sales of merchandise amounted to $120,000 and $180,000. On December 31, 1980 and December 31, 1981, unrealized profit on intercompany sales of merchandise remained in inventory as a result of one-third of each year's intercompany sales remaining in that year's ending inventory. Intercompany sales were made at the same rate of gross margin as sales to nonaffiliates. January 1, 1980 inventories contained no unrealized intercompany profits.

The following data are taken from the financial statements of the two companies for 1980 and 1981:

	CALCULATOR COMPANY		TECHTRONICS, INC.	
	1980	1981	1980	1981
Sales	$1,500,000	$2,200,000	$900,000	$1,200,000
Cost of Sales	1,000,000	1,540,000	540,000	780,000
Expenses[a]	300,000	360,000	160,000	170,000

[a]Not including income tax expense.

The average income tax rate for both companies is 45%, and separate income tax returns are filed.

Required:

Prepare the journal entries recorded by Calculator Company in 1980 and 1981:

(a) Assuming that the intercompany sales were upstream.

(b) Assuming that the intercompany sales were downstream.

Problem 6–9

Fritzemeyer Company owns 30% of the voting stock of Barnett Company. Barnett Company reported net income of $200,000 in 1980 and $250,000 in 1981. Fritzemeyer Company's ending inventories included $60,000 in 1980 and $40,000 in 1981 of unrealized intercompany profit on merchandise it had purchased from Barnett Company. The average income tax rate for both companies is 40%. There were no intercompany sales prior to 1980.

Required:

A. Prepare in general journal form the entries to be recorded by Fritzemeyer Company to recognize its equity in the net income of Barnett Company for the years ending December 31, 1980 and December 31, 1981.

B. Assume that the intercompany sales of merchandise were downstream rather than upstream. Prepare in general journal form the entries to be recorded by Fritzemeyer Company to recognize its equity in the net income of Barnett Company for the years ending December 31, 1980 and December 31, 1981.

Problem 6–10

Crane Company owns 40% of the voting stock of Wiley Company. The investment in Wiley Company was made at the beginning of 1976 and is accounted for by use of the equity method. On the date the investment was made, the cost of the investment exceeded the book value of the equity interest acquired by $160,000. Crane Company is amortizing this difference over 20 years, the average remaining life of the property and equipment of Wiley Company on January 1, 1976.

    The January 1, 1980 inventory of Crane Company included merchandise in the amount of $400,000 which cost Wiley Company $320,000. During 1980, Crane Company purchased merchandise from Wiley Company in the amount of $800,000. The December 31, 1980 inventory of Crane Company includes merchandise in the amount of $500,000 that cost Wiley Company $375,000. Wiley Company reported net income of $250,000 in 1980. The average income tax rate for both companies is 40%.

Required:

A. Prepare in general journal form the entries to be recorded by Crane Company to recognize its equity in the net income of Wiley Company for the year ending December 31, 1980.
B. Assume that the intercompany sale of merchandise was downstream rather than upstream. Prepare in general journal form the entries to be recorded by Crane Company to recognize its equity in the net income of Wiley Company for the year ending December 31, 1980.

Problem 6–11

Union Corporation owns 90% of the common stock of Carter Company. The stock was purchased for $540,000 on January 1, 1976, when Carter Company's retained earnings were $100,000. This investment is accounted for under the equity method. Preclosing trial balances for the two companies at December 31, 1980, are presented below:

	UNION CORP.	CARTER CO.
Cash	$ 80,000	$ 50,000
Accounts Receivable (net)	213,000	112,500
Inventory—1/1	150,000	110,000
Investment in Carter Co.	542,250	
Other Assets	500,000	400,000
Dividends Declared	100,000	60,000
Purchases	850,000	350,000
Other Expenses	120,000	90,000
Income Tax Expense	87,000	47,500
	$2,642,250	$1,220,000
Accounts Payable	$ 70,000	$ 30,000
Other Liabilities	75,000	40,000
Common Stock	800,000	500,000
Retained Earnings	545,500	120,000
Sales	1,100,000	530,000
Equity in Subsidiary Earnings	51,750	
	$2,642,250	$1,220,000
Inventory—12/31	$ 140,000	$ 115,000

The January 1, 1980 inventory of Union Corporation includes $30,000 of profit recorded by Carter Company on 1979 sales. During 1980, Carter Company made intercompany sales of $200,000 with a markup of 25% on cost. The ending inventory of Union Corporation includes goods purchased in 1980 from Carter Company for $50,000.

The affiliates file separate tax returns, and the average income tax rate for both companies is 50%. Carter Company uses the FIFO cost flow assumption.

Required:
A. Prepare the entries made on the books of Union Corporation during 1980 to record its interest in Carter Company.
B. Prepare consolidating workpapers for the year ended December 31, 1980.
C. Compare the consolidated balances from Part B with the consolidated balances arrived at in Problem 6–6, Part B.

Problem 6–12
(Note: This problem is the same as Problem 6–11 except that in this problem it is assumed that the affiliates filed a consolidated income tax return.)

Union Corporation owns 90% of the common stock of Carter Company. The stock was purchased for $540,000 on January 1, 1976, when Carter Company's retained earnings were $100,000. This investment is accounted for under the equity method. Preclosing trial balances for the two companies at December 31, 1980, are presented below:

	UNION CORP.	CARTER CO.
Cash	$ 80,000	$ 50,000
Accounts Receivable (net)	213,000	112,500
Inventory—1/1	150,000	110,000
Investment in Carter Co.	537,750	
Other Assets	500,000	400,000
Dividends Declared	100,000	60,000
Purchases	850,000	350,000
Other Expenses	120,000	90,000
Income Tax Expense	87,000	47,500
	$2,637,750	$1,220,000
Accounts Payable	$ 70,000	$ 30,000
Other Liabilities	75,000	40,000
Common Stock	800,000	500,000
Retained Earnings	532,000	120,000
Sales	1,100,000	530,000
Equity in Subsidiary Earnings	60,750	
	$2,637,750	$1,220,000
Inventory—12/31	$ 140,000	$ 115,000

The January 1, 1980 inventory of Union Corporation includes $30,000 of profit recorded by Carter Company on 1979 sales. During 1980, Carter Company made intercompany sales of $200,000 with a markup of 25% on cost. The ending inventory of Union Corporation includes goods purchased in 1980 from Carter Company for $50,000.

The affiliates file a consolidated income tax return. Carter Company uses the FIFO cost flow assumption.

Required:

A. Prepare the entries made on the books of Union Corporation during 1980 to record its interest in Carter Company.

B. Prepare consolidating workpapers for the year ended December 31, 1980.

C. Compare the consolidated balances from Part B with the consolidated balances arrived at in Problem 6–7, Part B.

Problem 6–13

Alpha Company owns 70% of the outstanding common stock of Beta Company and all of the outstanding common stock of Cesta Company. During 1981 the affiliates engaged in intercompany sales as follows:

	SALES OF MERCHANDISE
Alpha to Beta	40,000
Beta to Alpha	60,000
Beta to Cesta	75,000
Cesta to Alpha	50,000
Total	225,000

The following amounts of intercompany profits were included in the December 31, 1980 and December 31, 1981 inventories of the individual companies:

	INTERCOMPANY PROFIT IN DECEMBER 31,1980 INVENTORY OF			
SELLING COMPANY	ALPHA	BETA	CESTA	TOTAL
Alpha Company		7,000		7,000
Beta Company	5,000		3,000	8,000
Cesta Company	8,000			8,000
Total	13,000	7,000	3,000	23,000

	INTERCOMPANY PROFIT IN DECEMBER 31,1981 INVENTORY OF			
SELLING COMPANY	ALPHA	BETA	CESTA	TOTAL
Alpha Company		2,000		2,000
Beta Company	6,000		9,000	15,000
Cesta Company	4,000			4,000
Total	10,000	2,000	9,000	21,000

The three companies reported net income from their independent operations for the year ending December 31, 1981 as follows:

Alpha Company	200,000
Beta Company	150,000
Cesta Company	125,000

The companies file separate income tax returns and are taxed at an average combined federal and state income tax rate of 40%.

Required:

A. Prepare in general journal form the workpaper entries necessary to eliminate intercompany sales and intercompany profit in the December 31, 1981 consolidated financial statement workpaper, assuming that
   (1) Alpha Company records its investments in Beta Company and Cesta Company using the cost method.
   (2) Alpha Company records its investments in Beta Company and Cesta Company using the equity method. Assume Alpha Company has adequate information as to sales between Beta Company and Cesta Company and the amounts of unrealized intercompany profit on December 31, 1980 and December 31, 1981 related thereto.
B. Calculate the balance to be reported in the consolidated income statement for the following line items:
   Combined income
   Minority interest in combined income
   Consolidated net income

Problem 6–14
Able Company, on January 1, 1980, issued 40,000 shares of its common stock for 90% (40,500 shares) of the outstanding common stock of Baker Company. All criteria for the use of the pooling of interests method were met. Trial balances for Able and Baker Companies on December 31, 1980 are as follows.

	ABLE COMPANY		BAKER COMPANY	
	DR.	CR.	DR.	CR.
Cash	$ 690,000		$ 110,000	
Inventory—1/1/80	469,000		301,000	
Other Current Assets	1,620,000		450,000	
Investment in Baker Co.	701,100			
Property & Equip. (net)	1,080,000		540,000	
Liabilities		$ 781,000		$ 549,000
Common Stock—$10 par		2,250,000		450,000
Premium on Common Stock		421,000		90,000
Retained Earnings—1/1/80		1,062,000		180,000
Dividends Declared	210,000		70,000	
Sales		2,450,000		1,330,000
Equity in Subsidiary Income		116,100		
Purchases	1,505,000		630,000	
Other Expenses	560,000		392,000	
Income Tax Expense	245,000		106,000	
	$7,080,100	$7,080,100	$2,599,000	$2,599,000
Inventory—12/31/80	$ 574,000		$ 273,000	

During 1980, Baker Company made intercompany sales of merchandise to Able Company of $500,000, and Able Company's December 31, 1980 inventory included $225,000 of these goods. Baker Company's markup on all sales is 50% of cost. The affiliates file separate tax returns and the average income tax rate for both companies is 40%. Able Company uses the FIFO cost flow assumption for inventories.

Required:

A. Reconstruct the entry to record the initial investment in Baker Company.

B. Reconstruct the entries recorded by Able Company during 1980 in respect to its investment in Baker Company.

C. Prepare a consolidated financial statements workpaper for 1980.

D. Prepare consolidated workpaper entries for 1981 with respect to the 1980 intercompany sales of merchandise.

Problem 6–15 (appendix)

On January 1, 1980, Nilo Company purchased 90% of the common stock of Call Company. At that time the retained earnings of Call Company were $240,000. Selected financial information for the affiliated companies on December 31, 1981 is presented below:

	DECEMBER 31, 1981	
	NILO CO.	CALL CO.
Sales	$752,000	$354,000
Purchases	400,000	208,000
Expenses	32,000	16,000
Inventory—January 1	144,000	64,000
Inventory—December 31	192,000	96,000
Retained Earnings—January 1	736,000	344,000
Dividends Declared	80,000	10,000
Dividend Income	9,000	–0–

During 1981, Nilo Company purchased merchandise from Call Company for $160,000. Call Company sells merchandise to Nilo Company at cost plus 20% of cost. On December 31, 1981, merchanidse purchased from Call Company for $48,000 remains in the inventory of Nilo Company. On January 1, 1981, Nilo Company's inventory contained merchandise purchased from Call Company for $28,000. The affiliated companies file a consolidated income tax return. There was no difference between cost and book value and no excess of cost over fair value on the date of acquisition.

Required:

A. Prepare the income statement and retained earnings statement sections of the consolidated financial statement workpaper for the year ended December 31, 1981 under each of the following assumptions:

    (1) Intercompany profits are eliminated using the 100% elimination method.

    (2) Intercompany profits are eliminated using the partial elimination method.

B. Compare the balances obtained using each method in Part A above for

    (1) Combined income

    (2) Minority interest in combined income

    (3) Consolidated net income

    (4) Consolidated retained earnings—December 31, 1981

    (5) Consolidated inventories—December 31, 1981

C. Determine the amount by which the minority interest reported in the December 31, 1981 consolidated balance sheet under the partial elimination method will be different from the minority interest reported in the consolidated balance sheet using the 100% elimination method.

7

Elimination of Unrealized Profit on Intercompany Sales of Property and Equipment

A company may sell property or equipment to an affiliate for a price that differs from its book value to the selling affiliate. In the year of the sale, the amount of intercompany profit (loss) recognized by the selling affiliate must be eliminated in consolidation. In subsequent years the purchasing affiliate will calculate depreciation on the basis of *its* cost. The depreciation recorded by the purchasing affiliate will, therefore, be excessive (deficient) from a consolidated point of view and will also require adjustment. From the point of view of the consolidated entity, the intercompany profit (loss) is considered to be realized as a consequence of the utilization of the property or equipment in the generation of revenue. Because such utilization is measured by depreciation, the recognition of the realization of intercompany profit (loss) is accomplished through depreciation adjustments.

In this chapter entries that are necessary in consolidated financial statement workpapers when an investment in a subsidiary is recorded at cost are presented first. Next, the effect of the elimination of intercompany profit on the recording and reporting of an investment under the equity method of accounting is considered. Finally, consolidated financial statement workpaper entries that are necessary when an investment in a subsidiary is recorded at equity are described and illustrated. Reporting complications relating to accounting for the difference between acquisition cost and book value are avoided in all illustrations by assuming that all acquisitions are made at the book value of the acquired interest in net assets, and that the book value of the subsidiary net assets equals their fair value on the date the parent company's interest is acquired.

ULTIMATE DISPOSITION

DEFERRED TAXES

UPSTREAM + DOWNSTREAM

CONSOLIDATING WORKPAPER—INVESTMENT RECORDED AT COST

Assume that P Company acquires a 70% interest in S Company for $980,000 in 1978 when S Company had retained earnings and capital stock in the amounts of $400,000 and $1,000,000, respectively. On January 1, 1980, P Company sells S Company equipment with a book value of $500,000 (original cost of $800,000 and accumulated depreciation of $300,000) for $600,000. On January 1, 1980, the equipment has an estimated *remaining* useful life of five years and is depreciated using the straight-line method. The average income tax rate for both companies is 40%, and S Company files a separate income tax return. Workpaper entries in the December 31, 1980 and December 31, 1981 consolidating workpapers (cost method) necessitated by this intercompany sale of equipment are presented in general journal form below.

December 31, 1980 workpaper entries

[handwritten: → ELIMINATE]

(1) Gain on Sale of Equipment   100,000
     Property and Equipment   100,000
       To eliminate the unrealized profit recorded on the intercompany sale and to reduce the carrying value of the equipment to its depreciated cost (500,000) on the date of the sale.

[handwritten: TO HIGH]

[handwritten: 600,000 ÷ 5 = 120,000]
[handwritten: 500,000 ÷ 5 = 100,000 ; 20,000]

(2) Accumulated Depreciation   20,000
     Depreciation   20,000
       To reverse the amount of excess depreciation recorded during the current year and to recognize an equivalent amount of intercompany profit as realized.

The purchasing affiliate will record depreciation in the amount of $120,000 (600,000/5) each year. From the point of view of the consolidated entity, only $100,000 (500,000/5) in depreciation on the intercompany equipment should be recognized. The effect of this entry is to increase consolidated net income by $20,000 and thus to treat an equivalent amount of intercompany profit as realized.

[handwritten: PREPAID →]

(3) Deferred Income Tax   32,000
     Income Tax Expense   32,000
       To defer income tax on unrealized intercompany profit.

[handwritten: 1/1 ; 100,000 6. ; (20,000)]

Assuming that the affiliates file separate income tax returns, their taxable income will reflect the $100,000 gain and the $20,000 added depreciation eliminated in consolidation. Income tax accrued or paid by the affiliates on the net difference of $80,000 (100,000 − 20,000) must therefore be deferred (.4 × 80,000 = 32,000).

(4) Property and Equipment   300,000
     Accumulated Depreciation   300,000
       Optional entry to restate property and equipment at original cost to the selling affiliate.

As shown in Illustration 7–1, on December 31, 1980, after adjustment by workpaper entries (1) and (2) above, the consolidated balance is $500,000 for property and equipment and $100,000 for accumulated depreciation. If we desire to show these amounts in the consolidated financial statements as they would have appeared if the intercompany sale of equipment had never taken place, however, they must be increased by the amount of the difference between the original cost of the equipment to the selling affiliate and its depreciated cost on the date of the intercompany sale $(800,000 - 500,000 = 300,000)$. Because this nicety is largely ignored in practice, it is treated as an optional entry in this text.

December 31, 1981 workpaper entries

(1) Beginning Retained Earnings—P Company   80,000

     Accumulated Depreciation   20,000

         Property and Equipment   100,000

[handwritten: GAIN NOW IN RETAINED EARNINGS — ALL FROM LAST YEAR]

         To reduce beginning retained earnings by the amount of unrealized intercompany profit on January 1, 1981, to reduce accumulated depreciation by the amount of excess depreciation accumulated at the beginning of the year, and to reduce the carrying value of the equipment to its depreciated cost on the date of the intercompany sale.

In this entry, reported retained earnings are reduced by the gross effect of prior-year workpaper reductions of consolidated income $(100,000 - 20,000 = 80,000)$. Further adjustment to beginning retained earnings for the tax effect on these amounts is accomplished in Entry (3) below.

(2) Accumulated Depreciation   20,000

     Depreciation   20,000

         To reverse the amount of excess depreciation recorded during the current year and to recognize an equivalent amount of intercompany profit as realized.

[handwritten: REDUCED EACH YEAR NOT BOOKED, ADJUSTED EACH YEAR]

(3) Deferred Income Tax   24,000

     Income Tax Expense   8,000

     Beginning Retained Earnings—P Company   32,000

[handwritten: INCOME TAX EXPENSE FROM 80 NOW HERE CLOSED OUT]

         To defer income tax on unrealized intercompany profit at December 31, 1981 $(.4 \times [100,000 - 20,000 - 20,000] = 24,000$, see Illustration 7–1), to recognize income tax expense on intercompany profit considered to be realized during the current year $(.4 \times 20,000 = 8,000)$, and to adjust beginning retained earnings for the income tax effects on the unrealized intercompany profit eliminated therefrom $(.4 \times 80,000 = 32,000)$.

(4) Property and Equipment   300,000

     Accumulated Depreciation   300,000

         Optional entry to restate property and equipment at original cost to the selling affiliate.

Entries similar to those summarized above would be made in the consolidating workpapers until the intercompany equipment is fully depreciated, at which time

ILLUSTRATION 7–1
Recorded and Consolidated Balances
For Equipment Transferred Between Affiliates
Investment Recorded at Cost

	DECEMBER 31				
PROPERTY AND EQUIPMENT	1980	1981	1982	1983	1984
On Records of Purchasing Affiliate	600,000	600,000	600,000	600,000	600,000
Workpaper Entry (1)	(100,000)	(100,000)	(100,000)	(100,000)	(100,000)
Consolidated Balance	500,000	500,000	500,000	500,000	500,000
Optional Workpaper Entry (4)	300,000	300,000	300,000	300,000	300,000
Optional Consolidated Balance	800,000	800,000	800,000	800,000	800,000
ACCUMULATED DEPRECIATION					
On Records of Purchasing Affiliate	(120,000)	(240,000)	(360,000)	(480,000)	(600,000)
Workpaper Entry (1)		20,000	40,000	60,000	80,000
Workpaper Entry (2)	20,000	20,000	20,000	20,000	20,000
Consolidated Balance	(100,000)	(200,000)	(300,000)	(400,000)	(500,000)
Optional Workpaper Entry (4)	(300,000)	(300,000)	(300,000)	(300,000)	(300,000)
Optional Consolidated Balance	(400,000)	(500,000)	(600,000)	(700,000)	(800,000)
BOOK VALUE					
On Records of Purchasing Affiliate	480,000	360,000	240,000	120,000	–0–
Consolidated	400,000	300,000	200,000	100,000	–0–
PROFIT RECOGNITION BEFORE ADJUSTMENT FOR TAX EFFECTS					
On Records of Selling Affiliate "Gain on Sale of Equipment"	100,000	–0–	–0–	–0–	–0–
In Consolidated Financial Statements "Reduction of Depreciation"	20,000	20,000	20,000	20,000	20,000
PROFIT RECOGNITION NET OF INCOME TAX					
On Records of Affiliates $(100,000 - 20,000) \times .6$	48,000	–0–	–0–	–0–	–0–
In Consolidated Financial Statements $20,000 \times .6$	12,000	12,000	12,000	12,000	12,000
UNREALIZED INTERCOMPANY PROFIT					
Gross Amount of Intercompany Profit Reported by Selling Affiliate in 1980	100,000	100,000	100,000	100,000	100,000
Less Cumulative Amount of Intercompany Profit Realized in Consolidation Through Depreciation	20,000	40,000	60,000	80,000	100,000
Unrealized Intercompany Profit Before Income Tax Effect	80,000	60,000	40,000	20,000	–0–
Less Deferred Income Tax (40 Percent)	32,000	24,000	16,000	8,000	–0–
Unrealized Intercompany Profit Net of Income Tax	48,000	36,000	24,000	12,000	–0–

ILLUSTRATION 7–2
Consolidated Statements Workpaper
P Company and Subsidiary
For Year Ending December 31, 1980

	P COMPANY	S COMPANY	ELIMINATIONS DR.	ELIMINATIONS CR.	MINORITY INTEREST	CONSOLIDATED BALANCES
INCOME STATEMENT						
Sales	3,400,000	2,100,000				5,500,000
Gain on Sale of Equipment	100,000		¹ 100,000			–0–
Total Revenue	3,500,000	2,100,000				5,500,000
Cost of Sales	1,800,000	1,130,000				2,930,000
Depreciation	380,000	330,000		² 20,000		690,000
Income Tax Expense	200,000	96,000		³ 32,000		264,000
Other Expense	820,000	400,000				1,220,000
Total Cost and Expense	3,200,000	1,956,000				5,104,000
Net	300,000	144,000				396,000
Minority Interest (.3 × 144,000)					43,200	(43,200)
Net Income to Retained Earnings	300,000	144,000	100,000	52,000	43,200	352,800
RETAINED EARNINGS STATEMENT						
1/1/80 Retained Earnings						
P Company	1,500,000			⁵ 186,200		1,686,200
S Company		666,000	⁶ 466,200		199,800	
Net Income from above	300,000	144,000	100,000	52,000	43,200	352,800
12/31/80 Retained Earnings						
to Balance Sheet	1,800,000	810,000	566,200	238,200	243,000	2,039,000
BALANCE SHEET						
Current Assets	1,210,000	570,000				1,780,000
Investment in S Company	980,000		⁵ 186,200	⁶ 1,166,200		
Land	1,000,000	200,000				1,200,000
Property and Equipment	3,800,000	2,700,000	⁴ 300,000	¹ 100,000		6,700,000
(Accumulated Depreciation)	(1,520,000)	(960,000)	² 20,000	⁴ 300,000		(2,760,000)
Deferred Income Tax			³ 32,000			32,000
Total Assets	5,470,000	2,510,000				6,952,000
Liabilities	670,000	700,000				1,370,000
Capital Stock						
P Company	3,000,000					3,000,000
S Company		1,000,000	⁶ 700,000		300,000	
Retained Earnings from above	1,800,000	810,000	566,200	238,200	243,000	2,039,000
Minority Interest					543,000	543,000
Total Liabilities & Equity	5,470,000	2,510,000	1,804,400	1,804,400		6,952,000

¹To eliminate unrealized gain on intercompany sale of equipment.
²To reverse the amount of excess depreciation recorded during the current year.
³To defer income tax on the net amount of unrealized intercompany profit.
⁴Optional entry to restate property and equipment at original cost to P Company.
⁵To establish reciprocity as of 1/1/80 (.7 × [666,000 − 400,000] = 186,200).
⁶To eliminate the investment account.

Purchase Accounting
Cost Method
70%-Owned Subsidiary
Downstream Sale of Equipment

ILLUSTRATION 7-3
Consolidated Statements Workpaper
P Company and Subsidiary
For Year Ending December 31, 1981

INCOME STATEMENT	P COMPANY	S COMPANY	ELIMINATIONS DR.	ELIMINATIONS CR.	MINORITY INTEREST	CONSOLIDATED BALANCES
Sales	4,000,000	2,200,000				6,200,000
Cost of Sales	2,100,000	1,180,000				3,280,000
Depreciation	380,000	330,000		² 20,000		690,000
Income Tax Expense	272,000	108,000	³ 8,000			388,000
Other Expense	840,000	420,000				1,260,000
Total Cost and Expense	3,592,000	2,038,000				5,618,000
Net	408,000	162,000				582,000
Minority Interest (162,000 × .3)					48,600	(48,600)
Net Income to Retained Earnings	408,000	162,000	8,000	20,000	48,600	533,400
RETAINED EARNINGS STATEMENT						
1/1/81 Retained Earnings						
P Company	1,800,000		¹ 80,000	³ 32,000		2,039,000
				⁵ 287,000		
S Company		810,000	⁶ 567,000		243,000	
Net Income from above	408,000	162,000	8,000	20,000	48,600	533,400
12/31/81 Retained Earnings						
to Balance Sheet	2,208,000	972,000	655,000	339,000	291,600	2,572,400
BALANCE SHEET						
Current Assets	1,400,000	790,000				2,190,000
Investment in S Company	980,000		⁵ 287,000	⁶ 1,267,000		
Land	1,600,000	200,000				1,800,000
Property and Equipment	3,800,000	2,700,000	⁴ 300,000	¹ 100,000		6,700,000
(Accumulated Depreciation)	(1,900,000)	(1,290,000)	¹ 20,000	⁴ 300,000		(3,450,000)
			² 20,000			
Deferred Income Tax			³ 24,000			24,000
Total Assets	5,880,000	2,400,000				7,264,000
Liabilities	672,000	428,000				1,100,000
Capital Stock						
P Company	3,000,000					3,000,000
S Company		1,000,000	⁶ 700,000		300,000	
Retained Earnings from above	2,208,000	972,000	655,000	339,000	291,600	2,572,400
Minority Interest					591,600	591,600
Total Liability & Equity	5,880,000	2,400,000	2,006,000	2,006,000		7,264,000

¹To eliminate unrealized intercompany profit at the beginning of the year.

²To reverse the amount of excess depreciation recorded during the current year.

³To defer income tax on unrealized intercompany profit and to recognize income tax on intercompany profit realized during the current year.

⁴Optional entry to restate property and equipment at original cost to P Company.

⁵To establish reciprocity as of 1/1/81 (.7 × [810,000 − 400,000] = 287,000).

⁶To eliminate the investment account.

workpaper adjustments will no longer be required. A comparison of the amounts recorded on the records of the affiliated companies with the consolidated balances for each of the remaining five years of the intercompany equipment's useful life is presented in Illustration 7–1. Consolidated financial statement workpapers for the years ending December 31, 1980 and December 31, 1981 are presented in Illustration 7–2 and Illustration 7–3, respectively.

Calculation of Minority Interest (Investment Recorded At Cost)

In the preceding example the selling affiliate was the parent company. Accordingly, even though 100% of the unrealized intercompany profit was eliminated, no modification in the calculation of minority interest in combined income or consolidated net assets was necessary. Had the selling affiliate been the 70%-owned subsidiary, however, workpaper modifications in the determination of minority interest would have been necessary if the majority and minority interest were to be adjusted in proportion to their interest in the amount of unrealized intercompany profit eliminated.

Calculations of minority interest in combined income would be modified as follows:

> December 31, 1980:
> .3 × (reported income of S Company[1] − 48,000[a]).

> December 31, 1981:
> .3 × (reported income of S Company[1] + 12,000[b]).

[a](100,000 − 20,000) × .6 = 48,000 = unrealized intercompany profit net of tax eliminated from 1980 combined income (see Illustration 7–1).
[b]20,000 × .6 = 12,000 = intercompany profit considered realized in the current period net of tax (see Illustration 7–1).

As was explained in the discussion of unrealized intercompany profit in inventory, as a matter of workpaper procedure, minority interest in net assets is adjusted by debiting (decrease in minority interest) or crediting (increase in minority interest) the beginning retained earnings row of the subsidiary company. The amount of the adjustment to minority interest is equal to the minority interest's share (percentage) of unrealized intercompany profit at the beginning of the period that would otherwise be carried to the parent company's (majority interest's) beginning retained earnings. If S Company had been the selling affiliate, the workpaper eliminations on December 31, 1981 that were summarized in the preceding example would be modified as follows in order to adjust minority interest in net assets.

---

[1]Reported income of S Company will not be the same as that presented in Illustrations 7–2 and 7–3, because the income statement of S Company will now include the gain on the sale of equipment and related income statement effects.

(1) Beginning Retained Earnings—P Company (.70 × [100,000 − 20,000])	56,000	
Beginning Retained Earnings—S Company (.30 × [100,000 − 20,000])	24,000	
Accumulated Depreciation	20,000	
Property and Equipment		100,000
(2) NO CHANGE		
(3) Deferred Income Tax	24,000	
Income Tax Expense	8,000	
Beginning Retained Earnings—P Company (.70 × 32,000)		22,400
Beginning Retained Earnings—S Company (.30 × 32,000)		9,600
(4) NO CHANGE		

The net affect of these entries is to allocate the unrealized intercompany profit net of tax on January 1, 1981 of $48,000 (see Illustration 7–1) proportionately between consolidated retained earnings on January 1, 1981 (.7 × 48,000 = 33,600 = [56,000 − 22,400]) and minority interest (.3 × 48,000 = 14,400 = [24,000 − 9,600]).

Premature Disposal of Property and Equipment by the Purchasing Affiliate (Investment Recorded at Cost)

NO WAY TO RECORD GAIN OR LOSS PROPERTY FOR CONS. STANDPOINT

Assume that on January 1, 1982, S Company sells the equipment purchased from P Company to a party outside the affiliated group for $400,000. The book value of the equipment on January 1, 1982 is the same as the amounts shown for December 31, 1981 in Illustration 7–1. On the records of S Company, the book value of the equipment is $360,000, and S Company will record a $40,000 gain on the sale as follows:

Cash	400,000	
Accumulated Depreciation	240,000	
Property & Equipment		600,000
Gain on Sale of Equipment		40,000

However, the consolidated book value of the equipment on the date of the sale by S Company is only $300,000, and from the point of view of the consolidated entity a $100,000 gain on the sale (400,000 − 300,000) should be recognized. The workpaper entries on the December 31, 1982 consolidating workpaper necessary to accomplish this result are as follows:

REASON FOR DIFF IN GAINS IS REDUCTION OF DIFF OF B.V. BY EXCESS DEPR (100,000 − 20,000 − 20,000)

(1) Beginning Retained Earnings—P Company	60,000	
Gain on Sale of Equipment		60,000

To adjust the reported gain on the sale of equipment by S Company to a third party from

$40,000 to $100,000, and to adjust beginning retained earnings for the amount of unrealized intercompany profit included therein on January 1, 1982 (100,000 — 20,000 — 20,000).

(2) Income Tax Expense	24,000	
Beginning Retained Earnings—P Company		24,000

To adjust the entry above for the income tax effects associated with the adjustments to the gain on the sale of equipment and to beginning retained earnings.

[handwritten margin notes:]
100,000 × .40 = 40,000
40,000 × .40 = 16,000
24,000
16 ON BOOKS BUT CONS SEES TAXES AS 40

After December 31, 1982, no more workpaper entries relating to this equipment will be required, because by that date the amount of profit recorded by the affiliates is equal to the amount of profit considered to be realized in the consolidated financial statements. The equality of the recorded and consolidated amounts may be confirmed as follows:

	GROSS	NET OF TAX
Amount of profit recorded by the affiliates		
1980—Gain on sale from P Company to S Company	100,000	60,000
1982—Gain on sale by S Company to nonaffiliate	40,000	24,000
Total	140,000	84,000
Amount considered to be realized in the consolidated income statement		
1980—Reduction of depreciation	20,000	12,000
1981—Reduction of depreciation	20,000	12,000
1982—Gain on sale of equipment to nonaffiliate	100,000	60,000
Total	140,000	84,000

Analytical Calculation of Consolidated Net Income and Consolidated Retained Earnings

The application of the analytical approach to the calculation of consolidated net income and consolidated retained earnings in cases involving intercompany profit on depreciable assets may be demonstrated as follows:

Consolidated Net Income   On the basis of Illustration 7–3, the calculation of consolidated net income for the year ending December 31, 1981 is as follows:

P Company's net income from its independent operations		408,000
Plus profit net of tax on intercompany sale of equipment to S Company in 1980 considered to be realized in 1981 through depreciation		12,000
P Company's income from its independent operations that has been realized in transactions with third parties		420,000
Reported net income of S Company	162,000	
Amount of income of S Company not realized in transactions with third parties	–0–	
Reported subsidiary income that has been realized in transactions with third parties	162,000	
P Company's share thereof (.7 × 162,000)		113,400
Consolidated net income		533,400

This is the same amount of consolidated net income as that calculated in the consolidated financial statement workpapers presented in Illustration 7–3.

Consolidated Retained Earnings   On the basis of Illustration 7–3, the calculation of consolidated retained earnings on December 31, 1981 is as follows:

P Company's retained earnings on December 31, 1981		2,208,000
Less unrealized profit net of tax on sale of equipment to S Company on January 1, 1980 included therein ([100,000 − 20,000 − 20,000] × .6)		(36,000)
P Company's retained earnings that have been realized in transactions with third parties		2,172,000
Increase in retained earnings of S Company from 1978 to December 31, 1981 (972,000 − 400,000)	572,000	
Amount of increase not realized in transactions with third parties	–0–	
Increase in reported retained earnings of S Company since acquisition that has been realized in transactions with third parties	572,000	
P Company's share thereof (.7 × 572,000)		400,400
Consolidated retained earnings on December 31, 1981		2,572,400

NONCONSOLIDATED INVESTEES REPORTED IN THE FINANCIAL STATEMENTS USING THE EQUITY METHOD

As explained in Chapter 3, certain investments must be *reported* in the financial statements using the equity method. In addition, investments in consolidated subsidiaries are sometimes *recorded* in the records of the parent company using the equity method. For the same reasons cited in the discussion of intercompany sales of merchandise, adjustments to the investment account balance and to the amount of equity in investee income recognized by the investor must be made to recognize the effects of any intercompany profit on the sale of property and equipment.

In addition, recall that the percentage of intercompany profit to be eliminated under the equity method differs depending upon whether the investment is in a nonconsolidated subsidiary or in a less than 50%-owned investee. In the case of nonconsolidated subsidiaries, adjustment must be made for the entire amount of intercompany profit if the sale is downstream, whereas only the parent company's share of the intercompany profit is adjusted for if the sale is upstream. In the case of less than 50%-owned investees, the amount of the adjustment for the effects of intercompany profit is the same regardless of whether the sale is upstream or downstream, and it is based on the percentage interest of the investor in the voting stock of the investee.

To illustrate the case of a less than 50%-owned investee, assume that Investor Company owns 30% of the voting stock of Investee Company. Investee Company reports net income of $200,000 in 1980 and $300,000 in 1981. Intercompany sales of depreciable equipment amount to $600,000 during 1980, and unrealized profit thereon at the end of 1980 amounts to $80,000. As of December 31, 1980, the equipment has a remaining life of four years (straight-line depreciation). The income tax rate on the taxable income of both companies averages 40%. Investor Company accounts for its investment in Investee Company by use of the equity method.

Regardless of whether the sale of the equipment was upstream or downstream, the entries on Investor Company's books to record its equity in the income of Investee Company during 1980 and 1981 are as follows:

Entries on the Books of Investor Company—1980

(1) Investment in Investee Company 60,000
    Equity in Investee Income 60,000
      To record Investor Company's share of the net income reported by Investee Company (.3 × 200,000 = 60,000).

(2) Equity in Investee Income 14,400
    Investment in Investee Company 14,400
      To reduce the recorded equity in investee income by an amount based on the percentage interest of Investor Company in Investee Company times the amount of unrealized intercompany profit net of tax (.3 × [.6 × 80,000] = 14,400).

Notice that even if the intercompany sale is downstream, in which case Investor Company will have recognized a profit net of tax of $48,000 on the intercompany sale, only 30% of that profit is considered to be unrealized (.3 × 48,000 = 14,400) and subject to elimination from reported income.

Entries on the Books of Investor Company—1981

(1) Investment in Investee Company   90,000
    Equity in Investee Income   90,000
      To record Investor Company's share of the net income reported by Investee Company ($.3 \times 300,000 = 90,000$).

(2) Investment in Investee Company   3,600
    Equity in Investee Income   3,600
      To recognize the amount of intercompany profit net of tax on the 1980 intercompany sale of depreciable equipment considered to be realized through depreciation in 1981 ($.3 \times [(80,000/4) \times .6] = 3,600$).

[handwritten margin notes:]
INCOME SHOULD HAVE BEEN
320,000
300,000
+ EXCESS DEPR
320,000
P.O.T (.6 × 20,000)
12,000
INCREASE INCOME

CONSOLIDATING WORKPAPER—INVESTMENT RECORDED AT EQUITY

Assume that P Company acquires a 70% interest in S Company for $980,000 in 1978 when the retained earnings and capital stock of S Company amount to $400,000 and $1,000,000, respectively. The retained earnings of S Company on January 1, 1980 are $666,000. The reported net income of S Company is $144,000 in 1980 and $162,000 in 1981. On January 1, 1980, P Company sells S Company equipment with a book value of $500,000 (original cost of $800,000 and accumulated depreciation of $300,000) for $600,000. On January 1, 1980, the equipment has an estimated remaining useful life of five years and is depreciated using the straight-line method. The average income tax rate for both companies is 40%, and separate income tax returns are filed. Entries to record subsidiary income *on the books* of P Company under the equity method, as well as *workpaper entries* necessary in the consolidating workpapers, for the years ending December 31, 1980 and December 31, 1981 are summarized in general journal form below.

Entries on the Books of P Company—1980 (Equity Method)

(1) Investment in S Company   100,800
    Equity in Subsidiary Income   100,800
      To record P Company's share of the reported net income of S Company ($.7 \times 144,000 = 100,800$).

(2) Equity in Subsidiary Income   60,000
    Investment in S Company   60,000
      To reduce equity in subsidiary income by unrealized profit net of tax on the intercompany sale of equipment ($1.0 \times [.6 \times 100,000] = 60,000$).

[handwritten margin notes:]
NET 2 + 3
EFFECTIVELY ELIMINATING
$18,000

Notice that, since this is a downstream sale to a controlled affiliate, equity in subsidiary income is adjusted for the *entire amount* of unrealized intercompany profit.

(3) Investment in S Company   12,000
    Equity in Subsidiary Income   12,000
        To recognize the amount of intercompany profit net of tax on the January 1 intercompany sale of depreciable equipment considered to be realized through depreciation in 1980 $(1.0 \times [(100,000/5) \times .6] = 12,000)$.

Consolidating Workpaper Entries—December 31, 1980 (Equity Method)

(1) Gain on Sale of Equipment   100,000
    Property and Equipment   100,000
        To eliminate the unrealized profit recorded on the intercompany sale of equipment and reduce the carrying value of the equipment to its depreciated cost on the date of the sale.

(2) Accumulated Depreciation   20,000
    Depreciation   20,000
        To reverse the amount of excess depreciation recorded during the current year and to recognize an equivalent amount of intercompany profit as realized $(100,000/5 = 20,000)$.

(3) Deferred Income Tax   32,000
    Income Tax Expense   32,000
        To defer income tax on the net amount of unrealized intercompany profit at December 31, 1980 $(.4 \times [100,000 - 20,000] = 32,000)$.

(4) Property and Equipment   300,000
    Accumulated Depreciation   300,000
        Optional entry to restate property and equipment at original cost to the selling affiliate.

(5) Equity in Subsidiary Income   52,800
    Investment in S Company   52,800
        To adjust the investment account to the beginning-of-year balance and to eliminate equity in subsidiary income $(100,800 - 60,000 + 12,000 = 52,800)$.

(6) Beginning Retained Earnings—S Company   466,200
    Capital Stock—S Company   700,000
    Investment in S Company   1,166,200
        To eliminate the investment account.

    Entries (1), (2), (3), and (4) are identical to corresponding cost-basis eliminating entries (see Illustration 7–2). Since this is a downstream sale, no modification in the calculation of minority interest in combined income on December 31, 1980 is necessary $(.3 \times 144,000 = 43,200)$.

Entries on Books of P Company—1981 (Equity Method)

(1) Investment in S Company   113,400

     Equity in Subsidiary Income   113,400

         To record P Company's share of the reported net income of S Company ($.7 \times 162,000 = 113,400$).

(2) Investment in S Company   12,000

     Equity in Subsidiary Income   12,000

         To recognize the amount of intercompany profit net of tax on the 1980 intercompany sale of equipment realized through depreciation in the current year ($1.0 \times [(100,000/5) \times .6] = 12,000$).

Consolidating Workpaper Entries—December 31, 1981 (Illustration 7–4)

(1) Investment in S Company   80,000

     Accumulated Depreciation   20,000

         Property and Equipment   100,000

         To adjust the investment account by the amount of unrealized intercompany profit on January 1, 1981 that has been removed therefrom in entries recorded on the books of P Company, to reduce accumulated depreciation by the amount of excess depreciation at the beginning of the year, and to reduce the carrying value of the equipment to its depreciated cost on the date of the intercompany sale.

The only difference between this entry and the corresponding cost-basis workpaper entry is that in this entry P Company's share (100%) of the unrealized intercompany profit on January 1, 1981 ($80,000) is debited to the investment account rather than to the beginning retained earnings of P Company (see Illustration 7–3). If this had been an upstream sale, the $80,000 of unrealized intercompany profit on January 1, 1981 would be allocated proportionately between the minority and majority interests by debiting the beginning retained earnings of S Company for $24,000 ($.3 \times 80,000$) and the investment in S Company for $56,000 ($.7 \times 80,000$).

(2) Accumulated Depreciation   20,000

     Depreciation   20,000

         To reverse the amount of excess depreciation recorded during the current year and to recognize an equivalent amount of intercompany profit as realized.

This entry is identical to the corresponding cost-basis workpaper entry (see Illustration 7–3).

(3) Deferred Income Tax   24,000
    Income Tax Expense   8,000
        Investment in S Company   32,000

        To defer income tax on unrealized intercompany profit on December 31, 1981 $(.4 \times [100,000 - 20,000 - 20,000] = 24,000)$, to recognize income tax expense on intercompany profit considered to be realized during the current year through depreciation $(.4 \times 20,000 = 8,000)$, and to adjust the investment account for the income tax effects of unrealized intercompany profit removed therefrom in entries recorded on the books of P Company.

The only difference between this entry and the corresponding cost-basis eliminating entry is that the investment account rather than the beginning retained earnings of P Company is credited for the $32,000 tax effect. If this had been an upstream sale, the $32,000 tax effect would be allocated proportionately between the minority and majority interests by crediting the beginning retained earnings of S Company for $9,600 $(.3 \times 32,000)$ and the investment balance for $22,400 $(.7 \times 32,000)$.

(4) Property and Equipment   300,000
        Accumulated Depreciation   300,000
        Optional entry to restate property and equipment at original cost to the selling affiliate.

(5) Equity in Subsidiary Income   125,400
        Investment in S Company   125,400
        To adjust the investment account to the beginning-of-year balance and to eliminate equity in subsidiary income $(113,400 + 12,000 = 125,400)$.

(6) Beginning Retained Earnings—S Company   567,000
    Capital Stock—S Company   700,000
        Investment in S Company   1,267,000
        To eliminate the investment account.

Since this is a downstream sale, no modification in the calculation of minority interest in combined income on December 31, 1981 is necessary $(.3 \times 162,000 = 48,600)$. The consolidated financial statement workpaper for the year ending December 31, 1981 is presented in Illustration 7–4. A comparison of the consolidated balances in Illustration 7–4 with those in Illustration 7–3 will confirm that the consolidated balances are not affected by the method of accounting (cost or equity) used by P Company to record its investment in S Company.

Purchase Accounting
Equity Method
70%-Owned Subsidiary
Downstream Sale of Equipment

ILLUSTRATION 7–4
Consolidated Statements Workpaper
P Company and Subsidiary
For Year Ending December 31, 1981

INCOME STATEMENT	P COMPANY	S COMPANY	ELIMINATIONS DR.	ELIMINATIONS CR.	MINORITY INTEREST	CONSOLIDATED BALANCES
Sales	4,000,000	2,200,000				6,200,000
Equity in Subsidiary Income	125,400		⁵ 125,400			
Total Revenue	4,125,400	2,200,000				6,200,000
Cost of Goods Sold	2,100,000	1,180,000				3,280,000
Depreciation	380,000	330,000		² 20,000		690,000
Income Tax Expense	272,000	108,000	³ 8,000			388,000
Other Expense	840,000	420,000				1,260,000
Total Cost and Expense	3,592,000	2,038,000				5,618,000
Net	533,400	162,000				582,000
Minority Interest (162,000 × .3)					48,600	(48,600)
Net Income to Retained Earnings	533,400	162,000	133,400	20,000	48,600	533,400
RETAINED EARNINGS STATEMENT						
1/1/81 Retained Earnings						
P Company	2,039,000					2,039,000
S Company		810,000	⁶ 567,000		243,000	
Net Income from above	533,400	162,000	133,400	20,000	48,600	533,400
12/31/81 Retained Earnings						
to Balance Sheet	2,572,400	972,000	700,400	20,000	291,600	2,572,400
BALANCE SHEET						
Current Assets	1,400,000	790,000				2,190,000
Investment in S Company	1,344,400		¹ 80,000	³ 32,000		
				⁵ 125,400		
				⁶ 1,267,000		
Land	1,600,000	200,000				1,800,000
Property and Equipment	3,800,000	2,700,000	⁴ 300,000	¹ 100,000		6,700,000
(Accumulated Depreciation)	(1,900,000)	(1,290,000)	¹ 20,000	⁴ 300,000		(3,450,000)
			² 20,000			
Deferred Income Tax			³ 24,000			24,000
Total Assets	6,244,400	2,400,000				7,264,000
Liabilities	672,000	428,000				1,100,000
Capital Stock						
P Company	3,000,000					3,000,000
S Company		1,000,000	⁶ 700,000		300,000	
Retained Earnings from above	2,572,400	972,000	700,400	20,000	291,600	2,572,400
Minority Interest					591,600	591,600
Total Liabilities & Equity	6,244,400	2,400,000	1,844,400	1,844,400		7,264,000

[1]To adjust the investment account for unrealized intercompany profit at the beginning of the year, to reduce accumulated depreciation by the amount of excess depreciation at the beginning of the year, and to reduce the carrying value of equipment to its depreciated cost on the date of the intercompany sale.

[2]To reverse the amount of excess depreciation recorded during the year and to recognize an equivalent amount of intercompany profit as realized.

[3]To defer income tax on unrealized intercompany profit and recognize income tax expense on intercompany profit realized during the year.

[4]Optional entry to restate property and equipment at original cost to the selling affiliate.

[5]To adjust the investment account to the beginning-of-year balance and to eliminate equity in subsidiary income.

[6]To eliminate the investment account.

INTERCOMPANY SALES OF NONDEPRECIABLE ASSETS

When intercompany sales involve nondepreciable assets, any profit recognized by the selling affiliate will remain unrealized from the point of view of the consolidated entity in all subsequent periods or until the asset is disposed of. Accordingly, a constant amount of unrealized intercompany profit is eliminated each year.

Assume that land costing $800,000 is sold to an affiliate for $1,000,000 on January 1, 1980 and that the affiliates file consolidated income tax returns. Workpaper entries necessary in the consolidating workpapers in the year of the sale and in subsequent years are presented below.

December 31, 1980 (Year of Intercompany Sale)

	COST METHOD		EQUITY METHOD	
Gain on Sale of Land	200,000		200,000	
Land		200,000		200,000

All Subsequent Years Until Disposed Of Workpaper entries in all subsequent years will differ depending on whether the intercompany sale was a downstream or upstream sale and whether the cost method or the equity method is used to account for the investment in the subsidiary.

Downstream sale

	COST METHOD		EQUITY METHOD	
Beginning Retained Earnings—				
P Company	200,000		—	
Investment in S Company	—		200,000	
Land		200,000		200,000

The only difference between the workpaper entries is that, when the investment is carried at equity rather than at cost, the debit is to the investment account rather than to the beginning retained earnings of the parent company. The reason for this procedural difference was explained earlier.

Upstream sale

	COST METHOD		EQUITY METHOD	
Beginning Retained Earnings—				
S Company	40,000		40,000	
Beginning Retained Earnings—				
P Company	160,000		—	
Investment in S Company	—		160,000	
Land		200,000		200,000

The entries above assume that the selling affiliate is an 80%-owned subsidiary. The debit to the beginning retained earnings of the subsidiary is to reduce the minority interest in consolidated net assets for its share of the unrealized profit recorded by the subsidiary (.2 × 200,000 = 40,000).

CONSOLIDATIONS ACCOUNTED FOR AS POOLING OF INTERESTS

As was discussed in Chapter 6, the concept that only profits resulting from the sale of goods and services to parties outside the affiliated group should be recognized in the consolidated financial statements is not altered by concepts underlying the difference between pooling of interests and purchase accounting. Therefore, workpaper entries for the elimination of unrealized profit on intercompany sales of property and equipment are the same whether the consolidation is accounted for as a purchase or as a pooling of interests. Since a parent company will ordinarily record its interest in a subsidiary that qualifies for pooling of interests accounting by use of the equity method, intercompany profit workpaper eliminations similar to those presented in the section headed *Consolidating Workpaper—Investment Recorded at Equity* are ordinarily applicable to pooled subsidiaries. If, for some reason, the parent company maintains its investment in the subsidiary at an amount equal to the book value on the date its interest was acquired, intercompany profit workpaper eliminations similar to those presented in the section headed *Consolidating Workpaper—Investment Recorded at Cost* would be appropriate.

SUMMARY OF WORKPAPER ELIMINATIONS

Consolidated financial statement workpaper entries to eliminate unrealized profit resulting from intercompany sales of property and equipment differ depending upon whether

1. The selling affiliate is wholly owned or less than wholly owned.

2. The parent company uses the cost method or the equity method to record the investment in a subsidiary.

3. The affiliates file separate income tax returns or a consolidated income tax return.

4. The property sold is depreciable or nondepreciable.

As previously noted, workpaper entries to eliminate intercompany profit are the same whether the consolidation is accounted for as a pooling of interest or as a purchase.

Workpaper elimination entries for the various alternatives presented above are summarized for intercompany sales of depreciable property and equipment in Illustration 7–5. The entries illustrated therein are based on the assumption that the selling affiliate recorded a gain on the intercompany sale. If a loss was recorded by the selling affiliate, the accounts debited and credited in the entries presented in Illustration 7–5 would be reversed.

INTERCOMPANY PROFIT PRIOR TO PARENT-SUBSIDIARY AFFILIATION

Generally accepted accounting standards are silent as to the appropriate treatment of unrealized profit on assets that result from sales between companies prior to affiliation (preaffiliation profit). The question is whether or not preaffiliation profit should be eliminated in consolidation. In our opinion, workpaper entries eliminating preaffiliation profit are inappropriate.

If the selling company is the new subsidiary, the profit recognized by it prior to its acquisition is implicitly considered in determining the book value of the interest acquired by the parent company. Accordingly, such profit is automatically eliminated from consolidated retained earnings in the investment elimination entry. A second elimination would therefore result in a double reduction of the amount of preaffiliation profit from consolidated retained earnings on the date of acquisition. When the assets are sold to third parties in subsequent years, consolidated net income would be increased by a corresponding amount, thus restoring the amount of the second reduction to consolidated retained earnings. The net result is to make an unwarranted reduction of consolidated retained earnings on the date of acquisition in order to report preacquisition profit in consolidated net income in years subsequent to affiliation that has already been reported by the subsidiary prior to affiliation. In our opinion such effects lack both conceptual and practical merit.

ILLUSTRATION 7-5
Intercompany Profit—Equipment
Summary of Workpaper Elimination Entries

	SELLING AFFILIATE IS A PARENT OR WHOLLY OWNED SUBSIDIARY		SELLING AFFILIATE IS A LESS THAN WHOLLY OWNED SUBSIDIARY	
	INVESTMENT IN SUBSIDIARY IS RECORDED AT		INVESTMENT IN SUBSIDIARY IS RECORDED AT	
	BOOK VALUE (POOLING) OR COST (PURCHASE)	EQUITY (POOLING) OR EQUITY (PURCHASE)	BOOK VALUE (POOLING) OR COST (PURCHASE)	EQUITY (POOLING) OR EQUITY (PURCHASE)

ENTRIES IN YEAR OF INTERCOMPANY SALE

Gain on Sale

Equipment		SAME	SAME	SAME

To eliminate unrealized profit on intercompany sale in the year of the sale and to reduce the carrying value of equipment to its undepreciated cost on the date of the sale.

Accumulated Depreciation

Depreciation		SAME	SAME	SAME

To reverse the amount (if any) of excess depreciation recorded during the current year and to recognize an equivalent amount of intercompany profit as realized.

If the affiliates file separate income tax returns, an additional workpaper entry is necessary, as follows:

Deferred Income Tax

Income Tax Expense		SAME	SAME	SAME

To defer income tax on the amount of unrealized intercompany profit at the end of the year.

ENTRIES IN YEARS SUBSEQUENT TO THE YEAR OF INTERCOMPANY SALE

Beg. Ret. Earn.—P
    Investment in S
    Accumulated Depreciation
        Equipment

Beg. Ret. Earn.—P
Beg. Ret. Earn.—S
    Accumulated Depreciation
        Equipment

To adjust recorded balances by the amount of unrealized profit at the beginning of the year, to reduce accumulated depreciation by the amount of excess depreciation accumulated to the beginning of the year, and to reduce the carrying value of the equipment to its depreciated cost on the date of the sale.

To adjust recorded balances for the parent's share of unrealized profit at the beginning of the year, to adjust minority interest for its share of the unrealized profit at the beginning of the year, to reduce accumulated depreciation by the amount of excess depreciation accumulated to the beginning of the year, and to reduce the carrying value of the equipment to its depreciated cost on the date of the sale.

Accumulated Depreciation
    Depreciation

SAME   SAME

To reverse the amount of excess depreciation recorded during the current year and to recognize an equivalent amount of intercompany profit as realized.

If the affiliates file separate income tax returns, an additional workpaper entry will be necessary, as follows:

Deferred Income Tax
Income Tax Expense
    Beg. Ret. Earn.—P

Deferred Income Tax
Income Tax Expense
    Investment in S

Deferred Income Tax
Income Tax Expense
    Investment in S
    Beg. Ret. Earn.—P

Deferred Income Tax
Income Tax Expense
    Beg. Ret. Earn.—P
    Beg. Ret. Earn.—S

To defer income tax on unrealized profit at the end of the year, to recognize income tax expense on intercompany profit considered to be realized during the current year, and to adjust recorded balances for the the tax effect on the unrealized profit at the beginning of the year.

To defer income tax on unrealized profit at the end of the year, to recognize tax expense on intercompany profit considered to be realized during the current year, to adjust recorded balances for the parent's share of the income tax effect on unrealized profit at the beginning of the year, and to adjust minority interest for its share of the tax effect on unrealized profit at the beginning of the year.

If the selling company is the parent, the preaffiliation profit will ultimately be included in consolidated retained earnings in any case. However, a reduction of such profit from consolidated retained earnings on the date of affiliation simply results in the inclusion of the profit in the consolidated net income of subsequent years. Again, the effect of the elimination would be to report the profit twice, once prior to affiliation and once subsequent to affiliation. Again, we perceive no conceptual or practical merit in procedures that produce such a result. Support for the elimination of preaffiliation profit is based primarily on the application of conservatism to the valuation of consolidated assets on the date of acquisition.

Questions

1. From a consolidated point of view, when should profit be recognized on intercompany sales of depreciable assets? Nondepreciable assets?

2. In what circumstances might a consolidated gain be recognized on the sale of assets to a nonaffiliate when the selling affiliate recognizes a loss?

3. What is the essential procedural difference between cost-basis workpaper eliminating entries for unrealized intercompany profit and equity-basis workpaper eliminating entries?

4. What is the essential procedural difference in workpaper eliminating entries for unrealized intercompany profit when the selling affiliate is a less than wholly owned subsidiary and such entries when the selling affiliate is the parent company or a wholly owned subsidiary?

5. What is the essential procedural difference between the workpaper eliminating entries for unrealized intercompany profit when a consolidation is accounted for as a pooling of interests and when it is accounted for as a purchase?

6. Would you be more likely to make the workpaper entry to restate property and equipment at its original cost to the selling affiliate (optional entry) when a consolidation is accounted for as a pooling of interests or when it is accounted for as a purchase? Explain.

7. What problems do you perceive that auditors may have in verifying investment revenue because of the considerations discussed in this chapter?

8. Prior to its acquisition of its interest in a subsidiary, the parent company sold merchandise to the subsidiary. A portion of this merchandise remains in the ending inventory of the subsidiary at the date consolidated financial statements are being prepared. What treatment is required in the consolidated financial statements? If the subsidiary had been the selling company, what treatment would have been required in the consolidated financial statements?

Problems

Problem 7–1

Project Company owns 80% of the outstanding common stock of Sand Company. On June 30, 1980, Sand Company sold equipment to Project Company for $500,000. The equipment cost Sand Company $800,000 and had accumulated depreciation of $400,000 on the date of the sale. The management of Project Company estimated that the equipment had a remaining useful life of 5 years from June 30, 1980. In 1981, Project Company reported $300,000 and Sand Company reported $200,000 in net income from their independent operations. Project Company records its investment in Sand Company using the cost method.

Required:

A. Assume that the affiliates file consolidated income tax returns. Prepare in general journal form the workpaper entries necessary because of the intercompany sale of equipment in the
   (1) consolidated financial statements workpaper for the year ending December 31, 1980.
   (2) consolidated financial statements workpaper for the year ending December 31, 1981.
B. Assume that the affiliates file separate income tax returns and that the average combined state and federal income tax rate for both companies is 40%. Prepare in general journal form the entries necessary to reflect the income tax effects of the intercompany profit eliminations prepared in Part A.
C. Calculate the balances to be reported in the consolidated income statement for the year ending December 31, 1981 for the following items, assuming that consolidated income tax returns are filed:
   Combined income
   Minority interest in combined income
   Consolidated net income

Problem 7–2

On January 1, 1979, the Arba Company acquired a 90% interest in the common stock of Braginetz Company on the open market for $750,000, the book value at that date.

On January 1, 1980, Arba purchased new equipment for $14,500 from Braginetz. The equipment cost Braginetz $9,000 and had an estimated life of 5 years as of January 1, 1980. Arba uses the straight-line depreciation method for both financial and income tax reporting.

During 1981, Arba had merchandise sales to Braginetz of $100,000; the merchandise was priced at 25% above Arba's cost. Braginetz still owes Arba $17,500 on open account and has 20% of this merchandise in inventory at December 31, 1981. At the beginning of 1981, Braginetz had in inventory $25,000 of merchandise purchased in the previous period from the Arba Company. Braginetz uses the FIFO cost flow assumption.

Arba Company uses the cost method in accounting for its investment in Braginetz Company. The two companies file separate federal income tax returns, and each has an income tax rate of 40%.

Required:

A. Prepare all workpaper entries necessary to eliminate the effects of the intercompany sales on the consolidated financial statements for the year ended December 31, 1981.
B. Assume that Braginetz Company reports net income of $40,000 for the year ending December 31, 1981. Calculate the amount of minority interest to be deducted from combined income in the consolidated income statement for the year ending December 31, 1981.

Problem 7–3

The Miller Company owns 80% of the common stock of Edison Company. The stock was purchased for $1,600,000 on January 1, 1977, when Edison Company's retained earnings were $800,000. On January 1, 1979, the Miller Company sold fixed assets to the Edison Company for $540,000. These assets were originally purchased by the Miller Company for $600,000 on January 1, 1969, at which time their estimated depreciable life was 25 years. The straight-line method of depreciation is used.

On December 31, 1980, the trial balances of the two companies were as follows:

	MILLER CO.	EDISON CO.
Inventory—1/1	$ 150,000	$ 146,000
Fixed Assets	1,972,000	830,000
Other Assets	1,400,800	1,800,000
Investment in Edison Co.	1,600,000	
Dividends Declared	120,000	100,000
Purchases	960,000	720,000
Other Expenses		
(including depreciation)	145,000	90,000
Income Tax Expense	187,200	90,000
	$6,535,000	$3,776,000
Liabilities	$ 305,000	$ 136,000
Accumulated Depreciation	375,000	290,000
Sales	1,475,000	1,110,000
Dividend Income	80,000	
Common Stock	3,000,000	1,200,000
Retained Earnings	1,300,000	1,040,000
	$6,535,000	$3,776,000
Inventory—12/31	$ 168,000	$ 71,000

The average income tax rate for both companies is 40%, and Edison Company files a separate income tax return.

Required:

A. Prepare consolidating workpapers for the year ended December 31, 1980.
B. Assuming that on January 1, 1981, Edison Company sells the fixed assets purchased from Miller Company to a party outside the affiliated group for $400,000:
   (1) Prepare the entry that would have been entered on the books of Edison Company to record the sale.
   (2) Prepare workpaper entries for the December 31, 1981 consolidating workpaper necessitated by the sale of the assets.
   (3) Prepare any workpaper entries that will be needed in the December 31, 1982 consolidating workpapers in regard to these fixed assets.

Problem 7–4

Assume the same information as that presented in Problem 7–3 except that the affiliates filed a consolidated income tax return rather than separate income tax returns.

Required:

A. Prepare consolidating workpapers for the year ended December 31, 1980.

B. Assume that on January 1, 1981, Edison Company sells the fixed assets purchased from Miller Company to a party outside the affiliated group for $400,000.

   (1) Prepare the entry to be made on the books of Edison Company to record the sale.

   (2) Prepare workpaper entries for the December 31, 1981, consolidating workpaper necessitated because of the sale of the assets.

   (3) Prepare any workpaper entries that will be needed in the December 31, 1982 consolidating workpapers in regard to these fixed assets.

Problem 7–5

Tidwell Company owns 40% of the voting stock of Reneau Company. On January 1, 1980, Reneau Company sold equipment to Tidwell Company for $500,000. The equipment had a book value to Reneau Company of $400,000 on the date of the sale. The management of Tidwell Company estimated that the equipment had a 5-year remaining useful life on January 1, 1980. In 1980, Reneau Company reported net income of $300,000, and in 1981 it reported net income of $250,000. The combined state and federal income tax rate for Tidwell Company is 40%.

Required:

A. Prepare in general journal form the entries to be recorded by Tidwell Company to recognize its equity in the net income of Reneau Company for the years ending December 31, 1980 and December 31, 1981.

B. Assume that the intercompany sale of equipment was downstream rather than upstream. Prepare in general journal form the entries to be recorded by Tidwell Company to recognize its equity in the net income of Reneau Company for the years ending December 31, 1980 and December 31, 1981.

Problem 7–6

ABC Company owns a 40% interest in the voting stock of XYZ Company. XYZ Company reported net income after taxes of $200,000 in 1980 and $300,000 in 1981. In addition, XYZ Company's ending inventories included $40,000 in 1980 and $60,000 in 1981 of unrealized profit on intercompany merchandise sales.

An intercompany sale of land took place in 1980. XYZ Company had originally purchased the land in 1974 for $50,000 and sold the land to ABC Company for a bargain price of $65,000. In 1981, ABC Company sold the land in an arms-length transaction for $70,000.

The average income tax rate for both companies is 40%.

Required:

A. Prepare the entries made by ABC Company during 1980 and 1981 to record its investment in XYZ Company's income, using the equity method.

B. Assuming that the intercompany merchandise sales were upstream instead of downstream, and that the land sale was downstream instead of upstream, what entries would ABC Company have made during 1980 and 1981 to record its investment, using the equity method?

Problem 7–7

Pump Company owns 90% of the outstanding common stock of Sound Company. On January 1, 1980, Sound Company sold equipment to Pump Company for $200,000. Sound Company had purchased the equipment for $300,000 on January 1, 1975 and had depreciated it using a 10%

straight-line rate. The management of Pump Company estimated that the equipment had a remaining useful life of 5 years on January 1, 1980. In 1981, Pump Company reported $150,000, and Sound Company reported $100,000 in net income from their independent operations. The companies file consolidated income tax returns.

Required:

A. Prepare in general journal form the workpaper entries relating to the intercompany sale of equipment that are necessary in the December 31, 1980 and December 31, 1981 consolidated financial statements workpapers, assuming:

(1) Pump Company uses the cost method to record its investment in Sound Company.

(2) Pump Company uses the equity method to record its investment in Sound Company.

B. Calculate consolidated net income for 1981.

Problem 7–8

The Miller Company owns 80% of the common stock of the Edison Company. The stock was purchased for $1,600,000 on January 1, 1977, when Edison Company's retained earnings were $800,000. On January 1, 1979, the Miller Company sold fixed assets to the Edison Company for $540,000. These assets were originally purchased by the Miller Company for $600,000 on January 1, 1969, at which time their estimated depreciable life was 25 years. The straight-line method of depreciation is used.

On December 31, 1980, the trial balances of the two companies were as follows:

	MILLER CO.	EDISON CO.
Inventory—1/1	$ 150,000	$ 146,000
Fixed Assets	1,972,000	830,000
Other Assets	1,400,800	1,800,000
Investment in Edison Co.	1,726,400	
Dividends Declared	120,000	100,000
Purchases	960,000	720,000
Other Expenses		
(including depreciation)	145,000	90,000
Income Tax Expense	187,200	90,000
	$6,661,400	$3,776,000
Liabilities	$ 305,000	$ 136,000
Accumulated Depreciation	375,000	290,000
Sales	1,475,000	1,110,000
Equity in Subsidiary Earnings	115,200	
Common Stock	3,000,000	1,200,000
Retained Earnings	1,391,200	1,040,000
	$6,661,400	$3,776,000
Inventory—12/31	$ 168,000	$ 71,000

The average income tax rate for both companies is 40%, and Edison Company files a separate income tax return.

Required:

A. Prepare the entries made on the books of Miller Company during 1980 to record its interest in Edison Company.

B. Prepare consolidating workpapers for the year ended December 31, 1980.
C. Compare the consolidated balances from Part B with the consolidated balances arrived at in Problem 7–3, Part A.

Problem 7–9

This problem is the same as Problem 7–8 except that it is assumed that the affiliates filed a consolidated income tax return.

The Miller Company owns 80% of the common stock of the Edison Company. The stock was purchased for $1,600,000 on January 1, 1977, when Edison Company's retained earnings were $800,000. On January 1, 1979, the Miller Company sold fixed assets to the Edison Company for $540,000. These assets were originally purchased by the Miller Company for $600,000 on January 1, 1969, at which time their estimated depreciable life was 25 years. The straight-line method of depreciation is used.

On December 31, 1980, the trial balances of the two companies were as follows:

	MILLER CO.	EDISON CO.
Inventory—1/1	$ 150,000	$ 146,000
Fixed Assets	1,972,000	830,000
Other Assets	1,400,800	1,800,000
Investment in Edison Co.	1,664,000	
Dividends Declared	120,000	100,000
Purchases	960,000	720,000
Other Expenses		
(including depreciation)	145,000	90,000
Income Tax Expense	187,200	90,000
	$6,599,000	$3,776,000
Liabilities	$ 305,000	$ 136,000
Accumulated Depreciation	375,000	290,000
Sales	1,475,000	1,110,000
Equity in Subsidiary Earnings	120,000	
Common Stock	3,000,000	1,200,000
Retained Earnings	1,324,000	1,040,000
	$6,599,000	$3,776,000
Inventory—12/31	$ 168,000	$ 71,000

The affiliates filed a consolidated income tax return.

Required:
A. Prepare the entries made on the books of Miller Company during 1980 to record its interest in Edison Company.
B. Prepare consolidating workpapers for the year ended December 31, 1980.
C. Compare the consolidated balances from Part B with the consolidated balances arrived at in Problem 7–4, Part A.

Problem 7–10

Plaines Company purchased 80% of the outstanding common stock of Georgia Company on December 31, 1977 for $540,000. At that date, Georgia Company had common stock outstanding at a stated value of $450,000 and retained earnings of $135,000. Plaines Company purchased the Georgia Company stock from Georgia Company's major stockholder to acquire control of the rights to certain technical patents held by Georgia Company. Except for the patents, the book value of the recorded assets and liabilities of Georgia Company were equal to their fair value on December 31, 1977. On that date, Plaines Company executives estimated that the patent rights, which expire on December 31, 1982, had a fair value $50,000 in excess of their book value. Trial balances for both companies on December 31, 1981 are presented below.

	TRIAL BALANCE DECEMBER 31, 1981	
DEBITS	PLAINES CO.	GEORGIA CO.
Cash	55,900	86,850
Accounts Receivable	360,000	342,000
Inventories	246,600	385,200
Other Current Assets	75,500	79,150
Investment in Georgia Co.	540,000	
Notes Receivable	36,000	
Land	112,500	50,000
Property and Equipment	900,000	180,000
Technical Patents (net of accumulated amortization of $151,200)		37,800
Cost of Goods Sold	1,417,500	1,080,000
Expenses	292,500	157,500
Total Debits	4,036,500	2,398,500
CREDITS		
Accumulated Depreciation	459,000	31,500
Accounts Payable	159,750	196,200
Dividends Payable		40,500
Other Current Liabilities	110,250	69,300
Notes Payable		36,000
Capital Stock	1,350,000	450,000
Retained Earnings	67,500	225,000
Sales	1,890,000	1,350,000
Total Credits	4,036,500	2,398,500

The companies file separate income tax returns, and the average combined federal and state income tax rate for both companies is 40%. Georgia Company intends to permanently reinvest all earnings not currently distributed in the form of dividends. Additional information is presented below:

1. Any excess of cost over fair value is amortized over sixteen years.

2. Plaines Company sells merchandise to Georgia Company at the same prices and terms offered to other customers. During 1981, Plaines Company's sales to Georgia Company totaled $450,000. Georgia Company had $135,000 of merchandise purchased from Plaines Company on hand on December 31, 1981, which was an increase of $45,000 over the previous year. Georgia Company had not paid Plaines Company for $94,500 of the merchandise in

inventory and also owed Plaines Company for a $67,500 cash advance which was in Georgia Company's cash account on December 31, 1981.

3. On July 1, 1978, Georgia Company purchased a parcel of land from Plaines Company for $50,000 and a building on the land for $180,000. Georgia Company paid $86,000 cash and gave a mortgage which called for four payments of $36,000 each plus interest at 10% to be paid annually on the anniversary of the sale. Plaines Company credits the interest paid by Georgia Company to interest expense. The land originally cost Plaines Company $50,000, and Plaines Company's book value of the building was $135,000 at the date of the sale. Georgia Company estimated that the building had a 20-year life and no salvage value when purchased and has computed depreciation on a monthly basis.

4. Georgia Company declared a 9% cash dividend on December 22, 1981, payable on January 10, 1982 to stockholders of record on December 31, 1981. Plaines Company has not recorded this dividend at December 31, 1981. Neither company paid a dividend during 1981.

Required:
Prepare a consolidated financial statements workpaper for Plaines Company and its subsidiary, Georgia Company, as of December 31, 1981.

(AICPA adapted)

Problem 7–11
Project Company acquired 90% of the outstanding common stock of Salt River Company on June 30, 1980 for $426,000. On that date Salt River Company had retained earnings in the amount of $60,000, and the fair value of its recorded assets and liabilities was equal to their book value. The excess of cost over the fair value of the recorded net assets was attributed to an unrecorded manufacturing formula held by Salt River Company which had an expected remaining useful life of 5 years from June 30, 1980. The companies file consolidated income tax returns, and all earnings of Salt River Company that are not distributed currently are expected to be permanently reinvested.

Trial balances of the two companies on December 31, 1982 are presented below:

	TRIAL BALANCES DECEMBER 31, 1982	
DEBITS	PROJECT COMPANY	SALT RIVER COMPANY
Cash	119,500	132,500
Accounts Receivable	342,000	125,000
Inventory	362,000	201,000
Other Current Assets	40,500	13,000
Land	150,000	–0–
Investment in Salt River Co.	524,250	–0–
Property & Equipment	825,000	241,000
Cost of Goods Sold	1,730,000	690,500
Expenses	654,500	251,000
Dividends Declared	100,000	60,000
Total Debits	4,847,750	1,714,000

CREDITS		
Accumulated Depreciation	207,000	53,500
Accounts Payable	295,000	32,000
Other Current Liabilities	43,000	19,000
Capital Stock	1,000,000	300,000
Additional Paid-in Capital	-0-	50,000
Retained Earnings	591,200	139,500
Sales	2,555,500	1,120,000
Equity in Subsidiary Income	156,050	-0-
Total Credits	4,847,750	1,714,000

On December 31, 1980, Project Company sold equipment to Salt River Company at a profit of $47,500. This equipment has since been depreciated at an annual rate of 20% of the purchase price. During 1981, Salt River Company sold land to Project Company at a profit of $15,000.

The inventory of Project Company on December 31, 1981 included goods purchased from Salt River Company on which Salt River Company recognized a profit of $7,500. During 1982, Salt River Company sold goods to Project Company for $375,000, of which $60,000 was unpaid on December 31, 1982. The December 31, 1982 inventory of Project Company included goods acquired from Salt River Company on which Salt River Company recognized a profit of $10,500.

Required:

Prepare a consolidated financial statements workpaper for the year ending December 31, 1982.

Problem 7–12

During 1980, Princeton Company acquired a controlling interest in Standard Company. The trial balance of each company at December 31, 1980 is presented below:

DEBITS	PRINCETON COMPANY	STANDARD COMPANY
Cash	$ 602,000	$ 300,000
Notes Receivable	400,000	
Accounts Receivable	800,000	400,000
Interest Receivable	8,000	
Inventories	3,696,000	500,000
Investment in Standard Company	1,694,000	
Property and Equipment	5,000,000	2,000,000
Deferred Charges	100,000	
Land		220,000
Cost of Sales	5,400,000	2,100,000
Operating Expenses	1,004,000	692,000
Interest Expense		8,000
Dividends Declared		20,000
Total	$18,704,000	$6,240,000

CREDITS

Accounts Payable	$ 1,696,000	$ 320,000
Notes Payable		300,000
Dividend Payable		20,000
Accumulated Depreciation	2,000,000	600,000
Capital Stock	1,200,000	400,000
Retained Earnings	6,600,000	1,600,000
Sales and Services	7,200,000	3,000,000
Interest Income	8,000	
Total	$18,704,000	$6,240,000

Additional information regarding intercompany transactions and the account balances of the companies is presented below:

1. The affiliated companies file a consolidated income tax return for the calendar year 1980.

2. Princeton Company acquired a 70% interest in Standard Company on January 1, 1980 for $1,302,000 and an additional 20% interest on September 30, 1980 for $392,000.

3. The net income of Standard Company for the nine months ending September 30, 1980 was $100,000.

4. The fair value of the assets and liabilities of Standard Company is equal to their book value except for the balance in the land account. The management of Princeton Company estimated that the land had a fair value of $80,000 during 1980.

5. Standard Company's sales consist primarily of engineering services that are billed at cost plus 40%. During 1980, $200,000 was billed to Princeton Company; of this amount $116,000 was charged to operating expense and $84,000 was treated as a deferred charge on Princeton's books at December 31, 1980.

6. Standard Company declared a dividend of $20,000 on December 31, 1980, payable on January 10, 1981.

7. During 1980, equipment manufactured by Princeton Company at a cost of $200,000 was sold to Standard Company for $250,000. Standard Company depreciates such equipment over a 5-year life and follows the policy of recording one-half year's depreciation in the year in which assets are acquired or disposed of.

8. Merchandise sales in the amount of $300,000 were also made by Princeton Company to Standard Company. Goods that were sold for $80,000, remained in the inventory of Standard Company on December 31, 1980. There were no intercompany sales of merchandise prior to 1980.

9. On September 30, 1980, Princeton Company lent Standard Company $400,000 on an 8% note. Interest and principal are payable in quarterly installments beginning on December 31, 1980.

Required:
Prepare a consolidated financial statement workpaper for the year ending December 31, 1980. Include schedules supporting the calculation of the amounts of your workpaper adjusting and eliminating entries.

(AICPA adapted)

8

Changes in Investor's Equity Interest in Investees

Two assumptions concerning the equity interest acquired have been followed in previous chapters dealing with consolidated statements. Although not expressly stated, these assumptions were:

    1. The interest in the subsidiary or other investee was obtained through a single purchase of stock.

    2. The percentage of ownership remained constant.

Obviously, these assumptions are not always valid. For example, control of a subsidiary may not be obtained until two or more stock acquisitions have been made. Similarly, the percentage of ownership may change for several reasons, such as: (1) additional shares of the subsidiary or other investee may be acquired; (2) some of the shares held by the investor may be sold; (3) the subsidiary or other investee may engage in capital transactions with outside parties that change the investor's percentage of ownership. The problems arising from these changes in the investor's percentage of ownership are discussed and illustrated in this chapter.

ACQUISITION OF STOCK THROUGH SEVERAL PURCHASES

Open-Market Purchases

Sometimes the controlling interest in a subsidiary is acquired through the initial stock purchase; at other times control is not achieved until two or more stock purchases have been made. When control is achieved on the first purchase, the date of acquisition is the purchase date. Some disagreement exists among accountants as to what constitutes the date of acquisition, however, where several purchases are made before control is obtained.

Determination of the date of acquisition is important under purchase accounting because subsidiary retained earnings accumulated prior to that time constitute a portion of the equity acquired, whereas the parent's share of retained earnings accumulated subsequent to acquisition is properly included in consolidated retained earnings. If two or more purchases are made over a period of time, the retained earnings of the subsidiary at acquisition should generally be determined on a step-by-step basis; however, if small purchases are made over a period of time and then a purchase is made that results in control, the date of the latest purchase, as a matter of convenience, may be considered as the date of acquisition.[1] The step-by-step method is preferred because it produces a conceptually better determination of consolidated retained earnings. Because the second approach excludes from consolidated retained earnings the investor's share of the undistributed income of the investee earned prior to the date control is achieved, it can be supported only on the basis of expediency or convenience.

Equity Method   To illustrate the problems associated with step-by-step acquisitions, assume that S Company had 10,000 shares of $10 par common stock outstanding during the 1980–82 period and retained earnings as indicated below:

	S COMPANY RETAINED EARNINGS
January 1, 1980	40,000
January 1, 1981	70,000
January 1, 1982	120,000
December 31, 1982	185,000

P Company acquired S Company common stock by cash purchase on the open market as follows:

DATE	SHARES ACQUIRED	COST
1/1/80	1,500 (15%)	21,000
1/1/81	1,000 (10%)	20,000
1/1/82	6,500 (65%)	168,000

Some additional simplifying assumptions are made in order to concentrate attention on the new issues introduced and because the issues covered by the assumptions have been discussed in detail in previous chapters. The assumptions are:

[1] *Accounting Research Bulletin No. 51,* "Consolidated Financial Statements" (New York: AICPA, 1959), Par. 10.

1. Any difference between cost and book value of the various purchases relates solely to the undervaluation of land owned by S Company and is, therefore, not subject to amortization.

2. S Company distributes no dividends during the periods under consideration. Thus, the increase in S Company retained earnings each year represents income earned during that year.

3. Income tax deferral on the investor's share of the undistributed income of the subsidiary or other investee is ignored.

4. P Company uses the equity method on its books to account for nonsubsidiary investments that must be reported under the equity method in accordance with *APB Opinion No. 18.*

As discussed earlier, the initial purchase of the 15% interest in S Company is recorded at its cost of $21,000 and reported at cost on P Company's balance sheet on December 31, 1980 because less than 20% of the stock is owned. No income on the investment would be reported for 1980 because no dividends were distributed by S Company. The second purchase on January 1, 1981 is also recorded at its cost of $20,000. Because P Company now has a 25% interest in S Company, however, the equity method of reporting is required, and P Company will restate its investment in S Company by the equity method on its books through the following entry:

Investment in S Company	4,500	
Retained Earnings		4,500

During 1980, S Company earned $30,000, 15% of which accrues to the benefit of P Company. *APB Opinion No. 18* provides:

> An investment in common stock of an investee that was previously accounted for on other than the equity method may become qualified for the use of the equity method by an increase in the level of ownership. . . . When an investment qualifies for use of the equity method, the investor should adopt the equity method of accounting. The investment, results of operations, and retained earnings of the investor should be adjusted retroactively in a manner consistent with the accounting for a step-by-step acquisition of a subsidiary.[2]

At the end of 1981, P Company will recognize investment income of $12,500 ($50,000 $\times$ .25) and will report its Investment in S Company at $58,000 ($21,000 + $20,000 + $4,500 + $12,500) on its December 31, 1981 balance sheet.

With the acquisition of an additional 65% interest on January 1, 1982, P Company has a 90% controlling interest in S Company and will normally consolidate S Company in its December 31, 1982 statements. Assume that P Company continues to employ the equity method on its books. In the preparation of a consolidated workpaper at December 31, 1982, it is necessary to compute the amount of S Company equity to

---

[2]*APB Opinion No. 18,* "The Equity Method of Accounting for Investments in Common Stock" (New York: AICPA, 1971), Par. 19m. (If comparative statements are prepared, all prior-year statements presented must be restated.)

eliminate, as well as the difference between cost and book value. On a step-by-step basis, the computation is as follows:

| | PURCHASE | | | |
	1ST	2ND	3RD	TOTAL
Cost	21,000	20,000	168,000	209,000
Equity Acquired:				
Common Stock	15,000	10,000	65,000	90,000
Retained Earnings	¹ 6,000	² 7,000	³ 78,000	91,000
Total	21,000	17,000	143,000	181,000
Difference Between				
Cost and Book Value	–0–	3,000	25,000	28,000

¹15% × $40,000
²10% × $70,000
³65% × $120,000

The Investment in S Company account is reproduced below as it would appear at the end of 1982:

INVESTMENT IN S COMPANY		
1/1/80 Purchase	21,000	
1/1/81 Purchase	20,000	
1/1/81 Adjustment 15% × 30,000	4,500	
12/31/81 Sub. Income	12,500	
1/1/82 Purchase	168,000	
12/31/82 Sub. Income	¹58,500	
Balance	284,500	

¹ 90% × $65,000

The workpaper eliminating entries on December 31, 1982, in general journal form, would be:

Equity in Subsidiary Income	58,500	
Investment in S Company		58,500
To eliminate subsidiary income.		
Common Stock—S Company	90,000	
Retained Earnings, 1/1 (.9 × 120,000)	108,000	
Land	28,000	
Investment in S Company		226,000
To eliminate investment in S Company.		

Cost Method   Assume now that P Company elected to account for its investment in S Company by the cost method.[3] The investment account would contain the total cost of all three purchases in the amount of $209,000. No particular problem is created by use of the cost method except that care must be used in determining the amount needed to establish reciprocity on the consolidated workpaper. At December 31, 1982, the first time that S Company would be included in the consolidated statements, reciprocity would be established by the following workpaper entry:

Investment in S Company	17,000	
Retained Earnings—P Company		17,000

The amount is computed as follows:

UNDISTRIBUTED INCOME OF S COMPANY			YEAR END	P COMPANY'S SHARE OF S COMPANY'S
YEAR	AMOUNT		% OF OWNERSHIP	UNDISTRIBUTED INCOME
1980	30,000	×	15%	4,500
1981	50,000	×	25%	12,500
Total				17,000

After reciprocity is established, the investment is eliminated by the same workpaper eliminating entry required under the equity method, that is:

Common Stock—S Company	90,000	
Retained Earnings—S Company	108,000	
Land	28,000	
Investment in S Company		226,000

Completion of the workpaper would be as illustrated in previous chapters. The computation of minority interest would continue to be made by multiplying the end-of-year minority interest percentage times subsidiary income and subsidiary equity amounts.

Purchase of Shares Directly from Subsidiary

The preceding example assumed that the subsidiary shares were purchased on the open market. It is possible, of course, to purchase the shares directly from the subsidiary, in which case care must be exercised in the determination of equity acquired and any difference between cost and book value. When the shares are acquired directly from the subsidiary, the proceeds flow to the subsidiary and increase its stockholders' equity.

---

[3]If the cost method were used on the books of P Company, an adjustment would be needed on P Company's individual workpaper at the end of 1981 to restate its investment in S Company to equity for reporting in P Company's financial statements, because P Company owned more than a 20% interest at that time.

In addition, the new issue of shares by the subsidiary may be purchased entirely by the parent company, partly by the parent and partly by the minority shareholders, or entirely by the minority shareholders.

New Shares Acquired by the Parent Only—Cost Method   Where the parent company holds less than a 100% interest and acquires the entire new issue of stock directly from the subsidiary, one of two situations must exist: (1) Either the preemptive right has been waived previously; or (2) The minority shareholders have elected not to exercise their rights. The acquisition of the entire new issue will increase the parent company's *percentage* of ownership with an equal reduction in the minority interest's percentage of ownership. The computation of the book value of the interest acquired requires determination of the parent's share of the book value of the subsidiary's equity immediately prior to and immediately after the new purchase.

To illustrate, assume that P Company acquired 14,000 shares (70%) of S Company at par value for cash ($140,000) when S Company was formed on January 1, 1975; thus, there is no difference between cost and book value. P Company uses the *cost method.*

On January 1, 1980, P Company acquired 4,000 additional shares of S Company stock directly from S Company for $20 per share. Minority shareholders elected not to participate in the new issue. On December 31, 1979, S Company's equity was as follows:

Common Stock, $10 par	$200,000
Retained Earnings	150,000
Total	$350,000

P Company's percentage of ownership after this acquisiton is 75% (18,000/24,000 shares). The computation of the book value of the interest acquired in this purchase is made as follows:

	BOOK VALUE OF P COMPANY'S SHARE OF S COMPANY'S EQUITY		BOOK VALUE OF INTEREST ACQUIRED
	BEFORE NEW PURCHASE (70%)	AFTER NEW PURCHASE (75%)	
Common Stock	[1]140,000	[2]180,000	40,000
Retained Earnings	[3]105,000	[4]112,500	7,500
Premium on Common Stock	–0–	[5] 30,000	30,000
Total	245,000	322,500	77,500

[1].7 × 200,000
[2].75 × 240,000
[3].7 × 150,000
[4].75 × 150,000
[5].75 × 40,000

The cost of the new shares was $80,000 (4,000 × $20), and the book value of the interest acquired was $77,500, as determined above; thus, a debit difference of $2,500 exists between cost and book value. The nature of this difference should be examined closely because it does not necessarily have any relationship in amount to an undervaluation of subsidiary assets or overvaluation of subsidiary liabilities. In essence, it results from a decision by the majority interest (the parent company) to provide some additional financing for the subsidiary via an equity transaction. In effect, the parent has transferred $2,500 of its share of S Company's equity to the minority interest. Although the minority shareholders did not participate in the new issue and their percentage of interest decreased, the amount of their total interest in S Company's net assets increased by $2,500. The amount can be verified as follows:

Minority Interest

Before the new issue	.30 × 350,000 = 105,000
After the new issue	.25 × 430,000 = 107,500
Increase in minority interest	2,500

Because it results from an equity transaction, the $2,500 is treated as a reduction in additional paid-in capital.

The workpaper entry to establish reciprocity for the preparation of a consolidated balance sheet immediately after the new purchase would be:

Investment in S Company	105,000	
Retained Earnings—P Company		105,000
To establish reciprocity: .7 × 150,000 increase in S Company retained earnings since date of acquisition.		

Reciprocity is established to January 1, 1980 on the basis of the percentage of ownership (70%) that existed prior to the acquisition of the additional shares. In subsequent years, reciprocity will be established on the basis of a 70% interest for the period prior to January 1, 1980 and 75% thereafter.

The December 31, 1980 workpaper entry to eliminate the investment account would be:

Common Stock—S Company	180,000	
Retained Earnings—S Company	112,500	
Premium on Common Stock—S Company	30,000	
Additional Paid-in Capital—P Company	2,500	
Investment in S Company		325,000
(140,000 + 105,000 + 80,000)		

It should be noted that the $2,500 increase in the minority interest arose because P Company acquired the additional shares from S Company at a price ($20) in excess of the book value per share of stock ($17.50). If the new shares had been issued at a price equal to their book value, total minority interest would have remained unchanged, and there would be no difference between cost and book value; if the new shares had been issued at a price less than their book value, total minority interest would have decreased, and there would be a credit to additional paid-in capital in the elimination entry. The reader may wish to make the appropriate computations to verify this.

If the *equity* method had been used in the situation above, the analysis and eliminating entry would be the same except, of course, there would be no need for the workpaper entry to establish reciprocity.

New Shares Acquired by Parent and Minority Shareholders—Cost Method   In the previous example, minority shareholders elected not to exercise their right to subscribe to the new issue of stock. If the minority shareholders had elected to exercise their right, the percentage of stock owned by the parent and minority shareholders after the new issue would be the same as their respective interests prior to the issue.

Assume, for example, the previous situation except that P Company is permitted to acquire only its ratable share of the new issue and the remaining shares are acquired by the minority shareholders. Thus, P Company would acquire 2,800 of the new shares and would retain its 70% (16,800/24,000 shares) interest in S Company. Determination of the book value of the interest acquired by P Company is as follows:

PAID MORE THAN BV BUT BV ACQUIRED IS THE SAME AS THAT PAID EQUAL PERCENTAGE BEFORE AFTER

	BOOK VALUE OF P COMPANY'S SHARE OF S COMPANY'S EQUITY		
	BEFORE NEW PURCHASE (70%)	AFTER NEW PURCHASE (70%)	BOOK VALUE OF INTEREST ACQUIRED
Common Stock	[1]140,000	[2]168,000	28,000
Retained Earnings	[3]105,000	[4]105,000	–0–
Premium on Common Stock	–0–	[5] 28,000	28,000
Total	245,000	301,000	56,000

[1].7 × $200,000
[2].7 × $240,000
[3].7 × $150,000
[4].7 × $150,000
[5].7 × $40,000

Note that the book value of the interest acquired is equal to cost (2,800 × $20), and no difference between cost and book value exists. This condition will always result if the shares are subscribed to ratably by the existing stockholders, regardless of whether the new shares are issued at a price below, equal to, or above their book value.

Workpaper entries to establish reciprocity and eliminate the investment account for the preparation of a consolidated balance sheet immediately after the new issue would be:

Investment in S Company	105,000	
Retained Earnings—P Company		105,000
To establish reciprocity: .7 × 150,000.		
Common Stock—S Company	168,000	
Retained Earnings—S Company	105,000	
Premium on Common Stock—S Company	28,000	
Investment in S Company		301,000
(140,000 + 105,000 + 56,000)		

Like the preceding situation, if the *equity* method were used, the analysis and eliminating entry would be the same as that above. Again, the entry to establish reciprocity would not be necessary.

New Shares Acquired by Minority Interest Only—Cost Method

    Occasionally, in order to obtain an additional capital increment for the consolidated entity, the subsidiary may issue new shares entirely to minority shareholders. Since any shares acquired by the parent would represent a transfer of funds within the affiliated group, purchases by the parent do not provide any additional capital to the group as a whole. As long as the number of new shares issued is not so large that it reduces the parent's percentage of ownership below that needed for control, new equity financing can be made available and control retained.

The issue of new shares to minority shareholders does, of course, reduce the parent company's percentage of ownership. However, the book value of the parent's interest in the subsidiary may increase or decrease depending upon the relationship of the issue price to book value per share of stock.

To illustrate, assume that P Company acquired, for $320,000 cash, 18,000 shares (90%) of the outstanding common stock of S Company on January 1, 1978 when S Company had $10 par common stock of $200,000 and retained earnings of $100,000. The $50,000 difference (320,000 − [.9 × 300,000]) between cost and book value relates to undervalued subsidiary land, and is, therefore, not subject to amortization. P Company uses the *cost method* to account for its investment in S Company on its books. By January 1, 1980, S Company's retained earnings had increased to $180,000.

On January 1, 1980, S Company issued 4,000 shares of its authorized stock to minority shareholdes for $25 per share. The new issue results in a decrease in P Company's percentage of ownership from 90% to 75% (18,000/24,000 shares). The change in the book value of P Company's interest in S Company is determined as before by an immediately "before" and "after" computation.

	BOOK VALUE OF P COMPANY'S SHARE OF S COMPANY'S EQUITY		
	BEFORE NEW ISSUE (90%)	AFTER NEW ISSUE (75%)	INCREASE (DECREASE)
Common Stock	[1]180,000	[2]180,000	–0–
Retained Earnings	[3]162,000	[4]135,000	(27,000)
Premium on Common Stock	–0–	[5] 45,000	45,000
Total	342,000	360,000	18,000

[1].9 × $200,000
[2].75 × $240,000
[3].9 × $180,000
[4].75 × $180,000
[5].75 × $60,000

[handwritten: INCREASE IN BV MAY OFFSET DECREASE IN OWNERSHIP PERCENTAGE]

Although P Company's ownership interest decreased from 90% to 75%, the book value of its interest in S Company after the new issue increased by $18,000. The workpaper adjusting entry to give effect to the increase is:

Investment in S Company	18,000	
Additional Paid-in Capital		18,000[4]

Note that this adjusting entry is a workpaper-only entry because the cost method is being used. If the *equity method* were used, the entry would be made on the *books* of P Company. In either case the increase must be added to the investment account, since it reflects an increase in P Company's share of S Company's net assets. Disagreement exists concerning the proper accounting treatment of the credit element of the entry. Some accountants argue that the increase (decrease) in equity should properly be reflected in net income of the parent company. This view has some merit in the preparation of parent-company-only statements. The other view, which we support, is a total entity view. If the two companies, parent and subsidiary, are considered to be one economic entity, then that entity should not recognize gain or loss from dealings in its own equity shares. Thus, the increase (decrease) should be treated as the result of an equity transaction and carried to additional paid-in capital.

[handwritten: BOTH ENTRIES NECCESSARY BOTH CHANGE VALUE OF INVESTMENT]

Workpaper entries to establish reciprocity and eliminate the investment account for the preparation of a consolidated balance sheet immediately after the new issue would be:

[handwritten: PICK UP % INCREASE IN R/E]

Investment in S Company	72,000	
Retained Earnings—P Company		72,000
To establish reciprocity: .9 × 80,000.		

[4]If the new issue had resulted in a decrease in P Company's equity in S Company, the entry would simply be reversed, unless P Company had no additional paid-in capital, in which case the debit would be to retained earnings.

As discussed earlier, in subsequent years reciprocity would be established on the basis of a 90% interest prior to January 1, 1980 and a 75% interest thereafter.

Common Stock—S Company	180,000	
Retained Earnings—S Company	135,000	
Premium on Common Stock—S Company	45,000	
Land	50,000	
Investment in S Company		410,000
(320,000 + 72,000 + 18,000)		

(Again, under the *equity method* the eliminating entry would be the same; the entry to establish reciprocity is not necessary.)

Note that in the example above the new shares were issued at a price in excess of book value, which resulted in an increase in P Company's share of S Company's net assets. If the new shares had been issued at a price below book value, a decrease in P Company's share of S Company's net assets would have resulted; if they had been issued at a price equal to book value, there would be no change in P Company's share of S Company's assets.

DISPOSALS OF SUBSIDIARY STOCK INVESTMENTS

The sale of all or a portion of its investment by the parent company is treated in a manner similar to that used to account for the disposal of any other corporate asset. The asset received is recorded, the portion of the investment sold is eliminated, and gain or loss is recognized on the sale as the difference between the value of the asset received and the carrying value of the investment sold. Because the value of the asset received is generally easily measured, the amount of any gain or loss recognized hinges upon the appropriate measurement of the carrying value of the investment sold. If only a portion of the investment is sold, federal tax law specifies that either specific identification or the first-in, first-out (FIFO) method must be used to determine the value of the shares disposed of. These methods are also acceptable for accounting purposes; we will assume use of the first-in, first-out method.

The amount of gain or loss on sale recorded by the parent company will vary, depending upon whether the investment has been accounted for under the cost method or the equity method. Book entries and workpaper elimination entries under both methods will be discussed and illustrated. The ultimate effect on consolidated income and retained earnings, however, will be the same under either method.

To illustrate the procedures involved in the sale of part of an investment, assume that P Company acquired shares of S Company as follows:

DATE	SHARES ACQUIRED	COST
1/1/79	12,000 (60%)	175,000
1/1/80	6,000 (30%)	100,000

S Company's stockholders' equity for 1979 and 1980 was:

	1979	1980
Common Stock, $10 par	200,000	200,000
1/1 Retained Earnings	60,000	100,000
Net Income	50,000	60,000
Dividends Declared, 10/30	(10,000)	(20,000)
12/31 Retained Earnings	100,000	140,000
Total Equity, 12/31	300,000	340,000

Comparison of cost with the book value of equity acquired for each stock purchase produces the following results:

	1ST PURCHASE	2ND PURCHASE
Cost	175,000	100,000
Book Value of Equity Acquired	[1]156,000	[2] 90,000
Difference Between Cost and Book Value	19,000	10,000

[1].6 × 260,000
[2].3 × 300,000

The $29,000 difference between cost and book value relates to the undervaluation of a nonamortizable fixed asset.

Assume further that on July 1, 1980, P Company sold 2,400 of its S Company shares for $25 per share. Under the first-in, first-out method, the shares sold represent 20% of those acquired in the first purchase on January 1, 1979. After the sale, P Company retains control with a 78% (15,600/20,000 shares) interest.

Equity Method

If P Company uses the equity method to account for its investment in S Company, the investment account would appear as follows on July 1, 1980, the date of the sale:

INVESTMENT IN S COMPANY

1/1/79 Purchase	175,000	10/30/79 Dividends	6,000
12/31/79 Sub. Income	30,000		
12/31/79 Balance	199,000		
1/1/80 Purchase	100,000		
6/30/80 Sub. Income*	27,000		
6/30/80 Balance	326,000		

*It is assumed that P Company received a 6-month interim income statement from S Company reporting $30,000 net income, of which P Company recognized 90%.[5]

P Company would make the following entry to reflect the sale of its S Company shares:

Cash	60,000	
Investment in S Company*		43,400
Gain on Sale of Investments		16,600

*Cost of 1st Purchase	175,000
1979 Income	30,000
1970 Dividends Received	(6,000)
1980 Income to July 1 (.6 × 30,000)	18,000
Total	217,000
Portion Sold	20%
Total Carrying Value Sold	43,400

[handwritten:] 27000 = 90% 18,000 = 60% ↑ AMOUNT ATTACHED TO FIRST PURCHASE

A workpaper for the preparation of consolidated financial statements on December 31, 1980 under the equity method is presented in Illustration 8–1. Data necessary to complete the workpaper, other than those previously provided, were simply assumed.

[5]If interim statements are not available near the date of sale, two options are available: (1) the sale of the stock may be credited to a suspense account until subsidiary statements are received, at which time the appropriate entry is made to eliminate the suspense account, reduce the investment account, and recognize gain or loss on the sale; or (2) the investment account may be credited at the time of sale for the carrying value of the shares sold as of the beginning of the year. In the latter case, the investment account would be credited for $39,800 (.2 × 199,000) in our example, and a gain on sale recognized in the amount of $20,200. This treatment will not change total consolidated income, although $3,600 will be reported as gain on sale of investments rather than as operating income. If this approach is used, subsidiary income at the end of the year would be recognized by P Company in an amount equal to reported subsidiary income times the end-of-year percentage of ownership, $46,800 (78% × 60,000) in this example.

ILLUSTRATION 8–1

Purchase Accounting   **Consolidated Statements Workpaper**
Sale of Part of Investment   **P Company and Subsidiary**
Equity Method   **For the Year Ended December 31, 1980**

	P COMPANY	S COMPANY	ELIMINATIONS DR.	ELIMINATIONS CR.	MINORITY INTEREST	CONSOLIDATED BALANCES
INCOME STATEMENT						
Net Income Before Sub. Income and Gain on Sale of Investment	120,000	60,000				180,000
Equity in Subsidiary Income	50,400		¹ 46,800			3,600
Gain on Sale of Investment	16,600					16,600
Total	187,000	60,000				200,200
Minority Interest (.22 × 60,000)					13,200	(13,200)
Net Income to Retained Earnings	187,000	60,000	46,800	–0–	13,200	187,000
RETAINED EARNINGS STATEMENT						
1/1 Retained Earnings						
P Company	306,000					306,000
S Company		100,000	² 78,000		22,000	
Net Income from above	187,000	60,000	46,800	–0–	13,200	187,000
Dividends Declared, 10/30						
P Company	(40,000)					(40,000)
S Company		(20,000)		¹ 15,600	(4,400)	
12/31 Retained Earnings to Balance Sheet	453,000	140,000	124,800	15,600	30,800	453,000
BALANCE SHEET						
Current Assets	220,000	100,000				320,000
Investment in S Company	290,400			¹ 31,200 ²259,200		
Other Assets	572,600	315,000				887,600
Difference Between Cost & Book Value			² 25,200			25,200
Total	1,083,000	415,000				1,232,800
Liabilities	130,000	75,000				205,000
Common Stock						
P Company	500,000					500,000
S Company		200,000	²156,000		44,000	
Retained Earnings from above	453,000	140,000	124,800	15,600	30,800	453,000
Minority Interest					74,800	74,800
Total	1,083,000	415,000	306,000	306,000		1,232,800

¹To reverse the effect of subsidiary income and dividends during the year.
²To eliminate investment in S Company.

Several items on the workpaper should be specifically noted:

1. Subsidiary income was recognized by P Company on December 31, 1980 for the second half of the year in the amount of $23,400 (78% × 30,000). Thus, total equity in subsidiary income is $50,400 (27,000 + 23,400). Dividends were declared by S Company after the sale; thus, P Company received 78% of the dividend, or $15,600. Verification of the investment account balance follows:

Balance, 7/1/80	326,000
Reduction for sale of stock	(43,400)
Increase for 7/1 to 12/31 income	23,400
Reduction for dividends received	(15,600)
Balance, 12/31/80	290,400

2. Minority interest in income is based on the December 31, 1980 percentage of 22%.

3. Although $50,400 of subsidiary income was recognized, only $46,800 is eliminated. The remaining $3,600 (.6 × 30,000 × .2) was sold to the minority interest with the sale of stock and is, therefore, extended to the consolidated column, after which the full minority interest in income of $13,200 is deducted. On the formal consolidated income statement the $3,600 is simply included as other income.

4. The elimination of S Company equity against the investment account is based on end-of-year equity owned, or 78%.

5. The difference between cost and book value is $25,200 rather than the originally computed amount of $29,000. This result reflects the fact that 20% of the $19,000 difference on the first purchase of stock was sold with the sale of stock. If the difference had been allocated to depreciable assets, the unamortized portion would have been reduced by 20%, and future adjustments to depreciation expense would be reduced accordingly.

Cost Method

If P Company uses the cost method to account for its investment in S Company, the following entry would be made to reflect the sale of stock:

Cash	60,000	
Investment in S Company (.2 × 175,000)		35,000
Gain on Sale of Investments		25,000

The $25,000 gain recorded by P Company contains three elements: (1) P Company's share of the undistributed profits of S Company from the date of acquisition to the beginning of 1980 on the shares sold, $4,800 (.2 × .6 × 40,000); (2) P Company's share of the undistributed profits of S Company for 1/1/80 to 7/1/80, $3,600 (.2 × .6 × 30,000); and (3) fluctuations in the value of the stock that come about from a variety of market factors other than accumulated earnings. Although the full gain is properly reflected in P Company's records, for consolidated statement purposes the gain must be allocated between that relating to the undistributed profits on the shares sold to the beginning of the year of sale and that arising from other factors. Such allocation is necessary because the undistributed profits to 1/1/80 on the shares sold have already been included in consolidated income during 1979. Because P Company uses the cost method, however, its share of the undistributed profits of S Company to 1/1/80 is not included in its beginning retained earnings as taken from its records. Inclusion of the full gain in income again would represent a double counting of the undistributed profits portion of the gain. Thus, an entry is made on the consolidated workpaper only as follows:

Gain on Sale of Investments	4,800	
Retained Earnings—P Company		4,800
(.2 × 24,000)		

During 1979, S Company's retained earnings increased by $40,000, $24,000 (60%) of which accrued to the benefit of P Company. Because 20% of the investment was sold, $4,800 represents undistributed profits on the shares sold.

A second entry may be made on the workpaper to reclassify the remaining portion of the gain ($20,200) between operating income and market gain. During the first six months of 1980, S Company earned $30,000, $18,000 (60%) of which related to the first purchase. Because 20% of the first purchase was held during the first six months of 1980, and then sold, $3,600 may be reclassified as operating income in the consolidated income statement. This entry is an optional one in that it has no effect on total consolidated income.

Illustration 8–2 presents a workpaper for the preparation of consolidated statements on December 31, 1980 under the cost method.

SUBSIDIARY TREASURY STOCK TRANSACTIONS SUBSEQUENT TO ACQUISITION

The parent company's percentage of ownership and total equity interest in its subsidiary may increase or decrease as a result of its subsidiary's dealings in its own shares. Although it is possible for a subsidiary to reacquire some of its own shares entirely from minority shareholders, entirely from the parent company, or in part from both, the latter two situations are relatively rare and, therefore, will not be discussed here. Subsidiary treasury stock transactions are generally open-market purchases under which the shares are reacquired from minority shareholders.

ILLUSTRATION 8-2

Purchase Accounting
Sale of Part of Investment
Cost Method

Consolidated Statements Workpaper
P Company and Subsidiary
For the Year Ended December 31, 1980

	P COMPANY	S COMPANY	ELIMINATIONS DR.	ELIMINATIONS CR.	MINORITY INTEREST	CONSOLIDATED BALANCES
INCOME STATEMENT						
Net Income Before Dividends and Gain on Sale of Investments	120,000	60,000		² 3,600		183,600
Dividend Income	15,600		³ 15,600			
Gain on Sale of Investment	25,000		¹ 4,800			16,600
			² 3,600			
Total	160,600	60,000				200,200
Minority Interest						
(.22 × 60,000)					13,200	(13,200)
Net Income to						
Retained Earnings	160,600	60,000	24,000	3,600	13,200	187,000
RETAINED EARNINGS STATEMENT						
1/1 Retained Earnings						
P Company	282,000			¹ 4,800		
				⁴ 19,200		306,000
S Company		100,000	⁵ 78,000		22,000	
Net Income from above	160,600	60,000	24,000	3,600	13,200	187,000
Dividends Declared, 10/30						
P Company	(40,000)					(40,000)
S Company		(20,000)		³ 15,600	(4,400)	
12/31 Retained Earnings to						
Balance Sheet	402,600	140,000	102,000	43,200	30,800	453,000
BALANCE SHEET						
Current Assets	220,000	100,000				320,000
Investment in S Company	240,000		⁴ 19,200	⁵259,200		
Other Assets	572,600	315,000				887,600
Difference Between Cost						
& Book Value			⁵ 25,200			25,200
Total	1,032,600	415,000				1,232,800
Liabilities	130,000	75,000				205,000
Common Stock						
P Company	500,000					500,000
S Company		200,000	⁵156,000		44,000	
Retained Earnings from above	402,600	140,000	102,000	43,200	30,800	453,000
Minority Interest					74,800	74,800
Total	1,032,600	415,000	302,400	302,400		1,232,800

[1]To adjust gain on sale of investment for portion included in income in prior years.
[2]To allocate remaining gain between operating income and gain on sale of investments.
[3]To eliminate intercompany dividends.
[4]To recognize P Company's share of S Company's undistributed income from the date of acquisition to the beginning of the current year on the first purchase shares retained (40,000 $\times$ .6 $\times$ .8).
[5]To eliminate investment in S Company.

Shares Reacquired Entirely from the Minority Shareholders

The reacquisition by a subsidiary of some of its shares from the minority shareholders results in an increase in the parent's percentage interest in the subsidiary. The parent's share of the subsidiary's net assets will increase or decrease depending upon whether the shares are reacquired at an amount below or above their book value per share.

RAISES OWNERSHIP PERCENTAGE

EFFECT ON BV ?

To illustrate, assume that P Company acquired 18,000 shares (75%) of the common stock of S Company on January 1, 1980 for $300,000 in cash when S Company had the following stockholders' equity:

Common Stock, $10 par	240,000
Retained Earnings	100,000
Total	340,000

The difference between cost and book value of $45,000 (300,000 $-$ [.75 $\times$ 340,000]) relates to the undervaluation of S Company land.

By January 1, 1981, S Company's retained earnings had increased to $140,000. On January 2, 1981, S Company reacquired 1,500 shares of its stock from minority shareholders at $20 per share, or a total of $30,000. Treasury stock is accounted for by the cost method.

On subsequent consolidated statements workpapers the offset entry to eliminate the treasury stock account would be:

EFFECTIVELY TREATING AS RETIRED STOCK

Common Stock—S Company	15,000	
Retained Earnings—S Company	15,000	
Treasury Stock		30,000

The acquisition of the treasury shares by S Company results in an increase in P Company's percentage interest from 75% to 80% (18,000/22,500 shares), and a decrease in the book value of its interest in S Company of $5,000 as computed below:

| | BOOK VALUE OF P COMPANY'S SHARE OF S COMPANY'S EQUITY | | |
	BEFORE THE TREASURY STOCK ACQUISITION (75%)	AFTER THE TREASURY STOCK ACQUISITION (80%)	INCREASE (DECREASE)
Common Stock	[1]180,000	[2]180,000	–0–
Retained Earnings	[3]105,000	[4]100,000	(5,000)
Total	285,000	280,000	(5,000)

[1] .75 × 240,000
[2] .8 × (240,000 − 15,000)
[3] .75 × 140,000
[4] .8 × (140,000 − 15,000)

Thus, an adjusting entry is required, on the books of P Company under the *equity method* and on the consolidated workpaper under the *cost method* as follows:

| Additional paid-in capital | 5,000 | |
| Investment in S Company | | 5,000 |

In the event P Company has no additional paid-in capital, the debit above would be to retained earnings. The entry must be made on the workpaper in each subsequent year if the cost method is used.

Workpaper entries for the preparation of a consolidated balance sheet immediately after the reacquisition of the treasury stock under cost and equity methods would be:

Under the cost method to establish reciprocity:

Investment in S Company	30,000	
Retained Earnings—P Company		30,000
(.75 × 40,000)		

Under both cost and equity methods, the eliminating entry for the investment would be:

Common Stock (.8 × 225,000)	180,000	
Retained Earnings (.8 × 125,000)	100,000	
Difference Between Cost and Book Value	45,000	
Investment in S Company		325,000

Note that reciprocity is established under the cost method on the basis of the percentage of ownership (75%) as of the beginning of the year, 1981. In workpapers for subsequent years, reciprocity is established under the cost method on the basis of a 75% interest for the period prior to January 2, 1981 and 80% thereafter. For example, assume that S Company earned $50,000 during 1981 and declared no dividends.

Entries to adjust the investment account for the decrease in equity from the treasury stock transaction and to establish reciprocity at the beginning of 1982 on the December 31, 1982 workpaper would be:

Additional paid-in capital	5,000	
Investment in S Company		5,000
Investment in S Company	70,000	
Retained Earnings—P Company		70,000

P Company's Share of the Undistributed Income of S Company

← ALWAYS DO IT

Prior to 1/1/81	.75 × 40,000 =	30,000
Subsequent to 1/1/81	.8 × 50,000 =	40,000
Total		70,000

The computation above is often included on the bottom of the workpaper so that it is readily available for reference in subsequent periods.

Workpaper preparation in subsequent periods under the equity method presents no problem. P Company will recognize 80% of S Company's income after January 1, 1981, and workpaper eliminating entries are made as usual by eliminating subsidiary equity on the basis of the end-of-year percentage of ownership.

Reissue of Treasury Shares by Subsidiary

The subsidiary may reissue some or all of its treasury stock entirely to the parent company, entirely to minority shareholders, or to both. In all of these treasury stock reissue situations the accounting is analogous to that concerning the issue of new shares of subsidiary stock as previously discussed. An immediately before-and-after computation of the parent's share of the book value of the subsidiary's equity is made in order to determine the amount of the increase or decrease in the book value of the parent company's interest in the subsidiary. The amount of the resulting increase or decrease is recorded as an adjustment to the investment account and to additional paid-in capital on the books under the equity method and treated as a workpaper only entry under the cost method.

SAME AS ISSUE OF NEW STOCK

OTHER EQUITY INVESTMENTS

Up to this point, the discussion in this chapter has concerned the appropriate treatment of changes in the investor's interest in its investees primarily in regard to their effect on parent-subsidiary relationships. Book entries similar to those described for parent-subsidiary relationships *where the equity method is used* are required for investors holding less than a 50% interest and using the equity method, in accordance with *APB Opinion No. 18*. Thus, the treatment developed earlier for disposals of a portion of the investment and changes in equity resulting from sales or purchases by the investee of its own shares to or from minority shareholders is applicable to all investments accounted for by the equity method.

CHANGE IN METHOD OF ACCOUNTING FOR NONCONSOLIDATED INVESTMENTS

Sometimes it becomes necessary to change the method of accounting for an investment in common stock of an investee company. For example, an investment that was accounted for by the cost method because it constituted less than a 20% interest may become qualified for use of the equity method because of an increase in the percent of ownership. The investor may acquire additional shares, or the investee may reacquire sufficient shares, to increase the investor's percentage of ownership to a level that requires use of the equity method. The procedures to be followed in converting to the equity method were discussed in the first section of this chapter dealing with step-by-step purchases. As you recall, the basic requirement is retroactive adjustment of the investment account, results of operations, and retained earnings of the investor.

Likewise, the level of an investment previously accounted for by the equity method may be reduced to a point where it no longer qualifies for reporting under the equity method. For example, the investor may sell part of its investment, or the investee may issue new shares to other parties, thereby reducing the investor's percent of ownership to less than 20%. If this occurs, the investor should discontinue use of the equity method. The earnings or losses that relate to the stock retained by the investor and that were previously accrued should remain as a part of the carrying amount of the investment; that is, the investment account *should not* be adjusted retroactively. However, dividends received by the investor in subsequent periods which exceed his share of earnings for such periods should be applied to reduce the carrying amount of the investment.[6]

Questions

1. Identify three types of transactions that result in a change in a parent company's ownership interest in its subsidiary.

2. Explain how the equity method of accounting is applied when the investment is acquired through a series of stock acquisitions and the initial acquisition was accounted for by the cost method.

___

[6]*APB Opinion No. 18*, "The Equity Method of Accounting for Investments in Common Stock" (New York: AICPA, 1971), Par. 19 (1).

3. P Company holds an 80% interest in S Company. Determine the effect (i.e., increase, decrease, no change, not determinable) on both the total book value of the minority interest and on the minority interest's percentage of ownership in the net assets of S Company for each of the following situations:
    a. P Company acquires additional shares directly from S Company at a price equal to the book value per share of the S Company stock immediately prior to the issuance.
    b. S Company acquires its own shares on the open market. The cost of these shares is less than their book value.
    c. Assume the same situation as in (b) except that the cost of the shares is greater than their book value.
    d. P Company and a minority shareholder each acquire 100 shares directly from S Company at a price below the book value per share.

4. When a subsidiary issues additional shares of stock and such issuance results in an increase in the book value of the parent's investment, what justification exists for crediting this increase to additional paid-in capital?

5. When a parent company has obtained control of a subsidiary through several purchases and subsequently sells a portion of its shares in the subsidiary, how is the carrying value of the shares sold determined?

6. When the cost method is used to account for an investment in a subsidiary, any recorded gain or loss on the sale of a portion of its investment during a fiscal period consists of three elements. What are they?

7. ABC Corporation purchased 10,000 shares (80%) of EZ Company at $30 per share and sold them several years later for $35 per share. The consolidated income statement reports a loss on the sale of this investment. Explain.

8. Explain the required accounting treatment when the sale of part of an investment reduces the investor's percent of ownership to less than 20%.

Problems

Problem 8-1

Prentice Company made open market purchases of the common stock of Sutter Company as follows:

DATE	NUMBER OF SHARES ACQUIRED	COST
1/1/80	5,000	$142,000
1/1/81	10,000	293,500
1/1/82	30,000	922,000

Any excess of cost over the book value of equity acquired relates to the undervaluation of Sutter Company's Relay Resistor patents, which had an estimated remaining economic life of 10 years on January 1, 1980.

Sutter Company had $1,000,000 of $20 par common stock outstanding at all times. Relevant retained earnings, income, and dividend data were:

	RETAINED EARNINGS
1/1/80 Balance	$320,000
1980 Income	110,000
1980 Dividends	(30,000)
12/31/80 Balance	400,000
1981 Income	90,000
1981 Dividends	(20,000)
12/31/81 Balance	470,000
1982 Income	100,000
1982 Dividends	(40,000)
12/31/82 Balance	$530,000

Prentice Company uses the equity method, where appropriate, to account for its common stock investments.

Required:

A. Prepare a schedue to compare investment cost with the book value of equity acquired for each stock purchase.

B. Prepare the general journal entries that Prentice Company would make regarding its investment in Sutter Company during 1980, 1981, and 1982.

C. Prepare, in general journal form, the eliminating and amortization entries that would be made for the preparation of a consolidated workpaper for Prentice Company and Sutter Company on December 31, 1982.

PATENT AMORTIZED OVER 10 YRS

Problem 8–2

Up to the time of its incorporation on April 1, 1977, Shaffer Company was an autonomous division of the Berkshire Corporation. The incorporation of the division was effected to permit an influx of needed equity capital without disturbing the existing owners' interests in the Berkshire Corporation. Berkshire contributed net assets with a fair value of $400,000 in return for 6,400 shares of Shaffer's common stock. The remaining 20% was purchased by Flagg Enterprises for $100,000.

Shaffer Company, although profitable, was experiencing working capital shortages because of expanded operations. In an attempt to relieve this problem, the two owners agreed that, on March 31, 1980, Berkshire Corporation would contribute an additional $175,000 cash in return for 2,000 shares to be issued directly by Shaffer Company. Immediately prior to this stock issue, Shaffer Company had the following equity balances:

Common Stock, $50 par	$400,000
Premium on Common Stock	100,000
Retained Earnings	100,000
Total	$600,000

8000

Required:

A. Prepare a schedule to show the book value of the interest acquired by Berkshire Corporation on March 31, 1980, and the effect the acquisition had on the minority interest's (Flagg's) share of Shaffer's equity.

B. What was the "consideration" given by Flagg for the incremental increase in its share of Shaffer's equity?

C. Assume that Berkshire Corporation uses the cost method to account for this investment. Prepare, in general journal form, all determinable workpaper entries that would be made in the preparation of a consolidated balance sheet workpaper on April 1, 1980.

Problem 8–3

On January 1, 1980, Pratt Company acquired 84% of the capital stock of Steven Company for $360,000. On that date Steven Company had stockholders' equity as follows:

Capital Stock, $20 par	$200,000	*8400*
Additional Paid-in Capital	80,000	
Retained Earnings	120,000	
Total	$400,000	

The difference between cost and book value of equity acquired relates to land owned by Steven Company.   *12000*

On January 2, 1982, Steven Company issued 2,000 shares of its authorized capital stock, with a market value of $60 per share, to Jack Minton in exchange for a patent. Steven Company's retained earnings on this date were $190,000; capital stock and additional paid-in capital balances had not changed during 1980 and 1981.

Pratt Company uses the cost method to account for its investment in Steven Company.

Required:

A. Prepare, in general journal form, the workpaper entries needed for the preparation of a consolidated balance sheet workpaper on January 2, 1982:

   (1) To reflect the change in the carrying value of the investment account resulting from the issue of the additional shares to Mr. Minton.

   (2) To establish reciprocity.

   (3) To eliminate the investment account.

B. Assuming that Pratt Company used the equity method to account for its investment in Steven Company, how should the effect of the new issue of shares by Steven Company be treated by Pratt Company?

C. Assuming that the market value of the stock issued for the patent was $40 per share, repeat Requirement A above.

Problem 8–4

Trial balances for Plato Company and its subsidiary Seto Company on December 31, 1981 are as follows:

	PLATO	SETO
Current Assets	$ 176,000	$ 89,000
Investment in Seto Company	254,000	
Other Assets	540,000	298,000
Dividends Declared	80,000	40,000
Cost of Goods Sold	610,000	260,000
Other Expense	190,000	55,000
	$1,850,000	$742,000
Liabilities	$ 88,000	$ 32,000
Capital Stock, $10 par	400,000	200,000
Retained Earnings, 1/1	360,000	110,000
Sales	970,000	400,000
Dividend Income	32,000	
	$1,850,000	$742,000

Plato Company acquired its investment in Seto Company through open-market purchases of stock as follows:

DATE	SHARES PURCHASED	COST	SETO RETAINED EARNINGS BALANCE
1/1/78	4,000	$ 50,000	$ 28,000
1/1/80	6,000	98,000	69,000
1/1/81	6,000	106,000	110,000
Total	16,000	$254,000	

Any difference between cost and book value of the interest acquired relates to Seto Company land.

Seto Company issued 20,000 shares of stock on July 1, 1976, its date of incorporation. No other capital stock transactions were undertaken by Seto Company after that time.

No intercompany transactions had occurred between Plato and Seto Companies prior to 1981. During 1981, however, Plato Company made sales of merchandise to Seto Company in the amount of $80,000. Plato Company sells merchandise to Seto Company at a markup of 25% above cost. One-fourth of the goods purchased from Plato were still in Seto's inventory on December 31, 1981. At the end of the year, Seto owed Plato $12,000 for goods purchased during the year.

Required:

Prepare a workpaper for the preparation of consolidated financial statements for Plato and Seto Companies on December 31, 1981.

Problem 8–5

The accounts of Pearson Company and its subsidiary, Lawler Company, are summarized below as of December 31, 1982.

DEBITS	PEARSON	LAWLER
Current Assets	$200,000	$115,000
Investment in Lawler Company	72,000	
Other Assets	400,000	128,000
Dividends Declared	8,000	7,000
	$680,000	$250,000
CREDITS		
Liabilities	$ 88,000	$ 35,000
Common Stock, $25 par	20,000	50,000
Premium on Common Stock	30,000	30,000
Retained Earnings, 1/1	500,000	100,000
Net Income	42,000	35,000
	$680,000	$250,000

Pearson Company made the following open-market purchase and sale of Lawler Company common stock: January 2, 1980—purchased 1,500 shares, cost $90,000; January 2, 1982—sold 300 shares, proceeds $30,000. Pearson Company uses the cost method to account for its investment in Lawler Company.

The book value of Lawler Company's net assets at January 2, 1980, $120,000, approximated the fair value of those assets. Subsequent changes in the book value of these net assets are entirely attributable to net income less dividends paid.

Required:
Prepare a workpaper for the preparation of consolidated financial statements for Pearson Company and Lawler Company as of December 31, 1982. Begin the income statement section of the workpaper with "Income before Gain on Sale of Investments and Dividend Income."

Problem 8–6
Rex Company acquired 16,000 shares of Still Company's common stock on January 1, 1979 for $496,000 when Still Company had common stock ($20 par) of $400,000 and retained earnings of $220,000.

On January 1, 1981, Still Company issued 10,000 additional shares of its common stock for $42 per share. The new shares were purchased ratably by Rex Company and the minority shareholders. Still Company's retained earnings had increased to $360,000 by this date. Rex Company uses the cost method to account for its investment in Still Company.

Required:
Prepare, in general journal form, the workpaper entries for the preparation of consolidated financial statements on December 31, 1981.

Problem 8–7
X Company purchased 36,000 shares of the capital stock of Y Company for $334,800 on January 2, 1978 when Y Company had the following stockholders' equity:

Capital Stock, $5 par	$300,000
Other Contributed Capital	120,000
Retained Earnings	88,000
Total	$508,000

Any difference between cost and book value relates to Y Company land.

On January 1, 1981, Y Company reacquired 10,000 of its own shares by direct purchase from Jake Smith, a minority shareholder, for cash of $140,000. Y Company's retained earnings had increased to $180,000 by this date; capital stock and other contributed capital balances had not changed since January 2, 1978. Y Company uses the cost method to account for its treasury shares.

X Company uses the cost method to account for its investment in Y Company.

Required:

A. Prepare, in general journal form, all workpaper entries at December 31, 1981 for the preparation of consolidated financial statements.

B. If X Company had used the equity method to account for its investment in Y Company, explain any differences that would exist in the solution you arrived at in Part A above.

Problem 8-8

On January 1, 1980, Pooltec Company purchased 5,000 shares of Sims Company capital stock (par $10) for $72,500 when Sims Company had capital stock of $200,000 and retained earnings of $90,000. On July 1, 1980, an additional 9,000 shares were acquired by Pooltec at a cost of $138,600. On November 1, 1980, 1,000 of the shares acquired on January 1, 1980 were sold for $18,000. Pooltec uses the cost method to account for its investment in Sims Company.

During 1980, Pooltec earned $76,000 and Sims earned $36,000 evenly throughout the year. Neither company declared dividends during the year. Pooltec's retained earnings were $176,000 on January 1, 1980.

Required:

A. Prepare a partial consolidated workpaper at December 31, 1980.

B. Prepare a computation to prove the amount reported as consolidated net income in Part A above.

Problem 8-9

The Peabody Company's purchases of Salem Company's 25,000 outstanding shares of $1.00 par value common stock are summarized below:

DATE	NUMBER OF SHARES ACQUIRED	CASH PAID	CARRYING VALUE OF SALEM'S NET ASSETS
1/2/80	2,500	$ 22,000	$200,000
1/2/81	5,000	50,000	240,000
1/2/82	7,500	93,000	300,000
Total	15,000	$165,000	

At the time of the initial purchase, the differences between the fair values and the book values of Salem Company's assets were:

ITEM	BOOK VALUE	FAIR VALUE	DIFFERENCE
Equipment	$ 37,500	$ 50,000	$12,500
Accumulated Depreciation	(7,500)	(10,000)	(2,500)
Equipment (net)	30,000	40,000	10,000
Land	70,000	80,000	10,000
Total	$100,000	$120,000	$20,000

The appraised value of the land did not change over the two-year period and was reflected in the cost of the subsequent purchases. However, the equipment was sold at the beginning of 1981. This equipment was depreciated at an annual rate of 10%, which assumed no salvage value.

Salem Company declared and distributed dividends of 80 cents per share during the years 1980 and 1981.

Required:
Prepare in good form Peabody Company's journal entries to record the step acquisition and the results of Salem Company's operations for the two-year period. When applicable, assume that Peabody Company records such investments under the equity method. Ignore income taxes.

9

Indirect Ownership and Reciprocal Stockholdings

In preceding chapters we have dealt only with situations in which one company, the parent, had a direct controlling interest in another company, the subsidiary. At times a parent may have an interest in a subsidiary that has an interest in a subsidiary of its own. For example, P Company may own 90% of S Company, which, in turn, owns 80% of R Company. Thus, P Company has a 90% direct interest in S Company and a 72% (90% $\times$ 80%) indirect interest in R Company. Ultimately, therefore, P Company is entitled to 90% of S Company's income from its individual operations and 72% of R Company's individual income. Or, if P Company owns 90% of S Company and 80% of R Company, and S Company owns a 10% interest in R Company, then P Company owns a direct interest in S Company of 90% and a combined direct and indirect interest in R Company of 89% (80% + [90% $\times$ 10%]). With relationships of this type it is often helpful to prepare an affiliation diagram identifying ownership relationships, with the direction of the arrow indicating the direction of ownership. The two situations described above may be diagrammed as follows:

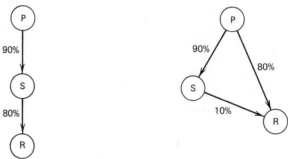

Occasionally two or more affiliates may have ownership interests in each other. For example, P Company may own 90% of S Company, which, in turn, owns 10% of

P Company. Or, P Company may own 90% of S Company, which owns 80% of R Company, which, in turn, owns 10% of S Company. Relationships of this type are generally termed reciprocal stockholdings. They may be diagrammed as follows:

Problems in preparing consolidated financial statements where there are indirect or reciprocal holdings are discussed in this chapter. Many indirect and reciprocal possibilities exist, and no attempt will be made to discuss them all. However, sufficient illustrations are presented to give the reader a basic understanding of the principles involved.

INDIRECT OWNERSHIP

In the process of preparing consolidated financial statements workpapers for a group of affiliates where there is some type of indirect ownership, it is important to start the elimination of intercompany investments with the lowest-level subsidiary and then simply proceed "up the ladder." For example, where P Company owns 90% of S Company, which owns 80% of R Company, S Company's investment in R Company should be eliminated first, and then P Company's investment in S Company. This "up-the-ladder" process is essential where the cost method is used in accounting for the investments.

Two illustrations of indirect ownership affiliations are presented, with appropriate affiliation diagrams. Since the date of acquisition of individual investments is an important consideration, the diagrams indicate both the degree of ownership and the date acquired.

Assume first, that on January 1, 1979, S Company acquired an 80% interest in R Company, and on January 1, 1980, P Company acquired 90% of S Company. The appropriate diagram would appear as follows:

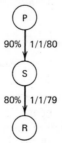

Relevant investment and stockholders' equity data are presented below. It is assumed further that both P Company and S Company account for their investments by the *cost method*. Consolidating workpaper procedures for investments recorded under the equity method will be discussed later.

Cost Method

	P COMPANY	S COMPANY	R COMPANY
Cost of Investment	290,000	125,000	
Common Stock	500,000	200,000	100,000
Retained Earnings 1/1/79	230,000	80,000	50,000
1979 Income	100,000	40,000	20,000
1979 Dividends Declared	(30,000)	(20,000)	(10,000)
Total Equity, 12/31/79	800,000	300,000	160,000
1980 Income	110,000	50,000	30,000
1980 Dividends Declared	(30,000)	(20,000)	(10,000)
Total Equity, 12/31/80	880,000	330,000	180,000

Note that consolidated statements for P Company, S Company, and R Company are not appropriate on December 31, 1979, because P Company had not yet acquired its investment in S Company; however, consolidated statements for S Company and R Company were appropriate and may have been prepared.

Computation of the difference between cost and book value for each investment may be made as follows:

	P COMPANY'S INVESTMENT IN S	S COMPANY'S INVESTMENT IN R
Cost of Investment	290,000	125,000
Book Value of Equity Acquired	[1]277,200	[2]120,000
Difference between Cost & Book Value	12,800	5,000

[1].9 × $308,000*
[2].8 × $150,000

*S Company's equity on 1/1/80 was $300,000 plus its share, $8,000 (.8 × $10,000), of R Company's undistributed income from the date S Company acquired its interest in R Company to 1/1/80 (for 1979 only in this illustration).

Before illustrating workpaper preparation for this situation, it should be noted that S Company could prepare consolidated statements with its subsidiary, R Company. P Company could then take that set of statements and consolidate them with its own. In our illustrations, however, we will assume that each company prepares individual statements and that P Company's accounting staff prepares consolidated statements from the individual statements. In order to concentrate attention on the new issues involved, it is assumed further throughout this chapter that any difference between cost and book value relates to the undervaluation of nondepreciable subsidiary fixed assets.

A *partial* workpaper for the preparation of consolidated financial statements on December 31, 1980 is presented in Illustration 9–1. The remainder of the workpaper would be completed in the manner presented in previous chapters.

Workpaper eliminating entries, in general journal form, are summarized below for the convenience of the reader:

(1) Investment in R Company	8,000	
Retained Earnings—S Company		8,000
To establish reciprocity: .8 × 10,000.		

Note that there is no reciprocity entry for P Company's investment in S Company because the investment was acquired on January 1, 1980.

(2) Dividend Income	26,000	
Dividends Declared—S Company		18,000
Dividends Declared—R Company		8,000
To eliminate intercompany dividends.		
(3) Common Stock—R Company	80,000	
Retained Earnings—R Company	48,000	
Difference Between Cost & Book Value	5,000	
Investment in R Company		133,000
To eliminate investment in R Company.		
(4) Common Stock—S Company	180,000	
Retained Earnings—S Company*	97,200	
Difference Between Cost & Book Value	12,800	
Investment in S Company		290,000

*(.9 × 108,000)
To eliminate investment in S Company.

As discussed earlier, where the cost method is used to account for investments on the investors' books, a workpaper adjusting entry is made to give recognition, in retained earnings as of the beginning of the year, to the investor's share of the undistributed earnings of its subsidiary from the date of acquisition to the beginning of the current year. In this illustration S Company acquired its interest in R Company at the beginning of 1979. During 1979, R Company earned $20,000, distributed a dividend of $10,000 and, therefore, had $10,000 of undistributed income, 80% of which accrues to the benefit of S Company. After the adjustment above is made, the investment accounts are eliminated, as usual, against the related subsidiary equity. Note that in the elimination of P Company's investment in S Company, 90% of S Company's *adjusted* retained earnings of $108,000 on January 1, 1980 is eliminated.

Purchase Accounting
Partially Owned Subsidiaries
Cost Method
Indirect Ownership

ILLUSTRATION 9-1
P Company and Subsidiaries
Partial Consolidated Statements Workpaper
For the Year Ended December 31, 1980

INCOME STATEMENT	P COMPANY	S COMPANY	R COMPANY	ELIMINATIONS DR.	ELIMINATIONS CR.	MINORITY INTEREST	CONSOLIDATED BALANCES
Net Income Before Inter-company Dividends	92,000	42,000	30,000				164,000
Dividend Income	18,000	8,000		² 26,000			
Minority Interest						12,600	(12,600)
Net Income to Retained Earnings	110,000	50,000	30,000	26,000	–0–	12,600	151,400
RETAINED EARNINGS STATEMENT							
1/1 Retained Earnings							
P Company	300,000						300,000
S Company		100,000		⁴ 97,200	¹ 8,000	10,800	
R Company			60,000	³ 48,000		12,000	
Net Income from above	110,000	50,000	30,000	26,000	–0–	12,600	151,400
Dividends Declared							
P Company	(30,000)						(30,000)
S Company		(20,000)			² 18,000	(2,000)	
R Company			(10,000)		² 8,000	(2,000)	
12/31 Retained Earnings to Balance Sheet	380,000	130,000	80,000	171,200	34,000	31,400	421,400
BALANCE SHEET							
Investment in S Company	290,000				⁴290,000		
Investment in R Company		125,000		¹ 8,000	³133,000		
Difference Between Cost & Book Value—S Company				⁴ 12,800			12,800
Difference Between Cost & Book Value—R Company				³ 5,000			5,000
Common Stock							
P Company	500,000						500,000
S Company		200,000		⁴180,000		20,000	
R Company			100,000	³ 80,000		20,000	
Retained Earnings from above	380,000	130,000	80,000	171,200	34,000	31,400	421,400
Minority Interest						71,400	71,400
				457,000	457,000		

¹To recognize S Company's share of R Company's undistributed earnings from date of acquisition to the beginning of the current year (10,000 × .8).

²To eliminate intercompany dividends.

³To eliminate S Company's investment in R Company.

⁴To eliminate P Company's investment in S Company.

The remaining 10% constitutes the minority interest. The minority interest in combined income is computed as follows:

Minority Interest in Income of R Company:		
$30,000 × 20%		6,000
Minority Interest in Income of S Company:		
S Company's Reported Income	50,000	
Add: S Company's share of undistributed		
income of R Company during 1980,		
80% × $20,000	16,000	
S Company's Adjusted Net Income	66,000	
Minority Interest Therein	10%	6,600
Total Minority Interest in Combined Income		12,600

Consolidated net income can be verified as follows:

P Company's income from its own operations	92,000
Add: P Company's share of subsidiaries income	
from their own operations:	
S Company $42,000 × 90%	37,800
R Company 30,000 × 72%*	21,600
Consolidated Net Income	151,400

*(.90 × .80 = .72)

OR

P Company's reported income	110,000
Add: P Company's share of the *undistributed*	
income of its subsidiaries for 1980:	
S Company 90% × ($50,000 − $20,000)	27,000
R Company 72% × ($30,000 − $10,000)	14,400
Consolidated Net Income	151,400

Equity Method

If the equity method had been used to account for the investments on the books of the investor companies, the investment and stockholders data that were presented earlier would be adjusted to appear as follows:

	P COMPANY	S COMPANY	R COMPANY
Investment at Equity, 12/31/80	²331,400	¹149,000	
Common Stock	500,000	200,000	
Retained Earnings, 1/1/79	230,000	80,000	50,000
1979 Income	100,000	48,000	20,000
1979 Dividends Declared	(30,000)	(20,000)	(10,000)
Total Retained Earnings, 12/31/79	300,000	108,000	60,000
1980 Income	³151,400	⁴ 66,000	30,000
1980 Dividends Declared	(30,000)	(20,000)	(10,000)
Total Retained Earnings, 12/31/80	421,400	154,000	80,000

¹125,000 + (.8 × 10,000) + (.8 × 20,000)
²290,000 + (.9 × 46,000)
³ 92,000 + (.9 × 66,000)
⁴ 42,000 + (.8 × 30,000)

A partial workpaper for the preparation of consolidated financial statements on December 31, 1980 under the equity method is presented in Illustration 9–2.

Workpaper eliminating entries, in general journal form, are summarized below:

(1) Equity in Subsidiary Income   24,000
    Dividends Declared—R Company   8,000
    Investment in R Company   16,000
        To reverse effect of entries during the year.

(2) Equity in Subsidiary Income   59,400
    Dividends Declared—S Company   18,000
    Investment in S Company   41,400
        To reverse effect of entries during the year.

(3) Common Stock—R Company   80,000
    Retained Earnings—R Company   48,000
    Difference Between Cost & Book Value   5,000
    Investment in R Company   133,000
        To eliminate investment in R Company.

(4) Common Stock—S Company   180,000
    Retained Earnings—S Company   97,200
    Difference Between Cost & Book Value   12,800
    Investment in S Company   290,000
        To eliminate investment in S Company.

Note that the computation of minority interest in combined income can be computed directly here and, of course, is the same amount as it would be under the cost method.

$$\text{Minority Interest in R Company Income } 30{,}000 \times .2 = \underline{6{,}000}$$
$$\text{Minority Interest in S Company Income } 66{,}000 \times .1 = \underline{6{,}600}$$
$$\text{Total Minority Interest in Combined Income } \quad \underline{\underline{12{,}600}}$$

Also, consolidated income and consolidated retained earnings are the same as P Company income and retained earnings, and the minority interest and consolidated balances columns are the same as in Illustration 9–1.

As another illustration of indirect holdings, assume that on January 1, 1979, P Company acquired 90% and 70% interests in S Company and R Company, respectively. One year later, on January 1, 1980, S Company acquired a 20% interest in R Company. The affiliations may be diagrammed as:

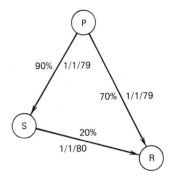

Relevant investment and stockholders' equity data are presented below. The data are essentially the same as in the preceding illustration with the exception of the cost of the investments.

	P COMPANY	S COMPANY	R COMPANY
Cost of Investment in R Company	115,000	35,000	
Cost of Investment in S Company	265,000		
Common Stock	500,000	200,000	100,000
Retained Earnings, 1/1/79	230,000	80,000	50,000
1979 Income	100,000	40,000	20,000
1979 Dividends Declared	(30,000)	(20,000)	(10,000)
Total Retained Earnings, 12/31/79	300,000	100,000	60,000
1980 Income	110,000	50,000	30,000
1980 Dividends Declared	(30,000)	(20,000)	(10,000)
Total Retained Earnings, 12/31/80	380,000	130,000	80,000

Purchase Accounting
Partially Owned Subsidiaries
Equity Method
Indirect Ownership

ILLUSTRATION 9–2
P Company and Subsidiaries
Partial Consolidated Statements Workpaper
For the Year Ended December 31, 1980

INCOME STATEMENT	P COMPANY	S COMPANY	R COMPANY	ELIMINATIONS DR.	ELIMINATIONS CR.	MINORITY INTEREST	CONSOLIDATED BALANCES
Net Income Before Equity in Subsidiary Income	92,000	42,000	30,000				164,000
Equity in Subsidiary Income	59,400	24,000		¹ 24,000 ² 59,400			
Minority Interest						12,600	(12,600)
Net Income to Retained Earnings	151,400	66,000	30,000	83,400	–0–	12,600	151,400
RETAINED EARNINGS STATEMENT							
1/1 Retained Earnings							
P Company	300,000						300,000
S Company		108,000		⁴ 97,200		10,800	
R Company			60,000	³ 48,000		12,000	
Net Income from above	151,400	66,000	30,000	83,400	–0–	12,600	151,400
Dividends Declared							
P Company	(30,000)						(30,000)
S Company		(20,000)			² 18,000	(2,000)	
R Company			(10,000)		¹ 8,000	(2,000)	
12/31 Retained Earnings to Balance Sheet	421,400	154,000	80,000	228,600	26,000	31,400	421,400
BALANCE SHEET							
Investment in S Company	331,400				² 41,400 ⁴290,000		
Investment in R Company		149,000			¹ 16,000 ³133,000		
Difference Between Cost & Book Value—S Company				⁴ 12,800			12,800
Difference Between Cost & Book Value—R Company				³ 5,000			5,000
Common Stock							
P Company	500,000						500,000
S Company		200,000		⁴180,000		20,000	
R Company			100,000	³ 80,000		20,000	
Retained Earnings from above	421,400	154,000	80,000	228,600	26,000	31,400	421,400
Minority Interest						71,400	71,400
				506,400	506,400		

¹To reverse the effect of intercompany income and dividend entries on S Company's investment in R Company during the year.
²To reverse the effect of intercompany income and dividend entries on P Company's investment in S Company during the year.
³To eliminate S Company's investment in R Company.
⁴To eliminate P Company's investment in S Company.

Computation of the difference between cost and book value for each investment is as follows:

	P COMPANY'S INVESTMENT IN S	P COMPANY'S INVESTMENT IN R	S COMPANY'S INVESTMENT IN R
Cost of Investment	265,000	115,000	35,000
Book Value of Equity Acquired:			
P Company in S Company			
(.9 × $280,000)	252,000		
P Company in R Company			
(.7 × $150,000)		105,000	
S Company in R Company			
(.2 × $160,000)			32,000
Difference Between Cost			
& Book Value	13,000	10,000	3,000

Cost Method

A partial workpaper for the preparation of consolidated financial statements on December 31, 1980 is presented in Illustration 9–3.

The process of adjustment and elimination follows the procedures previously employed. A summary of workpaper eliminating entries is presented below:

(1) Investment in S Company	18,000	
Retained Earnings—P Company		18,000
To establish reciprocity: .9 × 20,000.		
(2) Investment in R Company	7,000	
Retained Earnings—P Company		7,000
To establish reciprocity: .7 × 10,000.		
(3) Dividend Income	27,000	
Dividends Declared—S Company		18,000
Dividends Declared—R Company		9,000
To eliminate intercompany dividends.		

Purchase Accounting
Partially Owned Subsidiaries
Cost Method
Indirect Ownership

ILLUSTRATION 9–3
P Company and Subsidiaries
Partial Consolidated Statements Workpaper
For the Year Ended December 31, 1980

INCOME STATEMENT	P COMPANY	S COMPANY	R COMPANY	ELIMINATIONS DR.	ELIMINATIONS CR.	MINORITY INTEREST	CONSOLIDATED BALANCES
Net Income Before Inter-company Dividends	85,000	48,000	30,000				163,000
Dividend Income	25,000	2,000		³ 27,000			
Minority Interest						8,400	(8,400)
Net Income to Retained Earnings	110,000	50,000	30,000	27,000	–0–	8,400	154,600
RETAINED EARNINGS STATEMENT							
1/1 Retained Earnings							
P Company	300,000				¹ 18,000		325,000
					² 7,000		
S Company		100,000		⁶ 90,000		10,000	
R Company			60,000	⁴ 12,000		6,000	
				⁵ 42,000			
Net Income from above	110,000	50,000	30,000	27,000	–0–	8,400	154,600
Dividends Declared							
P Company	(30,000)						(30,000)
S Company		(20,000)			³ 18,000	(2,000)	
R Company			(10,000)		³ 9,000	(1,000)	
12/31 Retained Earnings to Balance Sheet	380,000	130,000	80,000	171,000	52,000	21,400	449,600
BALANCE SHEET							
Investment in S Company	265,000			¹ 18,000	⁶283,000		
Investment in R Company	115,000			² 7,000	⁵122,000		
Investment in R Company		35,000			⁴ 35,000		
Difference Between Cost & Book Value—S Company				⁶ 13,000			13,000
Difference Between Cost & Book Value—R Company				⁴ 3,000			13,000
				⁵ 10,000			
Common Stock							
P Company	500,000						500,000
S Company		200,000		⁶180,000		20,000	
R Company			100,000	⁴ 20,000		10,000	
				⁵ 70,000			
Retained Earnings from above	380,000	130,000	80,000	171,000	52,000	21,400	449,600
						51,400	51,400
				492,000	492,000		

[1]To recognize P Company's share of S Company's undistributed earnings from date of acquisition to the beginning of the current year (.9 × 20,000).

[2]To recognize P Company's share of R Company's undistributed earnings from date of acquisition to the beginning of the current year (.7 × 10,000).

[3]To eliminate intercompany dividends.

[4]To eliminate S Company's investment in R Company.

[5]To eliminate P Company's investment in R Company.

[6]To eliminate P Company's investment in S Company.

(4) Common Stock—R Company	20,000	
Retained Earnings—R Company	12,000	
Difference Between Cost & Book Value	3,000	
Investment in R Company		35,000
To eliminate S Company's investment in R Company.		
(5) Common Stock—R Company	70,000	
Retained Earnings—R Company	42,000	
Difference Between Cost & Book Value	10,000	
Investment in R Company		122,000
To eliminate P Company's investment in R Company.		
(6) Common Stock—S Company	180,000	
Retained Earnings—S Company	90,000	
Difference Between Cost & Book Value	13,000	
Investment in S Company		283,000
To eliminate P Company's investment in S Company.		

Adjusting entries are made to P Company's investments and retained earnings accounts as of the beginning of the year to recognize its share of the undistributed income of S Company and R Company from the date of acquisition to the beginning of the current year.[1] The investment accounts are then eliminated against the related subsidiary equity.

[1]In subsequent periods an adjusting entry to S Company's investment in R Company and retained earnings as of the beginning of the year, to recognize its 20% share of the undistributed income of R Company from the date of acquisition to the beginning of the year, will be needed to establish reciprocity. Adjustment for P Company's investment in S Company will be made after S Company's investment and retained earnings accounts have been adjusted for its share of the undistributed income of R Company. For example, the adjustments to establish reciprocity for a workpaper at December 31, 1981 in the situation above would be as follows:

Investment in R Company (.2 × 20,000)	4,000	
Retained Earnings—S Company		4,000
Investment in R Company (.7 × 30,000)	21,000	
Retained Earnings—P Company		21,000
Investment in S Company—.9 × (50,000 + 4,000)	48,600	
Retained Earnings—P Company		48,600

Minority Interest in Consolidated Income is computed as follows:

Minority Interest in Income of R Company:		
(.1 X 30,000)		3,000
Minority Interest in Income of S Company:		
S Company's Reported Income	50,000	
Add: S Company's share of the undistributed		
income of R Company during 1980,		
(.2 X 20,000)	4,000	
S Company's Adjusted Income	54,000	
Minority Interest Therein	10%	5,400
Total Minority Interest in Combined Income		8,400

Consolidated Net Income can be verified as:

P Company's income from its own operations	85,000
Add: P Company's share of its subsidiaries'	
income from their own operations:	
S Company 48,000 X .9	43,200
R Company 30,000 X .88˙	26,400
Consolidated Net Income	154,600

˙.7 + .9(.2) = .88

OR

P Company's reported income	110,000
Add: P Company's share of the *undistributed*	
income of its subsidiaries for 1980:	
S Company (90% X $34,000)	30,600
R Company (70% X 20,000)	14,000
Consolidated Net Income	154,600

Equity Method

Use of the equity method in this situation presents no particular problem. Investor companies, P and S, would recognize their respective shares of the income of R Company in the normal manner under the equity method. Note, however, that when P Company recognizes its share of S Company income for 1980, it should be after S Company has given effect to its share of R Company's income. Thus, P Company would make the following income entry for its investment in S Company:

Investment in S Company	48,600	
Equity in Subsidiary Income		48,600

S Company's individual income	48,000	
S Company's share of R Company		
Income (.2 × $30,000)	6,000	
Total S Company Income	54,000	
	× 90%	
P Company's Share	48,600	

Preparation of a consolidated workpaper on December 31, 1980 under the equity method would follow the same procedures as those in Illustration 9–2.

Indirect Ownership—Several Levels

In some situations a chain of ownership may exist in which the "primary" parent company actually has an indirect interest of less than 50% in one or more of the affiliates. Assume, for example, the following affiliation:

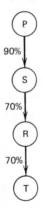

P Company has an indirect interest in T Company of only 44.1% (90% × 70% × 70%). Nonetheless, T Company is properly included in the consolidated group, because P Company effectively controls the operations of T Company through its ability to elect boards of directors of all three subsidiaries. Of course, only 44.1% of T Company's income will be included in consolidated net income. The remainder represents minority interest.

Intercompany Profit Eliminations with Indirect Ownership

Procedures related to the elimination of intercompany profits where direct ownership exists were discussed in Chapters 6 and 7. As you recall, there is general agreement among accountants that 100% of the gross intercompany profit should be eliminated. The effect of indirect ownership on the elimination of intercompany profits is discussed and illustrated in this section and clearly demonstrates the importance of "up-the-ladder" eliminations where the cost method is used.

To illustrate, assume that, on January 1, 1977, S Company acquired an 80% interest in R Company, and P Company acquired a 90% interest in S Company. The affiliation may be diagrammed as follows:

Relevant data concerning the investments and related stockholders' equity are:

	P COMPANY	S COMPANY	R COMPANY
Common Stock	500,000	200,000	100,000
Retained Earnings on *Date of Acquisition*		80,000	40,000
Cost of Investment in R Company		112,000	
Cost of Investment in S Company	252,000		
Net Income for 1980	90,000	60,000	30,000
Dividends Declared in 1980	–0–	–0–	–0–

The cost of both investments was purposely set equal to the book value of the interest acquired in order to simplify and direct attention specifically to the problems of the elimination of intercompany profits. Also, deferred income taxes are ignored. It is assumed further that the following intercompany profits existed in the inventory of S Company on merchandise acquired from R Company:

On January 1, 1980	$5,000
On December 31, 1980	2,000

Cost Method

A partial workpaper illustrating the consolidating procedures in this situation under the *cost method* is presented in Illustration 9–4.

Summarized eliminating entries for the workpaper are presented below:

(1) Retained Earnings—S Company   4,000
    Retained Earnings—R Company (minority interest)   1,000
        Cost of Goods Sold   5,000
        To eliminate intercompany profit in beginning inventory.

(2) Investment in R Company   24,000
    Retained Earnings—S Company   24,000
        To establish reciprocity: .8 × 30,000.

(3) Investment in S Company   54,000
    Retained Earnings—P Company   54,000
        To establish reciprocity: .9 × 60,000.

(4) Common Stock—R Company   80,000
    Retained Earnings—R Company   56,000
        Investment in R Company   136,000
        To eliminate S Company's investment in R Company.

(5) Common Stock—S Company   180,000
    Retained Earnings—S Company   126,000
        Investment in S Company   306,000
        To eliminate P Company's investment in S Company.

(6) Cost of Goods Sold   2,000
    Inventory   2,000
        To eliminate intercompany profit in ending inventory.

Because the $5,000 intercompany profit in beginning inventory is unrealized from a consolidated viewpoint, an adjusting entry is made first to adjust cost of goods sold and to reduce S Company's retained earnings for its share, $4,000 (.8 × 5,000), and to reduce R Company's retained earnings for the minority interest's share, $1,000 (.2 × 5,000), of the unrealized profit. Next, an adjusting entry in the amount of $24,000 is made to recognize S Company's share of the increase in reported retained earnings of R Company from the date of acquisition to the beginning of the year (30,000 × .8). Next, P Company recognizes its share of the increase in S Company's adjusted retained earnings from the date of acquisition in the amount of $54,000 (120,000 + 20,000 = 140,000 − 80,000 = 60,000 × .9). Thus, the significance of the "up-the-ladder" treatment is apparent.

Purchase Accounting
Partially Owned Subsidiaries
Cost Method
Indirect Ownership

ILLUSTRATION 9–4
P Company and Subsidiaries
Partial **Consolidated Statements Workpaper**
For the Year Ended December 31, 1980

INCOME STATEMENT	P COMPANY	S COMPANY	R COMPANY	ELIMINATIONS DR.	ELIMINATIONS CR.	MINORITY INTEREST	CONSOLIDATED BALANCES
Sales	300,000	200,000	160,000				660,000
Cost of Goods Sold	160,000	110,000	90,000	⁶ 2,000	¹ 5,000		357,000
Other Expense	50,000	30,000	40,000				120,000
Total Cost and Expense	210,000	140,000	130,000				477,000
Net	90,000	60,000	30,000				183,000
Minority Interest						15,240	(15,240)
Net Income to Retained Earnings	90,000	60,000	30,000	2,000	5,000	15,240	167,760
RETAINED EARNINGS STATEMENT							
1/1 Retained Earnings							
P Company	250,000				³ 54,000		304,000
S Company		120,000		¹ 4,000			
				⁵126,000	² 24,000	14,000	
R Company			70,000	⁴ 56,000		13,000	
				¹ 1,000			
Net Income from above	90,000	60,000	30,000	2,000	5,000	15,240	167,760
12/31 Retained Earnings to Balance Sheet	340,000	180,000	100,000	189,000	83,000	42,240	471,760
BALANCE SHEET							
Investment in S Company	252,000			³ 54,000	⁵306,000		
Investment in R Company		112,000		² 24,000	⁴136,000		
Inventory, 12/31	40,000	30,000	20,000		⁶ 2,000		88,000
- - - - - - - - - - - - - -	- - - - - -	- - - - - -	- - - - - -	- - - - - -	- - - - - -	- - - - - -	- - - - - -
Common Stock							
P Company	500,000						500,000
S Company		200,000		⁵180,000		20,000	
R Company			100,000	⁴ 80,000		20,000	
Retained Earnings from above	340,000	180,000	100,000	185,000	79,000	42,240	471,760
Minority Interest						82,240	82,240
				523,000	523,000		

¹To eliminate intercompany profit in beginning inventory.
²To recognize S Company's share of the increase in retained earnings of R Company from the date of acquisition to the beginning of the year (.8 × 30,000).
³To recognize P Company's share of the increase in retained earnings of S Company from the date of acquisition to the beginning of the year (.9 × 60,000).
⁴To eliminate the investment in R Company.
⁵To eliminate the investment in S Company.
⁶To eliminate intercompany profit in ending inventory.

Minority interest in the beginning balance of retained earnings of R Company and S Company is entered as the balance existing after the elimination of the related investment accounts. Minority interest in combined income is computed as follows:

Minority interest in income of R Company		
realized in transactions with third parties		
($30,000 + $5,000 − $2,000) × .2		6,600
Minority interest in S Company income:		
S Company's reported income	60,000	
Add: S Company's share of undistributed		
income of R Company realized in		
transactions with third parties		
during 1980 ($33,000 × .8)	26,400	
S Company's adjusted income	86,400	
Minority interest therein	10%	8,640
Total minority interest in combined income		15,240

Equity Method

If the equity method had been used in this situation, the investor companies would have made one or more entries to recognize the investor's share of the realized income of its subsidiary. Some companies may recognize their share of the reported income of their subsidiary and follow with individual entries to give effect to the realization of the intercompany profits in beginning inventory and the unrealized profits in ending inventory. Other companies compute their share of the realized income and make one summary entry. The entries, summarized, with computations for P and S Companies for 1980 would appear as follows:

S COMPANY

Investment in R Company	26,400		
Equity in Subsidiary Income		26,400	
R Company's reported income			30,000
Add: Realized profit in beginning inventory			5,000
Less: Unrealized profit in ending inventory			(2,000)
R Company's realized income			33,000
S Company's interest in R Company			.8
S Company's share of R Company's income			26,400

P COMPANY

Investment in S Company	77,760		
Equity in Subsidiary Income		77,760	
S Company's income from individual			
operations			60,000
S Company's share of R Company income			26,400
Total			86,400
P Company's interest in S Company			.9
P Company's share of S Company's income			77,760

Illustration 9–5 presents a partial workpaper for the preparation of consolidated financial statements on December 31, 1980 under the equity method.

Purchase Accounting
Partially Owned Subsidiaries
Equity Method
Indirect Ownership

ILLUSTRATION 9–5
P Company and Subsidiaries
Partial Consolidated Statements Workpaper
For the Year Ended December 31, 1980

INCOME STATEMENT	P COMPANY	S COMPANY	R COMPANY	ELIMINATIONS DR.	ELIMINATIONS CR.	MINORITY INTEREST	CONSOLIDATED BALANCES
Sales	300,000	200,000	160,000				660,000
Equity in Subsidiary Income	77,760	26,400		[1]104,160			
Total Revenue	377,760	226,400	160,000				660,000
Cost of Goods Sold	160,000	110,000	90,000	[3] 2,000	[2] 5,000		357,000
Other Expense	50,000	30,000	40,000				120,000
Total Cost and Expense	210,000	140,000	130,000				477,000
Net	167,760	86,400	30,000				183,000
Minority Interest						15,240*	(15,240)
Net Income to Retained Earnings	167,760	86,400	30,000	106,160	5,000	15,240	167,760
RETAINED EARNINGS STATEMENT							
1/1 Retained Earnings							
P Company	304,000						304,000
S Company		140,000		[5]126,000		14,000	
R Company			70,000	[4] 56,000 [2] 1,000		13,000	
Net Income from above	167,760	86,400	30,000	106,160	5,000	15,240	167,760
12/31 Retained Earnings to Balance Sheet	471,760	226,400	100,000	289,160	5,000	42,240	471,760
BALANCE SHEET							
Investment in S Company	383,760				[5]306,000 [1] 77,760		
Investment in R Company		158,400		[2] 4,000	[4]136,000 [1] 26,400		
Inventory	40,000	30,000	20,000		[3] 2,000		88,000
Common Stock							
P Company	500,000						500,000
S Company		200,000		[5]180,000		20,000	
R Company			100,000	[4] 80,000		20,000	
Retained Earnings from above	471,760	226,400	100,000	289,160	5,000	42,240	471,760
Minority Interest						82,240	82,240
				553,160	553,160		

* 10 (86,400) + .20 (30,000 + 5,000 − 2,000) = 15,240
¹To reverse the effect of intercompany income on investment accounts during the year.
²To eliminate intercompany profit in beginning inventory.
³To eliminate intercompany profit in ending inventory.
⁴To eliminate investment in R Company.
⁵To eliminate investment in S Company.

Workpaper eliminating entries are summarized as:

(1) Equity in Subsidiary Income   104,160
     Investment in S Company   77,760
     Investment in R Company   26,400
       To reverse the effect of income entries during the year.

(2) Retained Earnings—R Company (Minority Interest)   1,000
    Investment in R Company   4,000
     Cost of Goods Sold   5,000
       To eliminate intercompany profit in beginning inventory.

(3) Cost of Goods Sold   2,000
     Inventory   2,000
       To eliminate intercompany profit in ending inventory.

(4) Common Stock—R Company   80,000
    Retained Earnings—R Company   56,000
     Investment in R Company   136,000
       To eliminate S Company's investment in R Company.

(5) Common Stock—S Company   180,000
    Retained Earnings—S Company   126,000
     Investment in S Company   306,000
       To eliminate P Company's investment in S Company.

RECIPROCAL STOCKHOLDINGS

Indirect ownership situations are relatively common; reciprocal stockholdings are not. Occasionally a subsidiary owns a small equity interest in its parent, or subsidiaries of the same parent own equity interests in one another. Where these reciprocal holdings exist, the reciprocal effect is often immaterial. The infrequency of occurrence of reciprocal stockholdings and the often relatively immaterial effect where they do exist suggests that this topic should receive less attention than others. Nevertheless, some familiarity with the problems created may be useful.

Two general approaches have been used to treat the effect of reciprocal holdings, a mathematical approach and a treasury stock approach. The mathematical approach gives explicit recognition to the effect of the reciprocal holding, whereas the treasury stock approach simply treats the reciprocal stockholding as treasury stock on the consolidated balance sheet. Because the treasury stock approach is generally used in practice, it is discussed and illustrated in the following section. Recent surveys of practice show that this is the approach most often used.[2] The mathematical approach is presented in the appendix for those who may be interested in its application.

Treasury Stock Approach

Subsidiary shareholdings in the parent company are generally treated the same as treasury stock, because the parent company is considered to have reacquired some of its own shares by using subsidiary resources. Under this approach, the reciprocal relationship is ignored, and the cost of the subsidiary's investment in the stock of the parent company is deducted from total stockholders' equity on the consolidated balance sheet. Although the parent's investment in its subsidiary could be accounted for under either the cost or equity methods, the subsidiary's investment in the stock of the parent company is generally accounted for at cost.[3] The subsidiary does not record an interest in the earnings of the parent, and the investment in the parent company remains at cost. Dividends distributed to the subsidiary are recognized by the subsidiary as dividend income.

To illustrate, assume that P Company acquired 90% of the common stock of S Company on January 1, 1980. On the same date S Company acquired 10% of the common stock of P Company. An affiliation diagram, along with relevant investment, equity, income and dividend data, is presented below:

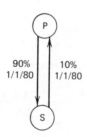

P

90%   10%
1/1/80   1/1/80

S

---

[2]Accountants International Study Group, *Consolidated Financial Statements,* 1973, par. 67.

[3]If the subsidiary owned 20% or more of the common stock of the parent, its investment in the parent company would have to be adjusted to the equity method when reporting to parties outside the affiliated group. In the event the subsidiary elected to use the equity method on its books to account for its investment in the stock of its parent, a workpaper entry to return the investment account to its cost would be required so that the investment account could be deducted at its cost from stockholders' equity on the consolidated balance sheet.

	P COMPANY	S COMPANY
Common Stock	500,000	200,000
Retained Earnings, 1/1/80	150,000	50,000
1980 Income	80,000	40,000
1980 Dividends Declared	(20,000)	(10,000)
Retained Earnings, 12/31/80	210,000	80,000
Investment in S Company	225,000	
Investment in P Company		65,000

Cost Method

If P Company used the cost method in this situation, the calculation of minority interest in S Company's income in the December 31, 1980 workpaper would be based on its reported income (10% × $40,000), and the workpaper adjustment for P Company's share of S Company's increase in retained earnings for a workpaper at the end of 1981 would be 90% of $30,000, or $27,000. In both cases, the reciprocal effect of the shareholdings is ignored. A partial workpaper on December 31, 1980 using the treasury stock approach is presented in Illustration 9–6.

The workpaper is prepared in the same manner as it normally would be under the cost method except that S Company's investment in P Company is not eliminated, but is extended to the consolidated balances column and labeled as treasury stock. Note also that the $2,000 dividend income received by S Company is eliminated against P Company dividends declared, and the remaining $18,000 is deducted from consolidated retained earnings because it represents dividends distributed to outside stockholders. The consolidated balance sheet resulting is presented in Illustration 9–7.

Equity Method

If the equity method were used by P Company on its books, it would be applied in the usual manner *ignoring the reciprocal relationship*. Thus, for example, during 1980, P Company would recognize $34,200 (.9 × [40,000 − 2,000 dividend income from P Company]) of subsidiary income and would reduce the investment in S Company for the $9,000 dividends received. A workpaper under the equity method would follow the same procedures illustrated in earlier chapters, except that S Company's investment in P Company would be carried to the consolidated column and labeled as treasury stock, as illustrated in this chapter.

Purchase Accounting
Reciprocal Stockholdings
Treasury Stock Approach
Cost Method

ILLUSTRATION 9–6
P Company and Subsidiary
Partial **Consolidated Statements Workpaper**
For the Year Ended December 31, 1980

INCOME STATEMENT	P COMPANY	S COMPANY	ELIMINATIONS DR.	CR.	MINORITY INTEREST	CONSOLIDATED BALANCES
Sales	300,000	170,000				470,000
Dividend Income	9,000	2,000	[1] 11,000			
Total Revenue	309,000	172,000				470,000
Cost of Goods Sold	160,000	90,000				250,000
Other Expense	69,000	42,000				111,000
Total Cost and Expense	229,000	132,000				361,000
Net	80,000	40,000				109,000
Minority Interest					4,000	(4,000)
Net Income to Retained Earnings	80,000	40,000	11,000	–0–	4,000	105,000
RETAINED EARNINGS STATEMENT						
1/1 Retained Earnings						
P Company	150,000					150,000
S Company		50,000	[2] 45,000		5,000	
Net Income from above	80,000	40,000	11,000	–0–	4,000	105,000
Dividends Declared						
P Company	(20,000)			[1] 2,000		(18,000)
S Company		(10,000)		[1] 9,000	(1,000)	
12/31 Retained Earnings to Balance Sheet	210,000	80,000	56,000	11,000	8,000	237,000
BALANCE SHEET						
Investment in S Company	225,000			[2] 225,000		
Investment in P Company		65,000				65,000 T/S
Common Stock						
P Company	500,000					500,000
S Company		200,000	[2] 180,000		20,000	
Retained Earnings from above	210,000	80,000	56,000	11,000	8,000	237,000
Minority Interest					28,000	28,000
			236,000	236,000		

[1] To eliminate intercompany dividends.
[2] To eliminate P Company's investment in S Company.

ILLUSTRATION 9–7
P Company and Subsidiary
Consolidated Balance Sheet
December 31, 1980

Assets	$1,086,000
Liabilities	$ 386,000
Minority Interest	28,000
Stockholders' Equity	
Common Stock	500,000
Retained Earnings	237,000
Less: P Company Shares Held	
by Subsidiary (at cost)	(65,000)
Total Equities	$1,086,000

APPENDIX—MATHEMATICAL APPROACH TO TREATING RECIPROCAL STOCKHOLDINGS

Where reciprocal holdings exist and the mathematical approach is used, the allocation of income between consolidated income and the minority interest must consider the interdependency of the relationship. In the situation described below (the same as that presented earlier under the treasury stock approach but restated here for the convenience of the reader), P Company is entitled to 90% of the income of S Company, but S Company's income is unknown until it has recognized 10% of P Company's income. Likewise, P Company's income is unknown until it has recognized its share of S Company's income; thus, the nature of the reciprocal shareholding problem. The mathematical approach uses algebraic calculation to determine their respective income. The following situation is used as an example of accounting procedures under both the cost and equity methods of accounting. Additional data are assumed as reflected on the partial workpapers that are illustrated.

Assume that P Company acquired 90% of the common stock of S Company on January 1, 1980. On the same date S Company acquired 10% of the common stock of P Company. Relevant investment, equity, income, and dividends data are presented below:

	P COMPANY	S COMPANY
Common Stock	500,000	200,000
Retained Earnings, 1/1/80	150,000	50,000
1980 Income	80,000	40,000
1980 Dividends Declared	(20,000)	(10,000)
Retained Earnings, 12/31/80	210,000	80,000
Investment in S Company	225,000	
Investment in P Company		65,000

Cost Method

Under the cost method in the year of acquisition, the only problem that arises is the allocation of earnings between consolidated income and the minority interest. A partial workpaper under the cost method for the year of acquisition, is presented in Illustration 9–8.

Purchase Accounting
Reciprocal Stockholdings
Mathematical Approach
Cost Method

ILLUSTRATION 9–8
P Company and Subsidiary
Partial Consolidated Statements Workpaper
For the Year Ended December 31, 1980

	P COMPANY	S COMPANY	ELIMINATIONS DR.	ELIMINATIONS CR.	MINORITY INTEREST	CONSOLIDATED BALANCES
INCOME STATEMENT						
Sales	300,000	170,000				470,000
Dividend Income	9,000	2,000	¹ 11,000			
Total Revenue	309,000	172,000				470,000
Cost of Goods Sold	160,000	90,000				250,000
Other Expense	69,000	42,000				111,000
Total Cost and Expense	229,000	132,000				361,000
Net	80,000	40,000				109,000
Minority Interest					4,956	(4,956)
Net Income to Retained						
Earnings	80,000	40,000	11,000	–0–	4,956	104,044
RETAINED EARNINGS STATEMENT						
1/1 Retained Earnings						
P Company	150,000		³ 15,000			135,000
S Company		50,000	² 45,000		5,000	
Net Income from above	80,000	40,000	11,000	–0–	4,956	104,044
Dividends Declared						
P Company	(20,000)			¹ 2,000		(18,000)
S Company		(10,000)		¹ 9,000	(1,000)	
12/31 Retained Earnings to						
Balance Sheet	210,000	80,000	71,000	11,000	8,956	221,044
BALANCE SHEET						
Investment in S Company	225,000			²225,000		
Investment in P Company		65,000		³ 65,000		
Common Stock						
P Company	500,000		³ 50,000			450,000
S Company		200,000	²180,000		20,000	
Retained Earnings from above	210,000	80,000	71,000	11,000	8,956	221,044
Minority Interest					28,956	28,956
			301,000	301,000		

¹To eliminate intercompany dividends.
²To eliminate P Company's investment in S Company.
³To eliminate S Company's investment in P Company.

Intercompany dividend income is eliminated as usual. Note, however, that only $18,000 of P Company dividends are deducted from consolidated retained earnings, since that is the amount that was distributed to outside stockholders. The other $2,000 is eliminated because it represents an interaffiliate dividend distribution. Both investment accounts are eliminated in the usual manner; $50,000 of P Company's common stock is eliminated as part of the intercompany investment. The determination of minority interest in income takes into account the reciprocal nature of the shareholdings and is computed by taking the affiliates' *income from their individual operations* and giving effect to their reciprocal interests. Thus, the computation is as follows:

Let P = Net income of P Company
S = Net income of S Company

The algebraic formulation and solution become:

$$
\begin{aligned}
P &= \$\ 71,000 + .9S \\
S &= 38,000 + .1P \\
P &= 71,000 + .9(38,000 + .1P) \\
P &= 71,000 + 34,200 + .09P \\
.91\ P &= 105,200 \\
P &= 115,604 \\
S &= 38,000 + .1(115,604) \\
S &= 38,000 + 11,560 \\
S &= 49,560
\end{aligned}
$$

As indicated, S Company's income after considering its investment in P Company is $49,560, and the minority interest therein is 10%, or $4,956. Consolidated income is 90% of $115,604, or $104,044. The other 10% represents intercompany income on shares held by S Company. The combined income is, therefore, $109,000, which is equal to the actual income of both companies resulting from transactions with third parties (71,000 + 38,000).

In years subsequent to the year of acquisition, an additional reciprocal computation must be made, that necessary to compute the investor's share of the investee's undistributed income (loss), or increase (decrease) in retained earnings, from the date of acquisition to the beginning of the year. Thus, for a workpaper prepared at

December 31, 1981, computations for the adjustment to beginning retained earnings and investment accounts for this factor are:

Let P = Increase in P Company's retained earnings since date of acquisition of P Company Stock by S Company

   S = Increase in S Company's retained earnings since date of acquisition of S Company Stock by P Company

Then:

$$
\begin{aligned}
P &= \$60,000 + .9S \\
S &= 30,000 + .1P \\
S &= 30,000 + .1(60,000 + .9S) \\
S &= 30,000 + 6,000 + .09S \\
.91\,S &= 36,000 \\
S &= 39,560 \\
P &= \$60,000 + .9(39,560) \\
P &= 60,000 + 35,604 \\
P &= 95,604
\end{aligned}
$$

Thus, workpaper entries on the December 31, 1981 workpaper, in general journal form, to recognize the investor's share of the investee's increase in retained earnings from the date of acquisition to the beginning of the current year are:

Investment in P Company	9,560	
Retained Earnings—S Company		9,560
(10% × $95,604)		
Investment in S Company	35,604	
Retained Earnings—P Company		35,604
(90% × $39,560)		

In all other respects, completion of a workpaper at December 31, 1981 would be the same as in Illustration 9–8.

Equity Method

If the equity method were used to account for investments in this situation, each investor would make entries in the investment account during the year to record dividends received and its share of the reciprocally computed income of its investee. The computation of income is, of course, the same as that shown earlier for the cost method. Thus, the investment accounts on December 31, 1980 would appear as follows:

INVESTMENT IN S COMPANY

1/1/80	225,000	Dividends	9,000
12/31/80 Sub. Income	44,604*		
12/31/80 Balance	260,604		

*.9(49,560)

INVESTMENT IN P COMPANY

1/1/80	65,000	Dividends	2,000
12/31/80 Investee Income	11,560*		
12/31/80 Balance	74,560		

*.1(115,604)

A partial workpaper for the preparation of consolidated financial statements on December 31, 1980 under the equity method is presented in Illustration 9–9. Workpaper preparation in subsequent years under the equity method would follow the same procedures as those used in Illustration 9–9.

Questions

1. Distinguish among direct, indirect, and reciprocal stockholder interests.

2. What is meant by "up-the-ladder" eliminations?

3. X Company owns 70% of Y Company, and Y Company owns 60% of Z Company. Are consolidated financial statements for X, Y, and Z Companies appropriate? Justify your answer.

4. A Company owns 90% of B Company, 80% of C Company, and 70% of E Company. B Company owns 75% of D Company, which, in turn, owns 60% of F Company. C Company owns 15% of E Company. E Company owns 5% of F Company. What percent of each company's income should be included in consolidated net income?

5. Describe two approaches to the treatment of reciprocal shareholdings in the preparation of consolidated financial statements.

6. How does the determination of minority interests differ in the two approaches to the treatment of reciprocal shareholdings?

Problems

Problem 9–1
X Company made an open-market purchase of 80% of the common stock of Y Company on January 1, 1980 at a cost of $290,000. On that date Y Company had common stock of $300,000 and retained earnings of $70,000. On January 1, 1981, Y Company made an open-market purchase of 70% of the common stock of Z Company for $110,000. Z Company's equity on

Purchase Accounting
Reciprocal Stockholdings
Mathematical Approach
Equity Method

ILLUSTRATION 9–9
P Company and Subsidiary
***Partial* Consolidated Statements Workpaper**
For the Year Ended December 31, 1980

INCOME STATEMENT	P COMPANY	S COMPANY	ELIMINATIONS DR.	ELIMINATIONS CR.	MINORITY INTEREST	CONSOLIDATED BALANCES
Sales	300,000	170,000				470,000
Equity in Subsidiary Income	44,604		¹ 44,604			
Equity in Investee Income		11,560	¹ 11,560			
Total Revenue	344,604	181,560				470,000
Cost of Goods Sold	160,000	90,000				250,000
Other Expense	69,000	42,000				111,000
Total Cost and Expense	229,000	132,000				361,000
Net	115,604	49,560				109,000
Minority Interest					4,956	(4,956)
Net Income to Retained Earnings	115,604	49,560	56,164	–0–	4,956	104,044
RETAINED EARNINGS STATEMENT						
1/1 Retained Earnings						
P Company	150,000		³ 15,000			135,000
S Company		50,000	² 45,000		5,000	
Net Income from above	115,604	49,560	56,164	–0–	4,956	104,044
Dividends Declared						
P Company	(20,000)			¹ 2,000		(18,000)
S Company		(10,000)		¹ 9,000	(1,000)	
12/31 Retained Earnings to Balance Sheet	245,604	89,560	116,164	11,000	8,956	221,044
BALANCE SHEET						
Investment in S Company	260,604		{²225,000			
			{¹ 35,604			
Investment in P Company		74,560	{³ 65,000			
			{¹ 9,560			
Common Stock						
P Company	500,000		³ 50,000			450,000
S Company		200,000	²180,000		20,000	
Retained Earnings from above	245,604	89,560	116,164	11,000	8,956	221,044
Minority Interest					28,956	28,956
			346,164	346,164		

¹To reverse the effect of intercompany income and dividends on investment accounts during the year.
²To eliminate P Company's investment in S Company.
³To eliminate S Company's investment in P Company.

1/1/81 consisted of common stock of $100,000 and retained earnings of $40,000. X Company and Y Company both use the equity method to account for their investments. Stockholders' equity accounts for the three companies on December 31, 1981 were:

	X COMPANY	Y COMPANY	Z COMPANY
Common Stock	$600,000	$300,000	$100,000
Retained Earnings, 1/1	325,000	100,000	40,000
Net Income Before Equity in			
Subsidiary Income	140,000	65,000	36,000
Dividends Declared	40,000	25,000	10,000

Any difference between cost and the book value of equity acquired represents an over (under) valuation of land.

Required:
A. Prepare journal entries on the books of X Company and Y Company to recognize subsidiary income and dividends for 1981.
B. Prepare eliminating entries, in general journal form, for the preparation of a consolidated statements workpaper on December 31, 1981.
C. Compute:
  (1) Minority interest in combined income.
  (2) Consolidated net income for 1981.

Problem 9–2
Baker Company purchased a 70% interest in Carter Company on the open market for $215,000 on January 1, 1980. On that date Carter Company had capital stock of $200,000 and retained earnings of $85,000. One year later, on January 1, 1981, Albert Company purchased a 90% interest in Baker Company on the open market for $620,000. Relevant account balances for the three companies on December 31, 1981 were:

	ALBERT	BAKER	CARTER
Capital Stock	$700,000	$400,000	$200,000
Retained Earnings, 1/1	480,000	260,000	110,000
Net Income for 1981	175,000	86,000	50,000
Dividends Declared	60,000	30,000	20,000
Investment in Baker Company	620,000		
Investment in Carter Company		215,000	

Any difference between cost and the book value of equity acquired is assignable to subsidiary land holdings.

Required:
A. Prepare a schedule to compute the difference between cost and book value acquired for each investment.
B. Prepare, in general journal form, reciprocity and elimination entries for the preparation of a consolidated statements workpaper on December 31, 1981.
C. Compute:
  (1) Minority interest in combined income for 1981.
  (2) Consolidated net income for 1981.
  (3) Consolidated retained earnings at December 31, 1981.

Problem 9–3

The following investments were all made on January 1, 1981:

ACQUIRING COMPANY	ACQUIRED COMPANY	% INTEREST ACQUIRED	COST
P	R	90%	$580,000
R	S	80%	309,760
S	T	60%	130,000

Stockholders' equity, earnings, and dividend data for the affiliated companies at the end of 1981 were:

	P	R	S	T
Capital Stock	$500,000	$400,000	$200,000	$100,000
Retained Earnings, 1/1	348,500	216,000	187,200	106,500
1981 Net Income	117,400	96,320	84,200	60,500
1981 Dividends Declared	40,000	30,000	20,000	20,000
Retained Earnings, 12/31	425,900	282,320	251,400	147,000

Required:

Assuming use of the cost method for all investments, compute:
a. Consolidated net income for 1981.
b. Consolidated retained earnings at 12/31/81.
c. Minority interest in combined income for 1981.

Problem 9–4

Condensed balance sheets for M Company, N Company, and O Company on December 31, 1980 are as presented below:

	M COMPANY	N COMPANY	O COMPANY
Current Assets	$ 346,800	$242,600	$210,300
Investment in N Company	300,000		
Investment in O Company	80,000	250,000	
Other Assets	945,700	362,600	392,500
Total Assets	$1,672,500	$855,200	$602,800
Liabilities	$ 494,400	$247,200	$206,900
Capital Stock	600,000	300,000	200,000
Other Contributed Capital	190,600	87,400	102,500
Retained Earnings	387,500	220,600	93,400
Total Equities	$1,672,500	$855,200	$602,800

N Company purchased a 70% interest in O Company for $250,000 on January 1, 1976 when O Company had stockholders' equity consisting of Capital Stock, $200,000; Other Contributed Capital, $102,500; and Retained Earnings, $41,200.

On January 1, 1980, M Company purchased an 80% interest in N Company for $525,000 and a 20% interest in O Company for $80,000. Stockholders' equity for N and O Companies on 1/1/80 was:

	N COMPANY	O COMPANY
Capital Stock	$300,000	$200,000
Other Contributed Capital	87,400	102,500
Retained Earnings	240,000	62,300
Total	$627,400	$364,800

Required:
Prepare a workpaper for the preparation of a consolidated balance sheet for M, N, and O Companies on December 31, 1980. (Include a schedule to verify the difference between cost and book value of equity acquired, which in this problem is assumed to be assignable to Land.)

Problem 9–5
Proctor Company acquired 80% of the outstanding stock of Silo Company on January 2, 1980. On that date Silo Company held a 5% interest in Proctor Company. Summary account data for Proctor Company and Silo Company on December 31, 1980 were as follows:

DEBITS	PROCTOR	SILO
Assets	$ 578,000	$242,500
Investment in Silo Company	136,000	
Investment in Proctor Company		20,000
Cost of Sales and Expenses	440,000	190,000
Dividends Declared	50,000	30,000
Total	$1,204,000	$482,500

CREDITS		
Liabilities	$ 100,000	$ 60,000
Capital Stock, $10 par	200,000	50,000
Retained Earnings	280,000	120,000
Sales	600,000	250,000
Dividend Income	24,000	2,500
Total	$1,204,000	$482,500

Required:
Prepare a consolidated statements workpaper on December 31, 1980 using the treasury stock approach for the reciprocal investment in Proctor Company.

Problem 9–6
A Company owns 90% of B Company, 80% of C Company, 60% of D Company, and 70% of E Company. In addition, B Company owns 5% of C Company, D Company owns 20% of E Company, and E Company owns 80% of F Company.

Net income reported by each company for 1981 was:

A Company	$65,000
B Company	80,000
C Company	30,000
D Company	50,000
E Company	40,000
F Company	60,000

None of the companies declared dividends during 1981.

Required:
A. Draw a diagram of the affiliation.
B. Calculate consolidated net income for 1981.
C. Calculate minority interest in combined income for 1981.

Problem 9–7

On January 1, 1979, Bragg Company purchased 75% of the capital stock of Chuck Company. On January 1, 1980, Addis Company purchased 80% of the capital stock of Bragg Company. On January 1, 1981, Addis Company purchased 15% of the capital stock of Chuck Company. Addis Company and Bragg Company use the cost method to account for their investments. The following data are relevant to the affiliates:

	ADDIS	BRAGG	CHUCK
Capital Stock	$400,000	$250,000	$100,000
Retained Earnings, 1/1/79	120,000	80,000	50,000
Reported Net Income:			
1979	70,000	40,000	30,000
1980	90,000	50,000	20,000
1981	100,000	50,000	30,000
Dividends Declared and Paid:			
1979	30,000	10,000	10,000
1980	40,000	20,000	10,000
1981	40,000	20,000	10,000

Required:
Calculate
a. Consolidated retained earnings on January 1, 1981.
b. Consolidated retained earnings on January 1, 1982.
c. Consolidated net income for 1981.

Problem 9–8

On January 1, 1979, X Company purchased a 90% interest in Y Company for $380,000 when Y Company had capital stock of $300,000 and retained earnings of $90,000.

On January 1, 1980, Y Company purchased an 80% interest in Z Company for $260,000 when Z Company had capital stock of $200,000 and retained earnings of $110,000.

Both X Company and Y Company account for their investments by the cost method. Any difference between the cost of the investments and the book value of equity acquired relates to subsidiary land.

Data relevant to the preparation of consolidated financial statements on December 31, 1981 follow:

	X CO.	Y CO.	Z CO.
Capital Stock	$600,000	$300,000	$200,000
Retained Earnings, 1/1/81	560,000	160,000	140,000
Net Income for 1981	180,000	70,000	50,000
Dividends Declared, 1981	50,000	20,000	20,000

During 1981, Z Company sold merchandise to Y Company at a billed price of $80,000. Z Company bills merchandise to Y Company at its regular markup rate of 100% on cost.

Y Company's inventory included goods acquired from Z Company as follows: 12/31/80 $200,000; 12/31/81 $50,000.

Required:
Prepare, in general journal form, all eliminating entries required for the preparation of a consolidated statements workpaper for X, Y, and Z Companies on December 31, 1981.

Problem 9–9 (Appendix)
X Company owns 90% of Y Company, and Y Company owns 20% of X Company. During 1981 the companies earned net income from their independent operations of:

X Company	$80,000
Y Company	$30,000

Required:
A. Compute consolidated net income.
B. Compute minority interest in combined income.

Problem 9–10 (Appendix)
A Company owns 90% of B Company and 80% of C Company. B Company owns 10% of C Company, and C Company owns 10% of B Company. During the current year the companies earned the following from their independent operations:

A Company	$50,000
B Company	9,500
C Company	4,000

Required:
A. Compute the minority interest in the net income of each company.
B. Compute consolidated net income.

Problem 9–11 (Appendix)
On January 1, 1978, the date of incorporation of S Company, P Company purchased 16,000 shares of S Company capital stock at par value of $160,000. On January 1, 1979, S Company purchased 4,000 shares of P Company capital stock at $20 per share.

The capital stock of each company is $200,000, consisting of 20,000 shares with a par value of $10 per share. Retained earnings balances on January 1, 1978, and earnings and dividends for each company for 1978, 1979, and 1980, were:

	P COMPANY	S COMPANY
Retained Earnings, 1/1/78	$ 80,000	–0–
Net Income, 1978	30,000	$20,000
Dividends Declared, 1978	(10,000)	(10,000)
Net Income, 1979	40,000	10,000
Net Income, 1980	50,000	20,000
Retained Earnings, 12/31/80	$190,000	$40,000

Required:

A. Assuming that both companies use the equity method, prepare the entries on the books of each company to recognize equity in investee net income for 1980.

B. Assuming that both companies use the cost method, prepare workpaper entries to establish reciprocity and eliminate the investment accounts for the preparation of consolidated financial statements on December 31, 1980.

10

Consolidated Financial Statements – Miscellaneous Topics

60% – 7-10
40% – 1-6
MULT. CHOICE

In this chapter we discuss several areas related to the preparation of consolidated financial statements including:

1. Intercompany bond holdings

2. Intercompany notes receivable discounted

3. Stock dividends issued by a subsidiary company

4. Liquidating dividends declared by a subsidiary company

5. Preferred stock of a subsidiary.

The chapter concludes with a section on alternative workpaper formats. In order to concentrate on the new issues introduced, we have precluded reporting complications relating to accounting for the difference between acquisition cost and book value in all illustrations by assuming that all acquisitions of voting stock are made at the book value of the acquired interest in net assets, and that the book value of the subsidiary net assets equals their fair market value on the date the parent's interest is acquired.

INTERCOMPANY BOND HOLDINGS

WANT TO RECORD A GAIN OR LOSS

An affiliate company may purchase bonds issued by another affiliate directly from the issuing company or from outsiders subsequent to the original issue. Bonds acquired by one company directly from another create no special problems, since the book value of the investment equals the book value of the liability. In the consolidating workpaper the reciprocal bond investment and bond payable are eliminated, along with the reciprocal interest expense and income accounts. Although an intercompany bond investment and liability are created by the acquisition of the outstanding bonds of an affiliate from outsiders, the analysis of the events and the required eliminating entries in the consolidating workpaper are generally more complex, because the purchase price in most cases differs from the recorded book value of the bonds (i.e., the balance in the reciprocal bond investment account does not equal the related bond liability account balance). A brief review of accounting for bond transactions is presented in the next section before the preparation of consolidated financial statement workpapers involving intercompany bond holdings is illustrated.

Accounting for Bonds—A Review

To review accounting for bonds, assume that a company issued $100,000 par value bonds on January 1, 1980, for $90,000. The bonds mature 10 years later and pay 6% interest each December 31. The bonds were all acquired by the same lender, and the fiscal year-end of both entities is December 31. The journal entries for the first year of operations, assuming straight-line amortization of the discount, are:[1]

ISSUING COMPANY

January 1, 1980

Cash	90,000	
Discount on Bonds Payable	10,000	
Bonds Payable		100,000

December 31, 1980

Interest Expense	6,000	
Cash		6,000
Interest Expense	1,000	
Discount on Bonds Payable		1,000

INVESTOR COMPANY

January 1, 1980

Investment in Bonds	90,000	
Cash		90,000

December 31, 1980

Cash	6,000	
Interest Income		6,000
Investment in Bonds	1,000	
Interest Income		1,000

[1]For simplicity, it is assumed in this chapter that straight-line amortization policies are adopted by the reporting entities. However, the reader is reminded that the interest rate method is preferred unless the straight-line amortization method does not result in a material difference.

From the point of view of the issuing company, $90,000 was received, but the company must pay $100,000 to the bondholders when the bonds mature 10 years later. Instead of deferring the $10,000 discount as a loss to be reported in the year that the bonds mature, one-tenth of the discount ($1,000) is amortized each year as an increase in interest expense. The increase in expense results in a reduction of $1,000 in net income each year, which also reduces the retained earnings balance. At the end of 10 years, the issuing company's retained earnings is reduced $60,000 for the cash interest paid and $10,000 for the discount amortization. In effect, the $10,000 discount is recognized as a loss over the life of the bonds. From the investor's point of view, $90,000 is paid for the bonds, but if the bonds are held to maturity, $100,000 will be received. One-tenth of this $10,000 gain is added to interest income each period, which results in an increase in reported income. As a result of acquiring the bond investment at a discount, retained earnings is increased $1,000 each year for a cumulative total of $10,000 over the life of the bonds.

If, in the example above, the bonds had been issued for $110,000, the issuing company receives $10,000 more on the date of issue than must be paid when the bonds mature, while the investor will receive $10,000 less than the purchase price when the bonds mature. The investor (issuing) company, rather than reporting a loss (gain) when the bonds mature, records one-tenth of the loss (gain) each year as the premium on the bonds is amortized to interest income (expense) over the remaining life of the bonds. The effect is that the net income of the investor (issuing) company is $1,000 less (greater) each year as a result of amortizing the premium. The effect on income is, of course, also reflected in the reported retained earnings balance.

Constructive Gain or Loss on Intercompany Bond Holdings

The purchase of an affiliate's bonds does not alter the accounting in the books of the individual companies. As noted in the preceding section, the issuing company and the purchasing company recognize a gain or loss on the bond transaction indirectly as an adjustment to interest income and interest expense over the remaining life of the bonds. Thus, on the books of the individual companies the bonds are accounted for as if the transactions were with independent parties. In the preparation of consolidated statements, however, the acquisition of an affiliate's outstanding bonds from outsiders is considered a constructive retirement of the bond obligation. The generally accepted practice of accounting for the early extinguishment of debt is to compute a gain or loss equal to the difference between the carrying value of the bonds and the reacquisition price of the bonds and to report such gain or loss in the current income statement as an extraordinary item.[2] Thus, the constructive gain or loss on the bond retirement is recognized in consolidation prior to the recognition of the gain or loss on the books of the individual companies. In contrast (see Chapter 6), a gain or loss on the

---

[2]A gain or loss on the early extinguishment of debt is reported as an extraordinary item net of related income tax effects. *Statements of Financial Accounting Standards No. 4* "Reporting Gains or Losses From Extinguishment of Debt" (Stamford, Conn.: Financial Accounting Standards Board, March, 1975), par. 8.

intercompany sale of inventory or other assets is recognized currently on the books of the selling company, but the gain or loss is deferred for consolidation purposes until the profit or loss is confirmed by an arm's-length transaction with an independent party.

As noted in the preceding paragraph, the gain or loss on the bond retirement is computed as the difference between the carrying value of the liability and the cost of the bonds. There is general agreement on the amount of the gain or loss to be reported, but not on how the gain or loss should be allocated between the affiliated companies involved in the bond transaction for purposes of calculating minority interest.

Four methods are supported in practice and in the accounting literature. They are: (1) the gain or loss is assigned to the company that issued the bonds; (2) the gain or loss is assigned to the company that purchased the bonds; (3) the gain or loss is assigned to the parent company; or (4) the gain or loss is allocated between the purchasing and issuing companies. Support for the first method is based on the contention that the purchasing company, as a member of the consolidated group operating under the control of the parent company's management, was simply acting as an agent for the issuing company. Supporters of the second method contend that the purchasing company initiated the transaction and should be allocated the full gain or loss.

The third method views the companies as a single operating entity. The purchase of the other company's bonds by either company is considered a retirement of outstanding debt by the consolidated entity. Thus, the gain or loss is assigned to the parent company in the year of the purchase and, accordingly, has no effect on the computation of the minority interest. The fourth method recognizes that if the bonds are held to maturity, a gain or loss will be recognized by both companies when any related discount or premium is amortized as a reduction or increase in interest income or expense. In the year of the bond purchase, the loss (gain) is allocated to the two companies, the basis being a comparison of cost and par value for the acquiring company and book value and par value for the issuing company at the date of acquisition. A loss (gain) is allocated to the issuing company if the bonds were originally issued at a discount (premium). A loss (gain) is allocated to the purchasing company if the bonds were acquired at a premium (discount). Under this method, the amount allocated to the individual companies, and thus to the majority and minority interest in the year of the bond purchase, is equal to the adjustment to net income eventually recorded on the books of the individual companies.

The authors consider the fourth method to be the soundest conceptually. It is consistent with the allocation of a gain or loss between the minority and majority interest on other types of intercompany transactions. However, in practice, the holding of an affiliate company's bonds occurs infrequently. Furthermore, the allocation of the gain or loss between companies is necessary only for the purpose of computing the minority interest in net income and retained earnings. In the case of intercompany bond holdings this normally results in an immaterial affect on the computation of each year's consolidated net income. Because intercompany bond holdings are not often encountered in practice, and when they do exist, the allocation of a portion of the constructive gain or loss to the minority interest does not normally have a material impact on operating results, the assignment of the total constructive gain or loss to the controlling interest is illustrated in this chapter. In should be noted that over the remaining life of the bonds, use of either of the two methods will result in the same amount of *total* consolidated net income and *total* minority interest in net income. In the case of a constructive loss, consolidated (minority interest in) net income will be less (greater) in the year of the constructive retirement and greater (less) in subsequent years if the loss is assigned to the controlling interest than it would be if the loss had been allocated between the parent and subsidiary.

Consolidating Workpaper—Date of Bond Purchase by Affiliate

To illustrate the eliminations required in the consolidated financial statement workpaper, the following facts are assumed:

1. P Company acquired an 80% interest in S Company for $1,360,000 on January 1, 1980.

2. P Company uses the cost method to account for the investment.

3. On December 31, 1980, P Company acquired $300,000 of S Company's par value bonds on the open market for $310,000. At the time of purchase there were $500,000 par value bonds outstanding with a book value of $480,000. The bonds mature in four years on January 1, 1985, carry a nominal interest rate of 9%, and pay interest on December 31.

4. Straight-line amortization is used by both companies.

5. The fiscal year-end of both companies is December 31.

A consolidated financial statement workpaper for the year ending December 31, 1980 is presented in Illustration 10–1. The first two workpaper entries are the normal entries to eliminate the investment and dividend income accounts and are not repeated here. The entry to eliminate the intercompany bond holding is based on the following analysis.

On December 31, 1980, P Company records the bond acquisition as follows:

Investment in S Company Bonds	310,000	
Cash		310,000

Purchase Accounting
Cost Method
80%-Owned Subsidiary
Purchase of Subsidiary's Bonds
  By Parent Company—
  Date of Reacquisition

ILLUSTRATION 10–1
Consolidated Statements Workpaper
P Company and Subsidiary
For Year Ending December 31, 1980

	P COMPANY	S COMPANY	ELIMINATIONS DR.	ELIMINATIONS CR.	MINORITY INTEREST	CONSOLIDATED BALANCES
INCOME STATEMENT						
Sales	3,104,000	2,200,000				5,304,000
Dividend Income	16,000		² 16,000			
Total Revenue	3,120,000	2,200,000				5,304,000
Cost of Goods Sold	1,700,000	1,360,000				3,060,000
Interest Expense		50,000				50,000
Other Expense	1,124,000	665,000				1,789,000
Loss on Intercompany Reacquisition of Bonds			³ 22,000			22,000
Total Cost and Expense	2,824,000	2,075,000				4,921,000
Net	296,000	125,000				383,000
Minority Interest (.2 × 125,000)					25,000	(25,000)
Net Income to Retained Earnings	296,000	125,000	38,000		25,000	358,000
RETAINED EARNINGS STATEMENT						
1/1/80 Retained Earnings						
P Company	1,650,000					1,650,000
S Company		700,000	¹ 560,000		140,000	
Net Income from above	296,000	125,000	38,000		25,000	358,000
Dividends Declared						
P Company	(150,000)					(150,000)
S Company		(20,000)		² 16,000	(4,000)	
12/31/80 Retained Earnings to Balance Sheet	1,796,000	805,000	598,000	16,000	161,000	1,858,000
BALANCE SHEET						
Investment in S Company Bonds	310,000			³ 310,000		
Investment in S Company Stock	1,360,000			¹1,360,000		
Other Assets	5,260,000	2,620,000				7,880,000
Total	6,930,000	2,620,000				7,880,000
9% Bonds Payable		500,000	³ 300,000			200,000
Discount on Bonds Payable		(20,000)		³ 12,000		(8,000)
Other Liabilities	2,134,000	335,000				2,469,000
Capital Stock						
P Company	3,000,000					3,000,000
S Company		1,000,000	¹ 800,000		200,000	
Retained Earnings from above	1,796,000	805,000	598,000	16,000	161,000	1,858,000
Minority Interest					361,000	361,000
Total Liabilities and Equity	6,930,000	2,620,000	1,698,000	1,698,000		7,880,000

¹To eliminate the investment account.

²To eliminate the intercompany dividends.

³To eliminate the intercompany bond investment and liability, and to report the constructive loss on bond retirement.

After this entry is recorded, the account balances in the ledgers of P Company and S Company (related to the intercompany bond holdings) at December 31, 1980 are:

P COMPANY

INVESTMENT IN S COMPANY BONDS

310,000

S COMPANY

DISCOUNT ON BONDS

9% BONDS PAYABLE	PAYABLE	INTEREST EXPENSE
500,000	20,000	Nominal
		Interest 45,000
		Discount
		Amortiza-
		tion 5,000
		50,000

On the basis of these account balances the constructive loss is computed as follows:

Par Value 500,000 × .60° =	300,000
Unamortized discount 20,000 × .60 =	12,000
Book value of bonds purchased	288,000
Cost of bonds to P Company	310,000
Gain (Loss)	(22,000)

°Bonds purchased/Total bonds outstanding = 300,000/500,000 = .60

A constructive loss of $22,000 on the bond retirement is recognized in the consolidated income statement because the purchase price ($310,000) was greater than the book value of the constructively retired debt ($288,000). Had the bonds been acquired for less than $288,000, a gain would be reported and included in consolidated income.

Once the foregoing information is accumulated and analyzed, the workpaper eliminating entry can be made. The entry in general journal form is:

(Entry (3) in the 12/31/1980 workpaper)

Loss on Intercompany Reacquisition of Bonds	22,000	
Bonds Payable (500,000 × .60)	300,000	
Discount on Bonds Payable (20,000 × .60)		12,000
Investment in S Company Bonds		310,000

The entry combines the elimination of intercompany accounts with the recording of the loss on the bond retirement. The difference between the book value of the debt ($288,000) and the investment ($310,000) is the loss on the bond retirement, and it is recognized currently in the determination of consolidated income, but deferred in the books of the individual companies. Since the bonds could be reissued and are, in effect, treasury bonds, the amount of the bonds held should be disclosed.

In this example, the bonds were purchased at year-end, and no elimination of intercompany interest expense and interest income is required in the 1980 workpaper. However, if bonds of an affiliated company are purchased during the year, it is also necessary to eliminate any effects of the intercompany bondholdings from the nominal accounts. This means that each period the reported intercompany interest income and expense (adjusted for the related discount and premium amortized during the period) must also be eliminated.

Calculation of Minority and Majority Interest   The computation of the minority interest in combined net income is unaffected by the purchase of the bonds, since none of the loss is assigned to the minority interest. Consolidated net income is computed as follows:

Reported net income—P Company		296,000
Less: Constructive loss on bond retirement	22,000	
Intercompany dividends	16,000	38,000
Adjusted net income		258,000
Parent's share of S Company's		
net income (125,000 × .80)		100,000
Consolidated net income		358,000

Consolidating Workpapers—Subsequent to Constructive Retirement of Bonds

During 1981, the two companies record (on their individual books) the following entries related to the bond transactions:

P COMPANY			S COMPANY		
Cash	27,000		Interest Expense	45,000	
Interest Income		27,000	Cash		45,000
To record receipt of interest.			To record payment of interest.		
Interest Income	2,500		Interest Expense	5,000	
Investment in S Company Bonds		2,500	Discount on Bonds Payable		5,000
To amortize premium on bond investment.			To amortize discount on bonds outstanding.		

During this period, $2,500 of the total constructive loss was recognized on the books of P Company as a result of amortizing the premium on the investment. The same is true for S Company, except that only $3,000 (.60 × 5,000) of the discount amortization relates to the intercompany bonds held. This means that the ending retained earnings balances reported by each company reflect the recognition of $5,500 of the constructive loss. In future periods through 1984 the ending retained earnings balance of P Company is further reduced by $2,500 each period. The December 31, 1984 retained earnings balance will reflect the fact that $10,000 of the constructive loss has been recorded as a reduction of P Company's income. By the end of 1984, the net income reported and the ending retained earnings balance of S Company will also have been reduced by $12,000 ($3,000 each year).

The relevant account balances at the end of 1981 are:

P COMPANY

INVESTMENT IN S COMPANY BONDS

		Premium	
Balance 12/31/80	310,000	Amortization	2,500
Balance 12/31/81	307,500		

INTEREST INCOME

Premium		Nominal	
Amortization	2,500	Interest	27,000
		Balance 12/31/81	24,500

S COMPANY

9% BONDS PAYABLE

	500,000

DISCOUNT ON BONDS PAYABLE

		Discount	
Balance 12/31/80	20,000	Amortization	5,000
Balance 12/31/81	15,000		

INTEREST EXPENSE

Nominal Interest	45,000	
Discount Amortization	5,000	
	50,000	

On the basis of these account balances and the constructive loss computed earlier, the 1981 bond elimination entry becomes:

(Entry Number 4 in 12/31/1981 workpaper. See Illustration 10–2.)

Beginning Retained Earnings—P Company	22,000	
Bonds Payable (500,000 × .60)	300,000	
Interest Income	24,500	
Interest Expense (50,000 × .60)		30,000
Investment in S Company Bonds		307,500
Discount on Bonds Payable (15,000 × .60)		9,000

The entry may be analyzed in three stages. *First,* one part of the entry eliminates the intercompany bond investment and bond payable balances. Note, however, that the credits to the investment and the discount accounts are lower by $2,500 and $3,000, respectively, as compared with the December 31, 1980 workpaper entry. These

Purchase Accounting
Cost Method
80%-Owned Subsidiary
Purchase of Subsidiary's Bonds
 by Parent Company—
 One Year After Reacquisition

ILLUSTRATION 10–2
Consolidated Statements Workpaper
P Company and Subsidiary
For Year Ending December 31, 1981

INCOME STATEMENT	P COMPANY	S COMPANY	ELIMINATIONS DR.	ELIMINATIONS CR.	MINORITY INTEREST	CONSOLIDATE BALANCES
Sales	3,546,000	2,020,000				5,566,000
Dividend Income	48,000		³ 48,000			
Interest Income	24,500		⁴ 24,500			
Total Revenue	3,618,500	2,020,000				5,566,000
Cost of Goods Sold	2,040,000	1,200,000				3,240,000
Interest Expense		50,000		⁴ 30,000		20,000
Other Expense	1,124,500	630,000				1,754,500
Total Cost and Expense	3,164,500	1,880,000				5,014,500
Net	454,000	140,000				551,500
Minority Interest (.2 × 140,000)					28,000	(28,000)
Net Income to Retained Earnings	454,000	140,000	72,500	30,000	28,000	523,500
RETAINED EARNINGS STATEMENT						
1/1/81 Retained Earnings						
P Company	1,796,000		⁴ 22,000	¹ 84,000		1,858,000
S Company		805,000	² 644,000		161,000	
Net Income from above	454,000	140,000	72,500	30,000	28,000	523,500
Dividends Declared						
P Company	(150,000)					(150,000
S Company		(60,000)		³ 48,000	(12,000)	
12/31/81 Retained Earnings						
to Balance Sheet	2,100,000	885,000	738,500	162,000	177,000	2,231,500
BALANCE SHEET						
Investment in S Company Bonds	307,500			⁴ 307,500		
Investment in S Company Stock	1,360,000		¹ 84,000	²1,444,000		
Other Assets	5,652,500	2,690,000				8,342,500
Total	7,320,000	2,690,000				8,342,500
9% Bonds Payable		500,000	⁴ 300,000			200,000
Discount on Bonds Payable		(15,000)		⁴ 9,000		(6,000,
Liabilities	2,220,000	320,000				2,540,000
Capital Stock						
P Company	3,000,000					3,000,000
S Company		1,000,000	² 800,000		200,000	
Retained Earnings from above	2,100,000	885,000	738,500	162,000	177,000	2,231,500
Minority Interest					377,000	377,000
Total Liabilities and Equity	7,320,000	2,690,000	1,922,500	1,922,500		8,342,500

[1]To establish reciprocity as of 1/1/1981 ([805,000 − 700,000] × .80 = 84,000).

[2]To eliminate the investment account.

[3]To eliminate intercompany dividends.

[4]To eliminate intercompany bond investment and bond payable, to eliminate the intercompany interest income and expense, and to record the constructive loss on bond retirement not reflected in the beginning retained earnings balance.

amounts are the losses recognized currently in the income statements of the individual companies. The account balances will decline by these amounts each year if a straight-line amortization policy is adopted. The difference ($16,500) between the book value of the debt ($291,000) and the bond investment account ($307,500) is the remaining loss to be amortized in future periods on the books of the individual companies. It reflects the amount of the adjustment to the beginning retained earnings of P Company on the following year's workpaper.

Second, the intercompany interest income and expense accounts are eliminated. The difference between the balance in these accounts is the loss of $5,500 recognized this year by the two companies, but which, in effect, is eliminated since the credit to interest expense is greater by $5,500 than the debit to interest income. Of the total consolidated loss of $22,000, $5,500 is recognized currently in income of the individual companies, and $16,500 is still to be amortized. Third, the debit to P Company's beginning retained earnings is necessary since the loss was recognized last year for consolidated purposes, but the recorded balance in the beginning retained earnings account of P Company has not been adjusted.

It should be observed that after the adjustment to beginning retained earnings (see Illustration 10–2), the minority and majority interests are equal to their respective interests in the ending retained earnings balances reported in the December 31, 1980 workpaper.

The definitions of consolidated net income and consolidated retained earnings developed in Chapters 6 and 7 in conjunction with the discussion of intercompany profits on inventory and fixed assets is adequate to define these concepts when a gain or loss is confirmed on the retirement of bonds.

Consolidated net income is computed as follows:

	P COMPANY
Reported net income	454,000
Less: Intercompany dividends	48,000
Reported net income from independent operations	406,000
Add back loss on bond retirement recognized currently in income of the affiliated companies	5,500
Income from independent operations that has been realized in transactions with third parties	411,500
Majority interest in S Company's reported net income (140,000 × .8)	112,000
Consolidated net income	523,500

The full loss on bond retirement was recognized in 1980 for consolidation purposes. To avoid double accounting for the loss, the amortization of the discount and premium must be added back to the reported net income in order to verify consolidated net income.

On the basis of Illustration 10–2, the calculation of consolidated retained earnings on December 31, 1981, using the analytical approach, may be demonstrated as follows:

P Company's retained earnings on December 31, 1981		2,100,000
Constructive loss on bond retirement not recorded by P Company	22,000	
Less: Loss recorded by affiliated companies during 1981	5,500	16,500
P Company's retained earnings that have been realized in transactions with third parties		2,083,500
Increase in retained earnings of S Company from January 1, 1980 to December 31, 1981 (885,000 − 700,000)	185,000	
P Company's share thereof	× .80	148,000
Consolidated retained earnings on December 31, 1981		2,231,500

A comparison of the consolidated retained earnings balance computed above with the consolidated retained earnings calculated in the consolidating workpaper (Illustration 10–2) will confirm that the balances are the same.

The end of 1981 was the first full year that the bonds were held as an investment. Assuming that the bonds are held to maturity, the eliminating entries for the rest of the period that the bonds are outstanding are as presented below. (The letters in parentheses refer to computations in Illustration 10–3.)

	DECEMBER 31			
DEBITS	1981	1982	1983	1984
Beginning Retained Earnings—P Company (c)	22,000	16,500	11,000	5,500
Bonds Payable	300,000	300,000	300,000	300,000
Interest Income	24,500	24,500	24,500	24,500
CREDITS				
Interest Expense	30,000	30,000	30,000	30,000
Investment in S Company Bonds (b)	307,500	305,000	302,500	300,000
Discount on Bonds Payable (a)	9,000	6,000	3,000	–0–

ILLUSTRATION 10–3
Account Balances Related to Intercompany Bond Holdings

	DECEMBER 31			
UNAMORTIZED DISCOUNT ON S COMPANY'S BOOKS	1981	1982	1983	1984
Balance Beginning of Year	12,000	9,000	6,000	3,000
Amortization—Current Year	3,000	3,000	3,000	3,000
Adjustment Needed (a)	9,000	6,000	3,000	–
INVESTMENT IN BONDS **ON P COMPANY'S BOOKS**				
Balance Beginning of Year	310,000	307,500	305,000	302,500
Amortization—Current Year	2,500	2,500	2,500	2,500
Book Value—End-of-Year (b)	307,500	305,000	302,500	300,000
DIFFERENCE BETWEEN RECORDED **AND CONSOLIDATED RETAINED EARNINGS**				
Bond Retirement Loss Not Recognized on the Books (c)	22,000	16,500	11,000	5,500
Loss Currently Recognized Through Amortization	5,500	5,500	5,500	5,500
Overstatement in Ending Retained Earnings Balance for Consolidation	16,500	11,000	5,500	–0–

The debit to the beginning retained earnings of P Company is $5,500 less each year. This is the result of a combination of two factors. First, the reported net income of P Company is reduced $2,500 each year as the premium on the bond investment is amortized. The retained earnings of the parent will reflect the loss as the account is reduced on a cumulative basis by $2,500 each year. Second, S Company is also recognizing a loss of $3,000 through amortization each year. The parent's share of the loss reported by the subsidiary is automatically treated when the entry to establish reciprocity (which is based on undistributed reported earnings) is recorded in the workpaper. For example, the amount of the December 31, 1982 workpaper entry to establish reciprocity is computed as follows:

Reported net income—S Company		
1980	125,000	
1981	140,000	265,000
Less: Dividends		
1980	20,000	
1981	60,000	80,000
Undistributed earnings		185,000
Majority Interest		.80
Credit to beginning retained earnings— P Company (to establish reciprocity)		148,000

A portion of the retained earnings section from the December 31, 1982 workpaper would appear as follows:

	P COMPANY	S COMPANY	ELIMINATIONS DR.	ELIMINATIONS CR.	MINORITY INTEREST	CONSOLIDATED BALANCES
1/1/1982 Retained Earnings—						
P Company	2,100,000		³ 16,500	¹148,000		2,231,500
S Company		885,000	²708,000		177,000	

¹To establish reciprocity as of 1/1/1982.
²To eliminate the investment account (885,000 × .80 = 708,000).
³To record the unrecorded loss on bond retirement.

The $16,500 debit to beginning retained earnings is the total constructive loss of $22,000 less the $5,500 loss recognized through amortization to date. Again, note that the beginning consolidated retained earnings balance agrees with the ending consolidated retained earnings balance reported at December 31, 1981. (See Illustration 10–2.)

By the end of 1984, the loss recognized in the consolidated financial statements in 1980 will also have been recorded by each company, and no further adjustments to retained earnings will be needed. The investment account and bonds payable account will have been adjusted to par value of $300,000. When the bonds mature, the companies record a transfer of cash and reduce the investment and liability accounts.

Income Tax Effects

In the preceding illustration the income tax effects were ignored in order to focus on the issues of accounting for intercompany bond holdings. If the affiliates file separate tax returns, a timing difference will result as a consequence of reporting currently in consolidated income the gain or loss on bond retirement, but deferring the gain or loss to future periods in computing the taxable income of the individual companies.

To illustrate accounting for income tax effects the preceding illustration will be used. The introduction of tax effects requires that one additional workpaper entry be made in the first year to record the tax deferral and that one additional workpaper entry be made in each future period to record the amortization of the deferred tax. It is necessary to establish the deferred tax account each year, since this is only a workpaper account that is not formally recorded in the ledgers of the affiliated companies.

Year of the Loss   In the year that the loss is reported in the consolidated financial statements, a deferred asset is reported in the consolidated financial statements to recognize that the sum of the tax paid by the affiliates in 1980 was greater than the tax expense related to consolidated income because the full loss was deducted in determining consolidated income. Assuming a 40% tax rate, the following entry is made in the December 31, 1980 workpaper:

Deferred Income Tax (22,000 loss × .40)   8,800
   Loss on Intercompany Reacquisition of Bonds   8,800
     To recognize the prepayment of taxes that results from the deferral of a loss for tax purposes that is reported currently in consolidated income as an extraordinary loss.

The effect of the allocation of the net of tax loss on the consolidated net income is that net income is reduced by $13,200 rather than by the total loss of $22,000.

If there had been a net gain on the transaction, the deferred entry would have been reversed, since the consolidated income would be greater than the sum of the individual companies' taxable income. In the year of acquisition a deferred credit is reported in the consolidated statements which will be reduced in future periods when taxable income exceeds consolidated income. The recognition of tax effects will result in a reduction of the total gain recognized on the bond retirement.

In the loss year the elimination entries previously presented (Illustration 10–1) are unaffected by the recognition of tax effects.

Subsequent to the Year of Purchase   Subsequent to the year of loss, the deferred tax account is amortized as the timing difference reverses. After the loss year, taxable income will be less than consolidated income as the individual companies amortize the bond premium ($2,500) and the discount on the bonds payable ($3,000). The following entry is made in the December 31, 1981 to December 31, 1984 workpapers to amortize the deferred tax account:

	DECEMBER 31			
	1981	1982	1983	1984
Deferred Income Tax	6,600	4,400	2,200	—
Income Tax Expense (5,500 × .40)	2,200	2,200	2,200	2,200
Beginning Retained Earnings—P Company	8,800	6,600	4,400	2,200

The procedures followed for the elimination of intercompany bond holdings are the same whether the purchasing affiliate is the parent (illustrated above) or the subsidiary.

Nonconsolidated Subsidiaries

As discussed in detail in Chapter 6, if an investment in a subsidiary that is not consolidated is accounted for by use of the equity method, then the parent's net income for the period and ending retained earnings balance should equal consolidated net income and ending retained earnings balance as if the subsidiary had been consolidated. To obtain the same results, the constructive gain or loss on the purchase of bonds issued by an affiliate company must be recognized currently on the books of the parent company. In subsequent periods, the effects of any gain or loss recorded by the individual companies, as the discount and/or premium is amortized, must be eliminated from the reported income to avoid double accounting for the gain or loss.

To be consistent with the alternative adopted in this chapter, the entire amount of the constructive gain or loss on the bond retirement is assigned to the parent company. Accordingly, the adjustment to equity in subsidiary net income and to the investment account is for 100% of the constructive gain or loss.

To illustrate, assume that P Company owns 75% of the voting stock of S Company. The subsidiary is not consolidated. S Company reports net income of $200,000 in 1980 and $300,000 in 1981. At the end of 1980, P Company purchased on the open market $200,000 of S Company's par value bonds for $188,000. At the date of acquisition the bonds have six years to maturity and a book value of $194,000. The companies file separate tax returns, and the income tax rate on taxable income averages 40%. The procedures outlined below would also be followed if the subsidiary acquired bonds issued by the parent company.

The computation of the gain or loss follows:

	CONSTRUCTIVE GAIN OR LOSS
Book value of bonds acquired by affiliate	194,000
Cost of bonds to P Company	(188,000)
Gain (loss)	6,000

The early extinguishment of the bonds at less than book value results in a constructive gain of $6,000. Assuming that the bonds will be held to maturity, P Company will recognize a gain of $2,000 each year for a total of $12,000 as the discount is amortized as additional interest income. Each period S Company will recognize a loss of $1,000 for a total of $6,000 as the discount is amortized as an increase in interest expense. Thus, between the two companies a net gain of $6,000 is recorded over the life of the bonds, which is equal to the constructive gain of $6,000.

Entries on the Parent Company's Books in 1980 If P Company's net income for the period and ending retained earnings balance is to be the same amount that would be reported as consolidated net income and retained earnings if the firms were consolidated, then P Company must recognize the net of tax gain of $3,600 on the constructive retirement of the bonds. As discussed in Chapter 6, a number of alternative procedures have been suggested with regard to recognizing the parent company's interest in intercompany gain or loss when the subsidiary is not consolidated. Several alternatives were considered acceptable. The method selected for use in this text is the one in which the parent company's intercompany gain or loss is adjusted directly to its reported equity in the net income of the subsidiary. Thus, all adjustments to recognize the intercompany gain or loss on the bond transaction are made directly to the equity in the subsidiary income and the investment accounts. The total adjustment net of tax is computed as follows:

Gain on the constructive retirement of the bonds	6,000
Less: Income tax effect (6,000 × .40)	2,400
Net of tax gain on bond retirement	3,600

On the basis of this calculation, the parent's net income is increased by $3,600 by adding the gain to equity in subsidiary income.

The journal entries recorded by the parent in 1980 are:

(1) Investment in S Company   150,000
    Equity in Subsidiary Income   150,000
      To record P Company's share of the reported income of S Company (200,000 × .75).

(2) Investment in S Company   3,600
    Equity in Subsidiary Income   3,600
      To record the constructive gain, net of tax on the purchase of S Company bonds.

The effect of the entries is to increase both the assets and ending retained earnings balance of P Company by $3,600. The reported net income of P Company (including the equity in subsidiary company) and the ending retained earnings balance will now equal the consolidation balances that would be reported if the firms were consolidated.

Entries on the Parent Company's Books in 1981   During 1981 the net income of P Company was increased $1,200 after tax from the amortization of the one-sixth ($2,000) of the discount on the bond investment. The reported income of S Company is reduced $600 after tax as a result of a $1,000 discount amortization. The net increase in income of $600 must be eliminated this period to avoid double counting of the gain, inasmuch as the full gain of $3,600 was considered last year in determining P Company's reported net income. The journal entries are:

(1) Investment in S Company   225,000
    Equity in Subsidiary Income   225,000
      To record P Company's share of the reported net income of S Company (300,000 × .75).

(2) Equity in Subsidiary Income   600
    Investment in S Company   600
      To eliminate the net gain on bond holdings recorded currently in income but reported in 1980.

Assuming that the bonds are held to maturity and the use of straight-line amortization, the second entry will be the same each year until the bonds mature.

(handwritten margin notes:)
$\frac{6000}{6}$

GAIN GETS ON BOOKS BECAUSE THE DIFF. BETWEEN INT. INCOME – ACQ AND INT. EXPENSE – SELLING

$\frac{3600}{6}$ SHOWS THAT 3600 FLOWS THROUGH IN SIX YRS.

Less Than 50%-Owned Investees

A transaction under which an investor makes an open-market purchase of some of the outstanding bonds of a less than 50%-owned investee is different from a transaction under which one affiliate purchases inventory from another affiliate. The bond purchase transaction is made with an independent party, whereas the inventory transaction is between related parties. Where bonds are acquired on the open market, the cost of the bonds is established by the market and generally is not subject to manipulation by the investor or investee companies. For this reason, the bond investment should be accounted for as a normal transaction with an independent party. Accordingly, no adjustments are made to the equity in investee income or investment in investee accounts as a result of the bond transaction.

Consolidating Workpaper—Investments Recorded at Equity

When the parent company selects the equity method of accounting for an investment in a subsidiary company, the constructive gain or loss from the bond retirement is recorded in the year of the bond acquisition on the books of the parent by adjusting the equity in subsidiary income and investment accounts. Since this gain or loss recognition will also be reflected in the ending retained earnings balance reported by the parent (which will also equal consolidated retained earnings), no workpaper adjustments to the parent company's beginning retained earnings are necessary subsequent to the year of bond purchase. Because the parent has recorded the constructive gain or loss, the only procedural change in the workpaper entries in relation to the intercompany bond holdings is that the unrecorded constructive gain or loss on bond retirement is debited or credited to the investment account rather than the beginning retained earnings balance of the parent, as it is in cost-basis workpapers.

To illustrate the accounting for intercompany bond holdings when the investment is accounted for using the equity method, the set of facts used in the cost method illustrations will be used. This will enable the reader to compare the consolidated balances under both the cost and equity methods. The assumptions of the illustration are:

1. P Company acquired an 80% interest in S Company for $1,360,000 on January 1, 1980, when the retained earnings and capital stock of S Company were $700,000 and $1,000,000, respectively.

2. P Company uses the equity method to account for the investment.

3. The reported net income of S Company is $125,000 in 1980 and $140,000 in 1981.

4. S Company paid dividends of $20,000 in 1980 and $60,000 in 1981.

5. On December 31, 1980, P Company acquired $300,000 of S Company's par value bonds on the open market for $310,000. At the time of purchase there were $500,000 par value bonds outstanding with a book value of $480,000. The bonds mature on January 1, 1985 and pay interest on December 31.

6. The straight-line method of amortization is used by both companies.

7. Income taxes are ignored.

Entries to record subsidiary income *on the books* of P Company under the equity method, as well as *workpaper entries* necessary in the consolidated workpapers for the years ending December 31, 1980, and December 31, 1981, are summarized in general journal form below:

Entries on the Books of P Company—1980

(1) Investment in S Company   100,000

      Equity in Subsidiary Income   100,000

         To record P Company's share of the reported net income of S Company (125,000 × .80).

(2) Cash   16,000

      Investment in S Company   16,000

         To record receipt of dividends from S Company (20,000 × .80).

(3) Equity in Subsidiary Income   22,000

      Investment in S Company   22,000

         To recognize the amount of intercompany loss considered realized on the December 31, 1980 purchase of S Company bonds by P Company.

Notice that the loss is treated as a downstream transaction with a controlled affiliate. The equity in subsidiary income is adjusted for the full amount of the $22,000 realized loss assigned to P Company.

Consolidating Workpaper Entries—December 31, 1980

(1) Equity in Subsidiary Income   78,000

      Investment in S Company   62,000

      Dividends Declared   16,000

         To adjust the investment account to the beginning-of-year balance and to eliminate equity in subsidiary income.

(2) Beginning Retained Earnings—S Company   560,000

      Capital Stock—S Company   800,000

      Investment in S Company   1,360,000

         To eliminate the investment account.

(3) Loss on Intercompany Reacquisition of Bonds 22,000

Bonds Payable 300,000

    Discount on Bonds Payable 12,000

    Investment in S Company Bonds 310,000

        To eliminate the intercompany receivable and payable and recognize the constructive loss on bond retirement.

SAME AS COST

Entry (3) is identical to the corresponding cost-basis elimination entry (see Illustration 10–1).

Entries on the Books of P Company—1981

(1) Investment in S Company 112,000

    Equity in Subsidiary Income 112,000

        To record P Company's share of the reported net income of S Company (140,000 × .80).

(2) Cash 48,000

    Investment in S Company 48,000

        To record the receipt of dividends from S Company (60,000 × .80).

(3) Investment in S Company 5,500

    Equity in Subsidiary Income 5,500

        To reverse the amount of the loss on bond retirement recorded during the current year by the individual companies (2,500 by P Company + 3,000 by S Company = 5,500 or simply 22,000/5 = 5,500).

INT. EXPENSE HIGHER THAN INT. INCOME

Consolidating Workpaper Entries—December 31, 1981
(Illustration 10–4)

(1) Equity in Subsidiary Income 117,500

    Investment in S Company 69,500

    Dividends Declared 48,000

        To adjust the investment account to the beginning-of-year balance and to eliminate equity in subsidiary income.

SAME AS COST EXCEPT

(2) Investment in S Company 22,000

Bonds Payable 300,000

Interest Income 24,500

    Interest Expense 30,000

    Investment in S Company Bonds 307,500

    Discount on Bonds Payable 9,000

        To adjust the investment account by the amount of the constructive loss on the bond retirement recorded on the books of P Company, to eliminate the intercompany bond investment and bond payable, and to eliminate the intercompany interest expense and income.

(3) Beginning Retained Earnings—S Company	644,000	
Capital Stock—S Company	800,000	
Investment in S Company		1,444,000
To eliminate the investment account.		

The only difference between Entry (2) and the corresponding cost-basis workpaper entry [Entry (4) in Illustration 10–2] is that in the equity-basis workpaper entry the loss of $22,000 is debited to the investment account, rather than to the beginning retained earnings of P Company.

The consoliating workpaper for the year ending December 31, 1981 is presented in Illustration 10–4. A comparison of the consolidated balances in this illustration with those in Illustraion 10–2 will confirm that the consolidated balances are the same whether the investment is accounted for using the cost or the equity method.

NOTES RECEIVABLE DISCOUNTED

Occasionally a company may issue a note to an affiliated company which may then discount the note with an outside party, or a company holding a note receivable from an outside party may discount the note with an affiliated company. The affiliate acquiring the note may subsequently discount the note again with an outside party. From a consolidation point of view, a receivable held by one of the affiliated companies should be reported in the consolidated balance sheet only if the note is due from an outside party. A contingent liability should be disclosed if a note has been discounted with an outside party and the endorsement was with recourse.

To illustrate the workpaper elimination that may be required, assume that P Company issued a $100,000 note to its subsidiary, S Company, for cash. The two companies record the transaction as normal on their own books, i.e., P Company debits cash and establishes a note payable account and S Company credits cash and records a note receivable. Assume further that S Company discounted the note at a nonaffiliated bank before maturity. Ignoring interest, there are two methods commonly used to record the discounting of a note. These methods are:

Method 1: Cash	100,000	
Notes Receivable		100,000
Method 2: Cash	100,000	
Notes Receivable Discounted		100,000

If consolidated statements are prepared before the note matures, an elimination entry may be required, depending on the method used by S Company to record the discounting of the note. If Method 1 was used, the credit to notes receivable cancels the debit made to notes receivable when the note was received. The consolidated balance sheet will appropriately report the $100,000 note held by the bank and still reported on the books of P Company as a liability. If the second method was used, the notes

Purchase Accounting
Equity Method
80%-Owned Subsidiary
Purchase of Subsidiary's Bonds
  By Parent Company—
  One Year After Reacquisition

ILLUSTRATION 10–4
Consolidated Statements Workpaper
P Company and Subsidiary
For Year Ending December 31, 1981

	P COMPANY	S COMPANY	ELIMINATIONS DR.	ELIMINATIONS CR.	MINORITY INTEREST	CONSOLIDATED BALANCES
INCOME STATEMENT						
Sales	3,546,000	2,020,000				5,566,000
Equity in Subsidiary Income	117,500		¹ 117,500			
Interest Income	24,500		² 24,500			
Total Revenue	3,688,000	2,020,000				5,566,000
Cost of Goods Sold	2,040,000	1,200,000				3,240,000
Interest Expense		50,000		² 30,000		20,000
Other Expense	1,124,500	630,000				1,754,500
Total Cost and Expense	3,164,500	1,880,000				5,014,500
Net	523,500	140,000				551,500
Minority Interest (.2 × 140,000)					28,000	(28,000)
Net Income to Retained Earnings	523,500	140,000	142,000	30,000	28,000	523,500
RETAINED EARNINGS STATEMENT						
1/1/81 Retained Earnings						
P Company	1,858,000					1,858,000
S Company		805,000	³ 644,000		161,000	
Net Income from above	523,500	140,000	142,000	30,000	28,000	523,500
Dividends Declared						
P Company	(150,000)					(150,000)
S Company		(60,000)		¹ 48,000	(12,000)	
12/31/81 Retained Earnings						
to Balance Sheet	2,231,500	885,000	786,000	78,000	177,000	2,231,500
BALANCE SHEET						
Investment in S Company Bonds	307,500			² 307,500		
Investment in S Company Stock	1,491,500		² 22,000	¹ 69,500		
				³ 1,444,000		
Other Assets	5,652,500	2,690,000				8,342,500
Total	7,451,500	2,690,000				8,342,500
9% Bonds Payable		500,000	² 300,000			200,000
Discount on Bonds Payable		(15,000)		² 9,000		(6,000)
Liabilities	2,220,000	320,000				2,540,000
Capital Stock						
P Company	3,000,000					3,000,000
S Company		1,000,000	³ 800,000		200,000	
Retained Earnings from above	2,231,500	885,000	786,000	78,000	177,000	2,231,500
Minority Interest					377,000	377,000
Total Liabilities and Equity	7,451,500	2,690,000	1,908,000	1,908,000		8,342,500

To adjust the investment account to the beginning-of-year balance and to eliminate equity in subsidiary income.
To adjust the investment account by the amount of the constructive loss on the bond retirement recorded on the books of P Company, to eliminate the intercompany bond investment and bond payable, and to eliminate the intercompany interest expense and income.
To eliminate the investment account.

receivable and the notes receivable discounted accounts must be eliminated, because the consolidated group is not contingently liable for the note, but is the primary maker of the note held by an outside party.

Now assume that P Company discounts with S Company a note that had originally been received from one of its customers. Here it is P Company that may record the transfer in one of two ways. Again, if the first method was used, no elimination would be required, for the same reasons discussed in the preceding paragraph. However, if the second method was used, both companies would report the same note receivable as an asset, and P Company would show a contingent liability for a note receivable discounted. In the consolidating workpaper one note receivable must be eliminated, along with the note receivable discounted account, as shown below in the partial section of a consolidated workpaper:

	P	S	ELIMINATIONS		CONSOLIDATED
DEBITS	COMPANY	COMPANY	DR.	CR.	BALANCES
Notes Receivable	100,000	100,000		¹100,000	100,000
CREDITS					
Notes Receivable Discounted	100,000		¹100,000		–0–

The consolidated balance sheet would report one receivable from an outside party. The note was discounted to an affiliated company and, therefore, there is no contingent liability to an outside party.

To further complicate the situation, assume now that S Company discounted the customer's note with an outside firm. If both companies used Method 1 to record the two discounting transactions, no elimination entry would be required. If the second method was used, the accounts would appear as follows in the trial balances of the two companies:

	P	S
DEBITS	COMPANY	COMPANY
Notes Receivable	100,000	100,000
CREDITS		
Notes Receivable Discounted	100,000	100,000

In this case, one of the notes receivables and one of the notes receivable discounted should be eliminated. The consolidated balance sheet would report:

Notes Receivable	100,000	
Less: Notes Receivable Discounted	100,000	–0–

Alternatively, both notes receivable and both discount accounts could be eliminated and the contingent liability disclosed in a footnote to the consolidated statement.

In the examples above the notes were always transferred from the parent to the subsidiary. The same analysis is appropriate if the notes were transferred from the subsidiary to the parent.

STOCK DIVIDENDS ISSUED BY A SUBSIDIARY COMPANY

A subsidiary may issue stock dividends in the same class of stock that is held by the parent company. The parent company records the receipt of the shares in a memorandum entry only, since a dividend in like stock is not considered income to the recipient. An important fact to recognize in consolidation is that the stock dividend does not alter the investor's proportionate interest in the subsidiary. On the books of the subsidiary, the declaration of a stock dividend is recorded as a transfer from the retained earnings account to one or more contributed capital accounts. The amount transferred is dependent on whether the dividend is a large or small stock dividend. (Recall from intermediate accounting that a large stock dividend is one in which the number of shares issued is greater than 20–25% of the outstanding shares.) From the consolidated entity point of view, the issuance of a stock dividend does not affect the consolidated financial statements. However, the issuance of a stock dividend does require some modification in the investment elimination entry and in the calculation of the undistributed profits of the subsidiary that have accumulated since the date of acquisition. For these reasons the problems created by the issuance of a stock dividend by a subsidiary are considered here.

To illustrate the effects of a stock dividend on the preparation of the consolidating workpaper, assume that P Company purchased 4,000 shares of S Company's $100 par value common stock on January 1, 1980 for $560,000. At the time of purchase, S Company reported common stock and retained earnings balances of $500,000 and $200,000, respectively. If consolidated statements were prepared on January 1, 1980, the eliminating entry would be:

Capital Stock—S Company	400,000	
Retained Earnings—S Company	160,000	
Investment in S Company		560,000

Now assume that S Company reports net income of $50,000 and declares a 30% stock dividend (1,500 shares) on December 31, 1980. S Company would record the dividend as follows, assuming that the company elected to capitalize the par value of the stock issued:

Stock Dividend Declared		
(1,500 shares $\times$ $100 par value)	150,000	
Capital Stock		150,000

Note that this entry has no effect on the total stockholders' equity. It changes only the composition of the account balances as shown below:

	S COMPANY'S CAPITAL ACCOUNT BALANCES	
	BEFORE THE STOCK	AFTER THE STOCK
ACCOUNTS	DIVIDEND	DIVIDEND
Capital Stock	500,000	650,000
Retained Earnings (200,000 + 50,000)	250,000	100,000
Totals	750,000	750,000

If the dividend had been considered a small stock dividend, the totals in the schedule above would not change. To record a small stock dividend, the retained earnings account is normally reduced by an amount equal to the number of shares to be issued times the fair market value per share, and contributed capital accounts are increased by the same amount.

The entries made during 1980 by P Company depend on whether the cost method or the equity method is used to record the investment. In either case, the receipt of the shares of stock is recorded by a memorandum entry only.

Cost Method If the cost method was selected to account for the investment, the only entry made in 1980 would be a memorandum entry to record the receipt of the 1,200 shares since no cash dividends were declared by S Company. A condensed consolidating workpaper for the year ended December 31, 1980 is presented in Illustration 10–5.

In the year that the stock dividend was declared, one additional workpaper eliminating entry would be made to eliminate the effects of the dividend on the parent's interest in the capital accounts of the subsidiary. The workpaper entries, in general journal form, are:

(1) Capital Stock—S Company   120,000
     Dividends Declared—S Company   120,000
      To reverse the effects of the stock dividend (150,000 × .80).

(2) Retained Earnings—S Company (.8 × 200,000)   160,000
    Capital Stock—S Company (.8 × 500,000)   400,000
     Investment in S Company   560,000
      To eliminate the investment account.

In the closing process the dividends declared account is closed to the retained earnings account. In subsequent periods the two entries are combined: a debit of $40,000 ($160,000 − $120,000) is made to the beginning retained earnings balance, and the capital stock is debited for $520,000 (400,000 + 120,000). The result is that the debit to capital stock is increased $120,000, and a corresponding decrease is made in the debit to the retained earnings account.

In the consolidated workpapers the entry to establish reciprocity is based on the undistributed income earned by the subsidiary since the date of acquisition. A cash dividend declared by the subsidiary is generally considered to be a distribution of the most recent profits, which, of course, reduces undistributed profits of the subsidiary accumulated after the date the parent obtained control of the subsidiary. Conversely, stock dividends are generally considered to be a distribution to the stockholders, the source of which is the earliest earnings accumulated in the retained earnings balance.

Purchase Accounting
Cost Method
80%-Owned Subsidiary
Subsidiary Issued Stock Dividend

ILLUSTRATION 10-5
Condensed Consolidated Statements Workpaper
P Company and Subsidiary
For Year Ending December 31, 1980

INCOME STATEMENT	P COMPANY	S COMPANY	ELIMINATIONS DR.	ELIMINATIONS CR.	MINORITY INTEREST	CONSOLIDATED BALANCES
Net	200,000	50,000				250,000
Minority Interest (50,000 × .20)					10,000	(10,000)
Net Income to Retained Earnings	200,000	50,000			10,000	240,000
RETAINED EARNINGS STATEMENT						
1/1/80 Retained Earnings						
P Company	460,000					460,000
S Company		200,000	²160,000		40,000	
Net Income from above	200,000	50,000			10,000	240,000
Dividends Declared						
S Company—Stock Dividend		(150,000)		¹120,000	(30,000)	
12/31/80 Retained Earnings						
to Balance Sheet	660,000	100,000	160,000	120,000	20,000	700,000
BALANCE SHEET						
Investment in S Company	560,000			²560,000		
Net Assets	1,000,000	750,000				1,750,000
Total	1,560,000	750,000				1,750,000
Capital Stock						
P Company	900,000					900,000
S Company		650,000	¹120,000			
			²400,000		130,000	
Retained Earnings from above	660,000	100,000	160,000	120,000	20,000	700,000
Minority Interest					150,000	150,000
Total Liabilities and Equity	1,560,000	750,000	680,000	680,000		1,750,000

¹To reverse the effects of the stock dividend.
²To eliminate the investment account.

In this illustration the procedures to compute the amount of the entry to establish reciprocity must be modified to recognize that the retained earnings balance at the date of acquisition has been reduced to $50,000 as a result of the stock dividend. The December 31, 1981 workpaper entries are:

(1) Investment in S Company	40,000	
Beginning Retained Earnings—P Company		40,000
To establish reciprocity as of 1/1/81 (50,000* × .80).		
*1/1/81 Retained earnings balance		100,000
Retained earnings balance—date of acquisition	200,000	
Less: Stock dividend	150,000	
Adjusted retained earnings balance—		
date of acquisition		50,000
Increase in retained earnings since		
date of acquisition		50,000
(2) Beginning Retained Earnings—S Company	80,000	
Common Stock—S Company	520,000	
Investment in S Company		600,000
To eliminate the investment account.		

The credit to the investment account is the sum of the ending balance ($560,000) on December 31, 1980 plus the debit made in Entry (1) above.

A portion of the retained earnings section of the December 31, 1981 workpaper is presented below:

	P COMPANY	S COMPANY	ELIMINATIONS DR.	ELIMINATIONS CR.	MINORITY INTEREST	CONSOLIDATED BALANCES
1/1/81 Retained Earnings						
P Company	660,000			¹40,000		700,000
S Company		100,000	²80,000		20,000	

Observe that the entries above result in beginning retained earnings balances that are equal to the ending retained earnings balances reported for minority interest and the consolidated retained earnings in the December 31, 1980 workpaper.

The issuance of a stock dividend does not affect the computation of consolidated retained earnings. As proof, the consolidated retained earnings balance as of December 31, 1980 is computed using the analytial approach as follows:

P Company's retained earnings balance at December 31, 1980	660,000
P Company's share of the change in the subsidiary's retained	
earnings since the date of acquisition (50,000 × .80)	40,000
Consolidated retained earnings—December 31, 1980	700,000

Equity Method   P Company will record the following entries in 1980 if the parent accounts for the investment using the equity method:

(1) Memorandum entry—Receipt of 1,200 shares
    of S Company common stock.
(2) Investment in S Company   40,000
        Equity in Subsidiary Income   40,000
          To record P Company's share of reported net income in S Company (50,000 × .80).

As has been discussed earlier in this text, the parent company records its share of the subsidiary's earnings each period as in Entry (2) if the equity method is used to account for the investment in the subsidiary. The percentage interest in the subsidiary and the entry to record the parent's equity in the subsidiary's operating results are unaffected by a stock dividend. As a result, no special workpaper problems are encountered, since the parent's retained earnings balance will reflect its share of the subsidiary's operations since the date of acquisition.

The only adjustment required in the workpaper procedures is to eliminate the effects of the stock dividend on the capital accounts in the year of the declaration, as was done in the cost method illustration. The entries to eliminate the investment account and the equity in subsidiary income account are made as before.

Stock Dividends Issued from Post-acquisition Earnings

In the illustration above the retained earnings capitalized ($150,000) was less than the retained earnings balance ($200,000) at the date of acquisition. If the stock dividend had been large enough, some of the post-acquisition earnings of the subsidiary may be capitalized. For example, assume that S Company made the following entry to record the stock dividend:

Retained Earnings   220,000
    Capital Stock   220,000

The entry capitalized $200,000 of the retained earnings that existed at the date of acquisition plus $20,000 of the net income reported after the date of acquisition. The capitalization of the current earnings does not affect consolidated retained earnings, which is still $700,000 as determined in Illustration 10–5, but it does result in the inclusion of earnings in the consolidated retained earnings balance which have been capitalized and are not available for the payment of dividends. The amount of the subsidiary's earnings that have been capitalized and included in the consolidated retained earnings should be disclosed in the consolidated financial statements. Some may contend that the portion of the retained earnings that has been capitalized should be reported as contributed capital in the consolidated balance sheet. In response to this contention the Committee on Accounting Procedures of the American Institute of Certified Public Accountants made the following comment:

Occasionally, subsidiary companies capitalize earned surplus [retained earnings] arising since acquisition, by means of a stock dividend or otherwise. This does not require a transfer to capital surplus on consolidation, inasmuch as the retained earnings in the consolidated financial statements should reflect the accumulated earnings of the consolidated group not distributed to the shareholders of, or capitalized by, the parent company.[3]

DIVIDENDS FROM PREACQUISITION EARNINGS

The nature of a liquidating dividend (dividend from preacquisition earnings) and the entries to record a liquidating dividend were discussed in Chapter 3. The objective of this section is to illustrate the effects of a liquidating dividend on the consolidating workpaper entries.

To illustrate the adjustment required in the workpaper procedures when a liquidating dividend is involved, assume that P Company acquired an 80% interest in S Company on December 31, 1979 for $560,000. At the time of purchase, S Company had capital stock and retained earnings in the amounts of $500,000 and $200,000, respectively. During the first year that the investment was held, S Company reported net income of $200,000. On December 31, 1980, the subsidiary declared and paid a cash dividend of $250,000. In this case, $50,000 of the declared dividend is a distribution of earnings accumulated before the controlling interest was obtained in the subsidiary.

As discussed in Chapter 3, there is general agreement that a liquidating dividend should be accounted for as a return of part of the original investment rather than income to the parent company. The entry made on the books of P Company depends on the method used (cost or equity) to account for the investment.

Cost Method   Recall that the source of a cash dividend is considered to be the most recent earnings. Under the cost method the following entry is made on the books of P Company to recognize that $200,000 of the dividend is based on the current earnings and $50,000 is a distribution of preacquisition earnings:

Cash	200,000	
Dividend Income (200,000 × .80)		160,000
Investment in S Company (50,000 × .80)		40,000
To record receipt of a cash dividend from S Company.		

This entry reduces the investment account balance to $520,000. In the year of the liquidating dividend one additional workpaper entry must be made to reverse the effects of the liquidating dividend, since the dividend has been adjusted to the

[3]Committee on Accounting Procedure, American Institute of Certified Public Accountants, *Accounting Research and Terminology Bulletin, Final Edition* (New York: AICPA, 1961), Bulletin No. 51, par. 18.

investment account, but the dividends declared are still shown as a separate amount in the trial balance of S Company. Although the consolidating workpaper is not presented, the December 31, 1980 eliminating entries are:

(1) Dividend Income	160,000	
Dividends Declared—S Company		160,000
To eliminate intercompany dividends.		
(2) Investment in S Company	40,000	
Dividends Declared		40,000
To reverse out the liquidating dividend.		
(3) Retained Earnings—S Company	160,000	
Capital Stock—S Company	400,000	
Investment in S Company		560,000
To eliminate the investment account.		

In the workpapers prepared in subsequent years, the amount of the entry made to establish reciprocity is based on the difference between the current year's beginning retained earnings balance and the retained earnings balance at the date of acquisition reduced by the $50,000 liquidating dividend. The investment elimination entry is a combination of Entry (2) and Entry (3) above. The December 31, 1981 workpaper entry would be:

(1) Retained Earnings—S Company	120,000	
Capital Stock—S Company	400,000	
Investment in S Company		520,000
To eliminate the investment account.		

No entry is needed to establish reciprocity because all of the earnings of the subsidiary since acquisition have been distributed, and the parent's share thereof was recorded by and is reported in the retained earnings balance of P Company.

Equity Method   If the equity method is used to account for the investment, all dividends including liquidating dividends are automatically recorded as credits to the investment account. Thus, no modification to the workpaper eliminating entries is necessary when the investment is recorded using the equity method of accounting.

SUBSIDIARY WITH BOTH PREFERRED AND COMMON STOCK OUTSTANDING

A subsidiary company may have both common and preferred stock outstanding. To justify consolidation the parent must hold a controlling interest in the outstanding voting stock, which is usually the common stock. At the same time, the parent may or may not hold shares of the preferred stock. In either case, in the preparation of consolidated financial statements, the shares of the preferred stock not held by the parent company are considered part of the minority interest.

The existence of preferred stock creates special problems in the preparation of consolidated financial statements. In preparing consolidated financial statements, it must be recognized that both classes of stockholders have an interest in the total stockholders' equity of the firm. Therefore, to determine the amounts of the beginning retained earnings balances to be eliminated, the balance at the date of acquisition must be apportioned between the preferred and common stock interest. In doing so, the provisions of the preferred stock issue, in particular the liquidating value and dividend provisions, must be analyzed and provided for in making the apportionment. Subsequent to the date of acquiring the controlling interest, the operating results of the subsidiary must also be allocated to determine the interests of the two classes of stock in the changes in the retained earnings balance. The dividend preference of the preferred stock issue will determine the amounts so apportioned.

The effects that the various rights and priorities granted to the preferred stockholders have on the determination of the book value interests and the claim to earnings are discussed in detail in the intermediate accounting text in this series. The rules for determining such allocations for some of the more common alternatives are summarized in Illustration 10–6.

ILLUSTRATION 10–6
Apportionment of Retained Earnings Balance and Net Income
When Subsidiary Has Both Common and Preferred Stock Outstanding

	ACCUMULATED RETAINED EARNINGS BALANCE		ALLOCATION OF NET INCOME	
	PREFERRED STOCK[a]	COMMON STOCK	PREFERRED STOCK	COMMON STOCK
Noncumulative, Nonparticipating	Zero	Balance in retained earnings account	Assigned to preferred only if a preferred dividend is declared	Balance of net income after preferred dividend is subtracted, if declared
Cumulative, Nonparticipating	Dividends in arrears	Residual after subtracting dividends in arrears	Current year's dividend whether declared or not	Residual net income to common stock
Noncumulative, Fully Participating	Apportioned between preferred and common stock[b]		Apportioned between preferred and common stock[b]	
Cumulative, Fully Participating	Dividends in arrears		Current year's dividend	Current year's dividend
	Balance is apportioned between preferred and common stock[b]		Net income remaining after current year's dividend is apportioned between preferred and common stock[b]	

[a] Assumes that the par value of the preferred stock is equal to the stock's liquidation value. If the liquidation value is greater, the preferred stock interest in retained earnings is increased by the amount of the liquidation premium and a corresponding reduction made in the common stock interest.

[b] Apportionment is based on ratio of capital balances.

The illustration does not describe the treatment of a deficit balance in the retained earnings account or a subsidiary reporting a net loss during an operating period. If the preferred stock is noncumulative, nonparticipating, and has a liquidation value equal to par value, the full deficit or net loss is allocated totally to the common stock interest. If the preferred stock is cumulative and nonparticipating, a deficit balance in retained earnings is assigned to the common stock, unless there are dividends in arrears, in which case the amount of dividends in arrears is added to the deficit and assigned to the common equity. In the case of a net loss, the current year's dividends on the preferred stock are added to the preferred interest and added to the net loss (which reduces the common interest) to determine the interest of the common stockholders in current operations. In the case of deficit operations, the participating provision can be ignored.

Consolidating a Subsidiary with Preferred Stock Outstanding

Cost Method   To illustrate the accounting for a subsidiary, and the consolidating workpaper procedures to be followed when the subsidiary has both preferred stock and common stock outstanding, the following information concerning the capital accounts of S Company as of January 1, 1980 is assumed:

8%, $100 par value preferred stock, cumulative nonparticipating, no dividends in arrears, liquidation value equal to par value	500,000
$10 par value common stock	1,000,000
Retained earnings	200,000
Total stockholders' equity	1,700,000

On January 1, 1980, P Company acquired 80% of the outstanding common stock for $960,000 and 30% of the outstanding preferred stock for $200,000. The entry to record the purchase is:

Investment in S Company Preferred Stock	200,000	
Investment in S Company Common Stock	960,000	
Cash		1,160,000

During the year, S Company reported net income of $200,000 and declared no cash dividends during the year. On the books of P Company no journal entries are required, assuming that the cost method is used.

The consolidating workpaper at December 31, 1980 is contained in Illustration 10–7. The balances are assumed except for the ones given above.

Purchase Accounting
Cost Method
80%-Owned Subsidiary
Subsidiary Has Preferred
Stock Outstanding

ILLUSTRATION 10–7
Consolidated Statements Workpaper
P Company and Subsidiary
For Year Ending December 31, 1980

INCOME STATEMENT	P COMPANY	S COMPANY	ELIMINATIONS DR.	ELIMINATIONS CR.	MINORITY INTEREST	CONSOLIDATED BALANCES
Net	800,000	200,000				1,000,000
Minority Interest						
Preferred Stock (40,000 × .70)					28,000	
Common Stock						
([200,000 − 40,000] × .20)					32,000	(60,000)
Net Income to Retained Earnings	800,000	200,000			60,000	940,000
RETAINED EARNINGS STATEMENT						
1/1/80 Retained Earnings						
P Company	1,500,000		¹ 50,000			1,450,000
S Company		200,000	² 160,000		40,000	
Net Income from above	800,000	200,000			60,000	940,000
Dividends Declared						
P Company	(500,000)					(500,000)
12/31/80 Retained Earnings						
to Balance Sheet	1,800,000	400,000	210,000		100,000	1,890,000
BALANCE SHEET						
Investment in S Company						
Preferred Stock	200,000			¹ 200,000		
Investment in S Company						
Common Stock	960,000			² 960,000		
Other Assets	4,640,000	2,500,000				7,140,000
Total	5,800,000	2,500,000				7,140,000
Liabilities	1,000,000	600,000				1,600,000
Preferred Stock						
S Company		500,000	¹ 150,000		350,000	
Common Stock						
P Company	3,000,000					3,000,000
S Company		1,000,000	² 800,000		200,000	
Retained Earnings from above	1,800,000	400,000	210,000		100,000	1,890,000
Minority Interest					650,000	650,000
Total Liabilities and Equity	5,800,000	2,500,000	1,160,000	1,160,000		7,140,000

¹To eliminate the investment account.
²To eliminate the investment account.

The eliminating entries in general journal form are:

(1) Preferred Stock—S Company	150,000	
Retained Earnings—P Company	50,000	
Investment in S Company Preferred Stock		200,000
To eliminate the investment account.		

Note that the excess of cost over the equity interest acquired on the preferred stock investment (200,000 − .3 [500,000] = 50,000) is treated as a reduction in consolidated retained earnings rather than allocated to undervalued assets.[4] The excess paid for a preferred stock interest is generally not related to the market value of the assets, but is more closely associated with the relationship of the preferred dividend rate to the market rate of interest for this risk class of preferred stock. In essence, the market factors that cause movements in the market value of the preferred stock are similar to the market factors that cause movements in the market value of a firm's bonds. The major difference is, of course, that the preferred stock does not normally have a maturity date. Thus, the period selected to amortize the excess would be arbitrary. This treatment is also supported by the view that the acquisition is a constructive redemption of the outstanding preferred stock by the consolidated entity at a cost greater than its book value. The excess is accounted for in consolidation as a reduction in consolidated retained earnings that results from the retirement of outstanding stock. In other words, as with the accounting for the purchase of treasury stock, the excess is viewed as a special dividend distribution to the selling stockholders.

(2) Beginning Retained Earnings—S Company	160,000	
Common Stock—S Company	800,000	
Investment in S Company Common Stock		960,000
To eliminate the investment account.		

Observe in the workpaper that the net income of S Company is first allocated between the preferred ($40,000) and the common stock ($160,000) in the computation of minority interest. The total minority interest in combined income is computed as follows:

CLASS OF STOCK	NET INCOME ALLOCATION	PERCENTAGE INTEREST HELD BY MINORITY	MINORITY INTEREST IN NET INCOME
Preferred	40,000	70%	28,000
Common	160,000	20%	32,000
Total Minority Interest in 1980 Combined Income			60,000

[4]If there had been an excess of book value interest acquired over cost of the preferred stock, the credit difference would have been carried to contributed capital.

Consolidated retained earnings is computed analytically as follows:

P Company's December 31, 1980 retained earnings balance		
from own operations		1,800,000
Less: Excess of cost of preferred stock		
over book value of interest acquired		50,000
		1,750,000
Plus: Undistributed income of subsidiary earned		
since date of acquisition		
Preferred	40,000 × .30 = 12,000	
Common	160,000 × .80 = 128,000	140,000
December 31, 1980 Consolidated Retained Earnings Balance		1,890,000

Now assume that S Company reported net income of $300,000 in 1981 and paid cash dividends of $80,000 to the preferred stockholders and $50,000 to common stockholders. Note that the dividend to preferred is $40,000 for the arrearages and $40,000 for the current year. P Company would record receipt of the dividends as follows:

(1) Cash	24,000	
Dividend Income		24,000
To record receipt of dividends on preferred stock investment (80,000 × .30).		
(2) Cash	40,000	
Dividend Income		40,000
To record receipt of dividends on common stock investment (50,000 × .80).		

A consolidating workpaper for December 31, 1981 is contained in Illustration 10–8.

The eliminating entries, in general journal form, are:

(1) Dividend Income	64,000	
Dividends Declared—S Company (Preferred)		24,000
Dividends Declared—S Company (Common)		40,000
To eliminate intercompany dividends.		

In subsequent periods a workpaper entry is made to establish reciprocity for both the preferred and common stock interests in the undistributed profits of S Company earned since the date of acquisition. The entry in the December 31, 1981 workpaper is:

(2) Investment in S Company Preferred Stock	12,000[a]	
Investment in S Company Common Stock	128,000[b]	
Beginning Retained Earnings—P Company		140,000
To establish reciprocity as of 1/1/81.		

[a](40,000 − 0) × .30 = 12,000
[b](360,000 − 200,000) × .80 = 128,000

Purchase Accounting
Cost Method
80%-Owned Subsidiary
Subsidiary Has Preferred
Stock Outstanding

ILLUSTRATION 10–8
Consolidated Statements Workpaper
P Company and Subsidiary
For Year Ending December 31, 1981

INCOME STATEMENT	P COMPANY	S COMPANY	ELIMINATIONS DR.	ELIMINATIONS CR.	MINORITY INTEREST	CONSOLIDAT BALANCES
Net (including dividend income of $64,000)	700,000	300,000	¹ 64,000			936,000
Minority Interest						
Preferred Stock (40,000 × .70)					28,000	
Common Stock (260,000 × .20)					52,000	(80,000
Net Income to Retained Earnings	700,000	300,000	64,000		80,000	856,000
RETAINED EARNINGS STATEMENT						
1/1/81 Retained Earnings						
P Company	1,800,000		³ 50,000	² 140,000		1,890,000
S Company—Preferred Stock		40,000	³ 12,000		28,000	
—Common Stock		360,000	⁴ 288,000		72,000	
Net Income from above	700,000	300,000	64,000		80,000	856,000
Dividends Declared						
P Company	(500,000)					(500,000
S Company—Preferred Stock		(80,000)		¹ 24,000	(56,000)	
—Common Stock		(50,000)		¹ 40,000	(10,000)	
12/31/81 Retained Earnings						
to Balance Sheet	2,000,000	570,000	414,000	204,000	114,000	2,246,000
BALANCE SHEET						
Investment in S Company						
Preferred Stock	200,000		² 12,000	³ 212,000		
Investment in S Company						
Common Stock	960,000		² 128,000	⁴1,088,000		
Other Assets	4,840,000	2,670,000				7,510,000
Total	6,000,000	2,670,000				7,510,000
Liabilities	1,000,000	600,000				1,600,000
Preferred Stock						
S Company		500,000	³ 150,000		350,000	
Common Stock						
P Company	3,000,000					3,000,000
S Company		1,000,000	⁴ 800,000		200,000	
Retained Earnings from above	2,000,000	570,000	414,000	204,000	114,000	2,246,000
Minority Interest					664,000	664,000
Total Liabilities and Equity	6,000,000	2,670,000	1,504,000	1,504,000		7,510,000

[1]To eliminate intercompany dividends.
[2]To establish reciprocity as of 1/1/81.
[3]To eliminate the investment account.
[4]To eliminate the investment account.

To facilitate making the elimination entries, the retained earnings of S Company are apportioned between the two classes of stock in the trial balance of the subsidiary.

(3) Beginning Retained Earnings—S Company		
(Preferred) (40,000 × .30)	12,000	
Preferred Stock—S Company	150,000	
Retained Earnings—P Company	50,000	
Investment in S Company Preferred Stock		212,000
To eliminate the investment account.		
(4) Beginning Retained Earnings—S Company		
(Common)	288,000	
Common Stock—S Company	800,000	
Investment in S Company Common Stock		1,088,000
To eliminate the investment account.		

On the basis of Illustration 10–8, consolidated net income and retained earnings for the year ending December 31, 1981, using the analytical approach, are computed as follows:

CONSOLIDATED NET INCOME

P Company's net income from independent			
operations (700,000 − 64,000)			636,000
P Company's share of S Company's net income:			
Allocated to Preferred Stock	40,000 × .30 =	12,000	
Allocated to Common Stock	260,000 × .80 =	208,000	220,000
Consolidated Net Income, December 31, 1981			856,000

CONSOLIDATED RETAINED EARNINGS

P Company's retained earnings on December 31, 1981			2,000,000
Less: Excess of cost of preferred stock over			
book value interest acquired			50,000
			1,950,000

Increase in retained earnings of S Company from January 1, 1980 to December 31, 1981:

	PREFERRED STOCK	COMMON STOCK	
Balance January 1, 1980	–0–	200,000	
Retained earnings December 31, 1981	–0–	570,000	
Increase in retained earnings	–0–	370,000	
Majority percentage interest	.30	.80	296,000
Consolidated retained earnings December 31, 1981			2,246,000

The computation above of consolidated retained earnings recognizes that the distribution of earnings accumulated after the date of acquisition is recorded in the retained earnings of P Company. Therefore, the majority interest in the retained earnings of S Company is based on undistributed earnings that were accumulated after January 1, 1980.

Equity Method   A company that holds a controlling interest in the voting stock of another company and at the same time holds an interest in the preferred stock of the same company may elect to account for both investments by use of the equity method.[5] If so, then the parent will record on its own books its share of the subsidiary's reported income (or loss) allocated to the common stock, as well as its share of the operating results allocated to the preferred stock. For example, the entries in 1980 on the books of P Company to record its share of the $200,000 net income reported by S Company in the illustrations above are:

(1)   Investment in S Company Preferred Stock   12,000
        Equity in Subsidiary Income   12,000
             To record P Company's share of the reported net income of S Company allocated to preferred stock (40,000 × .30).

(2)   Investment in S Company Common Stock   128,000
        Equity in Subsidiary Income   128,000
             To record P Company's share of the reported net income of S Company allocated to common stock (160,000 × .80).

P Company will record the receipt of dividends as reductions in the respective investment accounts.

The apportionment of beginning retained earnings and the results of operations between the common and preferred interest, as illustrated in the preceding section, are unaffected by the use of the equity method. Workpaper procedures are also similar to those illustrated in earlier sections of this text. The only difference is that additional workpaper entries must be made to adjust the investment in the preferred stock

[5]The method to be used (cost or equity) to account for an investment in preferred stock when the investor holds a controlling interest in the voting stock of the investee has not been specified by accounting authorities. In the opinion of the authors, the equity method is appropriate for accounting for an investment in preferred stock when the investor holds a sufficient number of *voting shares* to significantly influence the operating and financial policies of the investee. This position extends the criteria relating to use of the equity method for investments in common stock established in *Accounting Principles Board Opinion No. 18* (par. 17) to include accounting for investments in preferred stock of the investee. The equity method is preferred over the cost method, because it recognizes that there may be little relationship in the amount or the timing of income or loss and the declaration of dividends. An investor holding a sufficient number of voting shares of stock may be in a position to influence the amount and the period in which the earnings are distributed in the form of cash dividends. An investor who can influence the dividend policy on common stock can also influence the dividend policy on preferred stock. Thus, it seems logical that the investor record its share of the investee earnings allocated to preferred stock on the same basis that it recognizes earnings allocated to common stock investors. Furthermore, when the equity method is used, the financial statements of the investor report the same net income and retained earnings balance that would be reported for the majority interest if the subsidiary had been consolidated. This fact implies that the provisions of *Opinion No. 18* (par. 19), should also apply to preferred stock holdings.

account to the beginning-of-year balance and to eliminate the preferred stock investment account. Because there is little change in what has been discussed in detail in earlier sections of this text, the equity-method workpaper is not illustrated here. The reader may want to use the set of facts presented in the preceding section to prepare a set of workpapers based on the assumption that the equity method was used to account for the investment. The consolidated balances should equal the consolidated balances derived in Illustrations 10–7 and 10–8.

ALTERNATIVE WORKPAPER FORMATS

The practicing accountant may encounter a variety of formats in the workpapers used in the preparation of consolidated statements. The various forms may be classified into two categories, the three-division workpaper form used in this text, and the trial balance format. In the three-divisional form the account balances of the individual firms are first arranged into financial statement format. In contrast, in the trial balance format, columns are provided for the trial balances, the elimination entries, and, normally, each financial statement to be prepared, except for the statement of changes in financial position.

The consolidated balances derived in a workpaper are the same regardless of the formats selected. If the statement preparer has a sound understanding of consolidation principles, he should be able to adapt quite easily to alternative workpaper formats. However, the reader may want to develop a familiarity with the trial balance format, since this format is frequently preprinted on forms to be used in solving CPA examination problems. Although it would probably be acceptable to classify the trial balance into the three-divisional workpaper format, valuable examination time may be lost in doing so or in reasoning your way through the trial balance workpaper format.

To illustrate the trial balance workpaper format, and at the same time to verify that the results are the same as they would be if the three-divisional format were used, the same facts used in the preparation of Illustration 6–5 are assumed in Illustration 10–9. The facts of the case are:

1. P Company acquired an 80% interest in S Company for $1,360,000 on January 1, 1980.

2. The average tax rates for both companies is 40%, and S Company files a separate tax return.

3. S Company sold merchandise to P Company as follows:

YEAR	TOTAL SALES OF S COMPANY TO P COMPANY	INTERCOMPANY MERCHANDISE IN 12/31 INVENTORY OF P COMPANY	UNREALIZED INTERCOMPANY PROFIT
1980	700,000	400,000	100,000
1981	1,000,000	500,000	125,000

4. P Company uses the cost method to account for its investment in S Company.

5. The December 31, 1981 trial balances for P Company and S Company are contained in the first two columns of Illustration 10–9 on pages 372–373.

The steps in the preparation of the statement are: (1) The trial balances of the individual affiliates are entered in the first two columns. In this case the debit account balances are separated from the credit account balances. Or, the accounts can be listed as they appear in the ledger. A debit column and a credit column may be provided for each firm, or one column may be used and the credit balances identified by parentheses.[6] (2) The account balances are analyzed, and the required adjustments and eliminations are entered in the next two vertical columns. (3) The net adjusted balances are extended to the appropriate columns. A column is provided to accumulate the account balances needed for the preparation of the consolidated income statement, retained earnings statement, and the balance sheet. In addition, an optional column is provided for the identification of the minority interest. (4) Once the accounts are extended, the combined income is computed from the income statement column and allocated between the minority and majority interest. (5) The consolidated retained earnings balance and total minority interest can now be computed. The amounts are extended to the final column and should balance the liabilities and equities with the total assets. The alert reader will observe that these procedures are similar to the preparation of an 8-column work sheet developed to facilitate the preparation of financial statements for an individual firm.

Questions

1. Define "constructive retirement of debt." How is the gain or loss determined?

2. The realized gain or loss on constructive retirement of debt is subsequently recognized by the individual companies. Explain.

3. Allocating the gain or loss on constructive bond retirement between the purchasing and issuing companies is preferred conceptually. Describe how this allocation would be made.

4. Give arguments for assigning the *total* gain or loss on constructive bond retirement to the parent company *only*.

5. Under the assumptions followed in this text, how is the calculation of minority interest affected by intercompany bondholdings?

[6]For an example of this form see, Accounting Practice Part II, *Uniform Certified Public Accountants Examination,* Problem 5, May 1975.

6. If affiliates file separate tax returns, a timing difference will arise from the gain or loss on constructive bond retirement. Describe the workpaper adjustments relating to the timing difference for the year of retirement and subsequent years.

7. Investor Company purchases 70% of the outstanding bonds of Investee Company, a 40%-owned investee. What portion of a resulting gain or loss on constructive bond retirement should Investor Company recognize? What journal entry would be made to recognize the gain or loss?

8. In regard to the elimination of intercompany bondholdings, how would the use of the equity method differ from the cost method on a consolidating workpaper?

9. Outside party issues a note to Affiliate X, who then sells the note to Affiliate Y. Y discounts the note at an unaffiliated bank, endorsing it with recourse. Who is primarily liable and who is contingently liable for the note?

10. Cash dividends are viewed to be a distribution of the most recent earnings. How are stock dividends viewed? Explain how the reciprocity calculation is modified subsequent to a stock dividend.

11. How does the existence of preferred stock affect the calculation of minority interest?

12. Explain how to account for the difference between cost and book value of an investment in preferred stock of a subsidiary.

13. What effect would cumulative preferred stock have on the allocation of a net loss to the common stockholders?

14. Give support for the use of the equity method to account for investments in preferred stock of subsidiaries.

Problems

Problem 10-1
P Company issued 10-year, 7% bonds with a par value of $1,000,000 on January 1, 1978 for 106. On December 31, 1980, $600,000 of the par value bonds were purchased by S Company for $607,000. S Company is an 80%-owned subsidiary.

   P Company accounts for the investment in S Company using the cost method. S Company declared cash dividends of $50,000 each year during the period 1980–1981.

Required:
A. Prepare in general journal form the eliminating entries required on the consolidating workpaper as of December 31, 1980, December 31, 1981, and December 31, 1982. (Ignore income tax effects.)

Purchase Accounting
Cost Method
80%-Owned Subsidiary
Trial Balance Format

ILLUSTRATION 10-9
Consolidated Statements Workpaper
P Company and Subsidiary
For Year Ending December 31, 1981

	P COMPANY	S COMPANY	ELIMINATIONS DR.	ELIMINATIONS CR.	CONSOLIDATED INCOME STATEMENT	CONSOLIDATED RETAINED EARNINGS STATEMENT	MINORITY INTEREST	CONSOLIDATED BALANCE SHEET
DEBITS								
Inventory	480,000	310,000		[4] 100,000	690,000			
Investment in S Company	1,360,000		[6] 84,000	[8] 1,444,000				
Other Assets	5,450,000	2,330,000						7,780,000
Deferred Taxes			[3] 50,000					50,000
Dividends Declared								
P Company	150,000					(150,000)		
S Company		60,000		[7] 48,000			(12,000)	
Purchases	2,070,000	1,250,000		[1] 1,000,000	2,320,000			
Other Expense	798,000	587,000			1,385,000			
Income Tax Expense	302,000	93,000	[5] 40,000	[3] 50,000	385,000			
Total	10,610,000	4,630,000						
Inventory 12/31/81	510,000	360,000		[2] 125,000				745,000
Total Assets								8,575,000
CREDITS								
Liabilities	2,220,000	805,000						3,025,000
Capital Stock								
P Company	3,000,000							3,000,000
S Company		1,000,000	[8] 800,000				200,000	
Retained Earnings								
P Company	1,796,000		[4] 80,000	[5] 32,000 [6] 84,000		1,832,000		
S Company		805,000	[4] 20,000 [8] 644,000	[5] 8,000			149,000	
Sales	3,546,000	2,020,000	[1] 1,000,000		(4,566,000)			
Dividend Income	48,000		[7] 48,000					
Totals	10,610,000	4,630,000						

Inventory 12/31/81	510,000	360,000	² 125,000	(745,000)	
			2,891,000		2,891,000
Combined Net Income				531,000	
Minority Interest					
(.2 [140,000 +					
(100,000 − 40,000) −					
(125,000 − 50,000)])				25,000	25,000
Consolidated Net Income				506,000	
				506,000	
Consolidated Retained					
Earnings				2,188,000	2,188,000
Total Minority Interest				362,000	362,000
Total Liabilities					
and Equity					8,575,000

¹To eliminate intercompany sales.

²To eliminate unrealized intercompany profit in ending inventory.

³To defer recognition of income tax paid on unrealized intercompany profit.

⁴To recognize intercompany profit in beginning inventory realized during the year and to reduce consolidated retained earnings and minority interest at beginning of year for unrealized intercompany profit at the beginning of the year.

⁵To recognize tax effects on intercompany profit in beginning inventory.

⁶To establish reciprocity as of 1/1/81 ([805,000 − 700,000] × .80).

⁷To eliminate the intercompany dividends.

⁸To eliminate the investment account.

B. Calculate the minority interest in the net income of S Company and the consolidated net income for 1980 and 1981, assuming that the two companies reported net income from their independent operations as follows:

	P COMPANY	S COMPANY
1980	200,000	100,000
1981	210,000	90,000

C. Assuming that each company files separate income tax returns, and the average tax rate for each company is 40%, prepare in general journal form the eliminating entries required in the consolidating workpaper as of December 31, 1980, and December 31, 1981.

Problem 10-2

P Company issued 10-year, 7% bonds with a par value of $1,000,000 on January 1, 1978 for 106. On December 31, 1980, $600,000 of the par value bonds were purchased by S Company for $607,000. S Company is an 80%-owned subsidiary.

P Company accounts for the investment in S Company using the equity method. S Company declared cash dividends of $50,000 each year during the period 1980–1981.

Required:

A. Prepare the entries made on the books of P Company during 1980 and 1981 to record its interest in S Company. Assume that the two companies reported net income from their independent operations as follows:

	P COMPANY	S COMPANY
1980	200,000	100,000
1981	210,000	90,000

(Ignore income tax effects.)

B. Prepare in general journal form the intercompany bond eliminating entries required on the consolidating workpaper as of December 31, 1980, December 31, 1981, and December 31, 1982. (Ignore income tax effects.)

C. Assuming that each company files separate income tax returns and the average tax rate for each company is 40%, prepare in general journal form the intercompany bond eliminating entries required in the consolidating workpaper as of December 31, 1980 and December 31, 1981.

Problem 10-3

Hope Corporation owns 80% of the common stock of Ford Company. The stock was purchased for $480,000 on January 1, 1978 when Ford Company's retained earnings were $100,000. Preclosing trial balances for the two companies at December 31, 1980 are presented below:

DEBITS	HOPE CORP.	FORD COMPANY
Current Assets	367,000	498,000
Investment in Ford Company Common Stock	480,000	—
Investment in Ford Company Bonds	191,000	—
Other Assets	1,100,000	600,000
Dividends Declared	100,000	60,000
Operating and Financing Expenses	970,000	440,000
Income and Other Tax Expenses	87,000	48,000
	3,295,000	1,646,000

CREDITS		
Current Liabilities	145,000	70,000
Bonds Payable	200,000	400,000
Premium on Bonds Payable	2,000	6,000
Common Stock	1,200,000	500,000
Retained Earnings	600,000	140,000
Sales	950,000	500,000
Other Income	150,000	30,000
Dividend Income	48,000	—
	3,295,000	1,646,000

On January 1, 1979, Hope Corp. purchased 50% of Ford Company's outstanding bonds for $188,000. The book value of the bonds outstanding on this date were $408,000. The bonds are 7% bonds and mature December 31, 1986.

Required:
A. Prepare consolidating workpapers for the year ended December 31, 1980. (Ignore income taxes.)
B. Calculate consolidated net income using an analytical approach and compare your answer to the consolidated net income arrived at on the workpaper.

Problem 10–4
Hope Corp. owns 80% of the common stock of Ford Company. The stock was purchased for $480,000 on January 1, 1978 when Ford Company's retained earnings were $100,000. Preclosing trial balances for the two companies at December 31, 1980 are presented below:

DEBITS	HOPE CORP.	FORD COMPANY
Current Assets	367,000	498,000
Investment in Ford Company Common Stock	509,600	—
Investment in Ford Company Bonds	191,000	—
Other Assets	1,100,000	600,000
Dividends Declared	100,000	60,000
Operating and Financing Expenses	970,000	440,000
Income and Other Tax Expenses	87,000	48,000
	3,324,600	1,646,000

CREDITS		
Current Liabilities	145,000	70,000
Bonds Payable	200,000	400,000
Premium on Bonds Payable	2,000	6,000
Common Stock	1,200,000	500,000
Retained Earnings	646,000	140,000
Sales	950,000	500,000
Other Income	150,000	30,000
Equity in Subsidiary Income	31,600	—
	3,324,600	1,646,000

On January 1, 1979, Hope Corp. purchased 50% of Ford Company's outstanding bonds for $188,000. The book value of the bonds outstanding on this date was $408,000. The bonds are 7% bonds and they mature December 31, 1986. (Ignore income taxes.)

Required:

A. Prepare the entries made on the books of the Hope Corp. during 1980 to record its interest in Ford Company.

B. Prepare consolidating workpapers for the year ended December 31, 1980.

Problem 10–5

In this problem you are to assume the same trial balances and set of facts as those in Problem 10–3 except that the affiliates file separate tax returns. Assume that the average income tax rate for both companies is 40%.

Required:

A. Prepare consolidating workpapers for the year ended December 31, 1980.

B. Calculate consolidated net income using an analytical approach and compare your answer to the consolidated net income arrived at on the workpaper.

Problem 10–6

Hope Corp. owns 80% of the common stock of Ford Company. The stock was purchased for $480,000 on January 1, 1978, when Ford Company's retained earnings were $100,000. Preclosing trial balances for the two companies at December 31, 1980 are presented below:

DEBITS	HOPE CORP.	FORD COMPANY
Current Assets	367,000	498,000
Investment in Ford Company Common Stock	504,800	—
Investment in Ford Company Bonds	191,000	—
Other Assets	1,100,000	600,000
Dividends Declared	100,000	60,000
Operating and Financing Expenses	970,000	440,000
Income and Other Tax Expenses	87,000	48,000
	3,319,800	1,646,000

CREDITS		
Current Liabilities	145,000	70,000
Bonds Payable	200,000	400,000
Premium on Bonds Payable	2,000	6,000
Common Stock	1,200,000	500,000
Retained Earnings	640,400	140,000
Sales	950,000	500,000
Other Income	150,000	30,000
Equity in Subsidiary Income	32,400	—
	3,319,800	1,646,000

On January 1, 1979, Hope Corporation purchased 50% of Ford Company's outstanding bonds for $188,000. The book value of the bonds on the date was $408,000. The bonds are 7% bonds and they mature December 31, 1986.

The affiliates file separate tax returns. Assume that the average income tax rate for both companies is 40%.

Required:

A. Prepare the entries made on the books of the Hope Corporation during 1980 to record its interest in Ford Company.

B. Prepare consolidating workpapers for the year ended December 31, 1980.

Problem 10–7
Condensed financial information for the Patterson Company and Wilson Company is given below:

Balance Sheet
December 31, 1980

	PATTERSON CO.	WILSON CO.
Current Assets	730,000	700,000
Investment in Wilson Company Common Stock	1,040,000	—
Investment in Wilson Company Bonds	404,000	—
Other Assets	1,276,000	1,400,000
	3,450,000	2,100,000
Bonds Payable (10%)	300,000	500,000
Premium on Bonds Payable	20,000	40,000
Other Liabilities	400,000	160,000
Common Stock	2,000,000	1,000,000
Retained Earnings	730,000	400,000
	3,450,000	2,100,000

Retained Earnings Statement
For Year Ending December 31, 1980

Balance—1/1/80	600,000	300,000
1980 Net Income	380,000	200,000
1980 Dividends	(250,000)	(100,000)
	730,000	400,000

Income Statement
For Year Ending December 31, 1980

Sales	3,000,000	2,000,000
Dividend Income	80,000	—
Other Income	100,000	200,000
Total Revenue	3,180,000	2,200,000
Expenses	2,800,000	2,000,000
Net Income	380,000	200,000

Patterson Company purchased 80% of Wilson Company's common stock at the beginning of 1980 and uses the cost method to account for the investment. On July 1, 1980, Patterson Company purchased from outsiders the total $500,000 bond issue of Wilson Company for $380,000. The bonds mature in 2½ years on January 1, 1983.

Required:
Prepare a workpaper for the preparation of consolidated financial statements on December 31, 1980. (Ignore income taxes.)

Problem 10–8

On January 1, 1980, Golden Corporation purchased a 70% interest in the Rosy Corporation. The liabilities of Rosy Corporation on this date included the following:

	CARRYING VALUE
6% Debentures (due 6/30/84, interest payable annually on 6/30)	$382,000
8% Mortgage Bonds (due 1/1/93, interest payable semi-annually on 1/1 and 7/1)	513,000

Golden Corporation made the following acquisitions of Rosy Corporation bonds during 1980:

	COST
6/30—100% of the 6% debentures	$392,000
12/31—50% of the 8% mortgage bonds	238,000

Additional information:

1. Rosy Corporation issued the $400,000 face value debenture on July 1, 1974 at 90; the $500,000 mortgage bonds were issued on January 1, 1973 at a premium of $20,000.

2. Both companies have December 31 year-ends.

3. Both companies amortize bond discounts and premiums using the straight-line method of amortization.

4. The average tax rate of both companies is 40%.

5. Golden Corporation uses the cost method to account for its investment in Rosy Corporation.

Required:

A. Compute the extraordinary gain or loss from early extinguishment of debt to be shown on the consolidated income statement for 1980.

B. Prepare the necessary workpaper entries to eliminate the effects of the intercompany bondholdings on the consolidated financial statements for the year ended December 31, 1980.

C. Repeat Requirement (B) for 1982.

Problem 10–9

Investor Company holds a 70% interest in the voting stock of Investee Company, an unconsolidated subsidiary. The interest was acquired in 1977 when Investee Company reported capital stock of $200,000 and a retained earnings balance of $50,000. On December 31, 1980, Investor Company purchased $100,000 of Investee Company's par value bonds for $120,000. On this date (the fiscal year-end for Investor Company) the book value of the bonds was $110,000. Investee Company, using straight-line method of amortization, amortized $2,000 of the issue premium each year. During 1980, Investee Company reported a net loss of $40,000 and declared no cash dividends. In 1981, the subsidiary reported a net income of $30,000 and declared a cash dividend of $10,000. Both companies file separate tax returns, and the income tax rate averages 40%.

Required:

Journalize the entries necessary on the books of Investor Company to account for the investment in Investee Company for 1980 and 1981.

Problem 10–10

An analysis of the retained earnings account of B.G. Railroad, an 80%-owned subsidiary of R.R. Enterprises, disclosed the following information:

Balance 1/1/1980	160,000
Net income earned during 1980	45,000
Par value of stock dividends declared	
during 1980	30,000
Cash dividends declared during 1980	10,000
Balance 12/31/1980	165,000
Balance 12/31/1981	175,000

The investment in B.G. Railroad was acquired on January 1, 1980 for $220,000 and is accounted for using the cost method. On the date of acquisition, B.G. Railroad had $100,000, $10 par value common stock outstanding.

Required:

A. Prepare the general journal entries for 1980 to account for the investment in the subsidiary.
B. Compute R.R. Enterprises' equity in the 1980 undistributed net income of B.G. Railroad.
C. Prepare all determinable workpaper entries that would be made in the preparation of the 1980 consolidating workpaper.
D. Prepare the entries that would be made on the December 31, 1981 consolidating workpaper to establish reciprocity at January 1, 1981 and to eliminate the investment account.
E. Assuming that the equity method is used to account for the investment, repeat Requirements A and C above.

Problem 10–11

On January 1, 1980, X Company acquired a 60% interest in Y Company for $200,000. On this date, Y Company reported common stock of $100,000 and retained earnings of $200,000. Other information pertaining to Y Company follows:

1980 Net Income	$40,000
1980 Cash Dividends	60,000
1981 Net Income	70,000
1981 Cash Dividends	40,000

X Company uses the cost method to account for its investment in Y Company.

Required:

A. Prepare the general journal entries for 1980 and 1981 to record the receipt of the cash dividends.
B. Prepare all determinable workpaper entries that would be made in the preparation of the 1980 consolidating workpaper.
C. Prepare all determinable workpaper entries that would be made in the preparation of consolidated statements for 1982.

Problem 10–12

On January 2, 1980, Lewis Corporation purchased 80% of the outstanding common stock and 40% of the outstanding cumulative, nonparticipating, preferred stock of Wesley Company for $360,000 and $120,000, respectively. At this date, Wesley Company reported account balances of $500,000 in common stock, $200,000 in preferred stock, and $5,000 in retained earnings. No other contributed capital accounts exist. Dividends on the 6% cumulative preferred stock (par $10) were not paid during 1979. Lewis uses the cost method to account for all of its investments. Other information:

	LEWIS CORPORATION	WESLEY COMPANY
1/1/1980 Retained Earnings	$45,000	$ 5,000
1980 Reported Net Income	75,000•	30,000
1980 Dividends Declared	25,000	30,000

•Includes dividend income.

Required:

A. Compute consolidated net income for 1980, minority interest in Wesley Company's net income, and consolidated retained earnings at December 31, 1980 using the analytical approach.

B. Prepare workpaper entries to eliminate the investment accounts in the December 31, 1980, consolidating workpaper.

Problem 10–13

Pew Company reported the following stockholders' equity account balances on December 31, 1980:

Preferred Stock (7%, $100 par value, liquidation value equal to par value)	200,000
Premium on Preferred Stock	10,000
Common Stock, $10 par value	400,000
Other Contributed Capital	40,000
Retained Earnings	100,000
	750,000

On December 31, 1980, Nelson Co. acquired 70% of Pew Company's common stock for $400,000 and 40% of Pew Company's preferred stock for $100,000.

Any difference between the cost of common stock (preferred stock) and the book value interest acquired is assignable to land (consolidated retained earnings). The liquidation value of the preferred stock is equal to the par value of the preferred stock.

Required:

Prepare in general journal form the December 31, 1980 workpaper elimination entries for each of the following independent cases:

Case 1: The preferred stock is noncumulative and nonparticipating.

Case 2: The preferred stock is cumulative, nonparticipating, and dividends have not been paid for 1978, 1979, and 1980.

Case 3: The preferred stock is noncumulative and fully participating.

Problem 10–14

On January 1, 1980, Kearney Company acquired 80% of Pugh Company's $300,000 par value common stock for $200,000 and 40% of Pugh Company's 7% $100,000 par value preferred stock for $80,000. During 1980, Pugh Company reported net income of $50,000 and declared cash dividends of $20,000.

Required:
In each of the following independent cases, compute the minority interest in the net income of Pugh Company, assuming the following preferred stock provisions:
Case 1: The preferred stock is noncumulative and nonparticipating.
Case 2: The preferred stock is cumulative and nonparticipating. Dividends were in arrears two years as of January 1, 1980.
Case 3: The preferred stock is noncumulative and fully participating.
Case 4: The preferred stock is cumulative and fully participating. Dividends were in arrears two years as of January 1, 1980.

Problem 10–15

On January 1, 1979, High Company purchased an 80% interest in Low Company for $120,000. On this date, Low Company reported capital stock and retained earnings balances of $50,000 and $100,000, respectively. During 1979, Low Company reported net income of $20,000 and declared a cash dividend of $30,000. At the end of 1980, Low Company was facing a cash shortage. The board of directors accordingly elected to issue a 50% stock dividend. Low Company's accountant recorded the stock dividend as follows:

Stock Dividend Declared	25,000	
Common Stock		25,000

On December 31, 1980, High Company purchased on the open market bonds of Low Company with a par value of $100,000 for $92,000. Ignore tax effects on bonds.

Trial balances for the two companies as of December 31, 1980, are presented below:

DEBITS	HIGH COMPANY	LOW COMPANY
Current Assets	125,000	148,000
Investment in Low Company Stock	112,000	—
Investment in Low Company Bonds	92,000	—
Discount on Bonds Payable	—	4,000
Other Assets	300,000	250,000
Dividends Declared	30,000	25,000
Cost of Goods Sold	180,000	60,000
Other Expense	80,000	20,000
	919,000	507,000
CREDITS		
Accounts Payable	50,000	40,000
Long-term Bonds	250,000	200,000*
Common Stock	200,000	75,000
Retained Earnings 1/1	84,000	90,000
Sales	320,000	100,000
Dividend Income	15,000	2,000
Total	919,000	507,000

*8%, maturity date January 1, 1985.

Required:

A. Prepare a consolidated statements workpaper on December 31, 1980.

B. Prepare in general journal form the eliminating entries that would be required in the December 31, 1981, workpaper to (1) establish reciprocity as of January 1, 1981, (2) eliminate the balance in the investment account, and (3) eliminate the intercompany bondholding.

Problem 10–16

On January 1, 1980, Mesa Company purchased 90% of the common stock of Baker Company for $720,000. Condensed financial information for the companies is given below:

INCOME STATEMENT DATA—1980	MESA COMPANY	BAKER COMPANY
Sales	400,000	170,000
Subsidiary Income	30,600	—
Other Income	40,000	30,000
Cost of Goods Sold	(240,600)	(100,000)
Other Expense	(70,000)	(60,000)
Net Income	160,000	40,000

RETAINED EARNINGS—1980		
Balance 1/1/80	440,000	200,000
Net Income	160,000	40,000
Dividends		
Cash	(100,000)	(50,000)
Stock	—	(140,000)
Balance 12/31/80	500,000	50,000

BALANCE SHEET—12/31/80		
Current Assets	700,000	400,000
Investment in Baker Company Stock	705,600	—
Investment in Mesa Company Bonds	—	209,000
Other Assets	1,223,400	501,000
	2,629,000	1,110,000
Long-term Bonds	509,000*	200,000
Other Liabilities	150,000	100,000
Notes Receivable Discounted	70,000	20,000
Common Stock ($10 par value)	1,000,000	600,000
Other Contributed Capital	400,000	140,000
Retained Earnings	500,000	50,000
	2,629,000	1,110,000

*10% bonds, par value $500,000.

Other data:

1. At the end of 1980, Baker Company declared a cash dividend of $1.00 per share and issued a 20% stock dividend (10,000 shares). Market price of the stock was $14 per share.

2. On July 1, 1980, Baker Company purchased 40% (book value at date of acquisition was $510,000) of Mesa Company's outstanding bonds for $210,000. The bonds mature on July 1, 1985. Both companies use the straight-line method of amortization.

3. During October of the current year, Mesa Company advanced the subsidiary $50,000 and received short-term notes in exchange. The notes were subsequently discounted at a bank, and Mesa Company received $50,000 in cash.

4. Mesa Company accounts for the investment using the equity method.

Required:
A. Reconstruct in general journal form the entries required on the books of Mesa Company to account for the investment in Baker Company. (Ignore income taxes.)
B. Prepare consolidating workpaper for the year ended December 31, 1980.

Problem 10–17

In this problem you are to assume the same facts as those in Problem 10–16 except as noted below:

1. The subsidiary did not declare any stock dividends during 1981.

2. The discounted notes receivable matured during 1981.

Condensed financial statement data for 1981 are given below:

INCOME STATEMENT	MESA COMPANY	BAKER COMPANY
Net Income Before Recognition of Subsidiary Income	164,800	60,000
Subsidiary Income	55,200	—
Reported Net Income	220,000	60,000
RETAINED EARNINGS—12/31/81		
Balance 1/1/81	500,000	50,000
Net Income	220,000	60,000
Cash Dividends Declared	(100,000)	(50,000)
Balance 12/31/81	620,000	60,000
BALANCE SHEET		
Investment in Baker Company Stock	715,800	—
Investment in Mesa Company Bonds	—	207,000
Other Assets	2,031,200	913,000
	2,747,000	1,120,000
Long-term Bonds	507,000	200,000
Other Liabilities	220,000	120,000
Common Stock	1,000,000	600,000
Other Contributed Capital	400,000	140,000
Retained Earnings	620,000	60,000
	2,747,000	1,120,000

Required:
Prepare consolidating workpaper for the year ended December 31, 1981. (Ignore income taxes.)

Problem 10–18

On January 1, 1975, P Company acquired 80% of S Company's common stock and 40% of S Company's 6% preferred stock. P Company paid $760,000 for the common stock and $120,000 for the preferred stock. The preferred stock is cumulative, nonparticipating, and has a liquidation value equal to par value. On the date of acquisition there were no dividends in arrears. On January 1, 1975, S Company reported the following account balances:

Preferred Stock ($100 par)	300,000
Common Stock ($10 par)	600,000
Other Contributed Capital	
(Sale of common stock in excess of par value)	100,000
Retained Earnings	200,000
Total	1,200,000

Condensed preclosing trial balances for the two companies at December 31, 1980 are presented below:

	P COMPANY	S COMPANY
Current Assets	1,660,000	990,000
Investment in S Company Common Stock	760,000	—
Investment in S Company Preferred Stock	120,000	—
Other Assets	1,000,000	1,000,000
Dividends Declared	100,000	—
Expenses	360,000	220,000
	4,000,000	2,210,000
Current Liabilities	500,000	200,000
Long-term Liabilities	500,000	280,000
Preferred Stock	400,000	300,000
Common Stock	1,000,000	600,000
Other Contributed Capital	600,000	100,000
Retained Earnings	500,000	430,000
Sales	500,000	300,000
	4,000,000	2,210,000

On December 31, 1980, dividends on the preferred stock were in arrears for 1979 and 1980.

Required:

Prepare consolidating workpapers for the year ended December 31, 1980. (Assume that any difference between cost and book value interest acquired is attributable to an undervaluation in the land of S Company.)

Problem 10–19

On January 1, 1976, Brim Company purchased an interest in the capital stock of Cross Company for $550,000. At that time Cross Company had capital stock of $500,000 and retained earnings of $100,000. The difference between cost and book value on the date of acquisition was attributed to an understatement of land held by Cross Company. Preclosing trial balances for the two companies at December 31, 1980 are presented below:

	BRIM COMPANY	CROSS COMPANY
Cash	91,400	137,500
Accounts Receivable	260,400	111,000
Inventory—1/1	140,000	100,000
Investment in Cross Company	550,000	—
Investment in Brim Company Bonds	—	80,000
Other Assets	800,000	600,000
Dividends Declared		
Cash	100,000	66,000
Stock	—	71,500
Purchases	850,000	350,000
Other Expenses	120,000	90,000
Income Tax Expense	103,200	84,000
	3,015,000	1,690,000
Accounts Payable	90,000	60,000
8% Bonds Payable ($300,000 par		
value, maturity date January 1, 1985)	288,000	—
Other Liabilities	62,000	108,500
Common Stock ($10 par value)	700,000	605,000
Preferred Stock ($100 par value)	—	100,000
Additional Paid-in Capital	100,000	36,500
Retained Earnings	527,000	140,000
Sales and Other Revenue	1,200,000	630,000
Dividend Income	48,000	10,000
	3,015,000	1,690,000
Inventory 12/31	120,000	110,000

During 1978, Cross Company issued a 10% stock dividend (5,000 shares). The market value of the stock on this date was $14.00 per share. On October 1, 1978, Cross Company acquired $100,000 of Brim Company par value bonds.

The January 1, 1980 inventory of Cross Company includes $20,000 of profit recorded by Brim Company on 1979 sales. During 1980, Brim Company made intercompany sales of $100,000 with a markup of 25% on cost. The ending inventory of Cross Company includes goods purchased in 1980 from Brim Company for $40,000.

During 1980 Cross Company issued a 10% stock dividend. The market value of the stock on this date was $13.00 per share. Cross Company's preferred stock is 6%, noncumulative, and is nonparticipating. The affiliates file separate tax returns, and the average income tax rate for both companies is 40%. The affiliates use the FIFO cost flow assumption and straight-line amortization.

Required:
A. Prepare the entries recorded on the books of Brim Company during 1980 relating to its interest in Cross Co.
B. Prepare consolidating workpapers for the year ended December 31, 1980.

C. Calculate consolidated net income using an analytical approach and compare your answer to the consolidated net income arrived at on the workpaper.

Problem 10–20

On January 1, 1976, Brim Company purchased an interest in the capital sotck of Cross Company for $550,000. At that time Cross Company had capital stock of $500,000 and retained earnings of $100,000. The difference between cost and book value on the date of acquisition was attributed to an understatement of land held by Cross Company. Preclosing trial balances for the two companies at December 31, 1980 are presented below:

	BRIM COMPANY	CROSS COMPANY
Cash	91,400	137,500
Accounts Receivable	260,400	111,000
Inventory—1/1	140,000	100,000
Investment in Cross Company	690,800	—
Investment in Brim Company Bonds	—	80,000
Other Assets	800,000	600,000
Dividends Declared		
Cash	100,000	66,000
Stock	—	71,500
Purchases	850,000	350,000
Other Expenses	120,000	90,000
Income Tax Expense	103,200	84,000
	3,155,800	1,690,000
Accounts Payable	90,000	60,000
8% Bonds Payable ($300,000 par value, maturity date, January 1, 1985)	288,000	—
Other Liabilities	62,000	108,500
Common Stock	700,000	605,000
Preferred Stock ($100 par value)	—	100,000
Additional Paid-in Capital	100,000	36,500
Retained Earnings	615,000	140,000
Sales and Other Income	1,200,000	630,000
Equity in Subsidiary Income	100,800	—
Dividend Income	—	10,000
	3,155,800	1,690,000
Inventory—12/31	120,000	110,000

During 1978, Cross Company issued a 10% stock dividend. The market value of the stock on this date was $14.00 per share. On October 1, 1978, Cross Company acquired $100,000 of Brim Company par value bonds. The January 1, 1980 inventory of Cross Company included $20,000 of profit recorded by Brim Company on 1979 sales. During 1980, Brim Company made intercompany sales of $100,000 with a markup of 25% on cost. The ending inventory of Cross Company included goods purchased in 1980 from Brim Company for $40,000.

During 1980, Cross Company issued a 10% stock dividend. The market value of the stock on this date was $13.00 per share.

Cross Company's preferred stock is 6%, noncumulative, and is nonparticipating.

The affiliates file separate tax returns and the average income tax rate for both companies is 40%. The affiliates use the FIFO cost flow assumption and straight-line amortization.

Required:

A. Prepare the entries made on the books of Brim Company during 1980 to record its interest in Cross Company.

B. Prepare consolidating workpapers for the year ended December 31, 1980.

11

Accounting for Home Office and Branch Activities

A company seeking to grow or to diversify can do so by acquiring an interest in an established company or by acquiring a controlling interest in the common stock of a newly created entity. The preceding chapters on consolidated financial statements focused on the accounting issues related to consolidating the financial statements of two or more separate entities. One purpose of preparing consolidated financial statements is to provide information on the performance of separate companies controlled and operated under common management.

As an alternative to growth by acquisition, a company may achieve internal growth by establishing branch sales offices or branch production facilities. As it grows and expands into new marketing territories, a company may find it desirable to establish branch production or sales facilities with some degree of autonomy in order to provide a better service to its customers. The management of such branch facilities ordinarily reports to the management of the home office. The amount of autonomy that the branch management is granted by the home office and the accounting records maintained at the branch vary considerably from firm to firm.

In this chapter, we consider the problems associated with accounting for a branch facility. Although it is impossible to cover all of the possibilities, a general system is discussed and illustrated in sufficient detail to enable the reader to understand the basic procedures involved and to relate them to most systems encountered. In addition, the preparation of combined statements for the home office and and its branches is described and illustrated. Combined financial statements for the home office and branches are prepared in order to evaluate the financial position and operating performance of the firm as a whole. Procedures for preparing combined financial statements are much the same as those developed in earlier chapters on consolidated statements.

SALES AGENCY AND BRANCH CONTRASTED

Generally, a separate office is established to provide a sales outlet, and it most often takes the organizational form of either a sales agency or a branch. Factors such as the needs of the clientele, competition in the new territory, and type of product being marketed, dictate the form that best accomplishes the objectives established by management.

The term *sales agency* is commonly applied to an office that maintains samples of the firm's products. Orders for merchandise are taken by personnel of the agency, but the granting of credit, shipment of merchandise, and collection responsibility are all performed by the home office. The accounting records for an agency are kept simple, and transactions of the agency are generally recorded in the books of the home office. The agency may operate an imprest cash system, which would require the normal control procedure.

The term *branch* is used to describe a facility that carries an inventory of goods. The branch may or may not have the authority to grant credit terms and collect outstanding receivables. Although the branch is a separate unit and typically has greater independence than an agency, it is subject to the control of the home office and is governed by general corporate policies.

ACCOUNTING FOR A BRANCH OPERATION

Accounting System for a Branch

The accounting system created to account for the transactions of the branch can be quite flexible and varied. The system design may vary from a highly centralized system with the accounting done entirely by the home office to a system that is basically decentralized with most of the accounting for the branch transactions done by the branch. The system selected should be designed to satisfy the information needs of management. Management should also consider the cost of a particular system versus the benefits received. For example, the establishment of a full accounting system at a small branch may be too costly, even though it would provide the most timely information. In such a case, perhaps a centralized system should be used if it provides the needed information and is more economical to operate. In other cases, there may be a separation of the accounting function; some data may be accumulated and accounted for by the branch and other information kept by the home office. Generally, the accounting control exercised by the branch is directly related to the amount of responsibility granted to the branch manager. A manager who has been given a great deal of authority may also need a full accounting system in order to exercise adequate control over the branch operations.

In a centralized system the accounting records are maintained entirely by the home office. Supporting business documents are provided by the branch to the home office as a basis for the recording of the branch transactions. It may be useful for the home office to establish separate accounts for branch transactions in order to separate the activities of the branch from the activities of the home office. The branch management may operate a cash fund to pay some items that are more conveniently paid by the branch. Such a cash fund is similar to a petty cash fund operation, and no special accounting problems are involved.

If a decentralized accounting system is used by the firm, a few modifications are required in the accounting procedures to account for the branch operations. Because a decentralized system is more complex than a centralized system, it will be illustrated in the remainder of this chapter. It is assumed that the branch accounts for its activities using a double-entry accounting system with books of original entry and a fully self-balancing ledger. After a typical branch accounting system is reviewed, combined financial statements for the home office and branch are illustrated.

Accounting for a Branch Illustrated

Reciprocal Accounts[1] In a decentralized system, transactions between the home office and the branch are recorded on both the home office and the branch books. In the branch ledger, a *Home Office* account is created to record transactions between the home office and the branch. When the home office transfers cash or other assets to the branch, the home office acount is credited to offset the equal amount of debits made to the asset accounts. Conversely, the account is debited when assets are returned to the home office. The account is also credited (debited) for the amount of reported profit (loss) of the branch. As can be seen, the home office account is necessary if the branch is to use a double-entry accounting system and is a substitute for the equity section of the balance sheet, since the branch is established by a direct contribution of assets from the home office, rather than from assets received from the issuance of common stock.

On the home office books, a reciprocal account, *Investment in Branch,* is created for each branch established. If there are a number of branches, a control account in the general ledger could be used with supporting detail for each branch maintained in a subsidiary ledger. The Investment in Branch account is debited when assets are transferred to the branch or if the branch reports a net income. The account is credited when the branch returns assets to the home office or operates at a loss. The account serves as a record of the investment in the branch and also as a controlling account over the branch ledger, i.e., the amount of the net assets reported on the branch books should equal the balance in the Investment in Branch account.

After all adjustments and closing entries have been posted to the ledger, the balance in the Home Office account on the branch books and the balance in the Investment in Branch account on the home office books should be equal unless there are some transactions between the home office and the branch that are unrecorded on one set of books.

---

[1]Reciprocal accounts are related accounts on different sets of books that have equal but opposite balances, i.e., one account on one set of books has a debit balance while a related account on another set of books has an equal credit balance.

Inventory   When the branch is authorized to acquire goods for resale from outsiders, the normal journal entries are made to record such purchases. The purchases account is debited if a periodic inventory system is used; the inventory account is debited when a perpetual inventory system is used.

Inventory purchased by the home office and shipped to the branch for resale is normally billed to the branch at cost or some amount above cost. Accounting for goods billed in excess of cost is discussed later. The journal entry to record a shipment of inventory to the branch that is billed at cost depends on whether the firm uses a periodic or perpetual inventory system. To illustrate both systems, assume that the home office shipped goods that cost $5,000 to the branch.

Periodic Inventory System

HOME OFFICE			BRANCH		
Investment in Branch	5,000		Shipments from Home Office	5,000	
Shipments to Branch		5,000	Home Office		5,000

Perpetual Inventory System

Investment in Branch	5,000		Inventory—Home Office	5,000	
Inventory		5,000	Home Office		5,000

In both cases, the transfer of assets from the home office to the branch increases the accountability of the branch to the home office. Also note that the transaction does not affect revenue, since this is not an arm's-length transaction, but is merely the transfer of goods within the same firm. Any profit or loss on the sale of the inventory should be deferred until it is sold to an independent party by the branch.

The home office credits an account Shipments to Branch when a periodic inventory system is used by the firm. On the income statement of the home office, this account is subtracted from the sum of the beginning inventory and purchases to reflect the fact that the shipment of goods to the branch reduces the goods available for sale by the home office. On the books of the branch, the account Shipments from Home Office is equivalent to a purchases account. A different account title is used to distinguish goods received from the home office from goods purchased from outsiders. For the purpose of preparing combined financial statements, this distinction is not necessary when the goods are billed at cost. However, as will be demonstrated in a later section of this chapter, differentiation facilitates development of worksheet entries that are necessary to eliminate markups above cost on inventories acquired from the home office.

The inventory acquired from the home office is also recorded in a separate account, Inventory—Home Office, when the perpetual system is used. The entries made under the perpetual system are otherwise self-explanatory.

Freight charges incurred on the shipment of goods from the home office to the branch are considered normal inventoriable costs. The freight is an added cost of inventory, since the goods are presumably more valuable to the firm at the branch facility than in the home office warehouse. However, excessive freight that results from inefficiencies should be expensed. For example, if because of an error, a mode of transportation must be used that is more expensive than the mode normally used, only the normal freight charges should be recognized as an addition to the cost of inventory. The excessive freight charges should be expensed currently. As it is, from a practical point of view, immaterial freight charges are sometimes expensed currently rather than added to the cost of inventory.

Operating Transactions of the Branch   Transactions that involve only the branch and outsiders are normally reflected in the accounts of the branch only. For example, the collection of a receivable by the branch changes the composition of the branch assets, but not total branch assets. The accountability to the home office is not altered by such events; thus, the transactions are not normally recorded by the home office. Other types of transactions are initially recognized on the branch books and their net effect is recorded by the home office at a later date. For example, revenue (expense) transactions increase (decrease) the assets (or increase liabilities) of the branch and correspondingly increase (decrease) its accountability to the home office. These normal operating transactions are recognized currently by the branch, but recognition of the net change is deferred until the Income Summary account is closed to the Home Office account on the branch books. The home office will recognize the net change in the branch account when the net income or loss is reported by the branch.

Operating Expenses   The management of the branch is normally granted the authority to engage in most functions necessary for the conduct of branch operations. It may be more efficient and economical, however, for the home office to maintain a large, highly qualified staff centralized in one location to perform certain functions than to duplicate the functions at each branch. For example: (1) It may be more effective for the home office to conduct a national or regional advertising program than for branches to conduct individual advertising campaigns. (2) The company may obtain a lower insurance rate and receive better service if the contract is negotiated for company-wide coverage. (3) A central purchasing department acquiring items of equipment, inventory, and supplies for all branches may receive discounts on quantity purchases. Of course, branches may still be granted authority to acquire some of these goods and services from their own sources.

The services provided by the home office for the branch and expenses paid directly by the home office for the branch are factors that affect the profitability of the branch. The home office may adjust the financial statements provided by the branch when they are received, or the branch may be notified by the home office of the charges to be reflected on the branch financial statements. Some costs, such as property taxes, may be directly identified with each branch. Other costs incurred by the home office may benefit a number of branches. In such cases the home office is confronted with the problem of allocating joint costs to its branches. Problems involved in allocating joint costs are discussed in most managerial accounting textbooks.

Fixed Assets   In some branch operations, the home office maintains the records for all fixed assets even though the fixed assets are located at branch facilities. For control purposes, the home office may establish an individual fixed asset account for each branch. Thus, the journal entry to record the home office purchase of $10,000 of equipment for Branch #8 would be as follows:

Home Office Books

Equipment—Branch #8	10,000	
Cash		10,000

Note that the journal entry does not affect the branch books since the equipment is to be carried on the home office books. A journal entry must be made on both sets of books if the branch acquires equipment, but the asset is to be recorded on the home office books. The journal entries for both sets of books are as follows:

HOME OFFICE BOOKS			BRANCH BOOKS		
Equipment—Branch #8	10,000		Home Office	10,000	
Investment in Branch #8		10,000	Cash		10,000

In this latter case, the payment by the branch to acquire an asset to be carried on the home office books reduces the amount for which the branch is responsible to the home office. The result is the same as if the branch transferred assets to the home office. The reduction in the Home Office account by the branch requires a corresponding reduction in the Investment in Branch account by the Home Office and the concurrent recognition by the home office of the fixed asset.

The procedure for accounting for fixed assets described above facilitates computing depreciation charges when the company seeks to apply company-wide uniform depreciation policies. In particular, group depreciation rates can be computed more conveniently when the company follows the practice of grouping like assets for depreciation purposes or uses a composite depreciation method. The branch may or may not be informed of the amount of the depreciation charges on the fixed assets used by the branch.

Normal journal entries are made if the assets are to be recorded on the branch books. Purchases of equipment by the home office for the branch are recorded on both sets of books. The home office records the equipment purchase and then recognizes the transfer of the asset to the branch; upon receipt of the equipment, the branch records the asset with a corresponding increase in the Home Office account. Direct acquisitions of equipment by the branch are recorded on the branch books as an asset purchase.

Accounting for a Branch Illustrated

To illustrate the accounting for a branch that maintains a complete set of separate books, assume the following:

1. The branch files financial statements at the end of each month with the home office.

2. The branch began the month of January, 1980 with a $1,000 cash balance and $7,000 in inventory, all acquired from the home office.

3. The branch has the authority to purchase inventory and fixed assets from the home office or from other sources.

4. Inventory acquired from the home office is billed to the branch at cost to the home office.

5. Accounting records for the fixed assets of the branch are maintained by the home office.

6. The home office and branch use a periodic inventory system.

7. The branch is billed by the home office for services rendered and certain expenses incurred by the home office. These charges are to be reflected on the branch financial statements.

Transactions and journal entries related to the first full month of operations are shown in Illustration 11–1 for both the home office (ABC Company) and its Branch #1. The two most active ledger accounts (Investment in Branch #1 and Home Office) are reproduced in Illustration 11–2.

PREPARATION OF COMBINED FINANCIAL STATEMENTS

In the preceding discussion, it was assumed that the branch provided the home office with a complete set of financial statements and any supplementary information required by management. The financial statements prepared by the branch can take various forms since they are prepared for internal use and therefore need not be presented in accordance with generally accepted accounting principles. The statements, however, do generally follow the format of a publicly traded manufacturing or merchandising firm with a few differences, such as reporting the Home Office account in place of the owners' equity section on the balance sheet. These statements are used as the basis for performing the usual kinds of managerial evaluations, e.g., evaluating the financial position and the operating performance of the branch during the reporting period. Also, separate financial statements provide information that can be used to compare branches. Without separate statements, an unprofitable branch operation may be concealed by profitable operations of other branches. When evaluating the performance of the branch for the period under review, management should recognize that the net income is probably not reflective of a completely independent entity, because services performed by the home office may not be charged to the branch, or if they are charged, the services may be billed on some arbitrary basis.

The home office also prepares a balance sheet and income statement based on the results of the home office operations. The additional ledger accounts required to account for transactions with the branch may be reported separately. If so, then the Investment in Branch account is reported on the Home Office balance sheet as an asset. The Shipments to Branch account is reported as a subtraction from goods available for sale. The net income reported by the branches can be reported as a separate line item on the income statement. Separate home office statements provide a periodic record of the home office activities and also provide information for management to use in evaluating the performance of the home office without the inclusion of the branch activities. Again, one must recognize that some costs incurred by the home office may also benefit branch operations. The allocation of such costs may result in an over- or understatement in the home office operations.

Before issuing financial statements to users outside the firm, it is necessary to combine the assets, liabilities, revenues, and expenses of the individual branches with like accounts of the home office. Before the accounts are combined, however, transactions between the branch and home office must be eliminated. The presumption is that information provided to external statement readers should disclose the financial position and results of operation for the firm as a whole (i.e., as if the branches and home office had operated as one combined business entity).

Procedurally, it is easy to eliminate the intracompany transactions that occur during the period if the transactions are accounted for in reciprocal accounts. More specifically, most transactions between the home office and the branch are accounted for in the Home Office account and Investment in Branch account. These two accounts should have equal, but opposite, balances which are eliminated before the balance sheet accounts are combined. The result is that the assets and liabilities of the branch are substituted for the Investment in Branch account, which is reported as an asset in the trial balance of the home office. In other words, as noted earlier, the Investment in Branch account can be viewed as a control account, the balance of which equals the net assets (assets minus liabilities) of the branch. On the combined balance sheet, the individual assets and liabilities of the branch are included after being added to the like accounts of the home office.

On the income statement, the debit balance in the Shipments from Home Office account is eliminated by a credit; the offsetting debit is made against the credit balance in the Shipments to Branch account. The next step is to add the revenue and expense accounts of the branch to the respective home office accounts.

Inventory Billed to the Branch at Cost

Although the process of combining the financial statements of the branch and home office is normally not difficult, the use of a workpaper will facilitate the accumulation of the needed account balances. An example of one workpaper format, which takes the three-divisional format used in the consolidated financial statement workpapers, is presented in Illustration 11–3. The branch preclosing trial balance is developed from the journal entries presented in an earlier section of this chapter. The home office account balances are assumed except for the reciprocal account balances. Also note that within the retained earnings section of the workpaper, the branch reports no beginning retained earnings balance. This beginning balance will always be zero, because the net income or loss reported by the branch in prior years is closed to the Home Office account.

ILLUSTRATION 11–1
Journal Entries to Record Branch Transaction on Books of Home Office and Branch

TRANSACTION	HOME OFFICE			BRANCH		

(1) Home Office transferred $10,000 in cash and $20,000 of display equipment.	Investment in Branch
	  Cash
	Equipment—Branch
	  Equipment
		10,000
		
		20,000
			
			10,000
			
			20,000
				Cash
				  Home Office
					10,000	
						10,000

(2) Home Office shipped $30,000 inventory to branch.	Investment in Branch
	  Shipments to Branch
		30,000	
			30,000
				Shipments from Home
				  Office
				    Home Office
					
					30,000
						
						30,000

(3) Branch purchases equipment costing $5,000.	Equipment—Branch
	  Investment in Branch
		5,000	
			5,000
				Home Office
				  Cash
					5,000	
						5,000

(4) Branch makes $40,000 in credit sales and $20,000 in cash sales.	(NO ENTRY)			Accounts Receivable
				  Sales
				Cash
				  Sales
					40,000
					
					20,000
						
						40,000
						
						20,000

(5) Expenses of $7,000 are incurred and paid by the branch.	(NO ENTRY)			Operating Expenses Cash	7,000	 7,000
(6) Branch purchases $6,000 of inventory on account from an outside company.	(NO ENTRY)			Purchases Accounts Payable	6,000	 6,000
(7) Branch collects $15,000 of accounts receivable.	(NO ENTRY)			Cash Accounts Receivable	15,000	 15,000

(8) Cash of $20,000 is remitted to Home Office.	Cash
	  Investment in Branch
		20,000	
			20,000
				Home Office
				  Cash
					20,000	
						20,000

(9) Home Office bills branch $2,000 for services performed and for depreciation.	Investment in Branch
	  Operating Expenses
		2,000	
			2,000
				Operating Expenses
				  Home Office
					2,000	
						2,000

(10) End of the first month of operations—Branch has $1,000 of accrued expenses.	(NO ENTRY)			Operating Expenses Accrued Liabilities	1,000	 1,000

TRANSACTION	HOME OFFICE		BRANCH		
(11) Closing entries—Ending inventory balance is $6,000.			Income Summary	7,000	
			Inventory		7,000
			Inventory	6,000	
			Income Summary		6,000
	(Home Office follows normal closing procedures).		Sales	60,000	
			Income Summary		60,000
			Income Summary	46,000	
			Purchases		6,000
			Shipments from Home Office		30,000
			Operating Expenses		10,000
	Investment in Branch	13,000	Income Summary	13,000	
	Branch Net Income	13,000	Home Office		13,000

ILLUSTRATION 11–2
Transactions Recorded in Reciprocal Accounts

INVESTMENT IN BRANCH # 1

TRANSACTIONS	DEBIT	CREDIT	BALANCE
Beginning balance (Inventory, $7,000:			
Cash, $1,000)	8,000		8,000
Entry (1)	10,000		18,000
(2)	30,000		48,000
(3)		5,000	43,000
(8)		20,000	23,000
(9)	2,000		25,000
(11) Closing entry	13,000		38,000

HOME OFFICE

TRANSACTIONS	DEBIT	CREDIT	BALANCE
Beginning balance (Inventory, $7,000:			
Cash, $1,000)		8,000	8,000
Entry (1)		10,000	18,000
(2)		30,000	48,000
(3)	5,000		43,000
(8)	20,000		23,000
(9)		2,000	25,000
(11) Closing entry		13,000	38,000

ILLUSTRATION 11–3
Combined Statement Workpaper
ABC Company and Branch #1
January 31, 1980

| | TRIAL BALANCE | | ELIMINATIONS | | COMBINED |
	ABC COMPANY	BRANCH #1	DR.	CR.	BALANCES
INCOME STATEMENT					
Sales	100,000	60,000			160,000
Inventory—1/1/80	20,000	7,000			27,000
Purchases	95,000	6,000			101,000
Shipments from Home Office	—	30,000		¹30,000	—
	115,000	43,000			128,000
Shipments to Branch	30,000	—	¹30,000		—
Inventory—1/31/80	25,000	6,000			31,000
Cost of Goods Sold	60,000	37,000			97,000
Other Expense	25,000	10,000			35,000
Net Income to Retained Earnings	15,000	13,000	30,000	30,000	28,000
RETAINED EARNINGS STATEMENT					
1/1/80 Retained Earnings	57,000	—			57,000
Net Income from above	15,000	13,000	30,000	30,000	28,000
Dividends Declared	(10,000)	—			(10,000)
1/31/80 Retained Earnings to Balance Sheet	62,000	13,000	30,000	30,000	75,000
BALANCE SHEET					
Cash	33,000	14,000			47,000
Accounts Receivable	20,000	25,000			45,000
Inventory	25,000	6,000			31,000
Investment in Branch	25,000	—		²25,000	—
Plant and Equipment—Home Office (net of accumulated depreciation)	75,000	—			75,000
Plant and Equipment—Branch (net of accumulated depreciation)	24,000	—			24,000
Other Assets	30,000	—			30,000
Total	232,000	45,000			252,000
Current Liabilities	20,000	7,000			27,000
Long-term Notes Payable	50,000	—			50,000
Home Office	—	25,000	²25,000		—
Capital Stock	100,000	—			100,000
Retained Earnings from above	62,000	13,000	30,000	30,000	75,000
Total Liabilities and Equity	232,000	45,000	55,000	55,000	252,000

¹To eliminate intracompany transfer of inventory.

²To eliminate the investment account.

The workpaper eliminating entries are as discussed above and need not be explained here again. It should be noted, however, that the eliminating entries are made on the workpaper only.

Financial statements for ABC Company are prepared (see Illustration 11–4) from the combined column of the workpaper.

Inventory Billed to the Branch in Excess of Cost

The home office may use a system of pricing inventory shipped to the branch at some percentage above cost. In some cases, the mark-up is added by the home office to charge the branch for services performed in acquiring the inventory. It is sometimes maintained that keeping the amount of the mark-up unknown to the branch manager will improve the internal control over the branch operations by preventing the branch management from knowing the full profit earned by the branch. However, in most cases this is not a valid reason for using the method, since the branch management is usually aware of company policies concerning mark-ups or could probably approximate the cost rather closely.

Sometimes inventory is billed to the branch at its retail price. The procedures to operate such a billing system are similar to the retail inventory method. This procedure eliminates the need for a dual pricing system, one for billings to the branches and one for normal sales. The primary objective of the system is to provide information to management on the unsold inventory held by the branch, without the branch taking a physical count, and to improve internal control over the inventory. With such a system, management can approximate the ending inventory at retail by subtracting the sales of the branch from the goods available (beginning inventory at retail plus shipments from home office during the current period) for sale at retail. Management can then approximate the ending inventory at cost by multiplying the ending inventory at retail by a mark-up percentage of sales. A physical count of the inventory should be taken at least once a year to check on the reliability of the estimating procedure. The system will require more detailed records if the branch is permitted to alter the retail price and if goods are acquired from outside parties.

The mark-up on the inventory shipped to the branch is not realized until the goods are sold by the branch. To facilitate accounting for the mark-up and to maintain the cost of inventory shipped to the branch, the home office usually separates the unrealized profit from the cost of the goods. This can be done either by memorandum entry or by incorporation in the home office ledger. To illustrate the latter, assume that inventory costing the home office $30,000 is shipped and billed to the branch for $36,000 (120% of cost). The journal entry is:

Investment in Branch (billed price)	36,000	
Shipments to Branch (cost)*		30,000
Unrealized Profit in Shipment to Branch		6,000

*Inventory is credited if a perpetual inventory system is used.

ILLUSTRATION 11–4
Combined Financial Statements for ABC Company and Branch #1

ABC Company
Income Statement
For Month Ending January 31, 1980

Sales		$160,000
Cost of Goods Sold:		
Beginning Inventory	$ 27,000	
Purchases	101,000	
Goods Available for Sale	128,000	
Less: Ending Inventory	31,000	97,000
Gross Profit on Sales		$ 63,000
Operating Expenses		35,000
Net Income		$ 28,000

ABC Company
Retained Earnings Statement
For Month Ending January 31, 1980

Beginning Retained Earnings Balance	$ 57,000
Add: Net Income	28,000
Less: Dividends	10,000
Ending Retained Earnings Balance	$ 75,000

ABC Company
Balance Sheet
January 31, 1980

Cash	$ 47,000	Liabilities:		
Accounts Receivable	45,000	Current Liabilities		$ 27,000
Inventory	31,000	Long-term Note Payable		50,000
Plant and Equipment (net of		Total Liabilities		$ 77,000
accumulated depreciation)	99,000	Stockholders' Equity:		
Other Assets	30,000	Capital Stock	$100,000	
		Retained Earnings	75,000	
		Total Stockholders' Equity		175,000
		Total Liabilities and		
Total Assets	$252,000	Stockholders' Equity		$252,000

The "Unrealized Profit in Shipment to Branch" account is a contra to the Investment in Branch account if a balance sheet for the home office only is prepared. In other words, the balance in the Investment in Branch account is overstated by the amount of the unrealized profit. The account is eliminated when combined statements are prepared.

Accounting on the branch books when the inventory is billed to the branch in excess of cost to the home office is essentially the same as accounting procedures discussed earlier. However, since the ending inventory must be adjusted to cost on the combined financial statements, it is necessary for the branch to maintain sufficiently detailed inventory records to permit differentiating the ending inventory acquired from the home office from the ending inventory acquired from outsiders.[2] The branch records the $36,000 inventory shipment from the home office as follows:

Shipments from Home Office *	36,000	
Home Office		36,000

*Inventory—Home Office is debited if a perpetual system is maintained.

The branch will record the entry as if the goods had been billed at cost. Acquisitions from the home office are distinguished from purchases from outsiders to facilitate preparation of the combined statements.

The branch recognizes revenue on inventory acquired for resale when there is an arm's-length transaction with an outside party. The portion of the unrealized profit carried on the books of the parent that is related to the goods sold by the branch is considered earned. Generally, the home office defers recognition of the realized profit on individual sales until a periodic report is received from the branch. For example, assume that the only transaction of the branch during the year was the sale of three-fourths of the $36,000 in inventory acquired from the home office for $30,000. The branch would recognize $3,000 profit on the sale and report to the home office that one-fourth of the goods acquired from the home office is still on hand. The home office would record the net income reported by the branch and adjust the Unrealized Profit in Shipments to Branch account as follows:[3]

Investment in Branch	3,000	
Branch Net Income		3,000

[2]To avoid the necessity of maintaining separate inventory records, the ending inventory acquired from the home office is sometimes estimated by multiplying the ending inventory by a ratio of the goods acquired from the home office over total inventory purchases (from home office and outsiders).

[3]The similarity between this entry to record the branch net income and the equity method of accounting should be noted.

The net income is computed as follows:

Sales	30,000	
Cost of Sales (36,000 × .75)	27,000	
Net income reported by branch	3,000	

Unrealized Profit on Shipments to Branch	4,500	
Branch Net Income (6,000 × .75)		4,500

The required adjustment to the unrealized profit account can be verified as follows:

Balance in Unrealized Profit Account		6,000
Ending inventory reported by branch	9,000	
Cost of the ending inventory: $9,000/1.2	7,500	
Unrealized profit in ending inventory		1,500
Realized profit—Adjustment required		4,500

   The debit in the last entry reduces the balance in the Unrealized Profit account on the home office books to $1,500, which is equal to the unrealized profit in the inventory still held by the branch. This $1,500 will be recognized as income when the remaining one-fourth of the goods is sold by the branch. (As noted earlier, in the home office balance sheet, the $1,500 is offset against the Investment in Branch account.) The credit adds $4,500 to the $3,000 profit of the branch recorded in the first entry. This adjustment results in a branch net income of $7,500, which is the net income that would have been reported had the home office billed the branch for the cost of the inventory.[4] In other words, the net income as reported by the branch is understated by the amount of the mark-up on goods sold by the branch to third parties.

Inventory Billed to the Branch in Excess of Cost—Workpaper Illustration

Before combining the trial balances of the branch and home office, it is necessary to reduce to cost the inventory items reported on the income statement and balance sheet of the branch. To illustrate, assume the same set of transactions as recorded in the section where the goods were billed to the branch at cost, except that all goods acquired from the home office are billed to the branch at 20% above cost. To simplify the illustration, it is further assumed that all goods acquired from outsiders were sold

----

[4]The $7,500 can be verified as follows:

Sales price	30,000	
Cost of goods:		
30,000 × .75	22,500	
Net profit based on cost	7,500	

during the year. The branch beginning inventory is $8,400 ($7,000 times 120%) after the mark-up with a corresponding increase in the Home Office account. In the home office ledger the Investment in Branch account and Unrealized Profit in Shipments to Branch account beginning balances are $1,400 greater than the cost illustration. Journal entries to record the transfer of inventory and closing entries numbered to correspond with the earlier illustration are modified as shown in Illustration 11–5. All other journal entries are the same as those illustrated earlier. The Investment in Branch #1 and Home Office ledger accounts are presented in Illustration 11–6 to clearly show the effect of the transactions on these reciprocal accounts. In the closing process, the home office recognizes the net income of the branch as reported in the periodic reports submitted by the branch management. The unrealized profit account is adjusted to record the portion that was realized during the period. The adjustment is computed as follows:

Beginning balance	$1,400
Additions during the year	6,000
Balance before adjustment	$7,400
Balance needed*	1,200
Adjustment	$6,200

$\cdot$ $7,200 - ($7,200/1.2) = $1,200$ or

$(7,200/36,000) = .20; .20 \times 6,000$

$= $1,200$

It should be noted that the adjusted branch net income of $13,000 ($6,800 + $6,200) equals the net income reported in Illustration 11–3.

A combined workpaper is prepared in Illustration 11–7. Workpaper eliminating entries in Illustration 11–7 are summarized below in general journal form for the convenience of the reader.

January 31, 1980 workpaper entries in general journal form

(1) Unrealized Profit in Shipments to Branch   1,400

  Inventory—1/1/80 (Income Statement)   1,400

   To eliminate the intracompany profit in the beginning inventory. This reduces the branch beginning inventory to cost ($7,000).

(2) Shipments to Branch   30,000

  Unrealized Profit in Shipments to Branch   6,000

   Shipments from Home Office   36,000

   To eliminate the intracompany transfer of inventory and the unrealized profit recorded on the books of the home office.

ILLUSTRATION 11–5

Journal Entries to Record Branch Transactions in Books of Home Office and Branch

TRANSACTION	HOME OFFICE			BRANCH		
(2) Home Office ships inventory that cost $30,000 to branch; billing price is $36,000.	Investment in Branch	36,000		Shipments from Home Office	36,000	
	Shipments to Branch		30,000	Home Office		36,000
	Unrealized Profit in					
	Shipments to					
	Branch		6,000			
(11–16) Closing entries— Ending inventory balance is $7,200.	(The Home Office would follow the normal procedures to close other nominal accounts.)			Income Summary	8,400	
				Inventory		8,400
				Inventory	7,200	
				Income Summary		7,200
				Sales	60,000	
				Income Summary		60,000
				Income Summary	52,000	
				Purchases		6,000
				Shipments from Home		
				Office		36,000
				Operating Expenses		10,000
	Investment in Branch	6,800		Income Summary	6,800	
	Branch Net Income		6,800	Home Office		6,800
	Unrealized Profit in			(NO ENTRY)		
	Shipments to Branch	6,200				
	Branch Net Income		6,200			

(3) Inventory—1/31/80 (Income Statement)   1,200
         Inventory (Balance Sheet)   1,200
             To eliminate the unrealized profit in the branch ending inventory. This reduces the ending
             inventory to cost in the balance sheet and income statement.

(4) Home Office   32,400
         Investment in Branch   32,400
             To eliminate the investment account.

The purpose of the eliminating entries is to reflect the operations of one firm as if all the transactions had been recorded on one set of books. The same net income is derived as computed in Illustration 11–3 when the goods were billed at cost. This is a logical result since all the intracompany profit is eliminated from the branch inventory accounts.

The financial statements would appear as prepared in Illustration 11–4.

ILLUSTRATION 11–6
Transactions Recorded in Reciprocal Accounts

INVESTMENT IN BRANCH # 1

TRANSACTIONS	DEBIT	CREDIT	BALANCE
Beginning balance (Inventory, $8,400; Cash, $1,000)	9,400		9,400
Entry (1) Home Office transferred cash	10,000		19,400
(2) Shipment of inventory	36,000		55,400
(3) Branch purchased equipment		5,000	50,400
(8) Branch remitted cash to home office		20,000	30,400
(9) Expenses billed by home office	2,000		32,400
(11) Closing entry	6,800		39,200

HOME OFFICE

TRANSACTIONS	DEBIT	CREDIT	BALANCE
Beginning balance (Inventory, $8,400; Cash, $1,000)		9,400	9,400
Entry (1) Home Office transferred cash		10,000	19,400
(2) Shipment of inventory		36,000	55,400
(3) Branch purchased equipment	5,000		50,400
(8) Branch remitted cash to home office	20,000		30,400
(9) Expenses billed by home office		2,000	32,400
(11) Closing entry		6,800	39,200

INTERBRANCH TRANSFER OF ASSETS

In the preceding illustration, the home office established only one branch facility. Frequently, however, the home office may operate with a number of branch offices. To improve the operating efficiency of the firm, the home office may authorize the transfer of cash or other assets between branches. For example, one branch may transfer excessive inventory to another branch that has an inventory shortage. The branch that transfers the asset will recognize a decrease in the appropriate asset account. Rather than recording a receivable from another branch, the branch will typically recognize the transfer as a reduction in the accountability to the home office. The branch that receives the asset records the asset and increases the home office account. To maintain equal reciprocal balances, the home office must record appropriate adjustments to the investment accounts of the two branches involved in the tranfer.

ILLUSTRATION 11–7
Combined Statement Workpaper
ABC Company and Branch #1
January 31, 1980

	TRIAL BALANCES		ELIMINATIONS		COMBINED
	ABC COMPANY	BRANCH #1	DR.	CR.	BALANCES
INCOME STATEMENT					
Sales	100,000	60,000			160,000
Inventory—1/1/80	20,000	8,400		¹ 1,400	27,000
Purchases	95,000	6,000			101,000
Shipments from Home Office	—	36,000		²36,000	—
	115,000	50,400			128,000
Shipments to Branch	30,000	—	²30,000		—
Inventory—1/31/80	25,000	7,200	³ 1,200		31,000
Cost of Goods Sold	60,000	43,200			97,000
Other Expense	25,000	10,000			35,000
Net Income to Retained Earnings	15,000	6,800	31,200	37,400	28,000
RETAINED EARNINGS STATEMENT					
1/1/80 Retained Earnings	57,000	—			57,000
Net Income from above	15,000	6,800	31,200	37,400	28,000
Dividends Declared	(10,000)	—			(10,000)
1/31/80 Retained Earnings to Balance Sheet	62,000	6,800	31,200	37,400	75,000
BALANCE SHEET					
Cash	33,000	14,000			47,000
Accounts Receivable	20,000	25,000			45,000
Inventory	25,000	7,200		³ 1,200	31,000
Investment in Branch	32,400	—		⁴32,400	—
Plant and Equipment—Home Office (net of accumulated depreciation)	75,000	—			75,000
Plant and Equipment—Branch (net of accumulated depreciation)	24,000	—			24,000
Other Assets	30,000	—			30,000
Total	239,400	46,200			252,000
Current Liabilities	20,000	7,000			27,000
Long-term Notes Payable	50,000	—			50,000
Home Office	—	32,400	⁴32,400		—
Unrealized Profit in Shipments to Branch	7,400		{ ¹ 1,400 ² 6,000		—
Capital Stock	100,000				100,000
Retained Earnings from above	62,000	6,800	31,200	37,400	75,000
Total Liabilities and Equity	239,400	46,200	71,000	71,000	252,000

¹To eliminate the unrealized profit in the branch beginning inventory.
²To eliminate the intracompany shipment of inventory and unrealized profit thereon.
³To eliminate the unrealized profit in branch ending inventory.
⁴To eliminate the investment account.

ESTABLISHING RECIPROCAL BALANCES

In the preceding illustration, it was assumed that the balance in the Investment in Branch account was equal to the balance in the Home Office account. However, these accounts may not be in balance because of a delay in recording a transaction on one set of books. The two most common causes of differences in the accounts are cash transfers and inventory shipments in transit at year-end. For example, the branch records cash payments to the home office at the time the check is written and mailed to the home office. The home office will not record an entry until the check is received, which may be several days later. In the case of inventory, the home office will record inventory shipments to the branch when the goods are shipped. Depending on the mode of transportation and distance shipped, it may be a matter of weeks before the branch receives the goods and records the transaction. Between financial reports, there is no problem if the accounts are not in agreement. However, before combined financial statements are prepared, the full effect of the transaction should be recognized on both sets of books. Failure to do so will result in the assets of the firm being understated. In other words, cash and inventory in transit at the end of the period are not recorded on either set of books. The transaction will eventually be recorded on both sets of books; however, to bring the accounts up to date at year-end, the unrecorded side of the transaction should be entered in the elimination columns of the workpaper.

A COMPREHENSIVE ILLUSTRATION

It may be helpful at this point to prepare a comprehensive illustration for a home office with two branch operations. Preclosing trial balances of the three operations on December 31, 1980 are:

	HOME OFFICE		BRANCH #1		BRANCH #2	
	DEBIT	CREDIT	DEBIT	CREDIT	DEBIT	CREDIT
Cash	32,150		17,850		19,000	
Inventory 1/1/80	22,000		6,000		10,000	
Investment in Branch #1	26,850					
Investment in Branch #2	8,000					
Other assets	100,000		10,000		4,000	
Liabilities		30,000		10,000		10,000
Home Office				15,850		5,000
Unrealized Profit in Shipments to Branch		20,200				
Capital Stock		100,000				
Retained Earnings		28,800				
Dividends	10,000					
Sales		100,000		70,000		90,000
Purchases	130,000		19,000		13,500	
Freight-in	3,000		1,000		1,500	
Shipments from Home Office			32,000		45,000	
Shipments to Branch #1		29,600				
Shipments to Branch #2		38,400				
Operating Expenses	15,000		10,000		12,000	
Total	347,000	347,000	95,850	95,850	105,000	105,000
Inventory per count 12/31/80						
Purchased from Outsiders	18,000		4,000		2,000	
Purchased from the Home Office			4,000		3,000	

Other information:

1. The branches are permitted to acquire inventory from either the home office or outsiders. The home office marks-up inventory 25% above cost.

2. Inventory at a billed price of $5,000 was shipped by the home office to Branch #1 at year-end. The shipment was not received by the branch before December 31, 1980.

3. Branch #1 transferred cash of $6,000 to the home office. The payment was not received by the home office before December 31, 1980.

4. The home office directed Branch #1 to ship inventory to Branch #2. The goods were billed to Branch #1 for $3,000. Branch #2 had not recorded or received the goods.[5]

---

[5]In this illustration freight charges are ignored because accounting for them would distract from the main issues presented in the illustration. However, it should be noted that excess freight charges that are due to indirect routing of an asset are not properly charged to the cost of the asset, but should be recognized as an expense in the current period on the basis that the added cost incurred is a result of inefficient operations.

5. The beginning inventory of both branches was all acquired from the home office.

A workpaper for the preparation of the combined financial statements on December 31, 1980 is presented in Illustration 11–8. The adjusting entries and explanation for the entries follow:

(a) Shipments from Home Office   5,000
    Inventory (Balance Sheet)   5,000
        Home Office   5,000
        Inventory—12/31/80 (Income Statement)   5,000
            To record the shipment of inventory to Branch #1 in transit at year-end and not included in ending inventory count.

(b) Cash   6,000
        Investment in Branch #1   6,000
            To recognize the transfer of cash by Branch #1 that was not recorded by the home office.

(c) Shipments from Home Office   3,000
    Inventory (Balance Sheet)   3,000
        Home Office   3,000
        Inventory—12/31/80 (Income Statement)   3,000
            To record the shipment in transit at year-end that was unrecorded by Branch #2 and not included in ending inventory count.

It is assumed that the home office and Branch #1 made the appropriate journal entries. These entries are recorded in the appropriate home office or branch ledger.

The workpaper eliminating entries in Illustration 11–8 are summarized below in general journal form for the convenience of the reader.

December 31, 1980, workpaper entries in general journal form

(1) Unrealized Profit in Shipments to Branch   3,200
        Inventory—1/1/80 (Income Statement)   3,200
            To eliminate the intracompany profit in the beginning inventory—16,000 — (16,000/1.25).

(2) Shipments to Branch #1   29,600
    Shipments to Branch #2   38,400
    Unrealized Profit in Shipments to Branch   17,000
        Shipments from Home Office   85,000
            To eliminate the intracompany transfer of inventory and the unrealized profit recorded in the books of the home office.

ILLUSTRATION 11–8
Combined Statement Workpaper
Home Office and Branches #1 and #2
December 31, 1980
Trial Balances

INCOME STATEMENT	HOME OFFICE	BRANCH #1	BRANCH #2	ELIMINATIONS DR.	ELIMINATIONS CR.	COMBINED BALANCES
Sales	100,000	70,000	90,000			260,000
Inventory—1/1/80	22,000	6,000	10,000		[1] 3,200	34,800
Purchases	130,000	19,000	13,500			162,500
Freight-in	3,000	1,000	1,500			5,500
Shipments from Home Office	—	32,000	45,000	[a] 5,000 [c] 3,000	[2] 85,000	—
	155,000	58,000	70,000			202,800
Shipments to Branch #1	29,600				[2] 29,600	—
Shipments to Branch #2	38,400				[2] 38,400	—
Inventory—12/31/80	18,000	8,000	5,000	[3] 3,000	[a] 5,000 [c] 3,000	36,000
Cost of Goods Sold	69,000	50,000	65,000			166,800
Other Expense	15,000	10,000	12,000			37,000
Net Income to Retained Earnings	16,000	10,000	13,000	79,000	96,200	56,200
RETAINED EARNINGS STATEMENT						
1/1/80 Retained Earnings	28,800					28,800
Net Income from above	16,000	10,000	13,000	79,000	96,200	56,200
Dividends Declared	(10,000)					(10,000)
12/31/80 Retained Earnings to Balance Sheet	34,800	10,000	13,000	79,000	96,200	75,000
BALANCE SHEET						
Cash	32,150	17,850	19,000	[b] 6,000		75,000
Inventory	18,000	8,000	5,000	[a] 5,000 [c] 3,000	[3] 3,000	36,000
Investment in Branch #1	26,850				[b] 6,000 [4] 20,850	—
Investment in Branch #2	8,000				[5] 8,000	—
Other Assets	100,000	10,000	4,000			114,000
Total	185,000	35,850	28,000			225,000
Liabilities	30,000	10,000	10,000			50,000
Home Office		15,850		[4] 20,850	[a] 5,000	—
			5,000	[5] 8,000	[c] 3,000	—
Unrealized Profit in Shipments in Branch	20,200			[1] 3,200 [2] 17,000		—
Capital Stock	100,000					100,000
Retained Earnings from above	34,800	10,000	13,000	79,000	96,200	75,000
Total Liabilities and Equities	185,000	35,850	28,000	142,050	142,050	225,000

ᵃTo record the inventory in transit at year-end that was unrecorded by Branch # 1.

ᵇTo recognize the transfer of cash that was not recorded by the home office.

ᶜTo record the shipment in transit at year-end between the two branches.

¹To eliminate the intracompany profit in the beginning inventory.

²To eliminate the intracompany transfer of inventory and the unrealized profit recorded in the books of the home office.

³To eliminate the unrealized profit in the branch ending inventory.

⁴To eliminate the investment account.

⁵To eliminate the investment account.

(3) Inventory—12/31/80 (Income Statement)   3,000

    Inventory (Balance Sheet)   3,000

      To eliminate the unrealized profit in the branch ending inventory (15,000* −

      [15,000/1.25])

             *Inventory per count— 4,000 + 3,000 = 7,000

             Inventory in transit—   5,000 + 3,000 = 8,000

             Ending inventory purchased from

                home office   15,000

(4) Home Office   20,850

    Investment in Branch #1   20,850

      To eliminate the investment account.

(5) Home Office   8,000

    Investment in Branch #2   8,000

      To eliminate the investment account.

The workpaper eliminating entries are made on the workpaper only.

Questions

1. Distinguish between a sales agency and a branch.

2. What is a decentralized accounting system?

3. What type of an account is the "Home Office" account on the books of the branch?

4. Describe how to record the following transactions between a home office and its branch: (a) cash transfer; (b) inventory transfer (periodic inventory system); and (c) branch billed for services rendered by home office.

5. What type of an account is "Unrealized Profit in Shipments to Branch"? What does its balance represent?

6. Home office instructs Branch A to transfer $XXX of inventory to Branch B. Give the entries to be made on the books of both branches and the home office. (Assume periodic inventory system and inventory billed at cost.)

7. Reciprocal accounts on the home office and branch books may not always be equal. Why?

8. What eliminations are necessary for the preparation of combined financial statements?

9. What closing entries peculiar to branch accounting are made on the books of the home office?

Problems

Problem 11-1

On January 1, the Sun City Company, a recreational products manufacturer, opened a sales outlet in Phoenix. The following home office/branch transactions took place during January:

January 1 The Sun City Co. transferred $26,000 in cash to its Phoenix branch.

   2 Merchandise costing the home office $30,000 was shipped to the branch at an invoice price of $50,000. The home office and branch use a perpetual inventory system.

   8 The Phoenix branch received office equipment costing $37,000, purchased by the home office. The home office maintains all fixed asset accounts.

   11 The Phoenix branch purchased on account additional merchanidse from an outside wholesaler at a cost of $17,000.

   15 Branch sales for the period January 1-15: cash—$9,000; charge—$24,000. One-third of the goods sold were from the January 11 purchase and had an original cost to the Phoenix branch of $7,000. The remaining goods sold were from the January 2 home office shipment and were inventoried in the branch books at $15,000.

   29 Branch collections on charge sales—$7,000.

   30 Cash remitted to home office—$16,000.

   31 Branch sales for the period January 16-31: cash—$14,000; charge—$26,000. One-fourth of the goods sold were from the January 11 purchase and had an original cost to the Phoenix branch of $6,000. The remaining goods sold were from the January 2 home office shipment and were inventoried in the branch books at $25,000.

   31 Branch cash expenses for January:

Advertising	$500
Maintenance	375
Miscellaneous	25
Utilities	900

   31 Depreciation expense for January, recorded by Sun City Co. on assets at the Phoenix outlet, totaled $1,600. The branch is notified of the depreciation charge to be reflected on its branch financial statements.

Required:

A. Record the journal entries to be made by the home office and by its branch in regard to the transactions above.

B. The branch files financial statements at the end of each month with the home office. Prepare the necessary closing entries on the branch books.

Problem 11–2

The home office of Quick Company purchases blenders from a supplier at a cost of $13 a unit, and retails these same units at $20 in both its home office and Garden City branch retail outlets. During 1980 the home office purchased 10,000 units, of which 6,000 were sold at the home office outlet and 3,000 were shipped to the branch. During 1981 the home office purchased 12,000 units, of which 7,500 were sold at the home office outlet and 4,000 were shipped to the branch.

The Garden City branch sold 2,500 units in 1980 and 4,000 units in 1981. Both the home office and the branch office use a periodic inventory system. Beginning inventories were as follows: (in units)

	HOME OFFICE	BRANCH
1/1/80	–0–	–0–
1/1/81	1,000	500
1/1/82	1,500	500

Required:

A. Prepare journal entries, including closing entries, for the books of the Quick Company and its Garden City branch for 1980 and 1981. Inventory is billed to the branch at cost.

B. Assuming that the inventory is billed to the branch at a markup of 25% above cost, prepare the journal entries, including closing entries, for the books of the Quick Co. and its branch for 1980 and 1981.

Problem 11–3

The home office of the Hardy Sales Company is located in Boston. During the past ten years the home office established a number of branch operations in the New England states to sell canoes and other fishing equipment manufactured at the home office facility. The home office records inventory shipments to the branch operations at cost; the branch management is responsible for granting and collecting credit sales; fixed assets are carried on the home office books; and the company uses a perpetual inventory method for control purposes. The balance sheet on June 1, 1980 for Branch #8 is presented below:

Cash	20,260	Accrued Expenses Payable	2,430
Accounts Receivable (net)	18,420	Home Office	53,740
Inventory	16,860		
Prepaid expenses	630		
Totals	56,170	Totals	56,170

The transactions of Branch #8 which occurred during the second operating quarter (June, July, August) of 1980 are summarized below:

(1) Cash remitted to home office, $12,000.
(2) Sales on account, $7,200; Cash sales, $19,230: Cost of goods sold, $15,850.
(3) Cash paid on June 1, 1980 accrued liabilities, $1,680.
(4) Shipments received from home office, $8,240.
(5) Received display equipment with a useful life of 5 years from home office, $6,470.
(6) Collection of accounts receivable, $14,520.

(7) Paid salaries and other operating expenses, $7,970.
(8) End of quarter data:
   Balance of prepaid expenses, August 31, $420.
   Additional receivables estimated to be uncollectible, $165.
   Depreciation and other operating expenses charged to the branch by
      the home office, $860.

Required:

A. Assuming that the company completes the closing process at the end of each quarter, record the transactions above on both the home office and branch books including adjusting and closing entries.

B. Prepare a balance sheet for Branch #8 on August 31, 1980.

Problem 11–4

The Phoenix Company operates a number of branch offices in Arizona and Utah. Your firm is conducting the annual year-end audit of Phoenix Company and you are assigned the job of reconciling the Investment in Branch accounts and Home Office accounts. At the close of the current fiscal year, two of the reciprocal accounts appear as follows:

Home Office Books

INVESTMENT IN TUCSON BRANCH

1/1 Balance	26,500	1/4 Cash received from branch	4,500
4/10 Inventory shipments to branch	10,570	6/10 Cash received from branch	7,200
7/11 Inventory shipments to branch	11,600		
8/15 Equipment purchased for Tucson branch	17,000		
11/28 Operating expenses charged to branch	4,400		
11/30 Inventory shipments to branch	10,200		

Tucson Branch Books

HOME OFFICE

6/5 Remittance to home office	7,200	1/1 Balance	22,000
12/28 Remittance to home office	12,500	4/15 Inventory received from home office	10,750
		6/18 Collected an accounts receivable carried on home office books	420
		7/15 Inventory received from home office	11,600
		8/30 Equipment purchased by home office	17,000
		12/5 Inventory received from home office	10,200

In conducting other phases of the audit, you have verified that the amount of each entry recorded on the home office books is correct. The home office elected to use a periodic inventory system and accounts for the flow of goods using the FIFO method.

Required:
A. Prepare a statement to reconcile each of the accounts above to a correct balance as of the end of the year.
B. The procedures that your firm follows is to make workpaper entries to adjust the account balances provided by the client. Prepare in journal entry form the workpaper entries necessary to adjust the reciprocal accounts before combined financial statements can be prepared.

Problem 11–5
On July 1, 1980, the Crawford Co. established a branch office in a nearby city. To establish the branch, the home office sent the branch management $20,000 cash, furniture and fixtures that were carried on the home office books at a book value of $40,000, and 1,000 units of inventory that had cost $50 per unit. The home office bills inventory to the branch at 25% above cost. The management decided that furniture and fixtures are to be carried on the branch books and a periodic inventory system is to be used by the branch.

The branch transactions for the six-month period ending December 31, 1980 are summarized below:

Sales:	
Cash	$12,000
On account	55,200
Operating expenses paid by the branch (lease, salaries, utilities)	17,500
Purchase of inventory on account from outsiders—200 units	10,400
Collection of accounts receivable	52,000
Operating expenses paid by the home office and charged to the branch	4,500
Payment on accounts payable	8,200
Cash remittance to home office	20,000
Year-end data:	
Unpaid operating expenses	1,300
Depreciation expense for year	2,000
Inventory per physical count—360 units (40 of these units were purchased from outsiders)	

Required:
A. Prepare the journal entries on the branch books to record the transactions above.
B. Prepare adjusting and closing entries at year-end on the branch books.
C. Prepare a balance sheet for the branch as of December 31, 1980 after all closing entries have been posted to the ledger.
D. Prepare the journal entries needed on the home office books to record the branch transactions including the entry to record the branch net income (loss) and the entry to adjust the unrealized profit account and correct the branch reported net income (loss).

Problem 11–6

Kraft, Inc., of Atlanta, established a branch store in Columbus to distribute part of the goods purchased by the home office. The home office prices inventory shipped to the branch at 20% above cost. The following account balances were taken from the ledgers maintained by the home office and the branch:

ACCOUNT	KRAFT, INC.	COLUMBUS BRANCH
Revenues	$600,000	$210,000
Beginning Inventory	120,000	60,000
Purchases	500,000	—
Shipments to Columbus Branch	130,000	—
Shipments from Home Office	—	156,000
Operating Expenses	172,000	36,000
Ending Inventory	98,000	48,000

All of the branch inventory is acquired from the home office.

Required:

On the basis of these account balances, prepare a workpaper to determine the net income of the home office (excluding the branch net income), the net income reported by the branch, and the combined net income of the home office and branch.

Problem 11–7

On January 1, 1980, St. James Company opened a branch office, its first, in downtown Piedmont. The branch was given the responsibilities for granting credit and collecting receivables on its sales. The branch pays its own operating expenses. All merchandise was purchased from the home office at cost. Preclosing trial balances for the home office and branch at the end of the first year of operation are as follows:

	HOME OFFICE		BRANCH	
Cash	$ 485,000		$ 152,000	
Accounts Receivable (net)	1,205,000		263,000	
Inventory—1/1/80	906,000			
Property & Equipment— Home Office (net)	400,000			
Property & Equipment— Branch (net)	82,000			
Other Assets	120,000			
Accounts Payable		$ 411,000		$ 8,000
Other Liabilities		200,000		
Common Stock		1,500,000		
Retained Earnings		660,000		
Sales		4,100,000		960,000
Purchases	2,900,000			
Expenses	1,096,000		190,000	
Shipments to Branch		1,110,000		
Shipments from Home Office			950,000	
Investment in Branch	787,000			
Home Office				587,000
	$7,981,000	$7,981,000	$1,555,000	$1,555,000
Inventory—12/31/80	$ 559,000		$ 198,000	

A portion of the difference between the Home Office account and the Investment in Branch account is due to a transfer of $40,000 of cash by the Piedmont branch on December 30 that was not recorded on the home office books prior to the December 31 trial balance.

Required:
A. Prepare the closing entries at December 31, 1980 for the branch books.
B. Prepare the closing entries at December 31, 1980 for the home office books.
C. Prepare, in journal form, year-end adjustments pertaining to the branch operations that will appear on the combined workpapers.
D. Prepare a combined workpaper at December 31, 1980.

Problem 11–8
The Housewares Corporation is a merchandising company that sells its products through both a home office outlet and a branch outlet. The home office is the only supplier for the branch and bills goods to the branch at 25% above cost.

1980 preclosing trial balances for the home office and branch are as follows:

DEBITS	HOME OFFICE	BRANCH
Cash	$ 184,000	$ 124,000
Accounts Receivable (net)	180,000	267,000
Inventory—12/31/80	320,000	105,000
Fixed Assets—Home Office	1,200,000	
Fixed Assets—Branch	360,000	
Investment in Branch	578,000	
Cost of Sales	2,640,000	1,115,000
Expenses	840,000	592,000
Dividends Declared	100,000	
	$6,402,000	$2,203,000

CREDITS		
Accounts Payable	$ 171,000	
Notes Payable	450,000	
Unrealized Profit in Shipments to Branch	269,000	
Common Stock	1,000,000	
Retained Earnings—1/1/80	312,000	
Sales	4,200,000	1,800,000
Home Office		403,000
	$6,402,000	$2,203,000

Additional information:

1. The 1980 beginning inventories were $360,000 for the home office and $110,000 for the branch. Housewares Corp. uses a perpetual inventory system.

2. All expenses are paid by the home office, and the branch is notified of the charges they are to reflect on their trial balance.

3. On December 30, the branch forwarded a cash payment of $50,000 to the home office. As of the trial balance date the home office had not recorded the cash transfer.

4. On December 27 the home office shipped merchandise invoiced at $125,000 to the branch. As of the trial balance date the branch had not received the goods.

Required:
Prepare a combined statement workpaper at December 31, 1980.

Problem 11–9

Sales for the Mayer Company are made through the home office and a local branch. Although the branch is allowed to purchase locally from suppliers, the majority of its merchandise is received from the home office and billed to the branch at 120% of cost. The trial balances of the home office and branch at December 31, 1980 are as follows:

	HOME OFFICE	BRANCH
Cash	$ 846,400	$ 83,000
Short-term Securities	1,603,000	
Accounts Receivable (net)	1,208,900	390,100
Inventory—1/1/80	2,387,000	732,600
Investment in Branch	886,100	
Property and Equipment (net)	8,208,200	
Purchases	17,150,000	470,000
Expenses	2,667,000	546,700
Shipments from Home Office		5,648,400
Dividends Declared	300,000	
	$35,256,600	$7,870,800
Accounts Payable	$ 2,812,300	$ 98,700
Notes Payable	100,000	
Common Stock	7,000,000	
Retained Earnings	1,504,800	
Home Office		506,100
Sales	17,829,000	7,266,000
Shipments to Branch	4,907,000	
Unrealized Profit in Shipments to Branch	1,103,500	
	$35,256,600	$7,870,800
Inventory—12/31/80	$ 1,988,000	$ 600,000

Additional information:

1. The branch, owing to unexpectedly heavy post-Christmas sales, made three cash transfers to the home office within a one-week period.

DATE FORWARDED BY BRANCH	DATE RECORDED BY HOME OFFICE	AMOUNT
12/28	12/29	$ 50,000
12/30	1/3	140,000
1/3	1/5	100,000

2. At December 31, a shipment of merchandise from the home office, billed at $240,000, was in transit to the branch.

3. All goods purchased locally were for special orders and had been sold at year-end.

Required:
Prepare a combined workpaper at December 31, 1980.

Problem 11–10
The trial balances of the home office and branch office of the Azure Company appear below:

The Azure Company
Trial Balance
For the Year Ended December 31, 1980

DEBITS	HOME	BRANCH
Cash	$ 17,000	$ 200
Inventory—Home Office	23,000	
Inventory—Branch		11,550
Other Assets	200,000	48,450
Investment in Branch	60,000	
Purchases	190,000	
Purchases from Home Office		105,000
Freight-in from Home Office		5,500
Other Operating expenses	42,000	24,300
	$532,000	$195,000
CREDITS		
Liabilities	$ 35,000	$ 3,500
Home Office		51,500
Sales	155,000	140,000
Shipments to Branch	110,000	
Unrealized Profit in Shipments to Branch	1,000	
Capital stock	200,000	
Retained earnings	31,000	
	$532,000	$195,000

The audit at December 31, 1980 disclosed the following:

1. The branch office deposits all cash receipts in a local bank for the account of the home office. The audit worksheet for the cash cut-off revealed:

AMOUNT	DEPOSITED BY BRANCH	RECORDED BY HOME OFFICE
$1,050	December 27, 1980	December 31, 1980
$1,100	December 30, 1980	January 2, 1981
$ 600	December 31, 1980	January 3, 1981
$ 300	January 2, 1981	January 6, 1981

2. The branch office pays expenses incurred locally from an imprest bank account that is maintained with a balance of $2,000. Checks are drawn once a week on this imprest account, and the home office is notified of the amount needed to replenish the account. At December 31, an $1,800 reimbursement check was mailed to the branch office.

3. The branch office receives all of its goods from the home office. The home office bills the goods at cost plus a mark-up of 10% of cost. At December 31 a shipment with a billing value of $5,000 was in transit to the branch. Freight costs are typically 5% of billed values. Freight costs are considered to be inventoriable costs.

4. The trial balance opening inventories are shown at their respective costs to the home office and to the branch office. The inventories at December 31, excluding the shipment in transit, are

Home Office, at cost	$30,000
Branch Office, at billing value (i.e., excludes freight-costs)	$10,400

Required:
Prepare a three-divisional workpaper to combine the Azure Company and its branch. (Formal journal entries are not required. Supporting computations must be in good form. Disregard income taxes.)

(AICPA adapted)

Problem 11-11
The preclosing general ledger trial balances at December 31, 1980, for the Baltimore Wholesale Co. and its Atlanta branch office are presented below:

ACCOUNTS	HOME OFFICE DR. (CR.)	BRANCH OFFICE DR. (CR.)
Cash	$ 36,000	$ 8,000
Accounts Receivable	35,000	12,000
Inventory—Home Office	70,000	
Inventory—Branch Office		15,000
Fixed Assets (net)	90,000	
Branch Office	20,000	
Accounts Payable	(36,000)	(13,500)
Accrued Expenses	(14,000)	(2,500)
Home Office		(9,000)
Capital Stock	(50,000)	
Retained Earnings	(45,000)	
Home Office:		
Sales	(440,000)	
Purchases	290,000	
Expenses	44,000	
Branch Office:		
Sales		(95,000)
Purchases		24,000
Shipments from Home Office		45,000
Expenses		16,000
	-0-	-0-

Your audit disclosed the following:

1. On December 23 the branch office manager purchased $4,000 of furniture and fixtures but failed to notify the home office. The bookkeeper, knowing that all fixed assets are carried on the home office books, recorded the proper entry on the branch office records. It is the company's policy not to take any depreciation on assets acquired in the last half of the year.

2. On December 27, a branch office customer erroneously paid his account of $2,000 to the home office. The bookkeeper made the correct entry on the home office books but did not notify the branch office.

3. On December 30 the branch office remitted cash of $5,000 which was received by the home office in January 1981.

4. On December 31 the branch office erroneously recorded the December allocated expenses from the home office as $500 instead of $1,500.

5. On December 31 the home office shipped merchandise billed at $3,000 to the branch office, which was received in January 1981.

6. The entire opening inventory of the branch office had been purchased from the home office. Home office 1980 shipments to the branch office were purchased by the home office in 1980. The physical inventories at December 31, 1980, excluding the shipment in transit, are:

>Home Office—$55,000 (at cost)
>Branch Office—$20,000 (comprised of $18,000 from home office and
>$2,000 from outside vendors)

7. The home office consistently bills shipments to the branch office at 20% above cost. The sales account is credited for the invoice price.

Required:
Prepare a combined workpaper as of December 31, 1980. (Formal journal entries are not required. Supporting computations, including the computation of the ending inventories, must be in good form. Disregard income taxes.)

(AICPA adapted)

12

Accounting for Foreign Currency Transactions and the Translation of Financial Statements of Foreign Affiliates

Many large companies in the United States engage in international activities. The involvement of a United States company in foreign operations may entail transactions with a foreign company, such as the exporting or importing of goods, the establishment of a foreign branch, or holding an equity investment in a foreign company. Recording and reporting problems are encountered when transactions with a foreign company or the financial statements of a foreign branch or investee are measured in a currency other than American currency. *Foreign transactions* measured in a foreign currency must be translated into dollars before the transactions can be aggregated with the domestic transactions of the U.S. firm.

When a foreign branch or investee maintains its accounts and prepares its financial statements in terms of the currency of the country in which it is domiciled, the *accounts must be translated* into dollars before financial statements for the combined entity are prepared. To sum up, useful financial reports cannot be prepared until all transactions and account balances are stated in a common unit of currency.

Because of the widespread involvement of U.S. companies in foreign activities, accountants must be familiar with the problems associated with accounting for foreign activities. The purpose of this chapter is to examine the accounting standards for the translation of transactions measured in a foreign currency and financial statements prepared in terms of a foreign currency.

EXCHANGE RATES—MEANS OF TRANSLATION

Transactions that are to be settled in a foreign currency and financial statements of an affiliate maintained in terms of a foreign currency are translated into dollars by multiplying the number of units of the foreign currency by a foreign exchange rate. A foreign exchange rate "is the ratio between a unit of one currency and the amount of another currency for which that unit can be exchanged at a particular time."[1]

A *direct exchange quotation* is one in which the exchange rate is quoted in terms of how many units of the domestic currency can be converted into *one unit of foreign currency.* For example, a direct quotation of U.S. dollars for one British pound of 1.6715 means that $1.6715 can be exchanged for one British pound. The exchange rate can also be stated in terms of converting *one unit of the domestic currency* into units of a foreign currency, which is called an *indirect quotation.* Thus, in the example above, one U.S. dollar could be converted into .5983 pounds (1/1.6715). Direct quotations are preferred in this country and are used in this chapter.

Exchange rates may be quoted in terms of immediate delivery *(spot rate),* or a rate may be quoted for future delivery *(forward or future rate).* An example of direct exchange rate quotations for a particular day is contained in Illustration 12–1.

Before the 1970's, rates of exchange of free market countries were controlled to some extent by member countries of the International Monetary Fund.[2] Most of the member countries agreed to establish exchange rates in terms of U.S. dollars and gold. Although the actual rate was free to fluctuate, the countries that established official rates agreed to maintain the actual rate within 1% (2¼% after 1971) of the official rate by buying or selling U.S. dollars or gold. Because of pressure on the dollar, the United States in 1971 suspended its commitment to convert dollars into gold at $35 per ounce. The relationship between major currencies is now determined largely by supply and demand factors. As a result, significant realignments have occurred between the currencies of various countries over a relatively short period of time.

An unstable foreign exchange market increases the risk to companies doing business with a foreign company. After one rate change occurs, and until the next change occurs, all future transactions are conducted at the new rate. Because the amount to be received or paid is affected by a change in exchange rates, there is a direct economic impact on a company's operations. For example, if a company carried a receivable to be settled in pesos that had a current value of $1,000 and the value of the peso subsequently declined by more than 50%, as it did during 1976, then the number of dollars received by the company in exchange for the pesos received would be less than $500.

The selection of an exchange rate to be used in the translation process is complicated by the fact that some countries maintain multiple exchange rates. The

---

[1]*Statement of Financial Accounting Standards No. 8,* "Accounting for the Translation of Foreign Currency Transactions and Foreign Currency Financial Statements" (Stamford, Conn.: Financial Accounting Standards Board, 1975), par. 30.

[2]This section is based on information derived from Leonard Lorensen, "Reporting Foreign Operations of U.S. Companies in U.S. Dollars," *Accounting Research Study No. 12* (New York: AICPA, 1972), pp. 2–5.

government of a country may maintain official rates that differ from the market-determined rate depending on the nature of the transaction. For example, to discourage the outflow of cash from a country, the government may establish an exchange

ILLUSTRATION 12–1   Foreign Exchange Rates

Monday, October 23, 1978
Selling prices for **bank transfers** in the U.S. for payment abroad, as quoted at 3 p.m. Eastern Time (in dollars).

Country	Mon.	Fri.	Yr ago
Argentina (Peso) Finc'l	.00113	.00113	.00206
Australia (Dollar)	1.1755	1.1730	1.1255
Austria (Schilling)	.0759	.0750	.0621
Belgium (Franc)			
Commercial rate	.035100	.034819	.028378
Financial rate	.033000	.032950	.028430
Brazil (Cruzeiro)	.0527	.0527	.0670
Britain (Pound)	2.0070	2.0015	1.7790
30-Day Futures	2.0045	1.9991	1.7826
90-Day Futures	1.9962	1.9892	1.7882
180-Day Futures	1.9840	1.9756	1.7920
Canada (Dollar)	.8451	.8439	.8973
30-Day Futures	.8448	.8436	.8965
90-Day Futures	.8453	.8440	.8960
180-Day Futures	.8476	.8457	.8950
China-Taiwan (Dollar)	.028	.028	.0265
Colombia (Peso)	.0279	.0279	.0285
Denmark (Krone)	.1992	.1978	.1640
Ecuador (Sucre)	.0404	.0404	.0385
Finland (Markka)	.2570	.2562	.2415
France (Franc)	.2389	.2392	.2063
30-Day Futures	.2394	.2395	.2059
90-Day Futures	.2394	.2395	.2049
180-Day Futures	.2394	.2395	.2032
Greece (Drachma)	.0285	.0284	.0283
Hong Kong (Dollar)	.2111	.2115	.2131
India (Rupee)	.1310	.1300	.1180
Indonesia (Rupiah)	.002590	.002590	.00259
Iran (Rial)	.0144	.0144	.01416
Iraq (Dinar)	3.44	3.44	3.44
Israel (Pound)	.054434	.054908	.0948
Italy (Lira)	.001239	.001235	.001137
Japan (Yen)	.005501	.005498	.003966
30-Day Futures	.005534	.005528	.003981
90-Day Futures	.005597	.005588	.003998
180-Day Futures	.005692	.005682	.004028
Lebanon (Pound)	.3450	.3445	.3255
Malaysia (Dollar)	.4632	.4599	.4130
Mexico (Peso)	.04390	.04390	.04420
Netherlands (Guilder)	.5077	.5056	.4116
New Zealand (Dollar)	1.0800	1.0775	.9920
Norway (Krone)	.2052	.2042	.1826
Pakistan (Rupee)	.1020	.1020	.1025
Peru (Sol)	.0067	.0067	.01213
Philippines (Peso)	.1365	.1365	.1365
Portugal (Escudo)	.0225	.0224	.02485
Saudi Arabia (Riyal)	.3029	.3029	.2850
Singapore (Dollar)	.4700	.4668	.4159
South Africa (Rand)	1.1522	1.1522	1.1522
South Korea (Won)	.0021	.0021	.0021
Spain (Peseta)	.01454	.01446	.01197
Sweden (Krona)	.2352	.2346	.2092
Switzerland (Franc)	.6545	.6592	.4474
30-Day Futures	.6605	.6649	.4496
90-Day Futures	.6723	.6762	.4534
180-Day Futures	.6908	.6929	.4589
Thailand (Baht)	.05	.05	.05
Uruguay (New Peso) Finc'l	.1546	.1546	.1914
Venezuela (Bolivar)	.2331	.2331	.2331
West Germany (Mark)	.5517	.5529	.4422
30-Day Futures	.5551	.5562	.4433
90-Day Futures	.5616	.5622	.4458
180-Day Futures	.5722	.5719	.4495

Supplied by Bankers Trust Co., New York.

Source: Wall Street Journal, October 23, 1978.

rate for the conversion of dividend remittances to foreigners that is lower than the exchange rate established for the payment for exports by a foreign company. The appropriate exchange rate to use in the translation process when multiple rates exist is discussed later.

FASB STATEMENT NO. 8

The expansion of international business has been of particular concern to accountants because of developments in the worldwide monetary system during the last decade. These developments, coupled with the existence of a number of acceptable methods of translating foreign financial statements and of reporting gain or loss on foreign currency fluctuations, led the FASB to place the topic on its agenda in 1973. The result was the issuance of *FASB Statement No. 8,* "Accounting for the Translation of Foreign Currency Transactions and Foreign Currency Financial Statements."[3]

FASB Statement No. 8, issued in October, 1975, is effective for fiscal years beginning on or after January 1, 1976. The *Statement* supersedes all prior authoritative pronouncements. One objective of the *Statement* was to provide uniform accounting standards for the translation of foreign financial statements. A second objective was to fill the gap in the authoritative literature on accounting for transactions with foreign companies. The standards prescribed in *FASB Statement No. 8* are discussed and illustrated in the remainder of this chapter.

FOREIGN CURRENCY TRANSACTIONS

A U.S. company may engage in transactions with a foreign company for any number of reasons. In all transactions with a foreign company the invoice price is established in terms of the foreign currency of one party to the transaction, which is the domestic currency of the other party to the transaction.[4] For example, assume that a U.S. firm purchased goods from a French firm and the U.S. firm was to settle the liability by the payment of francs. The French firm would record the transaction as normal because the billing is in its domestic currency. Because the billing is in a foreign currency (francs), the U.S. firm must translate the foreign currency amount to dollars before the effects of the transaction can be entered in the accounts and combined with the other transactions of the firm. The U.S. firm must make payment in currency other than dollars and thus assumes the risk for unfavorable exchange rate changes that may

---

[3]*FASB Statement No. 8, op. cit.*

[4]A foreign currency transaction is a "transaction . . . whose terms are stated in a currency other than the local currency." *Ibid.,* Appendix E.

occur between the date the transaction is entered into and the date the account is settled. It is possible for the U.S. firm to hedge this exchange risk either by obtaining a forward contract or by making prepayment for the amount payable.

A hedge is a transaction entered into to protect the firm against a potential loss. A potential loss on a foreign exchange transaction is frequently reduced or eliminated by negotiating a forward exchange contract. A forward exchange contract (forward contract) is defined in *FASB Statement No. 8,* par. 22, as "an agreement to exchange at a specified future date currencies of different countries at a specified rate (the forward rate)." Thus, in this example, the U.S. firm could contract to buy in advance at a specified price the number of francs needed to satisfy the liability on the agreed settlement date. If the exchange rate for francs increases, the U.S. firm is protected by the forward contract to buy the francs at a specified contract price. The U.S. firm has shifted the risk that the franc may increase in value relative to the dollar to another party.

Some of the more common foreign currency transactions are:

1. Importing or exporting of goods or services.

2. Borrowing from or lending to a foreign company.

3. Obtaining a forward contract.

Each of the three types of transactions will now be examined.

Importing or Exporting of Goods or Services

Probably the most common form of a foreign currency transaction is the exporting or importing of goods or services. There are three stages in each foreign currency transaction of concern to the accountant. These stages and the appropriate exchange rate to use in translating the foreign currency measurements (except for forward contracts) are as follows:

1. At the *transaction date,* each asset, liability, revenue, or expense arising from the transaction shall be translated into (that is, measured in) dollars by use of the exchange rate (rate) in effect at that date, and shall be recorded at that dollar amount.[5]

2. At each *balance sheet date,* recorded dollar balances representing cash and amounts owed by or to the enterprise that are denominated in foreign currency shall be adjusted to reflect the current rate.[6]

3. At the *settlement date,* the foreign currency received or paid is converted into the domestic currency. Although translation is not required, an exchange gain or loss is recognized if the conversion to dollars is at a rate that is greater than, or less than, the rate at which the related receivable, or payable is recorded.

[5]*Ibid.,* par. 7(a).

[6]*Ibid.,* par. 7(b).

To illustrate, assume that a U.S. firm whose fiscal year-end is December 31, 1980 negotiates on December 1, 1980 to purchase from a French firm 100 units of inventory for $100,000, to be paid on March 1, 1981. It is further assumed that the U.S. firm did not engage in any form of hedging activity. The spot rate for francs at various points in time is as follows: $.20 at the date of purchase; $.23 at the balance sheet date; and $.22 on the settlement date. Assuming that the settlement is to be in dollars, the U.S. firm would record the transaction as follows:

December 1, 1980—Transaction Date

Purchases	100,000	
Accounts Payable		100,000

December 31, 1980—Balance Sheet Date

No entry is required.

March 1, 1981—Settlement Date

Accounts Payable	100,000	
Cash		100,000

This is a foreign currency transaction to the French firm, but not to the U.S. firm, since the purchase price is to be paid in dollars. Thus, the U.S. firm assumed no foreign currency risk because the dollars paid to settle the account were unaffected by the changes in the exchange rate. Accordingly, no exchange gain or loss arises for the U.S. firm. The journal entries to record the purchase and payment are recorded as a normal purchase transaction by the firm.

Now assume that the U.S. firm was billed 500,000 francs for the purchase of the 100 units of inventory from the French firm. The U.S. firm must translate the foreign currency to dollars before the transaction is recorded in the accounts. The translation is based on the exchange rate in effect at the transaction date.[7] The U.S. firm prepared the following journal entry on December 1, 1980, to record the purchase:

Purchases	100,000	
Accounts Payable (500,000 × .20)		100,000

At the balance sheet date the payable is adjusted using the exchange rate in effect at the balance sheet date. The entry is:

Exchange Loss	15,000*	
Accounts Payable		15,000

*Commitment at 12/31/80 (500,000 × .23)	115,000
Recorded liability (500,000 × .20)	100,000
Adjustment needed	15,000

---

[7]If multiple exchange rates exist for the foreign currency in which the transaction is denominated, the rate at which the transaction is to be settled should be used to translate and record the transaction and for valuations of receivables and payables at subsequent balance sheet dates. *Ibid.*, par. 30(a).

DAVE ERWIN

The exchange loss is reported as an operating loss in the current year's income statement even though it is unrealized and may reverse in a subsequent period. Reporting the loss in the period in which the exchange rate changes provides information to the statement reader when the event occurs, rather than delaying recognition of the loss until the account is settled. Furthermore, the adjustment results in reporting the liability in terms of the number of dollars that would be required to settle the account on this date. In other words, the U.S. firm would suffer an economic loss in 1980 if the account were settled on December 31, 1980 as a result of the unfavorable change in the exchange rate that occurred after the transaction date.

If the exchange rate declined below $.20 to, say, $.18, the U.S. firm would recognize a gain of $10,000 since it would take only $90,000 (500,000 × .18) to liquidate the $100,000 recorded liability.

Before the settlement date, the U.S. firm must buy 500,000 francs in order to satisfy the liability. With a change in the exchange rate to $.22, the firm will have to pay $110,000 on March 1, 1981 for the 500,000 francs. The journal entry to record the settlement on March 1, 1981 is:

Accounts Payable	115,000	
Exchange Gain		5,000
Cash		110,000

On the settlement date, accounts payable is debited for $115,000, the recorded basis of the liability after adjusting for the exchange rate in effect at December 31, 1980. The impact on the amount of currency to be paid as a result of fluctuations in the exchange rate is thus reported in the period in which the change occurs, that is, the gain or loss in this period is the result of management's decision to speculate in foreign currency by not obtaining francs or negotiating a forward exchange contract on January 1, 1981. The result of that decision on the financial position of the firm is reported in the period affected by the decision.

Over the three-month period the decision to delay payment cost the firm $10,000. This net amount was recognized as a loss of $15,000 in 1980 and a $5,000 gain in 1981.

Now assume that the U.S. firm sold 100 units of inventory to a French firm. All other facts are the same as stated above. The following journal entries are made assuming that: (1) settlement is made in domestic currency ($100,000), and (2) settlement is made in foreign currency (500,000 francs).

(1) Settlement in dollars

December 1, 1980—Transaction Date

Accounts Receivable	100,000	
Sales		100,000

December 31, 1980—Balance Sheet Date

No entry is required.

March 1, 1981—Settlement Date

Cash	100,000	
Accounts Receivable		100,000

In this alternative the account is settled in dollars. The journal entries are the same as those that would be made for a sale of goods to a domestic firm.

(2) Settlement in francs

December 1, 1980—Date of Transaction

Accounts Receivable	100,000	
Sales		100,000

December 31, 1980—Balance Sheet Date

Accounts Receivable	15,000	
Exchange Gain		15,000

March 1, 1981—Settlement Date

Cash	110,000	
Exchange Loss	5,000	
Accounts Receivable		115,000

On the transaction date the domestic firm will translate the 500,000 francs to $100,000 using the exchange rate in effect at that date. Because the billing is in a foreign currency, the U.S. firm will receive in payment 500,000 francs which may be exchanged for dollars, the amount of which is dependent on the exchange rate at the date of conversion. At the balance sheet date the receivable is adjusted on the basis of the exchange rate in effect at that date. At the settlement date the U.S. firm will exchange the francs received for $110,000, which is more than could have been received at the date of sale. Thus, there is a benefit to the firm of $10,000 ($15,000 gain in the first period minus the $5,000 loss in the second period) which results from a favorable change in the exchange rate that occurred between the transaction date and the settlement date.

How Should the Exchange Gain or Loss Be Reported? In the examples above the amounts recorded in the purchase or sale accounts were unaffected by subsequent changes in the exchange rates that occurred before the settlement date. Rather than adjusting the purchase or sale balances, the adjustments to the asset or liability were credited (debited) directly to a gain (loss) account. Under this approach, the purchase (sale) is viewed as a transaction separate from the commitment to subsequently buy (sell) foreign currency in order to settle a liability (receivable) created in the initial purchase (sale) transaction. This approach, the two-transaction method, is supported by the FASB in *Statement No. 8.*[8]

[8]An alternate view to the two-transaction approach is that the exchange gain or loss should be accounted for as an adjustment to the cost of the asset purchased or to the revenue recorded in a sale transaction. Supporters of this method, the one-transaction approach, contend that the transaction is incomplete until the firm knows the amount of the domestic currency to be received or paid. They contend that the initial amounts recorded are estimates until such time as the total benefits (units of domestic currency received) from the sale or the total sacrifice (units of currency paid) from the purchase are known. In the case of an asset acquisition, exchange rate adjustments are made to the asset account and they affect income when the asset is expensed rather than in the period when the rate changes. Revenue transactions are adjusted in the period of the sale for the difference between the amount previously recorded and the amount of domestic currency received upon settlement of the receivable. There is an obvious implementation problem with this method when the sale or purchase is recorded in one fiscal period and the receipt or payment occurs in another period.

Support for the two-transaction method rests primarily on the fact that an exchange gain or loss could be avoided either by making payment or by requiring payment on the transaction date, or by acquiring a forward exchange contract. Management's decision to assume the risk of a potential loss or to speculate in potential gains associated with fluctuations in the currency rate should be reported as a separate item in the operating section of the income statement in the fiscal periods in which the rate changes. In other words, the exchange gain or loss does not result from an operating decision to buy or sell goods or services in a foreign market, but from a financing decision to delay the payment or receipt of foreign currency and not to hedge the exposed receivable or payable against potential currency rate changes.

Should Unrealized Exchange Gains or Losses Be Reported?   In the examples above, and in accordance with the provisions of *Statement No. 8,* changes in the exchange rate were reported in the accounting period in which the rate change occurred. Before the issuance of *Statement No. 8,* several methods of accounting for the fluctuations in the exchange rate were considered acceptable. Some of the alternatives considered by the FASB were (1) to defer the recognition of any gain or loss until the settlement date, (2) to recognize an exchange gain or loss only if the change in the exchange rate exceeded a specified percentage, and (3) to record a gain or loss only if it was expected not to reverse in a subsequent period. These alternatives were all rejected by the FASB because it felt that current recognition of gains and losses provided better information to statement readers. It was argued further that deferring the gain or loss was an artificial process which delayed the recognition of historical fact. In addition, the establishment of a specified percentage was arbitrary and recognizing only rate changes that will not reverse requires subjective predictions of future events.

Foreign Borrowing or Lending

In the section on exporting or importing of goods the receivable and payable created were incidental to the operating transaction and were assumed to be short term in nature. The cost of granting extended credit or long-term borrowing in connection with the purchase or sale of goods is considered in this section, along with direct lending or borrowing to acquire cash or finance the purchase or sale of long-term assets.

Accounting for foreign borrowing or lending transactions is similar to accounting for the exporting or importing of goods, i.e., the two-transaction approach is followed in which the initial transaction is accounted for separately and does not reflect subsequent fluctuations in the foreign exchange rate. Accordingly, exchange gains or losses are reported currently in income, and receivables or payables are adjusted on the basis of the exchange rate in effect at the balance sheet date. For example, if a fixed asset is acquired in the transaction, the cost of the asset is the agreed foreign currency commitment translated into dollars using the exchange rate in effect at the transaction date. The cost of the asset is not adjusted for subsequent changes in the exchange rate, but the liability is adjusted at each balance sheet date on the basis of the exchange rate in effect at that date.

Forward Exchange Contracts

A forward exchange contract (forward contract) is a contract to deliver or receive at a specified rate (the forward rate) and on a stipulated future date currency of a foreign country. At the inception of the contract the forward rate normally varies from the spot rate. The difference between the two rates is referred to as a discount (premium) if the forward rate is less than (greater than) the spot rate. Although there are a number of reasons why the rates may not be the same, the FASB considered the difference normally to reflect the interest rate differential between the two countries.[9]

There are a number of business situations in which a firm may desire to acquire a forward exchange contract. *Statement No. 8* (par. 22) classified forward contracts as follows:
- I. Hedges:
  1. To hedge a foreign currency exposed net asset position or exposed net liability position.[10]
  2. To hedge an identifiable foreign currency commitment.
- II. Speculation:
  1. To speculate in foreign currency in anticipation of a gain.

The classification above is important because the accounting for a particular type of forward contract depends on the purpose for which a forward contract was obtained. The difference in accounting relates primarily to two questions. These are:

1. How is any exchange gain or loss on the forward contract computed and when should the gain or loss be reported?

2. How is any difference between the spot rate and the contracted forward rate at the inception of the contract accounted for over the life of the contract?

Accounting for the three classes of forward contracts is illustrated below.

Hedge of a Foreign Currency Exposed Net Asset or Exposed Net Liability Position It has been demonstrated that a U.S. firm buying goods on account from a foreign company or selling goods on credit to a foreign customer in a transaction denominated in a foreign currency is exposed to an added risk that the exchange rate

---

[9]*Ibid.*, par. 212.

[10]A company is in an exposed asset position if it holds receivables that are to be settled in units of a foreign currency. A firm is in an exposed *net* asset position if the units of foreign currency to be received in settlement of the receviables are greater than the same foreign currency units owed to foreign creditors. An exposed net liability position is the reverse. A U.S. firm with a foreign branch or equity interest in a foreign company which conducts its activities in a foreign currency may also be in an exposed net asset (liability) position if the foreign affiliate's monetary assets exceed (or are less than) its monetary liabilities.

will change unfavorably before the receivable or payable is settled. To eliminate or reduce this risk, the firm may acquire a forward contract at the transaction date. For example, assume that a U.S. firm purchased inventory on account for 500,000 francs, payable in francs 90 days later. If the exchange rate was $.20 on the settlement date, the U.S. firm could acquire 500,000 francs for $100,000 to liquidate the accounts payable. However, if the exchange rate was $.25, it would require $125,000 (500,000 × .25) to satisfy the firm's obligation. To eliminate the risk, the firm could acquire 500,000 francs when the goods were purchased, but by doing so, it would lose the use of the money for 90 days and the effect would be a cash purchase.

Another approach that the firm can take is to shift the risk of a possible unfavorable rate change by negotiating a forward contract to buy francs in 90 days at a specified price. Conversely, assume that the firm had sold goods to a foreign customer for 500,000 francs to be received in francs 90 days later. A decrease in the exchange rate of $.05 would reduce by $25,000 (500,000 × .05) the value of the francs received upon settlement of the receivable balance. To hedge this exposed net asset position, the firm may negotiate a forward contract to sell the foreign currency received at some future date at an established rate. In either case, by obtaining a forward contract a firm is able to eliminate or reduce the risk of exchange rate fluctuations and fix the number of dollars that are to be received or paid at the settlement date.

To illustrate the accounting for a forward contract that is a hedge of an exposed liability position, we will use the same set of assumptions that we used in the section on exporting and importing of goods so that the reader can compare the effects on the operating position of the firm when a forward contract was not acquired. For convenience the assumptions are restated here as follows:

1. On December 1, 1980, a U.S. firm purchases on account 100 units of inventory for 500,000 francs payable on March 1, 1981.

2. Spot rates were as follows:

> Date of purchase (12/1/80)—$.20
> Balance sheet date (12/31/80)—$.23
> Settlement date (3/1/81)—$.22

3. The transaction is denominated in francs.

4. On the date of purchase the U.S. firm enters into a forward contract to buy 500,000 francs on March 1, 1981, for $.205.

It should be noted that in the series of journal entries that follow, the purchase transaction and the forward contract are accounted for separately as independent transactions. The entries to record the purchase transaction were discussed earlier and will not be elaborated on in the discussion that follows.

The entries to record the purchase and forward exchange contract are:

December 1, 1980—Transaction Date

(1) Purchases   100,000
   Accounts Payable   100,000
      To record the purchase of goods on account.

(2) Deferred Cost of Forward Contract   2,500
   Obligation to Exchange Broker   2,500
   (500,000 × [.20 − .205])
      To record the premium on the forward contract.

At the transaction date a deferred cost is recorded ($2,500) equal to the difference between the current spot rate ($.20) and the contracted forward rate ($.205).[11] At the same time a liability to the exchange broker is recognized which will be liquidated when the forward contract matures. The deferred cost account is reported as a current asset, while the related obligation is reported as a current liability on the firm's balance sheet since the contract matures in 90 days. The asset can be viewed as an insurance contract acquired to protect the firm against unfavorable changes in the exchange rate that may occur before the liability for the goods purchased on account is settled by the payment of 500,000 francs. The cost of this contract is the number of foreign currency units multiplied by the difference between what the firm will pay for the francs 90 days later and what the firm could acquire the francs for at the date of purchase. The cost of obtaining this protection is subsequently accounted for separately from any gain or loss on the forward contract and is recognized as an expense over the life of the contract.

[11]In the set of journal entries above the contract to receive 500,000 francs upon the payment of $102,500 was not recorded when the contract was negotiated, because it represents an executory contract that does not require a formal journal entry in the ledger of the firm. Although the contract was negotiated on the transaction date, payment is not made to the exchange broker until the contract matures and the foreign currency is received from the broker. If one party to a forward contract does not perform, the other party to the contract does not have to perform. Within the framework of generally accepted accounting standards, executory contracts are not normally recorded until such time as one party to the contract at least partially performs his part of the agreement.

Some accountants contend, however, that a forward contract is both an economic resource (i.e., the firm has either a claim to dollars or foreign currency) and an economic liability (i.e., the firm must either deliver dollars or units of foreign currency). This position is supported by the fact that the unperformed forward contract may have a market value, and the rights and the related obligation can normally be assigned. See Lorensen, *Accounting Research Study No. 12, op. cit.*, pp. 65–66. In the authors' opinion, reporting both the asset and liability is at variance with the current accepted practice of accounting for executory contracts, and, therefore, such contracts are not recorded.

December 31, 1980—Balance Sheet Date

(3) Exchange Loss (500,000 × [.23 − .20])   15,000
    Accounts Payable   15,000
      To record loss on liability denominated in foreign currency.

(4) Receivable on Forward Contract Due to
    Increase in Spot Rate   15,000
    Exchange Gain (500,000 × [.23 − .20])   15,000
      To record gain on forward contract.

(5) Amortization of Deferred Cost of
    Forward Contracts ([30/90] × 2,500)   833
    Deferred Cost of Forward Contract   833
      To record amortization of forward contract cost using straight-line method.

On subsequent balance sheet dates and on the settlement date the firm accrues as a separate asset or liability an exchange gain or loss on the forward contract. The gain or loss is computed and reported currently in income by "multiplying the foreign currency amount of the forward contract by the difference between the spot rate at the balance sheet date and the spot rate at the date of inception of the contract (or the spot rate last used to measure a gain or loss on that contract for an earlier period)."[12] The recording of a net receivable on the forward contract recognizes that a firm can assign the rights along with the related obligation of an unperformed forward contract and will receive "as consideration an amount in money equal to the anticipated gain less a discount."[13] Stated another way, at the time the contract is negotiated, it has no value (the value of the right is offset by the obligation) and is not recorded, but as the exchange rate increases, the value of the right to acquire foreign currency at a specified price becomes greater than the exposure to pay dollars to the exchange broker. This net increase in value of the contract should be reflected in an increased market value for the forward contract which can be assigned. In this illustration an increase in the exchange rate in 1980 from $.20 to $.23 would probably result in some increase in the value of the exchange contract, the amount of which is measured by the change in the spot rate.

[12]*FASB Statement No. 8*, par. 25. The gain or loss on a forward contract in this section of the chapter is computed from changes in the spot rate in accordance with provisions of *Statement No. 8*. However, the change in the value of the forward contract is more closely related to the difference between the contracted forward rate and the forward rate available for the remainder of the original contract period. The FASB in the exposure draft proposed "accrual of the difference between the original market value of an unperformed forward contract (zero) and its current market value" (par. 209). The Board rejected this method, however, in the final statement and accepted the argument of certain respondents to the draft who maintained that it was inconsistent to use the forward rate to compute a gain or loss on a contract acquired with the intent to hold until maturity and hedge an exposed net asset or liability position, while using the current exchange rate to translate the exposed asset or liability position.

[13]Lorensen, *Accounting Research Study No. 12, op. cit.,* p. 6.

An initial decrease in the spot rate would be reported as an exchange loss. In the same entry a net liability is accrued to reflect the probable decline in the value of the forward contract.

March 1, 1981—Settlement Date

(6) Exchange Loss (500,000 × [.22 − .23])   5,000
    Receivable on Forward Contract Due to Increase in Spot Rate   5,000
      To record loss on forward contract from 12/31/1980 to 3/1/1981.

In 1981 the decrease in the exchange rate from $.23 to $.22 is reported as an exchange loss on the forward contract and is adjusted to the receivable recorded at the balance sheet date, since the loss is related to the same contract.

(7) Obligation to Exchange Broker   2,500
  Investment in Foreign Currency (500,000 × .22)   110,000
    Receivable on Forward Contract Due to Increase in Spot Rate   10,000
    Cash (500,000 × .205)   102,500
      To record the payment to exchange broker and receipt of foreign currency (500,000 francs).

(8) Accounts Payable   5,000
  Exchange Gain (500,000 × [22 − .23])   5,000
    To record gain on exposed net liability position from 12/31/1980 to 3/1/1981.

(9) Accounts Payable   110,000
  Investment in Foreign Currency   110,000
    To recognize payment of liability upon transfer of 500,000 francs.

(10) Amortization of Deferred Cost of
  Deferred Contract ([60/90] × 2,500)   1,667
  Deferred Cost of Forward Contract   1,667
    To record amortization of forward contract cost.

By obtaining the forward contract the firm was able to establish at the transaction date the number of dollars ($102,500) that it would take to acquire the 500,000 francs needed to settle the account with the foreign firm. In contrast to the illustration on the importing of goods, when a forward contract was not obtained, the net gain of $10,000 on the forward contract offsets the net loss of $10,000 on the net exposed liability position. The net income of the firm is lower by only $2,500 as a result of amortizing the cost of the forward contract.

Although the loss on the exposed net liability position is offset by the gain on the forward contract, the two were accounted for separately since they are based on what are considered independent transactions. For reporting purposes, however, the two may be combined. The firm is required to disclose the aggregate exchange gain or loss included in the determination of net income for the period. A gain or loss on a forward contract is considered an exchange gain or loss.[14]

The foregoing discussion illustrated the problems when a firm was involved in transactions with a foreign company. A domestic firm with a foreign branch or an interest in a foreign company is in a similar risk position. Since the transactions of the foreign affiliates are normally conducted in the currency of the country in which the affiliate is domiciled, monetary assets held by the affiliate are subject to the risk that the foreign currency will be convertible into fewer dollars at some future date. The settlement of foreign affiliate liabilities may require more dollars to be transferred if the exchange rate changes unfavorably before the liabilities are liquidated. The firm could obtain forward contracts to hedge an exposed net asset or net liability position. Accounting for such contracts would follow the same procedures outlined above.

Hedging an Identifiable Foreign Currency Commitment   In the foregoing discussion on the importing or exporting of goods, the purchase or sale of an asset was recorded on the transaction date. This date is considered the point at which title to the goods is transferred, which is consistent with the recording of a transaction with another domestic company. However, if the U.S. firm made a commitment to a foreign company to sell goods or buy goods at a date earlier than the transaction date, and the price was established at the commitment date, changes in the exchange rate between the commitment date and transaction date are reflected in the cost or sales price of the asset. For example, assume that a U.S. firm made an agreement on June 1 to buy goods from a French company for 500,000 francs. At this date the spot rate was $.20, but on the transaction date, when title to the goods transferred, the spot rate was $.22. The entry to record the purchase is:

Purchase (500,000 × .22)	110,000	
Accounts Payable		110,000

Thus, the change in the exchange rate that occurred between the commitment and the transaction dates becomes a part of the cost of inventory, rather than being reported as a separate gain or loss item as rate changes are when they occur between the transaction and settlement dates. The company, however, may still acquire a forward contract to hedge against unfavorable rate changes that may occur after the commitment date even though the rate change is not separately accounted for in the records.

A forward contract is considered a hedge of an identifiable foreign currency commitment if *all* of the following conditions are met:
- (a) The life of the forward contract extends from the foreign currency commitment date to the anticipated transaction date.
- (b) The forward contract is denominated in the same currency as the foreign currency commitment and for an amount that is the same or less than the amount of the foreign currency commitment.
- (c) The foreign currency commitment is firm and uncancelable.[15]

[14]*FASB Statement No. 8, op. cit.,* par. 32.

[15]*FASB Statement No. 8, op. cit.,* par. 27.

The contract is not a hedge of an identifiable commitment if the life of the contract extends beyond the transaction date or to the extent that the amount of the contract exceeds the amount of the commitment.

To illustrate the accounting for a forward contract acquired to hedge an identifiable foreign currency commitment, the following facts are assumed:[16]

1. On March 1, 1980, a U.S. firm contracts with a U.S. customer to sell for $100,000 certain equipment to be delivered on March 1, 1981.

2. On March 1, 1980, the U.S. firm also negotiates a noncancelable contract with a West German firm to manufacture the equipment for 200,000 German marks (spot rate is $.40).

3. On March 1, 1980, the U.S. firm enters into a forward contract to receive 200,000 German marks in 12 months at the forward rate of $.41.

4. The spot rate for German marks at December 31, 1980 (end of the firm's fiscal year) is $.395.

5. The spot rate for German marks at March 1, 1981 is $.38.

The journal entries to record the forward contract during 1980 are:

March 1, 1980

(1) Deferred Cost of Forward Contract	2,000	
Obligation to Exchange Broker		2,000
(200,000 × [.40 − .41])		
To record premium on forward contract.		

December 31, 1980

(2) Deferred Exchange Loss	1,000	
Liability on Forward Contract Due to		
Decrease in Spot Rate		1,000
(200,000 × [.395 − .40])		
To record loss on forward contract.		

There are two major differences in accounting for the forward contract as compared with the accounting for a contract to hedge a foreign currency exposed net asset or net liability position. First, the exchange loss (or gain if the spot rate was greater than $.40) is deferred rather than reported currently. As will be seen in the March 1, 1981 entry, the loss (or gain) is included in the determination of the dollar basis of the foreign transaction on the transaction date. Second, the discount or premium on the

[16]The illustration is adapted from an example developed in *Statement No. 8,* par. 208.

forward contract "that relates to the commitment period may be included in the measure of the dollar basis of the related foreign currency transaction when recorded."[17]

On March 1, 1981 (the transaction date) the journal entries are:

(3) Deferred Exchange Loss   3,000
    Liability on Forward Contract Due to Decrease
      in Spot Rate (200,000 × [.38 − .395])   3,000
        To record loss on forward contract from 12/31/1980 to 3/1/1981.

(4) Obligation to Exchange Broker   2,000
    Liability on Forward Contract
      Due to Decrease in Spot Rate   4,000
    Investment in Foreign Currency (200,000 × .38)   76,000
      Cash (200,000 × .41)   82,000
        To record payment to exchange broker and receipt of foreign currency.

(5) Inventory   76,000
    Investment in Foreign Currency   76,000
        To record the acquisition of the manufactured equipment from the German firm.

(6) Inventory   6,000
    Deferred Cost of Forward Contract   2,000
    Deferred Exchange Loss   4,000
        To close the deferred loss and deferred cost accounts to the asset acquired.

(7) Cash   100,000
    Sales   100,000
        To record the sale to the U.S. customer.

(8) Cost of Goods Sold   82,000
    Inventory   82,000
        To record the cost of goods sold.

Most of the entries on March 1, 1981 are self-explanatory. It should be emphasized that the exchange gain or loss on a forward contract acquired to hedge a specific commitment or an exposed asset or liability position are computed on the basis of changes in the spot rates that occurred during the current operating period. In this case the spot rate for German marks decreased from $.395 at the last balance sheet date to $.38 at the transaction date. The exchange loss of $3,000 plus the $1,000 loss from 1980, along with the premium ($2,000), is included as an adjustment to the cost of the manufactured equipment.

The effect of these transactions on the firm's profitability is as follows:

Sales	$100,000
Cost of Goods Sold	82,000
Gross Profit	$ 18,000

[17] *Ibid.*, par. 25.

Thus, the forward contract permitted the U.S. firm to lock in its desired profit (less the premium) on the sales contract. If the forward contract had not been obtained, the profit on the contract would have been affected by the exchange rate in effect when payment was made to the German manufacturer. An exchange rate of $.50 would have eliminated any gross profit on the contract (200,000 × .50 = 100,000).

Forward Contracts Acquired to Speculate in the Movement of Foreign Currencies A forward contract may be acquired for speculative purposes in anticipation of making a gain. For example, assume that on December 1, 1980, the spot rate for the British pound is $1.67 and that the 90-day futures rate is $1.63. Further assume that a company expecting the exchange rate to increase to, say, $1.70 buys a 90-day contract on December 1 to acquire £100,000. The firm's fiscal year ends on December 31, and on that date the 60-day futures rate for pounds to be purchased on March 1, 1981 is $1.67, and the spot rate was $1.69 on March 1, 1981. The journal entries to record the transactions are:

December 1, 1980

(1) No entry is required to record the forward contract.

December 31, 1980

(2) Net Receivable on Forward Contract	4,000	
Exchange Gain (100,000 × [1.67 − 1.63])		4,000
To record the gain on the forward contract.		

March 1, 1981

(3) Net Receivable on Forward Contract	2,000	
Exchange Gain (100,000 × [1.69 − 1.67])		2,000
To record the gain on the forward contract from 12/31/1980 to 3/1/1981.		
(4) Investment in Foreign Currency	169,000	
Cash (100,000 × 1.63)		163,000
Net Receivable on Forward Contract		6,000
To record payment to the exchange broker and receipt of the foreign currency.		
(5) Cash (100,000 × 1.69)	169,000	
Investment in Foreign Currency		169,000
To record conversion of pounds into cash.		

The gain or loss on a forward contract held for speculation is based on the forward exchange rates and changes in the forward rates. The exchange gain or loss is reported currently in income and is computed by multiplying the units of foreign currency by the difference between the forward rate available over the remaining life of the forward contract and the rate last used to value the contract. The FASB reasoned that the forward rate should be used because a firm speculating in foreign currency changes is exposed to the risk of movements in the forward rate.

The total gain recognized over the life of the contract is $6,000. This is a reasonable amount, since it is also equal to the difference between the value of the foreign currency received ($169,000) when the forward contract was exercised and the amount paid ($163,000) to the exchange broker. Since the entries are based on the forward rates, there is no separate accounting for the discount or premium. The discount or premium are, in effect, netted against the exchange gain or loss.

The accounting for forward contracts in accordance with the provisions of *Statement No. 8* is summarized in Illustration 12–2.

ILLUSTRATION 12–2
A Summary of Accounting for Forward Contracts

PURPOSE OF THE FORWARD CONTRACT	BASIS FOR VALUATION OF FORWARD CONTRACT AT BALANCE SHEET DATE	REPORTING EXCHANGE GAIN OR LOSS	ACCOUNTING FOR DISCOUNT OR PREMIUM ON FORWARD CONTRACT
I. Hedge of an exposed net asset or net liability position and other hedges not classified as a hedge of an identifiable foreign currency commitment.	Spot rate at balance sheet date	Reported currently in determination of income	Expensed over life of forward contract
II. Hedge of an identifiable foreign currency commitment.	Spot rate at balance sheet date	Deferred and adjusted to cost of asset acquired or cost of asset sold	May defer and adjust to cost of asset acquired or cost of asset sold or expensed over life of forward contract
III. Speculation.	Forward rate at balance sheet date available over the remaining life of contract	Reported currently in determination of income	Not accounted for separately

TRANSLATING FINANCIAL STATEMENTS OF FOREIGN AFFILIATES

A domestic company maintaining a branch office in a foreign country or holding an equity interest in a foreign company must translate the account data expressed in foreign currency into the currency of the reporting entity before the financial statements can be combined or consolidated. Furthermore, if the statements are not consolidated, and if the equity method of accounting is used to account for the investment in a foreign affiliate, the financial statements of the affiliate must be translated into dollars before the investor's share of the investee's reported net income or loss is properly determinable. In addition, if the foreign statements are not in conformity with generally accepted accounting standards in the United States, they must be adjusted to conform to U.S. standards before translation into U.S. currency.

Translating the Accounts of a Foreign Affiliate

Before the issuance of *Statement No. 8,* three methods, or some modifications thereof, were commonly used to translate the financial statements of foreign affiliates into dollars. These methods were (1) the current-noncurrent method, (2) the monetary-nonmonetary method, and (3) the temporal method. Under the current-noncurrent method, all current assets and current liabilities are translated at the current exchange rate in effect at the balance sheet date, and all other assets and liabilities are translated using the historical exchange rate in effect at the date of the transaction. Under the monetary-nonmonetary method, the monetary assets and liabilities are translated at the current exchange rate, and other assets and liabilities are translated at historical exchange rates. When using the temporal method, accounts such as cash, receivables, and payables stated at current prices and other assets or liabilities stated at future prices are translated using the current exchange rate. Assets and liabilities stated at historical prices are translated at the historical rate in effect at the time of the transaction.[18] In practice, the first two methods described were the most popular.[19]

The FASB rejected the current-noncurrent method and the monetary-nonmonetary method in favor of the temporal method. However, the results obtained from use of the temporal method may not differ significantly from those obtained under the monetary-nonmonetary method. The two methods yield similar results because a foreign branch or subsidiary must conform its accounting to U.S. generally accepted accounting standards before the accounts are translated into dollars. In doing so, most nonmonetary assets are reported in terms of historical cost and, accordingly, are translated using the historical rate under both methods. The FASB found the temporal method to be the most useful in meeting the objective that the translation process "should not affect either the measurement bases for assets and liabilities or the timing of revenue and expense recognition otherwise required by generally accepted accounting principles."[20] Under the temporal method the principle of measurement employed by the foreign affiliate is retained if the principle is in accordance with generally accepted accounting principles of this country. Thus, if an asset should be measured in terms of historical cost in the foreign financial statement, the translation is performed using the historical exchange rate; if an asset is stated at replacement cost and it is acceptable to do so in the United States, then the item is translated into dollars using the current rate.

[18]Lorensen proposed the use of the temporal method in *Accounting Research Study No. 12, op. cit.*

[19]In the 1976 edition of *Accounting Trends and Techniques* of the 394 companies disclosing foreign operations, 175 (44%) used the current-noncurrent method, 84 (21%) used the monetary-nonmonetary method, and 85 (22%) used the current rate for all accounts except fixed assets. *Accounting Trends and Techniques—1976 Edition* (New York: AICPA, 1975), p. 322.

[20]*FASB Statement No. 8, op. cit.,* par. 6.

The following general rules are prescribed in *Statement No. 8* (pars. 11, 12, and 13) for translating financial statements of foreign affiliates:

I. Translating balance sheet accounts:

In preparing foreign statements, balances representing cash and amounts receivable or payable that are denominated in other than the local currency shall be adjusted to reflect the current rate between the local and the foreign currency. Those adjusted balances and other balances representing cash and amounts receivable or payable that are denominated in the local currency shall be translated into dollars at the current rate.

For assets and liabilities other than those described in the preceding paragraph, the particular measurement bases used shall determine the translation rate. Several measurement bases are used in financial accounting under present generally accepted accounting principles. A measurement may be based on a price in a past exchange (for example, historical cost), a price in a current purchase exchange (for example, replacement cost), or a price in a current sale exchange (for example, market price). Foreign statements may employ various measurement bases. Accordingly, accounts in foreign statements that are carried at exchange prices shall be translated in a manner that retains their measurement bases as follows:

a) Accounts carried at prices in past exchanges (past prices) shall be translated at historical rates.

b) Accounts carried at prices in current purchase or sale exchanges (current prices) or future exchanges (future prices) shall be translated at the current rate.

II. Translating income statement accounts:

Revenue and expense transactions shall be translated in a manner that produces approximately the same dollar amounts that would have resulted had the underlying transactions been translated into dollars on the dates they occurred. Since separate translation of each transaction is usually impractical, the specified result can be achieved by using an average rate for the period. However, revenue and expenses that relate to assets and liabilities translated at historical rates shall be translated at the historical rates used to translate the related assets or liabilities.

Account balances that are stated in a foreign currency are translated either using a current rate or a historical rate.[21] Rates used to translate certain common balance sheet accounts are presented in Illustration 12–3.

When the current rate is used to translate cash, receivables, and payables, these accounts are restated to an amount that approximates that which the home office or investor would receive if the current rate were to remain unchanged. The use of the historical exchange rate to translate accounts carried at historical cost preserves the original cost of the account in conformity with generally accepted accounting standards. In effect, the account is restated as if dollars had been used to measure and record the asset or liability on the transaction date. Fluctuations in the exchange rate that occur after the acquisition date have no effect on the translation of such accounts on subsequent balance sheets.

---

[21]Par. 30(b) of *Statement No. 8* provides the following if multiple rates exist: In the absence of unusual circumstances, the rate applicable to conversion of a currency for purposes of dividend remittances shall be used to translate foreign statements.

ILLUSTRATION 12–3
Rates Used to Translate Assets and Liabilities

	TRANSLATION RATES	
ASSETS	CURRENT	HISTORICAL
Cash on hand and demand and time deposits	X	
Marketable equity securities:		
Carried at cost		X
Carried at current market price	X	
Accounts and notes receivable and		
related unearned discount	X	
Allowance for doubtful accounts and		
notes receivable	X	
Inventories:		
Carried at cost		X
Carried at current replacement price or		
current selling price	X	
Carried at net realizable value	X	
Carried at contract price		
(produced under fixed price contracts)	X	
Prepaid insurance, advertising, and rent		X
Refundable deposits	X	
Advances to unconsolidated subsidiaries	X	
Property, plant, and equipment		X
Accumulated depreciation of property, plant,		
and equipment		X
Cash surrender value of life insurance	X	
Patents, trademarks, licenses, and formulas		X
Goodwill		X
Other intangible assets		X
LIABILITIES		
Accounts and notes payable and overdrafts	X	
Accrued expenses payable	X	
Accrued losses on firm purchase commitments	X	
Refundable deposits	X	
Deferred income		X
Bonds payable or other long-term debt	X	
Unamortized premium or discount on bonds		
or notes payable	X	
Convertible bonds payable	X	
Accrued pension obligations	X	
Obligations under warranties	X	

Source: *Statement of Financial Accounting Standards No. 8*, p. 20.

Reporting Foreign Exchange Gain or Loss

In accounting for foreign exchange transactions, an exchange gain or loss is computed for each accounting period. The gain or loss results from fluctuations in the exchange rate during the period. The amount of the gain or loss reported currently in income is the difference between the receivable or payable balance which was translated into dollars at two different points in time using the exchange rate in effect at each balance sheet date. In accordance with *Statement No. 8,* certain assets and liabilities reported in foreign statements are also translated using the exchange rate in effect at the balance sheet date. If assets or liabilities are held by an affiliate during a period when the exchange rate fluctuates, a gain or loss results as a consequence of the translation process. The gain or loss is reported currently in the determination of net income in the period that the rate changes.

Translating Statements of Foreign Branches

Accounting for a domestic branch when both branch and home office maintain their accounting records in the same currency was discussed in an earlier chapter. The home office may adopt a similar accounting system to record the transactions of a foreign branch. Whereas the branch records the transactions in terms of the local currency of the country in which it is domiciled, however, the home office measures the branch transactions in terms of the domestic currency. Before combined financial statements are prepared, or before the home office can record the income or loss of the foreign branch, the trial balance of the branch must be translated into the reporting currency of the home office. The appropriate exchange rates to be used in translating most of the accounts that would be included in a branch trial balance were discussed in an earlier section of this chapter. The reciprocal accounts were not considered in the discussion because such accounts are peculiar to a branch operation.

In the translation process, a reciprocal account on the books of the branch is set equal to the dollar amount reported in the reciprocal account on the books of the home office so that the accounts can be eliminated in the combined workpaper. To facilitate this procedure and to provide information to management concerning the value of the foreign currency and dollars transferred between the home office and branch, separate reciprocal accounts are typically created to record the transfers. In other words, instead of using one single reciprocal account on each set of books (Investment in Branch and Home Office), two separate sets of reciprocal accounts are used to record remittances to and from the branch on the books of the home office and the branch. The various remittance accounts on the home office books are closed at the end of the period to the Investment in Branch Account, and the remittance accounts on the branch books are closed to the Home Office account.

In the case of a domestic branch, a disparity between the balance in the Home Office account and the balance in the Investment in Branch account would indicate that there were errors or unrecorded transaction(s) between the home office and the branch on one set of books at year-end. If the reciprocal account balances on the branch books are set to equal the related reciprocal account balance on the home office books, this automatic check is not available. Therefore, transactions between the home office and the branch must be reconciled to insure that there are no unrecorded transactions on one set of books at year-end. In order to perform the reconciliation, the branch must provide the home office with a summary of transactions recorded in the reciprocal accounts.

The following illustration is presented in order to focus on accounting for a home office and a foreign operation when two different currencies are involved. It is assumed that a U.S. firm established a branch in London to sell inventory manufactured by the home office. The branch is also permitted to acquire certain inventory items from English suppliers. Transactions and journal entries to record the first month of operations are shown in Illustration 12–4 for both the home office and the branch. The exchange rate in effect at each transaction date is given in parentheses after each transaction if the rate is needed for subsequent translations.

At the end of each period the home office typically requires the branch to furnish copies of the adjusted trial balance, completed financial statements, a summary of transactions recorded in the reciprocal accounts, and a breakdown of the ending inventory between goods acquired from outside suppliers and goods shipped from the home office. Since this information is in pounds, the home office must translate the data into U.S. currency before combined financial statements are prepared or before the home office records the branch net income or loss for the period. An adjusted trial balance before the closing entries are recorded by the branch is included in Illustration 12–5. In the illustration the accounts stated in pounds are translated into dollars following the procedures discussed earlier in this chapter. It is assumed that the exchange rate at the end of the month was $1.66 and the average exchange rate during the month was $1.68. As permitted by *Statement No. 8* (pars. 13 and 29), averages are used to translate the sales, purchases, and expense accounts.

When the trial balance of the foreign branch is translated, the use of different exchange rates normally results in an inequality between the total of the debit account balances and the total of the credit account balances. The difference between the sum of the balances is an exchange gain or loss. There is an exchange loss (gain) if a debit (credit) is required to reconcile the two balances. The exchange gain or loss is thus a balancing amount that reconciles the total debit balances with the total credit balances after the individual branch accounts have been translated. An error in translating one or more of the accounts would, of course, result in an error in the exchange adjustment.

The exchange adjustment results from the fact that the account debited in a certain entry is translated using an exchange rate that differs from the rate used to translate the account credited in the same entry. For example, the $10,000 debit in the accounts receivable account is translated to $16,000 using the current exchange rate of 1.66, while the $10,000 credit included in the sales account is translated to $16,800 ($10,000 × 1.68) using the average exchange rate for the month. In this transaction there is a loss of $200 since the accounts receivable could be converted into $16,600 at the balance sheet date, as opposed to $16,800 at the time of the sale. The net $2,479 gain could be accounted for by performing a similar analysis of other transactions and account balances.

ILLUSTRATION 12–4
Journal Entries to Record Branch Transactions
on Books of Home Office and Branch

	JOURNAL ENTRIES			
TRANSACTION	HOME OFFICE (DOLLARS)		BRANCH (POUNDS)	

1. The home office sent a draft for £15,000. ($1.70)	Remittance to Branch
	  Cash (15,000 × 1.70)
		25,500
		25,500
			Cash
			  Remittance from Home Office
				15,000
				15,0

2. The branch acquired a building for £60,000, paying £12,000 down and giving a long-term mortgage for the remaining balance. ($1.71)	No entry.		Building
			  Cash
			  Mortgage Payable
				60,000
				12,0
				48,0

3. The branch purchased fixed assets from English supplier for £2,400. ($1.69)	No entry.		Equipment Cash	2,400 2,4
4. The branch purchased inventory on account from an English supplier for £15,000. The firm uses a periodic inventory system.	No entry.		Purchases Accounts Payable	15,000 15,0

5. The home office shipped the branch $51,000 in inventory at cost. ($1.70)	Investment in Branch
	  Shipments to Branch
		51,000
		51,000
			Shipments from Home Office
			  Home Office (51,000/1.70)
				30,000
				30,0

6. The home office sent a draft to the branch for $16,700. The branch deposited the draft when the exchange rate was $1.67.	Remittance to Branch
	  Cash
		16,700
		16,700
			Cash
			  Remittance from Home Office
			  (16,700/1.67)
				10,000
				10,0

7. The branch sold inventory during the month for £30,000.	No entry.		Accounts Receivable Sales	30,000 30,0
8. The branch collected £20,000 during the month on account.	No entry.		Cash Accounts Receivable	20,000 20,0
9. The branch paid operating expenses of £10,000.	No entry.		Expense Cash	10,000 10,0

10. The branch remitted £10,000 to the home office. The exchange rate was $1.68 when the home office received the draft.	Cash
	  Remittance from Branch
	  (10,000 × 1.68)
		16,800
		16,800
			Remittance to Home Office
			  Cash
				10,000
				10,0

JOURNAL ENTRIES

TRANSACTION	HOME OFFICE (DOLLARS)	BRANCH (POUNDS)		
Adjusting entries:	(The home office would follow the normal	Expense	360	
Accrued interest—£360	procedures to adjust and close its own	Accrued Interest		360
Depreciation expense:	nominal accounts. In addition, the remittance	Depreciation Expense	300	
Equipment—£100	to and remittance from the branch accounts	Accumulated Depreciation—		
Building—£200	are closed to the Investment in Branch	Equipment		100
	account)	Accumulated Depreciation—		
		Building		200
Closing Entries: Ending		Inventory	30,000	
inventory balance is		Income Summary		30,000
£30,000—£10,000 from		Sales	30,000	
English suppliers, £20,000		Income Summary		30,000
from home office.				
		Income Summary	55,660	
		Shipments from Home Office		30,000
		Purchases		15,000
		Expense		10,360
		Depreciation Expense		300
		Income Summary	4,340	
		Home Office		4,340
		Remittance from Home Office	25,000	
		Remittance to Home Office		10,000
		Home Office		15,000

    Once the translation process is complete, the workpaper to combine the operations of the home office and branch can be prepared, since both trial balances are stated in the domestic currency. The exchange gain is included in the trial balance of the branch, since exchange gain or loss is to be reported currently in the determination of income. Completion of the workpaper would proceed as illustrated in Chapter 11.

    In the closing process the home office closes the remittance accounts and records the net income or loss of the branch. In this illustration the entries are:

ILLUSTRATION 12–5
Workpaper to Translate Trial Balance
of Foreign Branch into U.S. Dollars

DEBITS	ADJUSTED TRIAL BALANCE (POUNDS)	TRANSLATION RATE[a]	ADJUSTED TRIAL BALANCE (DOLLARS)
Cash	10,600	1.66 (C)	17,596
Accounts Receivable	10,000	1.66 (C)	16,600
Equipment	2,400	1.69 (H)	4,056
Building	60,000	1.71 (H)	102,600
Remittance to Home Office	10,000	— (R)	16,800
Shipments from Home Office	30,000	— (R)	51,000
Purchases	15,000	1.68 (A)	25,200
Expense	10,360	1.68 (A)	17,405[b]
Depreciation Expense:			
Equipment	100	1.69 (H)	169
Building	200	1.71 (H)	342
	148,660		251,768
CREDITS			
Accumulated Depreciation—Equipment	100	1.69 (H)	169
Accumulated Depreciation—Building	200	1.71 (H)	342
Accrued Interest	360	1.66 (C)	598[b]
Accounts Payable	15,000	1.66 (C)	24,900
Mortgage Payable	48,000	1.66 (C)	79,680
Remittance from Home Office	25,000	— (R)	42,200
Home Office	30,000	— (R)	51,000
Sales	30,000	1.68 (A)	50,400
	148,660		249,289
Exchange Gain			2,479
			251,768
ENDING INVENTORY			
Home Office	20,000	1.70 (H)	34,000
English Supplier	10,000	1.68 (A)	16,800
			50,800

[a]Translation rate:

(C) = Current exchange rate end of period.

(H) = Historical exchange rate date of transaction.

(A) = Average exchange rate during period.

(R) = Set equal to reciprocal balance on home office books.

[b]Rounded to nearest dollar.

| Investment in Branch | 9,563 | |
| Branch Net Income | | 9,563* |

To record the branch-reported net income.

Investment in Branch	25,400	
Remittance from Branch	16,800	
Remittance to Branch		42,200

To close the remittance accounts to the investment account.

*Computation of the branch net income is as follows:

Sales		50,400
Beginning Inventory	–0–	
Shipments from Home Office	51,000	
Purchases	25,200	
	76,200	
Ending Inventory (34,000 + 16,800)	50,800	
Cost of Goods Sold		25,400
Gross Profit		25,000
Expense	17,405	
Depreciation Expense (169 + 342)	511	17,916
		7,084
Exchange Gain		2,479
Net Income		9,563

ACCOUNTING FOR EQUITY INVESTMENTS IN FOREIGN AFFILIATES

A domestic company may hold an equity interest in a foreign company. The same criteria that determine the appropriate method of accounting for a domestic investee apply to accounting for a foreign investee. These criteria were discussed in earlier chapters, but will be mentioned briefly here.

If a foreign subsidiary is to be consolidated, the following requirement must be satisfied:

1. Parent company must control more than 50% of the voting stock of the subsidiary.

2. Intent of control should be permanent.

3. Control should rest with the majority owners.

In the case of a foreign subsidiary, there is one other factor to consider, the governmental policies of the country in which the subsidiary is domiciled. In some countries, the government restricts the withdrawal of assets. In recent years there have been a number of cases where a foreign government has completely expropriated the assets of United States companies. In view of the problems of determining the ultimate realization of assets maintained in foreign countries, the appropriate recording and reporting of foreign operations require careful consideration. In *Accounting Research Bulletin No. 43,* Chapter 12, the Committee on Accounting Procedures states:

> A sound procedure for United States companies to follow is to show earnings from foreign operations in their own accounts only to the extent that funds have been received in the United States or unrestricted funds are available for transmission thereto. Appropriate provision should be made also for known losses.
>
> Any foreign earnings reported beyond the amounts received in the United States should be carefully considered in the light of all the facts. The amounts should be disclosed if they are significant, and they should be reserved against to the extent that their realization in dollars appears to be doubtful.
>
> As to assets held abroad, the accounting should take into consideration the fact that most foreign assets stand in some degree of jeopardy, so far as ultimate realization by United States owners is concerned. Under these conditions it is important that especial care be taken in each case to make full disclosure in the financial statements of United States companies of the extent to which they include significant foreign items.[22]

The four methods listed below are considered acceptable methods of disclosing the operations of foreign subsidiaries:

(a) To exclude foreign subsidiaries from consolidation and to furnish (1) statements in which only domestic subsidiaries are consolidated and (2) as to foreign subsidiaries, a summary in suitable form of their assets and liabilities, their income and losses for the year, and the parent company's equity therein. The total amount of investments in foreign subsidiaries should be shown separately, and the basis on which the amount was arrived at should be stated. If these investments include any surplus of foreign subsidiaries and such surplus had previously been included in consolidated surplus, the amount should be separately shown or earmarked in stating the consolidated surplus in the statements here suggested. The exclusion of foreign subsidiaries from consolidation does not make it acceptable practice to include intercompany profits which would be eliminated if such subsidiaries were consolidated.

(b) To consolidate domestic and foreign subsidiaries and to furnish in addition the summary described in (a) (2) above.

(c) To furnish (1) complete consolidated statements and also (2) consolidated statements for domestic companies only.

(d) To consolidate domestic and foreign subsidiaries and to furnish in addition parent company statements showing the investment in and income from foreign subsidiaries separately from those of domestic subsidiaries.[23]

Adequate disclosure of the equity interest in a foreign firm should be made whether consolidation is considered appropriate or the investment is accounted for using the cost or equity method.

---

[22]*Accounting Research Bulletin No. 43,* "Restatement and Revision of Accounting Research Bulletins" (New York: AICPA, 1953), Ch. 12, pars. 4, 5, and 6.

[23]*Ibid.,* par. 9.

APB Opinion No. 18 extended the equity method to accounting for unconsolidated subsidiaries with certain exceptions, such as when the subsidiary is in legal reorganization or where a foreign government has placed restrictions on the withdrawal of assets. In other words, the APB considered it misleading to include in operations the investor's equity interest in the investee's net income if the income might not be distributed because of governmental restrictions. Unconsolidated foreign subsidiaries that are not accounted for using the equity method are accounted for using the cost method and appropriate provisions are made for known losses. If the equity method is appropriate, the investor may also encounter the problems of determination of fair values at the date of acquisition, allocation and amortization of the difference between cost and book value, and the elimination of intercompany profits.

The discussion in the preceding paragraph also applies if the investor can exert significant influence (i.e., holds a 20–50% interest in the voting stock) over the investee.[24]

Translating the Trial Balance of a Foreign Subsidiary

The trial balance of a foreign subsidiary is translated into dollars following the same basic procedures that were used to translate the trial balance of a foreign branch. The asset, liability, revenue, and expense account balances included in the trial balance of the subsidiary that are not reciprocal to an account balance on the books of the parent are translated using either a current or historical exchange rate. However, in the case of a foreign subsidiary, the historical rate used to translate certain account balances is affected by the method of accounting (purchase or pooling of interest) used by the parent to consolidate the subsidiary. *Statement No. 8* provides the following:

> If a business combination with a foreign operation is accounted for by the *pooling-of-interest* method, the assets and liabilities of the foreign operation shall be translated as if the foreign operation had always been a subsidiary of the enterprise. Therefore, assets and liabilities that are translated at historical rates shall be translated at the rates in effect at the date the foreign operation recognized the specific transactions or events.[25]

> If a business combination with a foreign operation is accounted for by the *purchase method,* assets and liabilities that are translated at historical rates shall be translated at the rates in effect when the enterprise acquired its interest in the assets or liabilities. Thus, assets and liabilities of a foreign operation at the date of its acquisition shall be adjusted to their fair values in local currency and then translated at the rate in effect at the date of acquisition. A difference between the translated net assets and the dollar cost of acquisition by the enterprise is *goodwill* or *an excess of acquired net assets over cost* as those terms are used in APB Opinion No. 16. Translation at the date of acquisition, as described, establishes the dollar measures of the asset acquired and liabilities assumed as of the date of acquisition that are translated at historical rates in subsequent balance sheets.[26]

[24]*FASB Statement No. 8, op. cit.,* par. 2.

[25]*Ibid.,* par. 40.

[26]*Ibid.,* par. 41.

The nonreciprocal account balances of a foreign subsidiary are translated into dollars using the rules discussed earlier. As with a foreign branch, the rules discussed did not treat translating reciprocal accounts of a subsidiary that result from recording transactions between the parent and subsidiary. A parent and a foreign subsidiary may conduct many of the same intercompany transactions as those between a parent and a domestic subsidiary, which were illustrated in earlier chapters of this book. Transactions, such as exporting or importing of goods, are recorded on the books of each entity, as illustrated in an earlier section of this chapter: the subsidiary records such transactions as an independent entity in terms of its domestic unit of currency, and the parent or subsidiary recognizes a gain or loss on the transaction depending on the unit of currency in which the transaction is billed. For example, assume that a U.S. firm sold goods on account to a French subsidiary for 100,000 francs when the exchange rate was $.20. Journal entries to record the transaction on both sets of books are:

P COMPANY (DOLLARS)			S COMPANY (FRANCS)		
Accounts Receivable	20,000		Purchases	100,000	
Sales		20,000	Accounts Payable—P Company		100,000

The entries to record the settlement of the account, assuming an exchange rate of $.21, are as follows:

Cash	21,000		Accounts Payable—		
Accounts Receivable		20,000	P Company	100,000	
Exchange Gain		1,000	Cash		100,000

Thus, since in this case the billing was in a foreign currency to the parent, a gain or loss upon settlement is recognized on the books of the parent.

For consolidation purposes, reciprocal account balances are eliminated. Before the accounts can be eliminated, however, equal balances must be reported in the reciprocal accounts by restating the balance in the subsidiary's reciprocal account equal to the balance reported by the parent. Before doing so, both accounts must be reconciled to insure that there are no unrecorded transactions or errors. In the example above, if consolidated financial statements were prepared before the settlement date, the accounts payable to the parent would be restated to the balance in the accounts receivable account on the books of the parent, and the portion of the purchases account represented by the purchases from the parent would be set equal to $20,000, as recorded by P Company in the sales account.

When consolidating a foreign subsidiary, there are additional reciprocal balances to translate that were not encountered when translating a foreign branch. These are the accounts that make up the stockholders' equity section of the subsidiary which are eliminated against the investment account on the books of the parent. The paid-in capital accounts (capital stock and other contributed capital) are translated using a historical rate.[27] The rate selected again depends on the method of accounting. If the purchase method is used, the paid-in capital accounts are translated using the exchange rate in effect when the investment was made. If the investment is accounted for as a pooling of interests, the rate in effect at the date a particular account was recorded by the subsidiary is used. At the date of acquisition, the retained earnings balance is a balancing amount after the other accounts have been adjusted in accordance with the rules of translation. Of course, the balance in retained earnings is zero in the case of a newly created subsidiary. If the acquisition is accounted for as a purchase, the balancing amount at the acquisition date should also equal the foreign currency retained earnings balance times the current rate, since the other accounts are all adjusted using the exchange rate in effect at the date of acquisition. In subsequent consolidated workpapers the beginning retained earnings balance for the period will be equal to the ending retained earnings balance at the end of the last reporting period.

If the foreign subsidiary is not wholly owned, the minority interest in the subsidiary should be computed on the basis of the translated statements.

Once the accounts of the subsidiary are fully translated into the reporting currency of the parent, the consolidated financial statements can be prepared. The workpaper and financial statements are prepared as illustrated in earlier chapters.

Questions

1. Define currency exchange rates and distinguish between "direct" and "indirect" quotations.

2. Name the three stages of concern to the accountant in accounting for import/export transactions. Briefly explain the accounting for each stage.

3. Explain what FASB *Statement No. 8* refers to as the "two transaction method." What support is given for this method?

4. What pervasive accounting principle requires that foreign currency be translated?

[27]Concerning preferred stock, par. 44 of *Statement No. 8* provides: "Preferred stock that is essentially a permanent stockholder investment shall be translated in the same manner as common stock, that is, at historical rates. However, if preferred stock not owned by the enterprise is carried in the foreign operation's balance sheet at its liquidation or redemption price, and liquidation or redemption is either required or imminent, that preferred stock shall be translated at the current rate. If translation at the historical rate would result in stating a preferred stock above its stated liquidation or redemption price in foreign currency translated at the current rate, the preferred stock shall be carried at the lesser dollar amount."

5. Describe a forward exchange contract.

6. Explain the effects on income from hedging a foreign currency exposed net asset position or net liability position.

7. The FASB classifies forward contracts as those for the purpose of hedging and those for the purpose of speculation. What main differences are there in accounting for these two classifications?

8. How are unrealized exchange gains and losses from hedging an identifiable foreign currency commitment reported?

9. How are assets and liabilities that are stated in a foreign currency in financial statements translated?

10. When multiple exchange rates exist, what rate should be used for (a) translation of import/export transactions, and (b) translation of foreign currency financial statements?

11. How are revenue and expense items in foreign currency financial statements translated?

12. Describe how the financial statements of a foreign branch are translated.

13. What requirements must be satisfied if a foreign subsidiary is to be consolidated?

14. How does the method of accounting for a business combination (purchase vs. pooling) affect the translation of a foreign affiliate's financial statement?

Problems

Problem 12–1

Prepare journal entries to record the following transactions on the books of Beckenbach Corporation, a sports equipment dealer. Beckenbach Corp. uses a periodic inventory system. All exchange rate quotations are direct.

Feb. 1	Purchased skis from a Stockholm, Sweden wholesaler, on account, at an invoice cost of 30,000 kronor. On this date the exchange rate for the krona was $.24.
Feb. 3	Sold ski accessories on account to a Swiss retail outlet. The invoice price was $3,500. The exchange rate for Swiss francs was $.41.
Feb. 5	Sold baseball equipment to a Copenhagen, Denmark retailer. The invoice price was 40,000 kroner, and the exchange rate was $.17.
Feb. 6	Purchased sleds from a Canadian manufacturer on account. The billing was for 15,000 Canadian dollars, and the exchange rate for Canadian dollars was $.97.
Feb. 13	Paid 10,000 kronor on account to the Stockholm wholesaler, when the exchange rate was $.25.
Feb. 18	Paid the entire amount due the Canadian manufacturer. The exchange rate was $.96.
Feb. 23	Received a $2,000 payment from the Swiss retailer. The exchange rate was $.44.

Feb. 27   Received a 15,000 kroner payment from the Copenhagen retailer. The exchange rate was $.15.

Feb. 29   Completed payment on the Stockholm invoice. The exchange rate was $.27.

Problem 12–2

During the year a United States company engaged in the following transactions with British companies:

DATE	TRANSACTION	BILLING AMOUNT	DIRECT RATE OF EXCHANGE
6/10	Purchased inventory from a British company.	$12,000	1.65
6/15	Sold inventory to a British company.	£ 4,000	1.67
6/25	Purchased inventory from a British company.	£ 3,200	1.68
6/30	Close of the firm's fiscal year.		1.665
7/10	Paid $12,000 to the British supplier for June 10 purchases.		1.685
7/20	Received £4,000 for the goods sold on June 15th.		1.675
7/20	Paid £3,200 on account to British supplier for goods purchased June 25.		1.67

The U.S. company uses a periodic inventory system.

Required:

Record, in general journal form, the required entries on the books of the U.S. company to record the transactions listed above and adjust the accounts on June 30.

Problem 12–3

Atlantic Distributors is an East Coast wholesaler engaged in foreign trade. The following transactions are representative of its business dealings. Atlantic uses a periodic inventory system, and is on a calendar-year basis. All exchange rate quotations are direct.

Dec. 1   Atlantic purchased merchandise from Transatlantic, Ltd., a British manufacturer. The invoice total was £40,000, payable in 90 days. On this same date Atlantic acquired a forward contract to buy £40,000 in 90 days for $1.70.

Dec. 29   Atlantic sold merchandise to London Retailers for £30,000, receivable in 60 days. No hedging was involved.

Feb. 28   Atlantic received £30,000 in full payment of London Retailers receivable.

Mar. 1   Atlantic submitted full payment of £40,000 to Transatlantic, Ltd., subsequent to obtaining the £40,000 on its forward contract.

Spot rates for the British pound were as follows:

Dec. 1	$1.670
Dec. 29	1.660
Dec. 31	1.665
Feb. 28	1.700
March 1	1.710

Required:

A. Prepare journal entries for the transactions, including any December 31 adjustments necessary.

B. Explain the income statement treatment given to any exchange gains and losses recognized at December 31.

Problem 12–4

Moose Company, an American importer and exporter, negotiated the following transactions with various foreign companies:

June 1, 1980	Sold merchandise on account to a Stockholm retailer. The sales price was negotiated in kronor, and the parties to the contract agreed that 80,000 kronor were to be paid by the Stockholm company on September 1, 1980.
June 1, 1980	Entered into a forward contract to sell 80,000 krona on September 1, 1980 for $.24.
July 1, 1980	Purchased on account merchandise from a Swedish supplier. Moose Company is to settle the account on November 1, 1980 by the payment of 100,000 krona.
July 1, 1980	Entered into a forward contract to buy 100,000 kronor on November 1, 1980 for $.23.

July 31 is Moose Company's fiscal year-end.

Direct exchange quotations for the krona on specific dates are presented below:

DATE	SPOT RATES
June 1, 1980	$.25
July 1, 1980	.22
July 31, 1980	.24
Sept. 1, 1980	.26
Nov. 1, 1980	.23

Required:

A. Prepare journal entries for all significant dates to account for Moose Company's foreign transactions. You are to include journal entries after the July 31 year-end to record the settlement of the open accounts.

B. Compute the exchange gain or loss to be reported on the 1980 income statement.

Problem 12–5

On July 1, 1980, American Cargo, Inc. placed an order with a Greek shipbuilder for a cargo vessel, to be delivered on June 1, 1981. The vessel was for use in American Cargo's shipping business. The agreed-upon sales price was 8,000,000 drachmas, to be paid on delivery. To protect itself against fluctuations in the foreign exchange rate, American Cargo entered into a forward contract on July 1 for the delivery of 8,000,000 drachma, on June 1, 1981, at a price of $.029.

Direct exchange quotations for drachmas on specific dates are presented below:

7/1/80	$.027
12/31/80	.028
6/1/81	.031

Required:
Prepare the necessary journal entries to be made by American Cargo, Inc., including December 31, 1980 adjusting entries.

Problem 12–6
Penny Becken, chief finance officer for Transoceanic Freight, suggested that the company buy a 90-day contract to acquire 500,000 West German marks as a speculative venture. The possibility that the exchange rate would increase seemed good, so the company bought the contract. On November 1, 1980, the purchase date, the spot rate for the mark was $.417 and the 90-day future rate was $.40.

At December 31, 1980, the end of the firm's fiscal year, the 30-day future rate for marks to be purchased on February 1, 1981 was $.385 and the spot rate was $.38. On February 1, 1981, the spot rate was $.39.

Required:
Prepare all necessary journal entries in regard to the forward contract.

Problem 12–7
Presented below are direct exchange quotations for the Mexican peso on specific dates:

June 30, 1974	.08	Jan. 1, 1980	.10
Jan. 1, 1976	.09	Oct. 15, 1980	.115
Jan. 1, 1979	.07	Dec. 31, 1980	.12
Sept. 1, 1979	.06	Average for 1980	.11

Indicate the appropriate exchange rate to be used in translating the following December 31, 1980 accounts which are measured in pesos. The accounts were taken from the ledger of a Mexican subsidiary in which the controlling interest was acquired on January 1, 1976; the acquisition was initially accounted for using the purchase method of accounting.

A. *Balance Sheet Accounts*
1. Cash on hand.
2. Accounts receivable balance due on sales made during 1980.
3. Fixed assets purchased June 30, 1974.
4. Fixed assets purchased January 1, 1980.
5. Marketable equity securities stated at December 31, 1980 market value.
6. Prepaid insurance acquired September 1, 1979.
7. Allowance for bad debts.
8. Accumulated depreciation on fixed assets purchased June 30, 1974.
9. Accumulated depreciation on fixed assets purchased January 1, 1980.
10. Long-term notes payable due on equipment purchased January 1, 1980.
11. Accounts payable to nonaffiliated companies.
12. December 31, 1980 inventory carried at cost—purchased October 15, 1980.
13. Accounts payable to the parent company for inventory received October 15, 1980.
14. Current installment due on notes payable issued on January 1, 1979.
15. Remainder of notes payable (No. 14 above) due December 31, 1983.
16. Unamortized premium on notes issued to purchase equipment on January 1, 1980.
17. Common Stock.

B. *Income Statement Accounts*
   18. Sales made evenly during the year.
   19. Purchases from nonaffiliated companies made evenly during the year.
   20. Depreciation expense on equipment purchased June 30, 1974.
   21. Depreciation expense on equipment purchased January 1, 1980.
   22. Beginning inventory purchased September 1, 1979.
   23. Salary expense incurred evenly during the year.

Problem 12–8

Big Ten Company, a multinational company based in the United States, operates a branch office in Sydney, Australia. The branch was established in January, 1978 as a sales outlet for products manufactured by the home office. The December 31, 1980 branch trial balance in Australian dollars is presented below:

	DEBIT	CREDIT
Cash	10,430	
Accounts Receivable	16,270	
Inventory—1/1	14,380	
Land	25,630	
Building (net)	40,000	
Equipment (net)	30,730	
Remittance to Home Office	59,110	
Accounts Payable		7,520
Long-term Notes Payable (6%)		52,460
Home Office		111,980
Sales		120,590
Shipments from Home Office	72,640	
Operating Expenses	18,290	
Depreciation Expense	5,070	
Total	292,550	292,550
Ending Inventory	12,880	

Other information:

1. Rates of exchange:

DATE	SPOT RATE*
1/1/78	1.05
1/1/80	1.08
12/31/80	1.10
Average for 1980	1.09

*U.S. dollars per one Australian dollar.

2. Investment in Branch account on the home office books disclosed the following transactions during 1980:

Beginning Balance	118,699	Remittance from Branch	64,310
Inventory Shipments to Branch	78,814		

3. The land, building, and equipment were all acquired on January 1, 1978. The assets were partially financed by the 6% long-term note.

4. The branch inventory is acquired totally from the home office. The ending inventory was acquired from the home office during the current year, and the beginning inventory was translated to $15,460 on a December 31, 1979 workpaper.

Required:
On the basis of the information above, translate the trial balance of the Australian branch to U.S. dollars.

Problem 12–9
Boulder Corporation is an American-based firm with a branch outlet in London. Boulder has successfully carried on overseas trade through its London outlet for several years. The following are the account balances (in pounds) for the branch at January 1, 1980. Historical exchange rates applicable to the individual accounts are given in parentheses where necessary.

	DEBIT	CREDIT
Cash	163,000	
Accounts Receivable	220,000	
Allowance for Doubtful Accounts		5,500
Merchandise Inventory—1/1 (1.64)	275,000	
Property and Equipment (1.60)	110,000	
Accumulated Depreciation—Property & Equipment		11,000
Accounts Payable		143,000
Home Office		608,500
	768,000	768,000

The Investment in Branch account, as recorded on the home office books at January 1, 1980, was $1,000,600.

The following transactions were completed by the branch during 1980. Current exchange rate quotations are given in parentheses where necessary.

1. Home office shipped new equipment costing $132,000 to the branch. (1.65)

2. Home office shipped merchandise costing $835,000 to the branch. (1.67)

3. Branch made purchases totaling £85,000 on account. The firm uses a periodic inventory system.

4. Branch made sales totaling £660,000, £400,000 of which was on account.

5. Collections on account by the branch were £320,000.

6. Payments on account by the branch were £90,000.

7. Branch paid expenses of £15,000.

8. Branch remitted £350,000 to home office, which was immediately transferred into cash. (1.68)

9. December 31 adjustments—
    (a) depreciation for 1980—£4,000 (3,000 on pre-1980 prop. & equip.)
    (b) bad debts expense—£6,000
    (c) uncollectible accounts receivable written off—£5,000.

The current exchange rate at December 31, 1980 was $1.72 and the average rate of exchange for 1980 was $1.68. Boulder and its branch use a FIFO inventory cost flow assumption. All January 1, 1980 inventory was purchased from the home office. The branch's ending inventory was 320,000 pounds (300,000 purchased from home office). Assume that the sales, expenses other than depreciation and bad debts, and purchases from outsiders accrued evenly during the year.

Required:

A. Prepare journal entries for the transactions above on the books of the home office and the branch.
B. Prepare a workpaper to translate the branch's adjusted trial balance into U.S. dollars.
C. Compute branch net income from the adjusted trial balance (in dollars).
D. Prepare closing entries for both the branch and home office.

Problem 12–10

Riviera Enterprises, a French corporation, is an 80%-owned subsidiary of Colt Industries, a U.S. corporation. Colt purchased the 80% interest in Riviera on January 1, 1977, paying an amount equal to the book value acquired, and accounted for the business combination by the purchase method. The trial balance of Riviera at December 31, 1980 is presented below (in francs):

Cash	360,000
Accounts Receivable (net)	600,000
Equipment	1,000,000
Cost of Sales	780,000
Depreciation Expense	160,000
Other Expense	190,000
	3,090,000
Accounts Payable	260,000
Notes Payable	100,000
Common Stock	400,000
Premium on Common Stock	200,000
Retained Earnings—1/1	800,000
Sales	1,330,000
	3,090,000

Colt accounts for its investment by the equity method. Riviera was organized on January 1, 1975 and purchased all of its equipment on March 1, 1975. The note payable was given to a financial institution on July 1, 1976. Foreign exchange rates at varying times during the life of Riviera were as follows—

1/1/75	$.25
3/1/75	.24
7/1/76	.22
1/1/77	.23
1/1/80	.22
12/31/80	.20
Average for 1980	.21

The retained earnings balance in the December 31, 1979 balance sheet (in dollars) of Riviera was $185,000.

Required:
A. Prepare a trial balance in dollars for Riviera Enterprises at December 31, 1980.
B. Calculate Riviera Enterprise's 1980 net income in dollars.
C. Prepare the journal entry made by Colt Industries at December 31, 1980 to record its equity in Riviera Enterprise's 1980 earnings.

Problem 12–11
The Carter Company, a U.S. firm, has a 100%-owned subsidiary in Switzerland, purchased in 1975 for an amount equal to book value. The Carter Co.'s investment is recorded using the equity method. Trial balances of the two companies as of December 31, 1980 are presented below.

DEBITS	CARTER CO. (DOLLARS)	SWISS SUB. (FRANCS)
Cash	$ 153,900	109,700
Accounts Receivable (net)	279,000	333,580
Inventory—12/31/80	168,600	111,000
Long-term Assets (net)	351,000	212,570
Investment in Swiss Subs.—12/31/79	212,800	
Dividends Declared	35,000	10,500
Cost of Sales	1,530,400	984,400
Other Expense	602,500	351,300
	$3,333,200	2,113,050·
Accounts Payable	$ 78,800	93,600
Common Stock	700,000	525,000
Retained Earnings—12/31/79	266,800	72,750
Sales	2,283,400	1,421,700
Dividends Received	4,200	
	$3,333,200	2,113,050
Inventory—12/31/79	$ 147,900	$97,000·

·Purchased 12/31/79

All purchases by the Swiss subsidiary were from the parent company, at cost. Its ending inventory was from an October 15, 1980 purchase. The subsidiary has purchased long-term assets with a current net value of 50,000 francs since acquisition.

77,000 francs of the Swiss subsidiary's accounts payable are to Carter Company, which shows $30,750 as accounts receivable due from its subsidiary. The parent's Sales account contains $400,358 sales (at cost) to its subsidiary.

The following exchange rate quotations are given:

Date of subsidiary acquisition	$.420
Date of post-acquisition long-term asset purchases	.415
12/31/79	.408
10/15/80	.400
12/31/80	.397
1980 average	.401

The Swiss subsidiary is the only dividend source of Carter Company.

Required:

A. Translate the trial balance of the Swiss subsidiary into dollars.

B. Prepare a consolidated statements workpaper at 12/31/80.

Problem 12–12

On January 1, 1979, the Franklin Company formed a foreign subsidiary which issued all of its currently outstanding common stock on that date. Selected captions from the balance sheets, all of which are shown in local currency units (LCU), are as follows:

	DECEMBER 31,	
	1980	1979
Accounts receivable (net of allowance for uncollectible accounts of 2,200 LCU at December 31, 1980 and 2,000 LCU at December 31, 1979)	40,000 LCU	35,000 LCU
Inventories, at cost	80,000	75,000
Property, plant and equipment (net of allowance for accumulated depreciation of 31,000 LCU at December 31, 1980 and 14,000 LCU at December 31, 1979)	163,000	150,000
Long-term debt	100,000	120,000
Common stock, authorized 10,000 shares, par value 10 LCU per share, issued and outstanding 5,000 shares at December 31, 1980 and December 31, 1979	50,000	50,000

Additional information:

Exchange rates are as follows:

Jan. 1, 1979–July 31, 1979	2 LCU to $1
Aug. 1, 1979–Oct. 31, 1979	1.8LCU to $1
Nov. 1, 1979–June 30, 1980	1.7LCU to $1
July 1, 1980–Dec. 31, 1980	1.5LCU to $1
Average monthly rate for 1979	1.9LCU to $1
Average monthly rate for 1980	1.6LCU to $1

An analysis of the accounts receivable balance is as follows:

	1980 LCU	1979 LCU
ACCOUNTS RECEIVABLE		
Balance at beginning of year	37,000	—
Sales (36,000 LCU per month in 1980 and 31,000 LCU per month in 1979)	432,000	372,000
Collections	423,600	334,000
Write-offs (May 1980 and December 1979)	3,200	1,000
Balance at end of year	42,200	37,000
ALLOWANCE FOR UNCOLLECTIBLE ACCOUNTS		
Balance at beginning of year	2,000	—
Provision for uncollectible accounts	3,400	3,000
Write-offs (May 1980 and December 1979)	3,200	1,000
Balance at end of year	2,200	2,000

An analysis of inventories, for which the first-in, first-out (FIFO) inventory method is used, is as follows:

	1980 LCU	1979 LCU
Inventory at beginning of year	75,000	—
Purchases (June 1980 and June 1979)	335,000	375,000
Goods available for sale	410,000	375,000
Inventory at end of year	80,000	75,000
Cost of Goods Sold	330,000	300,000

On January 1, 1979, Franklin's foreign subsidiary purchased land for 24,000 LCU and plant and equipment for 140,000 LCU. On July 4, 1980, additional equipment was purchased for 30,000 LCU. Plant and equipment is being depreciated on a straight-line basis over a 10-year period with no salvage value. A full year's depreciation is taken in the year of purchase.

On January 15, 1979, 7% bonds with a face value of 120,000 LCU were sold. These bonds mature on January 15, 1985, and interest is paid semiannually on July 15 and January 15. The first payment was made on January 15, 1980.

Required:
Prepare a schedule translating the selected captions above into United States dollars at December 31, 1980 and December 31, 1979, respectively. Show supporting computations in good form.

(AICPA adapted)

Problem 12–13
The Wiend Corporation acquired the Dieck Corporation on January 1, 1979 by the purchase at book value of all outstanding capital stock. The Dieck Corporation is located in a Central American country whose monetary unit is the peso (P). The Dieck Corporation's accounting records were continued without change; a trial balance, in pesos, of the balance sheet accounts at the purchase date follows:

The Dieck Corporation
Trial Balance (in pesos)
January 1, 1979

	DEBIT	CREDIT
Cash	P 3,000	
Accounts receivable	5,000	
Inventories	32,000	
Machinery and equipment	204,000	
Allowance for depreciation		P 42,000
Accounts payable		81,400
Capital stock		50,000
Retained earnings		70,600
	P244,000	P244,000

The Dieck Corporation's trial balance, in pesos, at December 31, 1980 follows:

The Dieck Corporation
Trial Balance (in pesos)
December 31, 1980

	DEBIT	CREDIT
Cash	P 25,000	
Accounts receivable	20,000	
Allowance for bad debts		P 500
Due from the Wiend Corporation	30,000	
Inventories, December 31, 1980	110,000	
Prepaid expenses	3,000	
Machinery and equipment	210,000	
Allowance for depreciation		79,900
Accounts payable		22,000
Income taxes payable		40,000
Notes payable		60,000
Capital stock		50,000
Retained earnings		100,600
Sales—domestic		170,000
Sales—foreign		200,000
Cost of sales	207,600	
Depreciation	22,400	
Selling and administration expenses	60,000	
Gain on sale of assets		5,000
Provision for income taxes	40,000	
	P728,000	P728,000

The following additional information is available:

1. All of the Dieck Corporation's export sales are made to its parent company and are accumulated in the account, Sales—Foreign. The balance in the account, Due from the Wiend

Corporation, is the total of unpaid invoices. All foreign sales are billed in U.S. dollars. The reciprocal accounts on the parent company's books show total 1980 purchases as $471,000 and the total of unpaid invoices as $70,500.

2. Depreciation is computed by the straight-line method over a 10-year life for all depreciable assets. Machinery costing P20,000 was purchased on December 31, 1979, and no depreciation was recorded for this machinery in 1979. No other depreciable assets have been acquired since January 1, 1979, and no assets are fully depreciated.

3. Certain assets that were in the inventory of fixed assets at January 1, 1979 were sold on December 31, 1980. For 1980 a full year's depreciation was recorded before the assets were removed from the books. Information regarding the sale follows:

Cost of assets	P14,000
Accumulated depreciation	4,900
Net book value	9,100
Proceeds of sale	14,100
Gain on sale	P 5,000

4. Notes payable are long-term obligations that were incurred on December 31, 1979.

5. No entries have been made in the Retained Earnings account of the subsidiary since its acquisition, other than the net income for 1979. The Retained Earnings account at December 31, 1979 was converted to $212,000.

6. The ending inventory was acquired evenly during the year.

7. Prepaid expenses are advance payments made on November 1, 1980 for newspaper ads to be run in 1981.

8. The prevailing rates of exchange follow:

	DOLLARS PER PESO
January 1, 1979	2.00
1979 average	2.10
December 31, 1979	2.20
1980 average	2.30
November 1, 1980	2.38
December 31, 1980	2.40

Required:
Prepare a worksheet to convert the December 31, 1980 trial balance of the Dieck Corporation from pesos to dollars. The worksheet should show the unconverted trial balance, the conversion rate, and the converted trial balance. (Do not extend the trial balance to statement columns. Supporting schedules should be in good form.)

(AICPA adapted)

13

Reporting for Segments of a Business Enterprise

In previous chapters we have dealt with the process of aggregating the financial data relating to the activities of an affiliated group of companies. Investors and lenders holding equity or creditor interests are aware of the importance of consolidated statements in reporting the financial position and results of operations of a group of companies under common control. At the same time, investors, creditors, and other users of financial statements also need disaggregated data that provide information about the various segments of an enterprise or affiliated group of companies.

HISTORICAL BACKGROUND

Although concern for disclosure of at least some types of segment information has existed for many years, the topic did not receive major attention until the 1960's.[1] During this period, which was marked by high business combination activity, many of the combinations were of the conglomerate type, involving firms in various industries. In addition, during this period, domestic companies increased their involvement in foreign operations. As a result, the need for some type of additional disclosure about a firm's operations in different markets, industries, and/or foreign countries became a primary concern of the business community. Several professional organizations, including the Financial Executives Research Foundation, the Financial Analysts Federation, and the National Association of Accountants, sponsored major research

---

[1] For example, *Accounting Research Bulletin No. 43*, Chapter 12, contained suggestions for disclosures related to an enterprise's foreign operations.

projects to study the desirability and feasibility of disclosing information about lines of business, or segments, of the enterprise for external reporting purposes.[2] These studies resulted in the issue of pronouncements by the sponsoring organizations encouraging business enterprises to provide voluntarily some type of segment financial data in their annual reports to stockholders.

At the same time, the Securities and Exchange Commission and the American Institute of Certified Public Accountants were also actively studying the need for and problems associated with segment reporting. In September, 1968, the SEC proposed the amendment of its registration forms to require disclosure of revenues and income before tax and extraordinary items by line of business. The proposal was adopted in 1969 for Forms S-1, S-7, and 10, and, in 1970 was extended to Form 10-K. The SEC did not specify the basis for determining appropriate "lines of business," but provided that consideration be given to such factors as profitability, degrees of risk, and opportunities for growth. Additional SEC reporting requirements included:

1. Revenues (in dollars or percentages) by "class of similar products and services" with the same materiality tests as for "line-of-business" information. (Basically, a line of business was deemed material if, during either of the most recent two years, it accounted for at least 10% of revenues or 10% of income or loss before income taxes and extraordinary items; for companies with revenues of $50,000,000 or less, the applicable percentage test was 15% rather than 10%.)

2. Information as to the identity and importance of any single or few customers on whose business the registrant is materially dependent.

3. Information about the nature, risks, and (if practicable) volume and relative profitability of foreign operations.

In April, 1974, the SEC issued *Accounting Series Release No. 154*, relating to consolidated financial statements, which provided that disclosure in annual reports to stockholders might be improved by including condensed information about consolidated subsidiaries engaged in financial activities as supporting financial statements or as lines-of-business disclosure.

The Accounting Principles Board, in September, 1967, added its support to additional segment disclosure by stating, "For the present, the Board urges diversified companies to review their own circumstances carefully and objectively with a view

---

[2]The major studies conducted and published by these organizations were:

Financial Executives Research Foundation:
R. K. Mautz, *Financial Reporting by Diversified Companies,* June, 1968.

Financial Analysts Federation:
Staff, *Evaluation of Corporate Financial Reporting in Selected Industries for the Year 1971,* March, 1972.

National Association of Accountants:
Backer and McFarland, *External Reporting for Segments of a Business,* April, 1968.
Rappaport and Lerner, *A Framework for Financial Reporting by Diversified Companies,* September, 1969.
Rappaport and Lerner, *Segment Reporting for Managers and Investors,* May, 1972.

toward disclosing voluntarily supplemental financial information as to industry seg-ments of the business."[3] In addition, the Accountants International Study Group issued the results of its study on segment reporting in June, 1972. The study's primary conclusions were:

1. Financial statements of diversified companies should include information on separate segments, and that information should be examined and reported upon by independent auditors.[4]

2. Consideration should be given by the participating Institutes to issuing technical pronouncements on the problems of examining and reporting on segmented information to facilitate reporting by independent auditors.[5]

Thus, the business community and the accounting profession, through their profes-sional organizations, provided considerable research data and other information to support the need for segment disclosure and for standards of implementation. As a result of the research studies, many companies began, on a voluntary basis, to include some type of segment disclosure in their annual reports to stockholders. As would be expected, however, definitions of "segments," the nature and extent of the information disclosed, and the methods of presentation varied widely. In addition, the information was generally included in the annual report in sections other than the financial statements section and was, therefore, not subject to independent audit.

Recognizing the importance of "segment" data and the necessity of establishing standards for disclosure, the Financial Accounting Standards Board included the topic on its initial agenda. Two research reports were issued by the FASB staff and they, along with the other research studies available, were the basis for the preparation of a Discussion Memorandum and Exposure Draft. After giving consideration to com-ments received through public hearings and position papers, the Board issued *Statement of Financial Accounting Standards No. 14*, "Financial Reporting for Segments of a Business Enterprise," in December, 1976.

NEED FOR DISAGGREGATED FINANCIAL DATA

The research studies discussed earlier concluded that financial statement users want information to aid them in evaluating prospective investments. If return on investment is computed on the basis of expected cash flows, the evaluation of risk requires an

---

[3]*APB Statement No. 2*, "Disclosure of Supplemental Financial Information by Diversified Compan-ies" (New York: AICPA, 1967), par. 11.

[4]Accountants International Study Group, *Reporting by Diversified Companies: Current Recom-mended Practices in Canada, the United Kingdom and the United States* (Birmingham, England: AISG, 1972), par. 86.

[5]*Ibid.*, par. 87.

assessment of the uncertainty surrounding both the timing and amount of those expected cash flows. Uncertainty results, in part at least, from factors unique to the company in which an investment is being considered. Uncertainty also results from factors related to the industries and geographical areas in which the firm operates, as well as related national and international economic and political factors.

Statement users use financial statement information to determine conditions, trends, and ratios that assist them in predicting cash flows of firms. These factors are often compared with those of other firms, as well as with industry-wide data, and general national and international economic information is considered in making an overall evaluation of the risk involved. When a firm engages in activities in several industries and/or geographic areas, analysis and the process used to predict future cash flows become more complex. The different industries or geographic areas may have different rates of profitability, opportunities for growth, and types of risk. Thus, many statement users reported that, although consolidated financial information is important, it would be more useful if supplemented with disaggregated information to assist them in analyzing the uncertainties surrounding the timing and amount of expected cash flows.

STANDARDS OF FINANCIAL ACCOUNTING AND REPORTING

FASB Statement No. 14, as amended by *FASB Statement No. 21,* requires that information concerning (1) the enterprises's operations in different industries (segments), (2) its foreign operations and export sales, and (3) its major customers be included in its financial statements when a complete set of financial statements is issued in conformity with generally accepted accounting principles for a fiscal period.[6] If statements are presented for more than one period, the required information must be presented for each period. The information required should be a disaggregation of *consolidated financial information* where the firm has consolidated subsidiaries, and a disaggregation of the individual firm data if it has no consolidated subsidiaries.

Disaggregation of financial information pertaining to unconsolidated subsidiaries or other unconsolidated investees is *not* required. Because these investments must normally be accounted for by the equity method, however, the requirements for disclosing information about equity method investees as expressed in *APB Opinion No. 18* must be complied with. Likewise, information must be presented concerning foreign subsidiaries as required by *ARB No. 43.* In addition, *FASB Statement No. 14* requires identification of both the industries and geographic areas in which equity method investees operate, even though none of the disclosures covered by the *Statement* are required for that enterprise.

Although transactions among affiliates are eliminated in the preparation of consolidated financial statements, intersegment transactions are *included* in the

---

[6]Nonpublic enterprises are not required to make these disclosures. A nonpublic enterprise is an enterprise other than (a) one whose debt or equity securities are traded in a public market on a foreign or domestic stock exchange or in the over-the-counter market (including securities quoted only locally or regionally), or (b) one that is required to file financial statements with the Securities and Exchange Commission.

segment information for purposes of the application of *Statement No. 14.* Thus, revenue reported for a segment includes both sales to outside parties and sales or transfers to other segments. The same principle applies to intersegment expenses. A reconciliation of segment information with amounts reported in consolidated financial statements is then required.

Disaggregation by Segment

FASB Statement No. 14 requires that financial statements include certain information about the industry segments of the firm. Before discussing procedures for determining (1) the types of information required, (2) appropriate segments, and (3) methods of presentation, some terms must be defined because they have been given specific definitions for purposes of reporting on industry segments. The terms and their definitions are:

a) *Industry segment.* A component of an enterprise engaged in providing a product or service or a group of related products and services primarily to unaffiliated customers for a profit. Because an industry segment is defined in terms of products and services that are sold primarily to unaffiliated customers, the disaggregation of the vertically integrated operations of an enterprise is not required.

b) *Reportable segment.* An industry segment (or, in certain cases, a group of two or more closely related industry segments) for which information is required to be reported.

c) *Revenue.* The revenue of an industry segment includes revenue both from sales to unaffiliated customers and from intersegment sales or transfers, if any, of products and services similar to those sold to unaffiliated customers. (Intersegment billings for the cost of shared facilities or other jointly incurred costs do *not* represent intersegment sales or transfers.) Interest from sources outside the enterprise and interest earned on intersegment trade receivables is included in revenue if the asset on which the interest is earned is included among the industry segment's identifiable assets, but interest earned on advances or loans to other industry segments generally is not included unless the advances or loans are made by a segment whose primary function is of a financial nature (bank, finance company, etc.). Revenue from intersegment sales or transfers is accounted for on the basis used by the enterprise to price the intersegment sales or transfers.

d) *Operating profit or loss.* The operating profit or loss of an industry segment is its revenue as defined above minus all operating expenses. Operating expenses include expenses that relate to both revenue from sales to unaffiliated customers and revenue from intersegment sales or transfers. Those operating expenses incurred by an enterprise that are not directly traceable to an industry segment must be allocated on a reasonable basis among those segments for whose benefit the expenses were incurred. Intersegment purchases are accounted for on the same basis as intersegment sales or transfers. The following items are *excluded* in computing the operating profit or loss of the segment:

1) Revenue earned at the corporate level (e.g., investment income) and not derived from the operations of an industry segment.

2) General corporate expenses.

3) Interest expense (unless the segment is a financial organization).

4) Income taxes.
5) Equity in income or loss from unconsolidated subsidiaries and other unconsolidated investees.
6) Gain or loss on discontinued operations.
7) Extraordinary items.
8) Minority interest.
9) The cumulative effect of a change in accounting principle.

e) *Identifiable assets.* Those tangible and intangible assets that are used by the industry segment, including (1) assets that are used exclusively by that segment and (2) an allocated portion of assets used jointly by two or more segments. Assets used jointly are allocated among the segments on a reasonable basis. Because the assets of a segment that transfers products or services to another segment are not used in the operations of the receiving segment, no amount of those assets *is* allocated to the receiving segment. Assets that represent part of an enterprise's investment in a segment, such as goodwill, are included in the industry segment's identifiable assets. Assets maintained for general corporate purposes (those not used in the operations of any segment) are not allocated. Advances or loans to or investments in another segment are not included unless they represent advances or loans from a financial segment to other segments. (Advances or loans from a financial segment are included because the income therefrom is included in computing the financial segment's operating profit or loss.) Asset valuation allowances are deducted in computing the amount of a segment's identifiable assets.[7]

Two of the most difficult tasks in applying the segment disclosure requirements of *Statement No. 14* are those of determining (1) an appropriate basis for the allocation of joint operating expenses, and (2) appropriate industry segments.

Joint Operating Expense Allocation *Statement No. 14* provides that, to compute operating profit or loss of segments, operating expenses that are not directly traceable to an industry segment must be allocated on a reasonable basis among those segments for whose benefit the expenses were incurred. Emphasis is upon *operating* expenses; general corporate expenses are not allocated. Unfortunately, no guidelines as to appropriate bases for allocation are provided; thus, the allocation process must depend to a large extent on the judgment of management.

Although judgment must be used, several of the research studies mentioned earlier contain recommendations concerning common cost allocation methods. Probably the most extensive study on appropriate allocation methods was conducted by the Cost Accounting Standards Board, and its recommendations were issued in *Cost Accounting Standard No. 403.* Although *Standard No. 403* concerns the problem of allocating joint home office expenses to segments of an organization involved in defense contracts, the general guidelines developed should be useful in applying the allocation provisions of *FASB Statement No. 14.* In essence, *Cost Accounting Standard No. 403* suggests that, where possible, joint costs should be accumulated into logical and relatively homogeneous expense pools. The pools are then allocated to segments on the basis of beneficial or causal relationships as measured by activity or output of the segments.

[7]*FASB Statement No. 14,* par. 10.

For example, joint data-processing expenses might be allocated on the basis of machine time or number of reports, joint personnel administration expenses on the basis of number of personnel or total labor hours, and joint centralized warehouse expenses on the basis of square footage, value of materials, or volume of transactions. Any remaining expenses that cannot be logically included in any of the homogeneous expense pools are allocated proportionately under a three-factor formula based upon payroll costs, revenue, and assets of the segments. That is, the percentage of the residual expenses to be allocated to any segment is the arithmetical average of the following three percentages:

1. The segment's payroll dollars to the total payroll dollars of all segments.

2. The segment's operating revenue to the total operating revenue of all segments.

3. The average net book value of the sum of the segment's tangible capital assets plus inventories to the total average net book value of such assets of all segments.

Determining Reportable Segments   *Statement No. 14* provides that reportable segments of the firm are to be determined by identifying the products and services from which the firm obtains its revenues, grouping those products and services by industry lines into industry segments, and selecting those segments that are significant with respect to the firm as a whole.

Determination of the firm's industry segments must depend to a large extent on the judgment of management. Many firms maintain profit centers for individual products and services, or groups of related products and services, to accumulate information about revenue and profitability. These profit centers represent a starting point for the determination of the firm's industry segments. If a profit center crosses industry lines, it is, of course, necessary to disaggregate that profit center into smaller groups of related products and services. If a firm operates in more than one industry, but does not maintain profit centers, it must disaggregate its operations along industry lines.

If the firm accumulates data along industry lines for its foreign operations, or if it is practicable to do so, segments should be determined on a worldwide basis. If it is impracticable to disaggregate part or all of its foreign operations, the firm should disaggregate its domestic operations and foreign operations for which disaggregation is practicable along industry lines, and treat the remainder of its foreign operations as a single industry segment. Disclosure should be made of the types of industries included in the foreign operations that have not been disaggregated. In addition, as discussed in a later section, data concerning significant foreign operations and export sales must also be disclosed.

Each segment that is significant to the enterprise as a whole must be identified as a reportable segment. A segment is considered to be significant if it meets *one or more* of the following tests, the tests being applied separately for each fiscal year for which financial statements are prepared:

    a) Its revenue, as defined earlier, is 10% or more of the combined revenue of all of the enterprise's industry segments.

b) The absolute amount of its operating profit or operating loss is 10% or more of the greater, in absolute amount, of:

    1) The combined operating profit of all industry segments that did not incur an operating loss, or

    2) The combined operating loss of all industry segments that did incur an operating loss.

c) Its identifiable assets are 10% or more of the combined identifiable assets of all industry segments.[8]

Revenue, operating profit or loss, and identifiable assets relating to those foreign operations that have not been disaggregated along industry lines on grounds of impracticability are included in computing the combined revenue, combined operating profit or loss, and combined identifiable assets of the firm's segments.

An example of the application of these tests for Papco, Inc. is presented in Illustration 13–1.

ILLUSTRATION 13–1
Significance Tests

(IN THOUSANDS OF DOLLARS)

REVENUE TEST	LUMBER	PAPER	PRINTING	FURNITURE	LEATHER	COMBINED
Sales to Unaffiliated Customers	16,000	3,000	2,000	1,500	1,000	23,500
Intersegment Sales	5,000	2,000	500	500	–0–	8,000
Total Revenue	21,000	5,000	2,500	2,000	1,000	31,500

The lumber and paper segments are reportable segments under the revenue test because their total revenues are at least 10% of combined total revenue of $31,500, whereas the other segments are not reportable segments under this test.

OPERATING PROFIT TEST						
Operating Profit (loss)	2,500	600	(300)	150	(100)	2,850

The lumber and paper segments are reportable segments under the operating profit test because the absolute amounts of their operating profit or loss are each at least 10% of the greater of (1) the combined profit of all industry segments that did not incur a loss (2,500 + 600 + 150 = 3,250), or (2) the combined loss of all industry segments that incurred a loss (300 + 100 = 400); the other segments are not reportable segments under this test.

IDENTIFIABLE ASSETS TEST						
Identifiable Assets	25,000	12,000	8,000	3,000	4,000	52,000

The lumber, paper, and printing segments are reportable segments because their identifiable assets are at least 10% of combined identifiable assets. The furniture and leather segments are not reportable segments under this test.

Thus, the lumber, paper, and printing segments are all reportable (subject to one further test discussed later) because they meet one or more of the three tests. The furniture and leather segments would be reported in combined form.

[8]*Ibid*, par. 15.

The results of the tests should be evaluated from the standpoint of comparability. Thus, a segment that has been significant in the past and is expected to be significant in the future should be treated as a reportable segment even though it fails to meet a test in the current year. Conversely, a segment that has been insignificant in the past and is expected to be insignificant in the future should be excluded as a reportable segment even though it may meet one of the tests in the current period because of abnormally high revenues or because the combined revenue or operating profit or loss of all segments is abnormally low.

In addition to the tests described above, the reportable segments taken together must represent a substantial portion of the firm's total operations. To determine whether a substantial portion of a firm's operations are explained by its segment information, the combined revenue from sales to unaffiliated customers of all reportable segments must constitute at least 75% of the combined revenue from sales to unaffiliated customers of all industry segments. The test is applied separately for each fiscal period for which financial statements are prepared. Revenue relating to those foreign operations that have not been disaggregated along industry lines on grounds of impracticability is included in the denominator of the computation and is included in the numerator if those operations have been identified as a reportable segment.

Application of this test to the situation presented in Illustration 13–1 produces the following:

$$\frac{\text{Combined sales to unaffiliated customers by the lumber, paper, and printing segments}}{\text{Combined sales to unaffiliated customers by all segments}} = \frac{(16{,}000 + 3{,}000 + 2{,}000)}{23{,}500} = 89\%$$

Thus, the 75% test is met, and the lumber, paper, and printing segments will be reported individually and the furniture and leather segments combined into one unit. If the 75% test had not been met, one or more of the segments that did not qualify as reportable segments under the previous tests would have to be included as reportable segments.

A firm may operate in only one industry, or a major portion of its operations may be in a single industry segment and the remaining portion in one or more other segments. In this case the segment information disclosures described in the next section need *not* be made, but financial statements should identify the industry in which the major portion of the firm's operations takes place. A major portion of its operations is considered to take place in a given industry segment if its revenue, operating profit or loss, and identifiable assets each constitute more than 90% of related combined totals for all industry segments.

Information To Be Presented   The following types of information must be presented for each of a firm's reportable segments, and in the aggregate for the segments that are not separately reported.

a) *Revenue.* Sales to unaffiliated customers and sales or transfers to other segments must be separately disclosed in presenting revenue of a reportable segment. The basis of accounting for intersegment sales or transfers must be disclosed. If the basis is changed, disclosure must be made of the nature of the change and its effect on the reportable segments' operating profit or loss in the period of change.

b) *Profitability.* Operating profit or loss as defined earlier must be presented for each reportable segment along with an explanation of the nature and amount of any unusual or infrequently occurring items reported in the consolidated income statement that have been added or deducted in computing operating profit or loss of the segment. In addition, a firm may elect to present some other measure of profitability for some or all segments, i.e., contribution margin, net income, or some measure of profitability between operating profit and net income. If presenting contribution margin, the firm must describe the difference between contribution margin and operating profit or loss. If presenting other measures of profitability, the nature and amount of each category of revenue or expense that was added to or deducted from operating income or loss should be disclosed.

c) *Identifiable Assets.* The aggregate amount of identifiable assets as defined earlier must be presented for each segment.

d) *Other Related Disclosures.* Other disclosures relating to each reportable segment must be made as follows:

1) The aggregate amount of depreciation, depletion, and amortization expense.

2) The amount of capital expenditures for the period, i.e., additions to property, plant and equipment.

3) The firm's equity in the net income from and investment in the net assets of unconsolidated subsidiaries and other equity method investees whose operations are vertically integrated with the operations of that segment, and the geographic areas in which those vertically integrated equity method investees operate.

4) The effect on the operating profit of a change in accounting principle in the period in which the change is made. (Pro forma effects of retroactive application on segments need not be disclosed.)[9]

---

[9]*Ibid,* pars. 23–27.

Methods of Presentation   Information about the reportable segments of a firm may be included in its financial statements in any of the following ways:

a) Within the body of the financial statements, with appropriate explanatory disclosures in the footnotes to the financial statements.

b) Entirely in the footnotes to the financial statements.

c) In a separate schedule that is included as an integral part of the financial sttements. If, in a report to securityholders, that schedule is located on a page that is not clearly a part of the financial statements, the schedule must be referenced in the financial statements as an integral part thereof and covered by the auditor's opinion.[10]

Financial information such as revenue, operating profit or loss, and identifiable assets must be presented in dollar amounts; related percentages may be shown if desired.

The information required to be presented for individual reportable segments, and in the aggregate for industry segments not deemed separately reportable, must be reconciled to related amounts in the financial statements for the enterprise as a whole as follows:

a) Revenue to revenue reported in the consolidated income statement.

b) Operating profit or loss to pretax income from continuing operations in the consolidated income statement.

c) Identifiable assets to consolidated total assets, with assets maintained for general corporate purposes separately identified in the reconciliation.[11]

As an illustration of segment reporting, assume the segment data presented in Illustration 13–1. In addition, assume that the consolidated income statements and balance sheets for 1980 and 1981 for Papco, Inc. are as follows:

PAPCO INC.
Consolidated Income Statement
(Thousands of Dollars)

| | YEAR ENDING DECEMBER 31 | |
	1981	1980
Sales	$23,500	$22,100
Cost of Goods Sold	16,400	15,300
Selling, General, and Administrative Expense	4,530	4,380
Interest Expense	600	570
Total Cost and Expense	21,530	20,250
Net	1,970	1,850
Equity in Income of B Company	150	120
Income Before Income Taxes	2,120	1,970
Income Taxes	1,020	980
Net Income	$ 1,100	$ 990

[10]*Ibid*, par. 28.

[11]*Ibid*, par. 30.

PAPCO INC.
Consolidated Balance Sheet
(Thousands of Dollars)

| | DECEMBER 31 | |
	1981	1980
Cash	$ 1,870	$ 1,785
Receivables	2,640	2,860
Inventories	6,400	6,345
Investment in B Company	700	600
Plant and Equipment (net of accumulated depreciation		
of $17,500 in 1981 and $16,200 in 1980)	41,500	40,400
Other Assets	690	970
Total Assets	$53,800	$52,960
Current Liabilities	$ 2,400	$ 2,320
Bonds Payable	12,000	12,000
Common Stock, $50 par	30,000	30,000
Additional Paid-in Capital	3,000	3,000
Retained Earnings	6,400	5,640
Total Liabilities and Stockholders' Equity	$53,800	$52,960

Disclosure of industry segment information might take the form of the following supporting schedules and footnotes:

PAPCO INC.
Data on Operations in Different Industries
(Thousands of Dollars)

	YEAR ENDED DECEMBER 31	
REVENUE	1981	1980
Lumber:		
Sales to Nonaffiliates	$16,000	$15,200
Intersegment Sales	5,000	4,800
	21,000	20,000
Paper:		
Sales to Nonaffiliates	3,000	2,800
Intersegment Sales	2,000	1,700
	5,000	4,500
Printing:		
Sales to Nonaffiliates	2,000	2,100
Intersegment Sales	500	300
	2,500	2,400
Other:		
Sales to Nonaffiliates	2,500	2,000
Intersegment Sales	500	460
	3,000	2,460
Total Sales	31,500	29,360
Elimination of Intersegment Sales	8,000	7,260
Total Consolidated Revenue	$23,500	$22,100
OPERATING PROFIT OR LOSS		
Lumber	$ 2,500	$ 2,460
Paper	600	580
Printing	(300)	(430)
Other	50	70
Total Operating Profit	2,850	2,680
Corporate Expense	(280)	(260)
Interest Expense	(600)	(570)
Equity in Net Income of B Company	150	120
Income Before Income Tax	$ 2,120	$ 1,970
IDENTIFIABLE ASSETS		
Lumber	$25,000	$24,460
Paper	12,000	11,500
Printing	8,000	7,900
Other	7,000	7,520
General Corporate Assets	1,100	980
Investment in Net Assets of B Company	700	600
Total Consolidated Assets	$53,800	$52,960

DEPRECIATION AND AMORTIZATION EXPENSE

Lumber	$ 1,300	$ 1,200
Paper	600	560
Printing	350	325
Other	240	225

CAPITAL EXPENDITURES

Lumber	$ 1,740	$ 1,280
Paper	420	360
Printing	30	20
Other	210	240

EQUITY IN B COMPANY

Equity in Earnings	$ 150	$ 120
Investment in Net Assets	700	600

Note D—Industry Segments

The Company operates in three main areas, lumber products, paper products, and printing. The principal products of these operations are described in the "Business Operations" section of this report.

Intersegment sales are made at the same prices as sales to nonaffiliates. Operating profit consists of total revenue less all operating expenses except interest and general corporate expense. Identifiable assets include those directly identified with the operations of each segment plus an allocated portion of assets used jointly. Corporate assets consist primarily of cash and investments.

The Company has a 30% interest in B Company, a domestic cattle-feeding venture.

Foreign Operations and Export Sales

Foreign Operations Statement No. 14 also requires that companies distinguish between domestic and significant foreign operations, and that foreign operations be broken down by country or groups of countries (geographic areas). Foreign operations are defined as those located outside the United States (or other "home country") that produce revenue from sales to unaffiliated customers or from intra-enterprise sales or transfers between countries or geographic areas. Foreign operations do *not,* however, include unconsolidated subsidiaries and investees. If operations are conducted in two or more foreign countries or geographic areas, information must be presented separately for each significant foreign country or geographic area and in the aggregate for all other foreign operations. Where the operations of some foreign countries are grouped into geographic areas, the groupings should be made on the basis of a consideration of (1) proximity, (2) economic affinity, (3) similarities of business environments, and (4) the nature, scale, and degree of interrelationship of the operations in the various countries.

"Significant" foreign operations are determined in a way similar to determining reportable industry segments, except that the operating profit test is not applied. Thus, foreign operations are considered to be significant if *either* of the following tests is met:

1. Revenue generated by the foreign operations from sales to unaffiliated companies is 10% or more of consolidated revenue.

2. Identifiable assets of the firm's foreign operations are 10% or more of consolidated assets.[12]

Information to be disclosed is similar to that reported for industry segments and includes, for domestic operations and for each foreign country or geographic area, the following:

Revenue, with separate disclosure of sales to nonaffiliates and intracompany sales or transfers. The basis of accounting for intracompany sales and transfers and the nature and effect of any change in method should be disclosed.

Operating Profit or Loss, or some other measure of profitability. A common measure of profitability must be used for all countries and/or geographic areas presented.

Identifiable Assets, using the same procedures for presenting industry segment information.

To illustrate, foreign operations information for Papco, Inc., might be presented as follows, assuming that the company conducts operations in the United States, Canada, and Mexico.

PAPCO INC.
Data on Operations in Different Geographic Areas
(Thousands of Dollars)

	YEAR ENDED DECEMBER 31	
REVENUE	1981	1980
United States:		
Sales to nonaffiliates	$18,000	$17,500
Intracompany sales and transfers	500	600
	18,500	18,100
Canada:		
Sales to nonaffiliates	4,000	3,500
Intracompany sales and transfers	200	300
	4,200	3,800
Mexico:		
Sales to nonaffiliates	1,500	1,100
Total Sales	24,200	23,000
Elimination of intracompany sales and transfers	700	900
Total Consolidated Revenue	$23,500	$22,100

Intracompany sales and transfers are made at the same prices charged for sales to nonaffiliates.

[12]*Ibid,* par. 32.

OPERATING PROFIT OR LOSS		
United States	$ 2,080	$ 2,000
Canada	570	530
Mexico	200	150
Total Operating Profit	2,850	2,680
Corporate Expense	(280)	(260)
Interest Expense	(600)	(570)
Equity in Income of B Company	150	120
Net Income Before Tax	$ 2,120	$ 1,970
IDENTIFIABLE ASSETS		
United States	$34,000	$33,600
Canada	12,200	12,000
Mexico	5,800	5,780
General Corporate Assets	1,100	980
Investment in Net Assets of B Company	700	600
Total Consolidated Assets	$53,800	$52,960

Export Sales   In addition to the foregoing disclosures concerning foreign operations, if sales by a company's *domestic* operations to *unaffiliated* foreign customers are 10% or more of consolidated revenues, the amount of those export sales should be disclosed and, where appropriate, broken down by foreign country or geographic area. Although *Statement No. 14* gives no guidance as to when it is appropriate to disclose by foreign country or geographic area, the prevalent use of the 10% or more guide throughout the *Statement* suggests that disclosure of export sales by individual foreign country or geographic area would be appropriate if the export sales to those countries or geographic areas are 10% or more of total consolidated revenues. Export sales disclosure is often presented in a separate footnote, or another section might be added to the preceding disclosure, such as:

UNITED STATES OPERATIONS EXPORT SALES	1981	1980
To Japan	$2,600	$2,300
Other	300	250

Information About Major Customers

If 10% or more of the revenue of a firm is derived from sales to any single customer, that fact and the amount of revenue from each such customer must be disclosed. (A group of customers under common control is considered to be a single customer.) Also, if 10% or more of the revenue is derived from sales to domestic government agencies in the aggregate or to foreign governments in the aggregate, that fact and the amount of revenue must be disclosed. Disclosure should include the amount of sales to each customer and the industry segment making the sale. Customers' names, however, need not be disclosed. These disclosures are required even though the firm may not be required to report information about operations in different industries or foreign operations.

SEC RULES ON REPORTING BUSINESS SEGMENTS

The SEC, in *Release No. 236,* December 23, 1977, changed its lines-of-business disclosure rules to conform to the industry segment reporting guidelines established in *FASB Statement No. 14,* with a few exceptions discussed below. The SEC also adopted *FASB Statement No. 14* requirements concerning disclosure of foreign and domestic operations, major customers, and export sales. In general, the required disclosures are to be made in annual reports to stockholders, although any information required by the SEC, but not by *FASB Statement No. 14,* can be presented outside of the audited financial statements.

Disclosures required include all of the data required by *FASB Statement No. 14* with the following exceptions:

1. *Reporting Period.* Data must be reported for a 5-year historical period, with segment data presented for fiscal years beginning after December 15, 1976 and lines-of-business information for the balance of the 5-year period. *Statement No. 14* requires disclosure of the data for each year for which a complete set of financial statements is presented.

2. *Major Customers.* If a material part of an industry segment is dependent upon a major customer or customers, and the loss of such customer or customers would have a materially adverse effect on the enterprise, the customer or customers must be *identified* and described for each segment. *Statement No. 14* does not require identification of major customers.

3. *Intra-enterprise Sales.* The basis of accounting for intra-enterprise transfers (i.e., between industry segments and geographic areas) and the effect of such transfers on the revenue and/or profit or loss of the segment or geographic area must be disclosed if transfers are made at prices substantially higher or lower than prevailing market prices for similar products or services or at prices substantially higher or lower than those charged to unaffiliated parties for similar products or services, and the effect of the pricing practice on the revenue and/or profit or loss of a segment or geographic area is quantitatively or qualitatively material to an understanding of the business as a whole.

4. *Dominant Segment. Release No. 236* does not include a requirement relating to financial information about a dominant segment because other SEC provisions already require appropriate disclosure.

A comparison of SEC rules with *FASB Statement No. 14* requirements is presented in Illustration 13–2, page 484.

FEDERAL TRADE COMMISSION LINES-OF-BUSINESS DISCLOSURES

The FTC also requires, on a selective basis, certain large manufacturing companies to report lines of business data annually on Form LB. The purpose of these reports, as expressed by the FTC, is to provide a data base for the compilation of aggregate industry data which can be used for various purposes. The type of information required is much the same as that required by the SEC and FASB. However, the FTC disclosures apply only to *domestic manufacturing* operations.

The FTC method of determining reportable segments is different from that required by the SEC and FASB. In essence the FTC requires that products and services be grouped by major Standard Industrial Classification (SIC) codes. At least 85% of the revenues of any reportable segment must be from a single SIC code group. FTC rules do not limit the number of reportable segments in the same way as the SEC and FASB; rather, the FTC requires separate reporting for all segments with ten million dollars (or more) of total revenue.

Before leaving this topic, the reader should recall that the units involved in the aggregation of financial data into consolidated financial statements are generally different from the units that must be disaggregated for segment reporting under SEC and FASB rules. The unit used to aggregate data in the preparation of consolidated financial statements is the affiliate (subsidiary) company. Disaggregation of data into segments is by industry, product or service line, or geographic area, which explains the need for the required reconciliation of segment data to consolidated financial statement data.

Questions

1. For what types of companies would segmented financial reports have the most significance? Why?

2. Why do financial statement users (financial analysts, for example) need information about segments of a firm?

3. List the three major types of information disclosures required by *FASB Statement No. 14*.

4. Define the following:
   (a) Industry segment.
   (b) Reportable industry segment.

5. Describe the guidelines to be used in determining whether a specific industry segment is a significant segment.

6. How does one determine whether a major portion of a company's operations occur within a single industry?

7. What type of disclosure is required of a firm when the major portion of its operations takes place within a single industry?

ILLUSTRATION 13-2
Significant Disclosure Requirements of
FASB Statement No. 14 **and SEC Rules**

REQUIREMENT	DISCLOSURES REQUIRED?	
	FASB STATEMENT NO. 14	SEC RULES
Applicability to annual statements	Years for which a complete set of financial statements is presented.	Most recent 5 years. Segment data for fiscal years beginning after December 15, 1976; lines-of-business data for the remainder of the 5-year period.
Applicability to interim statements	Voluntary	Only if, in the opinion of management, the 5-year segment data may not be indicative of current or future operations of the segment.
Industry segment data:		
Revenue	Yes	Yes
Operating profit (loss)	Yes	Yes
Identifiable assets	Yes	Yes
Depreciation expense	Yes	No
Capital expenditures	Yes	No
Equity in unconsolidated investments	Yes	Yes
Reconciliation of segment data to consolidated amounts	Yes	Yes
Foreign and domestic operations:		
Revenue	Yes	Yes
Operating profit, net profit, or other	Yes	Yes
Identifiable assets	Yes	Yes
Reconciliation of area data to consolidated amounts	Yes	Yes
Export sales	Yes	Yes
Major customers:		
Applicability	Disclose if amounts are at least 10% of total revenue.	Disclose if a material part of the industry.
Disclosures	Amount and segment.	Customer name, relationship, and material facts.
Intersegment or inter-area transfers:		
Revenue by segment or area	Yes	Yes
Purchases by segment or area	No	No*
Comparative pricing data	No	No*
Other Disclosures:		
Description of segment accounting policies	Identify major policies.	No

| | DISCLOSURES REQUIRED? | |
REQUIREMENT	FASB STATEMENT NO. 14	SEC RULES
Description of segment products and services	Briefly identify.	Lengthy description of major business factors.
Effect, by segment, or area, of change in accounting method or allocation method	Amount and nature of change.	No
Unusual or infrequently occurring items by segment	Amount and nature.	No

*Unless transfers are made at prices substantially higher or lower than prevailing market prices for similar products or services or at prices substantially higher or lower than those charged to unaffiliated parties for similar products or services, and the effect of the pricing practice on the revenue and/or profit or loss of a segment or geographic area is quantitatively or qualitatively material to an understanding of the business as a whole.

8. List the types of information that must be presented for each reportable segment of a company under the rules of *FASB Statement No. 14*.

9. Describe the methods that might be used to disclose reportable industry segment information.

10. How does one determine whether foreign operations constitute a significant portion of total enterprise operations?

11. What types of information must be disclosed about foreign operations under *FASB Statement No. 14?*

12. What factors should be considered in grouping foreign operations into "geographic area" operations?

13. What are the major differences between the requirements for industry segment disclosures under *FASB Statement No. 14* and SEC regulations?

Problems

Problem 13–1

Braden Industries operates in seven different industries. Information concerning the operations of these industries for the most recent fiscal period is:

INDUSTRY SEGMENT	REVENUE TOTAL	REVENUE INTERSEGMENT	OPERATING PROFIT (LOSS)	IDENTIFIABLE ASSETS
1	$ 600	$ 150	$ (75)	$ 1,200
2	1,500	300	300	1,800
3	9,000	1,500	300	7,500
4	12,000	–0–	1,650	9,750
5	14,250	–0–	750	12,750
6	2,400	600	600	2,250
7	2,250	750	(900)	3,000

Determine which of the above segments must be treated as reportable segments.

Problem 13–2

Kingston Industries is comprised of four separate profit centers which are distributed throughout the United States. Relevant data for each profit center is summarized below for 1980:

	PROFIT CENTER (IN THOUSANDS)				
	A	B	C	D	TOTAL
Sales to unaffiliated customers	$ 600	$1,450	$250	$200	$2,500
Intersegment sales	250	400	50	500	1,200
Operating profit (loss) before					
joint expense allocation	140	250	40	(10)	420
Identifiable assets	1,200	3,000	400	400	5,000
Labor hours worked	450	950	250	350	2,000

You determine that intersegment sales are distributed as follows:
Test for Harried—Chapter 13 aas/jk

	PROFIT CENTER (IN THOUSANDS)				
	A	B	C	D	TOTAL
Sales to unaffiliated customers	$ 600	$1,450	$250	$200	$2,500
Intersegment sales	250	400	50	500	1,200
Operating profit (loss) before					
joint expense allocation	140	250	40	(10)	420
Identifiable assets	1,200	3,000	400	400	5,000
Labor hours worked	450	950	250	350	2,000

You determine that intersegment sales are distributed as follows:

SELLER	BUYER A	B	C	D	E	TOTAL
A	-0-	200	25	25		250
B	200	-0-	100	100		400
C	25	25	-0-	-0-		50
D	300	175	25	-0-		500
Total	525	400	150	125		1,200

Administrative expenses of $400,000 were incurred at the corporate level during 1980. Management feels that total labor hours worked during the year provides a reasonable basis for allocation of these costs.

In each situation described below, an industry segment is comprised of different combinations of profit centers. Thus, the "AB" industry segment consists of profit centers "A" and "B." Consider the following five combinations of industry segments:

1. AB, CD

2. AB, C, D

3. A, B, CD

4. A, B, C, D

5. A, BD, C

Required:
A. For each combination listed, determine which industry segments are reportable segments under the provisions of *FASB Statement No. 14*. Apply all the required tests and indicate the results of each test separately.
B. For each combination given, indicate if the reportable segments determined in A above collectively represent a "substantial portion" of Kingston Industries' total operations as defined and required by *FASB Statement No. 14* by applying the 75% revenue test.

Problem 13–3
Saratoga Industries, a publicly held corporation, consists of several companies, each of which provides a diverse array of products and services to unaffiliated customers. In your opinion, each of these companies qualifies as a separate industry segment.

The corporation is in the process of completing its first-year financial statements. Although the directors of Saratoga Industries wish to comply with the provisions of *FASB Statement No. 14*, they believe that disclosing each individual industry segment would result in an unwieldy and cumbersome set of financial statements. For this reason, they request that when you prepare these statements, you keep the identified segments to the minimum number that would ensure compliance with *FASB Statement No. 14*.

Required:
A. To what extent does the management of Saratoga Industries have a "choice" in deciding whether an industry segment must be reported?
B. The directors of Saratoga Industries presumably feel that too much disclosure of financial information will impair the overall utility of the financial statements. What flexibility does the FASB allow that could invalidate this criticism? Explain.

C. Explain the needs for segment reporting. Why do consolidated financial statements fail to meet these needs?

D. Relate the concept of comparability to the required accounting treatment for intersegment transactions. What arguments would favor *excluding* the effect of intersegment transfers?

Problem 13–4

Carson Industries conducts operations in five major industries, A, B, C, D, and E. Financial data relevant to each industry for the year ending December 31, 1981 are as follows:

	(IN THOUSANDS)				
	A	B	C	D	E
Sales	$14,000	$38,000	$300,000	$12,000	$24,000
Cost of Goods Sold	6,000	24,000	160,000	2,800	14,000
Admin. Expenses	2,000	8,000	48,000	2,000	2,000
Selling Expenses	2,000	14,000	58,000	3,200	6,000
Total Cost & Expense	10,000	46,000	266,000	8,000	22,000
Operating Profit	4,000	(8,000)	34,000	4,000	2,000
Identifiable Assets	16,000	30,000	190,000	32,000	70,000
Depreciation and Amortization Expense	1,800	2,900	24,000	3,400	6,800
Capital Expenditures	1,200	2,000	12,000	6,000	8,000

Included in the sales of segments C and E are intersegment sales of $30,000 and $8,000, respectively. Corporate offices have assets of $26,000 and incurred general corporate expenses of $15,000.

Required:

A. Which industry segments should be separately reported in the segment report? Justify your answer.

B. Prepare a report to disclose required industry segment information under *FASB Statement No. 14.*

Problem 13–5

Textron Industries is a diversified company whose operations are conducted in five industries, L, M, N, O, and P. Segmented financial information is to be included with the December 31, 1980 annual report. Financial information pertaining to each segment for 1980 is as follows:

	L	M	N	O	P
Sales	$10,500	$28,500	$225,000	$ 9,000	$18,000
Cost of Sales	4,500	18,000	120,000	2,100	10,500
General and Admin. Expense	1,500	6,000	36,000	1,500	1,500
Selling Expense	1,500	10,500	43,500	2,400	4,500
Total Cost and Expense	7,500	34,500	199,500	6,000	16,500
Operating Profit (loss)	$ 3,000	$ (6,000)	$ 25,500	$ 3,000	$ 1,500
Identifiable Assets	$12,000	$22,500	$142,500	$24,000	$52,500

Other information:

1. In addition to the identifiable assets given above, the general corporate office has assets of $27,000 on December 31, 1980.

2. Included in the sales of segment P are $6,000 of sales made to segment N during the year. None of these goods remain in the ending inventory of segment N on December 31, 1980.

3. Income tax amounts to 25% of operating profit.

Required:
A. Determine which of the five segments must be treated as reportable segments and indicate the basis for your decision.
B. Prepare a financial report by segments which is reconciled to consolidated data.

14

Formation and Operation of a Partnership

A business organization may take the form of a sole proprietorship, a partnership, or a corporation. The next three chapters of this textbook deal exclusively with the accounting and reporting problems associated with the partnership form of business. These chapters cover the complete life cycle from formation and operation of a partnership to its dissolution. Partnerships are covered because (1) accountants often serve in an advisory capacity to partnerships and they need to be aware of the legal, organizational, and other problems that pertain to them; (2) although many of the accounting concepts applicable to a sole proprietorship or a corporation are also applicable to partnerships, some aspects of partnership formation, operation, and liquidation require additional consideration.

PARTNERSHIP DEFINED

A partnership is defined by the Uniform Partnership Act (UPA) as "an association of two or more persons to carry on as co-owners a business for profit."[1] Persons in this definition include individuals, partnerships, corporations, and other associations. Although the partnership agreement may be complex, all that is required legally for a partnership to exist is a co-ownership of assets that are used by a business to derive a profit.

---

[1]Uniform Partnership Act (UPA), Sec. 6. The UPA is integrated throughout the partnership chapters because it is the partnership law adopted by the majority of the states. A more in-depth study of the legal aspects of partnerships is generally contained in the typical business law course.

FEATURES OF A PARTNERSHIP

Each of the three basic legal forms of business organization has certain advantages and disadvantages. Partnerships are common for some or all of the following reasons:

1. *Pooling of Resources.* Partnerships permit the pooling of limited resources that may not be available to an individual proprietor. Resources may be in the form of operating capital, managerial ability, or physical capital.

2. *Ease of Formation.* Formation of a partnership can be very simple. The agreement can be oral; preferably it is in writing. Unlike a corporation, a partnership requires no government approval before it can be formed; thus, there may be a saving in organization cost.

3. *Possible Tax Advantage.* Tax laws are complex and should be considered carefully in deciding what form of business organization to adopt. A partnership is not subject to income tax; the individual partners report their share of the partnership income, whether distributed or not, on their respective individual income tax returns. This tax provision may be an advantage in the case of a partnership loss, since a partner may deduct his share of partnership losses on his individual tax return. In contrast, income of a corporation is subject to double taxation; the corporation is a taxable entity and dividends are taxed when distributed to the stockholders.

4. *Organization in Professional Fields.* Until recently, individuals in some professional fields were prohibited from organizing as a corporation either by state law or by their professional code of ethics. If professionals wanted to pool their resources, then their only alternative was the partnership form of organization. Now, in certain professional fields, individuals are permitted to incorporate if legal requirements are satisfied.[2]

There are other distinctive features of a partnership that may make the partnership form of business less attractive.

1. *Mutual Agency.* Every partner is an agent of the partnership and every other partner. A partner can bind the other partners to a contract if he or she is acting within the apparent scope of the business. Therefore, outside parties transacting business with a partner can assume the partner has the power to bind the partnership unless informed otherwise.

2. *Right to Dispose of a Partnership Interest.* A capital interest in a partnership is a personal asset of the individual partner which can be sold or disposed of in any legal way. However, the UPA, recognizing the highly personal relationship of the partners, provides that a purchaser of another partner's interest does not have the right to participate in management decisions unless he or she is accepted by all the partners.

---

[2]For example, individuals are now permitted to incorporate and conduct a public accounting practice if all provisions of the Code of Professional Ethics are satisfied. See Rule 505 and Appendix B, *Restatement of the Code of Professional Ethics,* (New York: American Institute of Certified Public Accountants), March 1, 1973.

The new partner is entitled to the profit allocation acquired and, in the event of liquidation, to receive whatever assets the selling partner would have received had he continued in the partnership.

3. *Unlimited Liability.* Partnerships can be classified in a number of different ways. One form of classification is by the type of partnership interest held by the individual partners. A general partnership is one in which all the partners have unlimited liability for partnership debts, i.e., in the case of liquidation, the creditors of the partnership, if not satisfied from assets of the partnership, can look to an individual partner's personal assets for recovery of any remaining debt balances. In a limited partnership, one or more of the partners have limited their liability for partnership debts to the amount invested or agreed to be invested in the partnership.

4. *Limited Life.* A partnership may be dissolved for any number of reasons, such as the death of a partner, the bankruptcy of a partner, or the dissolution of the partnership by a court if one partner becomes unable to carry out his part of the partnership agreement.

The prospective owners should carefully consider the advantages and disadvantages of the various forms of business organization before selecting the one that they believe best meets their organizational objectives and personal goals. It is possible for a firm to start as a sole proprietorship and, as the business and personal environment changes, to move to a partnership form of organization, and ultimately, to incorporate.

FORMATION OF A PARTNERSHIP

Partnership Agreement

As noted earlier, a partnership agreement may be oral, but for the protection of the partners the agreement should be in writing. Written agreements are generally referred to as the articles of partnership. The partnership agreement should fully reflect the intentions of the parties and be as unambiguous as possible. Legally the partners have a great deal of flexibility, but it may be wise for them to seek professional assistance (e.g., legal and accounting) to help them anticipate and attempt to avoid as many points of conflict as possible. If subsequent disagreements cannot be settled by the partners, it may be necessary to resort to litigation, in which case the courts will attempt to interpret the partnership agreement. The interpretation by the courts may be at variance with the original intentions of one or more of the partners.

The articles of partnership should be as explicit as possible and should include the following important points:

1. The partnership name and identity of the partners.

2. The nature, purpose, and scope of the business.

3. The effective date of organization.

4. The length of time the partnership is to operate.

5. Location of the place of business.

6. Provision for the allocation of profit and loss.

7. Provision for salaries and withdrawals of assets by partners.

8. Amount of time each partner will spend on business activities, and duties of each partner.

9. Authority of each partner in contract situations.

10. Provisions for the withdrawal of a partner.

11. Provisions to cover how operations are to be conducted and how the various partners' interests are to be satisfied upon the death of a partner.

12. Procedures to be followed in the event of disputes.

13. Fiscal period of the partnership.

14. Identification and valuation of initial asset contributions and the specification of capital interest that each respective partner is to receive.

Some of the items above will be discussed in more detail in subsequent sections.

Recording the Formation of a Partnership

Assets contributed to the partnership, any debts assumed by the partnership, and the capital interest each partner is to receive should be specified in the partnership agreement. A listing of partnership assets is important because creditors of the partnership must satisfy their claims from partnership assets before seeking recovery of unpaid claims from the personal assets of individual partners.

In drafting the partnership agreement, the partners must recognize that there is a distinction between a partner's interest in capital and his interest in profit and losses subsequently reported by the partnership. A partner's capital balance represents a respective interest in the net assets of the partnership; an interest in profit and loss determines how the partner's capital interest will increase or decrease as a result of subsequent operations. The partners may agree that an individual partner is to receive a one-third capital interest in the newly created partnership, but the same partner's interest in profits and losses may be greater than or less than one-third.

Assets contributed to the partnership can be either cash or noncash assets, such as land, equipment, or managerial talent. The contribution of noncash assets may create valuation problems. In fairness to the partners, since a gain or loss recognized on the sale of an asset is allocated in the agreed profit and loss ratio, assets contributed to the partnership should be recorded at fair value. For example, assume that X contributed land to a partnership that had a cost to X of $30,000 and a current fair market value of

$60,000. Further, assume that the partnership subsequently disposed of the land for $70,000. If the land had been recorded at $30,000 on the partnership books, the $40,000 gain, $30,000 of which occurred before the property was owned by the partnership, must now be shared with the other partners.[3] A more equitable treatment would be to have X receive a capital credit of $60,000 since he had assumed all risks or rewards of ownership before contributing the land to the partnership. An understatement in the value of the land would be detrimental to X, whereas an overstatement would be detrimental to the other partners.

Once the partners agree as to the identification and valuation of assets being contributed, liabilities being assumed by the partnership, and the capital interest that each partner is to receive, the assets, liabilities, and equities are recorded on the books of the partnership. To illustrate, assume that the following items are being contributed to form XY Partnership:

| | AGREED FAIR MARKET VALUES | |
	CONTRIBUTED BY X	CONTRIBUTED BY Y
Cash	10,000	10,000
Inventory	10,000	—
Land	—	20,000
Building	—	40,000
Equipment	20,000	—
Totals	40,000	70,000
Mortgage on building assumed by the partnership	—	20,000
Net assets contributed	40,000	50,000

The journal entry to record the initial contribution, assuming that X and Y agree that each partner is to receive a capital credit equal to the amount of the net assets he or she contributes, is:

Cash	20,000	
Inventory	10,000	
Land	20,000	
Building	40,000	
Equipment	20,000	
Mortgage Payable		20,000
X, Capital		40,000
Y, Capital		50,000

[3] For tax purposes, a partner's capital interest in the partnership is the amount of cash contributed. If noncash assets are contributed, his tax basis is the adjusted basis of the asset to him at the date of contribution reduced by the indebtedness assumed by the partnership.

A problem is encountered if the sum of the agreed net asset values does not equal the negotiated capital interest or if the agreement is unclear. For example, there are several possible interpretations of an agreement that each partner is to receive an equal capital interest. Two possible entries to record the formation, assuming the same facts as in the preceding paragraph, are as follows:

	I BONUS METHOD		II GOODWILL METHOD	
Cash	20,000		20,000	
Inventory	10,000		10,000	
Land	20,000		20,000	
Building	40,000		40,000	
Equipment	20,000		20,000	
Intangible*	—		10,000	
Mortgage Payable		20,000		20,000
X, Capital		45,000		50,000
Y, Capital		45,000		50,000

*Generally referred to as partnership goodwill.

Under the first method, there is a transfer of $5,000 from Partner Y to Partner X to equalize the capital balances. Such an entry is made if Y recognizes that X is contributing something to the firm other than tangible assets, but the partners are reluctant to recognize an intangible asset or a value for it cannot be objectively determined. The transfer is frequently referred to as a bonus from Y to X. Under the second method, the equalization is accomplished by recognizing an intangible asset with a corresponding increase in the credit to the capital account of X. It is assumed that the partners agree that X is contributing something of value to the partnership that is intangible in nature, and which could not be specifically identified. The value assigned to the intangible asset could have been more than $10,000. Partner Y may also be contributing an intangible asset to the partnership in addition to the tangible assets identified and valued. Unless the intangible is specifically identifiable, such as a patent, it should probably not be recognized. It is difficult to justify the recognition of an unspecified intangible such as goodwill on the books of a *new* partnership that does not have an established earnings record.

When recording goodwill, one must recognize the problems inherent in attempting to assign a value to an intangible. In particular, one can question whether the recognition of the intangible is based on an independent arm's-length transaction. Such a problem could be avoided if it had been anticipated when the articles of partnership were drafted. In the absence of such a provision in the articles of partnership, the interpretation of the agreement must ultimately be made by the partners. Other than the accountant's normal reluctance to recognize goodwill, there is no basis in accounting theory to settle the disagreement. The accountant could be of service to the partners by indicating the alternatives available and the impact of each alternative on future financial statements. For example, if the partners agree to share profits and losses equally, both methods will produce the same result, because the amortization of the intangible will eventually result in a $5,000 reduction of each partner's capital interest.

ACCOUNTING FOR A PARTNERSHIP SUBSEQUENT TO FORMATION

A partnership is not a separate entity for income tax purposes. It is frequently maintained a partnership is not even a legal entity. However, certain legal provisions (e.g., the title to partnership assets may be registered in the partnership name) suggest that the partnership may indeed be regarded as a separate legal entity. For accounting purposes, a partnership is considered a separate economic and accounting entity. The assets, liabilities, and residual capital interest, as well as the transactions and events that affect the accounts of the partnership, are areas of interest which require a separable accounting to provide information to the partners and other interested parties. Separation of these activities from the personal transactions of the individual partners is necessary in order to evaluate the performance of the partnership. This does not mean that other forms of statements cannot be prepared for other purposes. For example, a general partner has unlimited liability to the creditors of the partnership. Accordingly, the creditors may require information concerning the personal assets and debt position of individual partners, as well as the financial statements of the firm.

Accounting for a partnership basically follows the same procedures and adheres to the same generally accepted accounting principles as accounting for a sole proprietorship or a corporation. The primary difference in accounting for the three forms of organization is in the recording and reporting of capital transactions. Where a corporation's equity section purports to report the different sources of capital (e.g., capital stock, additional paid-in capital, and retained earnings), a partnership's equity section consists of one capital account and one drawing account for each partner. Practice varies as to which of the two accounts is changed by capital transactions. Generally, asset contributions and withdrawals considered to be other than temporary are recognized in the capital account. The drawing account is typically debited to record withdrawals of assets in anticipation of profitable operations or payments of personal expenses of a partner from partnership assets. It is common practice to close the income summary to either the drawing account or capital account. The drawing account may be closed periodically to the capital account. The various sources of capital may thus be combined into one account.

In order to provide a comparison with the corporate form of organization, it may be useful to accumulate undistributed profits in the drawing account and to reserve the capital account for permanent investment. This separation would recognize the distinction between capital originating from operations and capital contributed by the partners.

When closing the income summary account, the profit or loss must be allocated to each partner. Such an entry, assuming a $20,000 profit to be divided equally, takes the following form:

Income Summary	20,000	
A, Capital or Drawing		10,000
B, Capital or Drawing		10,000

If the partnership experienced an operating loss during the period, the capital or drawing account is debited.

The allocation of profit or loss between the partners is based on the profit and loss ratio. Such an allocation is not necessary if the organization is a sole proprietorship or corporation. Obviously, in a sole proprietorship, there is only one residual equityholder who has total claim to all the residual assets and all profits or losses. In a corporation, a holder of one share of stock has an interest equal to any other share in the assets of the firm and profit or loss of the firm. However, a partner's interest in profits will in most cases not be equal to his interest in assets. Therefore, it is necessary in the closing process to allocate the balance in the income summary account to the partner's capital account on the basis of their profit and loss agreement.

ALLOCATION OF PROFIT OR LOSS

The partners should include in the articles of partnership a provision indicating how profits or losses are to be allocated. The profit and loss agreement determines how much each partner's interest in the firm increases or decreases as a result of operations. Often one of the major problems of accounting for a partnership is to determine the intent of the partners as indicated in the partnership agreement. The partners have much flexibility in the area; however, if the intent of the partners is unclear, it may be necessary to settle the disagreement by litigation. To avoid disagreement and potential litigation, the profit and loss agreement should be explicitly stated even to the extent of including examples of application of the allocation agreement in the articles of partnership. In the absence of an agreement, courts have generally concluded that the intent of the parties was to allocate profits and losses equally. If a provision for profits, but not losses, is included in the agreement, the courts have generally concluded that losses should be allocated in the same ratio that profits are allocated. Therefore, if losses are to be allocated differently than profits, the agreement should so state.

The objective of the profit and loss agreement should be to reward the individual partners for their contributions to the partnership. Some of the more common agreements are based on some combination of the following:

1. Fixed ratio.

2. A ratio based on capital balances.

3. Interest on capital contribution.

4. A payment for time devoted to the partnership operation, either in the form of a fixed payment or a bonus as a percentage of income.

There are a number of possibilities, some of which will be illustrated in the following sections. Unless otherwise stated, income for the period of $20,000 is assumed.

Fixed Ratio

One of the simplest agreements is for each partner to be allocated profit or loss on the basis of an equal percentage or some other specified ratio each period. For example, A and B may agree that profit and loss is to be allocated in the ratio 7:3. A profit of $20,000 would be allocated $14,000 to A and $6,000 to B. Unless stated otherwise, a loss of $20,000 would also be allocated using a 7:3 ratio. If this is not the intent of the partners, a separate loss agreement should be negotiated.

Capital Balance

Assets invested in the partnership are important resources. The allocation of profits on the basis of the ratio of capital balances may result in an equitable distribution of profits where operation of the partnership requires little of the partner's time, e.g., the operation of an apartment building in which there is a hired manager. To avoid conflicts, the capital ratio to be used should be clearly stated as, for example, original investment, beginning-of-year balances, average, or end-of-year balances. The partners should recognize that distributions based on beginning and ending balances could be inequitable. For example, if the allocation ratio is based on ending balances, a partner could make a large capital contribution at the end of the year. To avoid such abuse, partners may want to provide for restrictions on contributions and withdrawals.

Assuming that the ratio is based on beginning capital balances and that A and B had balances of $60,000 and $40,000, respectively, the net income of $20,000 would be allocated as follows:

CAPITAL INVESTMENT	NET INCOME ALLOCATION
A 60,000	$(60,000/100,000) \times 20,000 = 12,000$
B 40,000	$(40,000/100,000) \times 20,000 = \underline{8,000}$
100,000	20,000

Frequently, net income allocation is based on a ratio of the weighted-average capital investment as computed in Illustration 14–1.

The first step in the computation is to multiply the various capital balances that each partner maintained during the year by the unit of time that a particular capital balance was maintained. In this illustration, the capital balances are weighted by the number of months. Other units of time, such as weeks, could be used as weights if the partners so specify. To derive the weighted-average capital investment, the sum of the weighted products is divided by the sum of the weights (12 months). The $20,000 net income is allocated on the basis of the ratio of the average capital investment.

AVERAGE INVESTMENT		NET INCOME ALLOCATION
A	77,500	$(77{,}500/115{,}000) \times 20{,}000 = 13{,}478$
B	37,500	$(37{,}500/115{,}000) \times 20{,}000 = 6{,}522$
Total	115,000	20,000

The allocation of a loss on the basis of the ratio of capital balances would mean that Partner A, who has contributed the most capital, would absorb the greatest amount of the loss, which may be considered an unreasonable allocation. If this is the case, the partners may want to negotiate a different ratio for the allocation of losses.

Interest on Capital Contribution

Using the ratio of capital balances as the basis for allocation of profit assumes that invested capital is the most important resource of the partnership. However, in many profit-making organizations, it is only one resource, and other factors should be recognized. To recognize other factors and still provide an equitable allocation, the partners may want to provide for interest on capital investment and allocate the remaining profit on some other basis. Such a provision may also provide an incentive for capital to be invested, if the firm has a use for added investment. Again the key is to be as explicit as possible to avoid problems in applying the agreement. The agreement should specify at least: (1) the interest rate, (2) which capital balance is to be used (beginning, ending, or average), (3) how remaining profits should be allocated, and (4) whether or not interest should still be allocated in case of loss or in case profits are less than the agreed interest allocation. It is easy to overlook provision No. 4, but as will be shown, in the event of disagreement between the partners, the lack of such an express provision would result in an interest allocation being made when there is a reported loss or when profits are insufficient to cover the interest allocation.

If interest is part of the profit allocation formula, the partners must be careful to distinguish between capital investments and loans. The UPA [Section 18(d)] provides that unless otherwise stated, a partner is not entitled to receive interest on capital investment except in cases where capital is not repaid on the due date. Then the partner is entitled to the legal rate. However, advances made in excess of the agreed contribution are considered creditor equity in the firm and subject to repayment with interest. Accountants also recognize this distinction and record interest on loan balances as expense, whereas interest on capital is recorded as an allocation of profit.

Frequently, the interest allocation is based on weighted-average capital investment. To illustrate, assume the same average investment as in Illustration 14–1.

ILLUSTRATION 14-1
Computation of Weighted-Average Capital Balances

A, CAPITAL	INCREASE (DECREASE) IN CAPITAL	CUMULATIVE BALANCE	NUMBER OF MONTHS BALANCE MAINTAINED	WEIGHTED TOTAL INVESTMENT
January 1 Beginning Balance		60,000	3	180,000
April 1 Added Investment	30,000	90,000	3	270,000
July 1 Withdrawal	(10,000)	80,000	6	480,000
				930,000

930,000 / 12 months = 77,500

B, CAPITAL				
January 1 Beginning Balance		40,000	9	360,000
October 1 Withdrawal	(10,000)	30,000	3	90,000
				450,000

450,000 / 12 months = 37,500

Interest is then computed on this amount. Assuming a net income of $20,000, an 8% rate of interest, and that any remaining profit is to be divided equally, the profit is allocated as follows:

INTEREST ALLOCATION	A	B	TOTAL
$77,500 × .08 =	6,200		6,200
$37,500 × .08 =		3,000	3,000
Total Interest Allocated	6,200	3,000	9,200
Remainder equally	5,400	5,400	10,800
Total to be Allocated	11,600	8,400	20,000

Salary

The UPA [Section 18(f)] provides that a partner is not entitled to remuneration for services performed for the partnership unless such remuneration is provided for by the partners in their profit and loss agreement. The partners may provide, as part of the profit and loss formula, a salary allowance to reward a partner(s) for personal services contributed in managing the partnership operations. The amount by which net income exceeds the salary allowances may then be divided using a ratio of other resources contributed by the partners. Traditionally, accountants have considered a salary allowance as a determinant in the allocation of net income, rather than as an expense to be considered in the determination of the amount of net income. For example, if A devotes full time to the business activity and B spends a limited amount of time, the partnership agreement may provide that A is to receive a salary of $1,000 per month and that the remaining profit is to be divided on the basis of the ratio of the beginning capital balances ($60,000 and $40,000, respectively). The allocation would be as follows:

	A		B	TOTAL
Salary allowance	12,000		–0–	12,000
Remainder 60,000/100,000	4,800	40,000/100,000	3,200	8,000
	16,800		3,200	20,000

A salary agreement is considered part of the profit and loss allocation formula and may be made independent of the agreement between the partners as to the right to withdraw cash or other assets from the partnership. However, since the term salary is normally understood to mean a cash payment for services received, it is important that the partners specify their intentions as to salaries or asset withdrawals. For example, assume that Partners A and B agree that they can withdraw $700 and $400 per month, respectively. The partnership agreement further provides that profit is to be divided equally. If the partners intend this to be a withdrawal agreement, then the $20,000 in net income is allocated equally ($10,000) to each partner. In this case the agreement to withdraw assets is not considered a part of the profit allocation. If their intention was that the withdrawals be considered salaries that could be withdrawn during the year in anticipation of profitable operations, then the $20,000 in income would be allocated as follows:

	A	B	TOTAL
Salary	8,400	4,800	13,200
Remainder equally	3,400	3,400	6,800
	11,800	8,200	20,000

Clearly, Partner A would prefer that the agreement to withdraw assets be considered a salary agreement as well. To avoid this potential conflict, the partnership agreement should be explicit as to the partner's intentions.

Instead of basing the salary allocation on a fixed amount, the partners may provide for a bonus arrangement as a percentage of profit. Since a number of interpretations can result, the partners should explicitly state the basis for calculating the amount of net income to be used in calculating the bonus. Some possibilities are:

1. Net income before any allocation of profit to partners (e.g., before interest on capital, salaries to partners, and any bonus).

2. Net income after other income allocations, but before subtracting the bonus.

3. Net income after subtracting the bonus, but before subtracting the other allocations.

4. Net income after subtracting the bonus and other allocations from net income.

Calculation of the bonus in the first two alternatives is straightforward. To illustrate, Nos. 3 and 4 assume that net income is $24,000 and a bonus of 20% is to be paid to A. Also, interest of $4,000 and $2,000 is to be allocated to A and B, respectively, and any remainder is to be allocated equally. The bonus and a proof of the calculation are as follows:

NO. 3	NO. 4
Bonus = .2($24,000 − B)	Bonus = .2($24,000 − $6,000 − B)
Bonus = $4,800 − .2B	Bonus = .2($18,000 − B)
1.2 Bonus = $4,800	Bonus = $3,600 − .2B
Bonus = $4,000	1.2 Bonus = $3,600
	Bonus = $3,000

Proof:

	NO. 3	NO. 4
Net income	24,000	24,000
Bonus	4,000	3,000
Interest	—	6,000
Income subject to bonus	20,000	15,000
	B = .2($20,000)	B = .2($15,000)
	B = $4,000	B = $3,000

The profit allocation for situation No. 3 is as follows:

	A	B	TOTAL
Bonus	4,000		4,000
Interest	4,000	2,000	6,000
	8,000	2,000	10,000
Remainder—equally	7,000	7,000	14,000
Total	15,000	9,000	24,000

Allocation of the income for situation No. 4 would be similar except the bonus would be $3,000 to A, and each partner would be allocated $7,500 in the residual calculation.

	A	B	TOTAL
Bonus	3,000		3,000
Interest	4,000	2,000	6,000
	7,000	2,000	9,000
Remainder—equally	7,500	7,500	15,000
	14,500	9,500	24,000

Frequently, to provide for an equitable allocation based on the various resources employed by the partnership, a profit and loss agreement may provide for a salary allowance and interest on capital invested and divide the remainder in some agreed ratio. For example, assume that A and B agree to divide $20,000 profits as follows:

1. Salary: A, $4,000; B, $2,000.

2. Interest: 8% on average capital balance (see Illustration 14–1).

3. Remainder: To be divided equally.

The profit allocation would be as follows:

	A	B	TOTAL
Salary	4,000	2,000	6,000
Interest	6,200	3,000	9,200
	10,200	5,000	15,200
Remainder	2,400	2,400	4,800
Totals	12,600	7,400	20,000

Insufficient Profits to Cover Allocation

In some cases, the partnership net income may be less than the allocation of interest and/or salary provided in the partnership agreement. If the partners fail to provide for such an occurrence in the profit and loss formula, the established practice is to allocate the interest and/or salary as if sufficient profit had been earned. The amount by which the salary and/or interest exceeds the net income is allocated to the individual partners in their agreed ratio for allocating residual profit. A net income of $11,000 would be allocated as follows, assuming the partnership agreement used in the previous example:

	A	B	TOTAL
Salary	4,000	2,000	6,000
Interest	6,200	3,000	9,200
	10,200	5,000	15,200
Excess allocation (11,000 − 15,200)	(2,100)	(2,100)	(4,200)
Profit allocation	8,100	2,900	11,000

The entry to close the Income Summary account is:

Income Summary	11,000	
A, Capital (Drawing)		8,100
B, Capital (Drawing)		2,900

As will be shown in the next section, this procedure produces the same results as if the partners' salary and interest had been expensed in the determination of the partnership net income or loss.

In the case of a loss of $20,000, the allocation would be as follows:

	A	B	TOTAL
Salary	4,000	2,000	6,000
Interest	6,200	3,000	9,200
	10,200	5,000	15,200
Excess allocation (− 20,000 − 15,200)	(17,600)	(17,600)	(35,200)
Loss allocation	(7,400)	(12,600)	(20,000)

To avoid such an allocation, the partners may elect to state an alternative allocation in the articles of partnership. Once again, this situation indicates a need for careful planning in drafting the partnership agreement.

SPECIAL PROBLEMS IN ALLOCATION OF PROFIT AND LOSS

Salaries and Interest as an Expense

In the foregoing illustrations, salaries and interest were accounted for as an allocation of net income rather than as an expense in the determination of net income. However, the partners may find the income statement more useful for evaluating the operating performance of the partnership if either or both salaries and interest were treated as an expense in the determination of net income. If the salary levels and interest rates are reasonable for the resources provided, the income statement for the partnership may be more comparable to income statements of nonpartnership forms of organizations. To illustrate, assume that the partnership reported net income of $11,000 before the interest and salary of the partners. The partners are to be allocated salaries and interest as follows:

	A	B
Salary	4,000	2,000
Interest	6,200	3,000

The partners agree to allocate residual profit and loss evenly. Journal entries to record the salary and interest are:

Salary Expense	6,000	
A, Capital (Drawing)		4,000
B, Capital (Drawing)		2,000
Interest Expense	9,200	
A, Capital (Drawing)		6,200
B, Capital (Drawing)		3,000

Net loss for the period after salaries and interest is $4,200, computed as follows:

Net income before salaries and interest		11,000
Less: Salary expense	6,000	
Interest expense	9,200	15,200
Net Loss		4,200

After the revenue and expense accounts are closed, the Income Summary would have a debit balance of $4,200 which would be allocated evenly to the partners as agreed. The following entry is recorded to close the income summary account:

A, Capital (Drawing)	2,100	
B, Capital (Drawing)	2,100	
Income Summary		4,200

Changes in the capital accounts are presented below:

A, CAPITAL

From Income Summary	2,100	Salary entry	4,000
		Interest entry	6,200
		Net change in capital	8,100

B, CAPITAL

From Income Summary	2,100	Salary entry	2,000
		Interest entry	3,000
		Net change in capital	2,900

This procedure results in the same change in the capital accounts as if the salary and expense were considered an allocation of profit. (See the illustration in the preceding section when profits were insufficient to cover salary and interest allocations.) The method of reporting that is selected should be the one that provides the most useful information to the partners. Since the normal practice is to recognize salaries and interest as an allocation of profit, any such amounts expensed should be adequately disclosed so the statement reader can properly evaluate the operating performance of the firm.

Adjustment of Income of Prior Years

Errors may occur in accounting for partnership operations, such as a failure to accrue or defer expenses or revenue, errors in the inventory count or pricing, and/or errors in the calculation or amortization of fixed assets. Problems in the allocation of profit and loss can result if (1) errors are discovered that occurred in specific prior years, and (2) the partners have altered the profit and loss agreement since the period in which the error occurred. In a corporation, an error correction is accounted for as an adjustment of the beginning retained earnings balance. However, in a partnership the correction is allocated to the individual partner's capital accounts. The allocation should be based on the profit and loss agreement in effect during the period of the error.

Other allocation problems may arise, such as market changes in assets being held for investment purposes that occur before a change in the allocation formula, or an adjustment for bad debts which cannot be attributed to any specific period. There is no clear-cut answer to such problems. Litigation can be avoided by providing for the treatment of such problems in the partnership agreement.

FINANCIAL STATEMENT PRESENTATION

The income statement, balance sheet, and statement of changes in financial position for a partnership are prepared in much the same manner as they are for a corporation. The following is a list of some of the differences in partnership reporting:

1. On the balance sheet each individual partner's equity in the business is reported.

2. Salaries are generally recognized as an allocation of net income, not as an expense in the determination of net income.

3. There is no income tax expense. The partners report their share of the partnership income or loss for the period on their individual income tax returns.

4. Interest is not recognized as an expense unless it is paid on contributions considered debt of the partnership. Interest paid on capital is considered an allocation of profit.

A statement of changes in partners' capital is prepared to disclose changes in the interest of each partner during the year as follows:

AB Partnership
Statement of Partners' Capital
For Year Ended December 31, 1980

	A	B	TOTAL
Capital Balance, January 1, 1980	$ 60,000	$40,000	$100,000
Add: Additional Investment	30,000	-0-	30,000
Net Income Allocation	16,800	3,200	20,000
	$106,800	$43,200	$150,000
Less: Withdrawals	10,000	10,000	20,000
Capital Balance, December 31, 1980	$ 96,800	$33,200	$130,000

For some external reporting purposes such detail may not be considered necessary. The partnership capital, for example, may be reported as one amount and the capital balance of each partner may be disclosed in a supplementary schedule or not disclosed at all.

Questions

1. How is a partnership defined by the Uniform Partnership Act? What does the term "persons" encompass in this definition?

2. Is a partnership required to pay income tax? Describe a specific tax advantage of the partnership form of business over the corporate form.

3. List some important provisions that should be included in a partnership agreement.

4. Distinguish between a partner's interest in capital and his interest in the partnership's profits and losses. Also, make a general distinction between a partner's capital account and his drawing account.

5. In 1980, Morris contributed land worth $50,000 in exchange for a 20% interest in the Hugh-Daley partnership. Morris paid $20,000 for this property in 1970. In 1981 the partnership sold the land for $60,000. How much gain should the partnership record in this transaction? Why would a recording of Morris's initial contribution of this land at his cost be inequitable?

6. Is there any difference in results between the goodwill method and the bonus method of recording a partner's capital contribution? What if the partners agree to share profits and losses equally? Would this affect your answer?

7. Explain why a partnership is viewed in accounting as a "separate economic entity."

8. Krikston, Gruber, and Baxter began the KGB partnership in 1980 with these contributions:

   Krikston—$10,000 cash and $10,000 worth of inventory.
   Gruber— Land worth $30,000 which cost Gruber $20,000.
   Baxter— A building that cost Baxter $20,000 with a mortgage unpaid of $20,000. This building has a fair market value of $30,000.

   Give the journal entry recording these initial partnership contributions, assuming that each partner is to receive an equal capital interest. If more than one interpretation of the agreement is possible, present at least two possibilities.

9. What are some of the methods commonly used in allocating profit and loss to the partners?

10. Is there any advantage to accumulating profits in the drawing accounts of the partners rather than in their capital accounts?

11. Describe the difference in the accounting treatment of "interest" on a partner's loan, and "interest" on his capital balance.

12. Explain the distinction between the terms "withdrawals" and "salaries."

13. Discuss some of the alternative methods of calculating a bonus which may appear in a partnership agreement.

14. What generally happens to interest and salary allocations to partners provided for in a partnership agreement when profits are insufficient to cover these payments?

15. How is the correction of a prior year's errors accounted for by a partnership?

16. Justify treating a partner's salary or his interest on capital as an expense.

17. Partners C and K share profits and losses equally after each has been credited in all circumstances with annual salary allowances of $15,000 and $12,000, respectively. Under this arrangement, C will benefit by $3,000 more than K in which of the following circumstances?
a. Only if the partnership has earnings of $27,000 or more for the year.
b. Only if the partnership does not incur a loss for the year.
c. In all earnings or loss situations.
d. Only if the partnership has earnings of at least $3,000 for the year.

(AICPA adapted)

Problems

Problem 14-1
Henry, Allen, and Dobbs decided to engage in a real estate venture as a partnership. Henry contributed $50,000 cash and Allen provided an office and furnishings valued at $60,000. (There is a $10,000 note payable remaining on the furnishings to be assumed by the partnership.) Although Dobbs has no physical assets to contribute, both Henry and Allen feel that Dobbs' expert salesmanship provides an adequte contribution to capital.

Required:
Assuming that each partner is to receive an equal capital interest in the partnership,
A. Record the partnership formation under the bonus method.
B. Record the formation under the goodwill method, and assume a total goodwill of $50,000.
C. Discuss the appropriateness of using either the bonus or goodwill methods to record the formation of the partnership.

Problem 14-2
A. The partnership of Wayne and Ellen was formed on February 28, 1980. At that date the following assets were contributed:

	WAYNE	ELLEN
Cash	$25,000	$ 35,000
Merchandise	—	55,000
Building	—	100,000
Furniture and equipment	15,000	—

The building is subject to a mortgage loan of $30,000, which is to be assumed by the partnership. The partnership agreement provides that Wayne and Ellen share profits or losses 25% and 75%, respectively. Compute Ellen's capital account at February 28, 1980.

B. Using the same facts stated above, if the partnership agreement provides that the partners initially should have an equal interest in partnership capital with no contribution of intangible assets, what would Wayne's capital account be at February 28, 1980?

(AICPA adapted)

Problem 14–3

On January 1, 1980, Andrews and Moorely formed the A and M Company with capital contributions of $40,000 and $25,000, respectively. The partners wanted to draft a profit and loss agreement that would reward each individual for the resources contributed to the partnership. Accordingly, the partnership agreement provides that profits are to be allocated as follows:

1. Annual salaries of $5,000 and $7,000 are granted to Andrews and Moorely, respectively.

2. In addition to the salary, Andrews is entitled to a bonus of 10% of net income after salaries and bonus but before interest on capital contributions is subtracted.

3. Each partner is to receive an interest credit of 5% on the original capital investment.

4. Remaining profits are to be allocated 30% to Andrews and 70% to Moorely.

On December 31, 1980, the partnership reported net income before salaries, interest, and bonus of $34,000.

Required:
Calculate the 1980 allocation of partnership profit.

Problem 14–4

Kuster and Manko formed an accounting partnership in 1980. Capital transactions for Kuster and Manko during 1980 are as follows:

DATE	TRANSACTION	AMOUNT
	KUSTER	
January 1	Beginning Balance	$40,000
April 1	Withdrawal	10,000
June 1	Investment	20,000
November 1	Investment	10,000
	MANKO	
January 1	Beginning Balance	$20,000
July 1	Investment	10,000
October 1	Withdrawal	5,000

Partnership net income for the year ended December 31, 1980 is $30,000 before considering salaries or interest.

Required:

Determine the amount of profit that is to be allocated to Kuster and Manko in accordance with each of the following independent profit-sharing agreements.

1. Kuster and Manko failed to provide a profit-sharing arrangement in the articles of partnership and fail to compromise on an agreement.
2. Net income is to be allocated 60% to Kuster and 40% to Manko.
3. Net income is to be allocated in the ratio of ending capital balances.
4. Net income is to be allocated in the ratio of average capital balances.
5. Interest of 8% is to be granted on average capital balances, salaries of $6,000 and $4,000 are to be allocated to Kuster and Manko, respectively, and the remainder is to be divided equally.
6. Manko is allocated a bonus of 25% on net income after the bonus, but before distributing salaries or interest. Interest of 8% is to be allocated in the ratio of beginning capital balances. A salary allowance of $6,000 is granted to Kuster and $4,000 to Manko. Any remainder is to be divided equally.

Problem 14–5

Able, Baker, and Carter are partners in a retail clothing store. The partnership was formed January 1, 1980, with each partner investing $30,000. They agreed that *profits* are to be shared as follows:

1. Monthly salaries are to be allowed as follows:

Able	$1,000
Baker	500
Carter	200

2. Baker is to receive a bonus of 10% of net income before subtracting salaries and interest, but after subtracting the bonus.

3. Interest of 5% is granted on the beginning-of-year capital balances.

4. Any remainder is to be allocated equally.

The partners provide that net income is to be divided in the ratio of 40:30:30 if net income is not sufficient to cover salaries, bonus, and interest. A net loss is to be allocated equally.
Operating performance and other capital transactions were as follows:

		CAPITAL TRANSACTIONS					
YEAR	NET INCOME	ABLE		BAKER		CARTER	
END	(LOSS)	INVESTMENT	WITHDRAWALS	INVESTMENT	WITHDRAWALS	INVESTMENT	WITHDRAW
12/31/80	($ 3,600)	$10,000	$12,000	$10,000	$6,000	$5,000	$2,400
12/31/81	$20,000	-0-	$12,000	-0-	$6,000	$5,000	$2,400
12/31/82	$50,000	-0-	$14,000	-0-	$8,000	$5,000	$2,400

Required:

A. Prepare a schedule of changes in partners' capital accounts for each of the three years.
B. Prepare the journal entry to close the income (loss) at the end of each year.

Problem 14–6
Hill, Mills, and Decker form a partnership and agree to share profits equally after recognition of 10% interest on beginning capital balances and monthly salary allowances of $1,000 to Hill and $500 to Decker. Capital balances on January 1 were as follows:

Hill	$30,000
Mills	20,000
Decker	30,000

Required:
Calculate the net income (loss) allocation to each partner under each of the following independent situations.
1. Net income is $38,000.
2. Net income is $17,000.
3. Net loss is $4,000.

Problem 14–7
Ford and Evans have been operating a business as a partnership for 5 years. The following capital accounts reflect the current year's capital transactions:

FORD, CAPITAL				EVANS, CAPITAL			
5/1	$5,000	1/1	$25,000	7/1	$10,000	1/1	$35,000
		3/1	10,000	9/1	5,000		

Required:
Prepare the journal entry to close a credit balance of $40,000 in the revenue and expense summary account, assuming that profits are allocated under each of the following independent agreements:
1. A salary allowance of $15,000 is granted to Ford, and any residual is to be allocated in the ratio of ending capital balances.
2. Interest of 6% is allowed on average capital balances, salary of $17,000 is granted to Ford, and any remainder is allocated equally.
3. Interest of 6% is allowed on ending capital balances, salaries of $1,200 and $800 per month are allocated to Ford and Evans, respectively, and any remainder is allocated equally.

Problem 14–8
S and T agree to form a partnership on January 1, 1980. S agrees to invest $30,000, and T agrees to invest $10,000. The partners agree that partnership profits are to be shared as follows:

1. Interest—5% on the beginning capital balance.

2. Salary—$6,000 to T.

3. Bonus—30% to T.

4. Residual—divided equally.

Required:
Prepare a schedule to allocate a profit of $34,000 under each of the following independent situations:

1. Bonus is to be based on net income before any profit allocations to partners for interest and salary.

2. Bonus is to be based on net income after subtracting the bonus, but before allocation to partners for interest and salary.

3. Bonus is to be based on net income after subtracting the bonus, interest, and salary.

Problem 14–9

Geller and Harden formed a partnership on January 2, 1980, and agreed to share profits 90% and 10%, respectively. Geller contributed capital of $25,000. Harden contributed no capital but has professional managerial skills which he employs in managing the firm full time. There were no withdrawals during the year. The partnership agreement provides for the following:

1. Capital accounts are to be credited annually with interest at 5% of beginning capital.

2. Harden is to be paid a salary of $1,000 a month.

3. Harden is to receive a bonus of 20% of income calculated before deducting his salary and interest on both capital accounts.

4. Bonus, interest, and Harden's salary are to be considered partnership expenses.

The partnership 1980 income statement follows:

Revenues	$96,450
Expenses (including salary, interest and bonus)	49,700
Net income	$46,750

Required:
Compute Harden's 1980 bonus.

(AICPA adpated)

Problem 14–10

M, N, and O have been partners throughout the year 1980. Their average balances for the year and their balances at the end of the year before closing the nominal accounts are as follows:

PARTNER	AVERAGE BALANCES	BALANCES 12/31/80
M	$90,000	$60,000
N	3,000	1,000*
O	7,000	10,000

*Debit Balance

The profit for 1980 is $75,000 before charging partners' salary allowances and before payment of interest on average balances at the agreed rate of 4% per annum. Annual salary allocations are $10,000 to M, $7,000 to N, and $5,000 to O. The balance of the profit is to be allocated at the rate of 60% to M, 30% to N, and 10% to O.

It is intended to distribute cash to the partners so that, after credits and allocations have been made as indicated in the preceding paragraph, the balances in the partners' accounts will be proportionate to their residual profit-sharing ratios. None of the partners is to pay in any money, but they wish to distribute the lowest possible amount of cash.

Required:
Prepare a schedule of partners' accounts, showing balances at the end of 1980 before closing, the allocations of the net profit for 1980, the cash distributed, and the closing balances.

(AICPA adapted)

Problem 14–11

Johnson and Turner are partners in a used car business. Their average capital balances for 1980 and their capital balances at the end of the year (before the nominal accounts were closed) are as follows:

	AVERAGE CAPITAL BALANCES	CAPITAL BALANCES 12/31/1980
Johnson	$60,000	$40,500
Turner	7,500	4,500

The partnership earned a net profit of $60,000 during 1980. The partners agree that net profit or loss is to be allocated as follows:

	JOHNSON	TURNER
Salary per year	$13,500	$9,000
Interest on average capital balances	5%	5%
Remaining profit	60%	40%

Required:
Compute the minimum amount of cash to be distributed to the partners so that the balance in each partner's capital account will be proportional to his profit-sharing ratio. The partners agree that no additional cash is to be contributed to the partnership.

Problem 14–12

Blake and Ellis have each been operating a separate business. A trial balance for each firm as of January 1, 1981, is presented below:

	BLAKE		ELLIS	
ACCOUNT	DEBIT	CREDIT	DEBIT	CREDIT
Cash	10,000		20,000	
Accounts receivable	20,000		25,000	
Inventory	25,000		20,000	
Equipment	40,000		50,000	
Building	80,000		–0–	
Land	50,000		–0–	
Accounts payable		40,000		30,000
Notes payable		90,000		50,000
Capital		95,000		35,000
Totals	225,000	225,000	115,000	115,000

Blake and Ellis agree to combine their operations and form a partnership effective January 1, 1981.

The two conducted an extensive review of the accounts. After some extended negotiations, the two agreed to the following adjustments:

The accounts receivable reported by Blake are to be contributed to the partnership at book value less a 10% adjustment. Blake used the FIFO method to account for inventory flows. The balance is considered to approximate replacement cost. Ellis had accounted for his inventory using the LIFO method. It is agreed that the inventory contributed by Ellis is understated by $7,000. Some of the duplicate equipment is to be sold by Ellis. Blake is to contribute to the business operated by Ellis cash equal to 50% of any loss on the equipment sale. Book value equipment of $30,000 is subsequently sold for $20,000. The remaining equipment is to be recorded at book value on the books of the partnership.

The appraised value of the building and land is $60,000 and $90,000, respectively. The accounts payable and the notes payable of Ellis are fairly valued. Blake's long-term note matures $30,000 each year on December 31 and bears a 6% rate of interest on the unpaid balance, also payable on December 31. If the partners were to obtain a similar loan today, the rate of interest would be 10%. All remaining assets and liabilities are to be assumed by the new partnership. Ellis is to contribute sufficient cash to give him a total capital balance equal to one-half of Blake's capital balance after giving effect to the loss allocation on the sale of the equipment by Ellis.

Required:

A. Record in general journal form the required adjustments on the books of the individual companies.
B. Journalize the contribution of assets and the assumption of the liabilities in separate entries for each partner on a new set of partnership books.
C. Journalize the cash contribution by Ellis.

Problem 14–13

A, B, and C, attorneys, agreed to consolidate their individual practices as of January 1, 1980. The partnership agreement included the following features:

1. Each partner's capital contribution was the net amount of the assets and liabilities taken over by the partnership, which were as follows:

	A	B	C
Cash	$ 5,000	$ 5,000	$ 5,000
Accounts receivable	14,000	6,000	16,000
Furniture and library	4,300	2,500	6,200
	23,300	13,500	27,200
Allowance for depreciation	2,400	1,500	4,700
Accounts payable	300	1,400	700
	2,700	2,900	5,400
Capital contributions	$20,600	$10,600	$21,800

Each partner guaranteed the collectibility of his receivables.

2. C had leased office space and was bound by the lease until June 30, 1980. The monthly rental was $600. The partners agreed to occupy C's office space until the expiration of the lease and to pay the rent. The partners concurred that the rent was too high for the space and that a fair

rental value would be $450 per month. The excess rent was to be charged to C at year-end. On July 1 the partners moved to new quarters with a monthly rental of $500.

3. No salaries were to be paid to the partners. The individual partners were to receive 20% of the gross fees billed to their respective clients during the first year of the partnership. After deducting operating expenses, the balance of the fees billed was to be credited to the partners' capital accounts in the following ratios: A, 40%; B, 35%; C, 25%.

On April 1, 1980, D was admitted to the partnership; he was to receive 20% of the fees from new business obtained after April 1 after deducting expenses applicable to that new business. Expenses were to be apportioned to the new business in the same ratio that total expenses, other than bad debt losses, bore to total gross fees.

The following information pertains to the partnership's activities in 1980:

1. Fees were billed as follows:

A's clients	$22,000
B's clients	12,000
C's clients	11,000
New business:	
Prior to April 1	3,000
After April 1	12,000
Total	$60,000

2. Total expenses, excluding depreciation and bad debt expenses, were $19,350, including the total amount paid for rent. Depreciation was to be computed at the rate of 10% on the gross asset value of $13,000. Depreciable assets purchased during 1980, on which one-half year's depreciation was to be taken, totaled $5,000.

3. Cash charges to the partners' accounts during the year were:

A	$ 5,200
B	4,400
C	5,800
D	2,500
	$17,900

4. Of A's and B's receivables, $1,200 and $450, respectively, proved to be uncollectible. A new client billed in March for $1,600 had been adjudged bankrupt, and a settlement of fifty cents on the dollar was made.

Required:

Prepare a statement of the partners' capital accounts for the year ended December 31, 1980. Supporting computations should be in good form. (Disregard income taxes.)

(AICPA adapted)

Problem 14–14

The partnerships of Down & Short and Need & Want started in business on July 1, 1977; each partnership owns one retail applicance store. It was agreed as of June 30, 1980, to combine the partnerships to form a new partnership to be known as Four Partners' Discount Stores.

The June 30, 1980 post-closing trial balances of the partnerships appear below.

The following additional information is available:

1. The profit and loss sharing ratios for the former partnerships were 40% to Down and 60% to Short, and 30% to Need and 70% to Want. The profit and loss sharing ratio for the new partnership will be Down, 20%; Short, 30%; Need, 15%; and Want, 35%.

2. The opening capital ratios for the new partnership are to be the same as the profit and loss sharing ratios for the new partnership. The capital to be assigned to Down & Short will total $225,000. Any cash settlements among the partners arising from capital account adjustments will be a private matter and will not be recorded on the partnership books.

3. The partners agreed that the allowance for bad debts for the new partnership is to be 3% of the accounts receivable balances.

4. The opening inventory of the new partnership is to be valued by the FIFO method. The inventory of Down & Short was valued by the FIFO method and the Need & Want inventory was valued by the LIFO method. The LIFO inventory represents 85% of its FIFO value.

5. Depreciation is to be computed by the double-declining balance method with a 10-year life for the depreciable assets. Depreciation for 3 years is to be accumulated in the opening balance of the Allowance for Depreciation account. Down & Short computed depreciation by the straight-line method, and Need & Want used the double-declining balance method. All assets were obtained on July 1, 1977.

6. After the books were closed, an unrecorded merchandise purchase of $4,000 by Need & Want was discovered. The merchandise had been sold by June 30, 1980.

7. The accounts of Down & Short include a vacation pay accrual. It was agreed that Need & Want should make a similar accrual for their ten employees, who will receive a two-week vacation at $100 per employee per week.

Required:

A. Prepare a worksheet to determine the opening balances of a new partnership after giving effect to the information above. Formal journal entries are not required. Supporting computations, including the computation of goodwill, should be in good form.

B. Prepare a schedule computing the cash to be exchange between Down & Short, and between Need & Want, in settlement of the affairs of each original partnership.

	DOWN & SHORT TRIAL BALANCE JUNE 30, 1980		NEED & WANT TRIAL BALANCE JUNE 30, 1980	
Cash	$ 20,000		$ 15,000	
Accounts receivable	100,000		150,000	
Allowance for doubtful accounts		$ 2,000		$ 6,000
Merchandise inventory	175,000		119,000	
Land	25,000		35,000	
Buildings and equipment	80,000		125,000	
Allowance for depreciation		24,000		61,000
Prepaid expenses	5,000		7,000	
Accounts payable		40,000		60,000
Notes payable		70,000		75,000
Accrued expenses		30,000		45,000
Down, Capital		95,000		
Short, Capital		144,000		
Need, Capital				65,000
Want, Capital				139,000
	$405,000	$405,000	$451,000	$451,000

(AICPA adapted)

Problem 14–15

The partnership of King, Gill, and Fisher engaged you to adjust its accounting records and convert them uniformly to the accrual basis in anticipation of admitting Wagner as a new partner. Some accounts are on the accrual basis and others are on the cash basis. The partnership's books were closed at December 31, 1980 by the bookkeeper, who prepared the general ledger trial balance that appears below.

King, Gill, and Fisher
General Ledger Trial Balance
December 31, 1980

	DEBIT	CREDIT
Cash	$ 10,000	
Accounts receivable	40,000	
Inventory	26,000	
Land	9,000	
Buildings	50,000	
Allowance for depreciation of buildings		$ 2,000
Equipment	56,000	
Allowance for depreciation of equipment		6,000
Goodwill	5,000	
Accounts payable		55,000
Allowance for future inventory losses		3,000
King, capital		40,000
Gill, capital		60,000
Fisher, capital		30,000
Totals	$196,000	$196,000

Your inquiries disclosed the following:

1. The partnership was organized on January 1, 1979 and no provision was made in the partnership agreement for the allocation of partnership profits and losses. During 1979, profits were allocated equally among the partners. The partnership agreement was amended, effective January 1, 1980, to provide for the following profit and loss ratio: King, 50%; Gill, 30%; and Fisher, 20%. The amended partnership agreement also stated that the accounting records were to be maintained on the accrual basis and that any adjustments necessary for 1979 should be allocated according to the 1979 allocation of profits.

2. The following amounts were not recorded as prepayments or accruals:

	DECEMBER 31	
	1980	1979
Prepaid insurance	$700	$ 650
Advances from customers	200	1,100
Accrued interest expense	—	450

The advances from customers were recorded as sales in the year the cash was received.

3. In 1980, the partnership recorded a provision of $3,000 for anticipated declines in inventory prices. You convinced the partners that the provision was unnecessary and should be removed from the books.

4. The partnership charged equipment purchased for $4,400 on January 1, 1980 to expense. This equipment has an estimated life of ten years and an estimated salvage value of $400. The partnership depreciates its capitalized equipment using the declining balance method at twice the straight-line depreciation rate.

5. The partners agreed to establish an allowance for doubtful accounts at 2% of current accounts receivable and 5% of past-due accounts. At December 31, 1979, the partnership had $54,000 of accounts receivable, of which only $4,000 was past due. At December 31, 1980, 15% of accounts receivable was past due, of which $4,000 represented sales made in 1979, and was considered collectible. The partnership had written off uncollectible accounts in the year the accounts became worthless as follows:

	ACCOUNT WRITTEN OFF IN	
	1980	1979
1980 accounts	$ 800	—
1979 accounts	1,000	$250

6. Goodwill was recorded on the books in 1980 and credited to the partners' capital accounts in the profit and loss ratio in recognition of an increase in the value of the business resulting from improved sales volume. The partners agreed to write off the goodwill before admitting the new partner.

Required:

Prepare a worksheet showing the adjustments and the adjusted trial balance for the partnership on the accrual basis at December 31, 1980. All adjustments affecting income should be made directly to partners' capital accounts. Supporting computations should be in good form. (Do not prepare formal financial statements or formal journal entries.)

(AICPA adapted)

15

Changes in the Ownership of the Partnership

A partnership is considered to be dissolved when there is a change in the membership of the partnership.[1] The partnership dissolution may be voluntary (e.g., mutual agreement by the partners to dissolve) or involuntary (e.g., by operation of the law as a result of a partner being shown to be of unsound mind). In dissolution, the old partnership is considered ended and a new partnership is established. For their protection, the partners that continue as members of the partnership should prepare a new partnership agreement. For example, if a new profit and loss formula is not agreed to when a new partnership is formed, and if there is disagreement concerning the profit and loss allocation after forming a new partnership, profits and losses will be shared equally.

In some forms of dissolution, the new partners may continue the normal operations of the partnership without much change. For example, a partnership is legally dissolved upon the addition of a new partner, but a new partnership may be formed without any visible interruption of the firm's operations. In other situations, such as bankruptcy of the partnership, the partnership may wind up its affairs and terminate operations.

In this chapter, we consider the accounting problems associated with changes in the membership of a continuing partnership. The form of changes in partnership membership that will be considered result from (1) admission of a new partner by purchase of an interest from one or more existing partners, (2) admission of a new partner by contribution of assets to the partnership, and (3) withdrawal of a partner by

---

[1]The UPA (Section 29) defines dissolution as "the change in the relation of the partners caused by any partner ceasing to be associated in the carrying on as distinguished from the winding up of the business." Although the provision specifically refers to a partner ceasing to be associated, other sections of the UPA and common practice recognize as a dissolution any change in the membership of the partnership, such as the admission of a new partner.

retirement or death. In the last section, accounting for a partnership when the partners decide to incorporate is illustrated. Dissolution of the partnership, in which the operations are eventually terminated, will be treated in the following chapter.

ACCOUNTING FOR A PARTNERSHIP DISSOLUTION

Valuation—A Central Issue

When there is a change in the membership of the partnership, the problem of assigning a fair value to the firm is encountered. For example, if a partner withdraws from the partnership and there are no express provisions in the partnership agreement for determining the settlement, an equitable payment for his interest must be negotiated between the existing partners. Similarly, before admission, an incoming partner must negotiate with the existing partners an equitable purchase price for the interest he acquires. The settlement or purchase price is based on a number of factors, one of which is the fair value of the partnership assets. However, the fair values of the partnership assets are generally not reflected on the partnership books. In accordance with generally accepted accounting standards, partnership assets are recorded at cost and subsequent increases in their market value are not recognized.

Technically, when there is a change in the membership of a partnership, the old partnership is terminated and a new one is formed. In order to provide an equitable measure of each partner's capital interest in the old partnership and an equitable starting point for the new partnership, unrecorded changes in the fair value of specific assets (whether tangible or identifiable intangible assets) and liabilities should be recognized before the admission or withdrawal of a partner is recorded. In practice, however, accountants are sometimes reluctant to recognize a change in the value of an asset, even though there may be objective evidence that the specific asset is undervalued. The partners should still be able to negotiate an equitable settlement price. When a new partner is admitted, the partners should be aware that unrecorded value changes subsequently realized will be allocated in the agreed profit and loss ratio.

The settlement price is frequently used to infer a value for the firm as a whole. Any difference between the value of the firm implied by the sales price and the sum of the market values of specific assets (book values if not restated) may be assigned to an intangible asset frequently referred to as partnership goodwill.

Accountants are generally hesitant to record goodwill unless it is purchased in a transaction involving arm's-length negotiation. In the absence of arm's-length negotiation, a settlement price may not necessarily provide objective evidence of the value of the firm and accordingly, such amounts should not be used as a basis for determining undervalued or unrecorded assets. Even so, from a practical point of view, the goodwill recognized may not have any impact on external parties. First of all, the partnership does not have to be concerned with reporting to stockholders. Second, most creditors follow the practice of eliminating goodwill from balance sheets in assessing the adequacy of protection for their loans. Thus, little harm may be done if the partners insist on the inclusion and amortization of the goodwill in the financial statements of the partnership.

Methods of Recording a Partnership Dissolution

Two methods are frequently used to record the changes in partnership membership. The two methods are:

1. *The Bonus Method.* When this method is used, the assets of the partnership are increased by the amount of the assets contributed by the partner being admitted. Any difference between the asset contributed and the credit to the new partner's capital account is adjusted to the capital accounts of the other partners involved in the negotiations. If a partner withdraws from a partnership, the partners may agree to settle his capital interest by permitting the withdrawal of partnership assets. If the bonus method is used to record the withdrawal, the difference between the recorded value of the assets withdrawn and the debit to the withdrawing partner's capital account is adjusted to the capital accounts of the remaining partners.

2. *The Goodwill Method.* When this method is used, a new asset is recorded which is based on the difference between the value implied by the amount of consideration negotiated in the admission or withdrawal of a partner and the values reported in the partnership books. When either method is used, unrecorded changes in the value of existing assets and liabilities that are objectively determinable may be recorded before the change in membership is recorded.

As will be demonstrated, if certain limited conditions related to the profit and loss agreement are satisfied, the bonus and goodwill methods will produce the same result. If these conditions are met, the use of the bonus method precludes the problem of recording an intangible asset.

There may be a question as to whether some of the subsequent illustrations in this chapter qualify as transactions resulting from arm's-length negotiation. Unless indicated otherwise, it will be assumed that before recording the admission or withdrawal of a partner, the existing net assets of the partnership have already been adjusted to reflect fair values on the basis of objective evidence and that the negotiation between existing partners and a prospective or withdrawing partner was arm's-length.

ADMISSION OF A NEW PARTNER

An individual can acquire an interest in a partnership (1) by purchasing all or part of an interest directly from one or more existing partners, i.e., the transaction is conducted by the individuals outside the partnership, and represents a transfer of assets between individuals, or (2) by being admitted as an additional partner upon the contribution of assets to the firm. Generally, the individual contributes cash and/or other assets (e.g., land, patent rights, equipment, marketable securities). A new partner could be admitted, however, by contributing a resource such as managerial talent. Because accountants ordinarily do not record such assets, unless the partners agree to transfer capital to the new partner's account, he will begin with a zero capital balance.

SALE OF AN INTEREST BY AN EXISTING PARTNER

A partner is entitled to sell his interest in the firm, but no partner can be forced to accept a new member to the partnership. The UPA (Section 27) provides that the purchaser of an interest in a partnership acquires only the right to receive the profit interest acquired and the interest in assets in the event of liquidation. The purchaser does not acquire the right to participate in management unless all remaining partners agree to grant him this right. The mere act of selling an interest does not dissolve the partnership, but if all the remaining partners agree to the admission of the new individual, the old partnership is ended and a new partnership is formed. Thus, in the case of disagreement, profits and losses will be shared equally unless a new partnership agreement is entered into. In some cases, such as when an old partner conveys his interest in the partnership to an individual, the partners may intend to continue the existing profit and loss agreement. If so, the agreement should be specifically stated.

In the following illustrations, it is assumed that the partnership currently consists of two partners, A and B, with respective capital interests of $60,000 and $40,000. A and B share profits and losses in the ratio of 6:4.

Acquisition of Interest by Payment to One Partner

If an individual acquires an interest in a partnership by making payment directly to an existing partner, the interest acquired is recorded in a new capital account by transferring a corresponding amount equal to the percentage interest acquired from the selling partner's capital account. For example, assume that A sold one-half of his interest in the firm to C for $36,000, and B agreed to the admission of C. The entry to record the transfer is:

A, Capital (½ × 60,000)	30,000	
C, Capital		30,000

The following should be noted:

1. Since this is a personal transaction between the two individuals, the entry is the same regardless of the amount paid by C directly to A.

2. Total assets and equities of the firm are not changed as a direct result of the transaction since the sale was negotiated outside the partnership. However, as noted earlier, the partners may choose to revalue assets and liabilities.

3. Since B agreed to the admission of C, a new profit and loss agreement should be made, even if it is an agreement to continue the existing formula.

4. C now has a capital interest of 30% ($30,000 of total interest of $100,000), but his profit interest does not have to equal this percentage.

A simplified balance sheet after the admission of C would be as follows:

Net Assets	$100,000	A, Capital	$ 30,000
		B, Capital	40,000
		C, Capital	30,000
Total	$100,000		$100,000

Acquisition of an Interest by Payment to More than One Partner

If C had purchased a 30% interest from each partner for $36,000, the entry would be:

A, Capital (.30 × 60,000)	18,000	
B, Capital (.30 × 40,000)	12,000	
C, Capital (.30 × 100,000)		30,000

The observations outlined above when the purchase was made from one partner apply in this case as well. Furthermore, this entry has no effect on how the cash payment made by C is to be distributed to A and B outside the partnership. The amount and distribution of cash is a negotiated transaction between individuals and does not affect the partnership accounts unless the amount is used as a basis for the revaluation of the firm.

Goodwill Implied from the Purchase Price

In the examples above, the amount paid by C to gain admission to the firm was ignored in recording the transfer of interest. This procedure is often referred to as the bonus method. Some would argue that the payment of $36,000 for a $30,000 interest in the partnership indicates that the firm has assets that are unrecorded or undervalued. The assumption is that the negotiated purchase price took into consideration such factors as the fair value of the firm's assets, the present value of the firm's liabilities, and the valuation of the firm on the basis of future prospects. Thus, the payment can be used to approximate the value of the firm. If C is willing to pay $36,000 for a 30% interest in the firm, then the implied value of the partnership net assets is $120,000 ($36,000/.30). Net assets and capital should be increased $20,000 from the recorded amounts of $100,000. Since this represents an unrecorded increase in the value of the firm's assets, the increase in assets of $20,000 is allocated to A and B on the basis of their agreed profit and loss ratio. In these illustrations, it is assumed that the assets and liabilities have already been revalued on the basis of the best information available at the time. However, if a specific asset(s) is still determined to be undervalued, then the increase should be assigned to the undervalued asset. To the extent that the excess cannot be assigned to specific identified recorded assets, the remaining amount is recorded as partnership goodwill. The entries to record the increase in assets and admission of C are:

Goodwill	20,000	
A, Capital (60%)		12,000
B, Capital (40%)		8,000
A, Capital (.30 × 72,000)	21,600	
B, Capital (.30 × 48,000)	14,400	
C, Capital (.30 × 120,000)		36,000

This results in account balances as follows:

	NET ASSETS	GOODWILL	CAPITAL A	B	C
Book values	100,000	–0–	(60,000)	(40,000)	–0–
Record goodwill		20,000	(12,000)	(8,000)	–0–
	100,000	20,000	(72,000)	(48,000)	–0–
Transfer of capital			21,600	14,400	(36,000)
Balance after					
admission of C	100,000	20,000	(50,400)	(33,600)	(36,000)

In the illustration, C is credited with a 30% interest in the firm under both the bonus and the goodwill methods. To assist the partners in making a decision between the two methods, it may be helpful to demonstrate the effects of the two methods on their respective capital balances. To compare the two methods, the goodwill is initially recorded in the accounts and is amortized in future periods. If the firm were forced to liquidate, the unamortized goodwill would probably be of no value and, therefore, would represent a loss to the partnership. In either case, the goodwill reduces the partners' capital accounts by their agreed profit- and loss-sharing ratio.

In order to isolate the effect of the goodwill allocation, all other capital changes are ignored. The bonus and goodwill methods will yield the same result only if two conditions related to the new profit and loss agreement are met. These are:

1. The new partner's profit-sharing percentage must be equal to his intial percentage interest in capital. In this illustration, C received a capital interest of 30%. His profit-sharing ratio must be 30%.

2. The old partners' profit-sharing ratio in the new partnership must be the same relatively as it was in the old partnership. Thus, if C is to receive 30% of the profits in

the new partnership, A and B must receive the remaining 70%. To be in the same relative ratio of 6:4, A must receive 42% (.6 × .70) of profits, and B must receive 28% (.4 × .70). The two methods are equivalent if, after amortizing goodwill, the account balances are the same as they would be under the bonus method. The balances for each method become:

GOODWILL METHOD	NET ASSETS	GOODWILL	CAPITAL A	B	C
Balances after recording					
goodwill and admitting C	100,000	20,000	(50,400)	(33,600)	(36,000)
Amortize goodwill					
20,000 × .42		(20,000)	8,400		
20,000 × .28				5,600	
20,000 × .30					6,000
Totals	100,000	–0–	(42,000)	(28,000)	(30,000)
BONUS METHOD					
Balances after recording					
admission of C	100,000	–0–	(42,000)	(28,000)	(30,000)

The two methods will yield the same results if the bonus method is used and the unrecorded assets ($20,000) are ultimately realized and allocated to the partners in the ratio of 42:28:30.

To illustrate a set of conditions that will not result in the same capital balances after the amortization of goodwill, assume that C is to receive a 30% capital interest but agrees to a 20% interest in subsequent profits; A and B share profits 48:32, respectively. After amortizing goodwill, the two methods result in the following capital balances:

GOODWILL METHOD	NET ASSETS	GOODWILL	CAPITAL A	B	C
Balances after recording					
goodwill and admitting C	100,000	20,000	(50,400)	(33,600)	(36,000)
Amortize goodwill					
20,000 × .48		(20,000)	9,600		
20,000 × .32				6,400	
20,000 × .20					4,000
Totals	100,000	–0–	(40,800)	(27,200)	(32,000)
BONUS METHOD					
Balances after recording					
admission of C	100,000	–0–	(42,000)	(28,000)	(30,000)

In this situation, A's and B's profit ratios are in the same relative proportion (6:4) as they were before the admission of C. However, C's interest in profits is less than his capital interest, which results in a greater capital balance for C and smaller capital balances for A and B when the goodwill method is used. The reader may wish to work out additional examples to determine the effect of varying the profit and loss ratios. The goodwill method, when compared with the bonus method, would be unfavorable (favorable) to C if he were to share profit and losses greater than (less than) 30%. The same general observation can be made for A and B using 42 and 28, respectively, as base percentages.

How Should the Cash Be Distributed?

A problem may be created when an individual purchases an interest from more than one partner. As we have discussed before, a partner's capital interest in the firm does not have to equal his profit ratio. Thus, the payment for an interest in a partnership represents two elements:

1. A claim to assets represented by the partner's capital balance.

2. The right to share in future profits.

If the two percentages are not equal, then there may not be an analytical solution to determine the appropriate distribution of cash. The allocation of the cash payment must be left to the partners to decide. Such a condition could be anticipated and provided for in the partnership agreement.

A frequently suggested solution is to distribute case to each selling partner in the amount of the capital transferred and distribute any excess in the selling partners' profit and loss ratio. However, a specific agreement of the partners would take precedence over this solution. Assuming that C purchased a 30% interest in the firm ratably from A and B for $36,000, the computation of an equitable distribution of cash paid becomes:

	A	B	TOTAL
Capital balances before sale	60,000	40,000	100,000
Capital transferred to C	18,000	12,000	30,000
Payment in excess of book value			
interest acquired: 6,000* × .60	3,600		
6,000 × .40		2,400	6,000
Payment by C	21,600	14,400	36,000

*36,000 − .30(100,000) = 6,000

In effect, this solution recognizes any excess payment over the book value interest acquired as a payment for unrecorded assets. This can be demonstrated by assuming that the goodwill is to be recorded on the partnership books as follows:

	A	B	TOTAL
Capital balances before sale	(60,000)	(40,000)	(100,000)
Goodwill implied from			
$36,000 sales price	(12,000)	(8,000)	(20,000)*
Capital after recognition			
of implied goodwill	(72,000)	(48,000)	(120,000)
Transfer of 30% interest to C	21,600	14,400	36,000

*Value of firm implied from	
sales price (36,000/.30) =	120,000
Book value of net assets	100,000
Goodwill	20,000

Relating the cash allocation to the capital interest transferred is only one possible solution, because the capital ratio may not equal the profit ratio.

This method is also subject to criticism because the distribution plan is based on existing capital balances on the partnership books, which ignores the independent nature of the negotiated transaction that took place outside the partnership.

ACQUISITION OF AN INTEREST BY CONTRIBUTING ASSETS

An individual may obtain a partnership interest by contributing something of value to the firm. If assets are contributed, the admission is recorded by recording the assets contributed and increasing the capital interest in the firm by a corresponding amount. It is important that the assets contributed be fairly valued. Any gain or loss recognized on sales subsequent to recording the admission will be distributed on the basis of the new profit and loss formula. For the same reason, the existing assets of the partnership should also be reviewed and revalued where necessary, since the partnership accounts may not reflect current values. It is also important to correctly reflect capital balances in accordance with the intention of the partners because, as we will see in the next chapter, the capital balances represent each partner's respective claim to the assets in the event of liquidation.

Three situations can exist when an individual contributes assets to a firm:

1. Book value of interest acquired is equal to the value of the assets contributed.

2. Book value of interest acquired is less than the value of the assets contributed.

3. Book value of interest acquired is greater than the value of the assets contributed.

The book value of the interest acquired is computed as follows:

$$\left(\begin{array}{c}\text{Capital balances of} \\ \text{existing partners}\end{array} + \begin{array}{c}\text{Contribution of} \\ \text{new partner}\end{array}\right) \times \begin{array}{c}\text{Percentage} \\ \text{interest acquired} \\ \text{by new partner}\end{array} = \begin{array}{c}\text{Book value of} \\ \text{interest acquired}\end{array}$$

To illustrate the three situations, assume that A and B have capital interests of $40,000 and $30,000, respectively. Assume further that the book values of the recorded assets of the firm have been previously adjusted to reflect their fair values. Profits are shared in the ratio of 6:4. C is to be admitted to the partnership, after which the profit ratio is to be 4:4:2. For simplicity, we will assume in all cases that C contributes cash.

Case 1: Book Value Acquired Equal to Asset Contributed

Assume that A, B, and C agree that C is to contribute $35,000 for a one-third capital interest in the partnership. The book value of C's interest is equal to the assets contributed and is computed as follows:

$$(70,000 + 35,000) = 105,000 \times \tfrac{1}{3} = 35,000$$

The entry to record the admission of C is simply:

Cash	35,000	
C, Capital		35,000

A's and B's capital accounts remain unchanged at $70,000, which represents the remaining two-thirds interest in the firm. C's capital account properly reflects a one-third interest of $35,000.

It should be noted that the ratio of the capital balance of 40:30:35 does not equal the agreed profit and loss ratio 4:4:2.

Case 2: Book Value Acquired Less than Assets Contributed

Assume now that C is to invest $50,000 for a one-third capital interest in the firm. Book value of the interest acquired is:

$$(70,000 + 50,000) = 120,000 \times \tfrac{1}{3} = 40,000$$

In this case, the amount contributed exceeds the book value interest acquired by $10,000. There could be a number of explanations for C's willingness to pay this $10,000 excess. It could be that, as a result of a profitable and favorable outlook for the firm's operations, A and B are in a strong bargaining position.

The accounting problem is to record the admission of C in accordance with the negotiated intentions of the parties involved. Obviously, if C's capital account is credited with $50,000, his interest would exceed one-third of the partnership's total capital. Either the bonus method or the goodwill method can be used to record the admission so that C will end up with a one-third capital interest.

Bonus Method   When the bonus method is used, the excess of the amount contributed over the book value interest received is considered a bonus payment to the existing partners. In this example, C contributed $10,000 more than the capital interest received. The $10,000 bonus is allocated to the old partners on the basis of their profit and loss ratio, since this is an increase in partnership assets. The entry to admit C becomes:

Cash	50,000	
A, Capital		6,000
B, Capital		4,000
C, Capital		40,000

A and B now have capital balances of $46,000 and $34,000 for a total capital interest of $80,000, which is a two-thirds interest in total capital of $120,000. C has the remaining one-third interest of $40,000.

The assets of the partnership may have been revalued prior to recording the admission of a new partner. The bonus method is frequently used when the parties consider that the accounts of the existing partnership reflect fair market value of the net assets. Notice in the entry to record the admission that the assets are increased only by the amount contributed. Any difference between the capital credit for C and the cash contributed is an adjustment to the capital accounts of A and B.

Goodwill Method   C may negotiate that he is to receive a capital credit equal to his investment. If C is to receive a capital credit of $50,000 for a one-third interest, the total capital interest implied by this contract is $150,000. A and B must have the remaining two-thirds interest, or $100,000. Since their current balances of $70,000 represent their interest in the net assets, assets and capital appear to be understated by $30,000.[2] Assuming that the specific assets are fairly valued, this understatement is recognized as partnership goodwill and is allocated to A and B on the basis of their current profit and loss ratios. The journal entry is:

Goodwill	30,000	
A, Capital (60%)		18,000
B, Capital (40%)		12,000

[2]An alternate way to calculate goodwill is as follows:

Net value of firm implied by contract	150,000
Minus: A's and B's capital balance + C's investment	120,000
Goodwill	30,000

The entry to record the admission of C is:

Cash	50,000	
C, Capital		50,000

Net Assets Undervalued The excess payment by C could mean that specific assets of the firm assumed to have been revalued in these illustrations are still undervalued, or that partnership liabilities are overstated. If so, the specific assets (whether tangible or identifiable intangible assets) and liabilities of the partnership should be adjusted instead of creating a goodwill account. However, the specific accounts should not be adjusted in the absence of objective evidence that there are unrecorded changes in value.

Case 3: Book Value Acquired Greater than Assets Contributed

Assume that C is to invest $20,000 for a one-third capital interest in the firm. Book value of the interest acquired is:

$$(70,000 + 20,000) = 90,000 \times \frac{1}{3} = 30,000$$

In this case, the book value acquired exceeds the value of the assets contributed by C, which could imply that assets are overvalued ($\frac{1}{3} X = 20,000; X = 60,000$) or that for some reason A and B are willing to grant C a capital credit greater than the amount of assets he is contributing. In some cases, for example, a partnership may be in need of operating capital and the partners may be willing to sacrifice their interest in existing assets to acquire the cash; or it could be that C is bringing some particularly needed talent or reputation to the partnership.

As with Case 2, the admission could be recorded either by the bonus method or by the goodwill method. Under either method, C will end up with a one-third total interest in the net assets and capital of the firm.

Bonus Method When the bonus method is used, assets are not increased above what the new partner is contributing, assuming that the firm's assets are fairly valued. If C is to receive a $30,000 capital credit upon investment of $20,000, then a bonus of $10,000 is being granted to C. This bonus reduces A and B capital balances in their agreed profit and loss ratio. The following entry reflects the bonus to C and a resulting one-third interest in the total capital of $90,000.

Cash	20,000	
A, Capital (60% $\times$ 10,000)	6,000	
B, Capital (40% $\times$ 10,000)	4,000	
C, Capital		30,000

A and B now have capital balances of $34,000 and $26,000, respectively, for a total of $60,000, or a two-thirds interest.

Goodwill Method   If A and B are unwilling to reduce their capital accounts upon the admission of C, then an alternative to the bonus method is to compute and record goodwill implicit in the agreement. Since A's and B's capital interests are to remain unchanged, the old partners' capital balances are used as the base to compute the value of the firm. If their interest represents a two-thirds interest in the net assets of the new partnership, then a three-thirds interest in the firm is $105,000, of which C is to receive a capital credit of $35,000 ($\frac{1}{3} \times 105,000$).[3] The $15,000 difference between the capital credit of $35,000 and C's investment of $20,000 is goodwill. The entry to record the admission of C is:

Cash	20,000	
Goodwill	15,000	
C, Capital		35,000

The goodwill relates to an intangible asset being contributed by the new partner. The amount recorded is based on the value implied by the partners' agreement.

Net Assets Overvalued   The payment of $20,000 by C for a $30,000 capital interest may provide evidence that the recorded value of the firm's net assets does not reflect fair values and that the use of the bonus method or the creation of a goodwill account is an effort to avoid a reduction in net assets. The $20,000 contribution by C for a one-third interest could be used to impute a value for the partnership net assets after the admission of C of only $60,000.[4] The journal entries to revalue the assets and admit C are as follows:

[3]An alternate way to calculate goodwill is as follows:
a.   First compute the capital interest implied from the agreement:

$$X = \text{total capital of the new partnership}$$
$$\tfrac{2}{3}X = 70,000$$
$$X = 105,000$$

b.   Compute the goodwill amount:

Implied value of net assets including C's investment	105,000
Recorded value of net assets plus C's investment (70,000 + 20,000)	90,000
Goodwill	15,000

[4]The amount of asset overstatement is calculated as follows:

$$\tfrac{1}{3}X = 20,000$$
$$X = 60,000$$

Implied value of net assets including C's investment	60,000
Recorded value of net assets including C's investment (40,000 + 30,000 + 20,000)	90,000
Overvalued assets	30,000

A, Capital	18,000	
B, Capital	12,000	
Assets		30,000
Cash	20,000	
C, Capital		20,000

The following balance sheets result from the admission of C for the three alternatives discussed:

DEBITS	BONUS METHOD	GOODWILL METHOD	OVERVALUED NET ASSETS
Net Assets	$90,000	$105,000	$60,000
CREDITS			
A, Capital	$34,000	$ 40,000	$22,000
B, Capital	26,000	30,000	18,000
C, Capital	30,000	35,000	20,000
Totals	$90,000	$105,000	$60,000

Subsequent events alone can indicate which method should have been used to record the admission. An examination of one of a number of events that could result will emphasize the importance of the initial asset valuation. Assume that the bonus method was used to record the admission of C and that the assets were overvalued and subsequently sold at a loss of $30,000. The agreed profit ratio is 4:4:2. After this transaction, the partners' capital balances are as follows:

	A	B	C
Balance after admission of C	(34,000)	(26,000)	(30,000)
Share of $30,000 loss	12,000	12,000	6,000
	(22,000)	(14,000)	(24,000)

The selection of the bonus method as opposed to reducing overvalued assets results in a gain in C's capital relative to B's. Additional comparisons of the three methods assuming various other subsequent events could be developed.

WITHDRAWAL OF A PARTNER

A partner cannot be prevented from withdrawing from a partnership by the other partners. Although some complex legal issues are involved, the partnership agreement may specify conditions for withdrawal and provisions for computing the settlement. If a settlement is not specifically provided for in the partnership agreement, Section 42 of the UPA states that "he or his legal representative . . . . may have the value of his interest ascertained and shall receive as an ordinary creditor an amount equal to the value of his interest."

If a partner withdraws in violation of the partnership agreement and without approval of the remaining partners, he is entitled only to his interest in the firm without consideration of goodwill. In such a case, the withdrawing partner is liable for damages sustained by the remaining partners for his breach of the partnership agreement. Any changes in partnership interest result in a dissolution of the old partnership and the formation of a new one. A partner who is forced to withdraw from a partnership, is entitled to compensation for his full interest including goodwill.

In the following examples, it is assumed that the partners mutually agree to the withdrawal: (1) The withdrawing partner may elect to sell his interest to an outside party; (2) the withdrawing partner may elect to sell his interest to one or more of the remaining partners; or (3) the partners may mutually agree to transfer partnership assets to the withdrawing partner for his interest in the firm. Case 1 has been discussed earlier and need not be reviewed again. The same considerations apply to Case 2, if negotiated outside the partnership. In Case 3, the partnership agreement may include requirements for determining the settlement price. In most cases, the capital account does not reflect the current value of the partner's interest. To be equitable, the assets and liabilities may need to be restated. It may be necessary to recognize unrecorded assets, correct the accounts for errors, or reflect changes in estimates such as the book value of depreciable assets. In the absence of a specific agreement, the partners may have to negotiate a settlement price at the date of withdrawal. Determination of an equitable value may be very difficult. The agreed settlement price may be equal to, greater than, or less than the book value interest of the withdrawing partner.

To illustrate the accounting for the withdrawal of a partner by transferring firm assets, assume a partnership consisting of three partners, A, B, and C, with capital balances of $30,000, $40,000, $30,000, and a profit and loss ratio of 5:3:2. Any agreed asset revaluation has already been recorded.

Payment to a Withdrawing Partner in Excess of Book Value

Assume now that A is withdrawing from the partnership and the partners have mutually agreed that he is to receive payment of $40,000. The partners may agree to use the bonus method or the goodwill method to record the withdrawal.

Bonus Method   If the bonus method is used, the remaining partners are charged with the amount of the payment that exceeds the book value of the retiring partner's capital balance. The amount of the bonus paid to the retiring partner is commonly allocated to the remaining partners on the basis of their relative profit and loss ratio (in this case the relative ratio of B to C is 3:2). Support for this method is based on the cost principle. The bonus method may also be justified when the remaining partners are simply anxious to get rid of a partner for various reasons. Any recognition of goodwill is difficult to justify in the absence of an arm's-length transaction. The entry to record the withdrawal would be as follows:

A, Capital	30,000	
B, Capital	6,000	
C, Capital	4,000	
Liability to A		40,000

Goodwill Method   The goodwill method is used if (1) B and C will not agree to a reduction in their capital balances; (2) the partners made specific provisions in the partnership agreement on how the withdrawal is to be recorded; or (3) the partners agree that an intangible asset should be recognized. If the partnership has been profitable, the firm as a whole may be worth more than the sum of the market values of the individual assets. One alternative is to calculate the implied goodwill from the price paid to the retiring partner. In our example, A receives a $10,000 excess payment over his capital balance. Since A's capital account is increased by 50% of any increase in assets, then a $10,000 excess payment implies a total goodwill of $20,000. The entries are:

Goodwill	20,000	
A, Capital		10,000
B, Capital		6,000
C, Capital		4,000
A, Capital	40,000	
Liability to A		40,000

Some would argue that, in accordance with the cost basis, only the goodwill of $10,000 that had been purchased should be recorded. Others would contend that the basis for recognizing goodwill should be "all or nothing at all."

It is probably difficult to justify recognition of any goodwill. If the goodwill is related to Partner A, it will not exist if he withdraws. However, as discussed before, if the goodwill is based on past operations, the withdrawal may provide the objective evidence necessary to recognize it in the partnership accounts.

Comparison of the Bonus and Goodwill Methods

The assets should be revalued before the partner withdraws. It may be difficult to determine fair values, however, or the partners may elect to recognize unrecorded goodwill. Once again, it may be helpful to the partners to see under what conditions the two methods will yield the same results. The only condition which must be met is that the remaining partners' profit and loss ratio must be in the same relative ratio as it was before the withdrawal of A. In the preceding illustration, this condition would be met if, after the withdrawal of A, B and C share profits 3:2.

	A	B	C
Capital balances before withdrawal	(30,000)	(40,000)	(30,000)
Allocate goodwill	(10,000)	(6,000)	(4,000)
	(40,000)	(46,000)	(34,000)
Withdraw A	40,000	—	—
	-0-	(46,000)	(34,000)
Amortize goodwill			
$20,000 × .60		12,000	
$20,000 × .40			8,000
	-0-	(34,000)	(26,000)
Capital balances using bonus method	-0-	(34,000)	(26,000)

Payment to a Withdrawing Partner Less than Book Value

A partner who is anxious to dispose of his interest in the partnership may agree to accept less than his book value interest in the partnership. He may do so for a number of reasons, such as (1) he may view the future of the company negatively, (2) he may need operating capital for personal reasons, or (3) the business association may no longer be acceptable to him and, in his opinion, a forced liquidation of the firm might be detrimental to his interest. In such cases, use of the bonus method is justified, since the settlement may not be based on the economic value of the firm.

To illustrate, assume that A withdraws from the ABC Partnership and agrees to settle his $30,000 interest for $25,000. A bonus of $5,000 accrues to the remaini.g partners. The common practice is to allocate the bonus on the basis of their rel. tive profit and loss ratio of 3:2. The entry would be:

A, Capital	30,000	
B, Capital		3,000
C, Capital		2,000
Liability to A		25,000

In the entry above, the net assets of the partnership were not revalued. However, a payment to a withdrawing partner that is less than his capital interest may be an indication that assets are overvalued. Assets should be written down to fair values if it is determined that they are overvalued and that the settlement price is based on the net assets' fair value. In particular, if goodwill was previously recorded, an agreement to accept a payment that is less than the partner's book value interest may provide evidence that the intangible is overstated. Accordingly, the intangible should be reduced by the difference between the settlement price and the capital interest being retired. Assuming that assets are overvalued by $10,000, the sequence of entries becomes:

A, Capital	5,000	
B, Capital	3,000	
C, Capital	2,000	
Asset		10,000
A, Capital	25,000	
Liability to A		25,000

Reducing the assets to fair value provides an equitable starting point for the new partnership formed by B and C. As long as B and C share profits in the same relative ratio, they will be indifferent as to the method used. However, it is more informative and conceptually preferred for the recorded asset values to reflect fair values if such values can be determined.

Death of a Partner

A partnership is dissolved upon the death of a partner. In the absence of specific settlement provisions, the surviving partners and the executor of the estate of the deceased partner must negotiate a settlement for the partner's interest in the firm. Attempting to determine a partner's interest in the firm can result in a number of controversies. To avoid litigation, partners should anticipate such an event and, in the articles of partnership, specify procedures for determining a deceased partner's interest and the method of settlement. Although the old partnership is dissolved, the agreement may provide that operations do not terminate, but may be continued by the surviving partners. If so, the method of settlement with the deceased partner should be specified in the partnership agreement.

INCORPORATION OF A PARTNERSHIP

After a partnership operates for a period of time, the partners may find that the partnership form of business is no longer satisfactory. The corporation, with its limited liability, continuity of existence, and ability to raise needed resources, may become more attractive. Upon incorporation, the assets and liabilities are transferred to the corporation and the partners receive capital stock in settlement of their interest. The partnership accounts should be restated to fair value to assure that the partners receive an equitable distribution of stock for their interest.

The partnership books may be retained for use by the corporation, or a new set of books may be established.

Retention of Partnership Books by Corporation

Assuming that the partnership books are used by the corporation, the steps to record the incorporation are as follows:

1. Assets and liabilities are adjusted to fair value. A valuation adjustment account is frequently created to accumulate the gains and losses.

2. The valuation adjustment account is closed to the partner's capital accounts in accordance with the profit and loss ratio.

3. The partners' capital accounts are closed upon the transfer of capital stock. Since the books are retained, offsetting entries are made to capital stock at par value for the number of shares issued. If the debit to partners' capital accounts exceeds the credit to capital stock, the difference is a credit to additional paid-in capital.

To illustrate, assume that AB Partnership is to incorporate. The new corporation is authorized to issue 5,000 shares of $10 par value stock. Book values of the partnership accounts and fair values for the assets are determined to be:

	BOOK VALUE		FAIR VALUES
	DEBIT	CREDIT	
Cash	$ 5,000		5,000
Accounts Receivable	4,000		3,600
Inventory	5,000		7,000
Land	10,000		15,000
Equipment (net of depreciation)	6,000		5,000
Accounts Payable		$ 7,000	
Notes Payable		10,000	
A, Capital		8,000	
B, Capital		5,000	
	$30,000	$30,000	

Other facts are: (1) Liabilities are assumed to be fairly valued; (2) A and B share profits equally; (3) A and B are to receive par value stock equal to their adjusted ending capital balances. The journal entries to incorporate are:

(1) Inventory	2,000	
Land	5,000	
Equipment		1,000
Accounts Receivable		400
Valuation Adjustment		5,600
(2) Valuation Adjustment	5,600	
A, Capital		2,800
B, Capital		2,800
(3) A, Capital	10,800	
B, Capital	7,800	
Capital Stock—$10 par		18,600

New Books Established by Corporation

If the corporation establishes a new set of books, then all accounts on the partnership books will end with a zero balance. The only difference in the illustration above is that upon receipt of the stock, asset and liability accounts are closed on the partnership books and transferred to the corporation. To balance the entry, an asset account is created for the capital stock received in the amount of $18,600. This balance should also equal the sum of the balances in the remaining capital accounts. The entry to record the distribution of the capital stock is:

A, Capital	10,800	
B, Capital	7,800	
Capital Stock From Corporation		18,600

The corporation records the assets received and the liabilities assumed on the new books at the net cost of the stock issued ($18,600), which is also equal to the net adjusted value on the partnership books. A credit of $18,600 to balance the entry is made to capital stock issued.

Questions

1. How does the UPA define "dissolution"? Why is it important for a continuing partnership to prepare a new partnership agreement after a dissolution?

2. What is goodwill? Why are accountants often hesitant to record goodwill?

3. Discuss the method used to record changes in partnership membership.

4. Explain why the purchase of a partnership interest from an existing partner would be recorded on the books of the partnership at an amount that differs from the purchase price. Does this transaction change the total assets and equities of the partnership?

5. Differentiate between the admission of a new partner through his purchasing an interest and through his investing in the partnership.

6. When might goodwill be implied from the purchase price of the partnership interest?

7. Under what two conditions will the bonus and goodwill methods of recording the admission of a partner yield the same result?

8. When a new partner is admitted to a partnership by his contributing something of value to the firm, how is the admission recorded? Describe the three situations which can exist when a new partner contributes assets to a firm.

9. Describe the situation when a new partner contributes goodwill.

10. George, Henrick, and Peterson are partners with capital balances of $50,000, $30,000, and $20,000, respectively. Freeman is to receive a one-fourth capital interest in the firm after making a capital contribution of $50,000 cash. What might this $50,000 contribution indicate about the firm?

11. Describe the circumstances where neither the goodwill nor the bonus method should be used to record the admission of a new partner.

12. How might a partner withdrawing in violation of the partnership agreement and without the consent of the other partners be treated? What about the partner who is forced to withdraw?

13. Can the partial recognition of goodwill to a withdrawing partner be justified?

14. Why might a withdrawing partner accept less than book value for his interest in a partnership?

15. What steps are taken to record the incorporation of a partnership, assuming that the partnership books are used by the corporation?

16. Pat, Helma, and Diane are partners with capital balances of $50,000, $30,000, and $20,000, respectively. The partners share profits and losses equally. For an investment of $50,000 cash, Mary Ann is to be admitted as a partner with a one-fourth interest in capital and profits. On the basis of this information, the amount of Mary Ann's investment can best be justified by which of the following?
   a. Mary Ann will receive a bonus from the other partners upon her admission to the partnership.
   b. Assets of the partnership were overvalued immediately prior to Mary Ann's investment.
   c. The book value of the partnership's net assets was less than their fair value immediately prior to Mary Ann's investment.
   d. Mary Ann is apparently bringing goodwill into the partnership and her capital account will be credited for the appropriate amount.

(AICPA adapted)

Problems

DO 15-8 ALSO
TRY 15-6 DON'T HAVE TO

Problem 15-1
Adams and Proctor are partners in the PA Company and have capital balances of $36,000 and $21,000, respectively. Adams and Proctor share profits 3:2.

Required:
Record in journal form the admission of Corey in each of the following independent cases.
1. Corey purchases a one-third interest of the existing partnership by paying $9,000 to each partner.
2. Corey invests $13,000 for a one-fifth interest in partnership capital. Total capital after the admission of Corey is to be $70,000.
3. Corey invests $18,000 for a one-fifth interest in partnership capital. Implicit goodwill should be recorded.

Problem 15-2

A florist shop is operated by Peterson, Ute, and Davis. The partners share profits in a ratio of 5:3:2 and have capital account balances of $143,000, $102,000, and $55,000, respectively. Tate is admitted to the partnership on January 1, 1980 after investing $50,000 for a one-fourth interest in capital and profits.

Required:

A. Prepare entries in journal form under each of the three methods of recording the admission of the new partner.

B. Assume that Tate ratably purchases an interest in the partnership from each of the existing partners. Prepare a cash transfer schedule for Peterson, Ute, and Davis.

Problem 15-3

The following balance sheet is for the partnership of Able, Bayer, and Cain:

Cash	$ 20,000	Liabilities	$ 50,000
Other Assets	180,000	Able, Capital (40%)	37,000
		Bayer, Capital (40%)	65,000
		Cain, Capital (20%)	48,000
	$200,000		$200,000

Figures shown parenthetically reflect agreed profit- and loss-sharing percentages.

Required:

Prepare the necessary journal entries to record the admission of Day in each of the following independent situations. Some parts may be recorded more than one way.

1. Day is to contribute sufficient cash to receive a one-sixth interest. The parties agree that the admission is to be recorded without recognizing goodwill or bonus.
2. Day is to contribute $50,000 for a one-fifth interest.
3. Day is to contribute $50,000 for a one-fourth interest.
4. Day is to contribute $50,000 for a 40% interest.

(AICPA adapted)

Problem 15-4

Lopes, Russell, and Garvey are partners sharing profit and loss in a 4:4:2 ratio. Their capital account balances are $42,000, $36,000, and $27,000, respectively. Cey is to invest $21,000 in the firm. Prepare the necessary journal entry or entries to record the admission under each of the following assumptions:

1. Cey is to receive a capital interest equal to his investment.
2. Cey is to receive a one-seventh capital interest, and a bonus is recorded.
3. Cey is to receive a one-seventh capital interest, and goodwill is recorded.
4. Cey is to receive a one-fifth capital interest, and bonus is recorded.
5. Cey is to receive a one-fifth capital interest, and goodwill is recorded.

Problem 15-5

Bassford and Cook have been partners in an audio equipment store for several years. In order to obtain volume discounts on their audio equipment purchases, the partners must open another store. To obtain sufficient capital to open the new store, the partners are currently negotiating with Wood to admit him as a partner with a one-third interest in capital and profits upon the investment of $250,000. Bassford and Cook currently have capital interest of $150,000 and $200,000, respectively. They share profits and losses in the ratio of 70:30.

The partners are unable to reach an agreement on how to record the $250,000 investment by Wood in the accounts. Wood contends that he should receive a capital credit equal to his investment of $250,000. Bassford argues that the total capital should not exceed $600,000, which is the capital interest of Bassford and Cook plus the investment by Wood. In the opinion of Cook, the payment by Wood is indicative of the undervaluation of land owned by the partnership since it was formed.

Required:
Prepare journal entries to record the admission of Wood in accordance with the position of each of the three partners.

Problem 15–6
Tidwell and Wyndelts have been operating a tax accounting service as a partnership for five years. Their current capital balances are $25,000 and $15,000, respectively, and they share profits equally. Because of the growth in their tax business, they decide that they need a new partner. Boyd is admitted to the partnership, after which the partners agree to share profits 35% to Tidwell, 35% to Wyndelts, and 30% to Boyd.

Required:
Prepare the necessary journal entries to admit Boyd in each of the following independent conditions.
1. Boyd contributes $20,000 in cash and receives a one-third capital interest.
2. Boyd contributes $30,000 cash for a two-sevenths capital interest. Total capital after his admission is to be $70,000.
3. Boyd agrees to contribute $23,000 cash for a one-third capital interest, but will not accept a capital credit for less than his investment.
4. Boyd contributes $10,000 cash for a one-fourth capital interest. The partners agree that assets and the firm as a whole should not be revalued.
5. Boyd contributes $9,000 cash for a one-fifth capital interest. The partners agree that total capital after the admission of Boyd should be $50,000.
6. Boyd contributes land to the partnership as a site for a new office building. The land originally cost Boyd $20,000, but now has a current market value of $30,000. Boyd is admitted with a one-third capital interest.
7. Boyd is admitted to the partnership with a one-fifth interest upon payment of $10,000 to Tidwell and Wyndelts. The $10,000 payment to Tidwell and Wyndelts is made outside the partnership and is split between them.

Problem 15–7
Record in general journal form the admission of Evans to the Heeter and Ford partnership in each of the following separate cases. Heeter and Ford share profits and losses in the ratio of 60:40; they have capital balances of $22,000 and $18,000, respectively. If more than one interpretation is possible, present all the possibilities.
1. Evans is admitted to a one-fifth interest in capital upon contributing $10,000 to the partnership. Total capital of the new partnership is to be $50,000.
2. Evans is admitted to a one-fourth interest in capital by the purchase of one-fourth of the interest of Heeter and Ford for $10,500. The new partnership capital is to be $40,000.

3. Same conditions as in 2 except the goodwill implied by the purchase price is to be recorded in the partnership books.
4. Evans is admitted to a one-fourth interest upon contributing $14,000 to the partnership. Total capital of the new partnership is to be $48,000.
5. Evans is admitted to a one-fourth interest in capital upon contributing $10,000 to the partnership. Total capital of the new partnership is to be $50,000.
6. Evans is admitted to a one-third interest in capital upon contributing $17,000, after which each partner is to have an equal capital equity in the new partnership.

Problem 15–8
The net assets of a partnership amount to $300,000. A's capital balance is $90,000, B's capital balance is $90,000, and C's capital balance is $120,000. The partners share profits 30:30:40.

    C is withdrawing from the partnership, and the partners agree to pay him $150,000 out of the partnership assets.

Required:
A. Illustrate in general journal form three different methods of recording the withdrawal of C. (Assume that tangible assets are already stated at values approximating their fair market values.)
B. Indicate under what conditions you would support or not support the use of either of the three methods presented in A.

Problem 15–9
Jackson, Kline, and Linstrom are partners in a construction company. Their respective capital balances and profit-sharing ratios are as follows:

As of December 31, 1980

PARTNERS	CAPITAL BALANCE	PROFIT-SHARING RATIOS
Jackson	$120,000	6
Kline	80,000	2
Linstrom	40,000	2

    Jackson wishes to withdraw from the partnership on January 1, 1981. Kline and Linstrom have agreed to pay Jackson $150,000 from the partnership assets for his 50% capital interest. This settlement price was based on such factors as capital contributions, sales performance, and earning capacity.

    Kline and Linstrom must decide whether to use the bonus method or the goodwill method to record the withdrawal, and they wish to compare the results of using the two methods.

Required:
Prepare a comparison of capital balances using the bonus and goodwill methods (and amortizing goodwill implied from the payment to Jackson), assuming that:
1. The new profit and loss ratio is in the same relative ratio as that existing before Jackson's withdrawal.
2. The profit and loss ratio is changed to 2:1. Kline is particularly interested in these results, because he feels that his present contribution of time and capital is better reflected by this new profit and loss ratio.

Problem 15–10

The balance sheet for ABC Partnership as of December 31, 1980, is as follows:

ASSETS		LIABILITIES AND CAPITAL	
Cash	$ 5,000	Accounts Payable	$ 25,000
Accounts Receivable	30,000	Other Current Liabilities	5,000
Inventory (at cost)	30,000	Long-term Note (8% due 1982)	25,000
Land	20,000	A, Capital	30,000
Building (net of depreciation)	35,000	B, Capital	20,000
Equipment (net of depreciation)	15,000	C, Capital	30,000
Total	$135,000		$135,000

The partnership, although operating profitably, has had a cash flow problem. Unable to meet their current commitment, the firm borrowed $25,000 from a bank giving a long-term note. During a recent meeting the partners decided to obtain additional cash by admitting a new partner to the firm. They feel that the firm is an attractive investment, but that proper management of their liquid assets will be required. D agrees to contribute cash to the firm, but only on the condition that his chief accountant can review the accounting records of the partnership.

The review by the two accountants results in the accumulation of the following information:

1. Approximately 10% of the accounts receivable are uncollectible. The old partnership had been using the direct write-off method of accounting for bad debts.

2. Current replacement cost of the inventory is $34,000.

3. The market value of the land based on a current appraisal is $35,000.

4. The partners had been using an unreasonably long estimated life in establishing a depreciation policy for the building. On the basis of sound value (current replacement cost adjusted for use), the value of the building is $25,000.

5. There are unrecorded accrued liabilities of $1,000.

The partners agree to recognize the foregoing adjustment to the accounts. A, B, and C share profits 40:30:30. After the admission of D, the new profit agreement is to be 30:20:30:20. D is to receive a 30% capital interest in the partnership after he contributes sufficient cash to increase the total capital interest to $110,000. Because of the uncertainty of the business, no goodwill is to be recognized before or after D is admitted.

Required:

A. Prepare the necessary journal entries on the books of the old partnership to adjust the accounts.

B. Record the admission of D.

C. Prepare a new balance sheet giving effect to the requirements above.

Problem 15–11

Miller and Walker operate a business as partners dividing profits equally. The partners decide to expand their product line and need additional capital. They agree to admit Pearce to the partnership as of January 1, 1980, with a one-third interest in profits and in the capital. Pearce is to pay cash into the business as additional capital in an amount equal to one-half of the combined capital of the two present partners, redetermined as follows:

The average partnership profits, after partners' salaries, for the past two years are to be capitalized at the rate of 10% per annum, which will redetermine the aggregate capital of the two present partners. Before such capitalization of profits, the accounts are to be adjusted for errors and omissions.

The business has not followed a strict accrual basis of accounting. As a result, the following items have been omitted from the books:

	BALANCE 12/31/77	BALANCE 12/31/78	BALANCE 12/31/79
Accrued expenses	$3,201	$2,472	$4,360
Prepaid expenses	1,010	1,226	872
Accrued income	—	250	475

In addition, no provision has been made for loss on uncollectible accounts. It is agreed that a provision of $4,500 is needed as of December 31, 1979, of which $600 is for 1978 accounts. Charge-offs have been made to expense in 1977 of 1976 and prior accounts, $1,200; in 1978 of 1977 accounts, $3,100; and of 1978 accounts, $400; in 1979 of 1978 accounts, $2,280; and of 1979 accounts, $525.

The inventory at December 31, 1979 contains some obsolete goods carried at cost of $4,300. A 20% write-down is to be made to reduce these items to their present value.

In 1978 and 1979, salaries of $3,000 for each partner were taken out of the business and charged to expense before determining profits. It has been agreed that the salaries should have been $4,000 each.

Balance Sheet
December 31, 1979

ASSETS		LIABILITIES AND CAPITAL	
Cash	$ 7,000	Accounts Payable	$ 43,200
Accounts Receivable	42,500	Notes Payable	25,000
Notes Receivable	6,000	Allowance for	
		Depreciation of Fixtures	5,300
Merchandise	64,000	Miller, Capital	22,000
Store Fixtures	12,400	Walker, Capital	36,400
Total	$131,900	Total	$131,900

	1977	1978	1979
Profits per books:	$ 8,364	$ 8,585	$10,497
Miller, Capital	20,000	24,000	22,000
Walker, Capital	25,000	33,000	36,400

Required:

A. Compute the amount that Pearce will pay into the partnership.

B. Prepare a balance sheet as it would appear after adjustments for errors and omissions and after redetermination of capital accounts and receipt of Pearce's capital contribution as of January 1, 1980.

(AICPA adapted)

Problem 15–12

The B & Q Company was organized on July 1, 1975. Under the partnership agreement, $900,000 was provided by Beke and $600,000 by Quinn as initial capital; income and losses were to be shared in the same ratio as the initial capital contributions. No additional capital contributions have been made.

The June 30, 1980 balance sheet follows:

ASSETS

Cash	$ 500,500
Accounts Receivable, net	950,000
Inventory (LIFO basis)	1,500,000
Prepaid Insurance	18,000
Land	58,000
Machinery and Equipment, net	1,473,500
Total	$4,500,000

LIABILITIES AND CAPITAL

Current Liabilities	$1,475,000
Beke, Capital	1,815,000
Quinn, Capital	1,210,000
Total	$4,500,000

Beke and Quinn are considering selling their business, but are concerned that the financial statements do not reveal its current worth. You have been requested to assist in determining the current value of the assets.

You compile the following information in addition to the asset section of the balance sheet:

1. An aging of accounts receivable disclosed the following:

FISCAL YEAR	AMOUNT	ALLOWANCE FOR DOUBTFUL ACCOUNTS
1977	$ 40,000	$ 35,000
1978	125,000	105,000
1979	160,000	67,500
1980	925,000	92,500
	$1,250,000	$300,000

A review of past experience shows that all receivables over two years old have been uncollectible, those over one year old have been 50% collectible, and those less than one year old have been 90% collectible.

2. The inventory level has been increasing and its cost has been determined using the LIFO flow assumption. The cost of the LIFO layers at the average price for the indicated year of aquisition and the inventory price increases have been as follows:

LIFO LAYERS		PRICE INCREASES	
FISCAL YEAR ACQUIRED	COST	PERIOD	INCREASE
1976	$ 60,000	1976–1980	20%
1977	150,000	1977–1980	18
1978	240,000	1978–1980	15
1979	350,000	1979–1980	11
1980	700,000	1980	5
	$1,500,000		

3. Machinery was purchased in fiscal years 1976, 1978, and 1979 for $500,000, $850,000, and $660,000, respectively. The straight-line depreciation method and a 10-year estimated life have been used for all machinery, and a half year of depreciation taken in the year of acquisition. The experience of other companies over the last several years indicates that the machinery can be sold at 125% of its book value.

4. An independent appraisal made in June 1980 valued land at $70,000.

Required:
Prepare a comparative statement of assets showing historical costs and current values at June 30, 1980. Supporting schedules should be in good form.

(AICPA adapted)

Problem 15–13
You have been engaged to prepare financial statements for the partnership of Alexander, Randolph, and Ware as of June 30, 1980. You have obtained the following information from the partnership agreement as amended and from the accounting records.

1. The partnership was formed originally by Alexander and Barnes on July 1, 1979. At that date:
   a. Barnes contributed $400,000 cash.
   b. Alexander contributed land, building, and equipment with fair market values of $110,000, $520,000, and $185,000, respectively. The land and building were subject to a mortgage securing an 8% per annum note (interest rate of similar notes at July 1, 1979). The note is due in quarterly payments of $5,000 plus interest on January 1, April 1, July 1, and October 1 of each year. Alexander made the July 1, 1979 principal and interest payment personally. The partnership then assumed the obligation for the remaining $300,000 balance.
   c. The agreement further provided that Alexander had contributed a certain intangible benefit to the partnership because of his many years of business activity in the area to be serviced by the new partnership. The assigned value of this intangible asset plus the net tangible assets he contributed gave Alexander a 60% initial capital interest in the partnership.
   d. Alexander was designated the only active partner at an annual salary of $24,000 plus an annual bonus of 4% of net income after deducting his salary but before deducting interest

on partners' capital investments (see below). Both the salary and the bonus are operating expenses of the partnership.

e. Each partner is to receive a 6% return on his average capital investment, and such interest is to be an expense of the partnership.

f. All remaining profits or losses are to be shared equally.

2. On October 1, 1979, Barnes sold his partnership interest and rights as of July 1, 1979, to Ware for $370,000. Alexander agreed to accept Ware as a partner if he would contribute sufficient cash to meet the October 1, 1979 principal and interest payment on the mortgage note. Ware made the payment from personal funds.

3. On January 1, 1980, Alexander and Ware admitted a new partner, Randolph. Randolph invested $150,000 cash for a 10% capital interest based on the initial investments at July 1, 1979 of Alexander and Barnes. At January 1, 1980, the book value of the partnership's assets and liabilities approximated their fair market value. Randolph contributed no intangible benefit to the partnership.

Randolph is to receive a 6% return on his average capital investment. His investment also entitled him to 20% of the partnership's profits or losses as defined above. However, for the year ended June 30, 1980, Randolph would receive one-half of his pro rata share of the profits or losses.

4. The accounting records show that on February 1, 1980, Other Miscellaneous Expenses had been charged $3,600 in payment of hospital expenses incurred by Alexander's eight-year-old daughter.

5. All salary payments to Alexander have been charged to his personal account. On June 1, 1980, Ware made a $33,000 withdrawal. These are the only transactions recorded in the partners' personal accounts.

6. Presented below is a trial balance which summarizes the partnership's general ledger balances at June 30, 1980. The general ledger has not been closed.

	DR. (CR.)
Current assets	$ 307,100
Fixed assets, net	1,285,800
Current liabilities	(157,000)
8% mortgage note payable	(290,000)
Alexander, capital	(515,000)
Randolph, capital	(150,000)
Ware, capital	(400,000)
Alexander, personal	24,000
Randolph, personal	—
Ware, personal	33,000
Sales	(872,600)
Cost of sales	695,000
Administrative expenses	16,900
Other miscellaneous expenses	11,100
Interest expense	11,700

Required:

Prepare a workpaper to adjust the net income (loss) and partners' capital accounts for the year ended June 30, 1980, and to close the net income (loss) to the partners' capital accounts at June

30, 1980. Supporting schedules should be in good form. Amortization of goodwill, if any, is to be over a 10-year period. *Ignore all tax considerations.* Use the following column headings and begin balances per books as shown.

DESCRIPTION	NET INCOME (LOSS)	PARTNERS' CAPITAL			OTHER ACCOUNTS	
		ALEXANDER	RANDOLPH	WARE	AMOUNT	NAME
	CR. (DR.)	CR. (DR.)	CR. (DR.)	CR. (DR.)	CR. (DR.)	
Book balances at June 30, 1980	$137,900	$515,000	$150,000	$400,000		

(AICPA adapted)

Problem 15–14

Wells and Williams formed a partnership on January 1, 1977. They have agreed to admit Meyer as a partner on January 1, 1980. The books for the year ending December 31, 1979 are closed. The following additional information is available:

1. Wells and Williams shared profits equally until January 1, 1979, when they agreed to share profits 40% and 60%, respectively. The profit-sharing ratio after Meyer is admitted will be 32% to Wells, 48% to Williams, and 20% to Meyer.

2. Meyer will invest $25,000 cash for a one-fifth interest in the capital of the partnership.

3. Wells and Williams reported earnings of $22,000 in 1977, $35,000 in 1978, and $32,000 in 1979.

4. The partnership of Wells and Williams did not use accrual accounting for some items. It was agreed that before Meyer's admission is recorded, adjustments should be made in the accounts retroactively to report properly the following items on the accrual method of accounting:
   a. The collections on installment sales were regarded as representing first the realization of the gross profit on the contract. After recognition of the full gross profit on each installment sale, all further collections were regarded as a recovery of cost. A minimum down payment equal to the gross profit was required on all installment sales. The full collection of the sales price on installment sales is not reasonably assured at the time of the sale, and there is no reasonable basis for determining the degree of uncollectibility. Data pertaining to installment sales are summarized below:

	1977	1978	1979
Installment contracts receivable per books on December 31 for sales made in:			
1977	$18,000	$10,000	
1978		24,000	$11,000
1979			19,000
Collection on installment sales	51,000	55,000	60,000
Gross profit percentage on installment sales	30%	32%	33%

b. Bad debts on trade accounts receivable were recorded when accounts were deemed uncollectible. It was agreed that an allowance for bad debts should be established and should include $250 from 1978 sales and $950 from 1979 sales. Bad debts previously recorded and years of sale were:

BAD DEBTS RECORDED		BAD DEBTS RECORDED FOR SALES MADE IN		
YEAR	AMOUNT	1977	1978	1979
1977	$ 800	$ 800		
1978	1,390	900	$ 490	
1979	1,575		750	$825
Totals	$3,765	$1,700	$1,240	$825

c. Salaries and insurance were recorded as expense when paid. The amounts of accrued salaries and prepaid insurance at the end of each year were:

	DECEMBER 31		
	1977	1978	1979
Accrued salaries	$600	$650	$820
Prepaid insurance	330	420	580

Required:

A. Prepare schedules presenting the computation of the overstatement or understatement of net income each year for each of the following items, because they were not recorded by the accrual method of accounting:
1. Gross profit on installment sales contracts.
2. Bad debts expense on trade accounts receivable.
3. Salaries expense.
4. Insurance expense.
B. Assume that your computations in part A resulted in net overstatements of net income of $7,000 in 1977 and $6,000 in 1978, and a net understatement of net income of $1,000 in 1979. Prepare a schedule presenting a computation of the adjustment necessary to properly report Wells' and Williams' capital account balances at December 31, for the years 1977, 1978, and 1979.
C. Assume that the adjusted capital balances on January 1, 1980 were $60,000 for Wells and $76,000 for Williams. Prepare a schedule presenting (1) the computation of Meyer's capital balance if he is admitted under the goodwill method, and (2) the amount of goodwill to be recognized.

(AICPA adapted)

Problem 15–15

The partnership agreement of Jones, McDill, Gilrey, Carter, and Adams contained a buy-and-sell agreement, among numerous other provisions, which would become operative in case of the death of any partner. Some provisions contained in the buy-and-sell agreement were as follows:

ARTICLE V. Buy-and-Sell Agreement

1. Purposes of Buy-and-Sell Agreement.
   (a) The partners mutually desire that the business shall be continued by the survivors without interruption or liquidation upon the death of one of the partners.
   (b) The partners also mutually desire that the deceased partner's estate shall receive the full value of the deceased partner's interest in the partnership and that the estate shall share in the earnings of the partnership until the deceased partner's interest shall be fully purchased by the surviving partners.

2. Purchase and Sale of Deceased Partner's Interest.
   (a) Upon the death of the partner first to die, the partnership shall continue to operate without dissolution.
   (b) Upon the decedent's death, the survivors shall purchase and the executor or administrator of the deceased partner's estate shall sell to the surviving partners the deceased partner's interest in the partnership for the price and upon the terms and conditions hereinafter set forth.
   (c) The deceased partner's estate shall retain the deceased partner's interest until the amount specified in the next paragraph shall be paid in full by the surviving partners.
   (d) The parties agree that the purchase price for the partnership interest shall be an amount equal to the deceased partner's capital account at the date of death. Said amount shall be paid to the legal representative of decedent as follows:
       (i) The first installment of 30% of said capital account shall be paid within 60 days from the date of death of the partner or within 30 days from the date on which the personal representative of decedent becomes qualified by law, whichever date is later, and
       (ii) The balance shall be due in four equal installments which shall be due and payable annually on the anniversary date of said death.

3. Deceased Partner's Estate's Share of the Earnings.
   (a) The partners mutually desire that the deceased partner's estate shall be guaranteed a share in the earnings of the partnership over the period said estate retains an interest in the partnership. Said estate shall not be deemed to have an interest in the partnership after the final installment for the deceased partner's capital account is paid, even though a portion of the guaranteed payments specified below may be unpaid and may be due and owing.
   (b) The deceased partner's estate's guaranteed share of the earnings of the partnership shall be determined from two items and shall be paid at different times as follows:
       (i) First, interest shall be paid on the unpaid balance of the deceased partner's capital account at the same date the installment on the purchase price is paid. The amount to be paid shall be an amount equal to accrued interest at the rate of 6% per annum on the unpaid balance of the purchase price for the deceased partner's capital account.
       (ii) Second, the parties agree that the balance of the guaranteed payment from the partnership earnings shall be an amount equal to 25% of the deceased partner's share of the aggregate gross receipts of the partnership for the full 36 months preceding the month of the partner's death. Said amount shall be payable in 48 equal monthly installments without interest, and the first payment shall be made within 60 days following the death of the partner or within 30 days from the date on which the personal representative of deceased becomes qualified, whichever date is

later; provided, however, that the payments so made under this provision during any twelve-month period shall not exceed the highest annual salary on a calendar-year basis received by the partner for the three calendar years immediately preceding the date of his death. In the event that said payment would exceed said salary, then an amount per month shall be paid which does not so exceed said highest monthly salary, and the term over which payments shall be paid to the beneficiary shall be lengthened out beyond the said 48 months in order to complete said payment.

Jones and Adams were killed simultaneously in an automobile accident on January 10, 1980. The surviving partners notified the executors of both estates that the first payment due under the buy-and-sell agreement would be made on March 10, 1980, and that subsequent payments would be paid on the tenth day of each month as due.

The following information was determined from the partnership's records:

PARTNER	PROFIT AND LOSS-SHARING RATIO	CAPITAL ACCOUNT ON JANUARY 10, 1980	ANNUAL SALARIES TO PARTNERS BY YEARS		
			1977	1978	1979
Jones	30	$25,140	$16,500	$17,000	$17,400
McDill	25	21,970	15,000	15,750	16,500
Gilrey	20	4,780	12,000	13,000	14,000
Carter	15	5,860	9,600	10,800	12,000
Adams	10	2,540	8,400	9,600	10,800

The partnership's gross receipts for the three prior years were:

1977	$296,470
1978	325,310
1979	363,220
	$985,000

Required:
Prepare a schedule of the amounts to be paid to the Jones Estate and to the Adams Estate in March 1980, December 1980, and January 1981. The schedule should identify the amounts attributable to earnings, to interest in the guaranteed payments, and to capital. Supporting computation should be in good form.

(AICPA adapted)

Problem 15–16
Gill and Miller have engaged successfully as partners in their law firm for a number of years. Soon after their state's incorporation laws are changed to allow professionals to incorporate, the partners decide to organize a corporation to take over the business of the partnership.

The after-closing trial balance for the partnership is as follows:

After-Closing Trial Balance
December 31, 1980

Cash	$10,000	
Accounts Receivable	30,000	
Allowance for Uncollectibles		$ 3,000
Prepaid Insurance	800	
Office Equipment	15,200	
Accumulated Depreciation		6,600
Gill, Loan (outstanding since 1978, at 5%)		6,400
Gill, Capital (50%)		20,000
Miller, Capital (50%)		20,000
	$56,000	$56,000

Figures shown parenthetically reflect agreed profit and loss sharing ratios.

The partners have hired you as an accountant to adjust the recorded assets and liabilities to their market value and to close the partners' capital accounts to the new corporate capital stock. The corporation is to retain the partnerships books.

Gill and Miller agree that the assets of the partnership should be taken over by the corporation in the following amounts:

Cash	$10,000
Accounts Receivable	25,000
Office Equipment	6,000
Prepaid Insurance	800

Gill's loan to be transferred to his capital account in the amount of $6,600.

Required:
A. Prepare the necessary journal entries to express the agreement above.
B. Prepare the entries to record the issuance of shares to G and M, assuming the issuance of 400 shares (par value $100) of stock to G and M.

16

Partnership Liquidation

In the preceding chapter, dissolution of a partnership in which the business affairs were continued without interruption was discussed. In this chapter, we will consider dissolutions in which the partnership is to be terminated. The phase of partnership operations that begins with the decision to dissolve and ends with the termination of partnership activities is referred to as "winding up the affairs." During this period some of the firm's noncash assets may be converted into cash (realization), liabilities are settled to the extent possible, and any remaining assets are distributed to the partners in settlement of their residual interest. These events may occur over a relatively short period of time (e.g., there may be a lump-sum sale of the assets and the liabilities may be assumed by the purchaser or discharged with the cash received), or over a period of several years if the assets are sold individually as the business affairs are gradually terminated.

In the first part of this chapter, we will assume that all noncash assets are converted into cash before any assets are distributed to creditors and partners; this procedure is referred to as a simple liquidation. In the second part of the chapter, we assume instead that noncash assets are sold in installments and cash is distributed to the various equity interests as it becomes available.

During the liquidation process, the accountant can provide service to the partners in a number of areas. He may assist in preparing financial statements and providing guidance to the partners to ensure that the liquidation proceeds in accordance with legal requirements and the partnership agreement. Much of the accounting for partnership liquidations depends on interpretation of the partnership agreement and the legal provisions governing partnership liquidation. The accountant needs to be familiar with pertinent statutory provisions, which may include the UPA and federal and state bankruptcy laws as well. In addition, for the protection of all parties concerned, it may be advisable to seek legal counsel.

STEPS IN THE LIQUIDATION PROCESS

The first step in the liquidation process is to compute any operating gain or loss up to the date of dissolution. The closing process should be completed and, as part of it, any operating gain or loss should be allocated to the partners in accordance with their profit and loss agreement.

In the first phase of the liquidation process, assets that are not acceptable for distribution in their present form are converted into cash. If the sales price of an asset is greater than (less than) the recorded book value, there is a gain (loss) from the sale. Procedurally, gains and losses on the realization of assets may be collected in one account and then closed to the capital accounts of the individual partners. The allocation of realization gains or losses should be based on the residual profit and loss formula, unless specific provisions for such allocation are made in the partnership agreement.[1] The rationale for this procedure is that since the changes in asset value are the result of risk assumed by the partnership, the gain or loss should be shared in the agreed profit and loss ratio.

In addition, it is very difficult to make an accurate income determination until the firm is liquidated. It may be difficult to separate gains and losses that result from liquidation from the under- or overstatement in book values that results from accounting policies followed in prior years. For example, a gain on the sale of an item of equipment could reflect the fact that the firm had used a conservative depreciation policy and recorded excessive depreciation in prior years. Other adjustments could result from the failure to recognize changes in market values in the appropriate year. Furthermore, any agreement as to interest and salaries in the profit allocation formula are ignored when allocating realization gains and losses. This is reasonable since interest and salaries are profit allocations for time and resources devoted to the normal operating activities of a going concern and are not directly associated with changes in market values of assets.

The next step is to distribute the available assets to creditors and partners. Section 40(b) of the UPA provides that

the liabilities of the partnership shall rank in order of payment, as follows:
  (I) Those owing to creditors other than partners,
  (II) Those owing to partners other than for capital and profits,
  (III) Those owing to partners in respect of capital,
  (IV) Those owing to partners in respect of profits.

Items III and IV are generally combined into one balance because of the practical problem of separating them. In other words, after several years of operation, a partner's capital contributions, withdrawals, and profit and loss elements may become combined into one balance and difficult to separate if the income summary account is closed to the capital accounts of each partner.

The UPA also provides for an order of payment that ranks partnership obligations to a partner ahead of asset distribution to a partner for capital contributions. However, in practice it is legally permissible to offset a partner's loan balance against his debit

---

[1]Section 18 of the UPA provides a list of rights and duties of partners, "subject to any agreement between them." Section 18(a) provides that "each partner . . . must contribute towards the losses, whether of capital or otherwise, sustained by the partnership according to his share in the profits."

capital balance. The courts have recognized that this "right of offset" is necessary in order to avoid the potential inequity of distributing cash to a partner to satisfy an outstanding loan balance when the partner has either a debit capital balance, or potential for a debit capital balance. A debit capital balance is considered an asset of the partnership.[2] If the partner is unable to honor this obligation to the partnership, and for some reason cannot be forced to do so, the debit balance in his capital account must be absorbed by the remaining partners in their relative profit and loss ratio. The residual claims of the remaining partners are reduced, as is the amount of cash they will receive. Thus, without modification for the right of offset, the order of payment established by the UPA may result in a payment to a partner who may eventually owe cash to the partnership as a result of a debit capital balance.

During the liquidation process, exercise of the "right of offset" results in the same amount of cash and the same order of distribution that would result if the partner's loan balance was combined with his capital account. Unless otherwise stated, this simplication will be recognized in the illustrations presented in this chapter and the problems at the end of the chapter. However, the accounts should not be combined in the ledger, since two different types of entity claims are represented. Furthermore, the distinction between loan and capital balances should be maintained, since the UPA [Section 18(c)] provides that a partner is entitled to accrued interest on a loan balance. In the ledger, distributions made to a partner with a loan balance should be recorded first as a reduction in the loan balance of that partner. As noted above, this is not meant to imply that the loan balance must be paid before any cash can be distributed to other partners for their capital interest. The "right of offset" may result in a partner receiving partial payment for a capital interest before a partner with a loan balance receives a distribution of cash.

SIMPLE LIQUIDATION ILLUSTRATED

Equity Interest of All Partners Adequate to Absorb Realization Losses

To illustrate the accounting for a simple liquidation, assume that the condensed balance sheet of ABC Partnership as reported below was prepared just before the liquidation:

---

[2]Section 40(a) of the UPA defines the assets of the partnership as:
  (I) The partnership property,
  (II) The contributions of partners necessary for the payment of all the liabilities specified in clause (b) of this paragraph.
Section 40(b), referred to above, specified that amounts owing to creditors and to partners for loans, capital, and profits are liabilities of a partnership. Thus, if a partner has a debit balance, there must be unsatisfied equity claims. The amount due from the deficit partner to settle the unsatisfied claim is an asset as defined in Section 40(a).

ASSETS		LIABILITIES AND CAPITAL	
Cash	20,000	Liabilities	70,000
Other Assets	180,000	C, Loan	10,000
		A, Capital (50%)	70,000
		B, Capital (30%)	40,000
		C, Capital (20%)	10,000
Totals	200,000	Totals	200,000

The profit and loss ratio is in parentheses.

The liquidation of the ABC Partnership is summarized in the realization and liquidation schedule presented in Illustration 16–1. Note that the loan to C of $10,000 has been combined with his $10,000 capital balance.

ILLUSTRATION 16–1
Schedule of Partnership Realization and Liquidation
All Partners' Capital Balances Sufficient to Absorb Share of Losses

	CASH	OTHER ASSETS	LIABILITIES	CAPITAL AND LOAN BALANCES		
				A	B	C
Profit and Loss Ratio				50%	30%	20%
Balances Before Realization	20,000	180,000	(70,000)	(70,000)	(40,000)	(20,000)
Sale of Assets and Allocation of $40,000 Loss	140,000	(180,000)		20,000	12,000	8,000
	160,000	-0-	(70,000)	(50,000)	(28,000)	(12,000)
Payment to Creditors	(70,000)		70,000			
Payment to C for Loan	(10,000)					10,000
Payment to Partners for Capital Interest	(80,000)			50,000	28,000	2,000
	—	—	—	—	—	—

In this and subsequent illustrations in this chapter (   ) means a credit to an account or a credit balance.

Although formal journal entries are not shown, they would be recorded in a journal in accordance with the tabular arrangement summarized in the realization and liquidation statement, except that the first $10,000 paid to C is recorded in the ledger as a reduction in the loan balance. In this illustration, it is assumed that assets with a book value of $180,000 were sold for $140,000. The net loss of $40,000 is distributed to the partners in their agreed profit and loss ratio of 5:3:2. In this case, no special problems are encountered in distributing the cash, since the capital interests of all the partners were adequate to absorb their respective shares of realization losses, and the cash balance is adequate to pay all creditors. The order of cash distribution is: (1) $70,000 is paid to the creditors, (2) Partner C receives $10,000 for his loan, and (3) remaining cash is distributed to partners for their capital interests. Partner C receives in total $12,000, $10,000 for his loan and $2,000 for his capital interest. Observe that the final cash distribution of $80,000 is based on capital balances, not profit and loss ratios. The rationale for doing so is that capital balance represents the partner's residual claims to the assets remaining after the settlement of the partnership obligations.

Now assume that the firm sells the other assets for $100,000 (see Illustration 16–2). In order to illustrate the justification for the "right of offset," the loan to C is not combined with his capital interest. Allocation of the $80,000 net loss results in a $6,000 balance in C's capital account.

ILLUSTRATION 16–2

Schedule of Partnership Realization and Liquidation

One Partner with a Debit Capital Balance

					CAPITAL BALANCES		
		OTHER		C	A	B	C
	CASH	ASSETS	LIABILITIES	LOAN	.5	.3	.2
Balances Before Realization	20,000	180,000	(70,000)	(10,000)	(70,000)	(40,000)	(10,000)
Sale of Assets and Allocation							
of $80,000 Loss	100,000	(180,000)			40,000	24,000	16,000
	120,000	–0–	(70,000)	(10,000)	(30,000)	(16,000)	6,000
Payment to Creditors	(70,000)		70,000				
	50,000	—	—	(10,000)	(30,000)	(16,000)	6,000
Offset Loan Against Capital Balance				6,000			(6,000)
	50,000	—	—	(4,000)	(30,000)	(16,000)	–0–
Payment to Partners	(50,000)			4,000	30,000	16,000	
	—	—	—	—	—	—	—

After the $70,000 payment to creditors, the partnership has assets of $50,000 cash and a $6,000 claim against C for the amount of the deficit. The cash balance is insufficient to satisfy the partners' loan and capital balances of $56,000. However, the "right of offset" should be exercised, because if C were first paid $10,000 to settle the loan the current balance in the cash account would be only $40,000 to satisfy A and B's claim of $46,000. If C fails to contribute the $6,000, then A and B would have to absorb a greater share of the losses than they agreed to. The cash distributed to the partners would be the same if the loan to C and his capital interest were combined. After allocating the loss of $180,000, C would have a net capital interest of $4,000 (20,000 − 16,000), which he would receive as settlement in the final cash distribution.

Equity Interest of One Partner
Inadequate to Absorb Realization Losses

Now assume that the noncash assets are sold and the partnership realizes cash of $70,000. Allocation of the $110,000 loss to the partners in their agreed profit and loss ratio results in a charge to Partner C of $22,000 (see Illustration 16–3).

ILLUSTRATION 16–3
Schedule of Partnership Realization and Liquidation
One Partner With Net Deficit

| | | | | CAPITAL AND LOAN BALANCES | | |
| | | OTHER | | A | B | C |
PART A	CASH	ASSETS	LIABILITIES	.5	.3	.2
Balances Before Realization	20,000	180,000	(70,000)	(70,000)	(40,000)	(20,000)
Sale of Assets and						
Allocation of						
$110,000 Loss	70,000	(180,000)		55,000	33,000	22,000
	90,000	–0–	(70,000)	(15,000)	(7,000)	2,000
Payment to Creditors	(70,000)		70,000			
	20,000	—	—	(15,000)	(7,000)	2,000
Receipt of Cash from C	2,000					(2,000)
	22,000	—	—	(15,000)	(7,000)	—
Payment to Partners	(22,000)			15,000	7,000	
	—	—	—	—	—	—
PART B						
Balances from Part A	20,000	—	—	(15,000)	(7,000)	2,000
Allocation of C's Deficit:						
To A—5/8				1,250		
To B—3/8					750	(2,000)
	20,000	—	—	(13,750)	(6,250)	–0–
Payment to Partners	(20,000)			13,750	6,250	
	–0–	—	—	—	—	—

At this stage, the liquidation is incomplete. Several alternatives could happen next. First of all, C has made an agreement with A and B to share 20% of all losses. To fulfill this agreement, he must pay $2,000 to the partnership. If he does so, the liquidation would be completed as shown, with A receiving $15,000 and B receiving $7,000. Second, if C is personally insolvent (i.e., he has no personal assets available to contribute to the firm), then A and B must absorb C's debit balance in the ratio of their respective profit and loss ratio (5:3), as shown in Part B of the statement. As discussed earlier, the debit balance is considered an asset for which no cash is realized and, thus, an added liquidation loss. This, of course, reduces the amount of cash that A and B receive.

A third possibility exists if at this point the partners are unsure what C will do, but they want to distribute all available cash. The problem is how to decide how to distribute $20,000 to satisfy their capital interest of $22,000. To determine a safe distribution, a conservative assumption is made that C will not contribute any of the $2,000 to the partnership. If C does not contribute any of the $2,000, the $2,000 debit balance must be absorbed by A and B in their respective profit ratio of 5:3. Cash should be distributed to maintain sufficient capital balances to do so. In order to determine the cash distribution, a pro forma allocation of the $2,000 loss is made as follows:

	A	B	C
Net capital balances before cash distribution	(15,000)	(7,000)	2,000
Allocate possible loss: 5/8	1,250		
3/8		750	(2,000)
Safe cash payment	(13,750)	(6,250)	–0–

The $20,000 should be distributed $13,750 to A and $6,250 to B. This distribution will result in capital balances of $1,250 and $750, respectively, for A and B. The balances are sufficient to absorb their respective shares of C's deficit in the event that C is unable to pay the $2,000 he owes the partnership. If C does contribute $2,000, then the capital balances of A and B represent their residual capital interest in the cash received.

Realization Losses Resulting in Two Capital Accounts with Debit Balances

In Illustration 16–3, the distribution of $110,000 realization losses resulted in a debit balance in Partner C's capital account only. However, a loss greater than $133,333 ($40,000/.30) would result in a debit balance for both Partners B and C. The liquidation process may also result in a debit capital balance when a partner's capital balance after realization losses is insufficient to absorb his share of losses that arise from failure to collect cash from another partner with a debit capital balance. In both cases, capital accounts with debit balances that are uncollectible or assumed uncollectible in the computation of safe payments are allocated to the remaining partners. The debit balances are allocated to the partners with credit balances on the basis of their relative profit and loss ratios.

To illustrate, assume the facts used in the previous illustrations except that the noncash assets are sold for $52,000. Liquidation would proceed as summarized in Illustration 16–4.

ILLUSTRATION 16–4
Schedule of Partnership Realization and Liquidation
One Partner with Net Deficit: Safe Payment

| | | OTHER | | CAPITAL AND LOAN BALANCES | | |
	CASH	ASSETS	LIABILITIES	A .5	B .3	C .2
Balances Before Realization	20,000	180,000	(70,000)	(70,000)	(40,000)	(20,000)
Sale of Assets and						
Allocation of $128,000 Loss	52,000	(180,000)		64,000	38,400	25,600
	72,000	—	(70,000)	(6,000)	(1,600)	5,600
Payment to Creditors	(70,000)		70,000			
	2,000	—	—	(6,000)	(1,600)	5,600
Payment to A	(2,000)			2,000		
		—	—	(4,000)	(1,600)	5,600

After allocating the $128,000 loss to the partners and paying $70,000 to the creditors, $2,000 cash remains. If the partners wish to distribute the $2,000 at this point, it will be necessary to calculate the capital balances needed to absorb all possible losses, as shown in Illustration 16–5.

ILLUSTRATION 16–5
Calculation of Safe Payment For Cash Distribution

		CAPITAL AND LOAN BALANCES		
		A	B	C
	CASH	.5	.3	.2
Balances	2,000	(6,000)	(1,600)	5,600
Allocation of C				
To A—5/8		3,500		
To B—3/8			2,100	(5,600)
Balances	2,000	(2,500)	500	–0–
Allocation of B		500	(500)	
Balances	2,000	(2,000)	—	—

To do so, it is assumed that any partner with a debit balance is personally insolvent. The objective of the computations is to determine the partner(s) whose capital balances are sufficient to absorb all potential liquidation losses. The first step is to allocate C's debit balance (after offsetting the loan) to A and B in the ratio of their respective profit and loss ratios. B's capital balance of $1,600 is insufficient to absorb the additional potential liquidation loss. If C does not contribute $5,600, then the partnership has a claim against B for $500. Thus, B should not receive any of the $2,000. The next step is to assume that B is personally insolvent and allocate the debit balance of $500 to the remaining partners in their respective profit and loss ratio. In this case, all of the $500 loss must be absorbed by A.

The $2,000 cash distribution to A results in a credit balance of $4,000 in A's capital account. At this point, any number of events may occur. At one extreme, C may contribute $5,600 to the partnership; if so, the cash would be distributed $4,000 to A and $1,600 to B. However, if first C and then B are unable to contribute any additional cash to the partnership to cover their debit balances, the $4,000 balance of A is sufficient to absorb the maximum amount of potential losses that may be charged to him. To complete the illustration, we will assume that something between the two extremes occurs and that C contributes $4,000 cash to the partnership. The liquidation is summarized in Illustration 16–6.

ILLUSTRATION 16-6
Schedule of Partnership Realization and Liquidation
Additional Contribution by Partner with Deficit Capital

		CAPITAL AND LOAN BALANCES		
		A	B	C
	CASH	.5	.3	.2
Balances After Cash Distribution to A				
(see Illustration 16-4)		(4,000)	(1,600)	5,600
Contribution from C	$4,000			(4,000)
Balances	4,000	(4,000)	(1,600)	1,600
Allocation of C's Remaining Deficit		1,000	600	(1,600)
Balances	4,000	(3,000)	(1,000)	
Payment to Partners	(4,000)	3,000	1,000	
	-0-	-0-	-0-	-0-

In summary, cash should not be distributed to any partner until all liquidation losses are recognized in the accounts or are provided for in determining the safe cash payment. Accordingly, a partner should not receive a cash distribution unless his net capital interest is sufficient to absorb his share of the maximum possible remaining losses.

PARTNERSHIP INSOLVENT

One of the disadvantages of the partnership form of business organization is that the partners generally have unlimited liability to partnership creditors. As a result, creditors of a partnership that were not paid in full from distribution of partnership assets can seek recovery from the personal assets of the individual partners. Conversely, personal creditors (i.e., nonpartnership obligations of a partner owed outside the partnership) of an individual partner can seek recovery of payment from personal assets of the respective partner or under certain conditions from partnership assets. Recognition of the rights of these two groups of creditors, and the classification of assets into personal and partnership categories, is referred to as "marshalling of assets." The rules as to the availability of assets for each class of creditors in states that have adopted the UPA are as follows:

A. Partnership creditors:
  1. Partnership creditors have first claim to partnership assets.
  2. The partnership creditors can seek recovery from personal assets of individual partners if partnership assets are insufficient to fully satisfy their claims. Such claims are subordinate to personal creditors and may be made against an individual partner regardless of whether the partner has a debit or credit equity balance in the partnership.

B. Personal creditors:
  1. Non-partnership creditors of a partner have first claim to the respective partner's personal assets. An amount owed by a partner to the partnership

by nature of a deficit capital interest is not included in this group of personal creditors. The UPA (Section 40-i) provides that a claim of the partnership against a partner for an amount "owing to the partnership by way of contribution" is subordinate to both personal creditors and partnership-creditors seeking recovery from personal assets.

2. To the extent that personal creditors do not recover from personal assets, they can seek recovery from the partnership assets still available after partnership creditors have been paid. However, recovery from partnership assets is limited to the extent that the partner has a credit interest in the partnership assets.

Because of the foregoing rules, the reader should understand the importance of properly recording all partnership assets, recognizing all liabilities to be assumed by the partnership, and recognizing the agreed interest of each partner in partnership assets.

To illustrate the marshalling of assets rules, assume that ABC Partnership reports the following balance sheet after the sale of all noncash assets:

DEBITS		CREDITS	
Cash	$ 50,000	Liabilities	$ 75,000
B, Capital	15,000	A, Capital	15,000
C, Capital	35,000	D, Capital	10,000
Total	$100,000		$100,000

Partners share profits and losses equally.

The personal status of each partner exclusive of partnership interest is as follows:

	PERSONAL ASSETS	PERSONAL LIABILITIES	ASSETS GREATER THAN (LESS THAN) LIABILITIES
A	20,000	50,000	(30,000)
B	33,000	30,000	3,000
C	90,000	40,000	50,000
D	40,000	10,000	30,000

The liquidation of the partnership is summarized in Illustration 16–7. After the cash of $50,000 is distributed to the creditors, the partnership has unpaid obligations of $25,000. Bankruptcy laws would dictate which of the partnership creditors would receive the $50,000. However, since this decision would have no impact on the total unpaid claims of the partnership, we will view the pool of creditors as if it were one obligation and will treat any cash payment as a reduction in the total liabilities.

The partnership creditors can proceed for judgment against Partner B, C, or D, even though D has a credit balance. It is assumed in this illustration that the partnership creditors obtained judgment against Partner C, and he is forced to contribute an additional $25,000 to the partnership. This contribution reduces his debit balance to $10,000.

ILLUSTRATION 16-7
Schedule of Partnership Liquidation
Partnership Insolvent

| | | | CAPITAL AND LOAN BALANCES | | | |
| | | | A | B | C | D |
	CASH	LIABILITIES	(¼)	(¼)	(¼)	(¼)
Balance Before Cash Distribution	50,000	(75,000)	(15,000)	15,000 *	35,000 *	(10,000)
Payment to Creditors	(50,000)	50,000				
	-0-	(25,000)	(15,000)	15,000	35,000	(10,000)
Contribution from C	25,000				(25,000)	
Payment to Creditors	(25,000)	25,000				
	—	—	(15,000)	15,000	10,000	(10,000)
Contribution from B	3,000			(3,000)		
	3,000		(15,000)	12,000	10,000	(10,000)
Allocation of B's Deficit			4,000	(12,000)	4,000	4,000
	3,000	—	(11,000)	—	14,000	(6,000)
Contribution from C	14,000				(14,000)	
	17,000	—	(11,000)	—		(6,000)
Payment to Partners	(17,000)		11,000			6,000
	—	—	—	—	—	—

*Debit capital balances.

Partners A and B are personally insolvent, that is, their obligations to the partnership and personal creditors exceed their personal assets. All of partner A's personal assets must go to partially satisfy his personal liabilities of $50,000. The personal creditors of A can also look for partial settlement of their claims through any distribution to A from final liquidation of the partnership. In this case, A receives $11,000, which would be distributed to the unpaid personal creditors. The first $30,000 of B's assets must be used to satisfy his personal liabilities. The remaining $3,000 in assets would be contributed to the partnership to partially reduce his capital deficit of $15,000.[3] The remaining $12,000 deficit balance is a liquidation loss and must be absorbed by the remaining partners in their relative profit and loss ratio. The

---

[3] In states in which the common law or federal bankruptcy laws are controlling, the personal assets of a partner with a debit capital balance are allocated between the personal creditors and the amount owed to the partnership. In this illustration, the personal assets of Partner B would be allocated as follows:

Total liabilities	
Personal liabilities	30,000
Amount owed to partnership	15,000
Total obligation of Partner B	45,000
Allocation:	
To personal creditors (30,000/45,000) × 33,000 =	22,000
To partnership (15,000/45,000) × 33,000 =	11,000
Total personal assets of Partner B	33,000

remaining step is to collect $14,000 cash from Partner C, who is the only partner with a deficit who is also personally solvent.

The same net result would be obtained if D were to pay $25,000 to the partnership. This payment would increase his interest in the firm and he would receive $31,000 in the final liquidation, as summarized in Illustration 16–8. The same net cash receipt from the partnership (additional investment) is obtained in both cases [A, $11,000; B, ($3,000); C, ($39,000); D, $6,000].

ILLUSTRATION 16–8
Schedule of Partnership Liquidation
Partnership Insolvent

	CASH	LIABILITIES	A (¼)	B (¼)	C (¼)	D (¼)
				CAPITAL AND LOAN BALANCES		
From Illustration 16–7		(25,000)	(15,000)	15,000	35,000	(10,000)
Contribution from D	25,000					(25,000)
Payment to Creditors	(25,000)	25,000				
	—	—	(15,000)	15,000	35,000	(35,000)
Contribution from B	3,000			(3,000)		
	3,000	—	(15,000)	12,000	35,000	(35,000)
Allocation of B's Deficit			4,000	(12,000)	4,000	4,000
	3,000	—	(11,000)	—	39,000	(31,000)
Contribution from C	39,000				(39,000)	
	42,000	—	(11,000)	—	—	(31,000)
Payment to Partners	(42,000)		11,000			31,000
	—	—	—	—	—	—

To illustrate further the order of distributing the partners' personal assets, assume that C is the only personally solvent partner with personal assets of $70,000 and personal liabilities of $40,000. The order of distribution is as follows:

1. Personal creditors—$40,000.

2. Partnership creditors—$25,000.

3. To partnership in partial settlement of $10,000 deficit—$5,000.

As summarized in Illustration 16–9, B's deficit of $15,000 and C's remaining deficit of $5,000 must now be absorbed by A and D equally, since they share profits equally. The end result is a $5,000 cash distribution to Partner A.

ILLUSTRATION 16–9
Schedule of Partnership Liquidation
Partnership Insolvent

	CASH	LIABILITIES	CAPITAL AND LOAN BALANCES			
			A (¼)	B (¼)	C (¼)	D (¼)
From Illustration 16–7		(25,000)	(15,000)	15,000	35,000	(10,000)
Contribution from C	25,000				(25,000)	
Payment to Creditors	(25,000)	25,000				
	—	—	(15,000)	15,000	10,000	(10,000)
Contribution from C	5,000				(5,000)	
	5,000	—	(15,000)	15,000	5,000	(10,000)
Allocation of B and C's Deficit			10,000	(15,000)	(5,000)	10,000
	5,000	—	(5,000)	—	—	—
Payment to Partner	(5,000)		5,000			
	—	—	—	—	—	—

INSTALLMENT LIQUIDATION

In the first part of the chapter, it was assumed that all of the noncash assets were converted into cash and the resulting gain or loss allocated before any distribution was made to the creditors or to the partners. It could be an advantage to the partnership, however, if conversion of noncash assets into cash were extended over several months. For example, in certain types of businesses, such as land development, more cash may be generated if the company completes construction projects it has started, or, as is frequently the case, the partnership may receive a greater cash price for the noncash assets if they are not sold at a forced liquidation. If the liquidation extends over a period of time, the partners will probably prefer that cash be distributed as it becomes available. If partners are to receive cash in installments before the total losses of liquidation and the total cash available are known, safeguards must be used to protect the interest of the creditors and the respective interest of each partner. In addition, the individual in charge of the liquidation must use safeguards to avoid potential personal liability for wrongful distributions.

The remainder of this chapter focuses on the problems associated with a liquidation in installments and the general rules governing such liquidations. Once again, many of the procedures followed are necessary to satisfy legal requirements and for the protection of the person in charge of the liquidation and the residual partners' interest.

General Rules for Installment Distributions of Cash

In Illustration 16–5, when the partners were unsure as to the collectibility of a debit balance from a deficit partner, the available cash was still distributed to the other partners. In computing the cash distribution, care was taken to ensure that the partners' remaining capital balances would be adequate to absorb the potential loss of the deficit partner. The same technique is used to compute the cash distribution in installments. The only difference is that all the assets have not been sold. At this point, the amount of cash to be generated on the unsold assets and the resulting gain or loss is not known. Therefore, the partners should view each cash distribution as if it were the final distribution.

One technique used to calculate a safe cash distribution is based on three assumptions. They are:

1. Any loan balances to partners are offset (or added if a credit capital balance) against the respective partners' capital accounts.

2. The remaining noncash assets will not generate any additional cash. In other words, the maximum remaining loss is equal to the book value of noncash assets. (This assumption will be modified later in the chapter.)

3. Any partner with a debit balance in his capital account will make no additional contributions to the firm.

The result of applying these assumptions is that cash will not be distributed to a partner whose capital account balance (including loan balance and drawing account) is insufficient to absorb his share of potential losses from either the write-off of assets or from the failure of a deficit partner to cover his deficit. Of course, no partner should receive cash until the liabilities have been liquidated or provided for through the retention of adequate cash to satisfy potential creditor claims.

Computation of Safe Payment Before Each Distribution

Application of the installment liquidation assumptions will bring the partners' capital balances into their profit and loss ratio as soon as possible. Any subsequent distributions are based on the profit and loss ratio. At this point, assuming that the maximum remaining loss is the book value of the noncash assets, the capital balances of the partners are sufficient to absorb their share of all potential remaining losses.[4]

---

[4]The maximum loss may exceed the book value of the recorded noncash assets (the sum of the capital balances) if the disposal costs of the remaining noncash assets are excessive. If this occurs, however, all partners will report debit capital balances.

To illustrate the assumptions developed in the preceding section, assume that the following condensed balance sheet was prepared prior to the partners' agreement to liquidate the partnership:

Cash	$ 10,000	Liabilities	$ 28,000
Other Assets	100,000	A, Capital	34,000
		B, Capital	30,000
		C, Capital	18,000
Total	$110,000	Total	$110,000

The realization of the noncash assets was as follows:

	SALES PRICE	BOOK VALUE
Sale No. 1	$20,000	$30,000
" No. 2	15,000	25,000
" No. 3	10,000	30,000
" No. 4	2,000	10,000
" No. 5	–0–	5,000

The realization and liquidation are summarized in Illustration 16–10. After the first sale of assets and payment to creditors, $2,000 remains to be distributed. In this case, the assumption that the remaining assets of $70,000 (Schedule A) will be worthless results in a debit balance in B's capital account. Allocation of the deficit results in a debit in the capital account of C, which must be absorbed by A. Thus, if $2,000 is paid to A, the person in charge of the liquidation can be assured that A will not be required to make additional contributions to the partnership unless significant amounts of unrecorded liabilities are discovered or significant amounts of liquidation expenses are incurred.

A safe payment schedule is prepared each time cash is to be distributed. The second payment to A and C brings their capital balances into a ratio of 3:2. The two partners now have capital balances sufficient to absorb their share of future losses up to $50,000. The capital balances of both A and C would be sufficient to absorb their share of the maximum possible losses that remain of $45,000. However, if the remaining assets were worthless, B's capital balance of $20,000 would be inadequate to absorb his share of the losses, which would be $22,500. The other cash distributions would proceed as illustrated.

Additional Losses, Discovery of Liabilities, and Liquidation Expense

Up to this point in this chapter, all available cash was distributed to (1) the partnership's creditors who were recorded on the partnership books, or (2) the partners. In the calculation of a safe payment, it was assumed that the potential loss was equal to the book value of the remaining noncash assets. In addition, no liquidation expenses were

ILLUSTRATION 16–10
Schedule of Partnership Realization and Liquidation
Installment Liquidation

	CASH	OTHER ASSETS	LIABILITIES	CAPITAL AND LOAN BALANCES A .3	B .5	C .2
Balance Before Realization	10,000	100,000	(28,000)	(34,000)	(30,000)	(18,000)
Sale of Assets	20,000	(30,000)		3,000	5,000	2,000
	30,000	70,000	(28,000)	(31,000)	(25,000)	(16,000)
Payment to Creditors	(28,000)	—	28,000			
Payment to Partners	2,000	70,000	—	(31,000)	(25,000)	(16,000)
(SCHEDULE A)	(2,000)			2,000		
	—	70,000	—	(29,000)	(25,000)	(16,000)
Sale of Assets	15,000	(25,000)		3,000	5,000	2,000
	15,000	45,000	—	(26,000)	(20,000)	(14,000)
Payment to Partners						
(SCHEDULE B)	(15,000)			11,000		4,000
	—	45,000	—	(15,000)	(20,000)	(10,000)
Sale of Assets	10,000	(30,000)		6,000	10,000	4,000
	10,000	15,000	—	(9,000)	(10,000)	(6,000)
Payment to Partners						
(SCHEDULE C)	(10,000)			4,500	2,500	3,000
	—	15,000	—	(4,500)	(7,500)	(3,000)
Sale of Assets	2,000	(10,000)		2,400	4,000	1,600
	2,000	5,000	—	(2,100)	(3,500)	(1,400)
Payment to Partners	(2,000)			600	1,000	400
	—	5,000	—	(1,500)	(2,500)	(1,000)
Write-off of Assets		(5,000)		1,500	2,500	1,000
	—	—	—	—	—	—

SCHEDULE A
COMPUTATION OF SAFE PAYMENTS

	A	B	C
	.3	.5	.2
Capital and Loan Balances	(31,000)	(25,000)	(16,000)
Allocation of Potential Loss—$70,000	21,000	35,000	14,000
	(10,000)	10,000	(2,000)
Allocation of B's Potential Deficit	6,000	(10,000)	4,000
	(4,000)	–0–	2,000
Allocation of C's Potential Deficit	2,000		(2,000)
Safe Payment	(2,000)	–0–	–0–

SCHEDULE B
COMPUTATION OF SAFE PAYMENTS

	A	B	C
	.3	.5	.2
Capital and Loan Balances	(26,000)	(20,000)	(14,000)
Allocation of Potential Loss—$45,000	13,500	22,500	9,000
	(12,500)	2,500	(5,000)
Allocation of B's Potential Deficit	1,500	(2,500)	1,000
Safe Payment	(11,000)	—	(4,000)

SCHEDULE C
COMPUTATION OF SAFE PAYMENTS

	A	B	C
	.3	.5	.2
Capital and Loan Balances	(9,000)	(10,000)	(6,000)
Allocation of Potential Loss—$15,000	4,500	7,500	3,000
Safe Payment	(4,500)	(2,500)	(3,000)

incurred. As the liquidation proceeds, some liabilities that had not been recorded previously may be reported. These creditors have claims that must be satisfied from the available cash before payments are made to partners for their capital interest.

Certain expenses, for example, such as the reasonable cost of carrying out the liquidation, have priority over payments to creditors. Furthermore, the disposal cost of assets may exceed the proceeds from the sale of the assets so that a loss results that is greater than the assets' recorded book value. Such items can be considered in the safe payment schedule by adding the estimated liquidation expenses, disposal cost, and unrecorded liabilities to the book value of noncash assets. To illustrate, assume the facts presented in Illustration 16–10 except that it is estimated that added expenses of $1,000 will be incurred in completing the liquidation. The safe payment calculation for the first cash distribution would be modified as follows:

	A	B	C
Capital and loan balances	(31,000)	(25,000)	(16,000)
Allocation of potential losses (70,000 + 1,000)	21,300	35,500	14,200
Balances	(9,700)	10,500	(1,800)
Allocation of B's potential loss	6,300	(10,500)	4,200
Balances	(3,400)	–0–	2,400
Allocation of C's potential loss	2,400		(2,400)
Balances	(1,000)	–0–	–0–

As can be seen, the effect of the adjustment is to hold back cash equal to the estimated expenses, which results in a corresponding reduction in the cash distributed to A.

ADVANCE PLAN FOR THE DISTRIBUTION OF CASH

In the installment liquidation illustrations presented thus far, a safe payment to each partner was calculated in a separate schedule before each cash distribution. This process was necessary until the capital accounts were in the profit and loss ratio. Although this method is feasible, it is more informative, and a simpler process as well, to prepare an advance schedule that specifies the order in which each partner will participate and the amount of cash each partner will receive as it becomes available for distribution. For example, from such a schedule, the personal creditors of an insolvent partner would be able to compute how much cash would have to be generated from the sale of the partnership assets before any cash is distributed to the insolvent partner.

To illustrate the procedures for the preparation of an advance cash distribution plan, assume the set of facts employed in Illustration 16–10. The objective of the procedure is to bring the balances of the partners' capital accounts into the agreed profit and loss ratio as soon as possible. The rationale for this procedure is that once the capital balances are in the profit and loss ratio, no one partner is in any better position to absorb losses than any other partner.

Steps in the development of an advance cash distribution plan are presented in Illustration 16–11 and explained below.

Step 1   Determine the net capital interest of each partner by combining the balance in the partner's capital account with obligations to or receivables from the partner.

	A	B	C
Capital Balance	34,000	20,000	18,000
Loan Balance	–0–	10,000	–0–
Net Capital Interest	34,000	30,000	18,000

Justification for this "right of offset" was explained earlier.

Step 2   Determine the order in which the partners are to participate in cash distributions. The objective of this step is to provide an order of cash distribution in which the ratio of the partners' capital interest will eventually be equal to their profit and loss ratio. Once this is accomplished, all partners will have an equal ability to absorb their share of partnership losses. Several approaches can be used to accomplish this objective. One systematic approach is to determine the loss absorption potential of each partner by dividing the net capital interest of each partner by his respective profit and loss ratio.

	A	B	C
Net Capital Interest	34,000	30,000	18,000
Profit and Loss Ratio	.30	.50	.20
Loss Absorption Potential	113,333	60,000	90,000
Order of Cash Distribution	1	3	2

This computation determines the maximum amount of loss each partner can absorb and provides a basis for ranking the partners in terms of each partner's capital interest relative to his loss ratio. Expressed another way, the partner with the largest positive difference between his percentage share of capital and his percentage share of losses should be the first to receive a cash distribution. Partner A has approximately 41% (34,000/82,000) of the total partnership capital, but absorbs only 30% of partnership losses. Partner B has about 37% (30,000/82,000) of the total partnership capital, but must absorb 50% of any loss. Partner C has 22% (18,000/82,000) of the total partnership capital and absorbs only 20% of losses. Thus, Partner A should receive a cash distribution before any cash is distributed to B or C, and Partner C should participate in cash distributions before any distribution to Partner B.

In summary, the partner with the largest loss absorption potential (Partner A) will receive the first distribution of cash (or other assets) after the creditors' claims have been satisfied. The partner with the lowest loss absorption potential (Partner B) will be the last partner to participate in the distribution of assets from the partnership.

ILLUSTRATION 16–11
Preparation of an Advance Plan for the Distribution of Cash

	A	B	C
STEP 1			
Capital Balances	34,000	20,000	18,000
Loan Balances	—	10,000	—
Net Capital Interest	34,000	30,000	18,000
Profit and Loss Ratio	30%	50%	20%
STEP 2			
Loss Necessary to Reduce			
Net Capital Balance to Zero	113,333	60,000	90,000
Order of Cash Distribution	1	3	2

	LOSS ABSORPTION POTENTIAL			ASSET DISTRIBUTION		
STEP 3	A	B	C	A	B	C
Profit and Loss Ratio	.30	.50	.20	.30	.50	.20
Loss Absorption Potential	113,333	60,000	90,000			
Distribution to A to reduce his capital interest so that his loss absorption potential is the same as C's.	23,333					
(113,333 − 90,000 = 23,333 × .30)				7,000		
Balances after Distribution to A	90,000	60,000	90,000			
Distribution to A and C to reduce their capital interest so that their loss absorption potential is the same as B's	30,000		30,000			
(90,000 − 60,000 = 30,000 × .30)				9,000		
(90,000 − 60,000 = 30,000 × .20)						6,000
Balances after Distribution to A and C	60,000	60,000	60,000			
Remainder of Asset Distributions				.30	.50	.20

STEP 4

CASH DISTRIBUTION PLAN

		A	B	C
ORDER OF CASH DISTRIBUTION	LIABILITIES	.3	.5	.2
1. First $28,000	100%			
2. Next $7,000		100%		
3. Next $15,000		60%		40%
4. Remainder		30%	50%	20%

Step 3 In Step 2, the order in which each partner is to participate in cash distributions was determined. The next step is to compute the amount of cash each partner is to receive as it becomes available for distribution. The objective is to determine the *amount* of cash to distribute to each partner to bring the ratios of their capital interests in the partnership into agreement with their profit and loss ratios. One way to compute this is to bring the loss absorption potential of each partner computed

in Step 2 into balance.[5] It was determined in Step 2 that A is in the strongest position relative to the other partners and is to receive the first cash distribution. A is capable of absorbing his share of $113,333 in losses, which is $23,333 greater than C's $(113,333 - 90,000)$, who is the next partner to participate in cash distributions. However, A must absorb only 30% or $7,000 $(23,333 \times .30)$ of such potential losses. Thus, a payment to A of $7,000 would reduce his loss absorption potential to $90,000 $(34,000 - 7,000 = 27,000/.30 = 90,000)$. A and C are now in the same relative position with respect to their ability to absorb their share of partnership losses. Also, note that a payment of $7,000 to A brings his capital interest into a ratio of 3:2 to that of C (27,000:18,000).

The next step in the process is to bring the loss absorption potential of A and C into balance with that of B, who is the last partner to participate in the distribution of cash. Using the same rationale, A and C are now capable of absorbing losses of $30,000 $(90,000 - 60,000)$ greater than B. Since they must absorb 30% and 20% of the losses, respectively, the distribution to each partner is computed as follows:

$$\text{To A: } 30,000 \times .30 = 9,000$$
$$\text{To B: } 30,000 \times .20 = 6,000$$

---

[5]An alternative method of determining the amount to be distributed at each level is to compute the capital account balances needed by each partner so as to bring the partners' capital balances into their agreed profit and loss sharing ratio. This is accomplished by bringing the ratio of the partners' capital account balances into their profit and loss sharing ratio in the same order that the partners are to participate in the distribution. In this case, the first step is to compute what the capital account balance of A should be so that his capital balance is in the profit and loss sharing ratio with that of C (3:2). This can be computed as follows:

$$\text{Let } X = \text{the desired capital balance}$$

$$\frac{\text{Loss ratio of } A}{\text{Loss ratio of } C} = \frac{X}{\text{Capital balance of C}}$$

$$\frac{3}{2} = \frac{X}{18,000}$$

$$2X = 54,000$$

$$X = 27,000$$

Since A has a capital balance of $34,000, it would take a distribution of $7,000 to reduce the balance to $27,000. The next level of payments should reduce the capital balances of A and C in such a way that their capital balances will be in the loss ratio to that of B which is 3:5 and 2:5, respectively.

$$\frac{3}{5} = \frac{X}{30,000} \qquad \frac{2}{5} = \frac{X}{30,000}$$

$$5X = 90,000 \qquad 5X = 60,000$$

$$X = 18,000 \qquad X = 12,000$$

A distribution of $9,000 to A $(27,000 - 18,000)$ and $6,000 to B $(18,000 - 12,000)$ will produce capital balances in the ratio of 3:5:2 (18,000:30,000:12,000). Although this method may be simple to use in some limited cases, the suggested approach may be more systematic when there are numerous partners.

Of the next $15,000, A is to receive $9,000 and B is to receive $6,000. Distributions of these amounts will bring the ratio of the partners capital balances into their agreed profit and loss ratio of 3:5:2 (18,000:30,000:12,000).

Step 4   A cash distribution plan is then prepared as follows:

ORDER OF CASH DISTRIBUTION	LIABILITIES	A	B	C
1. First $28,000	100%			
2. Next $7,000		100%		
3. Next $15,000		60%		40%
4. Remainder		30%	50%	20%

The first $28,000 available is, of course, paid to the creditors. Cash may be held back from distribution if it is anticipated that unrecorded liabilities will be discovered or if additional liquidation expenses will be incurred. The distribution of cash in excess of this reserve amount proceeds as determined. Partner A will receive all of any additional cash up to $7,000. Additional cash in excess of $7,000 and up to $22,000 is distributed 60:40 to A and C. After $22,000 (15,000 + 7,000) has been distributed to the partners, the capital accounts are in the desired profit and loss ratio of 3:5:2. Any further distributions to the partners are made in the profit and loss ratio.

The advance distribution plan developed above will yield the same cash distribution as will the process of computing a safe payment each time cash is available. As proof, in Illustration 16–12, the advance plan for distributing cash as developed in Illustration 16–11 is applied to determine the cash distribution in Illustration 16–10. Even though both methods produce the same results, the advance plan is more informative to creditors, both personal and partnership, and to the partners, because the interested parties now know the order in which individual partners will receive cash and the amounts that each may receive at each stage of the distribution process.

One requirement that must be satisfied in the development of the advance plan is that the partners must share profits in the same ratio that they share losses. If this were not the case, the allocation of liquidation gains could alter the order of cash distribution computed in the advance plan. To illustrate, assume that Partners A, B, and C, with capital balances of $45,000, $24,000, and $20,000, respectively, share losses in the ratio of 5:3:2, but share profits in the ratio of 3:5:2. The order of cash distribution based on the ratio of losses would be as follows:

	A	B	C
Net Capital Interest	45,000	24,000	20,000
Loss Ratios	.50	.30	.20
Loss Absorption Potential	90,000	80,000	100,000
Order of Cash Distribution	2	3	1

ILLUSTRATION 16–12
Cash Distribution Per Advance Plan

	LIABILITIES	A	B	C	TOTAL
First Distribution: $30,000					
First—$28,000	28,000				28,000
Next—$2,000		2,000			2,000
	28,000	2,000	—	—	30,000
Second Distribution: $15,000					
First—$5,000					
(Remainder of $7,000 level)		5,000			5,000
Next—$10,000		6,000		4,000	10,000
	—	11,000	—	4,000	15,000
Third Distribution: $10,000					
First—$5,000					
(Remainder of $15,000 level)		3,000		2,000	5,000
Next—$5,000		1,500	2,500	1,000	5,000
	—	4,500	2,500	3,000	10,000

Now assume that the partnership realizes a $50,000 gain. The allocation of the gain in the ratio of 3:5:2 and computation of the order of cash distribution follow:

	A	B	C
Net Capital Interest	(45,000)	(24,000)	(20,000)
Allocation of $50,000 Gain	(15,000)	(25,000)	(10,000)
Net Capital Interest	(60,000)	(49,000)	(30,000)
Loss Ratios	.50	.30	.20
New Loss Absorption Potential	120,000	163,333	150,000
New Order of Cash Distribution	3	1	2

In this illustration an allocation of the $50,000 gain moved B from being the last partner to receive cash to being the first partner to receive cash.

It is also necessary to recompute an advance plan if a certain classification of losses is shared in a different ratio than the one used in preparing the advance plan, or if adjustments are made to the capital balances in other than the loss ratio. For example, assume that it has been discovered that a cash withdrawal by a partner had been expensed instead of debited to his drawing account. The correction of the error would modify the loss absorption potential of that partner. If such adjustments occur frequently, then the computation of a safe payment may be less time-consuming and easier to use than the development of an advance cash distribution plan.

Questions

1. Why are realization gains or losses allocated to partners in their profit and loss ratios?

2. In what manner should the final cash distribution be made in a partnership liquidation?

3. Why does a debit balance in a partner's capital account create problems in the UPA order of payment for a partnership liquidation?

4. Is it important to maintain separate accounts for a partner's outstanding loan and capital accounts? Explain why.

5. Discuss the possible outcomes in the situation where the equity interest of one partner is inadequate to absorb realization losses.

6. During a liquidation, when should cash be distributed to any of the partners?

7. What is meant by the phrase "marshalling of assets"?

8. To what extent can personal creditors seek recovery from partnership assets?

9. In an installment liquidation, why should the partners view each cash distribution as if it were the final distribution?

10. Discuss the three basic assumptions necessary for calculating a safe cash distribution. How is this safe cash balance computed?

11. How are unexpected costs such as liquidation expenses, disposal costs, or unrecorded liabilities covered in the payment schedule?

12. What is the objective of the procedures used for the preparation of an advance cash distribution plan?

13. What is the "loss absorption potential"?

14. Q, R, S, and T are partners sharing profits and losses equally. Their partnership is insolvent and is to be liquidated; the status of the partnership and the status of each partner are as follows:

	PARTNERSHIP CAPITAL BALANCE	PERSONAL ASSETS (EXCLUSIVE OF PARTNERSHIP INTEREST)	PERSONAL LIABILITIES (EXCLUSIVE OF PARTNERSHIP INTEREST)
Q	$ 15,000	$100,000	$40,000
R	10,000	30,000	60,000
S	(20,000) Dr.	80,000	5,000
T	(30,000) Dr.	1,000	28,000
Total	$(25,000) Dr.		

Assuming that the Uniform Partnership Act applies, the partnership creditors:
a. Must first seek recovery against S, because he is solvent personally and he has a negative capital balance.
b. Will not be paid in full regardless of how they proceed legally, because the partnership assets are less than the partnership liabilities.
c. Will have to share R's interest in the partnership on a pro rata basis with R's personal creditors.
d. Have first claim to the partnership assets before any partner's personal creditors have rights to the partnership assets.

(AICPA adapted)

Problems

JUST AS WELL TO COMBINE LOAN INSTEAD OF RIGHT OF OFFSET

Problem 16–1

The BAD Company operated by Bass, Altose, and Dorm is being liquidated. A balance sheet prepared at this stage in the liquidation process is presented below:

Cash	40,000	Liabilities	30,000
Other Assets	55,000	Altose, Loan	10,000
		Bass, Capital	30,000
		Altose, Capital	10,000
		Dorm, Capital	15,000
	95,000		95,000

The partners share profits and losses 30%, 50%, and 20%, respectively. The partners are all personally insolvent.

Required:

A. The partners wish to distribute the $40,000 in cash. Record in journal entry form the distribution of the available cash. *ALLOCATE POT. LOSS OF 55,000 FOR SAFE PAY.*

B. Record in journal entry form the completion of the liquidation process, assuming that the other assets of $55,000 are sold for $13,000. *ALLOCATE LOSS OF 42,000*

Problem 16–2

The MNO Partnership is in the process of liquidation. The account balances prior to liquidation are given below:

DEBITS		CREDITS	
Cash	72,000	Liabilities	40,000
Macy, Drawing	10,000	Nolan, Loan	8,000
Nolan, Drawing	15,000	Oates, Loan	25,000
Oates, Drawing	20,000	Macy, Capital	49,000
Operating Loss	20,000	Nolan, Capital	18,000
Liquidation Loss	13,000	Oates, Capital	10,000
	150,000		150,000

The partners share profits in the following ratio: Macy, 1/6; Nolan, 2/6; Oates, 3/6.

Required:

Prepare a schedule showing the calculation of the distribution of cash under the Uniform Partnership Act, assuming that all three partners have personal liabilities in excess of their personal assets.

Problem 16–3

The four partners of the PORE Company agree to dissolve their partnership. Their capital balances are maintained at $100,000, $40,000, $20,000, and $20,000, respectively. Profits are distributed 50:20:20:10.

Noncash assets total $155,000, and unpaid liabilities at the date of dissolution amount to $13,000. During the first month of liquidation, assets having a book value of $70,000 were sold for $32,000. During the second month, assets having a book value of $52,000 were sold for $39,800. During the third month, the remaining unsold assets were determined to be worthless.

Required:

Prepare a schedule of liquidation showing cash distributions made during each month of liquidation. Compute a safe amount of cash that can be distributed before each payment is made to the partners.

Problem 16–4

W, X, Y, and Z do not anticipate favorable performance for their company and mutually agree to liquidate the partnership. Their capital and loan balances, after completing the closing process, are:

PARTNER	CAPITAL	LOANS	PROFIT AND LOSS RATIO
W	$30,000	$10,000	50%
X	36,000	–0–	30%
Y	15,000	5,000	10%
Z	9,000	–0–	10%

At this time the company assets consist of $10,000 cash and $110,000 of other assets, and $15,000 in partnership obligations in addition to the $15,000 outstanding loans to W and Y. The following data relate to the sale of the other assets:

ORDER OF SALES BY MONTHS	BOOK VALUE	MARKET VALUE
June	$30,000	$20,000
July	30,000	10,000
August	40,000	10,000
September	10,000	–0–

Required:

Compute the safe distribution of cash to be made to each partner at the end of each month.

Problem 16–5

The partnership of Johnson, McKenzie, and Reneau has operated profitably for the last five years. However, the partners anticipate that the development of solar energy will eliminate the demand for the natural gas pool heaters they sell. Unable to obtain a franchise for solar heaters, they decide to liquidate the firm. Just before the realization of the assets, the balance sheet shows the following balances:

ASSETS		EQUITIES	
Cash	$ 20,000	Liabilities	$ 18,000
		Johnson, Loan	10,000
Other Assets	100,000	Johnson, Capital	44,000
		McKenzie, Capital	30,000
		Reneau, Capital	18,000
Totals	$120,000		$120,000

The partners share profits and losses 30:50:20.

During the first month of liquidation they sell their inventory, which cost $30,000, for $20,000. The next week after the inventory sale they hold an auction to sell the office and display equipment. At the auction, assets with a book value of $20,000 are sold for $8,000. Being in no hurry to complete the liquidation process, they decide to hold the building and land owned by the partnership until an acceptable offer is received. Two months later the partners accept an offer for $65,000. The land and building were carried on the books at $50,000.

Required:

Prepare a schedule of partnership realization and liquidation. Cash is to be distributed as it becomes available. You are to prepare a safe payment schedule to support each cash distribution.

Problem 16–6

Barnett, Chapman, and Evans have operated a retail furniture store for the past thirty years. Their business has been unprofitable for several years, since several large discount furniture stores opened in their sales territory. The partners recognize that they will be unable to compete with the larger chain stores and decide that since all of the partners are near retirement, they should liquidate their business before it is necessary to declare bankruptcy. Account balances just before the liquidation process began were as follows:

Cash	$ 10,000	Liabilities	$110,000
Other Assets	218,000	Barnett, Capital	48,000
		Chapman, Capital	45,000
		Evans, Capital	25,000
	$228,000		$228,000

The partners share profits in the ratio of 4:3:3, respectively.

Rather than selling all of the assets in a forced liquidation and incurring selling expenses, the partners agree that some of the noncash assets may be withdrawn in partial settlement of their capital interest. The partners agree that if the market value of a withdrawn asset is less than book value, the difference should be allocated to all partners in their loss ratio. In the case where market value is greater than book value, the withdrawing partner must contribute cash equal to the difference. All the partners are personally solvent and can make additional cash contributions to the partnership up to $20,000 each. The following is a schedule of transactions that occurred in the liquidation process:

March 15, 1980:	During liquidation sale noncash assets with a book value of $100,000 were sold for $80,000.
March 16, 1980:	Sold accounts receivable with a book value of $35,000 to a factor for $30,000.
March 16, 1980:	Paid all recorded partnership creditors.
March 18, 1980:	Distributed all but $1,000 of available cash to partners.
March 19, 1980:	Chapman withdrew from inventory furniture with a book value of $10,000 and a market value of $13,000 to satisfy part of his capital interest. Chapman contributed $3,000 cash to the partnership.
March 21, 1980:	Sold remainder of inventory with a book value of $50,000 to a discount furniture store for $30,000 cash.
March 25, 1980:	Assigned for $12,000 cash the remaining term of the lease on the warehouse. The lease was accounted for as an operating lease.
March 25, 1980:	Distributed all available cash to partners.
April 1, 1980:	Barnett agreed to accept two vehicles with a book value of $10,000 and a market value of $8,000 in partial settlement of his capital interest.
April 5, 1980:	Remainder of furniture and fixtures, office equipment, and office supplies were sold for $4,000.
April 6, 1980:	Received additional cash from partners with debit capital balances.
April 6, 1980:	Distributed available cash to partners.

Required:

Prepare a schedule of partnership realization and liquidation in accordance with the sequence of the foregoing events. Compute a safe payment to support your cash distribution to partners.

Problem 16–7

The nonbusiness assets and liabilities of Kater, Blane, and Sands are as follows:

PARTNERS	LIABILITIES	ASSETS
Kater	$21,000	$20,000
Blane	26,800	37,600
Sands	13,200	42,000

Kater, Blane, and Sands are partners in KBS Insurance Company and share profits and losses 50:30:20.

Before liquidation, capital balances are Kater, $8,000 debit; Blane, $45,000 credit; Sands, $30,000 debit. The KBS Company has liabilities of $18,000 and noncash assets of $21,000 that were subsequently converted into $6,000 cash.

Required:

Prepare a partnership liquidation schedule according to the Uniform Partnership Act.

Problem 16–8

Allen, Berg, and Coe have operated a retail store for twenty years. The partners share profits 5:3:2 respectively. The partners decide to liquidate the partnership. The firm's balance sheet just before the partners sell the other assets for $20,000 is as follows:

ASSETS		EQUITIES	
Cash	$ 10,000	Liabilities	$ 40,000
Other Assets	100,000	Allen, Capital	50,000
		Berg, Capital	10,000
		Coe, Capital	10,000
	$110,000		$110,000

The personal status of each partner just before liquidation is as follows:

	PERSONAL ASSETS	PERSONAL LIABILITIES
Allen	$50,000	$80,000
Berg	30,000	10,000
Coe	30,000	50,000

The partnership operates in a state that has adopted the Uniform Partnership Act.

Required:
A. Determine the amount of cash each partner will receive in liquidation and how much cash each partner must contribute to the firm, given their personal positions.
B. Determine the amounts that the personal creditors will receive from personal assets and any distribution from the partnership.

Problem 16–9
Adams, Birch, Caldwell, and Dean operate a partnership and share profits and losses in the ratio of 2:1:1:1, respectively. The partnership is unable to meet its obligations and the partners decide to liquidate the partnership. A balance sheet prepared for the partnership just prior to liquidation follows:

BALANCE SHEET			
Cash	57,000	Liabilities	138,000
Noncash assets	184,000	Adams, Capital	23,000
		Birch, Capital	20,000
		Caldwell, Capital	26,000
		Dean, Capital	34,000
	241,000		241,000

Noncash assets of the partnership are sold for $55,000.

After the sale of the noncash assets, the personal assets and liabilities of each partner are determined to be the following:

	PERSONAL ASSETS	PERSONAL LIABILITIES
Adams	$138,000	$75,000
Birch	23,000	40,000
Caldwell	92,000	80,000
Dean	69,000	77,000

The partnership is located in a state in which the Uniform Partnership Act has been adopted.

Required:
Prepare a schedule of the partnership realization and liquidation. In a separate schedule determine the amount that personal creditors of each partner will receive after the final cash distribution is made from the partnership assets.

Problem 16–10

Allen, Baker, and Cole have been operating a partnership since 1965. During the current operating period the partnership was unprofitable and the partners decided to stop operations and liquidate the business after the close of this fiscal period. The following trial balance was prepared just prior to liquidation:

	DEBIT	CREDIT
Assets	150,000	
Liabilities		25,000
Allen, Capital (50%)		50,000
Baker, Capital (40%)		50,000
Cole, Capital (10%)		50,000
Income Summary	25,000	
Totals	175,000	175,000

Liquidation of the partnership is expected to take from 6 to 8 months. The partners want cash to be distributed as it becomes available.

Required:
A. Prepare an advance plan for the distribution of cash.
B. During the liquidation process, cash became available for distribution in the following order:

March	$30,000
April	35,000
June	20,000

In accordance with the plan developed in A above, prepare a schedule to show the amount of cash that should be distributed to the creditors and to each partner as it became available in March, April, and June.

Problem 16–11

X, Y, and Z share profits in the ratio of 4:4:2, respectively. All the partners are personally insolvent, so they decide to liquidate the partnership as of December 31, 1980. On this date the partnership account balances are as follows:

ASSETS		EQUITIES	
Cash	$ 5,000	Liabilities	$20,000
Other Assets	91,000	X, Capital	50,000
		Y, Capital	11,000
		Z, Capital	15,000
	$96,000		$96,000

The partners agree that cash is to be distributed at the end of each month.

Required:

A. Prepare a schedule to show the partners how the cash is to be distributed each month as the other assets are sold.

B. Prepare a schedule of partnership realization and liquidation, assuming the following sales of other assets:

MONTH OF SALE	SALES PRICE	BOOK VALUE
January	$30,000	$40,000
February	20,000	40,000
March	6,000	11,000

Distribute the cash in accordance with the advance plan prepared in A above.

Problem 16–12

The ABC Partnership is being dissolved. All liabilities have been liquidated. The balance of assets on hand is being realized gradually. The following are details of partners' accounts:

	CAPITAL ACCOUNT (ORIGINAL INVESTMENT)	DRAWING ACCOUNT (UNDISTRIBUTED EARNINGS NET OF DRAWINGS)	LOANS TO PARTNERSHIP	PROFIT AND LOSS RATIO
A	$20,000	$1,500 Cr.	$15,000	4
B	25,000	2,000 Dr.	–0–	4
C	10,000	1,000 Cr.	5,000	2

Required:

Prepare a schedule showing how cash payments should be made to the partners as assets are realized.

(AICPA adapted)

Problem 16–13

Hart, Griese, Stabler, and Jones form a partnership to purchase for $40,000 a franchise to market and sell unique needlework patterns and supplies. During 1980, they purchased large amounts of inventory and display equipment. After operating for two years, they decide that the venture is not producing an adequate rate of return and that the partnership should be dissolved. The partners' capital accounts and profit and loss ratios are as follows:

PARTNER	CAPITAL ACCOUNT	PROFIT AND LOSS RATIO
Hart	$40,000	50%
Griese	36,000	30
Stabler	14,000	10
Jones	8,000	10

The assets of the partnership are $4,000 cash and noncash assets of $110,000. The partners owe trade creditors $16,000, which is the only liability of the partnership.

The partners recognize that they need assistance and call upon you to advise them in "winding up the affairs" of the business. First you prepare an advance cash distribution plan to show the partners the order in which they will participate in the distribution of assets and how much each partner will receive. You advise the partners to hold in reserve $2,000 of cash in case unrecorded liabilities are discovered, or to cover liquidation expenses.

During the first month of liquidation, the partners sell assets with a book value of $30,000 for $20,000. The partners agree to distribute cash at the end of each month. During the second month you discover that a $2,000 withdrawal by Hart was incorrectly charged to Stabler. During this month, assets of $25,000 realize $12,000. During the final month of liquidation, the remaining assets realize $15,000 and the partners receive an invoice for $1,500. The invoice was for goods counted in the inventory, but for which the liability was unrecorded.

Required:

A. Prepare an advance distribution plan for the partners at the point in time when they decide to dissolve the partnership.

B. Prepare a realization and liquidation schedule in accordance with the sequence of the foregoing events.

Problem 16–14

The partners of Able, Bright, Cool, and Dahl have decided to dissolve their partnership. They plan to sell the assets gradually in order to minimize losses. They share profits and losses as follows: Able, 40%; Bright, 35%; Cool, 15% and Dahl, 10%. Presented below is the partnership's trial balance as of October 1, 1980, the date on which liquidation begins.

	DEBIT	CREDIT
Cash	$ 200	
Receivables	25,900	
Inventory, October 1, 1980	42,600	
Equipment (net)	19,800	
Accounts Payable		$ 3,000
Able, Loan		6,000
Bright, Loan		10,000
Able, Capital		20,000
Bright, Capital		21,500
Cool, Capital		18,000
Dahl, Capital		10,000
	$88,500	$88,500

Required:

A. Prepare a statement as of October 1, 1980 showing how cash will be distributed among the partners by installments as it becomes available.

B. On October 31, 1980, cash of $12,700 became available to creditors and partners. How should it be distributed?

C. Suppose that, instead of being dissolved, the partnership continued operations and earned a profit of $23,625. How should that profit be distributed if, in addition to the aforementioned profit-sharing arrangement, it was provided that Dahl receive a bonus of 5% of the net income from operations after treating such bonus as an expense?

(AICPA adapted)

Problem 16–15

Part A

Adams, Baker, and Crane have called upon you to assist them in winding up the affairs of their partnership.

You are able to gather the following information:

1. The trial balance of the partnership at June 30, 1980 is as follows:

	DEBIT	CREDIT
Cash	$ 6,000	
Accounts Receivable	22,000	
Inventory	14,000	
Plant and Equipment (net)	99,000	
Adams, Loan	12,000	
Crane, Loan	7,500	
Accounts Payable		$ 17,000
Adams, Capital		67,000
Baker, Capital		45,000
Crane, Capital		31,500
	$160,500	$160,500

2. The partners share profits and losses as follows: Adams, 50%; Baker, 30%; and Crane, 20%.

3. The partners are considering an offer of $100,000 for the accounts receivable, inventory, and plant and equipment as of June 30. The $100,000 would be paid to the partners in installments, the number and amounts of which are to be negotiated.

Required:

Prepare an advance cash distribution plan as of June 30, 1980. Prepare a schedule to show how the partners' available cash ($106,000) would be distributed as it becomes available.

Part B

Assume the facts in Part A except that the partners have decided to liquidate their partnership instead of accepting the offer of $100,000. Cash is distributed to the partners at the end of each month.

A summary of the liquidation transactions follows:

JULY

$16,500—collected on accounts receivable; balance is uncollectible.
$10,000—received for the entire inventory.
$ 1,000—liquidation expenses paid.
$ 8,000—cash retained in the business at the end of the month.

AUGUST

$ 1,500—liquidation expenses paid.
   As part payment of his capital, Crane accepted a piece of special equipment that he developed which had a book value of $4,000. The partners agreed that a value of $10,000 should be placed on the machine for liquidation purposes.
$ 2,500—cash retained in the business at the end of the month.

SEPTEMBER

$75,000—received on sale of remaining plant and equipment.
$ 1,000—liquidation expenses paid.
        No cash retained in the business.

Required:

Prepare a schedule of cash payments as of September 30, 1980, showing how the cash was actually distributed.

(AICPA adapted)

17

Introduction
Fund Accounting

Fund accounting concepts are generally associated with accounting for nonprofit organizations. Nonprofit organizations are economic entities that are organized to provide a socially desirable service without regard to financial gain. In contrast to commercial organizations, nonprofit organizations are not operated for the *financial* benefit of any specific individual or group of individuals.

The purpose of this chapter is to introduce the reader to fund accounting concepts and procedures. In order to do this, however, it is first necessary to present a brief introduction to the types and characteristics of organizations that utilize fund accounting concepts.

CLASSIFICATIONS OF NONPROFIT ORGANIZATIONS

There are five major classifications of nonprofit organizations.

1. Governmental Units. Governmental units include federal, state, and local governmental units. Local governmental units include counties, townships, municipalities, school districts, and special districts. Special districts include organizational units such as port authorities, industrial development districts, sanitation districts, and soil and water conservation districts.

2. Hospitals.

3. Colleges and Universities.

4. Voluntary Health and Welfare Organizations. Voluntary health and welfare organizations are organizations that derive their revenue from voluntary contributions

of the general public to be used for purposes connected with health, welfare, or community services. Examples of such organizations include heart associations, family planning councils, mental health associations, and foundations for the blind.

5. All Other Nonprofit Organizations. Other nonprofit organizations take a variety of forms and include such organizations as trade associations (Electrical Contractors Association), professional associations (Illinois Society of Certified Public Accountants), performing arts organizations (the Charlotte Symphony Society), museums, child care organizations, religious organizations, and research and scientific organizations.

DISTINCTIONS BETWEEN NONPROFIT AND PROFIT-ORIENTED ENTERPRISES

The most obvious characteristic that distinguishes a nonprofit organization from a profit-oriented enterprise is the absence of a deliberate or conscious effort to derive a profit. The performance of services by nonprofit organizations is based on social need rather than on the profit motive. Other characteristics of nonprofit organizations distinguish them from profit-oriented enterprises. For example, persons who contribute resources to a nonprofit organization receive no equity interest in the net assets of the organization and there is no equity interest therein that can be sold or exchanged. Nonprofit organizations do not often finance their operations through adequate charges to the direct beneficiaries of their services. Thus, they must rely on political action (e.g., tax levies) or fund-raising campaigns to sustain their activities and replenish their financial resources.

In addition, tax levies and voluntary contributions cannot ordinarily be justified on the basis of the value of the nonprofit organization's services to the individuals from whom such contributions come. Those who contribute resources to nonprofit organizations do not necessarily benefit proportionately or at all from the services provided by such organizations. Because of the characteristics identified above, the net income concept cannot be used to measure the effectiveness of the management of resources dedicated to nonprofit objectives. Therefore, the income determination model of accounting is generally not applicable to such organizations.

In profit-oriented enterprises, net income functions as an implicit regulator in the sense that (1) in the long run the organization must operate profitably to survive, and (2) in the short run, failure to operate profitably will affect management's decisions and actions and perhaps the constituency of management itself. In the absence of this implicit regulator, regulation of the allocation and utilization of the financial resources of nonprofit organizations is often achieved by the imposition of stringent controls. Such controls may be legally imposed (as in the case of governmental activities) or they may be imposed through formal action of the governing board.

Restrictions or limitations on the use of resources may also be directly imposed by the individuals or groups that contribute such resources. For example, most nonprofit organizations receive gifts, grants, or endowments that are to be used only for specific purposes designated by the donor, such as construction of buildings, research activities, scholarships, operation of parks, recreation programs, or the acquisition of land. In addition, the donor may stipulate that the principal of the gift is to remain intact and that only the income on the invested principal is to be used for the purposes designated by the donor.

In order to account for these legally imposed, externally imposed, and self-imposed restrictions or limitations on the utilization of their resources, nonprofit organizations have generally adopted the concepts of fund accounting. A fund has been defined by the National Council on Governmental Accounting as

> an independent fiscal and accounting entity with a self-balancing set of accounts recording cash and other financial resources, together with all related liabilities and residual equities or balances, and changes therein, which are segregated for the purpose of carrying on specific activities or attaining certain objectives in accordance with special regulations, restrictions, or limitations.[1]

In fund accounting, each fund consists of assets, liabilities, and a fund balance and constitutes a *separate accounting entity* created and maintained for a specific purpose. The inflow and outflow of resources of each fund must be accounted for in such a way that they can be compared with the approved or stipulated resource flows for that fund.

The potential users of the financial reports of nonprofit organizations include internal management, governing boards, legislators and legislative committees, interested citizens, individuals or donors, public interest groups, members, regulatory agencies, creditors, unions, and others. Historically, accounting reports have not been widely distributed to potential users other than management, governing boards, and legislative committees with limited distribution to creditors, bond rating services, and brokerage firms.

The financial reports of nonprofit organizations are used primarily to determine the fiscal responsibility and status of the organization and the compliance of administrators with the approved or stipulated receipt and utilization of financial resources. Until recently, there have been only limited attempts to measure or report on the efficiency or effectiveness of the utilization of the resources of nonprofit organizations. The lack of such measures and their exclusion from financial reports are probably major reasons for the apparent lack of interest of many potential users in the financial reports of nonprofit organizations.

FUND ACCOUNTING

Fund entities may be classified in a number of different ways. For example, they may be classified as expendable fund entities and proprietary fund entities. Expendable fund entities are the funds most closely associated with basic fund accounting concepts.

---

[1]National Council on Governmental Accounting, *Exposure Draft: GAAFR Restatement: Principles,* (Chicago: Municipal Finance Officers Association of the United States and Canada, 1978), p. 10.

Expendable Fund Entities

Expendable fund entities consist of net *current financial* resources that are dedicated to a specified use. Expendable assets are assigned to fund entities according to the purpose for which they may or must be used. The difference between expendable assets and any related current liabilities is referred to as the fund balance. The accounting model for the statement of financial position of an expendable fund entity is:

$$\text{Current Assets} = \text{Current Liabilities} + \text{Fund Balance}$$

At a particular point in time the fund balance represents the net current financial resources that are available for expenditure for the specified purposes or objectives for which the fund was created.

The financial resources of an expendable fund entity are not intended to be maintained intact. Rather, it is ordinarily intended that the financial resources of such entities be expended annually or over some other specified time period in order to carry out the objectives for which the fund was created.

The relevant measures of the operations of expendable fund entities are not, therefore, revenue, expense, and net income but rather increases in fund resources, decreases in fund resources, and the change in the fund balance. The accounting model for the operating statement of an expendable fund entity is:

LONG TERM ASSETS + LIABILITIES

$$\text{Financial Resource Inflows (by source)} - \text{Financial Resource}$$
$$\text{Outflows (by function)} = \text{Change in Fund Balance}$$

Increases in fund resources may be classified as revenues, debt issue proceeds, and transfers from other funds. Decreases in fund resources may be classified as expenditures or as transfers to other funds. Thus, the operating results of expendable fund entities is measured in terms of inflow, outflow, and balances of net current financial resources assigned to the fund, and the appropriate operating statement for such entities is essentially a statement of changes in net financial resources. To provide a basis for comparison, both budgeted and actual resource flows may be presented in the operating statement or in schedules relating thereto.

In summary, in accounting for expendable funds, the emphasis is changed from matching revenue and expense to the comparison of the actual inflow and outflow of financial resources with stipulated or approved resource flows. Thus, rather than attempting to measure the efficiency with which management has utilized resources, fund accounting is designed to measure the extent to which management has complied with the regulations or restrictions that govern the utilization of expendable fund resources.

Proprietary Fund Entities

Proprietary (nonexpendable) fund entities are used to account for the activities of nonprofit organizations that are similar to those of commercial enterprises. Many nonprofit organizations engage in quasi-commercial activities. The operation of an electric or water utility by a municipality and the rental of real estate by a religious organization are examples of such activities. Accordingly, even though these activities are accounted for in separate fund entities, relevant accounting measurements and reports are similar to those applicable to profit-oriented enterprises and focus upon the determination of net income, financial position, and changes in financial position.

The accounting model for the statement of financial position of a proprietary fund entity is:

Current Assets + Noncurrent Assets = Current Liabilities +
Long-term Liabilities + Nonprofit Organization Equity

The accounting model for the operating statement of a proprietary fund entity is:

Revenue — Expense = Net Income (Loss) plus (minus)
Transfers from (to) Other Funds = Change in Nonprofit
Organization Equity

Budgetary Fund Entities

In the traditional compliance model of reporting on the operations of governmental units, actual resource inflows and outflows are compared with stipulated or approved inflows and outflows of resources. Approved resource flows are incorporated into annual budgets. In some instances the budget for an expendable fund entity is so important to management control of fund resources that the budget is formally incorporated into the accounting records within the framework of the double-entry system. Fund entities in which the budget is formally incorporated into the accounting records are sometimes referred to as budgetary funds.

The preparation, use, and importance of such budgets for governmental units cannot be overemphasized. The annual budget for a governmental unit is usually prepared by the executive branch of the governmental unit. It is then presented to the legislative branch for consideration and enactment. In the case of annually levied taxes such as property taxes, adoption of budgeted revenue amounts may require the enactment of enabling legislation. In the case of continually levied taxes such as sales taxes and income taxes, no new enabling legislation is ordinarily required for the adoption of the budgeted amounts of revenue.

When budgeted expenditures are enacted into law, they are referred to as appropriations. Appropriations represent the maximum expenditures that are authorized by the legislature. As such, they represent (by budget category) amounts that cannot be legally exceeded. Accordingly, the accounting system must provide administrators of governmental units with timely information as to actual expenditures and allowable expenditures (appropriations) by budget category. In addition, financial statements must be prepared in such a way that the legislature or its representative can determine that the spending limits authorized by it have not been exceeded. The approved budget may, therefore, be formally recorded in the accounting records of the appropriate fund(s). Such formal budgetary account integration is for purposes of assisting in the control and administration of fund resources.

Restricted and Unrestricted Fund Entities

Expendable fund entities may be further classified as restricted and unrestricted. This classification is usually applicable to nonprofit organizations other than governmental units. The unrestricted expendable fund entity includes the net current financial resources of the nonprofit organization that are available to carry out the primary or general activities of the organization at the discretion of the governing board. Current financial resources that are restricted by donors or other outside agencies for specific current operating purposes are included in restricted expendable fund entities. The word *restricted* refers to resources which bear a legal restriction as to use imposed by parties outside the organization. The primary purpose of this distinction is to assist in the determination of the current financial resources that are available for use at the discretion of the governing board and those over which the governing board has little if any discretion as to use because of *externally* imposed restrictions. Most nonprofit organizations other than governmental units have one unrestricted fund and one or more restricted funds.

Within the framework of expendable fund entities, revenues are defined as inflows of net current financial resources, and expenditures are defined as outflows of net current financial resources. Because nonprofit organizations have different sources of revenues and different purposes and objectives, the recognition and classification of fund entity revenues and expenditures vary between different types of nonprofit organizations. However, there is general agreement in the authoritative literature that for financial reporting purposes:

1. Fund revenues should be classified by source, and transfers from other funds within the organization should be distinguished from and classified separately from revenue.

2. Fund expenditures should be classified by function or activity, and transfers to other funds within the organization should be distinguished from and classified separately from expenditures.

3. Fund revenues and expenditures should, where possible, be recognized using the accrual basis of accounting.

In the discussion that follows, these concepts are primarily developed within the framework of state and local governmental units. However, where such elaboration assists in the development of the concepts, reference will also be made to other types of nonprofit organizations, such as colleges and universities and voluntary health and welfare organizations.

Accrual Basis and Cash Basis Accounting Compared

In cash basis accounting, changes in assets and liabilities are recognized only when cash is received or paid. In accrual basis accounting, the effects of transactions and other events on the assets and liabilities of an accounting entity are recognized and reported in the periods to which they relate, rather than when cash is received or paid.

Financial resources of an expendable fund entity include cash, receivables, and securities that can be converted into cash. If an increase in net financial resources (revenue) is recorded when a valid receivable is established, rather than when the cash is ultimately collected, and if a decrease in net financial resources (expenditure) is recorded when a liability is incurred, rather than when cash is ultimately disbursed, then the accrual basis rather than the cash basis of accounting is being applied to the fund entity. Because some revenues of expendable fund entities are not susceptible to accrual and because some expenditures of expendable fund entities are not recognized in the period in which they are incurred, the application of accrual accounting to expendable fund entities is generally referred to as the modified accrual basis of accounting.

Before proceeding further, it may be useful to distinguish among the concepts of revenue, expense, and expenditure as they are used in relation to profit-oriented entities and expendable fund entities.

Profit-Oriented Entities (Income Determination)

Revenue—increase in net assets resulting from the sale of goods or services.

Expense—expired costs consumed in the production of revenues (as defined above).

Expendable Fund Entities

Revenue—increase in (source of) net current financial resources other than an increase resulting from debt issue proceeds or from the transfer of financial resources from another fund within the organization.

Expenditure—decrease in (use of) net current financial resources other than a decrease resulting from a transfer of financial resources to another fund within the organization. Expenditures represent the amount of financial resources expended during the period to carry out the operations and activities of the fund entity.

Classification of Revenue and Other Resource Inflows

Revenues are classified by source. Major sources of revenue for state and local governmental units, colleges and universities, and voluntary health and welfare organizations are summarized in Illustration 17–1. As is demonstrated therein, the number of sources of revenue available to nonprofit organizations is impressive when compared with those available to commerical enterprises.

ILLUSTRATION 17–1
Major Sources of Revenue for Three Types of Nonprofit Organizations

STATE AND LOCAL GOVERNMENTAL UNITS	COLLEGES AND UNIVERSITIES	VOLUNTARY HEALTH AND WELFARE ORGANIZATIONS
Property Taxes	Tuition and Fees	Public Contributions
Income Taxes	Federal, State, or Local	Special Events
Sales and Excise Taxes	Appropriations	Legacies and Bequests
Gift and Inheritance Taxes	Federal, State, or Local	Federated and Nonfederated Campaigns
Fines and Penalties	Grants and Contracts	Membership Dues
Gifts and Donations	Private Gifts, Grants,	Investment Income
Forfeits	and Contracts	Realized Gains on Investment Activities
Licenses and Permits	Endowment Income	
Grants from Federal, State, or	Sales and Services of	
Local Government Units	Educational Activities	
Shared Revenues from Federal, State,	(film rentals, testing	
or Local Government Units	services, etc.)	
Payments in Lieu of Taxes from	Sales and Services of	
Federal, State, or Local	Auxiliary Enterprises	
Government Units	(residence halls, food	
Sales of Property	services, etc.)	
Interest Earned on Loans and		
Investments		

Debt Issue Proceeds   Governmental units in particular may finance their operations through the issuance of bonds or other debt instruments. Although debt issue proceeds are sometimes classified as revenue of a particular fund entity, they are not revenue from the point of view of the issuing governmental unit because of the offsetting debt. Accordingly, debt issue proceeds should be classified separately from revenue for purposes of financial reporting.

Transfers of Resources from Other Funds   Transfers of resources from other fund entities within an organization do not represent an increase in the expendable financial resources of the organization as a whole. Accordingly, even though they represent an increase in the financial resources of the recipient fund entity, they should ordinarily be classified separately from revenue for financial reporting purposes.

Recognition of Revenue

In accounting for profit-oriented enterprises, revenue is ordinarily not recognized until (1) a transaction has taken place (i.e., the amount of revenue can be objectively measured), and (2) the earnings process is complete or substantially complete. Criterion (2) is not applicable to expendable fund entities. The revenue-recognition criteria for expendable fund entities can be stated as follows. In accounting for expendable fund entities, revenue is ordinarily not recognized until (1) it can be objectively measured, and (2) it is available to finance expenditures of the current period.[2]

Many sources of fund revenue do not meet the criteria of measurability and availability until they are received in cash. On the other hand, significant amounts of revenue (e.g., property taxes, pledges, regularly billed charges for routine services, and some types of grants) meet both criteria and are recognized as revenue prior to the receipt of cash. The application of these criteria to several significant sources of fund revenue may be illustrated as follows.

Property Taxes   Property taxes usually meet both criteria when levied. The amount of property tax is precisely determinable when levied and the amount of uncollectible taxes can ordinarily be reasonably estimated on the basis of previous experience. Thus, the amount of property tax revenue is objectively determinable at the time the taxes are levied. Ordinarily, taxes are also considered to be *available* in the period levied, even though they are collectible in a period subsequent to the levy, because (1) they provide a basis for obtaining cash resources through the issuance of tax anticipation notes,[3] and/or (2) they are usually collectible early in the subsequent period and thus available to finance current period operations.

Income Tax and Sales Tax   Self-assessed taxes such as the income tax and the sales tax are not ordinarily objectively measurable or available until the tax returns are filed with payment. Where the tax returns have been filed but payment is delayed, revenue should be recognized when the returns are filed, assuming that a reasonable estimate can be made of noncollectible amounts, if any. In addition, sales taxes held by merchants may be recognized as revenue prior to receipt by the fund entity if the measurability and availability criteria are met.

Fines and Forfeits   The amounts of fines, forfeits, inspection charges, parking meter receipts, etc. are not objectively determinable or available until assessed or collected and, accordingly, are not normally recognized as revenue until collected.

---

[2]These are the same criteria as those recommended by the National Council on Governmental Accounting in *Government Accounting, Auditing, and Financial Reporting.* They differ somewhat from the criteria recommended in the AICPA Industry Audit Guide, *Audits of State and Local Governmental Units,* which are stated as follows: "Revenues are recorded as received in cash except for (a) revenues susceptible to accrual and (b) revenues of a material amount that have not been received at the normal time of receipt." Since some types of revenue are not objectively measurable until received in cash, there is no necessary contradiction between these two statements of revenue-recognition criteria.

[3]Tax anticipation notes are notes or warrants issued in anticipation of the collection of taxes and are usually retirable only from the proceeds of the tax levy whose collection they anticipate.

Sales of Property   The entire amount of proceeds from the sale of property is treated as revenue because expendable assets are increased thereby and are available to finance current expenditures in the same manner as any other revenues would be.

Pledges and Grants   A pledge to contribute resources is considered revenue at the time it is made, so long as a reasonable estimate of uncollectible pledges can be made and there is no restriction on the time period in which the pledged resources can be expended. Grants may or may not be recognized as revenue at the time the grant is authorized. If the grant is dependent upon the performance of services, or if the expenditure of funds is the prime factor for determining the eligibility for the grant funds, revenue should not be recognized until the time the services are performed or the expenditures are made. Grants that are not dependent upon performance or expenditure of funds should be recognized in the period in which they are authorized.

Classification of Expenditures and Other Resource Outflows

Expenditures may be classified by function, by activity, by object, or by organizational unit. Since different classifications serve different purposes, multiple classification of expenditures is usually recommended.

Classification by Function and Activity   Typical functional classifications of expenditures for state and local governmental units, colleges and universities, and voluntary health and welfare organizations are presented in Illustration 17–2. Classification by function refers to the broad purposes for which expenditures are made. Classification by activity refers to the specific types of work performed to accomplish such purposes. For example, public safety is a major function of a municipality. The *function* of public safety may be divided into *subfunctions* such as police protection, fire protection, and protective inspection. The subfunction of police protection can be classified into *activities* such as criminal investigation, vice control, patrol, custody of prisoners, and crime laboratory.

Functional and activity classifications are particularly important and are the classifications ordinarily recommended for published financial reports. In addition, as noted by the National Council on Governmental Accounting,

> *Activity* classification is particularly significant because it facilitates evaluation of the economy and efficiency of operations by providing data for calculating expenditures per unit of activity. That is, the expenditure requirements of performing a given unit of work can be determined by classifying expenditures by activities and providing for performance measurement where such techniques are practical. These expenditure data, in turn, can be used in preparing future budgets and in setting standards against which future expenditure levels can be evaluated. Further, activity expenditure data provide a convenient starting point for calculating total and/or unit expenses of activities where that is desired, e.g., for "make or buy" and "do or contract out" decisions. Current activity expenditures (total

expenditures less those for capital outlay and debt principal retirement) may be adjusted by depreciation and amortization data ... to determine activity expense.[4]

Classification by Organizational Unit Classification of expenditures by organizational unit is important for management, control, and internal reporting purposes including responsibility accounting. Classification of expenditures by organizational unit is based on the departments, divisions, bureaus, or other administrative units that make expenditures to carry out their designated functions. Organizational units vary with the pattern of organization of the individual nonprofit organization. Examples include police department, attorney general's office, corporation commission, registrar's office, department of accountancy, dean of students office, etc. Each organizational unit may have responsibility for several functions or activities. In some instances a function or activity may cross organizational unit lines.

ILLUSTRATION 17-2
Functional Classification of Expenditures for Three Types of Nonprofit Organizations

STATE AND LOCAL GOVERNMENTAL UNITS	COLLEGES AND UNIVERSITIES	VOLUNTARY HEALTH AND WELFARE ORGANIZATIONS
General Government	Instruction	Research
Legislative	Academic Instruction	Public Health Education
Judicial	Community Education	Professional Education and Training
Executive	Research	Community Services
Elections	Institutes and Centers	Management and General
Financial Administration	Project Research	Fund Raising
Public Safety	Public Service	
Police	Community Service	
Fire	Conferences and Institutes	
Inspection	Extension Service	
Public Works	Academic Support	
Highways and Streets	Audiovisual Services	
Sanitation	Libraries	
Health and Welfare	Student Services	
Recreation—Cultural	Admissions	
Playgrounds	Counseling	
Swimming Pools	Financial Aid	
Golf Courses	Health and Infirmary	
Parks	Intramural Athletics	
Libraries	Student Organizations	
Urban Redevelopment and Housing	Registrar	
Economic Development and Assistance	Remedial Instruction	
	Institutional Support	

[4]National Council on Governmental Accounting, *Exposure Draft: GAAFR Restatement: Principles,* p. 42.

Classification by Object   Classification of expenditures by object identifies what is acquired in return for the expenditure. Typical object classifications are presented in Illustration 17–3.

ILLUSTRATION 17–3

Classification of Expenditures by Object

Personal Services
　　Salaries
　　Employee health and retirement benefits
　　Payroll taxes, etc.
Supplies
　　Office supplies
　　Operating supplies
　　Small tools
Other
　　Professional services
　　Telephone and telegraph
　　Travel
　　Rental (equipment, buildings, machinery)
　　Postage and shipping
　　Printing and publications
　　Repairs and maintenance
　　Insurance
　　Miscellaneous
Capital Expenditures
　　Land
　　Buildings
　　Improvements
　　Machinery and equipment
　　Motor vehicles
　　Furniture and furnishings
　　Office machines

Classification by object is useful primarily for internal management and may be omitted from published financial reports.

It is generally recommended that excessively detailed object classifications be avoided, since they may unnecessarily complicate accounting procedures and reports and because the control and reporting emphasis of the organization should be on functions, activities, and organizational units rather than on the object of expenditures per se.

With modern data-processing techniques, multiple classification of expenditures is easily accomplished. Multiple classification of expenditures by function, activity, organizational unit, and object facilitates the aggregation and analysis of data in different ways for different purposes.

Transfers to Other Funds   Transfers of resources to other fund entities within an organization do not represent decreases in the expendable financial resources of the organization as a whole. Accordingly, even though they represent a decrease in the financial resources of a particular fund, they ordinarily should be classified separately from expenditures for financial reporting purposes.

Recognition of Expenditures

An expenditure is one of four critical events in the use of the financial resources of an expendable fund entity. The sequence of events is as follows:

Appropriation or
Authorization $\longrightarrow$ Encumbrance $\longrightarrow$ Expenditure $\longrightarrow$ Disbursement

Appropriation   The appropriation process in governmental units has already been described. The necessity for giving accounting recognition to the next event, encumbrance, can be more clearly presented, however, if one recalls that it is the responsibility of administrators to use fund resources only in the amounts and for the purposes prescribed in the appropriations act or an equivalent authorization act of the governing board. In the case of governmental units, administrators are held strictly accountable for the provisions of the appropriation act, and stiff penalties are provided by law for those who fail to adhere to them. Thus, it is of great concern to administrators that they know how they stand relative to their appropriation authority and that they have accounting safeguards to prevent the utilization of fund resources in excess of that authority.

Encumbrance   Since the amount of an appropriation cannot be legally exceeded, the placing of purchase orders and the signing of contracts are critical events in controlling the expenditures of expendable fund entities. The financial resources of a fund are said to be encumbered when a transaction is entered into that requires performance on the part of another party before the nonprofit entity becomes liable to perform (expend financial resources) its part of the transaction. An encumbrance reduces appropriation authority and is formally recorded in the accounting records. Thus, at any particular time the accounting records will reflect management's remaining available appropriation authority as follows:

Appropriations $-$ (Encumbrances $+$ Expenditures) $=$ Unencumbered Balance

The unencumbered balance is the amount of resources that can still be obligated or expended without exceeding the legal or authorized limit.

Encumbrances are recorded as follows:

(1) Encumbrance (appropriately classified)   10,000
     Reserve for Encumbrance   10,000
       To record an order for goods in the amount of $10,000.

Expenditures   When the vendor or supplier performs on a contract or purchase order and goods or services are recieved, an expenditure has taken place. *Expenditures should ordinarily be recognized in the accounting period in which they are incurred.* Thus, an expenditure and a corresponding liability or cash disbursement will be recorded at the time goods or services are received or at the time funds are granted to an authorized recipient. When the goods ordered in (1) above are received, the following entries would be made.

(2) Expenditures (appropriately classified)   12,000
   Vouchers Payable   12,000
    To record the receipt of goods invoiced at $12,000.

(3) Reserve for Encumbrance   10,000
   Encumbrance   10,000
    To remove the encumbrance recorded in (1) for the good received and recorded as an
    expenditure in (2).

In this case, the goods cost $2,000 more than was estimated when the order was placed.

Disbursements   Disbursements represent the payment of cash for expenditures. Such payments may precede the expenditure (an advance), coincide with the expenditure (a direct payment), or follow the expenditure (the payment of a liability). The payment for the goods purchased in (2) above would be recorded as follows:

(4) Vouchers Payable   12,000
   Cash   12,000
    To record payment of vouchers payable.

Encumbrances and expenditures are classified on the same basis (by function, activity, object, and/or organizational unit) as appropriations. The effect on appropriation control of incorporating appropriations, encumbrances, and expenditures into the accounting records is demonstrated in Illustration 17–4.

In this illustration it is assumed that the appropriation for budget category 103 is $50,000 and that the amount of expenditures in this category prior to the entries illustrated above was $15,000. The effect of Entries (1), (2), (3), and (4) above on the subsidiary ledger card for budget category 103 are illustrated as indicated. The most important thing to note is that at any particular point in time information is available to administrators as to their unexpended and uncommitted appropriation authority.

Capital Expenditures   In accounting for profit-oriented enterprises, capital expenditures are recorded as assets and are distinguished from revenue expenditures. The cost of such assets is recognized in the operating statements (income statement) of such enterprises through the process of depreciation. *Neither fixed assets nor depreciation are recognized in the accounting records of an expendable fund entity.*

ILLUSTRATION 17–4
Subsidiary Ledger Control Card for One Budget Category
Function: Sanitation; Activity: Sanitary Sewer Cleaning; Object: Operating Supplies

BUDGET LINE 103	(A) APPROPRIATION	(B) ENCUMBRANCE	(C) EXPENDITURE	(D) TOTAL (B)+(C)	(E) UNENCUMBERED BALANCE (A)−(D)
Prior Balance	50,000	–0–	15,000	15,000	35,000
Purchase Order [Entry (1)]		10,000		10,000	(10,000)
Balance	50,000	10,000	15,000	25,000	25,000
Expenditure [Entries (2) & (3)]		(10,000)	12,000	2,000	(2,000)
Balance	50,000	–0–	27,000	27,000	23,000
Disbursement [Entry (4)]		–0–	–0–	–0–	–0–
Balance	50,000	–0–	27,000	27,000	23,000

In accounting for an expendable fund entity, capital expenditures (see Illustration 17–3), like other expenditures, are treated as an outflow of financial resources. The assets acquired do not represent expendable financial resources but rather reflect the purposes for which financial resources have been used. Thus, they are not recorded or reported as assets of the fund entity. This treatment is consistent with the primary purpose of fund accounting, which is to provide accounting control over the collection and expenditure of financial resources and to assure that no violations of authorized limits on expenditures occur. The operating statements of fund entities are therefore designed to reflect *all* of the sources and uses of its financial resources. The position statement of the fund entity is designed to present the status of its *financial resources,* the related liabilities, and the net financial resources available for subsequent appropriation and expenditure. This emphasis on the status and flow of net *financial resources* requires that capital expenditures be treated the same as any other classification of expenditures and that they not be reflected as assets of the fund entity. This is not to say that controls are not maintained over fixed assets acquired by means of expendable fund resources. The organization will establish records and controls outside of the records of the expendable fund entity. Accounting for and reporting on fixed assets of governmental units are illustrated in Chapter 18.

Depreciation is not accounted for in the records of an expendable fund entity for the same reason that fixed assets are excluded from the records of such entities. Expenditures, not expenses, are measured in fund accounting. Acquisitions of fixed assets required the *use* of financial resources and are accounted for as expenditures. Proceeds from the sale of fixed assets *provide* financial resources and are accounted for as revenues. Depreciation expense is neither a source nor a use of the financial resources of an expendable fund entity, and thus is not properly recorded in the accounts of such entities. Inclusion of depreciation expense in the operating statement of an expendable fund entity would confuse two fundamentally different measurements—expenditures and expense—and would result in misleading inferences relative to the operating activities of the expendable fund entity. This does not mean that the concept or measurement of depreciation is not important from the point of view of the organization as a whole. Indeed, if meaningful cost/benefit analysis is to be attempted for a particular activity, the operating expenditures of the activity must be adjusted by depreciation to determine total activity cost. However, the objective of fund accounting is not to provide information relative to the costs and benefits of activities but to control the collection and expenditure of financial resources. Accounting for and reporting on depreciation by state and local governmental units are further discussed in Chapter 18.

Inventory Items   In fund accounting, inventory items may be treated as expenditures when purchased (purchase method) or when used (consumption method). The use of the consumption method is a departure from the expenditure-recognition criteria stated above. However, it is argued that where inventories are material in amount, the consumption method results in more meaningful reporting and control.

Prepayments   Prepayments for items such as insurance that extend over several accounting periods are accounted for as expenditures in the period of acquisition.

Recording Budgeted and Actual Revenue and Expenditures

Condensed financial statements for an expendable fund entity are presented in Illustration 17–5. Entries that were recorded in the records of the expendable fund entity during 1980 are presented in summary form following Illustration 17–5.

ILLUSTRATION 17–5
Condensed Financial Statements of Expendable Fund Entity

BALANCE SHEET—JANUARY 1, 1980

Net Financial Resources (Assets — Liabilities)	$100,000
Fund Balance (Unreserved)	$100,000

STATEMENT OF CHANGES IN UNRESERVED FUND BALANCE

	BUDGET	ACTUAL	ACTUAL OVER (UNDER) BUDGET
Unreserved Fund Balance—1/1/80	$100,000	$100,000	$ –0–
Revenue	800,000	850,000	50,000
Total Resources Available	$900,000	$950,000	$ 50,000
Appropriation-Expenditures	$780,000	$600,000	
Encumbrances	–0–	170,000	
Total Resources Expended or Committed	$780,000	$770,000	$ (10,000)
Unreserved Fund Balance—12/31/80	$120,000	$180,000	$ 60,000

BALANCE SHEET—DECEMBER 31, 1980

Net Financial Resources (Assets — Liabilities)		$350,000
Fund Balance—December 31, 1980		
Unreserved	$180,000	
Reserved for Commitments (Encumbrances)	170,000	$350,000

(1) Estimated Revenue (classified)	800,000	
Appropriations (classified)		780,000
Unreserved Fund Balance		20,000

      To record budgeted revenues and expenditures adopted by the legislative body or governing board.

The excess of budgeted revenues over (under) budgeted expenditures is recorded as an increase (decrease) in the unreserved fund balance. In addition to this entry, postings would be made to subsidiary accounts for each source of revenue and each appropriation-expenditure category.

(2) Receivables or Cash	850,000	
Revenue (classified)		850,000

      To record revenues recognized during the year.

(3) Encumbrances (classified)	775,000	
Reserve for Encumbrances		775,000

      To record encumbrances.

As encumbrances are recorded, they are also posted to the appropriate appropriation-expenditure subsidiary account, thereby providing information as to the amount of each appropriation category that remains available for encumbrance or expenditure (see Illustration 17–4).

(4a) Expenditures (classified)	600,000	
Vouchers Payable or Cash		600,000

      To record receipt of encumbered goods and services.

(4b) Reserve for Encumbrances	605,000	
Encumbrances		605,000

      To remove encumbrances on goods and services that have been recorded as expenditures.

Two entries are required to record expenditures for goods or services that have been previously encumbered. Since the amount expended will not necessarily equal the amount encumbered, the dollar amounts in the two entries may not be the same. The reversal of the encumbrance is for the amount of the original encumbrance. The amount of expenditure is for the approved invoice price of the goods or services received.

(5) Revenue	850,000	
Estimated Revenue		800,000
Unreserved Fund Balance		50,000
To close the budgeted and actual revenue accounts.		

The excess of actual revenue over (under) budgeted revenue is recorded as an increase (decrease) in the unreserved fund balance. Postings would also be made to close out each subsidiary revenue account.

(6) Appropriations	780,000	
Expenditures		600,000
Encumbrances (775,000 − 605,000)		170,000
Unreserved Fund Balance		10,000
To close the appropriations, expenditures, and encumbrances accounts.		

The excess of appropriations over (under) expenditures plus encumbrances is recorded as an increase (decrease) in the unreserved fund balance. The balance of encumbrances at year-end is matched against appropriations because, although they are not expenditures, encumbrances do represent commitments made against the current year's appropriations and therefore represent the utilization of the appropriation authority of the current year. Postings would also be made to close each subsidiary appropriation-expenditure account.

After Entries (5) and (6) are posted, all account balances except assets, liabilities, the unreserved fund balance, and the reserve for encumbrances will have been closed. The balances in the unreserved fund balance and reserve for encumbrances accounts may be calculated as follows:

Reserve for Encumbrance—January 1, 1980	–0–
Total Amounts Encumbered During 1980—Entry (3)	775,000
Total Encumbrances Expended—Entry (4b)	605,000
Reserve for Encumbrance—December 31, 1980	170,000
Unreserved Fund Balance—January 1, 1980	100,000
Excess of Estimated Revenue over Appropriations—Entry (1)	20,000
Excess of Actual Revenue over Estimated Revenue—Entry (5)	50,000
Excess of Appropriations over Expenditures and Encumbrances—Entry (6)	10,000
Unreserved Fund Balance—December 31, 1980	180,000

The balance in the reserve for encumbrances account at December 31, 1980 represents the estimated amount of the net financial resources of the fund entity that will be needed in the subsequent year to liquidate obligations entered into under the authority of the current year's appropriation. As such, it represents a restriction on the availability of fund resources for future appropriation rather than a liability and is properly considered as a portion (reserved) of the total fund balance. The concept that the year-end balance in the reserve for encumbrance account is in reality a reserved fund balance would perhaps be clearer if an analysis of the change in the total fund balance were presented in the following form:

Total Fund Balance—January 1	100,000
Add Actual Revenue	850,000
Deduct Actual Expenditures	(600,000)
Total Fund Balance—December 31	350,000
Less Amount Reserved for Commitments	(170,000)
Unreserved Fund Balance—December 31	180,000

It is also instructive to note that the increase in the total fund balance is equal to the excess of actual revenues (inflows of net financial resources) over actual expenditures (outflows of net financial resources).

In the next year, the balance of the reserve for encumbrances will be charged by means of a separate expenditures account with the actual expenditures arising from the year-end commitments that are incurred in the subsequent year. A difference between the amount encumbered at the end of the year and the amount of the actual expenditures related thereto that are incurred in the subsequent year is debited or credited to the unreserved fund balance.

Comprehensive Illustration

The General Fund of Model City will now be used to illustrate the principles of fund accounting developed in this chapter.

The general fund of a municipality is used to account for all externally unrestricted financial resources of the municipality other than those required to be accounted for in another fund. It is established at the inception of the municipality and is continued as long as the municipality exists. Most of the current operations of a municipality are financed by the resources of this fund. The general ledger trial balance of the General Fund of Model City on January 1, 1980 is as follows:

Model City
The General Fund
General Ledger Trial Balance
January 1, 1980

Cash	45,000
Certificates of Deposit	100,000
Property Tax Receivable	190,000
Total Debits	335,000
Estimated Uncollectible Taxes	20,000
Vouchers Payable	65,000
Unreserved Fund Balance	95,000
Reserve For Encumbrances—1979	155,000
Total Credits	335,000

The Budget adopted by the City Council for the General Fund for the fiscal year ending December 31, 1980 is presented in summary form below.

Model City
The General Fund
1980 Fiscal-Year Budget

Estimated Revenue	
Licenses and Permits	188,250
Property Tax	1,158,750
State Grant—Education	300,000
Charges for Services	135,000
Proceeds from Sales of Equipment	78,000
Total	1,860,000
Appropriations	
Public Safety	416,000
General Government	193,500
Highways and Streets	135,500
Sanitation	75,000
Health	148,500
Cultural—Recreation	88,500
Education	687,000
Total	1,744,000
Excess of Estimated Revenue over Appropriations	116,000
Transfer from Enterprise Fund	150,000
Less Transfers to: Debt Service Fund	(60,000)
Special Assessments Fund	(200,000)
Excess of Revenue and Transfers from Other Funds Over	
Appropriations and Transfers to Other Funds	6,000

Summary entries to record the activities and transactions of the General Fund during 1980 are presented below. The assignment to specific subsidiary accounts of amounts credited to revenue or appropriations and of amounts debited to encumbrances, expenditures, or estimated revenue is not shown in these summary entries. The reader is reminded, however, that each entry to these general ledger control accounts also requires detailed postings by appropriate classifications to the related subsidiary accounts.

(1) Estimated Revenue	1,860,000	
Appropriations		1,744,000
Unreserved Fund Balance		116,000
To record budgeted revenue and expenditures.		

(2) Due from Enterprise Fund   150,000

      Transfers from Other Funds   150,000

         To record the authorization for the transfer of resources from other fund entities incorporated in the budget adopted by the City Council.

The reader is reminded that, for financial reporting purposes, transfers of resources from other fund entities of the same organization are distinguished from revenue of the recipient fund entity. Interfund transfers are properly recognized (accrued) in the period in which they are authorized. Control over authorized transfers from other fund entities is achieved by recording them as a receivable at the beginning of the year for which they are authorized (budgeted), rather than by including them in the budget entry for estimated revenue.

(3) Transfers to Other Funds   260,000

      Due to Debt Service Fund   60,000

      Due to Special Assessments Fund   200,000

         To record the authorization for the transfer of resources to other fund entities incorporated in the budget adopted by the City Council.

Although authorized transfers to other fund entities may be viewed as appropriation-expenditures from the point of view of the General Fund entity, for purposes of financial reporting they are distinguished from expenditures. Control over authorized transfers to other fund entities is achieved by recording them as liabilities at the beginning of the period for which they are authorized (budgeted), rather than by including them in the budget entry for appropriations.

(4) Property Tax Receivable   1,287,500

      Estimated Uncollectible Taxes   128,750

      Revenue   1,158,750

         To record property taxes at the time they are levied.

The estimate for uncollectible taxes is determined on the basis of collection policy and prior years' experience. It is recorded as a direct reduction of revenue, however, rather than as an expenditure, since the failure to collect taxes is not an outflow of net financial resources. Accordingly, there is no appropriation for the amount of estimated uncollectible taxes and it is, therefore, properly accounted for as a reduction of revenue rather than as an expenditure.

(5) Other Receivables   80,000

      Revenue   80,000

         To record billings for routine services.

(6) Expenditures—1979   148,000

      Vouchers Payable   148,000

         To record receipt of goods and services ordered in 1979.

A separate expenditure control account (and subsidiary ledger) is used to record expenditures during the current year that were encumbered in the prior year. At the end of the year, this expenditure account will be closed out against the Reserve for Encumbrance-1979 account and any difference taken to the unreserved fund balance [see Entry (25) below].

(7) Encumbrances	1,291,000	
Reserve for Encumbrances		1,291,000
To record encumbrances on goods and services ordered during the current year.		
(8) Cash	1,281,000	
Property Tax Receivable		1,201,000
Other Receivables		80,000
To record the collection of $170,500 of property taxes levied in 1979 and $1,030,500 of property taxes levied in 1980, and to record the collection of $80,000 in other receivables.		
(9) Estimated Uncollectible Taxes	19,500	
Property Tax Receivable		19,500
To record the write-off of uncollected 1979 property taxes authorized by the City Council (190,000 − 170,500 = 19,500).		
(10) Cash	221,000	
Revenues		221,000
To record collection of licenses, permits, fees, service charges, etc.		
(11) Expenditures	1,050,000	
Vouchers Payable		1,050,000
Reserve for Encumbrances	1,100,000	
Encumbrances		1,100,000
To record receipt of goods and services that had been previously encumbered [Entry (7) above] in the amount of $1,100,000.		
(12) Expenditures	210,000	
Vouchers Payable		210,000
To record receipt of goods and services that had *not* been previously encumbered.		

Not all expenditures go through the encumbrance process. Encumbrances are formally recognized in the accounts only when there is an extended period of time between the date the commitment is made and the date the expenditure is incurred. For example, expenditures for personnel services (payroll) are rarely encumbered.

(13) Receivable from State Government	275,000	
Revenue		275,000
To record municipal education grant authorized by the state legislature.		

The amount of revenue recognized is based on an approved grant application filed with the Department of Education and is not dependent upon the future performance of specific services or specified expenditures of financial resources.

(14) Encumbrances   250,000
    Reserve for Encumbrances   250,000
    To record a contract to acquire office furnishings and equipment.

(15) Cash   100,000
    Due from Enterprise Fund   100,000
    To record the receipt of a cash transfer from the Enterprise Fund.

(16) Expenditures   250,000
    Vouchers Payable   250,000
    Reserve for Encumbrances   250,000
    Encumbrances   250,000
    To record receipt of office equipment and furnishings and to remove encumbrance.

Capital expenditures, like other expenditures, represent the approved utilization of the financial resources of the General Fund and are therefore recorded as expenditures and not as assets in the records of the General Fund.

(17) Vouchers Payable   1,650,000
    Cash   1,650,000
    To record payment of liabilities.

(18) Cash   87,250
    Revenue   87,250
    To record proceeds from the sale of used office furniture and equipment.

Since the proceeds from the sale of Model City assets constitute expendable financial resources, they are recorded as revenue by the recipient general fund.

(19) Cash   275,000
    Receivable from State Government   275,000
    To record collection of grant from state government.

(20) Due to Debt Service Fund   60,000
    Due to Special Assessments Fund   200,000
    Cash   260,000
    To record the authorized transfers of cash to other Model City fund entities.

(21) Certificates of Deposit   6,000
    Revenue   6,000
    To record interest earned on certificates of deposit that has been or will be credited thereto.

(22) Estimated Uncollectible Taxes   76,000
    Property Tax Receivable   76,000
    To record write-off of 1980 property taxes authorized by the City Council.

Preclosing Trial Balance   The transactions summarized in the journal entries above are reflected in the December 31, 1980 general ledger trial balance for the General Fund of Model City presented below.

Model City
The General Fund
General Ledger Trial Balance
December 31, 1980

	DR.	CR.
Cash	99,250	
Certificates of Deposit	106,000	
Property Taxes Receivable	181,000	
Due from Enterprise Fund	50,000	
Estimated Revenue	1,860,000	
Expenditures	1,510,000	
Encumbrances	191,000	
Transfers to Other Funds	260,000	
Expenditures—1979	148,000	
Estimated Uncollectible Taxes		53,250
Vouchers Payable		73,000
Unreserved Fund Balance		211,000
Reserve for Encumbrances		191,000
Reserve for Encumbrances—1979		155,000
Appropriations		1,744,000
Revenue		1,828,000
Transfers from Other Funds		150,000
Total	4,405,250	4,405,250

Closing Entries   December 31, 1980 closing entries for the General Fund are as follows:

(23) Unreserved Fund Balance	32,000	
Revenue	1,828,000	
Estimated Revenue		1,860,000

To close out actual and budgeted revenue accounts.

(24) Appropriations	1,744,000	
Expenditures		1,510,000
Encumbrances		191,000
Unreserved Fund Balance		43,000

To close out appropriations and current year's expenditures and encumbrances accounts.

(25) Reserve for Encumbrances—1979   155,000

    Expenditures—1979   148,000

    Unreserved Fund Balance   7,000

      To close out expenditures for goods and services *ordered* and encumbered in prior year.

(26) Unreserved Fund Balance   110,000

Transfers from Other Funds   150,000

    Transfers to Other Funds   260,000

      To close out interfund transfers to the unreserved fund balance.

Financial Statements

In the past, three basic financial statements have been recommended for expendable fund entities: (1) a balance sheet, (2) a statement of revenue and expenditures and (3) a statement of changes in fund balance. More recently, it has been recommended by the National Council on Governmental Accounting that statements (2) and (3) be combined into a single statement of revenue, expenditures and other changes in fund balance. As stated by the Council, the major reasons for this recommendation are that such a statement will:

    (1) Provide a basic operating statement format for all funds. . . .

    (2) Present all changes in the fund balance . . . during the period, thus providing (a) an understandable summary of such changes and (b) a reconciliation of the beginning and ending balances in a single statement that is directly related to the beginning and ending balance sheets. Further, such statements may readily be cross-referenced to more detailed statements and schedules.

    (3) Embody the all-inclusive approach, thus eliminating questions as to whether certain changes in fund balance . . . should be reported directly in a statement of changes in equity while other changes are shown in the operating statement (e.g., transfers). Further, this format eliminates the need for separate statements of changes in fund balance . . . in most cases, since such changes usually are set forth clearly under this approach.[5]

Revenue should be classified by major sources and expenditures by major functions in the statement of revenue, expenditures and other changes in fund balance. In addition, comparative information for the prior year should be presented both in that statement and in the balance sheet.

The operating statement should be supported by schedules that present detailed financial data which support and amplify that summarized in the formal financial statements. Schedules may also be used to present budgetary data or to demonstrate compliance with legal provisions. Generally such schedules should include (1) a schedule of revenue, (2) a schedule of expenditures and encumbrances, and (3) unless such information can be presented in appropriate detail in the financial statements, a schedule of transfers and other changes in fund balance.

Examples of statements and schedules for the General Fund of Model City for the year ending December 31, 1980 are presented in the following illustrations.

[5]National Council on Governmental Accounting, *Exposure Draft: GAAFR Restatement: Principles,* pp. 55–56.

ILLUSTRATION 17–6
Model City
The General Fund
Balance Sheet December 31, 1980 and 1979

ASSETS	1980	1979
Cash	$99,250	$ 45,000
Time Certificates of Deposit	106,000	100,000
Property Tax Receivable (less allowance for uncollectible amounts, 1980—$53,250; 1979—$20,000)	127,750	170,000
Due from Other Funds	50,000	–0–
Total	$383,000	$315,000
LIABILITIES AND FUND BALANCE		
Vouchers Payable	$ 73,000	$ 65,000
Fund Balance:		
Unreserved	119,000	95,000
Reserved for Encumbrances	191,000	155,000
Total Fund Balance	310,000	250,000
Total	$383,000	$315,000

ILLUSTRATION 17–7
Model City
The General Fund
Statement of Revenue, Expenditures and Other Changes in Fund Balance
For the Years Ending December 31, 1980 and December 31, 1979

	1980			
	APPROPRIATED IN			
	CURRENT YEAR	PRIOR YEAR	TOTAL 1980	1979
Revenue				
Licenses and Permits			$ 170,500	$ 175,000
Property Tax			1,158,750	1,105,000
State Grant—Education			275,000	250,000
Charges for Services			136,500	130,000
Proceeds from Sales of Equipment			87,250	–0–
Total Revenue (Illustration 17–8)			$1,828,000	$1,660,000
Transfer from Enterprise Fund			150,000	–0–
Total Revenue and Transfers from Other Funds			$1,978,000	$1,660,000
Expenditures				
Public Safety	$ 376,000	$ 4,000	$ 380,000	$ 360,000
General Government	184,000	5,000	189,000	175,000
Highways and Streets	110,000	18,000	128,000	130,000
Sanitation	60,000	10,000	70,000	71,000
Health	135,000	6,000	141,000	132,000
Cultural—Recreation	80,000	–0–	80,000	82,000
Education	565,000	105,000	670,000	640,000
Total (Illustration 17–9)	$1,510,000	$148,000	$1,658,000	$1,590,000
Transfers to Other Funds				
To Debt Service Fund	$ 60,000	$ –0–	$ 60,000	$ 60,000
To Special Assessments Fund	200,000	–0–	200,000	–0–
Total	$ 260,000	$ –0–	$ 260,000	$ 60,000
Total Expenditures and Transfers to Other Funds	$1,770,000	$148,000	$1,918,000	$1,650,000
Excess (Deficiency) of Revenues and Transfers From Other Funds Over Expenditures and Transfers to Other Funds			$ 60,000	$ 10,000
Fund Balance—January 1			250,000	240,000
Fund Balance—December 31			$ 310,000	$ 250,000

ILLUSTRATION 17–8
Model City
The General Fund
Schedule of Estimated and Actual Revenue
For the Year Ending December 31, 1980

	ESTIMATED REVENUE	ACTUAL REVENUE	ACTUAL OVER (UNDER) ESTIMATED
Licenses and Permits			
Motor Vehicles	$ 103,000	$ 94,000	($ 9,000)
Hunting and Fishing	16,250	15,000	(1,250)
Marriage Licenses	24,000	27,500	3,500
Burial Permits	9,000	7,000	(2,000)
Animal Licenses	14,000	8,000	(6,000)
Other	22,000	19,000	(3,000)
Total	$ 188,250	$ 170,500	($17,750)
Property Tax	1,158,750	1,158,750	–0–
Intergovernmental Revenue[1]	300,000	275,000	(25,000)
Charges for Services[1]	135,000	136,500	1,500
Proceeds from Sale of Equipment[1]	78,000	87,250	9,250
Total	$1,860,000	$1,828,000	($32,000)

[1]Detail omitted for illustrative purposes. In practice, subcategories of these major revenue sources would also be presented as under Licenses and Permits in this illustration.

ILLUSTRATION 17-9
Model City
The General Fund
Schedule of Expenditures and Encumbrances Compared with Authorizations
For the Year Ending December 31, 1980

	RESERVE FOR ENCUMBRANCES 1979	EXPENDITURES 1979	CREDIT (CHARGE) TO FUND BALANCE	1980 APPROPRIATIONS	1980 EXPENDITURES	1980 ENCUMBRANCES	1980 UNENCUMBERED BALANCE
Public Safety							
Police							
Criminal Investigation	$ -0-	$ -0-	$ -0-	$ 24,000	$ 22,500	$ 750	$ 750
Vice Control	-0-	-0-	-0-	6,000	-0-	-0-	6,000
Patrol	-0-	-0-	-0-	80,000	75,000	1,500	3,500
Records	-0-	-0-	-0-	35,000	32,700	50	2,250
Custody of Prisoners	-0-	-0-	-0-	16,000	15,250	500	250
Crime Laboratory	3,500	3,000	500	31,000	26,000	2,500	2,500
Traffic Control	2,500	1,000	1,500	40,000	31,300	3,700	5,000
Training	-0-	-0-	-0-	15,000	14,250	-0-	750
Other	-0-	-0-	-0-	3,000	3,000	-0-	-0-
Total Police	$ 6,000	$ 4,000	$2,000	$ 250,000	$ 220,000	$ 9,000	$21,000
Fire	-0-	-0-	-0-	126,000	120,000	4,000	2,000
Inspection	-0-	-0-	-0-	40,000	36,000	-0-	4,000
Total Public Safety	$ 6,000	$ 4,000	$2,000	$ 416,000	$ 376,000	$ 13,000	$27,000
General Government[1]	5,000	5,000	-0-	193,500	184,000	8,000	1,500
Highways and Streets[1]	20,000	18,000	2,000	135,500	110,000	24,250	1,250
Sanitation[1]	8,000	10,000	(2,000)	75,000	60,000	12,500	2,500
Health[1]	6,000	6,000	-0-	148,500	135,000	8,250	5,250
Cultural—Recreation[1]	-0-	-0-	-0-	88,500	80,000	8,000	500
Education[1]	110,000	105,000	5,000	687,000	565,000	117,000	5,000
Total	$155,000	$148,000	$7,000	$1,744,000	$1,510,000	$191,000	$43,000

[1]For illustrative purposes, only major functions are presented in this schedule. In practice, each major function should be broken down by subfunctions and activities as was done for PUBLIC SAFETY (function); Police (subfunction); Criminal Investigation (activity).

Accounting for Supplies Inventory

Inventory items may be treated as expenditures when purchased (purchase method) or when used (consumption method). Under either method a portion of the fund balance may be reserved for the amount of supplies on hand on the balance sheet date. The creation and rationale for such reserves are illustrated as follows:

Assume that (1) the unreserved fund balance at the beginning of the period is $1,000,000, (2) the only transactions that occur during the period are the purchase and consumption of supplies, (3) there is no beginning inventory of supplies, and (4) budget and encumbrance entries are ignored. Entries and account balances relating to the purchase and consumption of supplies under each method are summarized below.

DESCRIPTION	JOURNAL ENTRY	PURCHASE METHOD DR.	PURCHASE METHOD CR.	CONSUMPTION METHOD DR.	CONSUMPTION METHOD CR.
Unreserved Fund Balance— Beginning of Period		1,000,000		1,000,000	
Purchase of Supplies	Expenditures	200,000		—	
	Supplies Inventory	—		200,000	
	Cash		200,000		200,000
Supplies in the amount of $50,000 are on hand at the end of the period	Expenditures	NO ENTRY		150,000	
	Supplies Inventory				150,000
Closing Entries	Unreserved Fund Balance	200,000		150,000	
	Expenditures		200,000		150,000
Unreserved Fund Balance		800,000		850,000	
Reserve for Supplies Inventory is established	Supplies	50,000		—	
	Unreserved Fund Balance	—		50,000	
	Reserve for Supplies Inventory		50,000		50,000
Unreserved Fund Balance			800,000		800,000
Reserve for Supplies Inventory			50,000		50,000
Fund Balance			850,000		850,000

Under the purchase method, the establishment of the reserve is a means of disclosing otherwise *unreported* supplies inventory. When the purchase method is used, significant amounts of inventory should be disclosed in this manner or by footnote. Under the consumption method, the supplies inventory is already recorded and *reported* as a fund asset and is included in the amount of the unreserved fund balance. Since such supplies cannot be expended except by consumption, they do not represent an expendable financial resource that is available for appropriation in a subsequent period. Accordingly, the unreserved fund balance is properly reduced and a reserve established for the amount of fund assets that are not available for appropriation.[6]

[6]In some applications of the consumption method, a reserve for supplies inventory is established only to the extent of the minimum amount of inventory that must be maintained and that is therefore not available for use.

Lapsing of Appropriations

The treatment illustrated in this chapter for encumbrances outstanding at the end of the period was based on the assumption (and generally followed practice) that encumbered appropriations do not lapse at the end of the fiscal year. It is possible, however, for the legislative body or governing board to impose a provision that causes unexpended appropriations to lapse at the end of the year. In this case, the reserve for encumbrances must be closed out at the end of the year, and if the encumbered items are to be purchased in the next year, the appropriation for the next year must contain authority for such expenditures.

If appropriations lapse, the closing entry for appropriations at the end of the year takes the following form.

Reserve for Encumbrances	XXX	
Appropriations	XXX	
Expenditures		XXX
Encumbrances		XXX
Unreserved Fund Balance		XXX

The subsequent year's appropriation should include authorization for the purchase of the encumbered items. Therefore, the reserve for encumbrances would be reestablished at the beginning of the next year by a debit to encumbrances, and subsequent expenditures for the items would be accounted for the same as any other expenditures of that year.

Questions

1. What characteristics distinguish nonprofit organizations from profit-oriented enterprises?

2. Define a fund as the term is applied in accounting for the activities of governmental units and other nonprofit organizations.

3. What is the significance of the "unreserved fund balance" of an expendable fund entity?

4. What are the major classifications of increases and decreases in expendable fund resources?

5. What are the revenue-recognition criteria for expendable fund entities? How do these criteria differ from revenue-recognition criteria for profit oriented enterprises?

6. Expenditures may be classified by function, activity, object, or organizational unit. Give an example of each classification for (a) a university; (b) a municipality. Which classification is the most appropriate for external financial reporting?

7. Distinguish between an appropriation, an encumbrance, an expenditure, and a disbursement.

8. Distinguish between an expense and an expenditure.

9. Explain and justify the difference between the treatment of estimated uncollectible taxes in fund accounting and the treatment of estimated bad debts in commercial accounting.

10. Explain the purpose of encumbrance accounting. Might encumbrance accounting be used by commercial enterprises?

11. Is the year-end balance in the reserve for encumbrances account a liability? Explain.

12. What columns would you suggest for a subsidiary ledger account in order that it might be a subsidiary not only to the "appropriations" control account but also to the "encumbrances" and the "expenditures" control accounts?

13. Why is depreciation on fixed assets not recorded in the records of expendable fund entities?

14. How does the adoption of a budget for a general fund entity differ from the adoption of a budget by a commercial unit?

15. Describe the principal financial statements used to report on the activities and status of expendable fund entities.

16. Why may it be difficult or impossible for a nonprofit organization to determine the total cost of performing a particular activity or function?

Problems

Problem 17–1

During 1980, the City of Meadville engaged in the following typical financial activities:

1. The City Council approved the budget for the general operating fund. The budget shows estimated revenues of $1,900,000 and appropriations for expenditures of $1,850,000.

2. Property tax assessments for 1980 were compiled and statements mailed to property owners. Assessments total $955,000. Past collection experience indicates that approximately 5% of assessed property taxes are delinquent or uncollectible during the year of billing.

3. A low bid of $5,500 was accepted for a new vehicle for the fire chief. A purchase order was issued providing for additional costs for painting and ancillary equipment (negotiated after the bid) prior to delivery. The estimate of additional costs is $400.

4. Additional purchase orders placed during the year amount to $140,000.

5. City employees are issued warrants for pay for the month of April. The total payroll amounts to $90,000.

6. The City received a statement from the State Treasurer that the City's portion of the state sales tax for the first half-year is $375,000.

7. Vouchers for expenditures totaling $135,000 are approved for payment. Encumbrances against these vouchers were recorded at a total of $137,000.

8. The vehicle for the fire chief was delivered and accepted. The invoice in the amount of $5,850 was approved for payment.

9. Property tax collections for the month of June amounted to $450,000.

10. The City Treasurer issued checks in payment of the vouchers totaling $135,000 and the invoice for the fire chief's vehicle.

11. A purchase order previously issued for an electric typewriter (estimated price $650) was cancelled when the vendor indicated a three-month delay in delivery.

Required:
Prepare journal entries to record and account for the foregoing transactions.

Problem 17–2
The following events relate typical activities in a municipality that affect the General Fund. Prepare the necessary journal entries to record each event in the General Fund general ledger accounts.

1. The Fairfax City Council passed an ordinance approving a general operating budget of $580,000 for fiscal year 1980. The city's only source of revenue is from property taxes. For 1980, these revenues are estimated at $565,000. (1 entry)

2. A property tax levy of $1 per $100 assessed valuation (total assessed valuation equals $60,000,000) is billed to property owners. Taxes are due in the current fiscal year. Experience indicates that 3% of taxes billed will be uncollectible. (1 entry)

3. A motorcycle for the Department of Public Safety is ordered by the purchasing department on the basis of a low bid of $4,200. (1 entry)

4. The motorcycle in (3) above is received and the invoice is approved for payment. Extra accessories not included in the bid price amount to $425. (2 entries)

5. Salaries and wages in the amount of $20,000 are paid by check to city employees for the two-week period ending on May 15. (1 entry)

6. The property division sold used typewriters and other office equipment at a public auction. Total receipts were $8,225. (1 entry)

7. Collected property taxes in the amount of $540,000.

8. Estimated revenue for the year totaled $565,000 (1 above). Actual revenue recorded equaled $590,225. Prepare an entry to close the revenue accounts at the end of the fiscal year.

Problem 17–3

The general ledger trial balance of the General Fund of the City of Avalon on January 1, 1980 shows the following:

	DR.	CR.
Cash	$150,000	$
Taxes Receivable	75,000	
Due from State	25,000	
Allowance for Uncollectible Taxes		35,000
Vouchers Payable		75,000
Unreserved Fund Balance		110,000
Reserve for Encumbrances—1979		30,000
Totals	$250,000	$250,000

A summary of activities and transactions for the General Fund during 1980 is presented below:

1. The City Council adopted a budget for the General Fund with estimated revenues of $1,560,000 and authorization for appropriated expenditures of $1,400,000. The budget authorized the transfer of $50,000 from the Water Fund to the General Fund for operating expenses as a payment in lieu of taxes. Cash for the payment of interest due for the year on the $1,000,000 6% bond issue for the Civic Center is approved for transfer from the General Fund to the Debt Service Fund.

2. The annual property tax levy of 10% on assessed valuation ($11,000,000) is billed to property owners. Two percent is estimated to be uncollectible.

3. Goods and services were ordered during the year amounting to $1,150,000.

4. Invoices for all goods ordered in 1979 amounting to $29,000 were approved for payment.

5. Transferred funds for bond interest on Civic Center bonds to the Debt Service Fund.

6. Recorded invoices for goods and services received during the year totaling $1,155,000. These were encumbered previously (see Item 3 above).

7. Received transfer of funds from the Water Co. in lieu of taxes.

8. Collected taxes from property owners in the amount of $1,050,000.

9. Charged off $17,000 of past-due tax bills determined to be uncollectible.

10. Issued checks in payment of invoices for goods and services ordered in 1979 and 1980. (See Items 4 and 6 above.)

11. Recorded revenues received from miscellaneous sources, other than property taxes, of $455,000.

12. Issued purchase order for two trash collection vehicle systems complete with residence trash containers for automatic pickup of trash. Bid price per system was $120,000.

13. Received payment from State of $25,000 due.

Required:

A. Prepare journal entries to record the summary transactions.

B. Prepare a preclosing trial balance.

C. Prepare closing entries.

D. Prepare a post-closing trial balance. You may find it necessary or convenient to post journal entries to ledger T accounts before and after making closing entries for the preparation of the required trial balances.

Problem 17-4

The following account balances, among others, were included in the preclosing trial balance of the General Fund of the City of Hopi on December 31, 1981.

Estimated Revenue	315,000
Expenditures	234,000
Encumbrances	60,000
Expenditures—1980	21,500
Reserve for Encumbrances (Note 1)	81,000
Appropriations	336,000
Revenue	348,000
Reserve for Supplies Inventory (Note 2)	36,000
Supplies Inventory	36,000
Unreserved Fund Balance	12,000

Note 1: The balance in this account was $21,000 on January 1, 1981. Purchase orders outstanding on December 31, 1981 total $60,000.

Note 2: Supplies on hand on December 31, 1981 amount to $30,000.

Required:

A. What was the balance in the Unreserved Fund Balance account on December 31, 1980? What was the total Fund Balance on December 31, 1980?

B. Prepare the necessary adjusting and closing entries for the year ended December 31, 1981.

C. Prepare a statement of revenue, expenditures and other changes in Fund Balance with comparative columns for "Budget," "Actual," and "Actual Over (Under) Budget."

Problem 17-5

The following account balances, among others, were included in the preclosing trial balance of the General Fund of the City of Glendale at December 31, 1981.

Estimated Revenue	1,860,000
Expenditures	1,510,000
Encumbrances	191,000
Transfers to Other Funds	260,000
Expenditures—1980	148,000
Reserve for Encumbrances	191,000
Reserve for Encumbrances—1980	155,000
Appropriations	1,744,000
Revenue	1,828,000
Transfers from Other Funds	150,000
Unreserved Fund Balance	211,000

Required:

A. Prepare the necessary closing entries on December 31, 1981.

B. Prepare a statement of revenue, expenditures and other changes in fund balance with comparative columns for: "Budget," "Actual," and "Actual Over (Under) Budget."

C. Assume that the ordinances of the City of Glendale require that unexpended appropriations lapse at the end of the fiscal year. How, if at all, will this provision change the closing entries at the end of the fiscal year?

Problem 17–6

The trial balance for the General Fund of the city of Pinetop as of December 31, 1980 is presented below.

City of Pinetop
The General Fund
Adjusted Trial Balance
December 31, 1980

	DEBIT	CREDIT
Cash	430,000	
Property Tax Receivable	45,000	
Estimated Uncollectible Taxes		20,000
Due from Trust Fund	50,000	
Vouchers Payable		60,000
Reserve for Encumbrances		30,000
Unreserved Fund Balance		415,000
	525,000	525,000

Transactions for the year ending December 31, 1981 are summarized as follows:

1. The City Council adopted a budget for the year with estimated revenue of $735,000 and appropriations of $700,000.

2. Property taxes in the amount of $590,000 were levied for the current year. It is estimated that $24,000 of the taxes levied will prove to be uncollectible.

3. Proceeds from the sale of equipment in the amount of $35,000 were received by the General Fund. The equipment was purchased ten years ago with resources of the General Fund at a cost of $150,000. On the date it was purchased it was estimated that the equipment had a useful life of fifteen years.

4. Licenses and fees in the amount of $110,000 were collected.

5. The total amount of encumbrances against fund resources for the year was $642,500.

6. Vouchers in the amount of $455,000 were authorized for payment. This was $15,000 less than the amount originally encumbered for these purchases.

7. An invoice in the amount of $28,000 was received for goods ordered in 1980. The invoice was approved for payment.

8. Property taxes in the amount of $570,000 were collected.

9. Vouchers in the amount of $475,000 were paid.

10. Fifty thousand dollars was transferred to the General Fund from the Trust Fund.

11. The City Council authorized the write-off of $30,000 in uncollected property taxes.

Required:

A. Prepare entries in general journal form to record the transactions for the year ending December 31, 1981.
B. Prepare a preclosing trial balance for the General Fund as of December 31, 1981.
C. Prepare the necessary closing entries for the year ending December 31, 1981.
D. Prepare a balance sheet and a statement of revenue, expenditures and other changes in fund balance for the General Fund for the year ending December 31, 1981.

Problem 17–7

The trial balance for the General Fund of the city of Centennial as of December 31, 1980 is presented below.

	DEBIT	CREDIT
Cash	300,000	
Supplies Inventory	75,000	
Unreserved Fund Balance		300,000
Reserve for Supplies Inventory		75,000
	375,000	375,000

Transactions of the General Fund for the year ending December 31, 1981 are summarized as follows:

1. The City Council adopted the following budget for 1981.

Estimated revenue	1,600,000
Transfer from Agency Fund	50,000
Appropriations	1,530,000
Transfer to Debt Service Fund	80,000

2. Property taxes of $1,500,000 were levied, of which it is estimated that $30,000 will not be collected.

3. Purchase orders in the amount of $1,400,000 were placed with suppliers and other vendors.

4. Property taxes in the amount of $1,450,000 were collected.

5. Cash was received from the Agency Fund in the amount of $50,000.

6. Invoices in the amount of $1,380,000 were approved for payment. The amount originally encumbered for these invoices was $1,360,000. The invoices included $25,000 net of trade-in allowance for the purchase of a new minicomputer and $400,000 for supplies. The City received a trade-in allowance of $4,000 on its old minicomputer, which had been purchased three years earlier for $16,000. At the time the old minicomputer was purchased, it was estimated that it would have a useful life of 4 years. The new minicomputer is expected to last at least 6 years.

7. Licenses and fees in the amount of $48,000 were collected.

8. Vouchers in the amount of $1,300,000 were paid.

9. Cash in the amount of $80,000 was transferred to the Debt Service Fund.

10. Supplies on hand at the end of the year amount to $100,000.

Required:

A. Prepare entries in general journal form to record the transactions of the General Fund for the year ending December 31, 1981. The City of Centennial uses the consumption method of accounting for its General Fund supplies inventory.

B. Prepare a preclosing trial balance for the General Fund as of December 31, 1981.

C. Prepare the necessary closing entries for the General Fund for the year ending December 31, 1981.

D. Prepare a balance sheet and a statement of revenue, expenditures and other changes in fund balance for the General Fund for the year ending December 31, 1981.

Problem 17–8

The January 1, 1980 trial balance, the calendar-year 1980 budget, and the 1980 transactions of the City of Lochinvar are presented below:

City of Lochinvar
Trial Balance
January 1, 1980

	DR.	CR.
Cash	155,450	
Certificates of Deposit	200,000	
Accounts Receivable	28,675	
Supplies Inventory	37,600	
Due from Federal Government	58,000	
Taxes Receivable	75,600	
Allowance for Uncollectible Taxes		32,150
Vouchers Payable		181,000
Unreserved Fund Balance		226,075
Reserve for Inventory		37,600
Reserve for Encumbrances		78,500
	555,325	555,325

Budget for General Fund
City of Lochinvar
Calendar Year 1980

Estimated Revenue:	
City vehicle and retail license fees	252,000
Property taxes	1,448,000
City sales tax	327,000
Collections for trash service	153,000
Sale of city-owned property	88,000
Total Estimated Revenue	2,268,000
Appropriations:	
General government	261,000
Public safety and security	875,000
Health and welfare	434,000
Recreation and parks	126,000
Street maintenance	367,000
Sanitation	162,000
Total Appropriations	2,225,000
Excess of Revenues over Appropriations	43,000
Transfer from Water & Sewer Fund	118,000
Less Payments (transfers) to Debt Service Funds	(55,000)
Excess of Revenue and Fund Transfers to General Fund over Appropriations and Fund Transfers out of General Fund	106,000

A summary of transactions of the City of Lochinvar affecting the General Fund during the year are:

1. The City Council approved the budget and it was recorded.

2. Orders for goods and services were issued for a total of $1,202,000 during the year.

3. Goods and services were delivered against orders placed with a total invoice amount of $1,165,600. Of this, $80,000 was for orders placed in the prior year.

4. The City accepted a low bid of $78,000 for a new street sweeper for the sanitation department. A purchase order was issued.

5. Sold an old street sweeper and one obsolete fire engine at public auction. Received $92,500 at high bid. The street sweeper cost $60,000 seven years ago, at which time it was estimated to have a useful life of 10 years. The fire engine cost $200,000 eight years ago, at which time it was estimated to have a useful life of 12 years.

6. Issued property tax statements. The tax levy was 8% of the assessed valuation of $18,500,000. An estimated 2% of the tax levy will be uncollectible.

7. Received payment of account from the federal government. This was a grant to be used for upgrading sanitation department equipment.

8. Transferred $55,000 to the Debt Service Fund for the payment of interest on the outstanding bond issue.

9. Billed city residents for trash service. Total billings amounted to $155,675.

10. Collected property taxes totaling $1,438,455, of which $34,200 was past-due collections from the prior year. Charged off $18,250 of past-due taxes as uncollectible.

11. Warrants were issued to employees during the year in payment of wages in total amount of $998,765.

12. City retail establishments remitted a total of $333,650 in sales tax collections for the year.

13. Other cash receipts during the year:

Vehicle license fees and parking fines	$ 98,682
Retail license fees	120,000
For trash services (includes $28,675	
due at end of prior year)	148,720
Transfer from Water & Sewer Fund	118,000

14. Received and paid for delivery of printed forms and other office supplies procured from a local office supply firm against an open purchase order. Billings for the year amounted to $57,680.

15. Received delivery of the street sweeper and an invoice for $78,000 plus freight charges of $1,280. The invoice was approved for payment and a check issued.

16. Issued checks in payment of outstanding vouchers totaling $1,207,100.

17. End-of-year activities: (adjustments)

Supplies Inventory 12/31/80	$38,250
Accrued interest on CD's at 6%	

City uses the consumption method in accounting for supplies expenditures.

Required:
A. Enter the opening trial balance data in T accounts.
B. Prepare journal entries for the year's transactions. Do not include entries for year-end adjustments.
C. Prepare a preclosing trial balance.
D. Prepare journal entries to adjust the Supplies Inventory and record the interest on the CD's.
E. Prepare journal entries to close the revenue, expenditures, and encumbrance accounts.
F. Prepare a comparative balance sheet for 1979–1980.
G. Prepare a statement of revenue, expenditure and other changes in fund balance for 1980.

Problem 17–9
The Sleepy Haven Township's adjusted trial balance for the General Fund at the close of its fiscal year ending June 30, 1981 is presented below.

Sleepy Haven Township
General Fund Trial Balance
June 30, 1981

Cash	11,000	
Property Tax Receivable—Current (Note 1)	82,000	
Estimated Uncollectible Taxes—Current		1,500
Property Tax Receivable—Delinquent	25,000	
Estimated Uncollectible Taxes—Delinquent		16,500
Accounts Receivable (Note 1)	40,000	
Allowance for Uncollectible Accounts		4,000
Due from Internal Service Fund (Note 5)	50,000	
Expenditures (Note 2)	755,000	
Encumbrances	37,000	
Revenue (Note 3)		60,000
Due to Enterprise Fund (Note 5)		10,000
Vouchers Payable		20,000
Reserve for Encumbrances—Prior Year		44,000
Reserve for Encumbrances		37,000
Surplus Receipts (Note 4)		7,000
Appropriations		720,000
Unreserved Fund Balance		80,000
	1,000,000	1,000,000

Note 1: The current tax roll and accounts receivable, recorded on the accural basis as sources of revenue, amounted to $500,000 and $200,000, respectively. These items have been recorded in the General Fund records subject to a 2% provision for uncollectible accounts.

Note 2: Includes $42,500 paid during the fiscal year in settlement of all purchase orders outstanding at the beginning of the fiscal year.

Note 3: Represents the difference between the budgeted (estimated) revenue of $700,000 and the actual revenue realized during the fiscal year.

Note 4: Represents the proceeds from the sale of equipment damaged by fire. The equipment originally cost $40,000 and had been held for 80% of its useful life prior to the fire.

Note 5: The interfund payable and receivable resulted from cash advances (loans) to and from the respective funds.

Required:
A. Prepare in columnar form a Statement of Changes in Unreserved Fund Balance for the year ending June 30, 1981 with column headings for "Budget," "Actual," and "Actual Over (Under) Budget."
B. Prepare a balance sheet for the General Fund at June 30, 1981.

(AICPA adapted)

Problem 17–10
Select the best answer for each of the following items:
1. When used in fund accounting, the term "fund" usually refers to
   a. A sum of money designated for a special purpose.
   b. A liability to other governmental units.

    c. The equity of a municipality in its own assets.

    d. A fiscal and accounting entity having a set of self-balancing accounts.

2. Authority granted by a legislative body to make expenditures and to incur obligations during a fiscal year is the definition of an

    a. Appropriation.

    b. Authorization.

    c. Encumbrance.

    d. Expenditure.

3. What type of account is used to earmark the fund balance to liquidate the contingent obligations of goods ordered but not yet received?

    a. Appropriations.

    b. Encumbrances.

    c. Obligations.

    d. Reserve for encumbrances.

4. A city's General Fund budget for the forthcoming fiscal year shows estimated revenues in excess of appropriations. The initial effect of recording this will result in an increase in

    a. Taxes receivable.

    b. Fund balance.

    c. Reserve for encumbrances.

    d. Encumbrances.

5. The reserve for encumbrances account is properly considered to be a

    a. Current liability if payable within a year; otherwise, a long-term debt.

    b. Fixed liability.

    c. Floating debt.

    d. Reservation of the fund's equity.

6. In preparing the General Fund budget of Brockton City for the forthcoming fiscal year, the City Council appropriated a sum greater than expected revenues. This action of the Council will result in

    a. A cash overdraft during that fiscal year.

    b. An increase in encumbrances by the end of that fiscal year.

    c. A decrease in the fund balance.

    d. A necessity for compensatory offsetting action in the Debt Service Fund.

7. What would be the effect on the General Fund balance in the current fiscal year of recording a $15,000 purchase for a new fire truck out of General Fund resources, for which a $14,600 encumbrance had been recorded in the General Fund in the previous fiscal year?

    a. Reduce the General Fund balance $15,000.

    b. Reduce the General Fund balance $14,600.

    c. Reduce the General Fund balance $400.

    d. Have no effect on the General Fund balance.

(AICPA adapted)

18

Introduction to Accounting for State and Local Governmental Units

The lifestyles and well-being of all people are significantly affected by the activities of both profit-oriented enterprises and nonprofit organizations. Of these, probably none is more important and pervasive in its impact on our daily lives than is the business of government. Today there are more than 40 *thousand* state and local governmental units, which employ more than 10 *million* people and collect annual revenues approaching 200 *billion* dollars. The well-publicized problems of some city governments have attracted great interest and concern in the last decade. They have focused attention on the need for (among other things) adequate accounting and financial reporting practices by cities and other government units as a basis for evaluating the extent of and the suggested solutions for such problems.

GENERALLY ACCEPTED GOVERNMENTAL ACCOUNTING STANDARDS

Like generally accepted accounting standards for profit-oriented enterprises, standards of accounting and reporting for governmental units are in a constant state of evolution and change. The pioneer organization in promulgating standards of accounting and reporting for state and local governmental units has been the Municipal Finance Officers Association (MFOA). Such standards were formulated by its National Committee on Governmental Accounting, which in 1974 was reconstituted as the National Council on Governmental Accounting (NCGA). Generally accepted governmental accounting standards are currently contained in the following authoritative sources: *Governmental Accounting, Auditing, and Financial Reporting* (GAAFR) published by the NCGA; *Audits of State and Local Governmental Units* published by the American Institute of Certified Public Accountants (AICPA); other pronouncements of the MFOA, NCGA, and AICPA, and pronouncements of the Financial Accounting Standards Board.

Examples of other pronouncements include the *Statement of Position on Accrual of Revenues and Expenditures by State and Local Governmental Units* published by the Accounting Standards Division of the AICPA and *Disclosure Guidelines for Offerings of Securities by State and Local Governments* published by the MFOA. Many of the pronouncements of the Financial Accounting Standards Board and its predecessor bodies are applicable to governmental units. For example, *Statement of Financial Accounting Standards No. 13,* "Accounting for Leases," and *Statement of Financial Accounting Standards No. 15,* "Accounting by Debtors and Creditors for Troubled Debt Restructurings," among others, are applicable to governmental units as well as to profit-oriented enterprises.

In 1978, the Financial Accounting Standards Board indicated that it was prepared to demonstrate its leadership in establishing and improving standards of financial reporting and accounting for nonbusiness enterprises. As a first step it commissioned a study entitled *Financial Accounting in Nonbusiness Organizations, An Exploratory Study of Conceptual Issues.* Upon completion of that study, the Board added financial reporting concepts for governments and private organizations to its agenda. Although the Board indicated that it intended to deal with broad conceptual issues rather than specific rules, we expect to see it expand its role in setting governmental accounting and reporting standards in the near future. It has also been suggested that the Securities and Exchange Commission should have a role in assuring adequate disclosure in connection with the issuance of securities by state and local governmental units. Thus, in time, pronouncements of the SEC may become another source of substantial authoritative support for governmental accounting and reporting standards.

THE STRUCTURE OF GOVERNMENTAL ACCOUNTING

A governmental unit, although a separate *legal* entity, is comprised of a number of separate fund and other *accounting* entities. The NCGA recommends the use of eight different types of fund entities and two different account group entities for accounting and reporting purposes, as follows:[1]

Fund Entities

Governmental Funds

(1) *The General Fund*—to account for all unrestricted resources except those required to be accounted for in another fund.

(2) *Special Revenue Funds*—to account for the proceeds of specific revenue sources (other than special assessments, expendable trusts, or for major capital projects) that are restricted by law or administrative action to expenditure for specified purposes.

[1]National Council on Governmental Accounting, *Exposure Draft: GAAFR Restatement: Principles* (Chicago: Municipal Finance Officers Association of the United States and Canada, 1978).

(3) *Capital Projects Funds*—to account for financial resources segregated for the acquisition of major capital facilities (other than those financed by Special Assessment and Enterprise Funds).

(4) *Debt Service Funds*—to account for the accumulation of resources for, and the payment of, interest and principal on general long-term debt.

(5) *Special Assessment Funds*—to account for the financing of public improvements or services deemed to benefit the properties against which special assessments are levied.

Proprietary Funds

(6) *Enterprise Funds*—to account for operations that are financed and operated in a manner similar to private business enterprises—where the stated intent is that the costs (expenses, including depreciation) of providing goods or services to the general public on a continuing basis be financed or recovered primarily through user charges—or where periodic determination of revenues earned, expenses incurred, and/or net income is deemed appropriate for capital maintenance, public policy, management control, accountability, or other purposes.

(7) *Internal Service Funds*—to account for the financing of goods or services provided by one department or agency to other departments or agencies of the governmental unit, or to other governmental units, on a cost-reimbursement basis.

Fiduciary Funds

(8) *Trust and Agency Funds*—to account for assets held by a governmental unit as trustee or agent for individuals, private organizations, and/or other governmental units. Expendable trust funds and agency funds are classified as governmental funds whereas nonexpendable trust funds are classified as proprietary funds.

Account Group Entities

(1) *The General Fixed Assets Account Group*—to account for all fixed assets of a governmental unit other than those fixed assets related to specific proprietary funds. Fixed assets related to specific proprietary funds or Trust Funds should be accounted for through those funds. All other fixed assets of a governmental unit should be accounted for through the General Fixed Assets Account Group.

(2) *The General Long-term Debt Account Group*—to account for all unmatured general obligation liabilities of a governmental unit other than noncurrent liabilities of proprietary funds and of Special Assessment Funds and certain fiduciary funds (e.g., Pension Trust Funds). Noncurrent liabilities of proprietary funds, Special Assessment Funds, and Trust Funds should be accounted for through those funds. All other unmatured general obligation long-term liabilities of the governmental unit should be accounted for through the General Long-Term Debt Account Group.

As indicated above, the three major classifications of accounting entities utilized in governmental accounting and reporting are (1) Governmental (Expendable) Fund Entities, (2) Proprietary (Nonexpendable) Fund Entities, and (3) Account Group Entities. Fiduciary funds are classified either as governmental (expendable) funds or as proprietary (nonexpendable) funds.

Expendable fund entities (see Chapter 17) of a governmental unit are designated by the NCGA as Governmental Funds. The accounting and reporting emphasis for these types of funds is on the inflow, outflow, and unexpended balance of net financial resources and on compliance with detailed legal provisions that specify the types of revenue to be raised and the purposes for which financial resources may be expended. The different types of governmental funds are distinguished by the sources of their financial resources and/or the types of activities financed by the resources of the fund.

Government operations that are similar to commercial business operations such as a water utility, an electric utility, or a central garage or central computer facility are accounted for in proprietary fund entities. Financial accounting and reporting for these entities closely parallel accounting and reporting for profit-oriented enterprises. Thus both current and fixed assets and current and noncurrent liabilities are accounted for in the records of proprietary fund entities. In addition, revenue, expenses (including depreciation and amortization expense), and net income are determined and reported for these fund entities.

The third classification of accounting entity utilized in accounting for governmental units is the account group entity. The two account group entities are not fund entities because they do not involve financial resources. Rather they represent self-balancing sets of accounts that are used to account for the general fixed assets and the unmatured general long-term debt of the governmental unit, the accounting for which is excluded from the governmental (expendable) fund entities. These self-balancing account groups are maintained for financial reporting and control purposes.

Each different type of fund entity and account group entity will now be discussed in more detail.

GOVERNMENTAL FUND ENTITIES

The General Fund

All revenues and expenditures of a governmental unit not accounted for in other governmental or proprietary funds are accounted for in the General Fund. The variety of revenue sources available to the General Fund and the variety of functions and activities financed by the resources of the General Fund are ordinarily more numerous than are those for any other fund entity. Accounting entries and reports for the General Fund of a governmental unit were illustrated in Chapter 17.

Special Revenue Funds

Special Revenue Funds are used to account for the proceeds of specific revenue sources that are required by statute, charter provisions, or local ordinance to be used to finance particular functions or activities of the governmental unit. Examples of Special Revenue Funds are those established to finance the operations of special facilities such as parks or museums or of particular activities such as the licensing and regulation of professions.

Although the sources of revenue for Special Revenue Funds in general are similar to those for the General Fund, a typical Special Revenue Fund will have only a single revenue source such as a single tax, or specified portion thereof, or a license fee, the proceeds of which must be used for a specific purpose, function, or activity.

Accounting entries and financial reports for Special Revenue Funds are analogous in all respects to the accounting entries and financial reports for the General Fund illustrated in Chapter 17, and no further illustration will be presented here. In Special Revenue Funds, as in the General Fund, (1) a budget is established and recorded in the accounts, (2) the encumbrance process is used to control budgeted expenditures, (3) fixed assets acquired by the expenditure of Special Revenue Fund resources are not reported as assets of the Special Revenue Fund but rather are recorded and reported in the General Fixed Assets Account Group, (4) depreciation of such assets is not recorded or reported by the Special Revenue Fund, and (5) the liability for long-term debt, the proceeds of which have been received and recorded by a Special Revenue Fund, is not recorded or reported as a liability of the Special Revenue Fund but is recorded and reported in the General Long-Term Debt Account Group.

Capital Projects Funds

Capital Projects Funds are initiated to account for the resources used by a governmental unit to acquire major capital facilities. Major capital facilities are permanent facilities such as buildings, streets and highways, storm drain systems, and sewer systems that have relatively long life. The primary purpose of accounting for the acquisition of major capital facilities in a separate Capital Projects Fund is to be able to show that the resources designated for such purposes were used for authorized purposes only and that any unexpended balances of such resources or resource deficits have been treated properly. Resources for the acquisition of major capital facilities include (1) proceeds of long-term debt issues, (2) grants or payments from other governmental units and agencies, (3) funds from private sources, (4) transfers of current revenues from other governmental funds, and (5) other sources.

Not all major capital facilities acquisitions are accounted for in Capital Project Funds. Construction and acquisition of capital facilities financed by Special Assessment Funds and Enterprise Funds are accounted for in the records of those funds. In addition, in some instances the resources of the General Fund or a Special Revenue Fund are appropriated for the acquisition of a major capital facility. So long as such acquisitions do not involve the issuance of general obligation long-term debt securities, they may be accounted for in the fund that appropriates the resources rather than in a separate Capital Projects Fund.

The operations of a Capital Projects Fund may extend over several accounting periods. Separate Capital Projects Funds are ordinarily created for each major capital project. When the project is completed, the associated Capital Projects Fund is closed out.

To illustrate accounting and reporting procedures for a Capital Projects Fund, assume that Model City authorizes the construction of a combination library and civic center that will be financed from the following sources:

General Obligation Bonds	2,000,000
State Government Grant	1,000,000
Total Authorized for Construction	3,000,000

Construction is to begin on September 1, 1980, and the bonds are to be issued on October 1, 1980.

Entries—1980 Entries to record the transactions of the Capital Projects Fund during 1980 are summarized and explained as follows.

(1) Due from State Government	1,000,000	
Revenue		1,000,000
To open Capital Projects Fund.		

There is no budget entry to incorporate estimated revenue and appropriations into the formal accounting records. Sources of estimated revenue for a capital project are few and predictable in amount. Thus, it would serve no useful purpose to incorporate budgeted revenue into the formal account system. Likewise, an appropriation account is not required as a formal control device, since the resources of the fund can be expended only for the single authorized project for which it was created. Thus, the fund balance itself serves as an adequate measure of and control over unexpended appropriation authority.

(2) Cash	2,100,000	
Bond Issue Proceeds		2,000,000
Bond Premium		100,000
To record receipt of proceeds from the issuance of long-term debt securities.		

Bond issue proceeds are distinguished from revenue for financial reporting purposes. Bond issue proceeds are recorded at par value, and the difference between the actual proceeds and par value is credited or debited to bond premium or bond discount. Since such differences represent an interest adjustment, they should result in a transfer of cash to (premium) or from (discount) the Debt Service Fund that is created to service the principal and interest on the debt. The entry to record the transfer of cash in the amount of bond premium to the Debt Service Fund is simply a debit to bond premium and a credit to cash. The entry to record a transfer of cash in the amount of bond discount to the Capital Projects Fund is simply a debit to cash and a credit to bond discount. In practice, the Debt Service Fund may not have sufficient resources to make up a discount on bonds in the year they are issued. Accordingly, bond discount is ordinarily disposed of by a debit to bond issue proceeds and a credit to bond discount.

(3) Bond Premium   100,000
         Cash   100,000
         To record transfer of cash in the amount of bond premium to the Debt Service Fund.

(4) Certificates of Deposit   1,000,000
         Cash   1,000,000
         To record investment of excess cash in temporary investments.

(5) Encumbrances   2,500,000
         Reserve for Encumbrances   2,500,000
         To record encumbrance created by the signing of a construction contract with Lloyd-Jones Construction Company.

(6) Cash   750,000
         Due from State Government   750,000
         To record the collection of part of the grant from the State Government.

(7) Expenditures   200,000
         Vouchers Payable   200,000
         To record unencumbered expenditures for architect and legal fees.

(8) Reserve for Encumbrances   1,300,000
         Encumbrances   1,300,000
     Expenditures   1,300,000
         Contracts Payable   1,300,000
         To record approved contract billings on construction completed to date and to remove encumbrance thereon.

(9) Vouchers Payable   150,000
     Contracts Payable   1,300,000
         Cash   1,450,000
         To record payment of liabilities.

(10) Interest Receivable   12,500
         Revenue   12,500
         To record interest earned on certificate of deposit to December 31, 1980.

The treatment of interest earnings on temporary investments depends on legal provisions or established policy. One alternative would be to transfer such earnings to the Debt Service Fund. A second alternative is to treat such earnings as revenue of the Capital Projects Fund. The latter treatment is justified on the grounds that resources allocated to the project are restricted exclusively to that project and, accordingly, any earnings on such resources are also restricted resources and should not be diverted to any other use.

December 31, 1980 Trial Balance   The December 31, 1980 trial balance for the Capital Projects Fund presented below reflects the transactions recorded in 1980.

	DEBIT	CREDIT
Cash	300,000	
Interest Receivable	12,500	
Certificates of Deposit	1,000,000	
Due from State Government	250,000	
Encumbrances	1,200,000	
Expenditures	1,500,000	
Vouchers Payable		50,000
Contracts Payable		–0–
Reserve for Encumbrances		1,200,000
Unreserved Fund Balance		–0–
Revenue		1,012,500
Bond Issue Proceeds		2,000,000
	4,262,500	4,262,500

CLOSING ENTRIES—DECEMBER 31, 1980

(11)	Bond Issue Proceeds	2,000,000	
	Revenue	1,012,500	
	Unreserved Fund Balance		3,012,500
	To close revenue and related accounts to unreserved fund balance.		
(12)	Unreserved Fund Balance	2,700,000	
	Encumbrances		1,200,000
	Expenditures		1,500,000
	To close expenditures and encumbrances accounts to unreserved fund balance.		

Since no budget accounts were formally recorded in the accounting records, there are no budget accounts to be closed at year-end. Hence, the nominal accounts are closed directly to the unreserved fund balance. As was true in the General Fund, the closing of the balance of the encumbrance account against the unreserved fund balance has the same effect as if an entry were made at year-end to reclassify an equal amount of the unreserved fund balance to a reserve for encumbrances.

At the end of each year, entries will also be made in the General Fixed Asset Account Group to record the cost of construction in progress represented by expenditures incurred by the Capital Projects Fund during the year.

Financial Statements   At the end of the first year, a balance sheet and a statement of revenue, expenditures and other changes in fund balance would be prepared. In addition, a schedule comparing estimated and actual revenues may be prepared if useful information is provided thereby. A schedule of expenditures and encumbrances compared to appropriations is not necessary, since all expenditures of a Capital Projects Fund are for capital outlays that relate to a single appropriation or authorization.

Completion of Project   Entries in 1981 to record the completion of the project are presented and explained below.

(13) Encumbrances	1,200,000	
Unreserved Fund Balance		1,200,000
To re-establish the contract encumbrance closed out at the end of the previous year.		

Since Capital Projects Funds are project-oriented rather than period-oriented, there is no need, as there is in accounting for the General Fund or a Special Revenue Fund, to identify expenditures with appropriation authority of a particular year. Thus, expenditures for amounts encumbered in prior years are not segregated from other expenditures of the current year. The effect of this entry is the same as if the amount in the reserve for encumbrance account was restored to the unreserved fund balance and encumbrances were then re-established for outstanding commitments at the beginning of the year, i.e., as if the following two entries were recorded:

Reserve for Encumbrances	1,200,000	
Unreserved Fund Balance		1,200,000
Encumbrances	1,200,000	
Reserve for Encumbrances		1,200,000
(14) Expenditures	225,000	
Vouchers Payable		225,000
To record unencumbered expenditures.		
(15) Cash	250,000	
Due from State Government		250,000
To record receipt of cash payment from the State Government.		
(16) Cash	1,020,000	
Certificate of Deposit		1,000,000
Interest Receivable		12,500
Revenue		7,500
To record redemption of certificate of deposit.		
(17) Reserve for Encumbrances	1,200,000	
Encumbrances		1,200,000
Expenditures	1,200,000	
Contracts Payable		1,200,000
To record approved final contract billings on completed construction and to remove remaining contract encumbrance.		
(18) Contracts Payable	1,200,000	
Contracts Payable—Retained Percentage		125,000
Cash		1,075,000
To record payment of contract except for the retention of 5% of the contract price pending inspection of the completed project.		

(19) Vouchers Payable	275,000	
Cash		275,000
To record payment of liabilities.		

December 31, 1981 Trial Balance   The preclosing trial balance of the Capital Projects Fund on December 31, 1981 is presented below.

	DEBIT	CREDIT
Cash	220,000	
Expenditures	1,425,000	
Contracts Payable—Retained Percentage		125,000
Unreserved Fund Balance		1,512,500
Revenue		7,500
	1,645,000	1,645,000

CLOSING ENTRY—DECEMBER 31, 1981

(20) Unreserved Fund Balance	1,417,500	
Revenue	7,500	
Expenditures		1,425,000
To close nominal accounts to unreserved fund balance.		

Financial Statements   A comparative balance sheet and a comparative statement of revenue, expenditures and other changes in fund balance for the years ending December 31, 1981 and December 31, 1980 are presented in Illustration 18–1 and Illustration 18–2.

ILLUSTRATION 18–1
Model City
Library—Civic Center Capital Projects Fund
Balance Sheet December 31, 1981 and December 31, 1980

ASSETS	1981	1980
Cash	$220,000	$ 300,000
Interest Receivable	–0–	12,500
Certificates of Deposit	–0–	1,000,000
Due from State Government	–0–	250,000
Total Assets	$220,000	$1,562,500
LIABILITIES AND FUND BALANCE		
Vouchers Payable	$ –0–	$ 50,000
Contracts Payable—Retained Percentage	125,000	–0–
Total Liabilities	$125,000	$ 50,000
Fund Balance:		
Unreserved	$ 95,000	$ 312,500
Reserve for Encumbrances	–0–	1,200,000
Total Fund Balance	$ 95,000	$1,512,500
Total	$220,000	$1,562,500

ILLUSTRATION 18–2
Model City
Library—Civic Center Capital Projects Fund
Statement of Revenue, Expenditures and Other Changes
in Fund Balance for the Years Ending December 31, 1981 and December 31, 1980

	1981	1980	CUMULATIVE
Fund Balance—January 1	$1,512,500	$ –0–	$ –0–
Revenue	7,500	1,012,500	1,020,000
Debt Issue Proceeds	–0–	2,000,000	2,000,000
Total Resources Available	$1,520,000	$3,012,500	$3,020,000
Expenditures	1,425,000	1,500,000	2,925,000
Fund Balance—December 31	$ 95,000	$1,512,500	$ 95,000

Closing Out a Capital Projects Fund Although it is intended that the cost of a capital project should equal the resources provided for its acquisition, actual expenditures normally are less than or they exceed the project authorization. If there is an unexpended fund balance remaining after the completion of the project, it should be distributed to the contributors of project resources in proportion to their contribution. For example, unless legal or policy decisions dictate otherwise, the capital projects fund of Model City illustrated above would be closed out as follows.

(21) Contracts Payable—Retained Percentage	125,000	
Cash		125,000
To record final payment on contract.		

(22) Transfer to Debt Service Fund	63,333[a]	
Expenditures	31,667[b]	
Cash		95,000
To record distribution of Fund Balance.		

[a](2,000,000/3,000,000) × 95,000 = 63,333
[b](1,000,000/3,000,000) × 95,000 = 31,667

For financial reporting purposes, transfers to other funds within a governmental unit are distinguished from expenditures. The return of $31,667 to the state government is treated as an expenditure because it reduces the financial resources of Model City.

When construction is completed, the assets acquired with Capital Projects Fund resources are recorded at cost in the appropriate accounts (land, building, etc.) of the General Fixed Asset Account Group.

Debt Service Funds

Debt Service Funds are created for the purpose of accounting for the accumulation of financial resources that will be utilized to make interest and principal payments on general obligation long-term debt. General obligation long-term debt consists of bonds, notes, or warrants that are secured by the general credit and revenue-raising powers of the governmental unit as a whole, rather than by the resources of a specific fund entity. Long-term debt that is the specific obligation of, and that will be paid out of the resources of, a Special Assessments Fund or an Enterprise Fund is a liability of those funds, and the accumulation of resources for its payment will be accounted for in those funds, rather than in a Debt Service Fund. Unmatured long-term debt that will be redeemed with the resources of the Debt Service Fund is not recorded or reported as a liability of the Debt Service Fund. Rather, the liability for general obligation long-term debt is recorded and reported in the General Long-term Debt Account Group. Payments of bond principal and interest are expenditures of (rather than reductions of liabilities of) the Debt Service Fund.

General obligation bonds may be serial bonds or term bonds. The principal of a term bond is repaid in one lump sum at a specified maturity date. The total principal of serial bonds is repaid in a specified number of annual (and usually equal) installments.

Debt Service Funds are usually financed by one or more of the following sources of revenue:

General Property Tax
Sales Tax or Other Specified Tax Revenues
Transfers of General Fund Revenues
Revenue from the Investment of Debt Service Fund Resources

It is generally recommended that the debt service for general obligation long-term debt be accounted for in as few Debt Service Funds as possible. However, for purposes of illustrating the difference between the debt service for serial bonds and for term bonds, two Debt Service Funds, Street Construction Serial Bonds Debt Service Fund and Library and Civic Center Term Bonds Debt Service Fund, will be illustrated for Model City.

Serial Bonds Accounting for the accumulation of resources and payment of annual installments of principal and interest on serial bonds is relatively simple. To illustrate, assume that in 1977 Model City issued $1,800,000 in 5% serial bonds, $300,000 of which come due on July 1 of each year beginning on July 1, 1978. On January 1, 1980, there is $1,200,000 in principal on these bonds outstanding, and $300,000 in principal and $60,000 in interest will come due on July 1, 1980. Annual installments of principal are financed from general property tax revenues, and annual interest payments are financed by the appropriation of resources of the General Fund. The trial balance of the Street Construction Serial Bonds Debt Service Fund on January 1, 1980 is as follows:

	DEBIT	CREDIT
Cash	3,000	
Taxes Receivable	2,000	
Fund Balance		5,000
Total	5,000	5,000

Transactions of the fund for 1980 are summarized in general journal form below.

(1) Estimated Revenue 315,000
    Authorized Transfer from the General Fund 60,000
        Appropriations 360,000
        Fund Balance 15,000
    To record budgeted revenue, transfers, and appropriations for the current year.

(2) Property Tax Receivable 320,000
    Estimated Uncollectible Tax 4,000
    Revenue 316,000
    To record general property tax levy earmarked for debt service on serial bonds.

(3) Due from the General Fund 60,000
    Transfer from General Fund 60,000
    To record the amount of resources authorized for transfer from the General Fund during the current period.

(4) Cash 318,000
    Property Tax Receivable 318,000
    To record the collection of property taxes.

(5) Cash 60,000
    Due from the General Fund 60,000
    To record the receipt of a cash transfer from the General Fund.

(6) Expenditures 360,000
    Bonds Payable 300,000
    Interest Payable 60,000
    To record the annual expenditure for principal and interest.

(7) Bonds Payable 300,000
    Interest Payable 60,000
    Cash 360,000
    To record the payment of interest and principal.

(8) Revenue 316,000
    Estimated Revenue 315,000
    Fund Balance 1,000
    Transfer from General Fund 60,000
    Authorized Transfer from the General Fund 60,000
    Appropriations 360,000
    Expenditures 360,000
    To close nominal and budget account balances at year-end.

(9) Estimated Uncollectible Taxes 4,000
    Property Tax Receivable 4,000
    To record the write-off of taxes authorized by the City Council.

The post-closing trial balance for this fund on December 31, 1980 is as follows:

	DEBIT	CREDIT
Cash	21,000	
Fund Balance		21,000
Total	21,000	21,000

A statement of revenue, expenditures and other changes in fund balance is presented in Illustration 18–3.

ILLUSTRATION 18–3
Model City
Street Construction Serial Bonds Debt Service Fund
Statement of Revenue, Expenditures and Other Changes
in Fund Balance for the Year Ending December 31, 1980

Revenue—General Property Tax	$316,000
Transfer from General Fund	60,000
Total Revenue and Transfers From Other Funds	$376,000
Expenditures	
Redemption of Serial Bonds	$300,000
Interest on Bonds	60,000
Total Expenditures	$360,000
Excess (Deficiency) to Fund Balance	$ 16,000
Fund Balance—January 1	5,000
Fund Balance—December 31	$ 21,000

Term Bonds Accounting for the debt service of term bonds is more complicated than accounting for serial bonds. Debt Service Funds for term bonds require annual additions to fund resources that, with compound interest, will provide the total amount of bond principal by the maturity date of the bonds. In addition, the Debt Service Fund for a term bond issue must provide for the payment of periodic interest on the bonds.

To illustrate, assume that the $2,000,000 in bonds issued on October 1, 1980 to finance the acquisition of the Library and Civic Center of Model City were 4% bonds that mature 5 years after their issue date. The calculation of the required annual additions to the Debt Service Fund presented in Illustration 18–4 is based on the assumption that fund resources can be invested at an average annual return of 6%. The required annual principal addition of $354,793 is calculated by dividing the term bond principal of $2,000,000 by the amount of an ordinary annuity of $1.000 for 5 periods at 6% (2,000,000/5.63709 = 354,793). Required annual earnings are based on the planned 6% return on invested fund resources.

The calculation in Illustration 18–4 does not take into account the $100,000 premium on the issue of the bonds that is transferred by the Capital Projects Fund to the Debt Service Fund in 1980. However, if the fund balance of a Debt Service Fund exceeds actuarial requirements, the excess is ordinarily carried forward without adjustment until the final addition to the fund is made. It is assumed that annual additions to the Library and Civic Center Term Bonds-Debt Service Fund are derived from an earmarked portion of the general property tax assessment.

ILLUSTRATION 18–4
Debt Service Fund—Term Bonds
Calculation of the Annual Required Additions and Annual
Required Earnings for the $2,000,000 Library-Civic Center Bond Issue

YEAR	REQUIRED PRINCIPAL ADDITIONS	REQUIRED EARNINGS	REQUIRED INCREASE IN FUND BALANCE	REQUIRED FUND BALANCE
1981	354,793[1]		354,793	354,793
1982	354,793	21,287[2]	376,080[3]	730,873[4]
1983	354,793	43,852[5]	398,645	1,129,518
1984	354,793	67,771	422,564	1,552,082
1985	354,793	93,125	447,918	2,000,000
Total	1,773,965	226,035	2,000,000	

Required Principal Addition	354,793
Required Interest Addition (.04 × 2,000,000)	80,000
Required Annual Addition	434,793

[1] $2,000,000/5.63709 = 354,793$
[2] $354,793 \times .06 = 21,287$
[3] $354,793 + 21,287 = 376,080$
[4] $354,793 + 376,080 = 730,873$
[5] $730,873 \times .06 = 43,852$

Transactions—1980 Transactions of the fund in 1980 are summarized in general journal form below.

(1) Cash	100,000	
Bond Issue Proceeds		100,000

To record the transfer of cash from the Capital Projects Fund in the amount of the premium received on the bond issue proceeds.

Had there been no transfer of cash to the Debt Service Fund by the Capital Projects Fund, no entries would have been required in the Debt Service Fund until the 1981 fiscal year.

(2) Investments	100,000	
Cash		100,000

To record the investment of cash in a certificate of deposit.

(3) Interest Receivable	2,000	
Interest Income		2,000
To accrue interest receivable on December 31, 1980.		

(4) Interest Income	2,000	
Bond Issue Proceeds	100,000	
Fund Balance		102,000
To close nominal accounts to fund balance.		

The post-closing trial balance on December 31, 1980 is as follows:

	DEBIT	CREDIT
Investments	100,000	
Interest Receivable	2,000	
Fund Balance		102,000
Total	102,000	102,000

Transactions—1981 Revenue and expenditure transactions for 1981 are summarized in Illustration 18–6. At the end of 1981 the post-closing trial balance for the fund is as follows:

	DEBIT	CREDIT
Cash	36,000	
Interest Receivable	2,000	
Property Taxes Receivable	6,000	
Investments	420,000	
Estimated Uncollectible Taxes		1,000
Fund Balance		463,000
Total	464,000	464,000

Transactions—1982 Transactions for 1982 are summarized in general journal form as follows.

(1) Required Additions	434,793	
Required Earnings	21,287	
Fund Balance		456,080
To record budgeted additions and budgeted income on invested resources of the fund for the current year (see Illustration 18–4).		

(2) Fund Balance	80,000	
Appropriations		80,000
To record budgeted expenditures for bond interest for the current year.		

(3) Property Tax Receivable   450,000
     Estimated Uncollectible Taxes   15,000
     Revenue   435,000
       To record property tax levy earmarked for debt service on the Library and Civic Center Term Bonds.

(4) Cash   432,000
     Property Tax Receivable   432,000
       To record the collection of property taxes.

(5) Investments   360,000
   Premium on Investments   15,000
     Cash   375,000
       To record investment of fund resources.

Debt service fund investments are closely regulated by law and are usually restricted to quality government and municipal securities. When such investments are expected to be held to maturity, they are recorded at their par value and premium or discount is recorded in a *separate* account and amortized by reducing or increasing investment income over the remaining life of the investment.

(6) Cash   16,000
     Interest Receivable   2,000
     Interest Income   14,000
       To record the receipt of interest on investments.

(7) Expenditures   80,000
     Interest Payable   80,000
       To record expenditure for current year's interest on bonds.

(8) Estimated Uncollectible Taxes   13,000
     Property Tax Receivable   13,000
       To record the write-off of property taxes authorized by the City Council.

(9) Interest Payable   80,000
     Cash   80,000
       To record payment of interest.

(10) Interest Receivable   13,000
     Interest Income   13,000
       To record interest accrued on investments to December 31, 1982.

(11) Interest Income   1,200
   Premium on Investments   1,200
       To record the current year's amortization of premium on investments.

(12) Revenue	435,000	
Required Additions		434,793
Fund Balance		207
Interest Income	25,800	
Required Earnings		21,287
Fund Balance		4,513
Appropriations	80,000	
Expenditures		80,000

To close budget and nominal account balances at year-end.

ILLUSTRATION 18–5
Model City
Library-Civic Center Term Bonds Debt Service Fund
Balance Sheet December 31, 1982 and December 31, 1981

ASSETS	1982	1981
Cash	$ 29,000	$ 36,000
Interest Receivable	13,000	2,000
Taxes Receivable (less allowance for uncollectible taxes, 1982—$3,000; 1981—$1,000)	8,000	5,000
Investments (at maturity value)	780,000	420,000
Unamortized Premium on Investments	13,800	–0–
Total	$843,800	$463,000
LIABILITIES AND FUND BALANCE		
Fund Balance	$843,800[1]	$463,000[2]

[1]Actuarial Requirement $730,873
[2]Actuarial Requirement $354,793

Comparative financial statements for the Library and Civic Center Term Bonds Debt Service Fund are presented in Illustrations 18–5 and 18–6. Two things should be noted about these statements as follows:

No Interest Payable Accrual on General Obligation Long-term Debt The perceptive reader may already have noted that there were no entries to record the accrual of interest payable on the bonds from the last interest payment date (July 1 for the serial bonds and October 1 for the term bonds) to the end of the fiscal year. This significant exception to expenditure accrual is justified because financial resources that are appropriated in other funds or from general tax levies for transfer to or receipt by Debt Service Funds are usually appropriated in the period the interest on the debt must be paid. To accrue the Debt Service Fund expenditure and liability in one year, but record the transfer or collection of the financial resources appropriated for this purpose in a later year, would be confusing and would result in an overstatement of fund liabilities and expenditures and an understatement of the fund balance. Thus,

ILLUSTRATION 18-6
Model City
Library and Civic Center Term Bonds Debt Service Fund
Statement of Revenue, Expenditures and Other Changes
in Fund Balance for the Years Ending December 31, 1982, 1981, and 1980

	1982	1981	1980
Revenue			
General Property Tax	$435,000	$435,000	$ –0–
Interest on Investments (net of amortization			
of premium and discount)	25,800	6,000	2,000
Total Revenue	$460,800	$441,000	$ 2,000
Debt Issue Proceeds	–0–	–0–	100,000
Total Revenue and Debt Issue			
Proceeds	$460,800	$441,000	$102,000
Expenditures			
Redemption of Term Bonds	$ –0–	$ –0–	$ –0–
Interest on Bonds	80,000	80,000	–0–
Total Expenditures	$ 80,000	$ 80,000	$ –0–
Excess (Deficiency) to Fund Balance	$380,800	$361,000	$102,000
Fund Balance—January 1	463,000	102,000	–0–
Fund Balance—December 31	$843,800[1]	$463,000[2]	$102,000[3]

[1]Actuarial Requirement $730,873
[2]Actuarial Requirement $354,793
[3]Actuarial Requirement $ –0–

it is considered appropriate and more informative to treat interest payable on general obligation long-term debt at the end of the year as an expenditure in the year of payment.

Actuarial Requirement An essential disclosure in the financial statements of Debt Service Funds for term bonds is the amount, actuarially determined, of resources that is necessary on the financial statement date for the accumulation of sufficient resources to redeem the debt on its maturity date. The actuarial requirements shown in Illustrations 18–5 and 18–6 are those determined in the "Required Fund Balance" column of Illustration 18–4.

Closing Out the Debt Service Fund Assume the following trial balance for the Library and Civic Center Term Bonds Debt Service Fund on September 15, 1985.

	DEBIT	CREDIT
Cash	2,140,000	
Fund Balance		2,140,000
Total	2,140,000	2,140,000

Entries to close the fund are as follows:

(1) Expenditures   2,080,000

    Matured Bonds Payable   2,000,000

    Interest Payable   80,000

      To record expenditure for redemption of term bonds and related interest.

(2) Matured Bonds Payable   2,000,000

    Interest Payable   80,000

    Cash   2,080,000

      To record the redemption of matured bonds and payment of interest.

(3) Transfer to X Fund   60,000

    Cash   60,000

      To record the transfer of unexpended fund resources to another Governmental Fund.

The unexpended balance of the fund after the final payment of interest and principal on the matured bonds should be disposed of in accordance with legal and/or bond indenture requirements. Usually the unexpended balance is transferred to another Debt Service Fund, but legal requirements may specify an alternative disposition. The accounts of the fund being terminated should be closed in such a way as to reflect compliance with applicable legal requirements.

(4) Fund Balance   2,140,000

    Expenditures   2,080,000

    Transfer to X Fund   60,000

      To close out the Debt Service Fund.

After the entries above have been posted, the balance of all accounts would be zero and the Debt Service Fund would effectively cease to exist.

Special Assessment Funds

Special Assessment Funds are used to account for the financing of certain public improvements which are paid for wholly or in part from special assessments levied against the property or property owners that are the direct beneficiaries of the improvements. Examples of special assessment improvements include the paving or widening of residential streets or the construction of sidewalks or storm sewers that are paid for in whole or in part by the property owners that are deemed to be the primary beneficiaries of the improvements. One function of the Special Assessment Fund is therefore to account for authorized expenditures for the construction of such improvements.

    Since the dollar amounts assessed to benefited property owners are usually substantial, they are frequently given the option of paying their share of the total assessment in installments over a specified number of years. A second function of the Special

Assessment Fund is, therefore, to account for the authorization and collection of special assessments and interest (if any) thereon.

A third function of the special assessment fund is to account for the issuance *and redemption* of debt issued to finance construction pending the collection of assessments. Such financing often takes the form of serial bonds. It is of particular importance to note that special assessment bonds are accounted for as a liability of the Special Assessment Fund. Since such debt must be paid out of special assessment revenues, it is considered to be a specific fund liability rather than a liability of the governmental unit as a whole. As installments on special assessments are collected, a corresponding amount of the serial bonds is retired.

Thus, a Special Assessment Fund usually combines the functions of (1) a Capital Projects Fund (by accounting for the proceeds from the issuance of debt and related construction expenditures), (2) a Debt Service Fund (by accounting for the interest payments on and the redemption of outstanding long-term debt), and (3) the General Long-term Debt Account Group (by accounting for unmatured long-term debt as a liability of the Special Assessments Fund).

The operations of a Special Assessment Fund requires accounting for several distinguishable events as follows.

1. The initial acquisition of financial resources through debt financing or other sources.

2. The construction of special assessment improvements.

3. The determination and imposition of the special assessment levy.

4. The collection of special assessments and interest (if any) thereon.

5. The payment of interest and principal on long-term debt.

A separate Special Assessment Fund is created for each separate special assessment project.

To illustrate, assume that Model City undertakes a $1,000,000 street widening and storm sewer installation project in one of the older residential sections of the city known as Paradise Valley. The construction is to be financed as follows:

Contribution from revenues of the General Fund	200,000
Special Assessment Serial Bonds	800,000
Total	1,000,000

It is also assumed that special assessments against property owners will not be levied until construction is completed and the exact cost of the project is known. As an alternative, a special assessments levy could be authorized for the estimated cost of the project prior to or at the time of the commencement of the project. This alternative is not recommended, however, since it usually requires the later determination of additional assessments or rebates.

Entries in 1980 to account for the operation of the Paradise Valley Special Assessments Fund are summarized in general journal form as follows.

(1) Cash	800,000	
Serial Bonds Payable		800,000

To record the issuance on February 15, of $800,000 in serial bonds at par.

It is assumed that the principal on the bonds is payable in equal annual installments of $80,000 beginning on February 15, 1981, and that interest in the amount of 4% of the face value is payable annually. If the bonds had been issued at a premium or a discount, such premium or discount would be separately recorded and amortized to interest expense.

(2) Due from the General Fund	200,000	
Transfer from the General Fund		200,000
Cash	200,000	
Due from the General Fund		200,000

To record the authorization for and the receipt of a cash transfer from the current year's appropriations of the General Fund.

The amount of the transfer is recognized in the period in which it is authorized, and the cash collection is recorded when received.

(3) Encumbrances	825,000	
Reserve for Encumbrances		825,000

To record the signing of a construction contract with Barnett Construction Company.

(4) Expenditures	120,000	
Vouchers Payable		120,000

To record unencumbered expenditures.

(5) Reserve for Encumbrance	825,000	
Encumbrances		825,000
Expenditures	825,000	
Contracts Payable		825,000

To record approved billings on the completed contract.

(6) Vouchers Payable	120,000	
Contracts Payable	825,000	
Cash		945,000

To record the payment of liabilities.

(7) Special Assessments Receivable—Current	57,000	
Special Assessments Receivable—Deferred	720,000	
Special Assessments Authorized (Revenue)		777,000

To record the amount of special assessments levied.

The amount of the levy was determined as follows:

Construction Contract Costs	825,000
Other Construction Costs	120,000
Total Construction Costs	945,000
One Year's Interest on Serial Bonds	32,000
Total	977,000
Provided by Transfer from the General Fund	(200,000)
Special Assessment Levy*	777,000

The current installment of \$57,000 is due on October 1, 1980, and the remaining \$720,000 will be collected in equal annual installments of \$80,000 plus interest of 4% on the unpaid balance.

(8) Cash	57,000	
Special Assessments Receivable—Current		57,000
To record the collection of special assessments.		

(9) Interest Expense	28,000	
Interest Payable		28,000
To accrue ten and one-half months interest to December 31, 1980 on the Serial Bonds Payable (800,000 × .04 × 21/24).		

The term *interest expense* rather than *interest expenditure* is used in accounting for interest in Special Assessment Funds. This is a matter of convention, not an attempt to make a conceptual distinction between an expenditure and an expense. Technically speaking, interest paid or accrued in the accounts of an expendable fund entity is more appropriately designated as an expenditure than as an expense.

(10) Interest Receivable	7,200	
Interest Revenue		7,200
To accrue three months interest to December 31, 1980 on deferred special assessments receivable (720,000 × .04 × 1/4).		

As an alternative to the accrual of interest illustrated in Entries (9) and (10), it is considered acceptable to ignore the accrual of interest expense and interest income at year-end in cases where the interest expense on special assessment debt is approximately offset by the interest income on special assessment levies.

(11) Special Assessments Authorized	777,000	
Transfer from the General Fund	200,000	
Interest Revenue	7,200	
Fund Balance		984,200
Fund Balance	973,000	
Expenditures		945,000
Interest Expense		28,000
To close nominal accounts to the fund balance at the end of the fiscal year.		

The post-closing trial balance of the Paradise Valley Special Assessment Fund as of December 31, 1980 is presented below.

	DEBITS	CREDITS
Cash	112,000	
Interest Receivable	7,200	
Special Assessments Receivable	720,000	
Serial Bonds Payable		800,000
Interest Payable		28,000
Fund Balance		11,200
Total	839,200	839,200

It is sometimes considered desirable for purposes of management control to subdivide the cash account into the portions designated for construction, bond principal payments, and interest payments. Such a segregation is optional for reporting purposes and is not illustrated in the entries presented herein.

Although construction of the improvement was completed during 1980, the Special Assessments Fund must be continued so long as there are assessments receivable and/or special assessment debt outstanding. The operations of the fund subsequent to the completion of construction is analogous to the operations of a Debt Service Fund. The activities of the Paradise Valley Special Assessment Fund for the first year (1981) subsequent to the completion of the project are summarized in general journal form as follows.

(1) Special Assessments Receivable—Current   80,000
        Special Assessments Receivable—Deferred   80,000
        To record the amount of special assessments receivable that is due in 1981.

(2) Serial Bonds Payable   80,000
    Interest Payable   28,000
    Interest Expense (800,000 × .04 × 3/24)   4,000
        Cash   112,000
        To record the annual payment of bond principal and interest.

(3) Cash   108,800
        Special Assessments Receivable—Current   80,000
        Interest Receivable   7,200
        Interest Revenue   21,600
        To record the collection of the annual installment of special assessments receivable and interest on the unpaid balance (80,000 + [720,000 × .04] = 108,800).

(4) Interest Expense   25,200
        Interest Payable   25,200
        To accrue ten and one-half months interest on outstanding serial bonds payable (720,000 × .04 × 21/24).

| (5) | Interest Receivable | 6,400 | |
| | Interest Revenue | | 6,400 |

To accrue three months interest on deferred special assessments receivable (640,000 × .04 × 1/4).

(6)	Fund Balance	1,200	
	Interest Revenue	28,000	
	Interest Expense		29,200

To close the nominal accounts at the end of the fiscal year.

Financial Statements   In addition to the two basic financial statements that are prepared for every governmental fund, it is recommended that a schedule of cash receipts and disbursements be prepared for Special Assessment Funds. Comparative financial statements for the Paradise Valley Special Assessments Fund are presented in Illustrations 18–7 and 18–8. A Schedule of Cash Receipts and Disbursements is presented in Illustration 18–9.

Closing the Special Assessment Fund   When all assessments have been collected and all special assessment debt has been redeemed, the Special Assessment Fund entity is closed out. Any remaining fund balance (deficit) should be disposed of in accordance with legal requirements or policy provisions.

ILLUSTRATION 18–7
Model City
Paradise Valley Special Assessment Fund
Balance Sheet—December 31, 1981 and 1980

ASSETS	1981	1980
Cash	$108,800	$112,000
Special Assessments Receivable—Deferred	640,000	720,000
Interest Receivable	6,400	7,200
Total Assets	$755,200	$839,200
LIABILITIES AND FUND BALANCE		
Interest Payable	$ 25,200	$ 28,000
Serial Bonds Payable	720,000	800,000
Fund Balance	10,000	11,200
Total Liabilities and Fund Balance	$755,200	$839,200

Expendable Trust and Agency Funds

Trust and Agency Funds are established to account for assets received and held by the governmental unit in the capacity of a trustee or agent for individuals, private organizations, and/or other governmental units. Trust Funds are classified as expendable or nonexpendable, depending on whether or not their resources must be maintained in-

ILLUSTRATION 18–8
Model City
Paradise Valley Special Assessment Fund
Statement of Revenue, Expenditures and Other Changes in
Fund Balance for the Years Ending December 31, 1981 and 1980
(Project Authorization $1,000,000)

	1981	1980
Interest Revenue	$28,000	$ 7,200
Special Assessments Authorized	–0–	777,000
Total Revenue	$28,000	$784,200
Transfers from the General Fund	–0–	200,000
Total Revenue and Transfers from Other Funds	$28,000	$984,200
Capital Outlay Expenditures	$ –0–	$945,000
Interest Expense	29,200	28,000
Total Expenditures	$29,200	$973,000
Excess (Deficiency) of Revenues and Transfers from Other Funds Over Expenditures	($ 1,200)	$ 11,200
Fund Balance—January 1	11,200	–0–
Fund Balance—December 31	$10,000	$ 11,200

ILLUSTRATION 18–9
Model City
Paradise Valley Special Assessment Fund
Schedule of Cash Receipts and Disbursements for the
Years Ending December 31, 1981 and 1980

	1981	1980
Cash Balance, January 1	$112,000	$ –0–
Current Special Assessments	$ 80,000	$ 57,000
Transfers from the General Fund	–0–	200,000
Proceeds from Sale of Serial Bonds	–0–	800,000
Interest on Assessments	28,800	–0–
Total Receipts	$108,800	$1,057,000
Total Cash Available	$220,800	$1,057,000
Capital Outlays	$ –0–	$ 945,000
Bonds Redeemed	80,000	–0–
Interest on Bonds	32,000	–0–
Total Disbursements	$112,000	$ 945,000
Cash Balance—December 31	$108,800	$ 112,000

tact. All of the principal and income of an expendable trust fund may be expended to carry out its designated activities. The principal (and in some cases the income) of a nonexpendable trust fund must be maintained intact. Expendable Trust Funds and Agency Funds are classified by the National Council on Governmental Accounting as Governmental Funds and are briefly illustrated below. Nonexpendable Trust Funds are classified as Proprietary Funds and are discussed in the next section.

Accounting procedures for agency funds and most expendable trust funds are virtually the same and are relatively simple.

Agency Funds   For example, assume that Model City collects property taxes on behalf of a legally separate governmental unit such as a water improvement district. The following entries are made to record the amount of taxes to be collected and their remittance to the water improvement district.

(1) Property Tax Receivable   250,000
    Tax Agency Fund Balance   250,000
      To record levy of taxes earmarked for the Valley Water Improvement District.

(2) Cash   250,000
    Property Tax Receivable   250,000
      To record collection of taxes earmarked for the Valley Water Improvement District.

(3) Tax Agency Fund Balance   250,000
    Cash   250,000
      To record the remittance to the Valley Water Improvement District of taxes collected on its behalf.

Expendable Trust Fund   Assume that Model City has an ordinance that requires all licensed contractors to deposit funds with the city to guarantee performance on their contracts. The deposits must be returned to the contractors when they relinquish their licenses. When a deposit is received, cash is debited and the fund balance is credited. When deposits are refunded, the fund balance is debited and cash is credited. Since the deposits may be held by the city for substantial periods of time, the resources of the trust fund are usually invested, and modest amounts of revenue may be earned thereon.

Accounting procedures for expendable trust funds may also be relatively complex. The most complex expendable trust funds of state or local governmental units are pension or retirement funds. The interested reader is referred to *Government Accounting, Auditing, and Financial Reporting* (GAAFR) or other reference texts on governmental accounting for a complete discussion and illustration of the problems and complexities of accounting for such funds.

PROPRIETARY FUND ENTITIES

Proprietary Funds employed in governmental accounting have been concisely described as follows.

> Proprietary Funds—sometimes referred to as "income-determination," "nonexpendable," or "commercial-type" funds—are used to account for a government's on-going organizations and activities which are similar to those often found in the private sector (Enterprise and Internal Services Funds). All assets, liabilities, equities, revenues, expenses, and transfers relating to the government's business and quasi-business activities—where *net income and capital maintenance are measured*—are accounted for through proprietary funds. The generally accepted accounting principles here are those applicable to similar businesses in the private sector; and the measurement focus is upon determination of *net income, financial position, and changes in financial position*.[2]

Thus, financial accounting and reporting for proprietary funds closely parallels commercial accounting and reporting. All assets *(including fixed assets)* and liabilities *(including long-term debt)* involved in the activities financed through the fund are accounted for therein. The normal commercial accounting distinction between capital and revenue expenditures is maintained, and depreciation is recorded. The operating results of Proprietary Funds are measured in terms of net income by applying the same accounting standards as those used to determine the net income of profit-oriented enterprises. In addition, the corporate accounting distinction between contributed capital and retained earnings is maintained.

Enterprise Funds

Enterprise Funds are used to account for the provision of goods or services to the *general public* on a continuing basis where all or most of the costs incurred are recovered from charges to users. The most common examples of governmental enterprises are public utilities that provide such services as water or electricity. Other activities of governmental units that are accounted for in Enterprise Funds include airports, transportation systems, parking lots and garages, and recreational facilities such as swimming pools.

The resources of an enterprise fund may come from contributions or from the proceeds of long-term debt issues or both. Contributions may be obtained from other governmental units, resources of the General Fund of the same governmental unit, property owners, subdivision developers, or customers.

Since accounting for the operations of Enterprise Funds closely parallels accounting for profit-oriented enterprises, a detailed illustration will not be presented. Instead, a condensed balance sheet of a typical Enterprise Fund is presented in Illustration 18–10, and several features of the Enterprise Fund are pointed out in connection therewith.

---

[2]National Council on Governmental Accounting, *Exposure Draft: GAAFR Restatement: Principles, op. cit.*, p. 11.

ILLUSTRATION 18–10
Model City
Enterprise Fund
Condensed Balance Sheet—December 31, 1980

ASSETS

Current Assets		$ 551,000
Restricted Assets		509,000
Utility Plant in Service (net of accumulated depreciation)		10,000,000
Construction in Progress		40,000
Total Assets		$11,100,000

LIABILITIES, CONTRIBUTIONS, AND RETAINED EARNINGS

Current Liabilities (payable from current assets)		$ 361,000
Current Liabilities (payable from restricted assets)		282,000
Revenue Bonds Payable		4,200,000
Total Liabilities		$ 4,843,000
Contributions		
From Municipality	$ 800,000	
From Customers	126,000	
From Subdividers	1,500,000	2,426,000
Retained Earnings		
Unappropriated	$3,331,000	
Reserve For Revenue Bond Retirement	500,000	3,831,000
Total Liabilities, Contributions, and Retained Earnings		$11,100,000

Restrictions on Enterprise Fund assets required by bond provisions or other arrangements are complied with through the use of restricted asset accounts, which represent earmarked portions of specified assets comprising "funds" in the narrow private-sector usage of that term (e.g., sinking fund). To avoid the confusion that may result from the use of the term "fund" in this context in the financial statements of a Fund Entity, the National Council on Governmental Accounting recommends the use of the term "restricted asset account group" rather than "fund."

In Illustration 18–10, the Restricted Assets consist of assets segregated in compliance with the sinking fund requirements of the revenue bonds,[3] and the Current Liabilities (Payable from Restricted Assets) consist of the current interest and principal installments due on the revenue bonds.

Contributions are classified by source and are segregated from retained earnings. Retained earnings are reserved in the same manner as in commercial accounting to indicate that assets in an amount equal to the reserve are not available for other purposes. Finally, both fixed assets and long-term debt are accounted for and reported as specific assets and liabilities of the Enterprise Fund, rather than in the General Fixed Asset Account Group and the General Long-term Debt Account Group, respectively.

[3]Revenue bonds are long-term obligations, the principal and interest of which are paid from the earnings of self-supporting enterprises on which the bond proceeds were spent.

Internal Service Funds

Internal Service Funds (formerly referred to as Working Capital Funds and then as Intragovernmental Service Funds) are created to account for the financing of goods and services provided by one department or agency to other departments or agencies of the same governmental unit on a cost reimbursement basis.

Typical examples of activities accounted for in Internal Service Funds include the operations of central computer facilities, central garages and motor pools, central purchasing and stores departments, and central printing departments.

Internal Service Funds are established with resources obtained from contributions from other funds, proceeds from the sale of general obligation bonds, or long-term advances from other funds. If an Internal Service Fund obtains resources from the proceeds of the issuance of general obligation bonds, the bond liability is *not* accounted for in the records of the Internal Service Fund. Rather a Debt Service Fund is established, and the bond liability is accounted for in the General Long-term Debt Account Group. Upon the receipt of the bond issue proceeds, the entry in the records of the Internal Service Fund is a debit to cash and a credit to "Contributions—General Obligation Bonds."

ILLUSTRATION 18–11
Model City
Internal Service Fund
Condensed Balance Sheet—December 31, 1980

ASSETS		
Current Assets		$122,500
Property and Equipment	$560,000	
Less Accumulated Depreciation	(140,000)	420,000
Total Assets		$542,500
LIABILITIES, CONTRIBUTIONS, AND RETAINED EARNINGS		
Current Liabilities		$ 27,500
Contributions		
From General Fund	$150,000	
From General Obligation Bonds	350,000	500,000
Retained Earnings		15,000
Total Liabilities, Contributions, and Retained Earnings		$542,500

Since accounting for the operations of Internal Service Funds closely parallels that of Enterprise Funds and profit-oriented enterprises, a detailed illustration is not presented. A condensed balance sheet for an Internal Service Fund is presented in Illustration 18–11. As indicated therein, fixed assets acquired with the resources of the Internal Service Fund and depreciation thereon are recorded in the accounting records of that fund. However, the National Council on Governmental Accounting does recommend that depreciation not be calculated on buildings provided through Capital Projects Funds, because such buildings are General Fixed Assets and their replacement would not normally be a responsibility of the Internal Service Fund. As in the financial statements of Enterprise Funds, the contributed capital of Internal Service Funds is accounted for by source and is distinguished from retained earnings.

Nonexpendable Trust Funds

There are two types of Nonexpendable Trust Funds: those in which principal must be retained intact but earnings may be expended, and those in which both the principal and the earnings of the fund must be retained intact. An example of the latter type of Nonexpendable Trust Fund is the Revolving Loan Fund where interest collected on loans outstanding increases the funds available for subsequent loans.

Nonexpendable Trust Funds may be established as a result of a gift, a bequest, or some other action that requires the governmental unit to act in a fiduciary capacity and to maintain and conserve cash or other assets which it does not own. Trust funds must be accounted for in accordance with the terms of the trust agreement and/or the applicable provisions of statutory and common law. Accounting procedures must result in a clear distinction between nonexpendable fund resources and expendable resources resulting from the earnings of the fund. Appropriate procedures are also necessary to insure that the expenditure of expendable resources is made in accordance with the trust agreement and/or other applicable legal provisions.

Where the earnings of a trust fund may be expended, they may be transferred to the General Fund (no restriction on expenditures) or to a Special Revenue or an Expendable Trust Fund (expenditures restricted to specified use). To illustrate, assume that a private donor granted Model City $300,000 fo the purpose of financing the purchase of rare classics for the public library. As a result of this grant, two funds were created: The Classics Endowment Fund to account for the nonexpendable fund principal and the investment thereof, and the Classics Acquisition Fund to account for the expenditure of the earnings of the endowment fund.

The general ledger trial balances for each fund on January 1, 1980 are presented below.

CLASSICS ENDOWMENT FUND	DEBIT	CREDIT
Cash	1,000	
Certificates of Deposit	300,000	
Interest Receivable	3,750	
Due to Classics Acquisition Fund		4,750
Fund Balance		300,000
Total	304,750	304,750
CLASSICS ACQUISITION FUND		
Cash	8,000	
Due from Classics Endowment Fund	4,750	
Fund Balance		12,750
Total	12,750	12,750

Transactions for 1980 for each fund are summarized below in general journal form.

CLASSICS ENDOWMENT FUND

(1) Cash   15,000
    Interest Receivable   3,750
    Interest Income   11,250
    To record interest collected on certificate of deposit.

(2) Interest Receivable   3,750
    Interest Income   3,750
    To accrue interest on certificate of deposit.

(3) Interest Income   15,000
    Due to Classics Acquisition Fund   15,000
    To record the amount of 1980 income transferable to the Classics Acquisition Fund.

(4) Due to Classics Acquisition Fund   16,000
    Cash   16,000
    To record cash payment to Classics Acquisition Fund.

For purposes of simplification, it is assumed that the trust agreement requires that the entire endowment principal be invested in a savings account earning 5% interest. Usually, the principal of an endowment fund is invested in various securities. If the securities are purchased at a premium or discount, such amounts should ordinarily be amortized to interest income, and only the net amount of investment income would accrue to the recipient Expendable Trust Fund. Accounting procedures for an endowment fund would be further complicated if the endowment includes depreciable income-producing assets such as rental properties. In that case, earnings accruing to the recipient expendable fund must also be reduced by depreciation if the trust principal is to be maintained "intact."

CLASSICS ACQUISITION FUND

(1) Due from Classics Endowment Fund   15,000
    Fund Balance   15,000
    To record expendable earnings due from endowment fund.

(2) Cash   16,000
    Due from Classics Endowment Fund   16,000
    To record receipt of cash from the endowment fund.

(3) Fund Balance   18,000
    Cash   18,000
    To record the acquisition of rare books.

In funds having few transactions, revenue, transfers, and expenditures may be debited or credited directly to the fund balance.

Financial statements for these trust funds are presented in Illustrations 18–12 and 18–13.

ILLUSTRATION 18–12
Model City
Classics Endowment Fund
Balance Sheet—December 31, 1980 and December 31, 1979

ASSETS	1980	1979
Cash	$ –0–	$ 1,000
Interest Receivable	3,750	3,750
Investments	300,000	300,000
Total	$303,750	$304,750
LIABILITIES & FUND BALANCE		
Due to Classics Acquisition Fund	$ 3,750	$ 4,750
Fund Balance	300,000	300,000
Total	$303,750	$304,750

Statement of Revenue, Expenditures and Other Changes in Fund Balance for the Years Ending December 31, 1980 and December 31, 1979.

	1980	1979
Revenue—Interest Income	$ 15,000	$ 15,000
Transfers to Expendable Trust Fund	(15,000)	(15,000)
Excess (Deficiency) to Fund Balance	$ –0–	$ –0–
Fund Balance—January 1	300,000	300,000
Fund Balance—December 31	$300,000	$300,000

ILLUSTRATION 18–13
Model City
Classics Acquisition Fund
Balance Sheet—December 31, 1980 and December 31, 1979

ASSETS	1980	1979
Cash	$ 6,000	$ 8,000
Due from Classics Endowment Fund	3,750	4,750
Total	$ 9,750	$12,750
LIABILITIES AND FUND BALANCE		
Fund Balance	$ 9,750	$12,750

Statement of Revenue, Expenditures and Other Changes in Fund Balance for the Years Ending December 31, 1980 and December 31, 1979.

Transfers from Endowment Trust Fund	$15,000	$15,000
Expenditures	(18,000)	(20,000)
Excess Deficiency to Fund Balance	($ 3,000)	($ 5,000)
Fund Balance—January 1	12,750	17,750
Fund Balance—December 31	$ 9,750	$12,750

ACCOUNT GROUP ENTITIES

General fixed assets and general long-term debt of a governmental unit are accounted for and reported in the financial statements of the two account group entities: The General Fixed Asset Account Group and the General Long-term Debt Account Group.

General fixed assets of a governmental unit are the fixed assets owned by it that are not accounted for in its proprietary (enterprise, internal service, and nonexpendable trust) funds. These assets are accouned for in the General Fixed Asset Account Group, which is essentially an "inventory" of the general fixed assets owned by the governmental unit balanced by accounts listing the sources of the resources used to acquire them.

General long-term debt of a governmental unit is the unmatured principal of general obligation indebtedness that is not properly accounted for in a Proprietary Fund, Special Assessment Fund, or Pension Trust Fund. Such debt is accounted for in the General Long-term Debt Account Group, which is essentially a listing of the amounts of unmatured long-term debt principal balanced by accounts that reflect the amount of resources available in Debt Service Funds for debt principal payments and the amount of resources that must be provided in future years for the payment of debt principal.

The General Fixed Assets Account Group

General fixed assets may be acquired through gift or foreclosure, or they may be acquired through the expenditure of resources of the General Fund, Special Revenue Funds, Capital Project Funds, or Special Assessment Funds.

The cost of constructed or purchased general fixed assets is determined using the same measurement standards as those applicable to commercial enterprises. Donated assets are recorded at their estimated fair value at the time they are received.

> The position of the National Council on Governmental Accounting is that "Depreciation of general fixed assets should not be recorded in the accounts of governmental funds. Depreciation of general fixed assets may be recorded in cost accounting systems or calculated for cost finding analyses; and accumulated depreciation may be recorded in the General Fixed Assets Account Group."[4]

The rationale for this position was discussed in Chapter 17.

The classification of general fixed assets is similar to that followed by commercial enterprises. The National Council on Governmental Accounting recommends the following classifications of general fixed assets and sources of general fixed assets for purposes of financial reporting.

[4]National Council on Governmental Accounting, *Exposure Draft: GAAFR Restatement: Principles, op. cit.,* p. 21.

CLASSIFICATION OF ASSETS	CLASSIFICATION OF SOURCES OF ASSETS
Land	Investments in General Fixed Assets from:
Buildings	Capital Projects Funds:
Improvements Other than Buildings	General Obligation Bonds
Machinery and Equipment	Federal Grants
Construction in Progress	State Grants
	Local Grants
	General Fund Revenues
	Special Fund Revenues
	Special Assessments
	Private Gifts

Accounting events in 1980 that affect the General Fixed Asset Account Group of Model City are summarized below in general journal form.

(1) Machinery and Equipment   250,000
        Investment from General Fund Revenues   250,000
            To record the expenditure for office equipment made by the General Fund in 1980 (see Chapter 17).

(2) Investment from General Fund Revenues   225,000
        Machinery and Equipment   225,000
            To record the sale of used office equipment.

The equipment was sold for $87,250, and the proceeds of the sale were accounted for as revenue of the General Fund (see Chapter 17). When a general fixed asset is sold, its original cost is simply removed from the records of the General Fixed Asset Account Group [see also Entry (6) below].

(3) Construction in Progress   1,500,000
        Investment from General Obligation Bonds   1,000,000
        Investment from State Grant   500,000
            To record expenditures incurred during 1980 for the construction of the Model City Library-Civic Center.

The investment in general fixed assets is allocated between general obligation bonds and state grants in relation to the relative contribution of each to the authorized project (Bonds—$2,000,000, State Grant—$1,000,000). When construction is completed in 1981, the following entry would be made in the records of the General Fixed Asset Account Group.

Land   200,000
Buildings   2,725,000
        Construction in Progress   1,500,000
        Investment from General Obligation Bonds   950,000
        Investment from State Grant   475,000

Expenditures incurred in 1981 amount to $1,425,000 and are allocated to investment from general obligation bonds and state grants in the same manner as in 1980. The total cost of the completed project is $2,925,000 (1,500,000 + 1,425,000) and is allocated to Land and Buildings in accordance with information supplied from the records of the Capital Projects Fund.

(4) Improvements	945,000	
Investments from Special Assessments		745,000
Investment from General Fund Revenues		200,000
To record Paradise Valley Improvement Project that was commenced and completed during 1980.		

Although special assessments of $777,000 were levied, $32,000 of this was for one year's interest on the special assessment serial bonds and not for construction expenditures.

(5) Reduction in Investment in General Fixed Assets		
Due to Accumulated Depreciation	306,000	
Accumulated Depreciation—Buildings		120,000
Accumulated Depreciation—Machinery and Equipment		55,000
Accumulated Depreciation—Improvements		131,000
To record depreciation on general fixed assets.		

As was previously explained, depreciation of general fixed assets is not measured or reported in the accounts of governmental (expendable) funds. However, if desired, depreciation may be measured and an allowance for accumulated depreciation may be deducted from the related assets in the General Fixed Asset Account Group with a contra reduction from the total investments in general fixed assets balance. It is assumed that Model City has elected to reflect accumulated depreciation on general fixed assets in this manner.

(6) Accumulated Depreciation—Machinery and Equipment	140,000	
Reduction in Investment in General Fixed Assets		
Due to Accumulated Depreciation		140,000
To adjust the accumulated depreciation and contra accounts for the amount of accumulated depreciation recorded on equipment sold during the year.		

This entry would ordinarily be made in conjunction with Entry (2) above. It was presented last here because it would not be required unless the governmental unit elects to reflect accumulated depreciation, as discussed on connection with Entry (5) above.

A comparative Statement of General Fixed Assets for the General Fixed Assets Account Group is presented in Illustration 18–14. Balances for 1979 in this illustration are assumed amounts. A Statement of Changes in General Fixed Assets should also be prepared, as may schedules detailing assets, depreciation, and accumulated depreciation by the activities in which the assets are utilized. The latter schedules would be of particular importance if any reasonable attempt were to be made to compare the benefits of governmental activities with their *cost*. Such statements and schedules are not illustrated here.

ILLUSTRATION 18–14
Model City
Statement of General Fixed Assets
December 31, 1980 and December 31, 1979

GENERAL FIXED ASSETS NET OF ACCUMULATED DEPRECIATION	1980	1979
Land	$ 500,000	$ 500,000
Buildings[1]	2,880,000	3,000,000
Improvements[2]	6,064,000	5,250,000
Machinery and Equipment[3]	660,000	550,000
Construction in Progress	1,500,000	–0–
Total	$11,604,000	$ 9,300,000
NET INVESTMENT IN GENERAL FIXED ASSETS		
Investments from:		
General Obligation Bonds	$ 2,800,000	$ 1,800,000
State Grants	500,000	–0–
General Fund Revenues	5,775,000	5,550,000
Special Revenue Fund Revenues	500,000	500,000
Special Assessments	5,395,000	4,650,000
Total	$14,970,000	$12,500,000
Less Reduction of Investment in General Fixed Assets Due to Accumulated Depreciation	(3,366,000)	(3,200,000)
Net Investment	$11,604,000	$ 9,300,000

[1]Less accumulated depreciation of $1,520,000 in 1980 and $1,400,000 in 1979.
[2]Less accumulated depreciation of $1,731,000 in 1980 and $1,600,000 in 1979.
[3]Less accumulated depreciation of $115,000 in 1980 and $200,000 in 1979.

General Long-Term Debt Account Group

General long-term debt of a governmental unit includes the unmatured principal on bonds, warrants, notes, and other long-term general obligations of the governmental unit. It is not limited to liabilities arising from debt issues, but may include noncurrent liabilities arising from pension plans, lease agreements, and similar commitments. It does not include long-term debt that is the specific liability of Proprietary Funds or Special Assessments Funds. However, where the full faith and credit of the governmental unit is pledged as additional assurance that specific proprietary or special assessment fund liabilities will be paid, the contingent liability should be disclosed in the notes to the Statement of General Long-term Debt.

Major credit account balances in the General Long-term Debt Account Group are Serial Bonds Payable, Term Bonds Payable, and Other General Long-term Liabilities. The two major divisions of the offsetting debit account balances are Amounts to be Provided for Payment of Long-Term Debt and Amounts Available in Debt Service Funds for Payment of Long-Term Debt.

The use of these accounts can be illustrated by summarizing in general journal form the accounting events in 1980 that affect the General Long-term Debt Account Group of Model City.

(1) Amounts to be Provided for Payment of Term Bonds   2,000,000
    Term Bonds Payable   2,000,000
        To record the issuance of $2,000,000 in par value of Term Bonds for the construction of the Model City Library-Civic Center.

(2) Amounts Available in Debt Service Fund—Term Bonds   102,000
    Amounts to be Provided for Payment of Term Bonds   102,000
        To record the increase in the balance of the Library-Civic Center Term Bonds Debt Service Fund available for payment of principal.

(3) Serial Bonds Payable   300,000
    Amounts to be Provided for Payment of Serial Bonds   300,000
        To record payment by the Street Construction Serial Bonds Debt Service Fund of the current year's installment of principal on the Street Construction Serial Bonds.

(4) Amounts Available in Debt Service Fund—Serial Bonds   16,000
    Amount to be Provided for Payment of Serial Bonds   16,000
        To record the increase in the balance of the Street Construction Serial Bonds Debt Service Fund during 1980.

Changes in the fund balances of serial bond debt service funds are often minimal. If the change is insignificant in relation to the oustanding liability, it need not be recorded in the accounts of the General Long-term Debt Account Group. A comparative Statement of General Long-term Debt is presented in Illustration 18–15.

INTERFUND TRANSACTIONS

Entries in the records of the Account Group Entities are initiated by transactions that are also recorded in the records of Governmental Fund Entities. In addition to this type of "reciprocal" transaction, fund entities may engage in interfund transactions. Interfund transactions are classified as quasi-external transactions, reimbursements, loans or advances, and interfund transfers.[5]

[5]National Council on Governmental Accounting, *Exposure Draft: GAAFR Restatement: Principles,* *op. cit.,* p. 38.

ILLUSTRATION 18–15
Model City
Statement of General Long-term Debt
December 31, 1980 and 1979

	1980	1979
AMOUNT AVAILABLE AND TO BE PROVIDED FOR THE PAYMENT OF GENERAL LONG-TERM DEBT		
Term Bonds		
Amount Available in Debt Service Fund	$ 102,000	–0–
Amount to be Provided	1,898,000	$ –0–
Total	$2,000,000	$ –0–
Serial Bonds		
Amount Available in Debt Service Fund	$ 21,000	$ 5,000
Amount to be Provided	879,000	1,195,000
Total	$ 900,000	$1,200,000
TOTAL AVAILABLE AND TO BE PROVIDED	$2,900,000	$1,200,000
GENERAL LONG-TERM DEBT PAYABLE		
Term Bonds Payable	$2,000,000	$ –0–
Serial Bonds Payable	900,000	1,200,000
TOTAL GENERAL LONG-TERM DEBT PAYABLE	$2,900,000	$1,200,000

Quasi-External Transactions

Quasi-external transactions are interfund transactions that would be treated as revenue, expense, or expenditures if they were consummated with organizations external to the governmental unit. Contributions in lieu of taxes from an Enterprise Fund to the General Fund and Internal Service Fund billings to government departments for services rendered are examples of quasi-external transactions. Quasi-external transactions are accounted for as revenue, expense, or expenditures of the funds involved. Accounting for quasi-external transactions in this manner is necessary for the determination of the operating results (net income) of Proprietary Funds.

To illustrate, assume that the Internal Service Fund bills the Police Department for $3,000 for services rendered. The corresponding entries to record this billing are:

INTERNAL SERVICE FUND

Due from General Fund	3,000	
Revenue		3,000

GENERAL FUND

Expenditures	3,000	
Due to Internal Service Fund		3,000

Reimbursements

Reimbursements are transactions that involve the transfer of resources from one fund to another in order to reimburse the recipient fund for expenditures made by it that are properly expenditures of the reimbursing fund. The recipient fund should record the transaction as a credit to expenditures, and the reimbursing fund should record the transaction as a debit to expenditures.

For example, assume that the General Fund performs services in the amount of $10,000 for a Special Assessment Fund. The corresponding entries to record the reimbursement are:

SPECIAL ASSESSMENTS FUND

Expenditures	10,000	
Due to General Fund (or cash)		10,000

THE GENERAL FUND

Due from Special Assessments Fund (or cash)	10,000	
Expenditures		10,000

Loans or Advances

Interfund loans or advances are self-explanatory. Assume that the General Fund advances $4,000 as a temporary loan to a Special Revenue Fund. Corresponding entries to record the advance are:

THE GENERAL FUND

Due from Special Revenue Fund	4,000	
Cash		4,000

SPECIAL REVENUE FUND

Cash	4,000	
Due to General Fund		4,000

Transfers

All interfund transactions other than quasi-external transactions, reimbursements, and loans or advances are interfund transfers. The importance of distinguishing interfund transfers from revenue and expenditures has already been explained. Interfund transfers may be classified as residual equity transfers or as other interfund transfers.

Residual Equity Transfers Residual equity transfers represent a transfer of equity of the funds involved. Examples include nonrecurring contributions from the General Fund to Proprietary Funds, the return of part or all of such contributions to the General Fund, and transfers of the residual balances of discontinued funds to the General Fund or to Debt Service Funds.

To illustrate, assume that an Enterprise Fund transfers $150,000 of excess resources to the General Fund. Corresponding entries to record the transfer are:

ENTERPRISE FUND

Transfer to General Fund	150,000	
Cash		150,000

THE GENERAL FUND

Cash	150,000	
Transfer from Enterprise Fund		150,000

Other Interfund Transfers Other interfund transfers consist of recurring transfers between funds for the purpose of shifting resources from the fund legally required to record the revenue to the fund legally required to expend the revenue. An example of this type of transfer is the annual transfer of revenue from an Endowment Trust Fund to an Expendable Trust Fund. To illustrate, the net effect of the entries to record the transfer of revenue from the Classics Acquisition Endowment Trust Fund of Model City to the Classics Acquisition Expendable Trust Fund may be summarized as follows.

ENDOWMENT TRUST FUND

Transfer to Expendable Trust Fund	15,000	
Cash		15,000

EXPENDABLE TRUST FUND

Cash	15,000	
Transfer from Endowment Trust Fund		15,000

Transfers are reported as separate items in the statement of revenue, expenditures and other changes in fund balance.[6]

FINANCIAL REPORTING

The development of financial reporting standards for state and local governmental units is currently in a state of flux. The reader can expect to see significant changes in the financial statements of governmental units as continued attention is given to means of enhancing public understanding of government activities and their financial implications.

[6]If a statement of changes in fund balance, equity, or retained earnings is presented separately from the operating statement, the AICPA Industry Audit Guide, *Accounting for State and Local Governmental Units* requires (pp. 11–12) that residual equity transfers not be reported in the separate operating statement, but that they be treated as a direct addition to or reduction of the fund or equity balance.

The Reporting Entity

Thus far in this chapter we have concentrated on appropriate financial reports for each separate fund entity. However, the governmental unit itself may be viewed as a separate reporting entity. A major reporting problem for state and local governments is finding a suitable way to aggregate the reports of the separate fund entities into a single set of integrated financial statements.

In the private sector, affiliated companies (separate legal entities) maintain separate records and may prepare separate financial statements, but the primary reporting entity is the consolidated group (economic entity), and the *primary* general purpose financial statements are the consolidated financial statements. If included in such reports, the financial statements of the individual affiliates are considered to be supplementary information.

The traditional reporting emphasis in the public sector is just the opposite. The separate funds (legal entities) are considered to be the *primary* reporting entities. Statements or schedules presenting combined or consolidated information for the fund entities are considered to be supplemental information rather than the primary financial statements. The following excerpts from the 1968 edition of *Government Accounting, Auditing and Financial Reporting* (GAAFR) and from the 1974 edition of *Audits of State and Local Governmental Units* (AG) reflect the view held by many that consolidated or combined financial statements for governmental units are also inherently misleading.

> The individual balance sheets of the respective funds may be presented in a combined balance sheet. In governmental financial statements, a combined balance sheet is a single statement that displays the separate balance sheets of individual funds, group of funds, or account groups of a governmental unit in separate, adjacent columns. A combined balance sheet may have a total column, which aggregates the amounts from all funds and account groups. If such a total column is shown, it should be captioned "Memorandum Only." The Total column on a combined balance sheet is not comparable to a consolidation; it does not fairly present financial position in conformity with generally accepted accounting principles, even if interfund eliminations were made. It is not customary to make such eliminations in the combined balance sheet.   (AG, pp. 20–21).
>
> Unlike a private corporation where the parent company has unlimited control over its subsidiary companies and where the entire group of companies constitute one economic entity, a government does not have unlimited control and flexibility over all of its financial operations; each fund is a completely independent entity, and very frequently the governmental unit's officials are limited by law in respect to what they can do or change in fund fiscal affairs. Moreover, the nature of financial operations and accounting requirements of some funds are so different from those of other funds that consolidations would only produce misleading results. . . . It will be noted that there is no "total" column (in the combined balance sheet) containing the aggregate balance for each identical account in all of the funds. Such a column should not be included because the figures in it can be grossly misleading.   (GAAFR, p. 111).
>
> A single set of consolidated financial statements for all funds and account groups will not fairly present financial position and results of operations in conformity with generally accepted accounting principles.   (AG, p. 20).
>
> Although a Combined Balance Sheet can and should be constructed for annual financial report purposes, no combined statement of operations for all funds can

be prepared. The reason for this is that such a statement would involve the comparison of revenues and expenditures for all funds of a governmental unit when, in fact, such comparisons cannot be legitimately made because of differences in fund fiscal operations and accounting requirements.   (GAAFR, p. 112).

Despite the views expressed above, there is an increasing and persistent demand for state and local governments to produce an understandable and meaningful set of integrated, overall financial statements.

Modest attempts are being made to accommodate this demand. For example, the reporting of interfund transfers and debt issue proceeds separately from revenues and expenditures is an attempt to distinguish revenues and expenditures of the governmental unit as a whole from revenue and expenditures of the individual fund entities.

There is also general agreement that where a conflict exists between legal requirements and generally accepted accounting standards, generally accepted accounting standards will prevail in the preparation of financial statements for external use.

The Pyramid Concept

The GAAFR restatement also reflects an attempt to present an integrated set of financial statements using a pyramid approach. The levels of the pyramid are:
(1) *Combined Statements—Overview.* These statements provide a summary overview of the financial position of all funds and account groups and of the operating results by fund types. They also serve as an introduction to the more detailed statements and schedules that follow ...
(2) *Combining Statements—By Fund Type.* Where a governmental unit has more than one fund of a given type (e.g., Special Revenue Funds), combining statements for all funds of that type should be presented in columnar format. The total columns of these combining statements should agree with the amounts presented in the Combined Statements—Overview ...
(3) *Individual Fund and Account Group Statements.* These statements present information on the individual funds and account groups where (a) a governmental unit has only one fund of a specific type, or (b) sufficient detail to assure adequate disclosure is not presented in the combining statements. These statements may also be used to present budgetary data, where the budget is prepared on a basis consistent with GAAP, and prior year comparative data.
(4) *Schedules.* Data presented in schedules may or may not be necessary for fair presentation of fund financial position or operating results. Schedules are used: (a) to provide details of data summarized in the individual fund and account group statements; (b) to demonstrate legal compliance (e.g., where the legal budget is prepared on a basis other than GAAP or where bond indentures require specific data to be presented); and (c) to present other information deemed useful by management (e.g., schedules of cash receipts, disbursements, and balances or other schedules that encompass more than one fund or account group).
All four pyramid levels of detail may be required for some funds. On the other hand, fair presentation and adequate disclosure of the financial position and

operating results of other funds may require only one or two levels. Determination of the appropriate level of detail—and the distinction as to what is presented in a statement as opposed to a schedule—is a matter of professional judgment.[7]

Recommended Financial Statements

The financial position and operating statements recommended by the National Council on Governmental Accounting within the framework of the pyramid approach are:

1. **Balance Sheets**
   (a) A Combined Balance Sheet—All Fund Types and Account Groups.
   (b) Combining balance sheets for all funds of each type.
   (c) Separate balance sheets and/or schedules for each fund and account group—as necessary to present fairly financial position of each fund and account group in conformity with generally accepted accounting principles and to demonstrate compliance with legal provisions.

2. **Operating Statements**
   (a) *Governmental Funds*
      (1) A Combined Statement of Revenues, Expenditures, and Changes in Fund Balances—All Governmental Fund Types.
      (2) Combining statements of governmental fund revenues, expenditures, and changes in fund balances by fund type.
      (3) Separate statements and/or schedules of revenues, expenditures, and changes in fund balances for each governmental fund—as necessary to present fairly operating results in conformity with generally accepted accounting principles and to demonstrate compliance with legal provisions.
   (b) *Proprietary Funds*
      (1) A Combined Statement of Revenues, Expenses, and Changes in Retained Earnings (or Equity)—All Proprietary Fund Types.
      (2) A Combined Statement of Changes in Financial Position—All Proprietary Fund Types.
      (3) Combining statements of proprietary fund revenues, expenses, and changes in retained earnings (or equity) by fund type.
      (4) Combining statements of proprietary fund changes in financial position by fund type.
      (5) Separate statements and/or schedules of revenues, expenses, and changes in retained earnings (or equity) and of changes in financial position for each proprietary fund—as necessary to present fairly fund operating results in conformity with generally accepted accounting principles and to demonstrate compliance with legal provisions.
   (c) *Fiduciary Funds*
      (1) Expendable Trust Funds are similar to governmental funds (modified accrual basis) and should be reported as indicated at 2(a) above; Nonexpendable Trust and Pension Trust Funds are similar to proprietary funds (accrual basis) and should be reported as indicated at 2(b) above.
      (2) Trust fund operating statements may be presented either within the combined operating statements of the governmental funds and the proprietary funds, as appropriate, or within separate fiduciary fund statements.

[7]National Council on Governmental Accounting, *Exposure Draft: GAAFR Restatement: Principles, op. cit.,* pp. 51 and 53.

       (3) A Combined Statement of Cash Receipts, Disbursements, and Balances—All Agency Funds.

   (d) *Account Groups*

       (1) Statement of Changes in General Fixed Assets.

       (2) Statement of Changes in General Long-Term Debt ...

Combined balance sheets show the data for each fund type and account group, whereas combining balance sheets present data for each fund of a given type. Both are ususally presented in columnar format. The Combined Balance Sheet—All Fund Types and Account Groups may contain a "memorandum only" total, with or without "memorandum only" interfund and similar eliminations. The total column of each combining balance sheet by fund type should agree with, and be cross-referenced to, the column for that fund type in the Combined Balance Sheet—All Fund Types and Account Groups ...

As in the case of the Combined Balance Sheet—All Fund Types and Account Groups, the separate fund type data in the Combined Statement of Revenues, Expenditures, and Changes in Fund Balances—All Governmental Fund Types preferably should be displayed in a series of columns; should be cross-referenced to the combining fund type and, if presented, separate fund statements; and may contain a "memorandum only" total column, with or without "memorandum only" interfund eliminations. Total columns of combining statements of governmental fund revenues, expenditures, and changes in fund balances by fund types should agree with the column for that fund type in the Combined Statement of Revenues, Expenditures, and Changes in Fund Balances—All Governmental Fund Types. Similar guidelines apply to the proprietary fund operating statements.[8]

A combined statement of revenue, expenditures and other changes in fund balances for all the governmental funds of Model City is presented in Illustration 18–16. A combining statement of revenue, expenditures and other changes in fund balances for all debt service funds of Model City is presented in Illustration 18–17.

Recommended financial statements for individual governmental fund entities and proprietary fund entities have been presented throughout this chapter in connection with the discussion of each fund entity.

COST-BENEFIT REPORTING

Reports that compare the cost of government programs with the benefits of such programs have long been the subject of suggested improvements in internal and external reporting for governmental units at all levels. Some consider it to be conceptually impossible to prepare reports on the overall effectiveness of a governmental unit but do consider it possible and useful to develop performance reports that provide information as to program costs and accomplishments. Cost-benefit reporting is viewed by some to be a more important consideration for governments than is the development of a single set of integrated financial statements, which was discussed in the preceding section.

The measurement of the cost of a program requires that all expenditures, including expenditures for fixed assets utilized in government programs, be allocated first to time periods and then to the program benefited. Such measurement, allocation,

---

[8]National Council on Governmental Accounting, *Exposure Draft: GAAFR Restatement: Principles, op. cit.,* pp. 53–56.

ILLUSTRATION 18–16

Model City
All Governmental Funds
Combined Statement of Revenue, Expenditures and Other Changes
in Fund Balance for the Year Ending December 31, 1980

	GENERAL FUND (17-7)[a]	CAPITAL PROJECTS FUND (18-2)[a]	DEBT SERVICE FUNDS (18-17)[a]	SPECIAL ASSESSMENT FUND (18-8)[a]	EXPENDABLE TRUST FUND (18-13)[a]	TOTAL MEMORANDUM ONLY
Revenue						
Property Tax	$1,158,750	$	$316,000	$	$	$1,474,750
Special Assessments				777,000		777,000
State Grants	275,000	1,000,000				1,275,000
Charges for Services	136,500					136,500
Licenses and Permits	170,500					170,500
Proceeds from Sales of Property	87,250					87,250
Investment Income		12,500	2,000	7,200		21,700
Total Revenue	$1,828,000	$1,012,500	$318,000	$784,200	$ -0-	$3,942,700
Debt Issue Proceeds	$ -0-	$2,000,000	$100,000	$ -0-	$ -0-	$2,100,000
Transfers From Other Funds						
From Proprietary Funds	$ 150,000	$	$	$	$15,000	$ 165,000
From Other Governmental Funds			60,000	200,000		260,000
Total Transfers from Other Funds	$ 150,000	$ -0-	$ 60,000	$200,000	$15,000	$ 425,000
Total Revenue, Debt Issue Proceeds, and Transfers From Other Funds	$1,978,000	$3,012,500	$478,000	$984,200	$15,000	$6,467,700
Expenditures						
General Government	$ 189,000	$	$	$	$	$ 189,000
Public Safety	380,000					380,000
Highways and Streets	128,000			945,000		1,073,000
Sanitation	70,000					70,000
Health	141,000					141,000
Cultural-Recreation	80,000	1,500,000			18,000	1,598,000
Education	670,000					670,000
Redemption of Principal of General Long-term Debt			300,000			300,000
Interest on Debt			60,000	28,000		88,000
Total Expenditures	$1,658,000	$1,500,000	$360,000	$973,000	$18,000	$4,509,000
Transfers to Other Funds						
To Proprietary Funds	$ -0-	$ -0-	$ -0-	$ -0-	$ -0-	$ -0-
To Other Governmental Funds	260,000					260,000
Total Transfers to Other Funds	$ 260,000	$ -0-	$ -0-	$ -0-	$ -0-	$ 260,000
Total Expenditures and Transfers to Other Funds	$1,918,000	$1,500,000	$360,000	$973,000	$18,000	$4,769,000
Excess (Deficiency) of Revenues, Debt Issue Proceeds, and Transfers From Other Funds Over Expenditures and Transfers to Other Funds	$ 60,000	$1,512,500	$118,000	$ 11,200	$ (3,000)	$1,698,700
Fund Balance—January 1, 1980	250,000	-0-	5,000	-0-	12,750	267,750
Fund Balance—December 31, 1980	$ 310,000	$1,512,500	$123,000	$ 11,200	$ 9,750	$1,966,450

[a]Illustration number for the source of information in this column.

ILLUSTRATION 18–17

Model City

All Debt Service Funds

**Combining Statement of Revenue, Expenditures and Other Changes
in Fund Balance for the Year Ending December 31, 1980**

	TOTAL	STREET CONSTRUCTION SERIAL BONDS (18-3)[a]	LIBRARY CIVIC CENTER TERM BONDS (18-6)[a]
Revenue			
General Property Tax	$316,000	$316,000	$ –0–
Investment Income	2,000	–0–	2,000
Total Revenue	$318,000	$316,000	$ 2,000
Debt Issue Proceeds	100,000	–0–	100,000
Transfers from Other Governmental Funds	60,000	60,000	–0–
Total	$478,000	$376,000	$102,000
Expenditures			
Redemption of Bonds	$300,000	$300,000	$ –0–
Interest on Bonds	60,000	60,000	–0–
Total	$360,000	$360,000	$ –0–
Excess (Deficiency) of Revenue, Bond Issued Proceeds and Transfers from Other Funds Over Expenditures	$118,000	$ 16,000	$102,000
Fund Balance—January 1	5,000	5,000	–0–
Fund Balance—December 31	$123,000	$ 21,000	$102,000

[a]Illustration number for the source of information in this column.

and cost accumulation are practical within the framework of present measurement techniques and accounting systems design capabilities.

The measurement of the cost of a program, however, may be of little use unless it can be compared with the benefits produced by such cost incurrence so as to provide an indicator of effectiveness. In the private sector, accomplishment is measured by revenue, which is matched with cost to determine net income (loss). Net income (loss) may be viewed as a measure of the effectiveness of performance.

Revenue of a governmental unit is generally unrelated to accomplishment and to the benefits of government programs. Thus, meaningful comparison of the costs and benefits of government programs is dependent upon the development of techniques to measure program accomplishments and benefits. In fact, the selection of relevant indicators with which to measure and evaluate accomplishment is probably as important as, if not more important than, efforts to compute the costs of the programs being evaluated.

Different measurements may be considered relevant, depending on different views as to objectives. If, for example, the objective of a particular government organizational unit is to build highways, one measure of accomplishment is the number of miles of highway constructed. Effectiveness indicators can be obtained by dividing the number of miles of highways constructed into total construction cost to determine the average cost per mile constructed. If, however, the objective of building highways is to transport goods and people effectively, efficiently, and safely, accomplishment might be measured in terms of the reduction of travel time, the decrease in the accident rate, the increase in the number of vehicles moved, or the increased average speed of movement.

A committee of the American Accounting Association described three different classifications of potential accomplishment measurements as follows.[9]

Operation Indicators. These measures are associated with outputs of activities. They are indicators in nonfinancial terms of what is produced for the money or effort expended. They are largely workload and performance statistics. Examples are number of licenses issued, number of tests administered, etc. These measures are often selected on the basis of simplicity of understanding and data availability rather than on the basis of relevance. They include the kind of data commonly used for the determination of unit costs by dividing the total cost of an activity for a period of time by the number of work units produced during the same period of time.

Program Impact Indicators. These indicators are related directly to a public need or policy. Examples of this type of indicator are (1) vehicle accidents averted, and (2) wages earned and welfare costs averted due to handicapped persons being made self-sufficient.

Social Indicators. This type of indicator relates to the "quality of life." Examples are family living and home conditions, personal security, and community livability. To the extent these indicators are available, they aid in answering such questions as: Are we getting healthier? To what extent is pollution increasing? Do children learn more now than they used to? Do people have more satisfying jobs?

Thus, the various performance indicators form a spectrum. At one end of the spectrum are indicators easily understood and applied (quantified) but giving little indication of accomplishment. As the spectrum is traversed, indicators of increasing relevance for program evaluation may be identified. However, they become increasingly more difficult to quantify.

The classification of expenditures by function and activity, the allocation of capital expenditures to functions and activities, and the development of operations indicators and workload statistics by many public sector organizations are encouraging steps in the development of the needed cost-benefit reporting model. The most pressing current need is research and innovation in the identification and measurement of program impact indicators.

Probably the greatest challenge for accountants in public sector organizations today is to find ways to measure and report program costs and accomplishments so that public officials and the electorate can evaluate and make informed policy decisions regarding alternative program and resource allocation opportunities and requirements.

---

[9]"Report of the Committee on Concepts of Accounting Applicable to the Public Sector," *The Accounting Review,* Supplement to Vol. XLVII, 1972, pp. 103–4.

Questions

1. Eight separate fund entities are recommended to account for the various activities and resources of a governmental unit. Identify these funds by title and type and briefly state (in two sentences or less) the basic purpose for which each fund is used.

2. In addition to fund entities, two nonfund "self-balancing" account group entities are recommended for use by governmental units. Identify these account groups and state the purpose of each. Prepare in general journal form an entry to record a typical "transaction" in the records of each.

3. What is the difference between a fund and an account group?

4. What is the difference between a governmental fund and a proprietary fund?

5. Are fiduciary funds governmental funds or proprietary funds? Explain.

6. A disbursement by the General Fund to another fund may be recorded as a receivable, an expenditure, or a fund transfer. Explain the circumstances that would result in each of these different treatments.

7. In what funds or account groups would you expect bonds payable to be included?

8. In what funds or account groups might property and other nonfinancial resources be recorded?

9. Why are budgeted revenues and expenditures formally recorded in the records of the General Fund but not in the records of a Capital Projects Fund?

10. Are all major capital facilities acquisitions accounted for in a Capital Projects Fund? Explain.

11. Describe the major activities accounted for in a Special Assessments Fund.

12. Under what circumstances would it be acceptable not to accrue interest on special assessment debt?

13. What exception to the normal expenditure recognition criteria is associated with Debt Service Funds and what is the justification for this departure?

14. Identify and describe four types of interfund transactions. Are interfund transactions the equivalent of intercompany transactions? Explain.

15. The following funds and account groups are recommended for use in accounting for state and municipal governmental financial operations:
    A. General Fund
    B. Special Revenue Fund
    C. Debt Service Fund
    D. Capital Projects Fund

    E. Special Assessment Fund
    F. Enterprise Fund
    G. Internal Service Fund
    H. Trust and Agency Fund
    I. General Fixed Asset Account Group
    J. General Long-Term Debt Account Group

Identify by the letters given above the funds and account groups in which each of the account titles below might properly appear.

    1. Bonds payable
    2. Reserve for encumbrances
    3. Equipment
    4. Appropriations
    5. Estimated revenue
    6. Property taxes receivable
    7. Construction work in progress
    8. Accumulated depreciation
    9. Depreciation expense
    10. Required earnings

Problems

Problem 18–1: Capital Project Fund—City of Ahern (Summary Transactions)

In the general election in November 1979, a bond issue for $1,000,000 was approved by the voters of the City of Ahern. Proceeds were used to defray part of the cost of the construction of a new municipal building.

In addition to the bond proceeds, other approved sources of financing consisted of:

Federal Government Civic Improvement Grant	$500,000
General Fund—City of Ahern	150,000

The fiscal year for the City of Ahern is from July 1 to June 30. The estimated completion date of the new building is December 1980.

On January 1, 1980, the Capital Project Fund—Municipal Building was established, and approved fund sources were recorded. One hundred thousand dollars was transferred from the General Fund to the new Capital Projects Fund.

Summary of Activities, January 1–June 30, 1980

1. Awarded contracts on low-bid basis to:
    a. Allen and Co., architects, for building design and specifications, $100,000.
    b. Baldwin Co. to remove trash and debris from city-owned site and grade to ground level, $18,000.

2. Accepted the high bid of Booz, Ross, and Merrill, underwriters, to purchase the bond issue at 103. Received cash proceeds from the bond sale on March 1. Half of the bond issue proceeds were immediately invested in 6-month CD's at 6% interest. Of the remaining proceeds, $250,000 was placed in a savings account at 5% interest. The premium on the bond sale was transferred to the Debt Service Fund.

3. Awarded a contract to Caldwell Co. who submitted the low bid of $1,255,000, for the construction of the building. Partial payments on the contract are to be made as the construction work progresses.

4. Received invoices which were approved and paid as follows:
   a. Baldwin Co. on completion of contract, $18,000.
   b. Allen and Co., architects, for work to date on contract, $70,000.
   c. Miscellaneous billings (printing, advertising, supervisory fees, travel), $133,000.
   d. Caldwell Co. on completion of 25% of construction work, $300,000.

5. The savings account was closed on June 1. Interest received amounted to $3,125.

Summary of Activities, July 1, 1980–January 15, 1981

1. Funds transferred from City of Ahern—General Fund, $50,000.

2. Funds received from Federal Government Civic Improvement Grant, $500,000.

3. The investment in CD's matured (August 30). Deposited $200,000 in a savings account at 5% interest. The balance including interest was held in the cash account.

4. Closed the savings account on October 2. Received interest of $850.

5. Approved and made payments for the following:
   a. Miscellaneous (legal, consulting and supervisory fees, etc.), $156,500.
   b. Caldwell Co., construction contract, $955,000.
   c. Allen and Co., architect, contract completion, $30,000.

6. All documentation on the project was completed and recorded. The balance in the Capital Project Fund was transferred to the Debt Service Fund. The Capital Project Fund was closed.

Required:
A. Prepare entries in general journal form to record the fund activities to June 30, 1980.
B. Prepare entries in general journal form to adjust and close appropriate accounts at June 30, 1980.
C. Prepare a balance sheet at June 30, 1980.
D. Prepare entries in general journal form to record the fund activites from July 1, 1980 to January 15, 1981.
E. Prepare necessary entries to close the fund on completion of the project.

Problem 18–2: Debt Service Fund—City of Ahern
The City of Ahern initiated a Debt Service Fund to manage and account for the accumulation of financial resources to insure the payment of principal when due and to make interest payments on the due dates for the General Obligation Bonds issued to construct the new Municipal Building (see Problem 18–1). The bonds were issued on March 1, 1980.
   Provisions of the bond indenture specified that:

(1) The semi-annual interest payments will be an obligation of the General Fund—City of Ahern.

(2) A first lien on the sales tax receipts of the City is exercisable to accumulate the necessary funds to be placed in the custody of a trustee for payment of the principal at maturity.

(3) The bond issue is in the principal amount of $1,000,000 for a term of 10 years with interest payable semi-annually on March 1 and September 1 at a stated rate of 6%.

(4) Sales tax receipts are to be deposited with the trustee every six months.

(5) Any premium on the bond issue will not be amortized during the term of the bond issue but will be held as additional security in the bond fund accounts. Earnings on premium, if any, may be applied to semi-annual bond interest payments.

Activities of the Debt Service Fund:
March 1–June 30, 1980:

(1) Recorded the transfer from the Capital Projects Fund of $30,000 of premium on the bond issue.

(2) Recorded the transfer of funds from the General Fund for the first 6 months' interest on the Bonds. This was a line item in City's 1980 budget.

(3) Completed negotiations with the Sinking Fund Trustee, 1st National Bank of Ahern, for semi-annual deposits to the trustee for the redemption of the bond issue at maturity, March 1, 1990. The first deposit is to be made on September 1, 1980. Earnings on the Sinking Fund deposits are guaranteed and will accumulate at 5% compounded semi-annually.

(4) Prepared a schedule of principal additions and earnings on the Bond Sinking Fund to the maturity of the trustee agreement—March 1, 1990.

(5) Purchased one-year renewable Certificates of Deposit with the premium on the bond issue ($30,000). Interest on CD's at 7% is payable annually on renewal of the principal amount (April 1, 1980). Interest earned on CD's reduces the amount due from the General Fund to pay interest on the bonds.

July 1, 1980–June 30, 1981:

(1) Recorded the receipt of sales tax collections due for the first half of the fiscal year.

(2) Paid semi-annual interest on the bonds—September 1, 1980 and March 1, 1981.

(3) Recorded the transfer of funds for bond interest due from the General Fund.

(4) Recorded the transfer of the $6,475 balance of funds from the Capital Projects Fund.

(5) Made the semi-annual deposit of funds with the trustee—September 1, 1980 and March 1, 1981.

(6) Renewed the Certificates of Deposit and recorded interest earned thereon.

Required:
A. Prepare a schedule of Deposits and Earnings for the Bond Sinking Fund (first 5 years only).
B. Prepare entries in general journal form to record the transactions and activities of the Debt Service Fund as they occur. Include adjusting and closing entries necessary on June 30, 1980 and June 30, 1981.
C. Prepare a balance sheet for the Debt Service Fund as of June 30, 1981, with comparative data for June 30, 1980.
D. Prepare a comparative statement of revenue, expenditures, and other fund balance changes for the Debt Service Fund for the years ending June 30, 1980 and June 30, 1981.

Problem 18–3: General Fixed Assets Account Group—City of Ahern

The City of Ahern accounts for its fixed assets in four major groupings: (1) Land; (2) Buildings; (3) Administrative Equipment; and (4) Vehicles and Road Equipment. Depreciation, which is recorded annually, is based on the cost reflected in these accounts at the end of each year at varying rates, i.e., Buildings 5% per year, Administrative Equipment 10% per year, and Vehicles and Road Equipment 15% per year.

On June 30, 1980, the Statement of General Fixed Assets reflected the following amounts:

	COST	ACCUMULATED DEPRECIATION
Land	$ 250,000	$
Buildings	4,550,000	1,235,000
Vehicles and Road Equipment	2,500,000	1,150,000
Construction in Progress	521,000	(Municipal Bldg.)
Administrative Equipment	850,000	375,000

During fiscal year 1981 (July 1, 1980—June 30, 1981), activities affecting the General Fixed Asset Accounts included the following:

1. The Municipal Building was completed at a total cost of $1,662,500.

2. Six electric typewriters were purchased for $350 each. These replaced non-electric typewriters which originally cost a total of $750 with accumulated depreciation of $600.

3. Purchased 2 new streetsweeper vehicles for $100,000 each.

4. Sold at annual auction:
   a. Non-electric typewriters for $125.
   b. Sanitation trucks and other vehicles for $125,000 (Original cost $530,000 with accumulated depreciation $425,000).

Required:

A. Prepare entries in general journal form relating to the General Fixed Asset Accounts for fiscal year 1981.

B. Record depreciation as applicable for the year. Compute depreciation on acquired assets for the full year.

C. Prepare a comparative statement of general fixed assets for June 30, 1981 and June 30, 1980.

Note: Sources of funds:

1. For equipment and vehicles acquired and sold—General Fund.

2. For Municipal Building:

General Fund	$ 150,000
Federal Government	500,000
General Obligation Bonds	1,012,500 ($521,000 at 6/30/80)

3. For General Fixed Assets Other than the Municipal Building—General Fund.

Problem 18–4: General Long-term Debt Accounts—City of Ahern

On March 1, 1980, the City of Ahern issued general obligation bonds (secured by a first lien on sales tax receipts) with principal in the amount of $1,000,000 and a stated interest rate of 6% payable semi-annually on March 1 and September 1. The bonds were sold at 103. The bonds were issued to construct the Municipal Building.

The following events with respect to this bond issue during the period March 1, 1980 to June 30, 1981 affect the accounts in the General Long-term Debt Account Group:

March 1, 1980:	(1) The bonds were issued at 103. (2) The premium on the bonds was transferred from the Capital Projects Fund to the Debt Service Fund.
September 1, 1980:	The semi-annual deposit with Sinking Fund trustee was made from the Debt Service Fund—$39,147.
January 15, 1981:	Construction on the Municipal Building was completed. The balance in the Capital Projects Fund was transferred to the Debt Service Fund—$6,475.
March 1, 1981:	The semi-annual deposit with the Sinking Fund trustee was made from Debt Service Fund Cash—$39,147; Interest earned on the Sinking Fund amounted to $979 for the period September 1, 1980 to March 1, 1981.
June 30, 1981:	Interest earned on the Sinking Fund amounted to $1,321 for the period March 1, 1981 to June 30, 1981.

Required:

A. Prepare entries in general journal form to record transactions that affect the General Long-term Debt Accounts.

B. Prepare a comparative statement of general long-term debt as of June 30, 1981 and June 30, 1980.

Problem 18–5

An administrative section of the County Assessor's Office of Crawford County serves as the billing and collection agency for all property taxes assessed in Crawford County. A charge of 1% of taxes and penalties collected is apportioned among recipients of the taxes for this service. All property tax records—current and delinquent—are maintained in this administrative unit. The 1% charge is included as revenue in the General Fund budget of the County government.

Information relative to the collection of property taxes for fiscal year 1980 is as follows:

Assessed valuation	$5,826,300
Tax rates per $100 assessed:	
County Government	1.20
State Government	.80
City of Midvale	2.80
Unified School District	3.20

Tax bills are issued on January 1; taxes are payable without penalty by April 30; taxes paid after April 30 are subject to a 5% penalty for late payment. Taxes not paid by June 30 are considered delinquent.

There are no delinquent taxes uncollected for years prior to 1980.

An estimated 3% of billed taxes for 1980 will be uncollectible.

A summary of the activities of the Tax Agency Fund for the period January 1, 1980 to June 30, 1980 includes the following:

January 1   Tax bills are mailed to property owners. Accounts are opened by the tax collection unit.
April 30   Taxes collected and deposited during first four months total $372,883.
             Distribution of taxes collected is made to the applicable governmental units.
June 30   Taxes collected and deposited during May and June including the 5% penalty total $73,412.
             Distribution of taxes and penalties collected is made to the applicable governmental units.

Required:
A. Prepare in general journal form entries to record the activities of the Tax Agency Fund from January 1 to June 30. Establish a Delinquent Account for taxes not collected.
B. Prepare a balance sheet for the Tax Agency Fund after adjusting the accounts on June 30.

Problem 18–6

The following activities and transactions are typical of those which may affect the various funds used by a typical municipal government.

Required:
Prepare journal entries to record each transaction and identify the Fund or Group of Accounts in which each entry is recorded.

1. The Baldwin City Council passed a resolution approving a general operating budget of $2,500,000 for the fiscal year 1980. Total revenues are estimated at $2,450,000.

2. The Baldwin City Council passed an ordinance providing a property tax levy of $6.25 per $100 of assessed valuation for the fiscal year 1980. Total property valuation in Baldwin City is $102,400,000. Property is assessed at 25% of current property valuation. Property tax bills are mailed to property owners. An estimated 3% will be uncollectible.

3. Calumet City sold a general obligation term bond issue for $500,000 at 105 to a major brokerage firm. The stated interest rate is 6%. Proceeds are to be used for construction of a new Central Law Enforcement Building.
   (Note: Entries are required in the Capital Project Fund and the General Long-term Debt Accounts.)

4. The premium on bond sale in (3) above is transferred to the Debt Service Fund. (3 entries required)

5. At the end of fiscal year 1980, the Baldwin City Council approves the write-off of $26,275 of uncollected 1979 taxes because of inability to locate the property owners. The tax bills have been referred to the legal department for further action.

6. The Calumet City Central Law Enforcement Building (3 above) is completed. Contracts and expenses total $494,500, and all have been paid and recorded in the Capital Projects Fund. Prepare entries to close this project and record the completion of the project in all other funds and/or account groups affected (4 entries). Any balance in the Capital Project Fund is to be applied to payment of interest and principal of the bond issue.

7. On May 1, 1980, Drennan City issued 5% serial bonds at par to finance street curbing in an area recently incorporated in the city limits. The face amount of the bonds is $300,000;

interest is payable annually, and bonds are to be retired in equal amounts over 5 years from collections from assessments against property owners affected.

   a. Record the issuance of the bonds on May 1, 1980.

   b. Record the payment to bondholders on May 1, 1981.

8. The curbing project in (7) above was completed on November 30 at a total cost of $295,000. Record summary entries for expenditure transactions May 1–November 30, 1980, and on completion of the project.

Problem 18–7

For each of the following transactions or events write the name of the fund(s) and or account group(s) in which the transaction or event would be recorded.

1. An issue of bonds, the proceeds of which were to be used for the erection of a new City Hall, was sold.

2. A sum of money was appropriated, to be advanced from moneys on hand, to finance the establishment of a City Garage for servicing city-owned transportation equipment.

3. A contribution was received from a private source. The use of the income earned on the investment of this sum of money was specifically designated by the donor.

4. Proceeds received from the sale of a bond issue were used for the purchase of the privately owned water utility in the city.

5. Property taxes designated to be set aside for the eventual retirement of the City Hall building bonds were collected.

6. Real estate and personal property taxes, which had not been assessed or levied for any specific purpose, were collected.

7. Payment was made to the contractor for progress made in the erection of the new City Hall.

8. Interest was paid on the bonds issued for the purchase of the water utility.

9. An issue of bonds to be used to pay for the improvement of streets in the residential district was authorized. The debt is to be serviced by assessments on the property benefited.

10. Salaries of personnel in the office of the mayor were paid.

11. Interest was paid on the City Hall building bonds.

12. Various amounts were paid by property owners for the benefits they received from the street improvement project.

13. Interest was paid on bonds issued for the payment of the improvement of streets in the residential district.

14. Interest was received on the investment of moneys set aside for the retirement of the City Hall building bonds.

15. Sums of money were received from employees by payroll deductions to be used for the purchase of United States government bonds for those employees individually.

16. City motor vehicle license fees, to be used for general street expenditures, were collected.

17. Materials to be used for the general repair of the streets were purchased.

18. The City Garage was reimbursed for services on the equipment of the fire and police departments.

19. The water hydrant rental was paid.

20. Excess funds were transferred from the water utility to the General Fund.

(AICPA adapted)

Problem 18–8

Prepare entries in general journal form to record the following transactions in the proper fund(s) and/or account group(s). Designate the fund or account group in which each entry is recorded.

1. The special assessment fund reimburses the General Fund for $20,000 in police protection and traffic direction services provided by the City Police Department.

2. Bond proceeds of $500,000 were received to be used in constructing a firehouse. An equal amount is contributed from general revenues.

3. $400,000 of serial bonds matured. Interest of $60,000 was paid on these and other serial bonds outstanding.

4. $4,000 was received as insurance proceeds from the accidental destruction of a year-old police car costing $6,000.

5. $60,000 in expendable funds were transferred from the City Parks Endowment Fund to the City Parks Special Revenue Fund.

6. Equipment purchased from general revenues at a cost of $100,000 was sold for $20,000.

7. The City Water Company (an enterprise fund) issued a bill for $400 for water provided to the street department's street cleaner.

8. The City Water Company transferred $200,000 in excess funds to the General Fund.

9. A central motor pool was established by a contribution of $60,000 from the General Fund, a long-term loan of $40,000 from the City Park Special Revenue Fund, and general obligation bond issue proceeds of $100,000.

10. The Motor Pool Fund billed the General Fund $5,000 and the City Park Fund $2,000 for the use of motor vehicles.

11. During the year, $300,000 of street improvements to be financed through a Special Assessment Fund were completed and approved for payment.

12. Special Assessment Bonds in the amount of $200,000 were retired.

13. Customers' deposits of $4,000 for water meters were received by the City Water Company during the year. The moneys are to be held in trust until the customers request that their services be disconnected, and the final bills are collected.

14. It is determined that the Debt Service Fund will require an annual contribution of $30,000 and earnings of $3,000 in the current year to accumulate the amounts necessary to retire general obligation term bonds.

Problem 18–9

In the early part of fiscal year 1980, the Town of Grissom officially annexed by council action a small unincorporated subdivision immediately adjacent to the town limits. The residents of the subdivision favored the annexation action because of their need to obtain administrative assistance from the Grissom government in the construction of street and sidewalk improvements in the subdivision. The residents would pay for such construction as improvements to their properties. Soon after annexation, the town council initiated action for the installation of sidewalks and curbing in the subdivision.

Prior to the annexation, the Grissom Town financial records had been satisfactorily maintained through the sole use of a General Fund to account for all its activities. This was continued through fiscal year 1980, at which time the council decided that the General Fund accounts were getting too cumbersome and the fund structure needed to be expanded.

The trial balance of General Fund at the end of fiscal year 1980 is presented below.

General Fund Trial Balance
Town of Grissom
June 30, 1980

	DR.	CR.
Cash	$ 78,160	
Cash—Street Project	221,000	
Property Tax Receivable	18,500	
Special Assessments Receivable—Deferred	300,000	
Supplies Inventory	40,500	
Improvement Project	15,000	
Estimated Revenue	2,215,000	
Interest Expense	18,000	
Encumbrances	160,000	
Expenditures	2,160,000	
Estimated Uncollectible Taxes		12,000
Vouchers Payable		31,500
Interest Payable		18,000
Bonds Payable		350,000
Reserve for Inventory		25,000
Reserve for Encumbrances		160,000
Appropriations		2,363,000
Interest Revenue		21,000
Revenue		2,050,000
Unreserved Fund Balance		195,660
Totals	$5,226,160	$5,226,160

Review of the records discloses the following:

1. Property tax receivable in the amount of $8,500 is uncollectible and should be written-off.

2. Office equipment acquired during the fiscal year 1980 cost $85,000. This was properly expended in the General Fund. Equipment acquired prior to fiscal year 1980 consists of: (1) Office Equipment $120,000, and (2) Vehicles and Street Machinery $530,000.

3. The consumption method is used in accounting for materials and supplies usage. Materials and supplies on hand on June 30, 1980 cost $28,500.

4. Bonds were issued in the amount of $350,000 with interest at 6% to pay for the street improvements. In addition, $15,000 from the General Fund was provided to defray initial costs for design and legal fees and was recorded in the Improvement Project account.

   Other information relative to the street improvement project:
   a. The bond issue is to be paid by assessments against property owners, who are obligated to retire $50,000 of bonds each year on August 20 and pay annual interest. Assessment for the first annual installment has been paid in full including $21,000 interest.
   b. Bond issue proceeds ($350,000) were incorporated in the fiscal year 1980 budget as Estimated Revenues and appropriated for the anticipated construction.
   c. Accrued interest expense on the bond issue on June 30 was $18,000. This was recorded as a liability in the General Fund accounts.
   d. A construction contract was awarded for $360,000. The balance to be paid on this contract on June 30, 1980 is in the Reserve for Encumbrances account. The contractor has been paid $200,000 for the work completed to date.
   e. The Cash-Street Project account was used for all receipts and payments for the project. This includes bond proceeds and assessment payments. The $200,000 paid to the contractor was deducted from this account and charged to General Fund Expenditures.
   f. The Special Assessments levy for the bond issue ($350,000) is recorded in the General Fund Revenue account. The bond principal due in the first year ($50,000) has been paid by assessed property owners. Interest collected is in the Interest Revenue account.

Required:
Prepare a worksheet to adjust the General Fund Trial Balance accounts and to establish and distribute balances as appropriate for a Special Assessment Fund. Initiate appropriate accounts to record the General Fixed Assets owned by the town.

Problem 18–10
The City of Bergen entered into the following transactions during the year 1981.

1. A bond issue was authorized by vote to provide funds for the construction of a new municipal building which it was estimated would cost $1,000,000. The bonds are to be paid in 10 equal installments from a Debt Service Fund, and payments are due March 1 of each year. Any premium on the bond issue and any balance of the Capital Projects Fund is to be transferred directly to the Debt Service Fund.

2. An advance of $80,000 was received from the General Fund to underwrite a deposit on the land contract of $120,000. The deposit was made.

3. Bonds of $900,000 were sold for cash at 102. It was decided not to sell all of the bonds because the cost of the land was less than expected.

4. Contracts amounting to $780,000 were let to Sandstone and Company, the lowest bidder, for construction of the municipal building.

5. The temporary advance from the General Fund was repaid and the balance on the land contract was paid.

6. On the basis of the architect's certificate, warrants were issued for $640,000 for the work completed to date.

7. Warrants paid in cash by the treasurer amounted to $620,000.

8. Because of changes in the plans, the contract with Sandstone and Company was revised to $880,000; the remainder of the bonds were sold at 101.

9. Before the end of the year, the building had been completed, and additional warrants amounting to $230,000 were issued to the contractor in final payment of the work. All warrants were paid by the treasurer.

Required:

A. Prepare entries to record the foregoing transactions (excluding the entries necessary to close out the fund) of the Capital Projects Fund.

B. Prepare a preclosing trial balance for the Capital Projects Fund.

C. Prepare entries necessary to close out the Capital Projects Fund upon the completion of construction.

D. Prepare a statement of revenue, expenditures and other changes in fund balance for the Capital Projects Fund.

E. Prepare preclosing trial balances at December 31, 1981 for the Debt Service Fund, General Fixed Assets Account Group, and General Long-term Debt Account Group, considering only the proceeds, expenditures, and transfers resulting from transactions of the Capital Projects Fund.

(AICPA adapted)

Problem 18–11

The following transactions represent practical situations frequently encountered in accounting for municipal governments. Each transaction is independent of the others.

1. The City Council of Bernardville adopted a budget for the general operations of the government during the new fiscal year. Revenues were estimated at $695,000. Legal authorizations for budgeted expenditures were $650,000.

2. Taxes of $160,000 were levied for the special revenue fund of Millstown. One percent was estimated to be uncollectible.

3. a. On July 25, 1983, office supplies estimated to cost $2,390 were ordered for the city manager's office of Bullersville. Bullersville, which operates on the calendar year, does not maintain an inventory of such supplies.

   b. The supplies ordered July 25 were received on August 9, 1983, accompanied by an invoice for $2,500.

4. On October 10, 1983, the general fund of Washingtonville repaid to the utility fund a loan of $1,000 plus $40 interest. The loan had been made earlier in the fiscal year.

5. A prominent citizen died and left ten acres of undeveloped land to Harper City for a future school site. The donor's cost of the land was $55,000. The fair value of the land was $85,000.

6. a. On March 6, 1983, Dahlstrom City issued 4% special assessment bonds payable March 6, 1988, at face value of $90,000. Interest is payable annually. Dahlstrom City, which operates on the calendar year, will use the proceeds to finance a curbing project.

b. On October 29, 1983, the full $84,000 cost of the completed curbing project was accrued. Also, appropriate closing entries were made with regard to the project.

7. a. Conrad Thamm, a citizen of Basking Knoll, donated common stock valued at $22,000 to the City under a trust agreement. Under the terms of the agreement, the principal amount is to be kept intact; use of revenue from the stock is restricted to financing college scholarships for needy students.
   b. On December 14, 1983, dividends of $1,100 were received on the stock donated by Mr. Thamm.

8. a. On February 23, 1983, the Town of Lincoln, which operates on the calendar year, issued 4% general obligation bonds with a face value of $300,000 payable February 23, 1993, to finance the construction of an addition to the City Hall. Total proceeds were $308,000.
   b. On December 31, 1983, the addition to the City Hall was officially approved, the full cost of $297,000 was paid to the contractor, and appropriate closing entries were made with regard to the project. (Assume that no entries have been made with regard to the project since February 23, 1983.)

Required:

For each transaction, prepare the necessary journal entries for all of the funds and groups of accounts involved. No explanation of the journal entries is required. Use the following headings for your workpaper:

TRANSACTION NUMBER	JOURNAL ENTRIES	DR.	CR.	FUND OR GROUP OF ACCOUNTS

In the far right column, indicate in which fund or group of accounts each entry is to be made, using the coding below:

Funds:
General	G
Special revenue	SR
Capital projects	CP
Debt service	DS
Special assessments	SA
Enterprise	E
Internal service	IS
Trust and agency (Governmental)	TAG
Trust and agency (Proprietary)	TAP

Groups of accounts:
General fixed assets	GFA
General long-term debt	LTD

(AICPA adapted)

Problem 18-12

The following summary of transactions was taken from the accounts of the Annaville School District General Fund before the books had been closed for the fiscal year ended June 30, 1981:

	POST-CLOSING BALANCES JUNE 30, 1980	PRECLOSING BALANCES JUNE 30, 1981
Cash	$400,000	$ 700,000
Property Tax Receivable	150,000	170,000
Estimated Uncollectible Taxes	(40,000)	(70,000)
Estimated Revenue	—	3,000,000
Expenditures	—	2,842,000
Expenditures—prior year	—	—
Encumbrances	—	91,000
	$510,000	$6,733,000
Vouchers Payable	$ 80,000	$ 408,000
Due to Other Funds	210,000	142,000
Reserve for Encumbrances	60,000	91,000
Unreserved Fund Balance	160,000	182,000
Revenue from Taxes	—	2,800,000
Miscellaneous Revenue	—	130,000
Appropriations	—	2,980,000
	$510,000	$6,733,000

Additional Information:

1. Property taxes in the amount of $2,870,000 were assessed for the year. Taxes collected during the year totaled $2,810,000.

2. An analysis of the transactions in the vouchers payable account for the year ended June 30, 1981 follows:

	DEBIT (CREDIT)
Current Expenditures	$(2,700,000)
Expenditures for Prior Year	(58,000)
Vouchers for Payment to Other Funds	(210,000)
Cash Payments During Year	2,640,000
Net Change	$ (328,000)

3. During the year the General Fund was billed $142,000 for services performed on its behalf by other city funds.

4. On May 2, 1981, commitment documents were issued for the purchase of new textbooks at a cost of $91,000.

Required:

On the basis of the data presented above, reconstruct the original detailed journal entries that were required to record all transactions for the fiscal year ended June 30, 1981, including the recording of the current year's budget. Do not prepare closing entries at June 30, 1981.

(AICPA adapted)

Problem 18–13: Capital Project Fund—City of Ahern (Detailed Transactions)

In the November 1979 general election, a proposed bond issue for $1,000,000 to finance the construction of a new city administration building was approved by the electorate of the City of Ahern. Total financing of the building was provided by:

Federal Government Civic Improvement Grant $500,000.
City of Ahern—General Fund—Architectural Design and Contract Supervision $150,000.
Proceeds from Bond Issue $1,000,000.

The terms of the federal government grant provided that half of the grant is to be paid when construction is 50% complete, and the balance is to be paid when the construction contract is 90% complete. The estimated completion date of the project was December 1980. The fiscal year for the City of Ahern ends on June 30 each year.

The sequence of events during 1980 was as follows:

January 1, 1980:	A Capital Projects Fund—Municipal Building is established. Cash in the amount of $50,000 is received by transfer of funds from the General Fund—City of Ahern. Two civil engineers from the City Engineer's Office are assigned full time to the project to supervise its completion.
January 15:	An $100,000 architectural contract was awarded to Allen & Co. for building design and specifications.
January 20:	A prospectus for the bond issue was offered to three brokerage firms for bid on the issue. Provisions of the bond proposal offer $1,000,000 10-year term bonds with tax-free interest at 6% payable semi-annually on March 1 and September 1. Date of issue is March 1, 1980.
	An $18,000 contract was awarded to a local firm, Baldwin Co., to remove trash and debris from a city-owned building site and grade to ground level.
February 20:	The high bid of Booz, Ross, and Merrill, underwriters, to purchase the bond issue at 103 was accepted. The effective date of purchase is March 1, 1980.
March 1:	Proceeds from the bond sale are received. The premium on sale of the bonds is transferred to the Debt Service Fund. Baldwin Co. completed work on the contract and submitted a bill for payment. A voucher was approved for payment to Baldwin Co. Half of the Bond Sale Proceeds were invested in 6-month CD's with interest at 6%. Of the remainder, $250,000, was placed in a savings account at 5% interest. Design specifications suitable for contract bidding were received from the architect. Allen and Co. submitted an invoice for $40,000 for architectural work completed to date. A voucher was approved for payment. A contract for building construction was advertised for bid. Payment was made on all items approved for payment.
April 1:	Caldwell Co. submitted the low bid of $1,255,000 for construction of the building. The contract was awarded. Provisions include partial payments on completion of 25%, 50%, and 75% of construction as determined by the architects and supervisory engineers.
	Invoices and internal billings are received for various expenses (printing, bid advertising, pay of civil engineers—reimbursement to City Engineer's office), $22,000.

	Received an invoice from the architect, Allen & Co., for $20,000 for work on contract specifications and contract award negotiations.
April 15:	Invoices of April 1 are approved for payment and warrants issued, $42,000. Received $50,000 from City of Ahern—General Fund.
May 15:	Expenses totaling $85,000 are approved for payment and payment made. (Legal fees, travel, etc.)
June 1:	The savings account is closed. Interest received amounts to $3,125.
June 15:	An invoice is received from the contractor for $300,000 for work completed to date (approximately 25%). On certification by the architect and engineers, the invoice is approved for payment and paid.
June 30:	Paid an invoice from the architect, Allen & Co., for additional work completed on contract, $10,000. Reimbursed the City Engineer's Office for pay of engineers and other work rendered on the project, $26,000.
August 1:	Vouchered invoices received and made payment for various expenses incurred, $55,000.
August 30:	Received cash including interest for the CD's at maturity. Deposited $200,000 in a savings account at 5% interest.
September 1:	Paid the contractor $325,000 on certification of the architect and engineers that 50% of work was completed. Filed a claim with the federal government for 50% of the grant.
September 30:	Received $250,000 due on federal grant. Paid invoices for various expenses and reimbursements to the City Engineer's office totaling $52,000. Paid the architect $15,000 for additional work on contract.
October 2:	Closed the savings account. Received interest of $850.
October 15:	Paid the contractor $310,000 on certification that 75% of the work is completed.
November 1:	Paid various expenses, $15,000. Received $50,000 (final amount due) from City of Ahern—General Fund.
December 1:	Received certification that 90% of the construction work is completed. Requested the federal government to pay the last portion of the grant. Paid invoices and reimbursements totaling $20,000.
December 15:	The architect and engineers certify completion of work on the contract—awaiting final inspection. Grant of $250,000 is received from the federal government.
December 20:	Final inspection on contract construction is completed. The contractor submits final bill for $320,000. The architect submits final bill on contract for $15,000. Final invoices and reimbursement billings are received totaling $14,500.
December 28:	All invoices and final billings are approved and paid: Contractor $320,000; Architect $15,000; Miscellaneous expenses $14,500.
January 15, 1981:	Final documentation on the project is completed and recorded. The balance in the Capital Project Fund is transferred to the Debt Service Fund. The Capital Project Fund is closed.

Required:

A. Prepare entries in general journal form to record fund transactions reported above to June 30, 1980.

B. Prepare necessary adjusting and closing entries at June 30, 1980.

C. Prepare a balance sheet at June 30, 1980.

D. Prepare entries to record fund transactions from July 1, 1980 to January 15, 1981.

E. Prepare necessary journal entries to close the fund on completion of the project.

Problem 18–14
Select the best answer for each of the following items:

1. Brockton City's water utility, which is an enterprise fund, submits a bill for $9,000 to the General Fund for water service supplied to city departments and agencies. Submission of this bill would result in:
   a. Creation of balances which will be eliminated on the city's combined balance sheet.
   b. Recognition of revenue by the Water Utility Fund and of an expenditure by the General Fund.
   c. Recognition of an encumbrance by both the Water Utility Fund and the General Fund.
   d. Creation of a balance which will be eliminated on the city's combined statement of changes in fund balances.

2. Brockton City has approved a special assessment project in accordance with applicable laws. Total assessments of $500,000, including 10% for the city's share of the cost, have been levied. The levy will be collected from property owners in 10 equal annual installments commencing with the current year. Recognition of the approval and levy will result in entries of:
   a. $500,000 in the Special Assessment Fund and $50,000 in the General Fund.
   b. $450,000 in the Special Assessment Fund and $50,000 in the General Fund.
   c. $50,000 in the Special Assessment Fund and $50,000 in the General Fund.
   d. $50,000 in the Special Assessment Fund and no entry in the General Fund.

3. Brockton City serves as collecting agency for the local independent school district and for a local water district. For this purpose, Brockton has created a single agency fund and charges the other entities a fee of 1% of the gross amounts collected. (The service fee is treated as General Fund revenue.) During the latest fiscal year, a gross amount of $268,000 was collected for the independent school district and $80,000 for the water district. As a consequence of the foregoing, Brockton's General Fund should
   a. Recognize receipts of $348,000.
   b. Recognize receipts of $344,520.
   c. Record revenue of $3,480.
   d. Record encumbrances of $344,520.

4. When Brockton City realized $1,020,000 from the sale of a $1,000,000 bond issue, the entry in its Capital Project Fund was

Cash	$1,020,000	
Bond issue proceeds		$1,000,000
Premium on bonds		20,000

   Recording the transaction in this manner indicates that:
   a. The $20,000 cannot be used for the designated purpose of the fund but must be transferred to another fund.
   b. The full $1,020,000 can be used by the Capital Project Fund to accomplish its purpose.
   c. The nominal rate of interest on the bonds is below the market rate for bonds of such term and risk.
   d. A safety factor is being set aside to cover possible contract defaults on the construction.

5. What will be the balance sheet effect of recording $50,000 of depreciation in the accounts of a utility, an Enterprise Fund, owned by Brockton City?
   a. Reduce total assets of the Utility Fund and the general fixed-assets account group by $50,000.
   b. Reduce total assets of the Utility Fund by $50,000 but have no effect on the general fixed-assets account group.
   c. Reduce total assets of the general fixed-assets account group by $50,000 but have no effect on assets of the Utility Fund.
   d. Have no effect on total assets of either the Utility Fund or the general fixed-assets account group.

6. The City of Paden should use a Capital Projects Fund to account for
   a. Structures and improvements constructed with the proceeds of a special assessment.
   b. Proceeds of a bond issue to be used to acquire land for city parks.
   c. Construction in progress on the city-owned electric utility plant, financed by an issue of revenue bonds.
   d. Assets to be used to retire bonds issued to finance an addition to the city hall.

7. Activities of a central print shop offering printing services at cost to various city departments should be accounted for in
   a. The General Fund.
   b. An Internal Service Fund.
   c. A Special Revenue Fund.
   d. A Special Assessment Fund.

8. Sanders County collects property taxes for the benefit of the state government and the local school districts and periodically remits collections to these units. These activities should be accounted for in
   a. An Agency Fund. — COLLECTS   REMITS   ALWAYS
   b. The General Fund.
   c. An Internal Service Fund.
   d. A Special Assessment Fund.

9. In order to provide for the retirement of general obligation bonds, the City of Osborn invests a portion of its receipts from general property taxes in marketable securities. This investment activity should be accounted for in
   a. A Capital Projects Fund.
   b. A Debt Service Fund.
   c. A Trust Fund.
   d. The General Fund.

10. The transactions of a municipal police retirement system should be recorded in
    a. The General Fund.
    b. A Special Revenue Fund.
    c. A Trust Fund.
    d. An Internal Service Fund.

11. The activities of a municipal golf course which receives three-fourths of its total revenue from a special tax levy should be accounted for in
    a. An Enterprise Fund.
    b. The General Fund.
    c. A Special Assessment Fund.
    d. A Special Revenue Fund.

12. Equipment in general governmental service that had been constructed ten years before with resources of a Capital Projects Fund was sold. The receipts were accounted for as unrestricted revenue. Entries are necessary in the
    a. General Fund and Capital Projects Fund.
    b. General Fund and general fixed-assets account group.
    c. General Fund, Capital Projects Fund, and Enterprise Fund.
    d. General Fund, Capital Projects Fund, and general fixed-assets account group.

13. An account for expenditures does not appear in which fund?
    a. Capital Projects.
    b. Enterprise. — EXPENSES NOT OUTFLOWS OF RESOURCES
    c. Special Assessment.
    d. Special Revenue.

14. Part of the general obligation bond proceeds from a new issuance was used to pay for the cost of a new city hall as soon as construction was completed. The remainder of the proceeds was transferred to repay the debt. Entries are needed to record these transactions in the
    a. General Fund and general long-term debt account group.
    b. General Fund, general long-term debt account group, and Debt Service Fund.
    c. Trust Fund, Debt Service Fund, and general fixed-assets account group.
    d. General long-term debt account group, Debt Service Fund, general fixed-assets account group, and Capital Projects Fund.

15. Cash secured from property tax revenue was transferred for the eventual payment of principal and interest on general obligation bonds. The bonds had been issued when land had been acquired several years ago for a city park. Upon the transfer, an entry would not be made in which of the following?
    a. Debt Service Fund.
    b. General fixed-assets account group.
    c. General long-term debt account group.
    d. General Fund.

16. Premiums received on general obligation bonds are generally transferred to what fund or group of accounts?
    a. Debt Service.
    b. General long-term debt.
    c. General.
    d. Special Revenue.

17. Of the items listed below, those most likely to have parallel accounting procedures, account titles, and financial statements are
    a. Special Revenue Funds and Special Assessment Funds.
    b. Internal Service Funds and Debt Service Funds.
    c. The general fixed-assets account group and the general long-term debt account group.
    d. The General Fund and Special Revenue Funds.

18. Recreational facilities run by a governmental unit and financed on a user-charge basis would be accounted for in which fund?
    a. General.
    b. Trust.
    c. Enterprise.
    d. Capital Projects.

19. Rogers City should record depreciation as an expense in its
   a. Enterprise Fund and Internal Service Fund.
   b. Internal Service Fund and general fixed-assets account group.   *— NOT NECESSARY*
   c. General Fund and Enterprise Fund.
   d. Enterprise Fund and Capital Projects Fund.

20. A performance budget relates a governmental unit's expenditures to
   a. Objects of expenditure.
   b. Expenditures of the preceding fiscal year.
   c. Individual months within the fiscal year.
   d. Activities and programs.

(AICPA adapted)

Appendix:
Tables of Amounts
and Present Values

Table 1 Amount of 1

$$s = (1 + i)^n$$

(n) PERIODS	2%	2½%	3%	3½%	4%	5%	6%	8%	10%
1	1.02000	1.02500	1.03000	1.03500	1.04000	1.05000	1.06000	1.08000	1.10000
2	1.04040	1.05063	1.06090	1.07123	1.08160	1.10250	1.12360	1.16640	1.21000
3	1.06121	1.07689	1.09273	1.10872	1.12486	1.15763	1.19102	1.25971	1.33100
4	1.08243	1.10381	1.12551	1.14752	1.16986	1.21551	1.26248	1.36049	1.46410
5	1.10408	1.13141	1.15927	1.18769	1.21665	1.27628	1.33823	1.46933	1.61051
6	1.12616	1.15969	1.19405	1.22926	1.26532	1.34010	1.41852	1.58687	1.77156
7	1.14869	1.18869	1.22987	1.27228	1.31593	1.40710	1.50363	1.71382	1.94872
8	1.17166	1.21840	1.26677	1.31681	1.36857	1.47746	1.59385	1.85093	2.14359
9	1.19509	1.24886	1.30477	1.36290	1.42331	1.55133	1.68948	1.99900	2.35795
10	1.21899	1.28008	1.34392	1.41060	1.48024	1.62889	1.79085	2.15892	2.59374
11	1.24337	1.31209	1.38423	1.45997	1.53945	1.71034	1.89830	2.33164	2.85312
12	1.26824	1.34489	1.42576	1.51107	1.60103	1.79586	2.01220	2.51817	3.13843
13	1.29361	1.37851	1.46853	1.56396	1.66507	1.88565	2.13293	2.71962	3.45227
14	1.31948	1.41297	1.51259	1.61869	1.73168	1.97993	2.26090	2.93719	3.79750
15	1.34587	1.44830	1.55797	1.67535	1.80094	2.07893	2.39656	3.17217	4.17725
16	1.37279	1.48451	1.60471	1.73399	1.87298	2.18287	2.54035	3.42594	4.59497
17	1.40024	1.52162	1.65285	1.79468	1.94790	2.29202	2.69277	3.70002	5.05447
18	1.42825	1.55966	1.70243	1.85749	2.02582	2.40662	2.85434	3.99602	5.55992
19	1.45681	1.59865	1.75351	1.92250	2.10685	2.52695	3.02560	4.31570	6.11591
20	1.48595	1.63862	1.80611	1.98979	2.19112	2.65330	3.20714	4.66096	6.72750
21	1.51567	1.67958	1.86029	2.05943	2.27877	2.78596	3.39956	5.03383	7.40025
22	1.54598	1.72157	1.91610	2.13151	2.36992	2.92526	3.60354	5.43654	8.14028
23	1.57690	1.76461	1.97359	2.20611	2.46472	3.07152	3.81975	5.87146	8.95430
24	1.60844	1.80873	2.03279	2.28333	2.56330	3.22510	4.04893	6.34118	9.84973

Table 1 Amount of 1

$$s = (1 + i)^n$$

(n) PERIODS	2%	2½%	3%	3½%	4%	5%	6%	8%	10%
25	1.64061	1.85394	2.09378	2.36324	2.66584	3.38635	4.29187	6.84847	10.83471
26	1.67342	1.90029	2.15659	2.44596	2.77247	3.55567	4.54938	7.39635	11.91818
27	1.70689	1.94780	2.22129	2.53157	2.88337	3.73346	4.82235	7.98806	13.10999
28	1.74102	1.99650	2.28793	2.62017	2.99870	3.92013	5.11169	8.62711	14.42099
29	1.77584	2.04641	2.35657	2.71188	3.11865	4.11614	5.41839	9.31727	15.86309
30	1.81136	2.09757	2.42726	2.80679	3.24340	4.32194	5.74349	10.06266	17.44940
31	1.84759	2.15001	2.50008	2.90503	3.37313	4.53804	6.08810	10.86767	19.19434
32	1.88454	2.20376	2.57508	3.00671	3.50806	4.76494	6.45339	11.73708	21.11378
33	1.92223	2.25885	2.65234	3.11194	3.64838	5.00319	6.84059	12.67605	23.22515
34	1.96068	2.31532	2.73191	3.22086	3.79432	5.25335	7.25103	13.69013	25.54767
35	1.99989	2.37321	2.81386	3.33359	3.94609	5.51602	7.68609	14.78534	28.10244
36	2.03989	2.43254	2.89828	3.45027	4.10393	5.79182	8.14725	15.96817	30.91268
37	2.08069	2.49335	2.98523	3.57103	4.26809	6.08141	8.63609	17.24563	34.00395
38	2.12230	2.55568	3.07478	3.69601	4.43881	6.38548	9.15425	18.62528	37.40434
39	2.16474	2.61957	3.16703	3.82537	4.61637	6.70475	9.70351	20.11530	41.14479
40	2.20804	2.68506	3.26204	3.95926	4.80102	7.03999	10.28572	21.72452	45.25926
41	2.25220	2.75219	3.35990	4.09783	4.99306	7.39199	10.90286	23.46248	49.78518
42	2.29724	2.82100	3.46070	4.24126	5.19278	7.76159	11.55703	25.33948	54.76370
43	2.34319	2.89152	3.56452	4.38970	5.40050	8.14967	12.25045	27.36664	60.24007
44	2.39005	2.96381	3.67145	4.54334	5.61652	8.55715	12.98548	29.55597	66.26408
45	2.43785	3.03790	3.78160	4.70236	5.84118	8.98501	13.76461	31.92045	72.89048
46	2.48661	3.11385	3.89504	4.86694	6.07482	9.43426	14.59049	34.47409	80.17953
47	2.53634	3.19170	4.01190	5.03728	6.31782	9.90597	15.46592	37.23201	88.19749
48	2.58707	3.27149	4.13225	5.21359	6.57053	10.40127	16.39387	40.21057	97.01723
49	2.63881	3.35328	4.25622	5.39606	6.83335	10.92133	17.37750	43.42742	106.71896
50	2.69159	3.43711	4.38391	5.58493	7.10668	11.46740	18.42015	46.90161	117.39085

Table 2 Present Value of 1

$$v^n = \frac{1}{(1+i)^n} = (1+i)^{-n}$$

(n) PERIODS	2%	2½%	3%	3½%	4%	5%	6%	8%	10%
1	.98039	.97561	.97087	.96618	.96154	.95238	.94340	.92593	.90909
2	.96117	.95181	.94260	.93351	.92456	.90703	.89000	.85734	.82645
3	.94232	.92860	.91514	.90194	.88900	.86384	.83962	.79383	.75132
4	.92385	.90595	.88849	.87144	.85480	.82270	.79209	.73503	.68301
5	.90573	.88385	.86261	.84197	.82193	.78353	.74726	.68058	.62092
6	.88797	.86230	.83748	.81350	.79031	.74622	.70496	.63017	.56447
7	.87056	.84127	.81309	.78599	.75992	.71068	.66506	.58349	.51316
8	.85349	.82075	.78941	.75941	.73069	.67684	.62741	.54027	.46651
9	.83676	.80073	.76642	.73372	.70259	.64461	.59190	.50025	.42410
10	.82035	.78120	.74409	.70892	.67556	.61391	.55839	.46319	.38554
11	.80426	.76214	.72242	.68495	.64958	.58468	.52679	.42888	.35049
12	.78849	.74356	.70138	.66178	.62460	.55684	.49697	.39711	.31863
13	.77303	.72542	.68095	.63940	.60057	.53032	.46884	.36770	.28966
14	.75788	.70773	.66112	.61778	.57748	.50507	.44230	.34046	.26333
15	.74301	.69047	.64186	.59689	.55526	.48102	.41727	.31524	.23939
16	.72845	.67362	.62317	.57671	.53391	.45811	.39365	.29189	.21763
17	.71416	.65720	.60502	.55720	.51337	.43630	.37136	.27027	.19785
18	.70016	.64117	.58739	.53836	.49363	.41552	.35034	.25025	.17986
19	.68643	.62553	.57029	.52016	.47464	.39573	.33051	.23171	.16351
20	.67297	.61027	.55368	.50257	.45639	.37689	.31180	.21455	.14864
21	.65978	.59539	.53755	.48557	.43883	.35894	.29416	.19866	.13513
22	.64684	.58086	.52189	.46915	.42196	.34185	.27751	.18394	.12285
23	.63416	.56670	.50669	.45329	.40573	.32557	.26180	.17032	.11168
24	.62172	.55288	.49193	.43796	.39012	.31007	.24698	.15770	.10153
25	.60953	.53939	.47761	.42315	.37512	.29530	.23300	.14602	.09230

Table 2 Present Value of 1

$$v^n = \frac{1}{(1+i)^n} = (1+i)^{-n}$$

(n) PERIODS	2%	2½%	3%	3½%	4%	5%	6%	8%	10%
26	.59758	.52623	.46369	.40884	.36069	.28124	.21981	.13520	.08391
27	.58586	.51340	.45019	.39501	.34682	.26785	.20737	.12519	.07628
28	.57437	.50088	.43708	.38165	.33348	.25509	.19563	.11591	.06934
29	.56311	.48866	.42435	.36875	.32065	.24295	.18456	.10733	.06304
30	.55207	.47674	.41199	.35628	.30832	.23138	.17411	.09938	.05731
31	.54125	.46511	.39999	.34423	.29646	.22036	.16425	.09202	.05210
32	.53063	.45377	.38834	.33259	.28506	.20987	.15496	.08520	.04736
33	.52023	.44270	.37703	.32134	.27409	.19987	.14619	.07889	.04306
34	.51003	.43191	.36604	.31048	.26355	.19035	.13791	.07305	.03914
35	.50003	.42137	.35538	.29998	.25342	.18129	.13011	.06763	.03558
36	.49022	.41109	.34503	.28983	.24367	.17266	.12274	.06262	.03235
37	.48061	.40107	.33498	.28003	.23430	.16444	.11579	.05799	.02941
38	.47119	.39128	.32523	.27056	.22529	.15661	.10924	.05369	.02674
39	.46195	.38174	.31575	.26141	.21662	.14915	.10306	.04971	.02430
40	.45289	.37243	.30656	.25257	.20829	.14205	.09722	.04603	.02210
41	.44401	.36335	.29763	.24403	.20028	.13528	.09172	.04262	.02009
42	.43530	.35448	.28896	.23578	.19257	.12884	.08653	.03946	.01826
43	.42677	.34584	.28054	.22781	.18517	.12270	.08163	.03654	.01660
44	.41840	.33740	.27237	.22010	.17805	.11686	.07701	.03383	.01509
45	.41020	.32917	.26444	.21266	.17120	.11130	.07265	.03133	.01372
46	.40215	.32115	.25674	.20547	.16461	.10600	.06854	.02901	.01247
47	.39427	.31331	.24926	.19852	.15828	.10095	.06466	.02686	.01134
48	.38654	.30567	.24200	.19181	.15219	.09614	.06100	.02487	.01031
49	.37896	.29822	.23495	.18532	.14634	.09156	.05755	.02303	.00937
50	.37153	.29094	.22811	.17905	.14071	.08720	.05429	.02132	.00852

Table 3 Amount of an Ordinary Annuity of 1

$$s_{\overline{n}|i} = \frac{(1 + i)^n - 1}{i}$$

(n) PERIODS	2%	2½%	3%	3½%	4%	5%	6%	8%	10%
1	1.00000	1.00000	1.00000	1.00000	1.00000	1.00000	1.00000	1.00000	1.00000
2	2.02000	2.02500	2.03000	2.03500	2.04000	2.05000	2.06000	2.08000	2.10000
3	3.06040	3.07563	3.09090	3.10623	3.12160	3.15250	3.18360	3.24640	3.31000
4	4.12161	4.15252	4.18363	4.21494	4.24646	4.31013	4.37462	4.50611	4.64100
5	5.20404	5.25633	5.30914	5.36247	5.41632	5.52563	5.63709	5.86660	6.10510
6	6.30812	6.38774	6.46841	6.55015	6.63298	6.80191	6.97532	7.33592	7.71561
7	7.43428	7.54743	7.66246	7.77941	7.89829	8.14201	8.39384	8.92280	9.48717
8	8.58297	8.73612	8.89234	9.05169	9.21423	9.54911	9.89747	10.63663	11.43589
9	9.75463	9.95452	10.15911	10.36850	10.58280	11.02656	11.49132	12.48756	13.57948
10	10.94972	11.20338	11.46388	11.73139	12.00611	12.57789	13.18079	14.48656	15.93743
11	12.16872	12.48347	12.80780	13.14199	13.48635	14.20679	14.97164	16.64549	18.53117
12	13.41209	13.79555	14.19203	14.60196	15.02581	15.91713	16.86994	18.97713	21.38428
13	14.68033	15.14044	15.61779	16.11303	16.62684	17.71298	18.88214	21.49530	24.52271
14	15.97394	16.51895	17.08632	17.67699	18.29191	19.59863	21.01507	24.21492	27.97498
15	17.29342	17.93193	18.59891	19.29568	20.02359	21.57856	23.27597	27.15211	31.77248
16	18.63929	19.38022	20.15688	20.97103	21.82453	23.65749	25.67253	30.32428	35.94973
17	20.01207	20.86473	21.76159	22.70502	23.69751	25.84037	28.21288	33.75023	40.54470
18	21.41231	22.38635	23.41444	24.49969	25.64541	28.13238	30.90565	37.45024	45.59917
19	22.84056	23.94601	25.11687	26.35718	27.67123	30.53900	33.75999	41.44626	51.15909
20	24.29737	25.54466	26.87037	28.27968	29.77808	33.06595	36.78559	45.76196	57.27500
21	25.78332	27.18327	28.67649	30.26947	31.96920	35.71925	39.99273	50.42292	64.00250
22	27.29898	28.86286	30.53678	32.32890	34.24797	38.50521	43.39229	55.45676	71.40275
23	28.84496	30.58443	32.45288	34.46041	36.61789	41.43048	46.99583	60.89330	79.54302
24	30.42186	32.34904	34.42647	36.66653	39.08260	44.50200	50.81558	66.76476	88.49733
25	32.03030	34.15776	36.45926	38.94986	41.64591	47.72710	54.86451	73.10594	98.34706
26	33.67091	36.01171	38.55304	41.31310	44.31174	51.11345	59.15638	79.95442	109.18177

Table 3 Amount of an Ordinary Annuity of 1

$$s_{\overline{n}|i} = \frac{(1+i)^n - 1}{i}$$

(n) PERIODS	2%	2½%	3%	3½%	4%	5%	6%	8%	10%
27	35.34432	37.91200	40.70963	43.75906	47.08421	54.66913	63.70577	87.35077	121.09994
28	37.05121	39.85980	42.93092	46.29063	49.96758	58.40258	68.52811	95.33883	134.20994
29	38.79223	41.85630	45.21885	48.91080	52.96629	62.32271	73.63980	103.96594	148.63093
30	40.56808	43.90270	47.57542	51.62268	56.08494	66.43885	79.05819	113.28321	164.49402
31	42.37944	46.00027	50.00268	54.42947	59.32834	70.76079	84.80168	123.34587	181.94343
32	44.22703	48.15028	52.50276	57.33450	62.70147	75.29883	90.88978	134.21354	210.13777
33	46.11157	50.35403	55.07784	60.34121	66.20953	80.06377	97.34316	145.95062	222.25154
34	48.03380	52.61289	57.73018	63.45315	69.85791	85.06696	104.18376	158.62667	245.47670
35	49.99448	54.92821	60.46208	66.67401	73.65222	90.32031	111.43478	172.31680	271.02437
36	51.99437	57.30141	63.27594	70.00760	77.59831	95.83632	119.12087	187.10215	299.12681
37	54.03425	59.73395	66.17422	73.45787	81.70225	101.62814	127.26812	203.07032	330.03949
38	56.11494	62.22730	69.15945	77.02889	85.97034	107.70955	135.90421	220.31595	364.04343
39	58.23724	64.78298	72.23423	80.72491	90.40915	114.09502	145.05846	238.94122	401.44778
40	60.40198	67.40255	75.40126	84.55028	95.02552	120.79977	154.76197	259.05652	442.59256
41	62.61002	70.08762	78.66330	88.50954	99.82654	127.83976	165.04768	280.78104	487.85181
42	64.86222	72.83981	82.02320	92.60737	104.81960	135.23175	175.95054	304.24352	537.63699
43	67.15947	75.66080	85.48389	96.84863	110.01238	142.99334	187.50758	329.58301	592.63699
44	69.50266	78.55232	89.04841	101.23833	115.41288	151.14301	199.75803	356.94965	652.64076
45	71.89271	81.51613	92.71986	105.78167	121.02939	159.70016	212.74351	386.50562	718.90484
46	74.33056	84.55403	96.50146	110.48403	126.87057	168.68516	226.50812	418.42607	791.79532
47	76.81718	87.66789	100.39650	115.35097	132.94539	178.11942	241.09861	452.90015	871.97485
48	79.35352	90.85958	104.40840	120.38826	139.26321	188.02539	256.56453	490.13216	960.17234
49	81.94059	94.13107	108.54065	125.60185	145.83373	198.42666	272.95840	530.34274	1057.18957
50	84.57940	97.48435	112.79687	130.99791	152.66708	209.34800	290.33590	573.77016	1163.90853

Table 4 Present Value of an Ordinary Annuity of 1

$$a_{\overline{n}|i} = \frac{1 - \dfrac{1}{(1+i)^n}}{i} = \frac{1 - v^n}{i}$$

(n) PERIODS	2%	2½%	3%	3½%	4%	5%	6%	8%	10%
1	.98039	.97561	.97087	.96618	.96154	.95238	.94340	.92593	.90909
2	1.94156	1.92742	1.91347	1.89969	1.88609	1.85941	1.83339	1.78326	1.73554
3	2.88388	2.85602	2.82861	2.80164	2.77509	2.72325	2.67301	2.57710	2.48685
4	3.80773	3.76197	3.71710	3.67308	3.62990	3.54595	3.46511	3.31213	3.16986
5	4.71346	4.64583	4.57971	4.51505	4.45182	4.32948	4.21236	3.99271	3.79079
6	5.60143	5.50813	5.41719	5.32855	5.24214	5.07569	4.91732	4.62288	4.35526
7	6.47199	6.34939	6.23028	6.11454	6.00205	5.78637	5.58238	5.20637	4.86842
8	7.32548	7.17014	7.01969	6.87396	6.73274	6.46321	6.20979	5.74664	5.33493
9	8.16224	7.97087	7.78611	7.60769	7.43533	7.10782	6.80169	6.24689	5.75902
10	8.98259	8.75206	8.53020	8.31661	8.11090	7.72173	7.36009	6.71008	6.14457
11	9.78685	9.51421	9.25262	9.00155	8.76048	8.30641	7.88687	7.13896	6.49506
12	10.57534	10.25776	9.95400	9.66333	9.38507	8.86325	8.38384	7.53608	6.81369
13	11.34837	10.98319	10.63496	10.30274	9.98565	9.39357	8.85268	7.90378	7.10336
14	12.10625	11.69091	11.29607	10.92052	10.56312	9.89864	9.29498	8.24424	7.36669
15	12.84926	12.38138	11.93794	11.51741	11.11839	10.37966	9.71225	8.55948	7.60608
16	13.57771	13.05500	12.56110	12.09412	11.65230	10.83777	10.10590	8.85137	7.82371
17	14.29187	13.71220	13.16612	12.65132	12.16567	11.27407	10.47726	9.12164	8.02155
18	14.99203	14.35336	13.75351	13.18968	12.65930	11.68959	10.82760	9.37189	8.20141
19	15.67846	14.97889	14.32380	13.70984	13.13394	12.08532	11.15812	9.60360	8.36492
20	16.35143	15.58916	14.87747	14.21240	13.59033	12.46221	11.46992	9.81815	8.51356
21	17.01121	16.18455	15.41502	14.69797	14.02916	12.82115	11.76408	10.01680	8.64869
22	17.65805	16.76541	15.93692	15.16712	14.45112	13.16300	12.04158	10.20074	8.77154
23	18.29220	17.33211	16.44361	15.62041	14.85684	13.48857	12.30338	10.37106	8.88322
24	18.91393	17.88499	16.93554	16.05837	15.24696	13.79864	12.55036	10.52876	8.98474
25	19.52346	18.42438	17.41315	16.48151	15.62208	14.09394	12.78336	10.67478	9.07704

Table 4 Present Value of an Ordinary Annuity of 1

$$a_{\overline{n}|_i} = \frac{1 - \dfrac{1}{(1+i)^n}}{i} = \frac{1 - v^n}{i}$$

(n) PERIODS	2%	2½%	3%	3½%	4%	5%	6%	8%	10%
26	20.12104	18.95061	17.87684	16.89035	15.98277	14.37519	13.00317	10.80998	9.16095
27	20.70690	19.46401	18.32703	17.28536	16.32959	14.64303	13.21053	10.93516	9.23722
28	21.28127	19.96489	18.76411	17.66702	16.66306	14.89813	13.40616	11.05108	9.30657
29	21.84438	20.45355	19.18845	18.03577	16.98371	15.14107	13.59072	11.15841	9.36961
30	22.39646	20.93029	19.60044	18.39205	17.29203	15.37245	13.76483	11.25778	9.42691
31	22.93770	21.39541	20.00043	18.73628	17.58849	15.59281	13.92909	11.34980	9.47901
32	23.46833	21.84918	20.38877	19.06887	17.87355	15.80268	14.08404	11.43500	9.52638
33	23.98856	22.29188	20.76579	19.39021	18.14765	16.00255	14.23023	11.51389	9.56943
34	24.49859	22.72379	21.13184	19.70068	18.41120	16.19290	14.36814	11.58693	9.60858
35	24.99862	23.14516	21.48722	20.00066	18.66461	16.37419	14.49825	11.65457	9.64416
36	25.48884	23.55625	21.83225	20.29049	18.90828	16.54685	14.62099	11.71719	9.67651
37	25.96945	23.95732	22.16724	20.57053	19.14258	16.71129	14.73678	11.77518	9.70592
38	26.44064	24.34860	22.49246	20.84109	19.36786	16.86789	14.84602	11.82887	9.73265
39	26.90259	24.73034	22.80822	21.10250	19.58448	17.01704	14.94907	11.87858	9.75697
40	27.35548	25.10278	23.11477	21.35507	19.79277	17.15909	15.04630	11.92461	9.77905
41	27.79949	25.46612	23.41240	21.59910	19.99305	17.29437	15.13802	11.96724	9.79914
42	28.23479	25.82001	23.70136	21.83488	20.18563	17.42321	15.22454	12.00670	9.81740
43	28.66156	26.16645	23.98190	22.06269	20.37079	17.54591	15.30617	12.04324	9.83400
44	29.07996	26.50385	24.25427	22.28279	20.54884	17.66277	15.38318	12.07707	9.84909
45	29.49016	26.83302	24.51871	22.49545	20.72004	17.77407	15.45583	12.10840	9.86281
46	29.89231	27.15417	24.77545	22.70092	20.88465	17.88007	15.52437	12.13741	9.87528
47	30.28658	27.46748	25.02471	22.89944	21.04294	17.98102	15.58903	12.16427	9.88662
48	30.67312	27.77315	25.26671	23.09124	21.19513	18.07716	15.65003	12.18914	9.89693
49	31.05208	28.07137	25.50166	23.27656	21.34147	18.16872	15.70757	12.21216	9.90630
50	31.42361	28.36231	25.72976	23.45562	21.48218	18.25593	15.76186	12.23349	9.91481

Index

707